Oil Injustice

Another World Is Necessary:
Human Rights, Environmental Justice, and Popular Democracy

Series Editor: Kenneth Gould

A better world is necessary, but also possible. A point of departure is that neoliberalism is imperiling humans, their societies, and the environments upon which they depend. Yet there are powerful countervailing forces. They include human rights and environmental movements, as well as movements for fair trade, a world parliament, redistribution of land and resources, alternative energy sources, sustainability, and many others. Another development has been the proliferation of forms of popular democracy, including social forums, e-governance, direct democracy, and worker self-management.

Books in this series will go beyond critique to analyze and propose alternatives, particularly focusing on either human rights, environmental justice, collective goods, or popular democracy.

Oil Injustice
    Patricia Widener
Global Obligations for the Right to Food
    Edited by George Kent
Latin America after the Neoliberal Debacle
    Ximena de la Barra and Richard A. Dello Buono

Oil Injustice

Resisting and Conceding a Pipeline in Ecuador

Patricia Widener

ROWMAN & LITTLEFIELD PUBLISHERS, INC.
Lanham • Boulder • New York • Toronto • Plymouth, UK

Published by Rowman & Littlefield Publishers, Inc.
A wholly owned subsidiary of The Rowman & Littlefield Publishing Group, Inc.
4501 Forbes Boulevard, Suite 200, Lanham, Maryland 20706
http://www.rowmanlittlefield.com

Estover Road, Plymouth PL6 7PY, United Kingdom

British Library Cataloguing in Publication Information Available

Library of Congress Cataloging-in-Publication Data
Widener, Patricia, 1966–
 Oil injustice : resisting and conceding a pipeline in Ecuador / Patricia Widener.
 p. cm. — (Another world is necessary: human rights, environmental justice, and popular democracy)
 Includes bibliographical references and index.
 ISBN 978-1-4422-0861-2 (cloth : alk. paper) — ISBN 978-1-4422-0863-6 (electronic)
 1. Petroleum pipelines—Ecuador—Case studies. 2. Environmental policy—Ecuador—Citizen participation—Case studies. I. Title.
 HD9580.E2.W532 2011
 388.5'509866—dc22   2011013489

♾™ The paper used in this publication meets the minimum requirements of American National Standard for Information Sciences—Permanence of Paper for Printed Library Materials, ANSI/NISO Z39.48-1992.

Printed in the United States of America

Contents

Preface

In January 2001, *Jessica*, an Ecuadorian oil tanker, struck a reef dumping 144,000 gallons of oil near the Galapagos Islands. At the time, the *Jessica* disaster warranted a sliver of newsprint. Tanker collisions, pipeline breaks, and oil spills are increasingly commonplace, but that one in particular was an opportune collision when I was a graduate student.

My master's thesis examined recovery following the 1989 *Exxon Valdez* oil spill, and I saw the chance to bridge from Alaska to the Galapagos a research project. I called a few contacts whom I knew to be knowledgeable on Ecuador to see how feasible such a comparison would be. At the time, one of them told me that the "real oil story" in Ecuador was with the persistent oil spills and leaks in the Amazon, which was flush with multinationals and debatable oil reserves. Over the course of the conversation, I also learned that a heavy crude pipeline, the Oleoducto de Crudos Pesados, or OCP, was going to be built from the edge of the Amazon rainforest, over the Andes Mountain range, to the Pacific Coast. I learned that the owners were multinationals, and that conflicts were beginning between environmental organizations, landowners, and communities along the proposed route and the Ecuadorian government and oil companies.

In 2001, with a misplaced sense of understanding, I went to Ecuador in anticipation that grassroots activism, particularly among the organized Indigenous communities, would delay, if not stop, the pipeline's construction. Though I had never been an activist, and perhaps because I had never been an activist, I idealized confrontational, streetwise, ecojustice activism. Perhaps I just wanted to investigate something as tangible and newsworthy as a pipeline, in a place as conflicted as South America.

I went back six more times for short periods over nine years. In the first two years, I felt a great deal of respect and admiration for the groups struggling against the lack of transparency and accountability in the oil process.

But in the next two years, I experienced more dismay and confusion at the concurrent, counterproductive infighting and slipperiness of their agendas. The more insidious impact of the oil project was its destructive impact on the communities and organizations and their scramble over each other for oil or international tokens.

At that time, I switched my attention from the activist-oriented, anti-oil environmental groups in two Andean towns, Mindo and Quito, and from the moderate, professional, conservation organizations in the capital Quito to the more somber community leaders in the oil hubs of Lago Agrio in the Amazon and Esmeraldas on the Pacific Coast. The oil-impacted communities were fighting a much longer environmental justice and community rights battle on the ground with the state as their primary target, rather than the individual oil companies.

I returned in 2007 and discovered that the crosscutting factions in Quito and Mindo had abated and both sites had been transformed over the years. Mindo's activists, in particular, became national environmental leaders in large part due to their antipipeline activities, while the affected communities in the Amazon and on the coast continued to demand greater and greater degrees of autonomy from the state and in oil revenue decisions. The conservation groups in Quito had also realized an environmental fund by this time.

The oil sector and oil executives warrant no compassion or leeway for providing jobs and a minimum number of basic projects to oil-affected communities. The vast majority are an exclusionary group, operating and living in nation-clubs—just a whisker beneath the authority of the state. Given the sector's wealth, the oil industry continues to "divide and conquer" from *campesinos* to state officials, and to treat the local population and ecosystems with a nonlocal disregard, which borders on wanton carelessness.

BP's oil spill in the Gulf of Mexico in 2010 encapsulates the industry's perception of the rest of us: with eleven workers killed; an ecosystem and coastal livelihoods ruined for perhaps decades; an audacity to discount the government's demand to stop using chemical dispersants; an overriding preference for deregulation, rapid production, and high profits; and a blatant indifference to contingency plans and disaster strategies even though breaks, spills, leaks, and explosions are inherent in the operating system.

In Ecuador, individuals and organizations spoke of being threatened, of having their phone lines tapped and their homes and workplaces videotaped. The police were called out, arrests were made, and international activists were deported. I believe the ubiquity of power and force that is held by the state and the oil industry, whether real or simply perceived, infiltrated my interviews with environmental and social rights organizations—and my own writing of their words—especially during the months of peak construction and peak confrontation.

But by and large, there were no individual villains or heroes in this conflict. There were grassroots leaders, environmentalists, and oil representatives with whom I would want to share a cup of Ecuadorian coffee—and oil executives, conservationists, and local activists with whom I would not. They would probably say the same about me. The rogue in this story is the global political economy that feeds upon the world's natural resources and the world's poor. This structure was never threatened by any campaign or mobilization effort during my research, and it is still not being questioned after the BP disaster.

I recall the experience as a time of observing tremendous transnational collaboration and courageous community-level protests, and absurd and defeating squabbles over scraps. Although layers of domestic motives were not easily revealed and were often ignored by international organizations working on global campaigns, transnational networks attempted to challenge the status quo of oil dominance in Ecuador and the global indifference of financiers and multinationals on impacted ecosystems and affected communities. The tally was two steps forward, one step back—resembling a racehorse at the starting gate, restrained by an eager, but inexperienced, jockey and held at a venue where the principal outcome was already predetermined. Nevertheless, I saw hope over and over again among the Ecuadorian activists and organizations.

That's why they stood together, initially, and said, "*Basta*, enough is enough, I want to be heard now." But it is the wife of one activist whom I remember more than the arrested tree sitters, beaten-up landowners, or well-known international activists, such as Bianca Jagger and Julia Hill, who flew to Ecuador to support two different anti-oil campaigns. In 2002, at the peak of activism when people were being arrested and community activists were receiving threatening phone calls, this woman was perpetually on the verge of tears when people talked about the construction of the pipeline and "the fight." Though I never interviewed her, I read on her face: "I married my husband, not this activist." And once when I was interviewing her husband, she corrected him when he chose to use the word *pelear*, which, and I am oversimplifying, means to fight, to scuffle, or to brawl. She told him to use *luchar*, which means to fight for something or with someone about something. He corrected himself.

The day when I asked if she was going to participate in the next day's "action" against OCP, she said, "No"—directly, and clearly. Her husband said, "She's not sure." She responded to him: "Our children?" He said, "Rosa can watch them." I empathized with her. At this action, some of the activists had no children, many others were just beyond childhood themselves, and I was a nonlocal researcher visiting for a few months each year. She just looked at me. I believe she wanted to say: "You don't understand. It's not okay now. You should leave." But she was too polite.

I dedicate much of my work to community residents who never wanted to be politically active but who were left little choice—by the actions and inactions of their government, by oil companies whether they are private or state owned, by oil demand in the United States, by global capitalism that treats people as disposable faceless liabilities and that treats the natural environment as an expendable, privately owned, profit-making stream, by the "polluter-industrial complex" identified by Daniel Faber, by the oil-industrial core that I present here, by the intrusion of researchers, by international advocates, by their neighbors, and by their own families and friends.

ACKNOWLEDGEMENTS

I cannot express enough gratitude to my advisor and mentor Phil Brown for supporting my research interests and for introducing me to the environmental justice movement. I would also like to thank Valerie Gunter and Steve Kroll-Smith for introducing me to the field of environmental sociology and to the importance of studying oil conflict. Ann Dill and Patrick Heller were also supportive and instrumental in guiding the early phases of this work. Series editor Kenneth Gould, editor Sarah Stanton, and editorial assistant Jin Yu were supportive and encouraging as well. More broadly, I am also grateful for the journal reviewers and conference audiences who offered helpful feedback when I presented my work. Finally, I thank, though I cannot thank them enough, everyone who met with me for an interview, who made sure I knew of upcoming events, and who gave me a tremendous amount of their time and insights so that I could better understand their experiences, arguments, and strategies with regard to the pipeline project. Others have provided essential financial support, including the National Science Foundation graduate student travel grant SES-0324956 and a series of grants made available through Brown University (Henry Luce Graduate Environmental Fellowship through Watson Institute for International Studies, Tinker Field Grant Fellowship through the Center for Latin American Studies, and the Graduate School's research grants and dissertation fellowship). At Florida Atlantic University, a Scholarly and Creative Accomplishment Fellowship permitted me time to write and the Lifelong Learning Society Research and Travel Fund allowed me to analyze more recent oil transitions in the Ecuadorian Amazon.

1

Oil Disasters and Conflicts

The study of global oil conflicts captures how three—potentially transnational—environmental movements compete and collaborate when affected people and organizations engage in resisting or conceding an oil project. In this case, the construction of an oil pipeline in Ecuador serves as a point to compare how each of these three movements—one based on conservation, another on healthy ecosystems for healthy bodies, and the other on social and economic justice—intersect.[1] It also reveals how each is interpreted, experienced, modified, and acted upon by people and organizations in the developing, lower-income South as well as the developed, higher-income North.[2]

Each of these environmental movements may have originated in the United States, which speaks to the degree of exploitation and contamination experienced in the United States, though they now influence and are influenced by decisions and actions made or enacted worldwide. The contemporary environmental movement, which launched in the United States from the conservation and preservation efforts in the late nineteenth century, remains strong in its primary focus of saving wildlife and wildlife habitat and corridors.[3] The majority of these campaigns are led primarily by white, formally educated professionals and members, who value the idea of pristine natural environments.[4]

A second movement, which developed in the 1960s, stresses the importance of healthy ecosystems. Emphasizing the interconnectedness between human health and the natural environment, this healthy ecosystems movement identified ecological hazards and human illnesses as being linked to the mass production, use, and disposal of synthetic chemicals and chemical combinations, such as pesticides and petrochemicals. It was led primarily by scientists, such as Rachel Carson, whose work *Silent Spring* is credited with popularizing concern,[5] raising awareness, inspiring a movement, as well as implementing greater environmental laws in the United States. Decades later

1

and with the growth rather than reduction of chemical production, *Silent Spring* was followed by *Our Stolen Future*, a scientists' detective work that travels from the laboratory to the natural environment and eventually identifies a pattern of birth defects and reproductive problems. *Living Downstream* was another important work at this time that offered "a scientist's personal investigation of cancer and the environment."[6] The early ecological movement was followed by and linked to a growing environmental health movement that is led by a coalition of activists and affected community members and scientists.[7] The tragedy is that with each significant bit of evidence that firmly links chemical exposure and human and ecological injury, chemical production has continued to climb.

Scientific research is still more likely to be used to confirm past harms than to predict future hazards or to protect communities.[8] "Those who spend their lives discovering links between health and the environmental can easily be seduced by the complexity of the analysis,"[9] warns Devra Davis, an epidemiologist who studied corporate environmental deception. To clarify, Davis adds that "the elegant equations employed to describe patterns of health and the environment can obscure the reasons for asking these questions in the first place."[10] In contrast, affected communities rarely lose sight of the most pressing issue. Adults in contaminated neighborhoods know that too many children have leukemia (and one is too many); they know that the smoke pumped nightly burns their eyes, nose, and throat; and they know that their local water supply irritates the skin. Given their personal experiences, they pursue answers from government, industry, and scientists, while trying to provide a healthy living, working, and playing space for their children, for themselves, and for their communities. They have too much to lose if they fail.

A third environmental movement speaks to, for, and through them. It is owned by them. Environmental justice (EJ) is both a paradigm and a movement that grew from the civil rights movement in the United States to incorporate people and justice into environmental policy and campaigns. By the 1980s, the practices of corporations that were enabled by government protection were identified as harming distinct and already marginalized populations: low-income and/or racial minority communities and households.[11] After a decade of contention, the delegates of the First National People of Color Environmental Leadership Summit in the United States identified seventeen principles of environmental justice. For them, environmental justice supports and empowers affected communities in their demands for ecological, social, and economic protection and equality, as well as for the recognition and safeguard of humankind's interconnectedness with nature and ecosystems.[12] Environmental justice emphasizes the critical role of communities in deliberating on their social and economic well-being, including the health of their communal and physical environments and the use of community and natural resources at their determination.

Environmental injustice implies unequal impact or burden on some groups imposed by others, including government agencies and corporations, due to differences in economic and political power arising from the inequalities associated with the race, ethnicity, or socioeconomic status of a people, workforce, or community. It also implies unequal responses, safeguards, and resolutions by government officials and industry. In other words, environmental injustice within and between nations identifies how histories, legacies, and contemporary practices of racism, sexism, and/or classism in the political economy has led to and continues to lead to "contaminated communities," poisonous worksites, "toxic struggles," and "collective trauma."[13]

Given the class distinctions in environmental justice struggles, labor groups, which have also been excluded from the machinations of political and economic power, have been a point of potential solidarity. They have collaborated when communities witnessed their homes as dumping sites and when workers identified the available employment to be hazardous.[14] "They see their communities used as dumping grounds for toxic wastes because they lack the power to prevent it; they find only the most hazardous jobs available, if they can find jobs at all; and they discover that the circumstances of their work are set by managers and engineers who do not have to suffer the hazards of the job floor" or live in contaminated communities, writes Robert Gottlieb.[15]

An additional component of the EJ movement is environmental racism, which emphasizes how racial minorities in the United States experience disproportionate residential exposure to chemical toxins and disproportionately slower responses of government and industry officials to respond to and to clean up known toxic sites.[16] Robert Bullard, a leading scholar on environmental racism, also identifies how government agencies fail to examine the "aggregate risks" of communities of color as well as the "synergistic risks" of multiple exposure points among "'contaminated-saturated' communities."[17] More recent research on environmental racism also indicates that racial tension exists within coalitions and networks due to the history and legacy of mistrust and misunderstanding in the United States, which has undermined a successful movement against the system of corporate pollution.[18] Environmental injustice and racism are also perpetuated within as well as between nations. Like systems of classism, the minority who possess economic and political power rule the majority in, as well as between, the Global North and the Global South, and developed and developing nations.[19]

Yet still absent in much of the contemporary struggles and research are the voices and collaborations of Native Americans, Native People, First Nations, or Indigenous communities.[20] Opportunities for them to contribute their ecological knowledge and practice of living sustainably are missing as well. But the language of the Environmental Justice Principles and its preamble point to an initial solidarity and to the global and structural focus that was initially demanded from the existing political economy. The preamble identifies as important components of environmental justice "[o]ur spiritual interdependence to the sacredness of our Mother Earth; to respect and celebrate each of our cultures, languages and beliefs about the natural world and our roles in healing ourselves" and the right "to secure our political, economic and cultural liberation that has been denied for over 500 years of colonization and oppression, resulting in the poisoning of our communities and land and the genocide of our peoples."[21] This call, if read, may have sent a chill over those controlling the world's political and economic systems as it is a truly wide-ranging structural adjustment to the historical and geopolitical violence and suffering that has been experienced. It is calling for the end of the capitalist-political system that has enabled a minority to rule for their own gains that have accrued over centuries.

In practice and in study, these three recognized environmental movements (conservation, ecology, and justice) and the fourth underrecognized Native ecological or ecospiritual movement are responding to local struggles against global decisions. Too frequently, however, their efforts are enacted and examined as disconnected endeavors mobilized against different entities for dissimilar causes and outcomes. At other times, these campaigns merge or collide. For example, one unintended harm of the success of the ecological and EJ struggles in the North—coupled with the global mobility of production and postconsumer waste—has been the relocation of burden onto other communities, laborers, and environments in the South.[22] As noted by David Pellow, North-South distinctions serve as a conceptual tool to organize communities within and between nations and to analyze the political, economic, social and historical influences, and power differences of communities within and between nations rather than as markers for geographical considerations alone.[23] A push for greater environmental regulation and community participation in the North, alongside greater industry responsibility and government authority, promoted the transfer of waste and industry to more impoverished communities, less vocal, less powerful, and less organized and without the political support to counter the worst offenses of industrial practices.[24] Indeed many industries, which are harmful to the environment and communities, are welcomed in developing nations, which continue to adhere to, or are forced to accept, trickle down and technology transfer arguments.[25] Likewise, some nations, such as India, are in the position of producing domestic postconsumer waste as well as receiving other's waste, while other nations are in debt arrangements that first created exposure pathways, including the adoption of the Green Revolution, and that then required cleanup operations, further spreading the risk of exposure.[26]

The ease and speed of injustice and a toxin's mobility point to how the operators and beneficiaries of the global political economy, and its current pace and breadth of expansion, have promoted conflict and the spread of pollution, while avoiding liability and accountability.[27] Though justice through local activism and transnational advocacy is the primary frame of this study, the causes of conflict and injustice are the practices and impacts of the global political economy, which currently allocates healthy and unhealthy ecosystems unevenly and unjustly. Even though this book examines how affected communities and their transnational allies resisted and conceded an oil pipeline in Ecuador, these conflicts are only a grounded expression of the global structures that systematically disadvantage some while advantaging others.

It could be argued that in the presence of industry-government coalitions,[28] the "polluter-industrial complex,"[29] and the "treadmill of production,"[30] civil society is leading a more contaminated life with more environmental disputes and illnesses than would be experienced in their absence. The polluter-industrial complex, as developed by Daniel Faber within an American context, identifies the industries and their financial backers who benefit from a political system that has been colonized by economic interests. The complex includes the beneficiaries of industry (not laborers), appointed and elected political leaders, and probusiness support centers (such as think tanks, lobbyists, scientists, and policy makers), who have consistently and successfully influenced and redesigned the political structure to serve business interests, which has led to weakened labor groups and insufficient environmental standards and regulations.[31] Though focused on the United States, this complex is certainly applicable to global dynamics, and how the American capitalist system has influenced the role of international institutions, such as the World Bank, the International Monetary Fund, and the World Trade Organization, in designing trade and lending policies and practices to facilitate Northern interests.

Another critical perspective recognized by Allan Schnaiberg and Ken Gould is the treadmill of production. The treadmill of production explains how a cyclical and reinforcing system has been orchestrated (by choice and direction of its beneficiaries) to increase production (and profits) by suppressing a workforce that remains committed to increased production (and therefore its own repression), by contaminating incidentally or intentionally the public that remains committed to consumption (and therefore its own risk of exposure), and by privatizing, degrading, and exploiting the natural environment.[32] The treadmill of production succeeds in hiding or denying the limits of nature, while being enabled, supported, and protected by boosters in political positions. This treadmill—operated by corporate activities and interests—is transnational,[33] and some would add racist.[34]

It could be argued that the treadmill of production is, or is part of, an advancing imperial process that is colonizing and exploiting the world's land, labor, and resources, while consumers, workers, and politicians compliantly permit these conquests and submissively accept colony as a way of life.[35] Paradoxically, activists and organizations in single-issue environment justice struggles appear to resist the local and isolated injuries of the political economic structure, while ignoring or even contributing to the global treadmill of production.[36] It is here, between the mill and the mall, where workers and consumers are facilitating the mobility of contamination and conflict.

In Southern places, these global arrangements press upon local political ecologies, or the right of the poor to defend their existence, their dignity, and their livelihoods against the interests of more powerful entities by exercising control over their own land and natural resources.[37] Incorporating an environmental justice frame into global and local perspectives lends analytical insight into the injustices, while supporting the justice efforts of affected peoples. Increasingly, the environmental justice struggle reaches beyond the United States to encompass local, national, and transnational campaigns and mobilization efforts in and between people and nations of the South and the North that are fighting against transnational polluters, national and international political acquiescence, global trade practices, or external debt pressures.

Indeed, "transboundary problems," such as climate change, the toxic waste trade, and the disposal of pollutants in soil, air, and waterways, create "communities of fate" and "circles of poison," in which communities across a broad geographical range are bound (and poisoned) together.[38] As argued by others, but forcefully by Pellow in terms of the environment, racism (and colonialism and neocolonialism that have been justified on racist classifications) eventually comes back to harm the racist individual and system.[39]

A transnational environmental justice movement has the potential to counter these forces, yet some have argued that it "is experiencing severe growing pains."[40] Points of overlap may be particularly strong in developing, low-income nations where Northern representatives of each movement operate and perhaps compete to influence the environmental course and discourse of a nation and a people. Indeed, successful site-specific efforts have not translated into a triumphant national, let alone transnational, movement. Early on, environmental justice scholars were some of the first to identify a national and global need for such a movement. They even appeared to express hope in its potential. "If justice is about equity and participatory democracy," writes Richard Hofrichter, "than any social movement designed to achieve environmental justice must be multicultural, multi-issue, and international."[41] Diversified grassroots groups of people of color are likely to be the most influential in expanding the environmental agendas and democratizing the movement, suggests Bullard.[42] Andrew Szasz describes community alliances with government officials, scientists, and professional organizations as "untroubled eclecticism,"[43] while Gerald Markowitz and David Rosner add that "future battles over regulation of the chemical industry would come from newer, less institutionally predictable community groups that could not as easily be manipulated by industry's lobbyists, lawyers, and political action committee money."[44] In another work, Faber argues that "the environmental justice movement must develop solidarity with those movements and governments in the Third World that appreciate that capitalist economic development, ecological degradation, and human poverty are different sides of the same general problem."[45]

One reason why a global EJ movement has failed to be sustained may be due to the Northern orientation of the movement. The North wanted to educate the South, or help the South "catch up," in the 1960s–1980s, and then sought to collaborate equally with the South in the 1990s–2000s. But perhaps the North still needs to listen and learn from, and perhaps be led by, the South. The North may need to say that it can be subordinate to the wisdom and knowledge of its Southern comrades. Indeed, Northern activists may now have more to learn from the South than to share,[46] and Northern humility may still be lacking, despite the impressive resistance and demands for justice and achievements of it coming from oppressed groups in the South. Moreover, a Northern or Euro-centric worldview constructed by political and economic interests and held by workers and consumers still fails to question the capitalist model, fails to permit discussions of alternatives, and fails to determine whether the harms associated with it outweigh the realized or visualized benefits.

Timmons Roberts and Bradley Parks identify how persistent global inequalities, the legacies of colonialism, and lopsided policy and trade agreements have created such a severe degree of mistrust between the North and the South so as to undermine climate change cooperation.[47] Their findings are insightful. Even though Roberts and Parks are discussing mistrust and noncooperation between national leaders and national scientists, mistrust of the North would likely infect Southern communities and organizations as well. At each level and over a tremendously long period, the North has benefited from the land, labor, and resources of the South without acknowledging, apologizing, or making reparations for this arrangement.

Many have also argued that environmental justice struggles may require or be aided by transnational cooperation, which is now deep into its second decade of practice.[48] Calls for human rights within EJ struggles may be a point to bridge North-South divisions and to strengthen the Southern role in such collaborations. Indeed, the North could learn from Southern efforts to end human rights abuses imposed by national and transnational forces. From within the environmental justice frame in particular, the "politics of pollution" and the identification and construction of "sacrifice zones" are human rights abuses imposed by the actions and inactions of the private and public sectors and by the beneficiaries of such violations.[49] Northern activists could learn from Southern activists who have framed their contention on human rights violations, while Northern consumers and audiences still need to understand how their role, as well as the role of their elected officials and corporations, contributes to the violations of the rights of others. They are linked. One body, community, or ecosystem is abused for another's gain or protection.

One guideline for how to act justly and humanely (if not learned at home or in school and then applied universally) is the first article of the United Nations Human Rights Declaration of 1948. This article calls for all human beings who are born "equal in dignity and rights" to "act towards one another in a spirit of brotherhood [*sic*]." Article 7 advocates "equal protection of the law," while Article 23 calls for "just and favourable conditions of work." Under Article 25, "Everyone has the right to a standard of living adequate for the health and well-being of himself and of his family." Article 30 concludes that not one "state, group or person" has a right "to perform any act aimed at the destruction of any of the rights and freedoms" of others.[50] This final article begs the question: is a multinational corporation a "group"? The United Nations Declaration of Social Progress and Development of 1969 expands upon the original Human Rights Declaration. Article 2, in particular, emphasizes that "social progress and development shall be founded on respect for the dignity and value of the human person and shall ensure the promotion of human rights and social justice, which requires: (a) The immediate and final elimination of all forms of inequality, exploitation of peoples and individuals, colonialism and racism."[51]

Economic inequality, exploitation of land and communities, beneficiaries of the legacies of colonialism, and practitioners of racism sound closely related to contemporary struggles between affected communities and extractive industries. The weaknesses of these two U.N. declarations are that they are proposed contracts between state governments or political leaders and individual citizens. Corporations, the private sector as well as the political-economic system, appear absolved of, and invisible in, any human rights violations. But this is not necessarily so in the hearts, eyes, and minds of Southern communities and some Southern leaders. Though globalization has enabled the pathways of goodwill among linked people, the impacts at points of oil extraction, production, and transportation remain spatially and socially removed and invisible from the end-product consumer and even further removed from, and hidden by, the structural systems that promote it.

Efforts to engage (rather than to punish) the private sector on human rights abuses has led to "corporate human rights reporting," which has encouraged corporations to report on their own efforts, best practices, and successful policies rather than to reveal existing violations or abuses, which has led to a corporate "silence on known human rights controversies."[52] Perhaps even more problematic, the emphasis is on individual corporations at specific locations rather than extractive industries in general and the oil-industrial core in particular. The use of the terms *oil-industrial core* or *oil-industrial complex* is an attempt to take Faber's "polluter-industrial complex" and make it more specific to the oil industry for this particular work. It is also to broaden and globalize Michael Watts's "oil complex," which emphasizes national-level operations, laws, and communities.[53] The oil-industrial core or complex links local production to national policies to global capitalism to Northern consumption and globally mobile workers, while acknowledging that oil's power, wealth, and influence is held by a few global interests, who never experience the burden of the industry. To be sure, petroleum, a critical lubricant in the treadmill of production, is an important driver of the polluter-industrial complex and producer of extreme environmental and human suffering.

Too frequently, the extraction, transportation, production, and consumption of petroleum and oil-based products are sites of environmental injustices and environmental, community, and human rights violations. In one noteworthy case, the death of Ogoni activist Ken Saro-Wiwa at the hands of the Nigerian government in 1995 shifted relations between international activists and the oil industry and revealed the industry's influence in oppressive state decisions and actions. Saro-Wiwa had waged a long-running struggle against Shell Oil's operations in Nigeria, but garnered influential and international scrutiny and outrage after his hanging by the state. Saro-Wiwa's killing was not just one component in a local "cycle of protest,"[54] or owned only by his family, friends, and Nigeria. His death was a global event and trigger, owned and utilized collectively and globally by human rights and anti-oil campaigners. It is imaginable that multinationals with concern of their international images took note of the immediate risk to Shell's reputation, due to the oil company's action and inaction in Nigeria and an international perception of Shell's apathy toward Saro-Wiwa's death.[55] Indeed, such depictions of oil-induced conflict by international activists and the media represented an acknowledged "political risk" for multinationals, according to one.[56]

Despite a list of oil-related conflicts and disasters, political figures, the media, and the global public cultivate an abbreviated response to them. The first ones have a vested interest in doing so, the owners of the second may have, and the third is kept unable or unwilling to engage these issues.[57] Boycotts and anti-oil campaigns have followed this nonexhaustive list: the *Exxon Valdez* oil spill off the coast of Alaska in 1989; a lawsuit in the early 1990s due to Texaco's oil operations in the Ecuadorian Amazon; Shell's presence in Nigeria, which instigated Saro-Wiwa's hanging in 1995; Unocal's construction of a gas line in Myanmar in the late 1990s; development of the oil or tar sands in Alberta, Canada; the subsequent pipeline and refinery projects throughout the United States to accommodate Canadian tar sands in the first decade of the twenty-first century; and the 2010 BP Deepwater Horizon oil disaster in the Gulf of Mexico. These major disasters generated a broad response. However, these campaigns were relatively short-lived and narrowly confined compared to the ongoing, and depth of, oil extraction, contamination, and consumption worldwide. Northern, primarily American, consumers have been raised on petroleum and oil-based products and have been discouraged from demanding alternatives, while the major oil companies remain some of the world's most influential corporations. At this time, it appears as if the treadmill is too vast and too embedded to be altered by disaster, nearby or afar. Wind, solar, and ocean wave energy are less toxic alternatives with an unlimited supply, unlike fossil fuels with a lethal quality and finite quantity, but as of yet, they have been underemphasized, underfinanced, underpromoted, underresearched, and underdemanded.

THIRTY YEARS OF OIL WEALTH AND POVERTY IN ECUADOR

Mapping oil conflict remains critical as the oil industry, whether run by private or public companies, remains a formidable economic and political power,[58] while the benefits and burdens associated with oil production remain vastly uneven and unjust. In this case, Ecuador is just one contemporary example, among many, of oil injustice. Like other oil-dependent places, Ecuador is an oil-led, export-oriented economy that is paying its external debt on the backs of its communities and ecosystems. And even though Ecuador contributes little to worldwide oil production,[59] and is not commonly known as an oil exporter, oil has driven Ecuador's politics and its economy for more than thirty years.[60]

In Ecuador, oil exploration began in the 1920s; yet large reserves of commercial quality went undiscovered until 1967 when a Texaco-Gulf consortium found oil beneath the Amazon rainforest. Shortly thereafter, oil roads and airstrips began to crisscross the northern region of the Amazon, where oil is found, and Ecuadorian military and civilian leaders committed the country and its citizens to an oil-led economy. To facilitate this transition, Ecuador's first cross-country pipeline, the Sistema del Oleoducto Transnacional-Ecuatoriano or SOTE, was completed in 1972. The SOTE originated on the edge of the Amazon, cut west across the Andean mountains to terminate on the Pacific Coast for export by tanker.

The SOTE's construction was a nonevent, occurring outside of public attention, with limited public debate, in sparsely populated areas. It occurred at a time when oil discovery was celebrated by economic and political elites, who were committed publicly to the belief that oil discovery would catapult their underdeveloped nation into the First World and that it was the only viable means toward modernization and development. The oil-industrial order argued that roads and bridges, schools and health care facilities built with oil revenues created a nation materially improved from what it was before oil discovery. In private, these oil boosters may have identified oil as an avenue to securing their own wealth and power, though publicly they propagated the perspective of advancement and prosperity.

Though many in Ecuador and the world still hold to the idea that oil produces growth and development—economic, that is—with greater experience the most affected communities in the Amazon began to challenge the social, economic, and environmental ills linked to the industry. By the late 1980s, relations between the oil sector and affected communities in the Amazon became increasingly contentious and volatile. Indigenous communities were finding their voice (or the North was beginning to hear them), and one community after another began fighting the oil-industrial system. They have been doing so ever since.

For the most part, oil struggles in Ecuador had remained isolated to the Amazon region and to one site on the Pacific Coast where oil is refined. Then in 2000, the Ecuadorian government announced plans for the construction of a second trans-Ecuadorian pipeline, the Oleoducto de Crudos Pesados or OCP, to transport oil from the fields of production in the Amazon, across the Andes Mountains to the Pacific Coast for shipping.

With OCP's announcement, oil disputes flowed beyond Indigenous and non-Indigenous struggles in the Amazon,[61] and along the pipeline's route. Given at least a decade of oil clashes and community articulations of lopsided distributions of oil benefit and burden, oil became a national issue for the first time along the pipeline's right-of-way. Then, when the pipeline's owners (seven multinationals) and its European and American financiers were made known, OCP became an international concern, rather than a single, narrowly defined community campaign against a specific oil entity.

The purpose of my research was not to determine whether the OCP pipeline would be built; it was. The OCP was built in two quick years, between 2001 and 2003, delayed only briefly with minimal alterations. Nor was my purpose to determine whether the construction of this particular pipeline benefited or harmed the country of Ecuador. The point of my research was to better understand how a broad spectrum of communities along an extract-to-export flow line, or from input to output, mobilized to press their long-running or first-time claims against the state and the oil sector, and how their demands were adopted or discarded by potential international support networks. I selected four sites within Ecuador to examine how the embodied environments of communities and organizations generated divergent responses to oil within both national and global contexts.[62] In particular, this book reflects the mobilization efforts of Ecuadorian society in one community in the Amazon, two in the Andean mountain range, and one on the Pacific Coast. It also analyzes the two transnational campaigns that they inspired: one of opposition and one of negotiation. Some of the Ecuadorian communities had been responding to the oil industry for at least a decade, while others were mobilizing for the first time, having just discovered the oil industry with the privately owned OCP project.

Though much has already been written on Indigenous-oil conflicts at the points of production in the Ecuadorian Amazon,[63] this pipeline project enabled a broader and richer analysis of community and environmental conflicts beyond Indigenous disputes and beyond the tropical rainforest of the Amazon. The OCP pipeline connected the diversity and complexities of Ecuadorian society from the Amazon, to the Andes, and onto the Pacific Coast. Research on it was able to capture, at the community and organizational levels, the competing and unifying perceptions of oil impacts as well as the competing and overlapping avenues of resistance and redress.

When construction began, disputes centered broadly on whether the extraction of oil in Ecuador hurt or benefited the nation's thirteen million people, 12–45 percent of whom are Indigenous.[64] Indeed with the announcement of OCP, there was an explosion of local and nuanced microresponses by affected communities and nongovernmental organizations (NGOs) to the pipeline's construction, fueled or inspired, undoubtedly, by the determined and decade-long claims of oil injustices made by Indigenous communities and organizers. To be sure, Ecuadorian communities and NGOs were responding locally, nationally, and internationally to the oil-industrial order, which had been enabled or aggravated and certainly not ameliorated by national leaders.

Collectively, a range of communities and organizations along the pipeline's route mobilized across the environmental spectrum: for wildlife habitat conservation, healthy and sustainable ecosystems, and global environmental justice. Some called for the economic and human rights of the laboring poor, for greater degrees of transparency and accountability in state and corporate practices and policies, and for a role in monitoring the oil sector and in influencing state decisions. They also mobilized for pedestrian material gains, including electricity, paved roads, and employment, and landowners demanded greater environmental care on their property, and still others wanted conservation funds.

Oil confrontations in Ecuador are also noteworthy as they represent a microcosm of the thousands of small, yet significant, local uprisings around the world against global decisions imposed upon underrepresented people, whose domestic campaigns have gained international traction and have been supported by transnational advocates. At the domestic heart of many oil-related conflicts in Ecuador and elsewhere were multinationals and oil-dependent states exporting the wealth of local people and leaving behind contaminated and impoverished communities. Resistance to the OCP pipeline represented people, who were not only demanding local change but were calling for global inclusion—not only for themselves but for their state—in influencing global, ecological, political, and economic decisions. Their positions were grounded in a thirty-year legacy of oil-tainted underdevelopment and ecological maladies.

But they may not have represented the majority of people in Ecuador. At the time of OCP, Ecuadorian opinion was being pulled in two directions. On the one hand, oil continued to be touted by state leaders—and perhaps adopted or accepted by the majority of citizens—as being tied to Ecuador's economic stability and its ability to pay back its debt, which totaled approximately US$14 billion in 2001.[65] Ecuador's oil impasse between wealth and debt was not new when construction began; it began in the late 1970s when the military government "made endeudamiento agresivo [aggressive indebtedness] an official component of economic policy," a policy that increased the nation's debt sevenfold in five years.[66] Yet at the time of OCP, Ecuador's debt was "the highest per capita in Latin America, at $1,100 per person,"[67] which pressured the Ecuadorian government to announce a second pipeline to double production and export capacity in order to pay off some of its debt. Extrapolating from these figures, the oil-affected communities were sacrificing local economic security and environmental health for a national debt from which they had yet to profit.

At the same time, pressure for alternatives was growing among people who had been affected by the first pipeline and the subsequent development of oil facilities in the Amazon and on the coast or by established NGOs that formed in the late 1980s or 1990s after the completion of the country's first pipeline. After decades of oil export, the status quo of oil production was being challenged by informed and globally connected societies seeking energy alternatives, healthy environments, sustainable economies, and human and environmental rights guarantees alongside just local employment and community-directed compensation projects. Affected people and grassroots activists were challenging a singular commitment to the anticipated benefit of oil production, while advocating for economic diversification, economic and environmental sustainability, and a social commitment toward higher and more just social standards. They countered that the persistent poverty, poor health, and low educational attainment in the areas closest to the oil industry indicated that oil wealth remained in the hands of a few, with little consideration for the needs of the many.[68]

Much was at stake in these struggles. For the past thirty years, Ecuador had been administered, nationally and internationally, as an oil economy. Like other oil economies, oil was its main source of foreign exchange. The country's second largest source of foreign exchange, at the time of OCP's construction, came from remittances from Ecuadorians who worked as day laborers in the United States and Spain, while its second most important exported item,[69] other than its citizens, remained the banana. You could say that Northern consumers preferred Ecuador's oil and bananas over the rights and experiences of Ecuadorians.

Ecuador's economy was also a volatile one through the twentieth century, culminating in 1999 in an economic crisis not witnessed since the 1920s. Banks closed, private accounts were frozen, and some people lost the bulk of their life savings. A year later, the country canceled its sucre currency and adopted the U.S. dollar. Prices appeared to fall haphazardly, among people who had previously calculated 2,500 sucres per one U.S. dollar. Following the demise of the sucre, political columnist Paul Krugman wrote, "Ecuador, by contrast [to Asia], has always been more or less a mess; its plunging currency is only the outward sign of an inward disgrace."[70]

Added to the financial instability, the people were governed, or not so well governed, by seven presidents between 1997 and 2006.[71] In 1997, former president Abdalá Bucaram was ousted, less than a year after taking office, and went into exile in Panama. In the reshuffle, Bucaram was replaced by former vice president Rosalía Arteaga, who presided for three days, before being replaced by interim president Fabián Alarcón. Jamil Mahuad was then elected in 1998. However, Mahuad was ousted in 2000 through an Indigenous uprising and went into exile in the United States. Mahuad's vice president Gustavo Noboa survived a two-year presidency, during the pipeline's construction, and then to evade a trial on financial mismanagement after his brief presidency he moved to the Dominican Republic in 2003. Lucio Gutierrez, who became president in January 2003 in a popular election, was forced out in April 2005. He moved to Brazil, and was replaced by vice president Alfredo Palacio, who remained in office until January 2007, when Rafael Correa, the eighth president in ten years, won the 2006 election on an antipoverty platform that challenged the policies and practices of national elites and Northern bodies. Correa identified allies in Venezuela's Hugo Chávez and Bolivia's Evo Morales.

At the time of OCP's construction, Ecuador was an oil nation, dependent on its oil reserves to pay back its external debt,[72] and suffering from political irregularities and leadership that lacked the will or commitment to redistribute its oil revenues for the benefit of its laboring poor, especially those in the oil-impacted communities. Since oil discovery, no political leader in Ecuador had wavered from the country's commitment to oil, or challenged the country's reliance on it, while even the vast majority of Ecuadorians saw few benefits or substitutes. To this, the Ecuadorian case supports suggestions that environmental and economic justice demands are increasingly bound within a capitalistic, political system,[73] in this case a global one, where the majority of community activists and professional NGOs seek local, distributive change and political representation, rather than attempting to defeat a disabling and unequal system that in large part is supported by the general public. To be sure, the choice of tools to combat the oil-industrial complex was not determined by the most affected, those who were directly impacted where they "live, work and play,"[74] or even by those with international connections. They were left to choose tactics from within a model not of their own design and not designed for their own interests.

Social and Economic Endangerment

To contextualize Ecuador's resistance to the OCP pipeline, it is helpful to offer a brief assessment of the social, economic, and environmental ills either brought on by the presence of the oil industry or not alleviated by its presence. In the Global South in general, oil dependency has been called a "resource curse,"[75] a "paradox of plenty"[76] and a "curse of the black gold."[77] Oil-led development has spurred crises of poverty, inequality, and political turmoil due to a nation's debts, military expenditure, internal security, and wanton waste of its resource royalties.[78] Democracy has been impaired,[79] and state institutions have been kept weak to prevent challenges to an oil-managed economy.[80] Among the oil states of the Organization of the Petroleum Exporting Countries (OPEC),[81] demonstrated dependence on a single, extractable commodity has also fostered neglect of domestic linkages, neglect of agricultural production for local consumption, and neglect of non-oil export activities.[82] Oil is also just a subsurface substance, possessed by nature—until it is purchased by the private sector or spoken for by the state.

A reduction or stagnation in social indicators following oil discovery is not always experienced and may be determined by the absence or presence of state-led initiatives. For example, Jean Dréze and Amartya Sen identify how "growth-mediated" security emphasizes economic-first initiatives with the secondary intent that economic prosperity will filter down to greater social development. On the other hand, a "support-led" path, also identified by Dréze and Sen, shifts the state's available resources to social support systems, such as free and compulsory education and the availability of and access to quality health care facilities and health care professionals in both urban and rural areas.[83] Each strategy has the potential to build social services for girls and boys, women and men, in rural and urban areas. However, growth-mediated strategies often stagnate at the economic level and at the benefit of the local, and historically, elite class.

In Ecuador one could argue that a growth-mediated path had been endorsed since oil discovery in the late 1960's, though Ecuador has toiled under international pressure, trade regulations, and neoliberal policies that influence how its oil dollars are spent. The ruling military in Ecuador, which came online in 1972 with the country's first cross-country pipeline and was maintained until 1979, entered into an oil arrangement that provided arguably greater benefit to the military than to the majority of citizens. In 2000, for instance, one source claimed that the Ecuadorian military received 50 percent of the nation's 18.5 percent royalty share from private oil production,[84] though oil agreements are periodically renegotiated. Moreover and perhaps more importantly in the absence of technology transfers and investments in oil's forward and backward linkages, Ecuador was an exporter of crude and an importer of refined oil and oil-based processed goods.[85] At the time of OCP's construction, Ecuadorian companies, including the national oil company PetroEcuador, actually lacked the capacity and capital to build their own trans-Ecuadorian pipeline and to produce and refine sufficient quantities to meet domestic need. This point may shed light on Northern practices of withholding technology transfers and knowledge rather than limited Ecuadorian capacity or desire.

Despite three decades of oil extraction, the majority of Ecuadorian communities remained impoverished with minimal economic and social opportunities even in (or particularly in) the oil-rich and oil-important provinces. On the ground, these structural failings led to the employment of one million children under the age of seventeen, an unemployment rate of 14 percent, an underemployment rate of nearly 57 percent, a rise in rural poverty from 50 to 70 percent between 1999 and 2003, and an increase in urban poverty from 69.7 to 78.5 percent between 1997 and 1999.[86] Positive indicators reveal that a cohort reaching grade five rose from 40.3 percent in 1990 to 78 percent in 2001; under-five mortality dropped from 57 per 1,000 in 1990 to 32 per 1,000 in 2001; while access to improved water sources rose from 71 to 85 percent and access to improved sanitation rose from 70 to 86 percent between 1990 and 2001.[87] However, the average number of years of schooling for adults varied slightly from 5.9 years in 1985 to 6.4 years in 2001, while enrollment in secondary education was only 50 percent in 2001.[88]

That a nation rich in oil still sets educational goals of six years is a collective cruelty that gets buried in national and international oil propaganda. Limited educational provisions diminish the skills and capacities of Ecuador's future workforce, disabling citizens from securing employment even in oil, if desired, which is a skilled, technical industry that frequently imports a more skilled labor force. Nevertheless, neglect of social and economic considerations is just one factor in a maelstrom of oil- and Northern-piloted harms experienced by citizens of oil-producing places. Environmental damage and poor health outcomes are others.

Environmental and Health Hazards

Since oil production and transportation began, Ecuador has experienced societal and environmental degradations, particularly in the Amazon, where oil spills, persistent leaks, wastewater dumping in the extraction and refining processes, and gas flares, in which gas by-products are burned off into the air, have damaged neighboring ecosystems. In oil-producing places, sites of exploration, drilling, extraction, storage, transportation, pipeline routes, and facilities for refining and loading tankers have been demonstrated to lead to distinct oil exposures for workers, communities, and ecosystems.[89] This research inserts process-specific points of community conflict as well. Though less research has been conducted on the impacts of pipeline construction, during the building of the Trans-Alaska pipeline, environmental damage, conflicts over Native land claims, employment booms and busts, the rise of transient labor, and an influx of people overwhelming public services were identified.[90] These known impacts pointed to a host of potential controversies within Ecuador, which operated with the additional burdens of peripheral global status, onerous foreign debt, and absolute poverty.[91] It was a nation attempting to clear itself of its underdeveloped status by operating within a political and economic system that put it there in the first place.

In Ecuador, the government estimated that the aboveground SOTE pipeline, the country's first transnational pipeline, discharged 16.8 million gallons of oil between 1972 and 1990,[92] which would be more than the *Exxon Valdez* oil spill of 10.8 million gallons yet less than the scale of the BP Deepwater Horizon spill in the Gulf of Mexico. Acción Ecológica, an ecoactivist organization in the capital Quito, documented more than forty breaks and oil spills along SOTE between 1972 and 2001, due mostly to earthquakes and landslides.[93] Likewise, the newspaper *El Universo* reported that a PetroEcuador representative claimed that there were 129 spills in 2000, due mostly to pipe corrosion, which the newspaper interpreted as a spill once every few days in the Amazon.[94] Even greater discharges were believed to have occurred in the Amazon as Texaco, using inferior technology in the 1970s and 1980s, dumped wastewater by-products into unlined pits and waterways at a time when the industry was self-regulating in Ecuador.[95]

Years later, health research in Ecuador demonstrated that communities near oil facilities experienced higher rates of illness, due in part to the inadvertent inhalation, ingestion, or absorption of petroleum-based carcinogens, including benzene.[96] Communities residing near oil facilities in the Amazon experienced greater risk of cancer,[97] childhood leukemia[98] and spontaneous abortion,[99] while in another study, Miguel San Sebastian and colleagues found that the community's water source for drinking, bathing, cooking, and washing clothes yielded chronic and severe exposure to petroleum hydrocarbons, exceeding the European Community's regulation limits by 10 to 288 times. The same study presented an overall cancer risk among men 2.26 times higher than expected, and an overall excess of deaths due to cancer among men 3.6 times higher than expected.[100] In a geographically expanded study, Anna-Karin Hurtig and San Sebastian found significantly elevated cancer rates for both women and men.[101] Malnutrition due to oil spills is also a concern for the rural poor. In 1989, for example, a secondary pipeline broke along the Napo River at a time of severe flooding, carrying petroleum into crop fields in thirty-one communities,[102] demonstrating the vulnerability of food security among marginalized Ecuadorian communities. Moreover, in gathering data and interpreting findings, these studies fail to account for any synergistic effects, including how smoking and inhalation of petroleum hydrocarbons may increase incidence of lung cancer, or how malnutrition and oil exposure may exacerbate or quicken a child's illness or death. Each is aggravated by the region's poverty and isolation relative to the political and economic centers of the country, Quito and Guayaquil respectively.

In the Amazon, an oil-funded physician and a public clinic physician claimed in 2003 that the three most frequent complaints by their clients were respiratory problems, skin rashes, and diarrhea.[103] However, the oil-supported physician claimed that the dust levels, unsanitary living conditions, and unsanitary water systems were the main causes, while the public physician attributed these illnesses to oil exposure and by-product releases of the petroleum industry.[104] Both were probably correct. While the public physician pointed directly to the oil industry as cause, the oil-funded physician acknowledged indirectly how oil presence failed to alleviate the unequal distribution of economic security and absolute poverty and may even magnify both.

In addition to the associations between direct oil exposure and poor health, oil dependency has a history of leading indirectly to lower health status for citizens of oil-rich places. John Caldwell demonstrated, for instance, how non-oil-producing nations, albeit developing ones, achieve lower mortality rates than oil-producing ones due to the political will to allocate a larger percentage of their revenues to citizen health.[105] It was not the absolute allocation but the relative allocation of state resources to female education, health care, health care access, and nutrition that determined health status.[106] One cause for the disparity in spending was a larger share going to the military among the oil producers, which supported Vandana Shiva's assessment that states may increase their policing role of citizens to protect the economic interests of multinationals at the expense of the social and health-related needs of its citizens.[107]

While oil discovery linked Ecuador to the global marketplace, the industry's economic, environmental, social, and health impacts mimicked that of other extractive economies in what Dréze and Sen call "unaimed opulence,"[108] or a wasted prosperity in which state leaders squander socially the nation's oil wealth and resource opportunities. This embodiment of global injustice represents the denial of social, political, and economic opportunities, including the failure to guarantee basic human rights, economic security, a transferable education, and healthy bodies. Paul Farmer documents how these global injustices are acts of "structural violence," while Sen identifies them as leading to a life of "unfreedoms."[109] A person suffers not only due to socioeconomic status, gender, race, ethnicity, and his or her nation's global position, but also due to physical proximity to oil and his or her nation's place in the global supply and consumption of oil. Indeed, it is the "dissonance between the promises" of the oil industry and its localized realities and outcomes that generate conflict.[110]

To clarify, *oil injustice* as experienced in Ecuador and applicable to other oil-exposed places is the absence of community participation, deliberation, and decision making at each leg of the oil process, on how oil revenues are to be used locally, and on each impact deemed important to the community (including social conditions and services, economic opportunities and employment, environmental health and safeguards, and food and water securities). If state and elected officials cannot make decisions for the good of people and ecosystems, oil justice would call for the public to make those determinations. Oil injustice is also the persistent inequalities—without attempts at redress—in experience and exposure between consumers in unpolluted neighborhoods and workplaces and the residents and workers of oil-processing towns. The uneven distribution of oil wealth is another injustice given the extreme differences between the oil elites (including executives, shareholders, politicians, lobbyists, and those who receive monetary gain from the industry in the North and the South) and the oil poor, or those who reside near oil facilities without witnessing the benefits of that association. Too few benefit from the exploitation of the public resource, while too many are harmed by it, and those injustices have always been at the crux of the conflicts between communities, workers, and the oil companies, whether they are private or state owned.

Finally, oil injustice is the absence of political will among state leaders to enforce an end to oil dependencies by keeping fossil fuels in the ground and committing to the development of alternative energy sources that lead to the healing of oil-contaminated places, to healthy and respectable workplaces, and to nourished and nourishing communities. Like environmental justice, it is not a call to redistribute burden and toxins, it is a call to end the production of environmental toxins and oil burdens. Oil justice requires a genuine social commitment and the steady political will of states, communities, and organizations to end fossil fuel use and to shift toward energy technologies with much less impact (and no toxic exposure) on communities, workers, and environments. Until petroleum use is stopped, oil justice requires affected communities and workers to have a guaranteed role in influencing and monitoring industry actions and state oil revenue spending and in requiring a cessation of production until the most advanced safeguards are ensured and community-based contingency plans are in place worldwide. Even standard petroleum operations should be seen and monitored like a potential fire—which would require constant vigilance (internal and external), an immediate response (internal and external), and the right of anyone to make the first emergency call when a spill, a leak, a break, or a fume is detected, triggering a full-assault emergency response.

Oil injustice as experienced in Ecuador laid the foundation and context within which domestic groups and transnational advocates mobilized for community-driven environmental and global justice with regards to the Ecuadorian state, to Ecuador's inferior and peripheral global position, to the oil industry in general, and to the OCP pipeline in particular. In this way, the pipeline served as an opportunity for some to restate long-running demands against the state and for others to either seek the rewards of the industry or to confront it for the first time. Until oil justice is achieved, states and individual companies should expect to be challenged. The OCP pipeline represented a new point of conflict and an opportunity to make some headway for the affected.

CONCURRENT OIL CONFLICTS

When the OCP pipeline project was announced, the Ecuadorian Amazon had been undergoing continuous and persistent flare-ups between the residents, the oil companies, and the state since oil extraction began. Though this book is not about Indigenous-oil conflict,[111] lowland Indigenous people in the Amazon have been confronting and negotiating with the oil industry since the beginning. Yet this time, the Indigenous communities with territories overlapped by oil blocks and the established and politically influential Indigenous organizations in Ecuador remained silent on the construction of this trans-Ecuadorian pipeline. During OCP's construction, Indigenous groups were more likely to respond to specific multinationals within their specific territories, rather than to participate in a national struggle against oil.[112] Even so, Indigenous organizations are likely to continue mobilizing, as OCP's transportation quotas push exploration and extraction efforts deeper into the southern Amazon and into untapped Indigenous territories and protected rainforest reserves, including the Yasuní National Park.[113] Moreover, they were instrumental in demonstrating the right of affected people in Ecuador to contest the actions and inactions of petroleum operators and the state.

To wit, a brief description of three concurrent and Indigenous-oil disputes is useful in locating OCP contention within the longer struggle to shift power in deliberations toward affected people and to hold oil and state projects up to community scrutiny. These cases are depicted here to indicate the endurance of oil disputes in the Oriente, as the Ecuadorian Amazon is called, and to provide a backdrop to the challenges that the OCP consortium would confront.[114]

Sarayacu: Inspiring an Anti-Oil Generation

The Indigenous community of Sarayacu, a lowland Kichwa community,[115] had been resisting oil exploration in its territories and subsistence and hunting grounds since 1988, when Los Angeles–based Atlantic Richfield Company

(ARCO) first acquired exploration rights. Since then, this community's resistance has placed them in conflict with the state, oil multinationals, and even neighboring Kichwa communities, while putting them in favor with Indigenous, human rights, and anti-oil supporters in the United States and Europe. Due to their impressive and steady resistance, Sarayacu's Indigenous leaders had succeeded at the time of OCP in blocking oil extraction from several multinationals, including Argentina-based Companía General de Combustibles (CGC) in Block 10 and CGC and Houston-based Burlington Resources in Block 23.

The international breadth of the Sarayacu community—they had spoken in Washington D.C., New York, Argentina, and multiple locations in Europe—was indicative of a well-connected and nearly untouchable Indigenous nation within the state of Ecuador. Yet in December 2003, after the OCP's completion, Sarayacu's leaders were threatened, assaulted, and detained by other communities. A month later, the Sarayacu community declared its own state of emergency when the government threatened to militarize the area to force the search and flow of oil.[116] At this point, the United Nations, the Inter-American Commission on Human Rights (IACHR), the Confederation of Indigenous Nationalities of Ecuador (CONAIE) as well as numerous Indigenous and environmental organizations declared their solidarity with this community of approximately fifteen hundred. Then, the oil company CGC declared that it too could not support the government's militarization of the area, which reduced some tension in the area.

To an outside observer of Sarayacu demonstrations in Quito and Puyo,[117] it appeared as if a generation had been born under a sporadic state of siege, their predecessor's way of life repeatedly threatened by oil and state interests in their living and hunting territories and by oil-fueled conflict with neighboring communities. Yet due to this warlike experience, the Sarayacu community was one of Ecuador's most singular Indigenous communities in orchestrating international responses. Their national and global actions, wide-ranging international alliances, and ongoing strife with neighboring communities point to the complexity of oil disputes and oil-community relations in Ecuador. That this community elected not to support any of the affected communities along OCP's right-of-way was also indicative of how they may manipulate their global actions to serve their localized demands, rather than to build a steady and collective commitment to national change—a point that also indicates the obstacles to linking Native and non-Native EJ struggles worldwide.

Texaco Lawsuit: Thirty Thousand Strong

A second battle against the oil industry and affected people in the Amazon was being waged in U.S. and Ecuadorian courts before, during, and after OCP's construction.[118] In October 2003, when OCP went online, the court case between thirty thousand affected Indigenous and non-Indigenous people of the Amazon and Texaco, spanning ten years of appeals and six motions to dismiss,[119] from New York to the oil town of Lago Agrio, finally went to trial. On the edge of the Amazon, the case was tried in a simple, muggy courtroom of wooden benches and folding chairs.[120] The sparsely furnished room belied the landmark case. The packed presence of Indigenous and non-Indigenous people, New York lawyers, international media, and human rights activist Bianca Jagger, however, testified to the trial's historic importance. In this courtroom, this case marked the first time that a case filed by non-American plaintiffs against a U.S. corporation in the U.S. courts had been returned to the place of impact for a local court's decision.[121]

Ten years earlier, non-Indigenous settlers, or *campesinos*, and Indigenous communities charged Texaco with the systematic destruction of their land, leading to multiple environmental and health damages, a price tag lawyers said totaled US$1 billion.[122] The plaintiffs' lawyers presented Texaco's profits during this time as "unjust enrichment" in the act of dumping oil and toxic waste, a by-product of oil extraction, rather than reinjecting it, and substandard drilling practices while it operated in Ecuador between 1971 and 1992. The civil action suit alleged that Texaco engaged in careless negligence and a reckless disregard for Latin American and Indigenous communities by refusing to adhere to accepted practices for the cleanup and disposal of oil and wastewater. Lawyers for the plaintiffs charged that Texaco was dumping 4.3 million gallons of wastewater per day in unlined open pits, rivers, and estuaries of the Amazon, which leached into the groundwater and water bodies used for drinking and bathing. They were demanding the cleanup of approximately 350 waste pits, the installation of reinjection technology in the wells, economic compensation, medical monitoring, and medical assistance for those people adversely impacted by oil-related activities.

In a twist that is heavily disputed, Texaco agreed to pay the Ecuadorian government $40 million in 1995 for cleanup costs in exchange for exemption from further cleanup costs. From the media press reports, it appeared as if there had been no public accounting of the money's use. Currently, the former Texaco fields are owned and operated by PetroEcuador, the state's oil company. Oil spews on or just below the surface in these fields and oil ponds thick with the viscous fluid are scattered throughout the edge of the Amazon, which is easily accessed by road or on foot. It appeared that PetroEcuador had absolved itself of cleanup responsibility and appeared protected politically from public accountability.

In this case, Texaco argued that it complied with Ecuadorian law at the time. On the other side, the plaintiffs' lawyers argued that Texaco developed the oil industry in Ecuador, which implies that Texaco's influence on Ecuador's oil laws may have been self-serving. Industry influencing government regulations of industry practices is not uncommon anywhere in the world. Texaco launched Ecuador's oil economy at a time when the country had no previous oil experience, no knowledge of minimizing environmental or social impact, no familiarity of laws to govern or regulate the industry, and no technology to extract oil for itself. This lawsuit then demonstrated the capacity of Ecuadorian society, with critical international assistance, to organize and to hold a multinational accountable for environmental health injustices even after its exit from the country. In particular, this case demonstrated the fortitude of Frente de Defensa de la Amazonia, whose cofounder along with the organization's lawyer won a Goldman Environmental Prize of US$150,000 each for their long-running campaign against Texaco and oil pollution in the Amazon.[123] The case also demonstrated an industry's manipulation of state law to protect itself, and the state and PetroEcuador's disregard of fellow Ecuadorians. But these factors do not necessarily translate into a legal win for the affected people. In 2011, Chevron, which acquired Texaco in 2001, was ordered to pay almost $9 billion in damages, though the lawyers for the plaintiffs had asked for considerably more. At the same time, Chevron responded with an appeal as well as a civil lawsuit of its own against the plaintiffs' lawyers. In a U.S. court, Chevron charged the plaintiffs' lawyers and consultants with fraud under a racketeering act. For evidence, Chevron cited the lawyers' comments on unseen portions of the documentary *Crude*, which an American judge had required to be turned over as possible evidence.[124]

Achuar and Shuar Conflicts in Block 23 and 24

A third, ongoing conflict during OCP's construction existed between Achuar and Shuar communities in the southern Amazon region, whose territories corresponded to oil blocks 23 and 24.[125] Houston-based Burlington Resources took exploration rights of Block 24 from ARCO in 1999, and at the time of OCP's construction, it held a 50 percent share with Perenco, a U.K. and French oil company, which also had shares in OCP.[126] Block 23 is within the Kichwa Sarayacu territory as well, and during OCP's construction its exploration rights were owned in shares by Burlington, CGC, Perenco, and ChevronTexaco.

Since 1998, when ARCO was granted mineral rights to explore in Block 24, these Indigenous communities have successfully resisted oil extraction within their territories. For the most part, their rejection of oil resided in their awareness of the environmental, health, and social impacts on communities in the northern region of the Amazon, where oil extraction began in the 1970s and 1980s. In 1999, they succeeded in obtaining a provincial judge's court order, which was eventually ratified by the Supreme Court,[127] prohibiting oil companies from conversing or negotiating with individual community members, thereby requiring all oil negotiations to be with authorized leaders of the Indigenous organizations. More recently, Achuar and Shuar Indigenous leaders reiterated their commitment to suspend dialogue with Burlington.[128] However, with the second pipeline in operation the oil companies and state officials are increasingly adamant for access, and in light of this increased pressure, five Indigenous communities in the southern Amazonian region formed an alliance to reject new oil concessions and to terminate existing contacts in Blocks 23 and 24.

International ties with advocates in the United States also facilitated the attendance of Indigenous leaders at Burlington's annual shareholders meetings.[129] Due in part to international pressures, ethical investment companies, which invest in socially and environmentally responsible companies and advocate for social justice at shareholders meetings, filed a resolution in 2004 requesting that local consent be obtained and suggesting that Burlington's activities posed a financial risk to the company. In addition, the resolution, filed by Boston Common Asset Management and Interfaith Center on Corporate Responsibility, called for the company to adhere to international law,[130] which recognizes Indigenous rights worldwide.[131]

These three conflicts are presented here to situate OCP's construction within national and international contexts and to establish how pockets of Ecuadorian society had a decade-long history making claims against oil impacts to the state, to specific oil companies, and at international sites. Yet despite these ongoing struggles, Indigenous organizations chose not to mobilize in response to OCP.[132]

Research on OCP suggests that Indigenous organizations and communities in Ecuador formed only weak and sporadic ties with non-Indigenous organizations and environmental groups.[133] At their initiative, Indigenous organizations utilize environmental groups for resources and contacts or to enlarge a roster of complaints and/or to broaden their number of demonstrators. However the bonds appear weak and easily dissolved at Indigenous discretion. This anecdotal, case-specific assessment is both supported and challenged by the findings of others. While some agree that alliances between Indigenous and environmental organizations are particularly tenuous,[134] others argue that such alliances have developed and strengthened since the early 1990s.[135] Yet in the case of OCP and despite the presence or absence and strengths or weaknesses of these ties, Indigenous actions in the 1990s served as a model for how non-Indigenous communities and environmental organizations would seize opportunities, utilize existing North-South connections, and develop new international avenues to contest OCP's construction in particular and oil expansion in the Amazon in general.

A NATIONWIDE RESPONSE TO A SECOND PIPELINE

Into this milieu, the construction of OCP, a second, trans-Ecuadorian pipeline, became very much a contested issue among a number of communities and domestic groups, some of which had observed only from a distance oil-community conflicts in the Amazon. Yet despite more than two years of national and transnational resistance to the decision-making and construction processes, construction of the US$1.4 billion, multinational project began in August 2001 and was completed two years later. Delayed by only a few months, heavy crude flowed through this line from the Amazon to the Pacific Coast in September 2003.

Though political and oil elites had discussed a second pipeline for more than ten years, one was not announced until February 1997, when the Ecuadorian government called for private bids under a twenty-year concession.[136]

The successful completion of this pipeline was presented by state officials as an economic savior, while national expectations included increased revenues paid by the barrel,[137] an international image of completing megaprojects, an increase in private investment in the oil sector, and state ownership after twenty years of private operation. Perhaps most importantly, pipeline revenues were central to paying a debt that was amassed on the nation's oil reserves. To the International Monetary Fund (IMF), for example, the pipeline was presented as a tangible example of the country's commitment to increase privatization and an assured debt payment.[138] To clarify, the Ecuadorian Congress passed into law the manner in which state revenues from OCP would be distributed: 70 percent for debt payment, 20 percent for an oil fund for unforeseen events, including natural disasters or drops in oil prices, and 10 percent for social spending.[139] Not only would a second pipeline double the country's export capacity and separate heavy, lower-priced crude from the state-owned lighter, higher-priced oil; a second line would protect the continuous flow of oil if stoppage should occur on any one line, as had been the case in the past with SOTE's repeated breaks.[140]

Bid Selection and Route Disputes

Initially, in November 1999, the Ecuadorian government announced that U.S.-based Williams Brothers, which built SOTE in the early 1970s, would build a US$500–$600 million pipeline to run parallel to SOTE, except for one diversion farther south of the SOTE line.[141] As Williams is a nonproducer, its pipeline would be accessible to any oil producer in the Amazon. However, in July 2000, the government opened the bidding process. Three groups tendered proposals, including Williams Brothers. A second bid came from a consortium of oil-producing multinationals in the Amazon, which aligned with the Argentine constructor Techint to propose an alternative route with use based on ownership. This consortium's proposed route also paralleled SOTE, except for a hundred-kilometer-long deviation north of Quito, which passed through ecological reserves and near communities previously unaffected by the oil process. This departure would mobilize established environmental NGOs in the capital and grassroots ecologists in the nature-based tourism town of Mindo to protect Andean ecosystems along the deviation. A third bid was presented by the Ecuadorian Army Corps of Engineers in conjunction with a Brazilian constructor and Petrobras, Brazil's state oil company with interests in the Ecuadorian Amazon. The Army Corps proposed two routes, one to parallel SOTE and the other to run closer to Ecuador's northern border with Colombia.

Discrepancies in bids, route selections, and environmental and social impact assessments fueled grassroots activists and NGOs in the Andes, which favored Williams's original southern route over the OCP oil consortium's northern one, resembling "not in my backyard" or NIMBY activists rather than comprehensive oil resisters. In November 2000, the Ecuadorian government accepted the bids of both private lines, which would have meant three trans-

Ecuadorian pipelines in total, at which point Williams pulled out. In February 2001, the OCP consortium signed a contract with the government to construct and own the OCP pipeline, and in April 2001, OCP presented its environmental impact assessment (EIA) to the Ministry of Energy and Mines.[142]

The OCP pipeline is 503 kilometers long (approximately 312 miles) and passes through seven national parks and protected areas, including a World Bank Global Environment Facility (GEF) biodiversity reserve, over ninety-four seismic fault lines, and near six active volcanoes, affecting an estimated 450,000 people living along its route.[143] To operate, there are four pumping stations to heat the oil and to control volume and pressure, and two pressure reduction stations. At the production and input terminal in Lago Agrio, storage tanks hold up to 1,250,000 barrels, while additional tanks retain up to 3,750,000 barrels at the output terminal, south of Esmeraldas on the Pacific Coast.[144] The right-of-way varies from less than seven meters in ecologically sensitive zones (determined by input from grassroots ecologists and environmental NGOs) to thirty meters, with the average right-of-way approximately nine meters; and the pipeline's diameter ranges from twenty-four to thirty-six inches.[145] Nearly 36 percent of OCP's route lies within SOTE's right-of-way, while nearly 99 percent of the pipeline is buried approximately one meter below the surface,[146] except where it bridges crevasse walls.

OCP's carrying capacity is 450,000 barrels per day (bpd), though it carries quantities below its capacity. The aboveground SOTE, for example, with a capacity of 400,000 bpd carried approximately 260,000 bpd in 2003. An underinvestment in exploration and production in the private oil blocks due in part to a tax rebate conflict between the private companies and the state explains some of the expected shortage for the new pipeline.[147] Given the tax dispute, which began in 2001 and amounted to approximately $200 million in 2003, private companies were reluctant to invest further in the country, and a lack of investment today in these types of fields is still felt five years later, which is the approximate lag between testing and production. In addition, the blocks of PetroEcuador commonly operate below capacity due in part to a lack of resources to develop new fields.[148]

The selected OCP consortium comprised seven multinationals, including EnCana Corporation of Canada, Repsol-YPF of Spain, Pecom Energía of Argentina, Occidental Petroleum of the United States, ENI-Agip of Italy, Perenco of France and Britain, and Techint, the Argentine constructor.[149] See table 1.1. Over the course of the pipeline's announcement and construction, the consortium underwent multiple changes of ownership and leadership. During the two-year construction process, for example, the head of OCP Ltd. changed in August 2002 from Hernan Lara of Colombia to Andy Patterson of Canada to Bernard Tobar of Ecuador in April 2003. Inconsistencies in personnel and firms arguably impeded dialogue between the individual companies, OCP personnel, state officials, affected communities, and NGO representatives as each repeatedly had to adjust to the other.[150]

Table 1.1. OCP Partner Companies and Percent of Ownership

1999	2000	2001	2002	2003	%
City Investing[a] (Canada)	Alberta Energy (Canada)	Alberta	EnCana (Canada)	EnCana	31.4
YPF (Argentina)	Repsol-YPF (Spain) *Repsol bought YPF*	Repsol-YPF	Repsol-YPF	Repsol-YPF	25.6
		Perez Com (Argentina)	Pecom (Argentina) *Acquired Perez's interests*	PetroBras (Brazil)	15.0
Occidental (Oxy) (U.S.)	Oxy	Oxy	Oxy	Oxy	12.2
ARCO (U.S.)	Agip Corp (Italy) *Acquired ARCO's interests*	ENI-Agip (Italy)	ENI-Agip	ENI-Agip	7.5
Oryx Energy (U.S.)	Kerr-McGee (U.S.) *Merged with Oryx*	Kerr-McGee	Perenco (French/British) *Acquired Kerr-McGee's interests*	Perenco	4.0
Williams Brothers (U.S.) [Constructor]	Williams	Williams or Techint (Argentina)	Techint	Techint	4.1

[a]City Investing, Alberta Energy of Canada (AEC), and EnCana were Canadian oil entities undergoing name changes and/or acquisitions. In Ecuador, regardless of which company was officially operating, it was commonly known as AEC or City Investing. In 2005, EnCana sold its oil operations in Ecuador to a Chinese consortium.

Moreover, unlike other large-scale projects, which may be funded by development banks,[151] OCP was privately financed. The lead financier, Westdeutsche Landesbank (WestLB) of Germany,[152] formed a lending consortium of banks, insurance companies, and pension funds to finance US$900,000 of OCP's costs. The loan was guaranteed by the projected oil reserves in each company's oil blocks and a ship-or-pay risk reduction agreement, such that the oil companies guaranteed to pay a transportation share whether they shipped their designated allotment or not.

This mix of private oil companies and private financiers offered at least eight international sites for transnational resistance and negotiation, while simultaneously impeding a cohesive movement against a single target. Unlike the class action lawsuit against Texaco or Sarayacu's mobilization against ARCO and Burlington Resources, professional and community organizations along OCP's right-of-way were confronting an unknown, multifirm consortium with private financing that lacked national or international name recognition.

FOUR SITES OF CONTENTION

Through one oil project in Ecuador, this book explores how grassroots groups, NGOs, and activist mayors at four sites of conflict mobilized to pressure the state and oil multinationals to redefine the country's oil path and to call for a potentially deeper form of democracy—a global yet Southern-led ecological and participatory democracy—within an entrenched oil economy.[153] This case typifies global struggles today. The multinational face of the oil industry and its worldwide extraction of a natural and national resource provided a powerful leverage to force community contention into national and international arenas with the intent to improve local realities and daily experiences of the most affected people. To be sure, their demands and actions were more profound than the technical description of the pipeline, which is a favored discourse of corporations and states, and which has been presented here in brief.

When affected communities launched their campaigns against the pipeline project in 2001, then-president Gustavo Noboa declared that "four birdwatchers and a couple of mayors" would not derail the project. He roared, "I'm not going to let anyone screw with the country. I'll give them war."[154] The resistance was on.

This research, which began at the first point of conflict in 2001, is grounded in the responses of communities along OCP's route, including the "four birdwatchers and a couple of mayors"—as well as an oil community in the Amazon, the professional conservation NGOs in the capital, a tiny town attempting to sustain itself through nature-based tourism in the Andes, and a community of African descent on the coast.[155] In particular, the OCP pipeline originated in Lago Agrio (site 1), an oil town on the edge of the Amazon, twenty miles south of the Colombian border. It followed the SOTE route, passing the active Reventador volcano and numerous rural towns dotting the Quito to Lago Agrio road, which was built with the discovery of oil. It broke from SOTE's route to cross north of Quito, where the country's largest conservation NGOs are based (site 2), through deforested and arid land, then through Andean cloud forests, previously not impacted by oil. In the Andean mountains, the pipeline passed through the Mindo-Nambillo protected forest and near private ecotourism reserves, including the nature-based tourism community of Mindo (site 3). The pipeline descended the mountains to terminate on the Pacific Coast, south of Esmeraldas (site 4), a port town of Ecuadorians of African descent, and a community nearly voiceless in its poverty and at the bottom of a national hierarchy. See map 1.1.

This work is an attempt to capture the sentiments and voices of the domestic and international activists and organizations as they formed a position to the pipeline project, and as they navigated each other's stances and tactics on the project over time and across local, national, and international spaces. I treated each site as a field of contention, a conceptual reference that utilizes Raka Ray's use of place- and political-bounded fields, identified as "a structured, unequal, and socially constructed environment *within* which organizations are embedded and *to* which organizations and activists constantly respond."[156] Viewing communities, organized by grassroots groups and NGOs, as fields of internal and external contention revealed how the social and economic configurations of each site, relative to its location in the oil process, influenced a community's domestic and international networks. A comparison across domestic sites along a resource supply chain provided additional insight into how domestic groups select targets, press their demands, and market themselves (or not), and how Northern ones select among competing campaigns—not only across nations, but within them as well, even when holding constant the source of conflict.[157]

Each site selected for analysis was notable in its unique position in the extract-to-export supply chain, and its spatial and social configurations relative to the oil industry.[158] A community's location in the petrochemical process, including direct and residual effects of oil and a community's oil history, gave rise to site-specific struggles, alignment with local political structures, leverage over designated targets, and formulation of demands, while facilitating or lessening a community's degree of transnational interconnectedness. The site-specific disputes and impacts also point to the importance of inserting the voices, eyes, hearts, and minds of affected Southern communities in deliberating, determining, and monitoring any oil project in their communal backyards.

Each community case and the single case of OCP also represented "flows stories,"[159] or the accounts, experiences, and perceived realities of the "environmental flows" of the material product and the local, national, and transnational campaigns against it.[160] By employing Arthur Mol and Gert Spaargaren's environmental flow perspective,[161] this analysis overlaps the tangible flow of oil with the accompanying and intangible resistance and deliberation flows of four

Map 1.1. *This map shows Ecuador's two trans-Ecuadorian pipelines, SOTE and OCP, built in 1972 and 2003 respectively. The input terminals for both OCP and SOTE are in Lago Agrio, on the edge of the Amazon, where oil is extracted. The two pipelines then run parallel until nearing the Andean capital of Quito, at which point the newer OCP pipeline diverges north of Quito, passing Andean communities, including Mindo, which had no previous experience with the oil industry. After descending the Andean slope, OCP rejoins near SOTE's right-of-way to end at export terminals on the Pacific Coast, south of Esmeraldas. The communities investigated here include Lago Agrio, Quito, Mindo, and Esmeraldas. This map is not an exact replica of Ecuador and these two pipelines. It is a drawing to approximate the two routes and location of the adjacent communities. The initial outline of this drawing was provided by the editorial team of* Mobilization: An International Quarterly; *see Widener 2007a.*

communities in Ecuador, which were accompanied by advocacy flows among Northern supporters in Europe and North America. This research explores how spatial location in the petrochemical process, or along oil's extract-to-export "commodity chain,"[162] gives rise to process-specific impacts, perceived injustices, community actions, and community networks.[163] By examining the absence or presence, and the strengths and weaknesses, of transnational ties at these four different sites in Ecuador, this work demonstrates how challenges to eradicate poverty while ensuring healthy environments and mutually beneficial workplaces remain largely a domestic issue among oil-important communities in the Amazon and on the Pacific Coast (an old social movement classification), while environmental protection is transformed into a global concern for the benefit of conservation groups in the Andean region, which is more fitting of a new social movement.[164]

In other words, environmental empathy bested economic empathy in this case, tilting efforts, solutions, and resources toward conservation and nature-based tourism projects rather than the more strident calls for environmental justice or oil justice. Comparisons along this supply chain offer insights into how distinct historical impacts and experiences led to competing interpretations of and resistance to the pipeline project, while supporting or discouraging national and transnational collaboration. This comparison reveals competing reactions, demands, and tactics, which highlight the importance of discerning community distinctions in oil conflicts. Indeed this work pushes for a geographically broader and historically deeper examination of community-oil conflicts, beyond the site of production (perhaps the most visibly noxious site) and toward other areas in the production-to-consumption chain.

A comparison between fields of contention within Ecuador and of the presence or absence of each site's networks is also important in understanding how norms of conservation and environmental protection may compete with global justice and human rights concerns—nationally and globally, despite global rhetoric of supporting communities affected by an increasingly global marketplace that is increasingly not accountable to the people and nations most affected. In this case, global binds on the Ecuadorian experience, which was tethered to a global political economy and the oil-industrial core, constrained both national leaders as well as local communities. I have dedicated a chapter to each site, followed by an analysis of the transnational networks, followed by a postscript, which presents the post-OCP changes and tensions in the country and in the oil fields. Presented here are brief summaries of each chapter.

Lago Agrio: Community-Driven Oil Justice

Lago Agrio, which is presented in chapter 2, is an oil frontier town on the edge of the Amazon settled by non-Indigenous residents in the 1970s and 1980s. It is also the site of two oil-receiving terminals, one for OCP and one for SOTE. Yet despite an oil history and a base of oil workers, the people remained persistently impoverished and a reminder to many observers what oil-led development looks like when it goes awry. With OCP's construction as a launching point and the state as primary target, the activist mayor and a range of community members and organizations mobilized to demand greater participation in oil decisions and greater autonomy in oil revenue spending after thirty years of monetary outflow from their oil-producing province. Located at the site of production, this community also had extensive knowledge of and access to oil facilities dotting the Amazon. Community residents, landowners, farmers, social justice activists, and oil workers executed this expertise by staging strikes, closing roads, stopping production, and "taking" airports to force the state and oil consortium to meet their demands. Unlike other sites along the route, this community had only peripheral ties with national and international organizations, in part due to their internal capacity, place-bounded demands, and national target, the state.

To them, development was not the isolated and narrowly focused extraction of oil and foreign debt payments, or even a US$1.4 billion dollar pipeline. Development meant participation in establishing the course of the nation's economy and how oil monies would be spent. In essence, they argued that "participation" was not manual labor alone and that they had a right to inform national and international decisions, given the social, economic, and ecological burden that they endured while residing alongside the oil industry. Development encompassed the inspirational, including their engagement in deliberating on and regulating oil revenue spending and transparency among local, national, and international bodies.[165] But development also meant instrumental improvements in their daily lives, including the prosaic, such as improved roads, sanitation systems, and health care facilities. Development purported healthy bodies, an eradication of poverty, and training for skilled jobs in the oil fields as well as state support for economic and environmental alternatives. In their ongoing class struggle with the state for redistributive benefit, OCP served as an opportunity of warning that the community, organized through established grassroots groups, would continue to resist the state and demand oversight over the state's use of the region's oil royalties and/or rents.

Quito's NGOs: Realizing an Environmental Fund

In contrast to the oil hub of Lago Agrio, Quito, presented in chapter 3, represented the professional conservation NGOs based in the capital. Situated in the chilly Andean highlands not impacted directly by the pipeline project, these NGOs discovered the oil industry with the construction of OCP, and then organized to incorporate the pipeline project into their environmental protection and research agendas. Unlike the Lago Agrio community, these NGOs had limited and certainly no direct experience with the oil industry or access to the oil fields. However, through their international partners and their own international experiences, they had boardroom access to the oil multinationals and other international bodies. In brief, the conservation community first opposed OCP's route, yet then transitioned to a position of negotiation in order to navigate a multimillion-dollar environmental fund. In the process, they formed a transnational coalition of negotiation, silenced their own initial objections, achieved greater environmental care in one section of the route, inserted themselves into oil debates, gained first-time experience negotiating with each other and with oil companies, and lost community allies among several grassroots activists.

Mindo: Oil and Tourism May Mix

Mindo, the third site of analysis, was a nature-based tourism community of national and nonnational landowners, farmers, and tourism operators, also situated in the Andean mountains, northwest of the capital. Discussed in chapter 4, the grassroots ecologists and activist groups of the greater Mindo region launched an ecowarrior, antipipeline campaign that included tree camps and subsequent arrests, and generated an extensive transnational campaign of opposition to the pipeline. With no previous oil experience, they feared that soil erosion from the construction process would destroy the natural environment and their livelihoods and that landslides and volcanic activity would eventually break the pipeline and pollute local watersheds. They based much of their concern on the industry's tarnished reputation in the Amazon.

In comparison to others long the route, Mindo's activists presented themselves as holding the most *environmental currency*—the Andean region's cloud forests and unique biodiversity—and therefore most representative of an exemplary, anti-oil, save the cloud forest campaign in Ecuador. Mindo's activists also represented the national voice for small-scale, eco-economic initiatives. Ironically, the town itself—due to its opposition to OCP—became a national site of nature-based, oil-inspired tourism for a domestic middle class.[166] Indeed, both the Quito-based NGOs and Mindo's grassroots ecologists represented most soundly the conservation position of Ecuador. They were the environmentally employed, and their livelihoods were tied to conservation and nature-based tourism respectively, even though they undertook polar positions—one of negotiation and one of opposition—on the pipeline project.

Though Mindo's activists failed to reroute or block the pipeline's construction, in the long term they may have achieved a much more lasting accomplishment: to have their small businesses in nature-based tourism and their environmental ideals valued as an economic and ethical alternative to natural resource extraction. Indeed Mindo's national and international achievements were made in tandem with local efforts to convert resistant residents to increasing their awareness of low-impact and environmentally protective lifestyles and economic opportunities. When taken together, their efforts and achievements may have realized the country's first organic environmental generation.

Esmeraldas: Finding Dignity through OCP

Esmeraldas, an industrial port town on the Pacific Coast with more than thirty years of experience with the state-owned oil refining, storing, and tanker loading facilities, is the final community analyzed. Like the community of Lago Agrio, it too had extensive oil experience and access to sites critical to oil export as well as to the refining facilities for domestic consumption. Historically, its workers and residents had been nearly voiceless in their poverty and their minority status as Ecuadorians of African descent. This community, which was led by their first mayor of African descent and organized through existing social justice groups and labor organizations, confronted a legacy of economic and social inequalities and oil contamination experienced in large part due to state and oil indifference. Given a history of deep marginalization, this community's experiences resembled environmental justice struggles in the United States. They coalesced around their activist mayor and found dignity in direct, self-determined negotiations with OCP for immediate community benefit including much-needed public works and employment for the province's underemployed. In this case, the pipeline project functioned as an occasion for the mayor to rebuild the community's dignity and capacity to advance their living conditions and to determine fair compensation at their own discretion. Their site-specific history, demands, achievements, and isolation are presented in chapter 5. For a summary of each site, see table 1.2.

Between these sites, mobilization efforts were not concerted, nor did they need to be. In this case, there was a burst of responses to the pipeline's construction, including communities with diverse oil histories formulating multiple agendas against multiple targets. Their call for an equal and ecological voice was not bounded by national borders as is common in environmental justice struggles in the United States. Here, they were calling for local, national, and global representation and participation given the local impacts and burdens due to national and international decisions and benefits. Yet when comparing across cases, the communities most critical to the supply of oil and with greatest links to the global marketplace and proximity to oil facilities, the communities of Lago Agrio and Esmeraldas, failed to have their agendas lifted beyond the particular site of contention. Indeed, the affected communities most embedded in the global oil supply, at sites of production and exportation, were locally bounded and least integrated into global networks. In contrast, grassroots ecologists and environmental NGOs in regions of least oil impact and with limited oil experience, in this case Quito and Mindo, established greater transnational ties to support their research and conservation efforts and their environmental employment initiatives. Though communities directly affected by oil processes demanded global justice, or considerations that incorporated economic redistribution alongside healthy communities and ecosystems, their complex demands, long-running disputes with the state, and acceptance of extractive industries failed to achieve sustained resonance with international audiences.

As another point of comparison, the tactics of the two oil important cases, Lago Agrio and Esmeraldas, were more radical in confronting global discriminatory practices than the actions of international advocates, yet their calls for

Table 1.2. Overview of Four Sites of Contention

Site	Organizational Type	Location in the Oil Process	Oil Experience	Perceived Externalities of Oil	Distributive Struggles	Targeted Adversaries
LAGO AGRIO Amazon's Edge	Community-based Social Justice and Labor Groups, Landowners, Local Government	Production, Extraction, Storage, Input Terminal	Thirty Years of Embodiment	Soil, Water, and Air Contamination, Continued Poverty, Health and Economic Impacts	Redistribution of Oil Revenue for Community, Local Determination of Oil Revenue, Just Compensation, Employment	State, OCP
QUITO Andean Capital	Professional Environmental, Conservation, and Social Justice NGOs	Policy, Conservation, Research	Inexperienced	Environmental Impact, Habitat and Species Loss	Land, Species, and Habitat Protection, Lack of Participation and Transparency in Oil Decisions, Access to Oil Revenues	OCP, International Institutions
MINDO Andean Cloud Forest, Tourism Town	Small Businesses, Grassroots Ecologists, National and Nonnational Landowners	Overland Transportation	Inexperienced	Economic Impact on Tourism Businesses, Environmental Impact, Habitat and Species Loss	Economic Alternatives, Land, Species, and Habitat Protection, Lack of Participation and Transparency in Oil Decisions	International Institutions, OCP
ESMERALDAS Pacific Coast	Community-based Social Justice and Labor Groups, Landowners, Local Government	Export Terminal, Storage, Refining	Thirty Years of Embodiment	Water and Air Contamination, Continued Poverty, Health and Economic Impacts	Redistribution of Oil Revenue for Community, Local Determination of Oil Revenue, Just Compensation, Employment	State, OCP

solutions or compensation were more pragmatic than the underrealized, anti-oil rhetoric of some nonlocal actors and more moderate than the initial impetus for the environmental justice movement.[167] Moreover, their calls remained domestic articulations, rather than global realizations. In contrast, international audiences welcomed and received calls for wildlife habitat and nature-based tourism protections, emanating from the Andean communities. This research would suggest that calls for global environmental justice arising from the Global South may not be responded to by the North until voiced with a Northern accent, and in this case it was not spoken loud enough or heard clearly enough.

Transnational Responses: Evidence for a Southern-Led Global Democracy

Chapter 6 shifts from a domestic analysis to a transnational one and finds that transnational advocates may provide important material and morale-boosting services, while also emphasizing Northern concerns and entities at the expense of local and Southern ones.[168] In this case, the contributions of transnational collaboration were mitigated by domestic burdens, even though individual transnational advocates held personal and professional commitments to global justice and a global democracy. Northern advocates unintentionally emphasized environmental concerns over calls for dignity in life, global justice, and global inclusion arising in the oil-important communities.

National and international NGOs parried Ecuador's oil conflict by struggle selection and by contrasting picturesque and polluted icons. In this case, environmental groups in Ecuador experienced the scaling up from the local to the global of their conservation concerns, while the environmental justice and economic rights claims of the oil-important communities failed to make a similar transition. It reveals, unexpectedly perhaps, that place-based oil conflicts may vary inversely in their integration within the global supply chain and within global networks. Lago Agrio and Esmeraldas, which were linked to global oil markets and of critical importance to Ecuador's production and exportation of oil, were locally bounded and least incorporated in transnational networks at the time of OCP's construction. In contrast, the environmental communities of Quito and Mindo, which were of nominal value to the production and/or transportation of oil and which were removed from oil-related environmental and health burden, established denser international ties and experienced the scaling up of their conservation and environmental concerns from the local to the international. Elsewhere I have referred to this as an *economic empathy gap* among international advocates and audiences, which facilitates a Northern-centric oil order. But more importantly, this chapter's analysis calls for informed communities and citizens to have the right, responsibility, and privilege to be able to accept, monitor, and reject any potentially toxic activity where they live, study, work, and play.

Post-OCP: Governing and Contesting Correa and China's Oil Operations

After OCP's construction, the oil fields and Ecuador's political system remained as turbulent as they had been before the project, and community-oil conflict remained as tense even though new faces occupied the oil blocks and state house. The final chapter advances how the OCP project was never just about a single oil pipeline. Globally, it represented the tremendous hurdles—girded by the political economy and regardless of political persuasion—that communities face to resist oil projects and the inherent realized and perceived disasters in the operating system. A few of the recent and high-profile disasters or conflicts include the BP oil explosion and spill in the Gulf of Mexico, Nigeria's prolonged human rights violations linked to the oil industry, the Burmese government's blatant disregard of communities along pipeline routes and oil fields, and the sinking of the *Prestige* tanker off the coast of Spain. Many more oil conflicts and disasters occur worldwide in the absence of international attention.

In Ecuador, Rafael Correa's election in late 2006 initiated a leftist shift in Ecuadorian politics. Correa's administration favored preferential treatment of state-owned oil companies, greater oversight of Northern oil entities, direct challenges to neoliberal influences as well as an escalation of state authority over oil contracts and revenue redistribution schemes. Yet the election of a socialist leader also pointed to the similarities of ecological and community impact between oil-led capitalism advocated by private multinationals and oil-fueled socialism governed by the state and enabled by state-run oil companies worldwide.

In addition, three of the seven members of the consortium sold or were forced to leave their Ecuadorian operations. A Chinese consortium purchased the holdings of the Canadian company, while the state took possession of the operations of the American and French companies. On China's presence in particular, the absence of independent Chinese activists, independent environmental NGOs, independent human rights scholars, and independent journalists to inform, monitor, and question Chinese oil operators and to support affected communities is a striking chasm. Consequently, the insertion of Chinese oil companies and state-owned oil operators in the Amazon is a test case for Ecuador's NGOs and communities to challenge a company's practices regardless of its place of origin and without the influence of Northern networks.

Each transition—whether toward a leftist government or Asian oil operators—reveals how ecological compensation or community agreements from a few receptive multinationals are short-term and impermanent endeavors. Moreover, each transition and the inherent potential of damages of the industry reaffirm the critical role of state leaders and state agencies to regulate all oil operators, including their own, at all stages of operation, to endorse and enforce equal economic opportunities and environmental justice for all citizens, and to push international bodies to do the same for global societies and ecosystems. Each transition also points to the even more crucial role of individuals, communities, and NGOs in governing political leaders to elevate people over oil.

OVERVIEW: AN EXACTING SOCIETY

Each community tells a unique story along the right-of-way. Together, they demanded bottom-up participation in the country's oil economy, which was critical to the transnational campaigns of negotiation and opposition. Local mobilization along the pipeline was indicative of a robust and engaged civil society, advancing in their efforts to hold the state and the oil industry accountable to an increasingly vocal and exacting public. A critical outcome of challenges to OCP was the emergence and engagement of a diverse contingent of civil society, at times alongside like-minded, local government officials, contesting the policies, actions, and inactions of the state, the oil industry, and international bodies. Indeed, the arrival of OCP represented a sharpening of democratic demand and environmental justice at local sites of contention, whether through transnational engagement, direct negotiations with the oil multinationals, or street-level conflict with state authorities. The state in this case is likely to continue to face constant challenges to its authority until it responds to community demands for community-driven oil justice in the oil-important, but underprivileged, provinces.

Global places of political and economic power are also likely to face constant challenges until a shared lifestyle is achieved within and between nations. That is, until communities of both the Global South and the Global North live and work in dignity, justice, and security without one group living in greater comfort due to the unequal use of the world's finite natural resources. This was the truly transnational commitment being asked by many of the Global South, but not so easily heard in the North. And because it had not been addressed previously, despite resounding articulations, another political, ecological, and economic dispute arose in Ecuador with the OCP project. Such struggles will continue to arise in Ecuador and worldwide until a people-centered and eco-centered global democracy is achieved and until global dependencies on oil and toxic petrochemicals are ended. The social catastrophe is that for some communities oil injustice is currently a way of life: they are born into it, they give birth in the middle of it, and they die a part of it.

2

Lago Agrio

Community-Driven Oil Justice

Lago Agrio is an oil frontier town on the edge of the Amazon, and the site of two oil-receiving terminals, one for OCP and one for SOTE, Ecuador's first cross-country pipeline. Lago Agrio's non-Indigenous residents settled the area alongside the oil industry; yet the oil-producing region has remained persistently impoverished relative to Quito, the Andean capital, and Guayaquil, Ecuador's coastal economic hub. With OCP's construction as a launching point and the state as primary target, the activist mayor and a diverse network of community members mobilized to demand greater participation in oil-siting decisions, greater autonomy in resource use and distribution, greater degrees of respect from the oil industry and the state, and greater tangible improvements to their daily lives. After thirty years of monetary outflow from their province, they were calling for a more just position in the country's economic hierarchy as well as among the oil operators in the Amazon. Located at the site of production, this community had extensive knowledge of and access to neighboring oil blocks and facilities; and they executed their expertise by staging strikes, closing roads, stopping production, and "taking" airports to force the state and the oil sector to meet some of their demands. However, unlike other sites along the route, this community had only peripheral ties with national and international organizations, in part due to their internal capacity, place-bounded demands, ties to the oil industry, and selection of a national target, the state.

This chapter speaks to "the struggle for ecological democracy," political participation, and locally determined development in a time of globalization, global inequality, and the endurance of poor communities in oil-rich economies.[1] Globalization, or the global integration of economies, people, and politics and the speed and ease of moving people and ideas, products and capital across time and space, is not only "enhancing our productive capacity" and "communication potential," as argued by globalization experts, but it is also "disfranchising societies" through loss of control and representation.[2] Indeed, the community of Lago Agrio embodies the opportunities and obstacles, and the sense of empowerment and disempowerment, linked to globalization and the global oil supply. Globalization, for instance, enables the expansion of extractive industries, alongside state policing of citizens to protect industry interests.[3] Simultaneously, globalization enables transnational networks to monitor the actions and inactions of states and international entities, while facilitating affected communities to press for greater degrees of local participation and discretion.

To counter the domination of national elites and international interests in local and global politics and to challenge the ill effects of globalization, Leonardo Avritzer suggests that civil society will begin to demand from the state and to build democratic "participatory publics," or public space for community deliberation and for community-guided decision making.[4] Jurgen Habermas's concept of "communicative action," or agreement in action and thought through dialogue,[5] would be a possible outcome of public forums for communities to address their economic insecurity, their political and social underdevelopment, and the environmental injustice that they experience daily. If realized, formerly disadvantaged and silenced communities would be creating and practicing forms of egalitarian democratization with the overall objective of improving community well-being. Though the theory of community-directed governance is well established, its realization is far from substantial in most marginalized places—especially perhaps in places with ties to the global oil supply.

Similarly, Guillermo O'Donnell and Philippe Schmitter frame the resurrection of civil society following authoritarian rule as a "recovery of personal dignity" through the "explosion of grass-roots movement" from the "layers of a reemergent society."[6] Though the formation of these new organizations were argued to be weak initially and assisted by outside groups, "they are numerous" and "their internal processes are quite often highly participatory and egalitarian."[7]

Community-based oil demands in oil-committed democracies may call for a recovery as well. In this case, state-oil collusion on the pipeline project represented an indignity to the people of the Amazon. It represented not just a personal humiliation, but a lack of community esteem and community respect. As will be heard from the voices of the affected, the right to a life lived in dignity was one of the community's more universal of demands.

Antonio Gramsci identifies how hegemony, or the "ideological subordination of the working class," is exercised to control the subordinated through consent, supported by minisacrifices or concessions of the dominant (national) class. As the argument claims, the state acts continuously to balance the differences between the subordinate and dominant classes, while continuously favoring the dominant group,[8] and justifying and maintaining the elite class's position.[9] The dominant group and the state act together to develop and maintain consent of the subordinate class, though Gramsci argues that the state will step in when the activities of the dominant class suppress too strenuously and too evidently the subordinate class. The state swings between reproducing inequality and enforcing policies to reduce those same inequalities.[10] As seen from a better light, an economically robust state may enter a state of "embedded autonomy," as argued by Peter Evans, in which the state has dense ties and a strong degree of cooperation with the economic elite, while, and if maintained by skilled and educated technocrats, it is also capable of making decisions independent of elite interests and for the well-being of non-elites.[11] In this position, the state is capable of directing capital, along with punishing it if necessary.

At the national level, South Korea and Taiwan speak to a state's successful balance for a population's social and economic development. At the community level, there have also been important examples of community-led decision making in marginalized places on which to model future achievements. In Brazil, the community of Port Alegre, in a collective effort of empowerment, formulated participatory budgeting governance for positive community outcome.[12] By controlling the decisions and direction of public funds, the community was able to redistribute state resources for community-determined needs. Indeed, Gianpaolo Baiocchi's study indicates that the participatory budgeting effort operated like a "school of deliberative democracy," in which the participants learned over time how to govern for more equitable results.[13] In another case, a Hispanos community of sheep farmers and weavers in northern New Mexico achieved sustainable development, community-generated labor opportunities, and "workplace democracy"—*only after* challenging mainstream environmentalists and government agencies.[14] In Kerala, India, state-labor synergy provided greater redistribution of social goods and services, gained through a reduction in labor militancy and a willingness to compromise, which resulted in citizen-driven social and democratic development.[15]

Though not specific to environmental considerations, these examples are informative of the importance of locally driven democratization and grassroots mobilization, in the absence or presence of state collaboration, for environmental, social, and economic gains. The popular sector, with whom environmental justice advocates clamor and consort, are people clustered in communities or associations, demanding a full participatory democracy as a means to other goals: to clean, improve, and make just the places that matter the most to them—their places of home, work, community, and surrounding environment.

Communities and organizations, which are willing to mobilize in order to control their own economic security and social development and to resist unsustainable resource use and environmental contamination, do exist. In an assessment on development, Richard Peet and Elaine Hartwick argue that "the dignity of the poor lies not in accepting their lot, learning to live simply with the constant possibility of death, but in the possibility too of life and resistance, silently or openly, locally and regionally, particularly and universally."[16] Linking political and economic experiences and inequalities, Peet and Hartwick support grassroots arguments for a democratic form of development, unencumbered and uncorrupted by the existing capitalist system. The faults of the capitalist system have been aggravated by globally competitive industries, while global communications have exposed its insults to a wider audience than in the past.

Charles Tilly approaches development by outlining the durability of inequalities, which are actively and collectively reproduced and maintained, and grounded in social dynamics in which resources for betterment are denied or hoarded by the elite at the expense of the less-than-elite class.[17] Ideally, social movements serve to challenge these inequalities, and may direct, guide, and monitor the state in a deliberative fashion so that the state responds to and implements the public's mandates.[18] A link between development and environmental justice was made, perhaps unknowingly, by Amartya Sen, who proposes a perspective on "development as freedom," or development (and justice) through the availability and capture of political, social, and economic choices and capabilities.[19] Limiting an individual's (or community's) choices, due to his or her lowly position in the local, national, or global social scale, is to ensure unfree and underdeveloped individuals (and communities). Freedoms enable development, and the intentional deprivation of choices and capabilities, or a life of "unfreedoms," of some imposed by others, hinders it.[20] Some communities within most nations are underdeveloped in some freedoms. "Unfreedoms," in Sen's use, are intrinsic to both individuals and collectives, such as the marginalized due to gender, race or ethnicity, locality, education, or income. Indeed, the empowerment and seizure of capabilities by subjugated groups will be achieved through collective endeavors, including campaigns against global environmental injustices.

In environmental management and protection, Fred Buttel and Dara O'Rourke argue that an engaged civil society pressuring and monitoring the state is the most effective route toward environmental reform.[21] Furthering the state's role in Latin America, it was found that governments will not take strong measures to decrease natural resource depletion unless pressured, and that environmental protection was successful only when endorsed and legitimized by government.[22] In addition, the Latin American state plays the lead role in road building, financing deforestation, and creating incentives for industries that deforest; therefore, the state's engagement on these trends, in order to reverse them, is essential.[23]

From this brief overview of some of the literature on the role of, and dynamics between, civil society and the state, it becomes apparent that community organizations are increasingly the agent that defines, or redefines in some cases, justice and democracy, and that pressures the state to acquiesce to society's decision-making capacities and role in governance, including control over community and natural resources. Such communities and community-based organizations need to be supported, and clearly not weakened by other national and transnational actors, including corporations, financiers, NGOs, and activists. To weaken them would be a contributing factor of oil injustice.

Societal place, geographical location, and the process of globalization, which risks magnifying global injustice and reducing relative choices and capabilities, are embodied in the people and communities most affected by the global supply of oil. In this case, the Lago Agrio struggle against the OCP pipeline project is but one campaign in the larger and longer-running anti-oil, antiglobalization, and increasingly, alternative energy movements. Inserted in a much more historical movement dominated by Indigenous communities in Amazon, this one also contributed to the "cycle of protest,"[24] or to the renewal of efforts, to confront oil and state practices and to seek greater local autonomy over the region's resources, including its oil profits. Though this analysis is not trying to reduce all protest actions to a single demand for greater participation, community challenges to OCP represent an advancing call to deepen local democracy by placing the development path of developing places into the hands of the affected communities. Community-driven demands from within extractive economies are a call for greater oil benefits by the people most affected in the deliverance of oil products to some and oil wealth to others.

Moreover, geography and location matter in these struggles.[25] Oil is found in the Amazon; communities of the Amazon are subordinated to the urban centers of Ecuador; and Ecuador is a budding semiperipheral nation in the world system. Spatial and temporal location along oil's supply chain give rise to site- and process-specific exposures and injustices, points of leverage, as well as potential solidarity campaigns. Lago Agrio's critical and visceral role in the global oil supply would seem to facilitate dense national and transnational anti-oil alliances. Yet its locally bounded and more importantly its locally owned demands, including equal voice and equal dignity, may dominate, inhibiting such ties.

SETTING: AN OIL FRONTIER

When the pipeline project began in 2001, Lago Agrio was a scrappy, muggy, oil town, with a notorious edge. On its outskirts, a billboard boasted in Texas-ese: "This Is Oil Country." Indeed, the Lago Agrio airport was testament to oil dominance—a living, breathing promotion of the petrochemical industry. Men wore company shirts and hats much like athletes and cheerleaders wear their school colors. However, on the backs of these men's T-shirts were the quantified details of their working lives: number of wells built, footage of wells built, and number of days to build.

This town of approximately thirty-five thousand was also known for its crime, assassinations, and a Colombian influence, including traders, refugees, and traffickers of arms and drugs.[26] The Colombian presence had been ignited in part by the U.S. Plan Colombia campaign to eradicate the production of coca leaves, which also forced farmers and Indigenous people from their land.[27] On the Ecuadorian side, Plan Colombia incited local anger at the state's inability to control border flows and the state's militarization of their communities, especially in Lago Agrio and Coca, the country's two most important oil-producing towns.[28] The military's presence was in anticipation of conflict along the Colombian border,[29] but their presence also heightened local resentment against an ineffective state and worsened antiforeign sentiment in this volatile region. At the time, the Ecuadorian military jogged down the main avenue at dawn, while the local police patrolled the streets dressed in urban fatigues of gray and black, rifles hung across their chests or shoulders. In the evenings, oil men, the Ecuadorian police or military, and Colombians gathered in segregated clusters at the outdoor cafés. Shoeshine boys stood quietly, reverently, at the men's tables, eating the men's discarded appetizers of popcorn and salted plantain or yucca chips, while the men drank warm Pilsener, an Ecuadorian beer. Young women dressed in bright skintight clothing whistled at these moneyed men.[30] The bars, such as Little Mermaid with wooden, swinging doors, were more reminiscent of oil towns in Texas in the early half of the twentieth century or Southeast Asian towns during the Vietnam conflict era than an Andean-Amazonian nation. It is not my intent to sensationalize the sex worker industry in oil towns and minimize the contributions of the other women.[31] Lago Agrio *is* a complete town. Women work as mothers and daughters, teachers and farmers, nurses and activists, market vendors and small shop owners. But the sex worker industry is an unjust and gendered repercussion of the presence of oil and requires acknowledgment.

If Lago Agrio resembled oil or conflict towns around the world, the rural towns outside of Lago Agrio embodied the frustration and provocation that exists when the truly local resides adjacent to the unmistakably global. After thirty years of oil work, rural communities in the Amazon watched globalization-in-practice from their doorways. Oil compounds were lit twenty-four hours a day, offering nonlocal meals and imported uniforms and equipment, while housing imported men. Nearby, the merely local still waited for telephone lines, electricity, and secured employment.

Questioning Oil-Led Development

Comparing Texan and Amazonian oil towns is an exercise in understanding oil-led development and the subsequent mix of pitfalls and profits. Indeed, Texan oil towns in the early twentieth century depict well the principal town and municipality of Sucumbios Province at the turn of the twenty-first century. A Texan comparison is also apt as Lago Agrio is said to have been named after Sour Lake, Texas, where Texas Company's, or Texaco's, third oil well was drilled in 1903.[32] More than sixty years after Sour Lake's discovery, the Texaco-Gulf consortium discovered oil in the Ecuadorian Amazon in 1967,[33] launching the South American agricultural country into a full-blown oil economy.

Back in Texas during Prohibition, Texan oil towns were described as rife with moonshine, honky-tonks, gambling halls, and brothels. Writing his memoirs as an oil worker in Texas in the late 1920s, Gerald Lynch describes presciently the Lago Agrio ambiance of today. The men had limited formal education, but worked long hours for good pay relative to their education and relative to the time and place, and therefore "counted themselves lucky."[34] In 2004, when an Ecuadorian community leader was asked why laborers in the Amazon asked for oil employment and why workers came from outside of the region seeking employment, he asserted, "Because oil is the best pay in the country."[35]

Of course, there were differences. In Texas in the late 1920s, workers were men from the region, not a volatile mix of national and nonnational workers, separated by culture, skill, education, and earnings. Individual property owners in Texas also became wealthy when oil was discovered, by leasing land or mineral rights to small oil companies; and by 1940 there were more than thirty-five hundred small and large oil operators.[36] In contrast, subsurface mineral rights are owned by the Ecuadorian state and only a handful of large multinationals and PetroEcuador, the state-owned company, own production rights, which consolidates oil prosperity among a few politicians, local elites, and oil multinationals.

In addition, Texas established the Permanent University Fund, which endowed the University of Texas a one-eighth royalty at that time on one oil find or field.[37] Then again, and at the same time in another budding Texas oil town, there were only six teachers for 150 primary and secondary students.[38] In these promising oil communities, schools followed in need after sewage, garbage disposal, wastewater management, and paved roads—much like Lago Agrio nearly a century later and despite decades of oil works. In Lago Agrio, the children of the national and nonnational, technical and skilled oil workers were also more likely to live and study outside of the country, or in Ecuador's urban centers, than they were to remain near Lago Agrio. Their absence further eroded the political will and social obligation of national leaders to serve the town's residents. Subsequently, the state's reluctance permitted the oil sector to fill in the gaps as they saw fit for promotional purposes. For instance, an oil spokesperson in the northern Amazon touted his company's educational commitment to paying the salaries of two secondary teachers, approximately $100 each per month.[39]

The state provided so little of its oil wealth to the oil-producing region that when an oil company paid a teacher's salary, it appeared to be a windfall, an act of benevolence. At least, this marginal contribution provided the children of the area one more teacher than they would have had otherwise. "Private companies were implicitly or explicitly charged with providing for the local population," wrote two social and human rights organizers when identifying a historical pattern of limited state resources for communities in the Amazon.[40] Left unasked in the initial gratitude in this particular case was why teachers were making $100 a month in the oil-rich region, and why the state was still paying for fewer teachers than the population needed.[41]

Almost a hundred years earlier on the labor side in Texas, there were periodic labor shortages for skilled and unskilled workers, which presented the men a window of opportunity to strike for better wages and better working and living conditions.[42] In contrast in more recent times in Ecuador, there was a shortage of employment opportunities at just wages for local men and women, who were mostly undereducated and underqualified for petroleum jobs.[43] Given the lopsided skill development in the rural reaches of Ecuador, and the absence of skill and technology transfers, oil multinationals typically hired nonlocal oil teams for short stints and skilled labor or technicians from the cities for permanent work.

An additional North-South resemblance is provided by William Freudenburg and Robert Gramling's analysis of oil perception in Louisiana.[44] Freudenburg and Gramling find that the people of southern Louisiana were receptive and oriented toward extraction of the natural environment. Even after the BP Deepwater Horizon disaster in 2010, Louisiana's oil workers and elected officials pushed to end offshore oil moratoriums.[45] Freudenburg and Gramling's analysis also presents the residents of Louisiana as having favorable contact experience with oil personnel. On the one hand, their assessment is similar to the greater Lago Agrio region where the people were amenable to the extraction of local resources. They hunted; they logged; they farmed. The land and the wildlife were their livelihoods. However in the Amazon, the extraction of a subsurface national and natural resource provided too few jobs for local people and impaired too extensively the local environment, while the very foreignness of the oil industry marked it further for attack and recriminations.

The American-Amazonian parallels—separated by a century—end with the divisions between national and nonnational, local and nonlocal distinctions. In this case, Lago Agrio residents had begun to reject the continued inequitable exchanges: exported oil wealth for imported environmental contamination, elevated human health risks, death of domestic farm animals due to oil exposure, communal disruption, and unrelenting residential poverty. Due to these persistent disparities, tension escalated and erupted on occasion in the border region of Ecuador and Colombia. In September 1999 for example, eight oil workers, including seven Canadians and one American, were taken hostage, and held in the jungle near the Colombian border for one hundred days.[46] A year later, in October 2000, ten foreign oil workers were kidnapped, one of whom was murdered. When he was found, a sheet covering him read, "I am a gringo. For nonpayment of ransom."[47] A few years later, I witnessed a foreign oil executive being driven commando-style, in a four-door, flatbed truck; the backseat overflowed with guards, wearing black fatigues, bulletproof vests, and machine guns across their chests.

The contrasts were unsettling. On the one hand, in 2003 a billboard outside of an oil guard post read: "Our commitment is to the environment and safety of the people working for us." On the other hand, the level of security near the oil facilities resembled a lockout. That is, most people were barred from entry. In this atmosphere, oil compounds mirror an economic enclave or an oil colony within a sovereign nation, with the multinationals appearing to be foreign occupiers, rather than neighbors. Ike Okonta and Oronto Douglas make a similar comparison of oil experiences in Nigeria, questioning whether transnational oil represented "partners in progress or just plain parasites?"[48] For local residents, this relationship is a daily reminder of their position in the global oil economy as well as their exclusion from the touted, immediate and local benefits of the petroleum industry.

Then again, and as politically awkward as a visible oil spill, oil multinationals provided needed and tangible services—which were not being fulfilled by the state or national or international NGOs. For instance, outside one of the compounds and along a pitted gravel road, locals gathered to wait for oil workers driving opened flatbed trucks to give them a lift. An oil ride was a free one, and anyway there was limited public transport and few car owners. In actuality, an oil spokesperson listed this service as one of their commitments to the neighboring communities, a not-so-subtle indication of the government's failure to provide public transportation despite the need and the oil revenues going to local and national coffers. As I watched, not all oil workers stopped and picked up a human load, but many routinely did. This microinteraction between multinationals and the community encapsulates the pervasiveness of the industry in people's lives, a presence unmatched by the state and national and international organizations, and one that alluded to the slight distinction between neighbor and occupier. If this constant give and take, and fluctuating acts of benevolence and violence between the community and the oil sector, appear confusing, imagine the insecurities of residing there, starting a family there, and growing old there.

Road into the Amazon

It is also worth noting the nonpetroleum pockets of the Amazon, as it is a tourist destination and home to numerous Indigenous communities, the original inhabitants of the Amazon. From Lago Agrio, travelers could easily take a two- to three-hour overland trip to an arm of the Cuyabeno River. On the ride, they would pass Tarapoa, an oil workers depot, an oil block, and an airstrip of Alberta Energy of Canada (since renamed EnCana Corporation and sold to a Chinese consortium). In 2001, a large billboard greeted traffic along this road reminding them of oil's presence: "408 days without worker injury or loss of production due to injury." That same year, the street was lined with abandoned cement or wooden stores and a scattering of oil bars. The road is an oil road—like many roads in this part of the country—built in conjunction with the SOTE pipeline and secondary flow lines. It was pitted and full of potholes, and if it was not dusty, it had probably been sprayed with oil. Along the unpaved roads, pipelines arched and curved, one to two feet above the ground, at times dipping belowground at the top of residential driveways.

Children walked them into town; women dried clothes on them; and they served as a bench to watch traffic. Within the oil blocks' immense factories of white pipe and tubing, dark smoke is pumped out of tall towers and gas flares burn off gas by-products daily.

Once off-road, a two-hour canoe ride could take the visitor away from the visual line of oil works and deeper into the Amazon, but it is an Amazon populated with Indigenous communities, tourist lodges, and canoes full of sightseers. The Cuyabeno River system is not remote. Nevertheless, the wildlife and natural scenery remain exceptional and manifest into an environmental and international desire to protect and preserve them. Indeed, tourists flock there for the Amazon's untamed image and wildlife viewing, promoted by the media, literary accounts, and rainforest protection groups. However, in this region, and further adding to the mix and turmoil, is the uncertain difference between an ecological reserve and an oil block, and between a local pet and an internationally protected species. The Limoncocha Lake and Reserve is a good example of such ambiguity. Limoncocha was at that time within Occidental's Block 15, so to access the lake tourists had to pass guarded checkpoints. Another example is the wildlife market. In the open-air general market of Lago Agrio, a live little monkey sold for approximately $25 in 2002, which sounded like the tourist price, given the teachers' salaries.

These assorted experiences between local and nonlocal users in the Amazon had created a precarious mix of sentiments and tensions when the construction of OCP was announced. Indeed, this brief historical comparison between Lago Agrio and a few oil towns nearly a century earlier in the United States and the descriptive account of the Amazon in general serve as harbingers for the demands and mobilization efforts of the oil-important Lago Agrio community. Even though strains in the oil-important provinces had already been identified between lowland Indigenous communities, the oil industry, and the state,[49] the construction of the OCP pipeline represented an opportunity for affected, non-Indigenous residents of the Amazon to mobilize against the ongoing underinvestment of the state and the careless practices of the oil industry in the region. Descriptions here point to the importance of analyzing an environmental conflict from a historical perspective of a place and its people,[50] while the upcoming sections identify how most large-scale projects of potential environmental and social impact provoke a multitude of competing opinions. In this case, some views will be articulated locally, while others will be heard more globally.

ON-GROUND TACTICS: AN ANNIVERSARY STRIKE

Due to the perceived and ongoing injustices, the oil-important region exploded in February 2002 at the height of OCP construction when residents, farmers, small business owners, activist mayors, and oil workers took to the

streets.[51] In Orellana and Sucumbios Provinces, the two most critically important oil provinces, the Bi-Provincial Strike Committee organized roadblocks,
the seizure of nearly sixty oil wells and domestic refineries, and the occupation
of two airports.[52] The eleven-day strike led to a state of emergency, a media
gag order, a night curfew, and the militarization of two regions to force the
flow of oil. Following the confrontation, reports differed on whether anyone
had been killed. One report claimed one adult was shot dead; another report
stated that two adults and two children were killed; another report alleged that
three children were asphyxiated by tear gas; and still another account noted
that four adults were killed.[53] Reports also indicated that approximately forty
people were arrested and nearly three hundred were injured.

When communities halt oil flows, they cut off the state's lifeline and serve
notice of their intolerance for the existing injustices. It is here and at these
times that Gabriela Valdivia's analysis that "Petroleum has become the body
through which state and citizen meet, contest, and legitimize each other"
gains traction.[54] After these "meetings," there is little misunderstanding of
the government's position; and in the case of the OCP pipeline, it was clear.
"Nobody is going to screw the country. OCP is going, because it's going," were
the often-quoted words of then-president Gustavo Noboa.[55] He added that his
government would fight anyone blocking the construction of OCP "trench by
trench."[56] Indeed by the 1990s, the Ecuadorian state's shift to neoliberal policies led to a decrease in its social vision and social responsibility to its citizens
and an increase in its "policing role" to protect oil exports,[57] a point made
more generally by Vandana Shiva.[58]

The OCP project, however, was only one reason for discontent in the Amazon.
The Bi-Provincial Strike Committee identified four justifications for the strike.[59]
One reason was the emergency situation in the agricultural sector as a response
to the falling produce prices due to the dollarization of the country's currency in
2000 and the indiscriminate fumigation of crops in the U.S.-led Plan Colombia
campaign. A second reason demanded the immediate resolution of the electrical crisis that included the limited supply and initiatives of the state to privatize
the power companies. State oil workers also joined to protest the state-led drive
to further privatize the oil sector. Although the strike was an anniversary strike
against the state, the OCP project served as an additional impetus to mobilize
and as an additional target to realize enduring demands. To this point, the third
demand called for a signed agreement of social compensation from the OCP
consortium, and guarantees that OCP would reduce environmental impacts in
the new installations. This demand also called for a stop in the repressive tactics
used by Techint, the Argentinean OCP constructor. In 2000 for example, Techint
had been accused of entering private property without authorization and cutting
trees and destroying vegetation to open a trench for the pipeline.[60] And the final
reason to mobilize was for the removal of obstructions to the Aguarico River,
due to the OCP construction, on the grounds of economic and ecological impact. For generations that have become accustomed to state provisions for clean

tap water and indoor plumbing at home, school, and work, the importance of access to fresh, running water outdoors is often overlooked. The divide between those who have experienced indoor water security for generations and those who have not highlights how far the world's understandings of injustice and dignity-in-life claims have diverged.

News reports estimated that 90 percent of the population of these two provinces was supportive of the strike and citizen "takes" of the streets and oil property, having been forced to live, work, and play in oil-contaminated areas with only marginal benefit. Widespread dissatisfaction with the social, economic, and environmental inequalities and insecurities between the oil-producing regions and the oil-benefiting ones, including the nation's monetary sinkholes, Quito and Guayaquil, was palpable. Noting the Amazon's importance to the state, Suzana Sawyer wrote in her work *Crude Chronicles*: "Although the state has marginalized the Oriente politically and socially, it still sees hydrocarbon and agro-industrial 'development' of the region as crucial for gaining modern status in the global arena."[61] The oil provinces, increasingly aware of the state's bind, found a collective voice and strength in challenging the state's mismanagement of oil wealth and neglect of the oil-producing regions in their efforts.

Importantly, the 2002 strike was an anniversary strike. A year earlier, the communities mobilized for paved roads, greater electricity, and farm subsidies following a drop in coffee prices.[62] At that time, Lago Agrio's electricity was shut off throughout the night, and smaller towns received only eight hours of electricity per day. Following the 2001 strike, the state made promises, which were not kept. The foundation of the strike a year later was to hold the state responsible for its promises and for just compensation,[63] given the region's oil importance and demonstrable cases of oil contamination.

Indeed, the community's leverage against the state was not international media attention or international support; it was the capacity to shut down oil production and block the construction of a new pipeline. During the strike, oil production was reduced to 19 percent, while a former president of OCP claimed the antigovernment strikes along the route cost OCP most of its lost construction days.[64]

Eventually a truce of sorts was called between the communities and the state with an agreement from the state of 125 miles of paved road, additional electrical supply to the towns and $5 million in credit for local farmers. OCP agreed to provide additional services to Sucumbios Province, including school materials and buildings, construction of a Red Cross facility, provisions of computers, printers, and chairs for schools and associations, sewage system improvement, medical supplies, sports uniforms, road access lanes to specific associations or facilities, and asphalt roads.[65] Despite these projects, communities outside of Lago Agrio, and closer to the sites of oil production, remained without a steady supply of electricity.

Of additional importance to Lago Agrio residents was the Amazonas Station, a pumping, heating, and storage facility of OCP that was sited within the urban perimeter, only 4.5 kilometers from the town center.[66] The community's outspoken mayor, Máximo Abad of the left-wing Popular Democratic Movement, specifically demanded that the pump station be relocated away from this "zone of rapid demographic expansion."[67] At the height of border tension, some organizers stated that the community believed that Colombian guerrillas would target OCP's facilities. After the mayor and the community's failure to relocate this station, the distrust and animosity between the residents, the state, and oil sector increased further. While Timmons Roberts and Bradley Parks identify how historical distrust between nations undermines cooperation,[68] this work supports calls for greater analysis of trust between actor groups and community responses to "development" projects.

Adding to the tension and distrust, and also not easily forgotten, was the military's access to and use of private oil vehicles and airstrips scattered throughout the Amazon. "Locals are not convinced of the difference between the company and the military's transportation," recalled one community leader. "They could be doing this to protect [workers], but also to intimidate and to demonstrate a relationship between the company and the military."[69] An apparent ease of access between the military and the oil companies underscored a communal perception that there existed little difference between the two, and between the military, police, and oil guards. Given these ties, community residents perceived that the state's allegiance was primarily with the oil sector and that the oil industry's protector was the military. According to one resident activist, describing the event in the 2003 documentary *Risky Business*:

> Special armed forces in an airplane arrived at the airport of Albert Energy. At the gateway of the airport they were there: pickup trucks of the company Alberta with drivers of the company Alberta, and they were transporting soldiers. They reached where we were and gave us five minutes to leave. But it seems that we didn't know what five minutes meant. They counted to three and started to throw tear gas and started to shoot, initially in the air. Two hundred soldiers for 150 men, women and children.

In the documentary, another resident, who was shot, substantiated these claims: "When the military came, they based themselves out of [Alberta Energy], and I believe the company gave them the opportunity to attack us in this way. I felt a sort of blow that hit me here." Given these accounts, multiple parties in Lago Agrio and Quito began documenting incidents of intimidation, harassment, threats, and detainment with regard to the pipeline's construction and other oil projects, sparking a temporary alliance between the grassroots groups and the more established social and human rights NGOs in Quito.

With a thirty-year history in oil and a base of oil workers and residents employed through subsidiary and contract work, the state and oil companies may have imagined the town's acceptance of expanded oil facilities, services, and temporary jobs. However, state and oil perceptions of oil benefit and a community's lived oil experience varied drastically. In spite of, or due to, oil extraction, the region remained impoverished, undereducated, and underemployed. Chronic oil contamination had already resulted in a transnational lawsuit against Texaco (now Chevron) and the poor health of many of the region's residents. When the OCP project was announced, affected residents, workers, and community leaders organized quickly. They already knew to do so.

RESISTANT RESIDENTS

Broad-based, grassroots groups, which were pitted against the state primarily and against the privatization of the oil industry secondarily, aligned to resist the continued misuse of oil revenues and the uneven allocations of oil benefit and burden. Social rights groups, community development groups, affected residents, local environmental groups, political supporters of the local mayor, landowners, and oil workers of the state-owned PetroEcuador allied to resist the pipeline or press for concessions. To be clear, the construction of OCP sparked animosities that had been smoldering between the greater Lago Agrio community, the state, and the oil industry for years. Nevertheless, many of these groups were not anti-oil per se. Rather they supported the redistribution of oil wealth and benefit.

Community Groups and an Activist Mayor: "Presente"

In Lago Agrio, community members, including those in surrounding rural areas, organized an eclectic and local movement against the state and its endorsement of the OCP pipeline.[70] Included in this movement were Asamblea de la Social Civil (Assembly of Civil Society), Frente de Defensa de la Amazonia (Defense Front of the Amazon, or Frente, a social, environmental and Indigenous rights organization), Frente de Mujeres de Sucumbios (Women's Front of Sucumbios, a collective of settler and Indigenous women), Red Amazonica por la Vida (Amazonian Network for Life, a landowner group), Federación Organisación Campesinos Agrinegroes (Federation Organization of Agricultural Campesinos, or FOCAN, an agricultural organization), and Fondo Ecuatoriano Populorum Progressio (Ecuadorian Popular Progress Fund, or FEPP, a national development organization).[71] Many of these established and recently formed organizations coalesced to demand the improvement of living conditions by joining the Bi-Provincial Strike Committee as well as their own local campaigns. Largely absent in this broad challenge to the state and the construction of OCP were oil-funded entrepreneurs, Indigenous organizations, and national and international environmental NGOs.

In the streets and on television, Lago Agrio's candid mayor challenged the location and construction practices of the pipeline project and the offers of compensation, arguing that the security and dignity of the people of Lago Agrio were nonnegotiable. "It's false to say that OCP is being generous," stated

Mayor Abad on national news. "It's a sign of their arrogance. . . . We are defending the dignity of this community."[72] His position won him loyalty from local organizations and the community, but cost him support within his own government, which attempted to negotiate directly with OCP in his absence. In this instance, a group of five in the council signed an agreement with OCP in August 2001 without the mayor's consent.[73] "OCP invited five councilors to a twelve-hour-long meeting in Quito. They took them out for dinner at a restaurant in Lago Agrio," recounted one activist. "The next morning, the councilors had reversed their decision, and they were all driving OCP pickup trucks."[74]

The agreement was for ten kilometers of pavement, US$1 million to be spent at the council's discretion, and an "ecological park" near the pipeline's Amazonas Station. This agreement was interpreted by the mayor and the majority of town residents as a giveaway of the region's resources. In 2002, the internal tension *within* the local government culminated in a city-bounded mayor, who was forced to remain in Lago Agrio or face a call-to-vote to revoke or rewrite his policy on the construction of the pipeline.

Oil Workers Union: A Nationalist, Antiprivatization Appeal

In addition to the mayor and the community groups, the National Federation of Oil Workers or FETRAPEC[75] joined OCP challengers in direct actions, providing undercurrents of pro-oil nationalism and antiprivatization globalism to this rural community's demands.[76] The oil union argued that the private pipeline would increase the country's dependency on raw export alone without increased investment in domestic refining or processing and that the state would lose transportation fees from the multinational corporations once OCP was built. In addition to calling the OCP project a "national humiliation," the president of FETRAPEC claimed that "during the last few years, the majority of Ecuadorians have been the victims of some of the worst deceits in the history of oil: the myth of a second oil boom that the private Heavy Crude Pipeline (OCP) offers."[77] In subsequent confrontations against the government's drive to privatize the industry, the government arrested eleven union leaders and fired fifty-two PetroEcuador workers.[78]

Nevertheless, Ecuador and PetroEcuador lacked the technology and expertise to construct a nationally owned pipeline, while Ecuador remained an importer of gasoline. To be fair to PetroEcuador, it has long demanded more investment from the state for repairs and equipment to boost production.[79] However, a consultant for the oil industry interpreted PetroEcuador's position somewhat differently. "PetroEcuador doesn't want to see competition and they use the nationalist card basically to keep foreign corporations out," the consultant said, before adding "and they're manipulating the population."[80]

Certainly, PetroEcuador served its own interests well. PetroEcuador targeted community mobilization efforts at multinationals rather than at the oil industry in general; while simultaneously lobbing mass demonstrations at the state for adhering to neoliberal policies and pressures to privatize certain public sectors and to diminish the role of labor unions. Indeed, PetroEcuador practiced little accountability, and was arguably one of the worst environmental offenders within the oil industry. Since 1992, PetroEcuador has owned and operated Texaco's oil fields; and it is PetroEcuador's fields of oiled ponds and visible oil seepage that are toured in awareness-building toxic tours. PetroEcuador operates with aging equipment and inferior investment and technology, some of which were acquired when multinational corporations left the country or their leases expired. Indeed, community and organizational alliances with PetroEcuador revealed both a successful smoke-and-mirror campaign orchestrated by the state-owned oil company as well as local solidarity and a prioritization of local demands.

This temporary alignment with state oil exposed a trace of nationalism, revealed a growing resentment over how the region's resources had been used, undermined a legitimate environmental concern, and weakened calls for greater environmental health considerations. Clearly, private- or state-generated contamination remains contamination for the affected people, farm animals, wildlife, and ecosystems. Nonetheless, this union-community alliance drove a powerful and organized assault at the state's intention of expanding private production without just compensation and greater public inclusion.

DEMANDS ON A CORRUPT STATE: DIGNITY AND SECURITY

The working-class community of Lago Agrio entrenched in the oil production and transportation processes employed the construction of OCP to lob long-running demands at the state, to profile the region's critical role in the nation's economic development plans, and to pressure the multinational oil consortium for greater public inclusion and greater assistance in establishing economic security for the community. Specific to the state, citizens were demonstrating against consecutive governments' actions and inactions in the region and oil-related corruption within the local municipalities. The community was demanding agricultural assistance, following a drop in coffee prices, as well as an improvement in the region's infrastructure, including paved roads and greater electrical supply. They were challenging the state's plans to privatize the oil and electrical systems, as well as demanding heightened regional security given the border tensions. Though a few of these demands seemed removed from the oil industry, they were intrinsically linked. Increased extraction leads to less land to cultivate, reduced water quality, poorer health, less state investment, which then converge to exacerbate the level of poverty. The resolution of oil conflicts cannot be addressed in isolation from the structural injustices experienced in a political and economic space where persistent inequality, grinding poverty, and limited democratic processes exist.

By the time of OCP, the well-being of the residents and the ecosystem had already become an unnecessary sacrifice.[81] Their particular grievances coalesced into a broader environmental justice stance: dignity, security, community safety, community participation, access and dialogue with the industry, just economic and community development, and environmental safeguards for the regional burden of living next to industrial pollution. Pragmatically, they demanded guarantees of minimum environmental and social impact, a monitoring role in the construction process, and a contingency plan should a break occur. On the whole, they wanted to reorient the region toward adopting community-driven economic and social development plans and community-driven participation in public health and environmental safeguards. They were too embedded with the petrochemical industry and too economically insecure, by and large, to present claims from an environmental protectionist point of view.

Lago Agrio pursued the state, in marked contrast to others along OCP's route. Their direct confrontation grew out of years of oil experience with limited social benefit and limited influence over the economic decisions of the petrostate. Encapsulating the community's ire in a television interview, Mayor Abad claimed, "OCP has some obligation to the municipality. . . . But in addition to these obligations, there is a moral obligation of the Ecuadorian government to develop this province. . . . This is our right, that we recover the redistribution of the wealth of this zone."[82]

As presented earlier, Ecuador mimics many petrostates. It has a centralized government, high degrees of corruption, unjust distribution of oil wealth, large external debt, and limited economic development outside of the oil industry. Terry Karl, a researcher of petrostates, captures the "perverse outcomes" of petrodollars when writing: "[R]evenues pouring into a highly-concentrated structure of power leads to further concentration, and they encourage rentier networks between politicians and capitalists."[83] In an earlier work, Karl wrote that over time petrostates "suffer from diminished state capacity," as their political and economic fortunes become bound.[84] In this regard, petrostates, tied to the mineral rents of a single product, begin to experience ineptness and a lack of public accountability, which translates into economic deterioration and arbitrary decision making.[85]

Thirty years of oil exploitation had created extreme dissatisfaction within Sucumbios Province with regard to the national government. The communities were flanked by oil multinationals, which had the resources to fund paved roads, provide greater electrical capacity, and install wastewater management systems. However, multinationals were not in the business to do so, and a negligent state lacked the political interest to convert oil revenues into an improved infrastructure for a peripheral region. A Lago Agrio social rights leader noted in an interview that challenging a "national project" became the community's strategic dilemma:

> Everyone says they don't want more oil exploration. Oil doesn't benefit one's health, the environment, the Amazon region. But nevertheless, we have to engage the other element, which is that oil is a national endeavor. We have to understand that the laws of the government are over the interests of the communities.[86]

Lending support to the affected people of the region, a human rights organizer in Quito criticized oil's position as a national priority: "Up until now, the fact that Ecuador has had petroleum, really it has not benefited the majority of the people, or the common good. . . . [So] when they say that it's a national project, you question for whom?"[87] Challenging the state's promotion that the pipeline was a necessity for the country's economic development, despite local perception to the contrary, another community activist added: "Oil in no way increases the economic situation of the people here."[88] Given this oil-nested political structure, Lago Agrio's community leaders identified the state's responsibility in improving the region's infrastructure, even though an oil compound appeared more visible, and perhaps more accessible, than the national government itself.

For its own protection perhaps, the oil industry even encouraged community agitation against the state. As noted earlier, an oil company's provision of small projects, including health and educational facilities, appeared more directly beneficial to the community than state provisions, and even more useful than some NGO projects. Multinationals also were quite receptive to publicizing their regional and state tax payments despite being such a secretive industry.[89] Throughout the Amazon, local government officials and oil company representatives hold joint town hall meetings to tell the communities of their annual contributions to the community's well-being. In this way, multinationals ultimately worked to make the local governments more accountable to its citizens, rather than the state forcing corporations to become more accountable to the state and the nation's citizens.

Paved roads and agricultural subsidies may be easy to envision and to provide, while calls for respect, a seat at the table, and dignity in life may be more difficult to imagine and to materialize. The distinctions however are not apparent to affected communities. In one instance, a community member identified how "in September [2003], there was an oil spill in the area, but the oil company didn't notify the people in the surrounding areas. Therefore, the people continued to eat fish."[90] Perhaps bitter by this degree of indifference to the community's health, the community spokesperson complained: "It is basic to inform the community." When community members complain, they are told by oil companies to contact the Ministry of the Environment or

Ministry of Energy and Mines. "[Yet] locals aren't aware of steps to take to file complaints to the ministry. But more importantly, they don't have the money to go there [to the capital], and they have lost faith in the ministries because they have received no response [in the past]," claimed one community spokesperson.[91]

Residing near oil compounds or oil facilities, these communities become pawns between the competitive orchestrations of the national government and the oil industry to establish a low bar of community compensation and protection. After identifying the inhabitants of two oil blocks as settlers and Indigenous people "with very little economic resources and low levels of education, who are suffering from the consequences of a deep agricultural crisis and weak government," one community leader claimed that an oil company was "taking advantage of this critical situation in order to carry out their work with low levels of investments in terms of payments made to landowners, compensation for damages causes, and environmental control."[92] Acknowledging this quandary, another local leader said, "Look, in the communities there is need. People live in poverty. Five hundred dollars, one thousand dollars is like the sky has fallen."[93]

Oil money in the Amazon was as slick as light crude. Yet the people were more pragmatic than radical in their demands, despite their ongoing frustration and their combative tactics. They were not organizing to overthrow the state or the oil industry.[94] They were organizing for more even, and more local, tangible and intangible reimbursements given the risks associated with residing near industrial facilities.

Against OCP: Jobs, Local Purchasing, Compensation, and Care

Locally and explicit to their oil history, laborers called for employment, shop owners requested local purchasing, and landowners mobilized for compensation for land use and greater care when operating on their land. The underemployed and economically insecure laboring class in particular demanded technical and skilled work. Yet in this semiremote area, oil companies argued that the people were too underskilled for the work required of the industry. Many of the adults in the area had only completed a sixth-grade education in the rural schools, which operated with too few teachers in multigrade classrooms. After the sixth grade, some children in remote communities attend weekend commuter schools, but it is not mandatory and many are unable to participate. Though education is accepted to be a responsibility of the state, some oil companies had constructed rudimentary primary or technical schools, paid teachers' salaries, and branded at least one classroom with bookshelves and paper supplies lined with company logos.[95] Though potentially helpful, educational attainment from oil-supported schools lacked conversion into skilled labor in the oil fields.

"The projects that might appear good are actually completely useless and don't distribute to the local development of the people," recalled one community leader. "For example, one project wanted to teach the women how to sew. But when the women learned how to sew, . . . the women approached the company and said, 'We want to make the uniforms for your employees.' The company didn't accept this proposal."[96] Though skill diversification was achieved, this type of training without subsequent employment linkages failed to translate into anything meaningful to former students. Mechanics and accounting classes were also offered without direct tie-ins to oil employment. "These projects merely serve to improve the company's image and to give the impression that they are working with the people," the community leader added.[97] In essence, there was an absence of essential training-for-hire programs and community-directed investment schemes specific to the region.

The petroleum industry's disconnectedness from its own geologically specific locality ranged from the daily and minute to the grand and global. For instance, EnCana, which funded a coffee-growing co-op, served Nescafé coffee in its compound, though boxes of packaged cooperative coffee were given to visitors as gifts.[98] Furthermore, shop owners wanted the oil workers to buy their drinks and supplies from them, while farmers wanted the companies to buy their produce of yucca, pineapple, and papaya. Yet work in the Amazon was considered a hardship post, which warranted residential compounds for nonnational oil workers, inclusive of meals. At this time, foreign workers were even discouraged from leaving the compounds, particularly those near the Colombian border,[99] and when they left the oil blocks, they left the region for weeks at a time.

Landowners were another local bloc justified in demonstrating against OCP action and state protection. In their roster of complaints, they identified cases of harassment and violence against them by local and OCP police, land expropriation, disproportionate settlement payments, property damage, and water pollution.[100] They described OCP personnel as coming onto their property accompanied by local police but without a government facilitator. To OCP, the police were viewed as security. To landowners, the police were viewed as a form of intimidation. Landowners were justifiably concerned. Landowners, who chose not to sign right-of-way access and receive compensation, watched as their land was expropriated, enforced by a contractual clause to construct and operate OCP.[101] According to one investigation of 111 landowners affected by OCP construction in Sucumbios Province, "More than half of those surveyed have been threatened, 42 of them by the military or police, 30 by OCP representatives and 18 by unknown people. For 73 percent of those interviewed, the construction of OCP generated the militarization of their region."[102]

Landowners were also angry over the damages done to their property and water sources, the discarded construction debris, and the loss of their domestic animals due to the constructor's poor work ethic on their land and inadequate support of the state. From the same study of landowners, 79 percent of them identified impacts on their livestock; 81 percent said their agriculture production was damaged, including loss of cocoa and coffee cultivation and timber production; 68 percent claimed that they or members of their family were experiencing physical and/or mental health problems, including the effects of increased noise and dust pollution.[103] Landowners perceived each slight as a reflection of the disregard and disrespect multinationals and the state had for them and their land.

Conflict also escalated between landowners and OCP on land value determination and unexplained disparities between landholdings.[104] On average, landowners in Sucumbios Province reported that they received US$1.59 for every square meter of affected land.[105] However, controversy arose when landowners realized some received or negotiated for higher prices than others. Wealthier landowners were determined by OCP to have higher use value of their land than campesinos, who believed the distinction was made between themselves and "important landowners," rather than actual land value and land use. Interviews indicated that people believed that some campesinos were paid $200 to $1,000 for use of their land, and some into the five figures. Unequal pay for comparable land held by different landowners was a well-known offense and part of a series of long-running disputes in the area. In the past, "when [one] company was starting their seismic testing project . . . , they offered the indigenous community of Pompeya US$11 per hectare; however, in previous seismic projects, they offered $20 to non-indigenous settlers," recalled one activist in 2004.[106]

Though it is not clear, it appears that in this case settlements for use of the right-of-way were determined not by land size alone, but by how the land was used. Land prices varied by the differences in agricultural and grazing land, the presence or absence of fruit-bearing trees, the value of a tree's production, and the presence or absence of fences, buildings, or humanmade structures. Landowners could have negotiated land price of the right-of-way. However, not all of them understood they had the right and the power to do so. In 2003, a state government representative told me unofficially that the state had agreed with OCP to permit negotiations up to 20 percent of the original land offer.[107] As it is a national project, land could be and was expropriated as needed if landowners refused OCP's offer, and since it was a national project, the route was nonnegotiable, except for minor alterations.

At this time, two landowner networks formed to contest these disparities. Over time, Red Amazonica por la Vida (Amazonian Network for Life), which included approximately 280 landowning families and the assistance of a local lawyer, began a national-level lawsuit to demand greater compensation for the use of the right-of-way after agreements between OCP and individual landowners had already been reached. In addition, landowners filed a petition through local courts against the expropriations and seemingly arbitrary detentions; however, the case was denied on the grounds that individuals cannot obstruct a project of national priority. The second landowner group was much smaller in number and sought assistance from Quito-based organizations and international allies to find international venues to present their claims and to launch an international lawsuit.[108]

An Essential Claim: Participation Is Not Manual Labor

Community groups and organizations in the oil region were not rejecting oil in most cases. They were primarily calling for mutually respectful dialogue and a redistribution of oil wealth, blanketed in dignity, transparency, and justice. They wanted their moderate voices heard, given their experience of the state and oil sector acting with audacity toward them and impunity from them. They wanted to deflate the control wielded over them by political and petroleum outsiders.

"Local participation has been reduced to only local manual labor, without civil society's active participation in the monitoring and control of the construction and operation of OCP, and the benefits that it will generate," wrote Frente de Defensa de la Amazonia (FDA).[109] "[Our strategy] is to train the people, so that they are prepared not just as monitors, but as participants," added an organizer in 2002.[110] A year later, another asserted, "We are not against oil exploration. But we believe that the relationship should be just and transparent. And the negotiations must be just and transparent."[111] Elaborating further the organizer said, "And if it's not just and transparent, no one passes through here. But first, we are not against them, we are not saying, 'No, to investment.' But first, this is our proposal: to study the situation, to analyze it, and to converse."[112]

An oil spokesperson countered that community meetings with affected residents were commonly held in what the spokesperson called a "process of information." "It's very clearly established," the oil representative said. "You sit down, you tell them [the community] what you are doing, you tell them what you want to do, they tell you what they want to do, then you decide whether it's feasible or not."[113]

In contrast, a resident and community leader near an oil block described consultations with the oil industry quite differently. "The company [not OCP] presents environmental impact assessments to the people when they are already done, when really they are supposed to carry out these consultations beforehand. And they end up misinforming people about the plans and what's going to happen," the attendee said. "They can't understand them; they can't read them. These are very technical documents, and so how can a local, in 24 hours, read this huge document when there is nobody there to support them?" Becoming angrier in recollection, the community spokesperson explained, "There's no democracy in this aspect. . . . This isn't a consultation; it's an imposition."[114] Another community organizer summed the plight of many in the Amazon when presenting the faults of one company at a shareholder's meeting: "The company does not allow communities to elaborate proposals for compensation according to their own [community] criteria, and they pressure communities to accept [the company's] own proposals through threats and deceit [sic]."[115] Though both individuals were not referring to OCP in particular, community anger and irritation with the oil industry in general carried over into OCP-community relations.

There is a long history of how government bodies shield themselves and corporations from community challenges and block community engagement on decisions that impact their lives. Michael Edelstein's study of contaminated communities found that the government's response to the communities' toxic exposure "disabled" communities by withholding information, distorting information, and preventing the public's attendance and/or participation at meetings, which greatly impaired the capacity of these burdened and disadvantaged community groups.[116] Phil Brown and Edwin Mikkelsen found that families exposed to toxic waste first sought information through government and scientific channels, before beginning to distrust these traditional sources.[117]

In Ecuador, community-based environmental justice issues may also be pivotal points at which oil-embedded communities stake demands on the state not only for greater participation on a single project, but for a participatory role on the community's development path. Indeed, there was a local perception that outsiders viewed Lago Agrio as incapable of, and an undesirable place for, hosting direct talks with the state and OCP. According to one grassroots leader, "All these negotiations have been in Quito because they are afraid to come here. So all the meetings are in Quito . . . for their security. Well, we don't have well-maintained primary roads. We don't have potable water."[118]

Lago Agrio's community groups were demanding the opportunity to create and practice forms of egalitarian democratization exclusive of national and international ties with the objective of improving community well-being, neglected by the state. But it was also these multifaceted concerns that opened them to multiple advocacy groups, while simultaneously disabling such networks.

OPPOSITION, INDIFFERENCE, AND ISOLATION

Tilly studied inequalities through the relational differences between categorical pairs (women-men, black-white) across time and place.[119] In the case of Lago Agrio, unequal categorical pairs include Indigenous people and non-Indigenous settlers; oil communities in the Global South and oil consumers in the Global North; and rural suppliers of raw resources in the Amazon and the political and economic beneficiaries in the Andean capital, Ecuador, and the Global North. Residents of the greater Lago Agrio area found allies among many, including their leftist mayor, social justice organizers, affected landowners, the nationalistic oil union, and human rights groups in Quito. But others in the region, as expected, sided with the oil industry or were indifferent to the pipeline's construction. Unsurprisingly, individuals who benefited economically from the industry were supportive, or at least not vocally against it, while—and perhaps this is surprising—Indigenous communities failed to mobilize an organized response to it. The environmental groups fractured around it, though a few supported the challengers on isolated positions rather than in direct action, while others united for their own environmental agendas rather than in support of the demands of the oil province. Yet both environmental sides, a radical and a conservation one, were considered outsiders by the local groups and people, who banded together around established local development and social rights organizations.

Oil-Supported Laboring and Professional Classes

A pro-oil voice was also heard among community residents and oil entrepreneurs in the Amazon who benefited economically from ties to multinationals. Among the professional class, oil companies paid the salaries of physicians, teachers, and locals, who became community leaders, when hired to manage oil-funded community centers, including small libraries, underused computer centers and closely guarded photocopy machines. Among the laboring class, the oil allies included trout farmers and coffee growers, who received start-up money from individual companies or through organizations established by the industry.

Fundación NanPaz, for one, was an organization set up and funded by the Canadian company Alberta Energy but which also received public funds through a collaborative aid agreement between the Canadian Ecuadorian Fund for Development and Canadian International Development Agency.[120] NanPaz provided basic services for neighboring communities including outdoor latrines for several villages, medicinal plant gardens, and art and recreation programs at local schools.[121] One of its largest projects was the establishment of an integrated farm as a demonstration model for local residents. Residents claimed that NanPaz gave $5,000 to people who wanted to start an integrated farm based on animal waste collection and reuse in the Amazon; however, community leaders said the availability of funds reached too few families, took too much time to obtain, and were accessible through "friendships" rather than demonstrated need.[122]

It could be argued that the oil-funded recipients exchanged their civic voice for petrodollars, and in turn became the unofficial ambassadors and goodwill spokespersons of oil's benevolence and generosity. They wrote, or at least signed, reports attesting to an oil company's community contributions. Moreover, they were on display—perhaps reluctantly—when public relations departments of oil companies entertained visitors.[123] While oil directors refused to criticize the state publicly, they willingly facilitated Ecuadorian nationals to do so. In this new role, teachers and directors of oil-supported schools told visitors, including myself, that the Education Ministry provided too little assistance to meet the demands of the population. Undoubtedly, it was the absence of state investment and participatory spaces for local determination that made residents and community leaders vulnerable to the purchasing power of oil.

The purchasing power of the private and public sectors is, as a rule, quite different. State-sponsored infrastructure is utilized by all community members whether deemed cooperative or uncooperative, deserving or not. In contrast, oil-funded services and projects are private endeavors, to which oil critics are excluded. To access oil funds, a person has to first acquiesce to the idea of oil benevolence. Indeed, community residents may be most susceptible to co-option in developing or low-income places, where state commitments favor large-scale extractive industries over the well-being of citizens. Moreover, the economic opportunities are so limited where oil operates that choice is nearly nonexistent. Notions that microentrepreneurs choose to support or to cooperate with the oil sector—given the absence of other economic opportunities or incentives—appears disingenuous to skeptical residents and visitors.

Presence and Absence of Indigenous Leadership

Indigenous positions on the oil industry are particularly perplexing and open to manipulation by various interested parties.[124] At the start of my research, I revealed myself to be a product of the Northern discourse on Indigenous communities of the Andean and Amazonian nations. I went to Ecuador for the first time in 2001, believing that if the Indigenous communities and organizations rejected the OCP pipeline, and I believed that they would, it would not be built. Two Indigenous uprisings in Ecuador, led by the Confederación de Nacionalidades Indígenas del Ecuador, or CONAIE, one of the most organized and effective Indigenous organizations in South America, were significant contributors to the overthrow of two presidencies, Abdalá Bucaram in 1997 and Jamil Mahuad in 2000. The panethnic Indigenous movement was also the strongest social movement in Ecuador, indeed stronger than the labor movement as argued by some.[125] Moreover, even a general reading of new accounts provided by Indigenous and environmental advocacy networks in the United States indicated Indigenous rejection of oil and alignment with environmental groups. The bulk of oil reserves in Ecuador were beneath the traditional living and hunting territories of at least eight lowland Indigenous communities, including the Cofan, lowland Kichwan, Secoya, Siona, Huaorani, Tagueri, Shuar, and Achuar.[126] In addition, in 2001, CONAIE along with six other organizations, including two human rights organizations and the association of professionals of PetroEcuador, signed an assessment arguing how the pipeline project violated the country's constitution.[127] So it seemed reasonable that they would unite to block the construction of a cross-country oil project. They did not.

Indigenous communities of the Amazon were both present and absent stakeholders in the country's oil dependence. They were always present, visibly or not, when discussing oil impacts in the Amazon and when international organizations identified oil conflict in the Amazon as Indigenous-oil conflict in the Amazon. However, they remained silent on the construction of OCP. For instance, one media report claimed that CONAIE *may* mobilize against OCP in the future. This threat, or acknowledgment of a potential but unlikely Indigenous campaign, served to remind the public that Indigenous leaders have a stake in the Amazon and to demonstrate media's awareness of impulsive international responses to Indigenous people fighting oil multinationals.

Despite these projections, and even though some communities would be experiencing the direct impacts of increased oil expansion and secondary pipelines across the Amazon and into untapped Indigenous territories and protected areas, they never mobilized directly against the OCP pipeline. Paraphrasing one Indigenous leader in the Amazon: the extraction is going to affect the Indigenous people, because they live where extraction occurs and where secondary lines flow. But for them, "It's not about OCP. It's about the companies that will extract oil to fill OCP. The Secoya are confronting Oxy.[128] The Siona are confronting City.[129] The Huaorani are confronting YPF. The Kichwa are confronting PetroEcuador."[130] It could also be argued that national-level Indigenous organizations were inundated with what they had determined as more pressing and urgent issues, including health, education, citizen rights, land rights, land titles, and political representation.

There was no single and unifying Indigenous position on the OCP project. *Some* Indigenous organizations were mobilizing in *some* cases to block secondary flow lines, and in other cases, to pressure for greater compensation. Others have called for a moratorium, but only in their territory.

Citing the member organizations of CONAIE and the Confederation of Indigenous Nationalities of the Ecuadorian Amazon, or CONFENAIE, as "legitimate" and "representative," one Quito-based advocate claimed, "All of those organizations are opposed to oil, or at least to oil under its current terms. [Some] have defined a very radical stance, that 'we don't want the oil, period.' The other organizations are saying, 'We don't want oil because we don't want to end up the way it is in the north. We don't want oil because we are not trained. We are not strong enough.'"[131] According to the same advocate, whose NGO has worked with Indigenous organizations since the mid-1990s, Indigenous leaders seek the training and experience to sit at the table with oil representatives and to decide as equal decision makers to accept, reject, or direct an oil project for community benefit.[132]

In clarification of "legitimate" organizations, this Indigenous advocate illustrated how and why some Indigenous communities support the oil industry and some do not.

There are smaller organizations, sometimes referred to as phantom, or ghost organizations, that have been created basically to work with the oil companies. That the oil companies always put up front to say that, "no, we are working with Indigenous communities." But in [one block] those communities are maybe one confirmed community and maybe as many as three or four out of a total of 40 or more communities that are just within the block. . . . And they are often created by one leader, who has an agreement with the oil company and then he has funding from the company to go out into the communities and talk about and promote oil development.[133]

Due to historical, political, and oil-related matters, divisions also existed between Indigenous organizations within Ecuador. For example, lowland Amazon communities that are more directly impacted by oil have viewed the national organizations, such as CONAIE, as favoring the more numerous and organized highland Indigenous communities of the Andes. Business ventures among some Indigenous communities and the agreements between them and the oil companies have exasperated this discord.[134]

For instance, the Huoarani, with previous little contact outside of their community before oil exploration began,[135] had agreements with the oil companies in their territory for simple, nonsustainable, noncapacity building projects, such as sports fields, community centers, and cash payments. In addition, the Huaorani Nation of the Ecuadorian Amazon (ONHAE) signed a five-year agreement of cooperation with Petrobras Energia of Brazil, an OCP member company, for $339,000 in community investment.[136] However, the Huaorani were predictably unpredictable in "negotiating." More commonly than not, they supported an oil agreement or an environmental organization's campaign one moment then canceled the agreement or commitment the next.

In general, agreements between Indigenous communities and NGOs and between Indigenous communities and oil companies have been established and broken in an ongoing pattern, resembling a situation in which Indigenous communities test their own agency with all outsiders, including oil companies as well as environmental groups. Worldwide, alliances between Indigenous groups and environmental organizations and between Indigenous people and conservation biologists appeared to be tenuous,[137] while others have argued that there were increasingly greater collaborative efforts between Indigenous and non-Indigenous communities.[138]

Sawyer balances perceptions by demonstrating both the extraordinary collaboration between environmental activists and Indigenous organizations in Ecuador in challenging the 1994 changes in the Hydrocarbon Law, as well as the deep divisions between Indigenous communities and between them and environmental organizations.[139] Amendments to the Hydrocarbon Law, which was supported by the World Bank, sought to facilitate private investment in the oil sector, which Indigenous and environmental activists opposed.[140] Their position, much like the experience of Lago's activist community with regards to OCP, would have made them temporary allies with PetroEcuador's oil union. From Marc Becker's assessment, Indigenous people in Ecuador have also had a long history of forming reciprocal bonds with socialists, anarchists, and more recently urban leftists.[141]

In this case, factionalism *within* the Indigenous communities created a space for oil companies and NGOs to select among them,[142] and then to reclaim a particular position as the Indigenous position for their own audience. "It is a tricky situation because definitely all Indigenous communities have the right to be active decision makers in their own future," remarked one Quito-based advocate. "But we recognize our partner organizations as legitimate, participatory organizations with power. The communities have created them for representation."[143]

Indigenous organizations in Ecuador also sought external alliances at their own discretion and control. However, when international or non-Indigenous concerns became increasingly dominant, Indigenous leaders and communities removed themselves from the collaboration, as in the case when Indigenous struggles for greater autonomy and economic independence in the Amazon pitted them against environmental groups. Though this research offers a very limited examination of Indigenous-environmental ties, I would suggest that Indigenous groups appear to rely more upon themselves and international Indigenous organizations and advocates, than on non-Indigenous organizations within Ecuador.

These inconsistencies of collaboration are problematic for all parties. For instance, while oil companies and environmental groups sought ties with Indigenous communities and organizations, they were also critical of them. Though not direct allies, members of the oil industry as well as the environmental profession objected to oil-Indigenous agreements. A representative of the oil industry interpreted payments to Indigenous communities as low-grade extortion: "Once you stop giving to them, because there's got to be a limit, then, is when the problems start. 'You build me a bridge here or you cannot pass.' Companies are not there for bridge-building, that's the job of the government."[144] The oil representative later added, "The constitution of my country says that oil belongs to the people. [It does] not belong to the tribes. [It does] not belong to the local people around where this oil is produced."[145]

In this case, the absence of Indigenous mobilization, and more specifically the absence of an Indigenous face or voice as symbol for an international market, limited international support against OCP in the Amazon. International audiences and advocates have demonstrated a preference for supporting Indigenous mobilization in the Amazon rather than the settler-campesino cases or causes.

FOR OIL ROADS, PETRODOLLARS, AND RADICALISM

Some of the past demands of the Indigenous groups and non-Indigenous settlers were also in direct conflict with the environmentalists' concepts of conservation. Regarding oil roads alone, there were vast disagreements between environmental outsiders and local Native and non-Native residents. For environmental NGOs with influential international alliances, oil roads destroy natural habitat and biodiversity by enabling human intrusion and increased deforestation into previously prohibited areas. Due to oil roads, one NGO director claimed that wildlife numbers were plummeting as communities moved beyond subsistent hunting to profitable hunting, eased by roads that expand hunting territory and market access. For Indigenous and settler communities, oil roads facilitated mobility to markets and hunting grounds and represented a veneer of development, which many commonly sought. States in general support road building,[146] and in Ecuador, the state relied on oil roads for land relief and to facilitate its own presence and governance in previously inaccessible zones. As for the oil industry, it can either build roads or treat the Amazon as an offshore site, bringing in by helicopter its men and equipment and positioning pipelines without permanent road work.[147]

Environmental NGOs, mimicking some in the oil industry, also oppose oil spending directly among affected communities and prefer greater state-level and NGO participation in oil-community negotiations and monetary use, particularly among the Indigenous of the Amazon. Nonlocal environmental and development NGOs want oil money to be spent on NGO-led development and/or conservation projects, as some believe the Indigenous communities and leaders are unable to understand the value of the money and how best to use it for long-term sustainability, rather than short-term pleasures.[148] Indeed, the largest environmental NGOs have voiced skepticism and suspicion that Indigenous communities once empowered with land rights and resources may not conserve their biodiversity.[149] According to one director of an international organization:

> You get in a situation in which those communities that know how to negotiate, and negotiate good deals with the companies that are in better shape. And there are others that do not have any experience and are at a disadvantage with the oil companies and they settle for whatever. Just nothing that really guarantees any long-term development alternatives for them.[150]

The Quito-based NGOs' positions may be in part paternalistic, but they also perpetuated a view that the acceptance of oil payment by local and/or Indigenous groups diluted their collective action. But it was a particularistic view.[151] During the construction of OCP for example, some Quito-based conservation NGOs found themselves in a similar situation. In their case, they also chose to accept oil money. They negotiated a US$16.9 million environmental fund with the OCP consortium, which, arguably, defused a transnational campaign against the pipeline's construction. Though negotiations on the conservation fund will be discussed in the next chapter, it is worth noting here that there was one important difference between oil negotiations between a categorical pair. One distinction between the Indigenous and settler communities in the Amazon and individual oil companies, and the Quito-based conservation NGOs and OCP was the dollar amount. The professional environmental NGOs with international partners received much more money. Besides the dollar amount, the variance between the NGOs and the affected communities is one of claims: one is based on conservation, Arcadian values, and environmental research, and the other is grounded in historical, territorial, equity, and/or justice claims. It is not clear, though worth pursuing, whether these competing and weak ties diminished the negotiating power and compensation packages of either the Amazonian communities or the conservation NGOs in the capital, or whether both parties were burdened by their separation.

As for a possible alliance with some of the radical ecologists in Quito, Lago Agrio's affected communities demanded something tangible and immediate in their lives, not necessarily a cessation of oil works or a harangue against global discrimination and inequality. "The groups have come here, gathered information, visited some communities, and well that's it," noted one grassroots leader. "They came for information,"[152] as did I.

Another NGO director in Lago Agrio further elaborated on the tensions between outsider groups and local ones. "I am also radical like them [the Quito-based ecologists]. But when I am with the social groups [in Lago Agrio], I cannot be radical, because the reality is something else," the director argued. "It's possible to be radical in the United States, in Europe or in Quito, because they don't live with contamination."[153]

This gap between ideological demonstration (by people removed from severe impact and danger) and entrenched pragmatism (alongside violent confrontations) splintered the Lago Agrio community from many of the environmentally specific and environmentally employed groups along OCP's route. In Lago Agrio, the NGO leader continued:

> If a community starts a dialogue with a company, to them [a Quito-based NGO] this is something very terrible, very bad. But for us, let's see if we can make the relationship better. Let's see if we can assist between the community and company. We cannot abandon the communities that enter into a dialogue with oil companies.[154]

Acknowledging the vast differences in their daily realities, a member of a human rights organization in Quito recalled that "there was a bit of a conflict there. And it's really difficult, because you know when you are here in Quito you say, 'No, no, no. . . . How are you going to [accept this oil project]?'" Continuing, the organizer added, "But [a community leader] said, 'Look, [the pipeline is] going to go through. There's no way it's not going to go through, so you help the people to get the best deal that they can.' Well, I suppose it's pragmatic and practical."[155]

At the height of tensions between the state and Lago Agrio, national ties were minimal, in large part due to Lago's demands to be treated as an equal player in regional politics and as a direct participant in state-oil decisions. However, outsider organizations including their international partners would cultivate the image of a contaminated Amazon and Indigenous communities under siege, in order to support their own environmental and conservation concerns without having dense ties with Lago Agrio's organizations or community groups or without facilitating the multifaceted demands of the oil-affected communities. This is not to say that Lago Agrio's social justice groups have never received Northern support for other oil campaigns in the Amazon; they have received a great deal. But in this case, at this time, and given their demands, they received little relative to other campaigns along the route.

INCORPORATING OCP INTO A LONGER FIGHT

In defining social movements, Donatella Della Porta and Mario Diani underscore four primary factors. Social movements are "(1) informal networks, based (2) on shared beliefs and solidarity, which mobilize about (3) conflictual issues, through (4) the frequent use of various forms of protest."[156] To these parameters, the community and laborers of the greater Lago Agrio area were in the middle of a movement to wrest social, political, economic, and ecological control from the state and the oil sector. The resistance campaigns of the Amazon would appear to resemble Andrew Szasz's depiction of the environmental justice movement as "untroubled eclecticism,"[157] or a robust gathering of multiple groups presenting multiple claims, as well as Manuel Castells's assessment of environmental movements as decentralized, multiform, network oriented, and pervasive.[158] From these depictions, national and international campaigns against oil and globalization and for the environment would appear to be suitable allies. But the community of Lago Agrio—in their struggle against the state and OCP—was quite alone.

The tactics of this oil important community were, for instance, *more* radical and direct in confronting global discriminatory practices than the more diffuse and paper-pushing actions of national and international advocates and environmental groups; while their calls for immediate concessions (electricity and roads) were more pragmatic than the anti-oil, antiglobalization rhetoric of some nonlocal actors. Yet despite, *or due to*, their limited connections to professional national and international NGOs, the oil communities sought a much more progressive standard of economic justice and poverty reduction by incorporating people-centered deliberations in oil revenue spending and oil decision making.[159]

The grassroots groups of Lago Agrio based their resistance to the state and the OCP pipeline on material demands for just reparation for existing and future impacts and an active and local role in directing oil decisions, monitoring oil activities, and distributing oil revenues. Their perspective was grounded in a legacy of being ignored and neglected by the state and the oil industry. Residing near production processes, including seismic testing, extraction, storage, and transportation sites, they wanted to be critical and active decision makers in the course of the country's oil-led development, in siting decisions, in a more equitable distribution of the country's oil monies, in protecting their environments, and in implementing job development strategies. Indeed, when Lago Agrio utilized the construction of OCP to challenge the state by blocking the daily flow of oil, the oil communities threw down the gauntlet and held the attention of the Andean capital. Calling for community-directed oil justice, these professional and grassroots groups let the political and economic elites know again that the oil communities would continue to challenge this history of unrelenting injustices.

Now we must wait and see whether the completion of OCP promoted greater arrogance among state leaders and oil companies to block community involvement or whether the Lago Agrio community will be taken as a legitimate voice and authority in influencing the oil sector and the state's use of oil wealth. The community's demonstrated strength in challenging the state in this round was significant as the construction of OCP, at least in Lago Agrio, was never really about the construction of a single trans-Ecuadorian pipeline. The successful completion of the OCP pipeline meant the availability of more work and more oil funds to be distributed locally to meet community-determined need; it meant the doubling of exploration in previously untapped areas in the Amazon, leading to greater environmental and health risks still needing to be addressed; and it may have also meant that state leaders and oil executives, after succeeding in the construction of this line, would marginalize the unresolved demands of the area's residents. Once again in February 2006, the Bi-Provincial Strike Committee organized a similar oil strike against the state, and will most likely continue to do so until the communities' demands are met, until economic security in the region is realized, until environmental safeguards are installed, and until a participatory role in oil decisions is achieved among affected communities. In oil towns, embodied conflicts are not fashionable slogans or icons (like "boycott BP"). In these communities, oil injustices persist across generations and personify the exploitation of people and ecosystems at the direction of the oil-industrial core and the negligence of political leaders worldwide to end their national dependencies on oil.

3

Quito's NGOs

Realizing an Environmental Fund

Conservation NGOs in the capital Quito were established, professional groups of formally educated employees with advanced degrees, secure offices, workday schedules, and moderate to strong national and international ties. One could say that they represented the managerial class or the *salariat* of Ecuador in contrast to the working poor of Lago Agrio and the Indigenous subaltern of the Amazon. Most of them formed initially to protect species habitats in the Andean mountain range and the Galapagos Islands, which for some were their bread and butter projects. They have also worked internationally to raise awareness of Ecuador's distinct wildlife and ecosystems. With offices a hundred miles west of the Amazon, some of these NGOs discovered the Oriente's oil fields when they learned of the construction of OCP. But even then, they were more concerned with the pipeline's impacts on the Andean reserves and forests that they had already designated as critically important habitats.

The presence of established and networked environmental organizations would at first indicate a potentially powerful resource to counterbalance the damaging impacts of the oil commitments of the state and the activities of the petroleum industry. To the average unaffected person, fossil fuels and the natural environment would appear to be two incompatible natural resources. Some environmental NGOs in the North and the South may even be supported by due-paying members with the implicit understanding that the NGOs are working to protect nature and to offset the activities of extractive and toxic industries. It is to these desires that oil disasters, spills in particular, serve as a startling wake-up call to armchair environmentalists because the connections between nature, industry, and lifestyle are revealed and because wildlife, coastlines, and landscapes are seen as being destroyed irreparably (though not necessarily needlessly). It is due to this lethal and visceral link that those culpable of the damage work so hard to erase the connection by controlling media's access, by making invisible the toxic nature of oil, and by emphasizing our own dependencies on oil.[1]

Yet some of the world's largest conservation NGOs, including The Nature Conservancy (TNC), Conservation International (CI), and World Wildlife Fund (WWF),[2] have become so closely intertwined with the oil sector that they may no longer be the most effective watchdog or protector of the natural environment—though this is not new to those who study environmental organizations.[3] In the United States, the environmental movement of the 1960s and 1970s gave rise to these NGOs that then in the 1980s and 1990s found a niche for themselves as partners of multinational corporations, including some oil companies. This transition to the corporate world began with the National Wildlife Federation,[4] though others quickly followed suit. The partnership is an exchange between money or charitable donations and environmental awards, environmental silence,[5] and/or environmental endorsements. By environmental endorsements, I am referring to NGO support or enablement—whether intentional or not—of the corporate practice of constructing ecologists as extremist radicals who undermine the economy, of greening a company's image through name, logo, and slogan changes to present itself as the true environmentalist or responsible corporate citizen out to save nature and people's jobs,[6] and by weakening their own environmental agendas to meet the political and economic goals of their sponsors.[7] Others have identified that corporations promote these partnerships to create dependency and to gather intelligence on the NGO community itself.[8] Such partnerships may also serve—before a disaster—to bifurcate landscapes and seascapes into either conserved or polluted patches rather than seeking an end to environmental pollution overall.

Environmental silence and endorsement encompass co-option, of which much has already been written. Co-option occurs when a dominant group assimilates a less influential or less powerful one into the institutions and values of the former.[9] In this regard, corporations have invited conservation NGOs into a corporate worldview, and through sustained interaction, the NGOs adopt corporate-friendly patterns of interaction and softer environmental demands. Once engaged with corporations and government agencies, environmental NGOs also run the risk of becoming bogged down in preparing reports on risk management assessments and cost-benefit analysis, which deflect environmental action and change.[10] Rachael Shwom argues that "cooperation and cooptation are two sides of the same coin" as each one requires compromise between organizations,[11] but her review undervalues the influence of corporate power and monetary influence on NGOs and sidelines the potential for environmental negligence, which are not inconsequential—even though, and correctly so, she identifies that interactions between organizations (including NGOs and the private sector) are active and emergent.[12]

The co-option stage of Northern NGOs is past, and so it would appear that today these NGOs may actually be in a position to practice the co-option of smaller environmental organizations both within and outside of the United States. Ensconced within the capitalist model and unable to see above or around it, they may be the ones diluting environmental discussions and minimizing environmental demands that are arising in the Global South. The three largest organizations, each based in the United States but with offices or projects worldwide, have been under pressure from the global community to address their wealth from corporate and government funds and their neglect of Indigenous and non-Indigenous communities, who are affected by corporate action.[13] As noted in chapter 1, the environmental justice movement rose in the United States as a grassroots backlash against what was perceived as the exclusionary efforts of mainstream environmental organizations, which mimicked corporations in being hierarchical and centralized, and which limited links with marginalized people fighting against housing and health inequalities.[14] As early as the 1970s, charges of elitist tendencies among conservation NGOs had begun,[15] though it would not be until the 1990s when the environmental justice movement formulated the perception of these organizations as "institutionally predictable" and easily manipulated by industry.[16] EJ activists departed from mainstream conservation groups due to the latter's compromises, which were not only believed to favor state and industry practices over community interests,[17] but which also granted multinational corporations authority over the environment in developing places.

Likewise, collaborations between Indigenous communities and the leading conservation organizations had also withered after NGOs began to view Indigenous people as "difficult" and environmentally destructive,[18] which is peculiar given the landscape-altering impacts of large-scale industries. Again, it points to the self-assigned task of NGOs in determining and permitting the distinction between conserved and polluted places. Shared definitions of "participation" between Indigenous communities and NGOs have also been difficult. For example, in one case in Mexico, environmental NGOs and government officials viewed Indigenous participation as managed contributions within the framework of NGO and government proposals, while the community itself viewed participation in terms of the "territorial politics of invitation."[19] In their view, Indigenous communities (or specifically their leaders) held territorial rights to the land, which was their home, so only they held the power to invite nonlocal guests, in this case WWF, to meet with them in their home territory.[20]

Pro-industry groups and communities have also criticized environmental NGOs. Affected communities have supported extractive industries that NGOs have rejected,[21] while trade unions and business associations have questioned the legitimacy of environmental NGOs in influencing workplace practices since such organizations appear to them to have "little to lose and lots to gain" in their positions.[22]

A pattern of preferring technical fixes, narrowly selecting singular campaigns, and protecting their brand names due in part to the wealth and professional nature of the NGOs today led Michael Shellenberger and Ted Nordhaus to claim an end to environmentalism as it was once known and an end to the political pressure that the movement once generated.[23] Indeed, environmental journalists, writers, and analysts have been some of the harshest critics of the largest NGOs.[24] Shellenberger and Nordhaus were not confronting the movement and its individual adherents or small, locally based organizations; they were challenging the largest of the professional NGOs, whose absence in grassroots activism and increasingly corporate ties (though not identified in their work) has undermined the larger, wider, and more progressive political work of the early movement. In response to Shellenberger and Nordhaus's analysis, a symposium of environmental sociologists was held and their replies were published in *Organization & Environment*.[25] But Shellenberger and Nordhaus and too many of those who responded to their call for greater value- and moral-laden environmentalism, ignore the increasingly prominent role of corporate-NGO partnerships in rewarding conservation efforts in certain places while discouraging more strident calls for universal political, economic, and environmental reforms. Shellenberger and Nordhaus identify NGOs as receiving "tens of millions of dollars every year from foundations and individuals,"[26] while Maurie Cohen in response calls TNC "a behemoth land trust with vast holdings."[27] Others call for women to revitalize and lead a new environmental movement,[28] while still others identify the absence of the political and economic context in Shellenberger and Nordhaus's analysis.[29] Yet, each one ignores the corporate ties of the largest NGOs.

This is not a critique of their work—each one has made invaluable contributions to a better understanding of the environmental movement today—but it is to suggest that corporate-NGO partnerships have succeeded in keeping themselves off the radar or that corporate-NGO partnerships are so undeniable that they no longer warrant a mention.

Corporate-sponsored research, which environmental NGOs conduct, is another area of concern. Corporate sponsorship influences the research questions, which shapes the findings that than directs what is or is not discussed in policy meetings.[30] The ethical considerations of corporate-funded NGO research are rarely asked,[31] though the impacts of such research may divert attention away from the most egregious industrial stressors on the environment. This practice is another component of environmental endorsement of corporate sponsors as the research itself accepts the oil-industrial core as a legitimate force that relegates conservation initiatives.

Furthermore, the maneuvering and outmaneuvering of the different stakeholders in environmental disputes hinges on the information produced, acquired, and exchanged—so to direct research or to block such exchanges greatly impairs the capacity of affected community groups. Gerald Markowitz and David Rosner document extensively how industry hoards industry-funded research, conducts sloppy research, and manipulates or falsifies findings, while challenging the "scientific expertise" of communities, demanding statistical significance, and presenting economic consideration as criteria in measuring the overall impact of industry location, production, and distribution.[32] Corporate-sponsored NGO research is likely to do the same. In contrast, grassroots groups engaged in EJ struggles (at least in the United States) have been—at times—assisted by university researchers or federal agencies in conducting environmental health studies. Unlike corporate-funded research, community groups involved in independent research, including collaborating in the data collection, data analysis, and presentation of findings, have succeeded in *owning* the research and using the information gathered for social change.[33] Jason Corburn refers to community-based participatory research as providing "actionable knowledge" for community education and learning, for political organizing and democratic participation, and for proactive strategies directed by the communities themselves.[34] Environmental research conducted by NGOs through corporate sponsorship would not likely be provided to affected communities or support their environmental claims against the industry. Likewise, NGO-corporate partners that have worked to disconnect conserved places from polluted ones conduct research and protection initiatives in areas cordoned away from industrial endeavors, which exclude communities and governments on the ground.

Less critically, James Speth identifies current environmentalism as pragmatic, incrementalist, and compromising: "It takes what it can get," while operating within the system.[35] What conservation NGOs get is an inverse or negative exchange: as revenues from corporate funders increase, political pressure on corporate polluters decreases. Three of the largest conservation NGOs, CI, TNC, and WWF, have "corporate partners" or "corporate collaborators,"[36] and according to one source, these three organizations earned US$1.28 billion in revenues in 2002.[37] Their fundraising endeavors encompass bilateral and multilateral agencies, the U.S. government, private foundations, members, and corporations. Some of the corporate partners include oil giants BP, ChevronTexaco, ExxonMobil, and Shell International, as well as agrochemical companies such as Monsanto[38] and Dow Chemical and timber-product suppliers such as IKEA.[39] Petro- and agrochemical partners are quite unlike smaller private sector companies, where coffee-NGO collaboration, for example, may increase sustainable practices in the field while creating and educating a new market on fair trade coffee and sustainable growing practices.[40]

If the corporate associations sound too risky for an environmental NGO, think again. Following the BP spill in the Gulf of Mexico in April 2010, TNC experienced some media scrutiny for its partnerships with BP.[41] But two months after the spill, a two-hour telethon to receive donations to clean up or to correct the spill raised US$1.8 million, which was considered a "meager amount" in philanthropic circles.[42] Of that, TNC received $400,000 and the National Wildlife Federation received US$835,000.[43] The irony of generating money from the public after an oil spill, while simultaneously being a partner of the corporate perpetrator that both wasted a public resource (oil reserves in the Gulf) while polluting another public resource (the Gulf of Mexico) is amazingly audacious. Part of their success was due to their past successes at branding; another part was due to limited public awareness. Applying Speth's general assessments to oil-NGO ties, I would suggest that environmental NGOs and their corporate sponsors succeed in part due to a "poorly informed public, and a pathetic level of public discourse on the environment."[44] Until an oil disaster occurs, it is much easier to minimize scrutiny of such alliances from uncritical members and to insist that donations from oil corporations are a workable arrangement for conservation initiatives. After an oil disaster, such efforts and exchanges appear irreversibly damaging (if not insulting) to affected ecosystems, cleanup crews, communities, due-paying members, and a public's natural resources. Even so, corporate liaisons protect environmental NGOs from charges of unethical conduct and unsavory choices made by smaller organizations and affected communities, while the public remains quite removed from national and global discussions on the environment and, even less so, on the oil-industrial complex.

What is new is that Northern NGOs are introducing Southern organizations to these practices for an increasingly wholesale adoption of corporate-environmental agreements and affiliations. This chapter suggests that environmental accommodations with corporations in the North have set a precedent for repeating this pattern in the South that may be even less beneficial to Southern organizations, communities, and ecosystems. The presence of Northern NGOs in Latin America is well established, but the transfer of corporate contacts may only be just beginning.

For example, CI, TNC, and WWF were instrumental in Latin America in arranging debt-for-nature swaps in the 1980s, for designing national environmental funds in the 1990s,[45] and for funding, directly or through secondary grants, domestic conservation organizations throughout these periods. Debt-for-nature swaps, first proposed by WWF in 1984,[46] entailed that the debtor nation, instead of paying back the foreign lender in foreign currencies, could pay conservation NGOs in local currencies to conserve parts of the country's natural environment or to develop national parks or reserves.[47] In 1987, WWF entered into Ecuador's first debt-for-nature swap and then in 1989 was joined by TNC and the Missouri Botanical Gardens for a larger swap that was managed by the domestic organization, Fundación Natura.[48] Parks included the Galapagos Islands, Cayambe-Coca, and Cotachachi-Cayapas ecological reserves of the Andes and Cuyabeno Wildlife Reserve and Yasuní National Park in the Amazon, as well as Machalilla National Park north of Esmeraldas on the Pacific Coast.[49] The two parks in the Amazon were reserves with Indigenous communities, oil workers, and new settlers, while the Andean parks also experienced the encroachment of loggers and farmers.[50] Yet, the debt-for-nature swaps failed to control new settlers or users, while also failing to account for the impacts the reserves and these new arrivals would have on the Indigenous populations. Moreover, Terisa Turner and Craig Benjamin assess that "the privatization of research findings by Northern firms is a central objective of the Ecuador swaps."[51] In particular, they identify that one of the projects organized by Fundación Natura, WWF, and TNC was to grant the U.S. research group, the Missouri Botanical Gardens, "exclusive rights to carry out research on genetic resources in the designated reserves and parks," without obligation to share the results with Ecuadorian groups, to incorporate local expertise or learning, or to engage in technology transfers.[52] In this case, the debt-for-nature swap granted Northern corporations access to novel genetic material, while domestic environmental NGOs were given greater control over physical landscapes inhabited by Indigenous people and recent settlers.

Then in the 1990s across Latin America, national environmental funds, conservation trusts, and environmental compensation packages were introduced as a long-term and national-level mechanism, with ties to the national government, to coordinate environmental financing schemes.[53] These funds or trusts, which were launched primarily in Latin America, were designed to create or expand national parks, access funds for conservation, support scientific research,[54] restore the environmental stock of nonimpacted areas,[55] and protect endemic ecosystems. Even in the mid-1990s, concerns were raised whether local governments would reduce their own environmental contributions and whether such funds would separate the environment from sustainable development plans and policies, while strengthening environmental considerations at the expense of the other concerns.[56] At that time, international donors to environmental funds in Latin America were governments and nonprofits, not corporations.[57] After nearly a decade, the Conservation Finance Alliance (CFA) was formed in 2002 to better formalize these funds and trusts in order to facilitate links between private and public funders and the worldwide conservation community.[58] Despite the expansion of such funds, it is not clear whether they are preempting environmental destruction, implementing contingency plans in the face of expanding extractive industries, or serving as a cover for the proliferation of capitalism's more destructive tendencies in more difficult to reach places. Indeed it has been argued that the outcome of environmental compensation accommodates the interests of developers and leaves unchallenged the environmental damage associated with economic growth.[59]

Though these funds or trusts were originally designed between government bodies, nonprofits, and international lenders or institutions, more corporations have begun contributing to them, which lessens further the autonomy of the fund recipients to pressure industry. To be sure, TNC in particular demonstrated its commitment to seeking corporate sponsorship for conservation projects in a 2004 report in *Nature Conservancy Magazine*:

> But with no clear end in sight to the world's thirst for hydrocarbons . . . , the Conservancy is forging a new approach to dealing with that threat: working directly with oil companies. By pushing for more careful site selection and stricter corporate controls, and by generating special funds for environmental protections, the Conservancy is seeking to minimize the footprint of energy extraction on the planet.[60]

The argument of minimizing impact is slightly disingenuous as environmental funds, typically, fail to address the direct environmental and community impacts of the petrochemical industry, while conserving land in non-oil-impacted areas, which contributes to the construction of natural environments as either worthy of protection or of pollution.

Research on the tensions between grassroots groups and professional NGOs due to class and power relations may also inform a richer understanding of the imbalances between professional domestic NGOs and international ones operating in Southern places.[61] Deep ideological differences between grassroots groups, which respond to community- and personal-level experiences (and cultural nuances in the case of domestic NGOs), and professional organizations (and international ones), which act from an institutional perspective, impede collective action. Likewise, the "detached identities" of professional (and perhaps international) NGOs may be in constant struggle with the "embedded identities" of community groups (and perhaps domestic NGOs), which live the experience daily.[62]

Through global interactions, the detached agendas and expert knowledge of international NGOs may dominate the embedded and localized knowledge of domestic NGOs and affected communities. Indeed, a Northern privilege to design and plan environmental sustainability programs in the South has been referred to as an "environmental truth."[63] When placed in a global context, the actions of leading conservation NGOs may also imperil developing communities and ecosystems by ignoring Northern or Western consumption patterns as cause for the pressing need to conserve,[64] and by weakening the bargaining power of affected communities,[65] and I would add: domestic NGOs. Vandana Shiva has labeled these one-sided influences as green imperialism, a persistent system of apartheid, in which "the South has no rights, but all responsibility" for conserving the world's resources.[66]

To clarify, this introduction to the environmental community is not meant to diminish the efforts and successes of the NGOs of Ecuador. It is however an effort to contextualize the international spaces, opportunities, and obstacles to which they were exposed or placed. These points of union and separation are particularly dynamic, both onerous and unfettering, for domestic groups, which not only shift but are pushed and pulled between the two sides (affected communities and Northern NGOs). Though domestic NGOs may have greater ties to affected communities due to shared local, cultural, and embedded perspectives, they are also at greatest risk of being pinched in the interface between community groups and international entities, including both Northern NGOs as well as oil multinationals. Southern NGOs are integral though underanalyzed actors in these community-international dialectics. Indeed, what are the organizational and relational impacts on domestic NGOs when first entering into a triangulated relationship with corporations and international NGOs, when collaborating with the country's oil sector for the first time, and when sanctioning oil funds for the environment? From the literature, we would expect these exchanges to be led by industry and Northern NGOs, to be particularly arduous on midsize Ecuadorian groups and ecosystems, to undermine calls for national-level environmental reform,[67] and to undercut the realization of oil justice for the most affected communities. This chapter demonstrates how Northern NGOs, which may be more amenable to industry than Southern ones, may introduce corporate-conservation protocol, which enables and disables, includes and excludes, and empowers and disempowers domestic groups—and to which Ecuadorian NGOs may not be immune.

SETTING: THE CAPITAL

Quito is a long, narrow string of a capital, situated in a valley in the central Andean highlands, approximately 2,850 meters above sea level. Quito's mayor and city council challenged the route of the pipeline, of which 103 kilometers (64 miles) passed through the outlying region of this metropolitan area, arguing that the city was expanding near the right-of-way and that the pipeline was placed through an area of high landslide and volcanic risk.[68] The mayor and city council were also concerned that a section of the route would affect the Papallacta River, the source of approximately 40 percent of Quito's water supply. For four months in 2001, Mayor Paco Moncayo, along with the mayors of Lago Agrio and Esmeraldas, put up strong resistance to the route, impact assessments, and compensation packages, delaying construction by two months. The city council, after its own impact analysis, asked for an increase in control valves to stop release at approximately 500 barrels, rather than the original 3,500 barrels, and microvariations in the route of 300 to 500 meters. By early October 2001, Mayor Moncayo approved the pipeline and accepted OCP's assurances of response and responsibility if a spill should occur. The city council's challenge of the pipeline's route was a test of the country's 1998 environment management law, which gave the Environment Ministry the responsibility to grant licenses to oil projects. A component of this law required the Environment Ministry to consult with local communities and local municipalities, which had jurisdiction within the project's territorial range.

Though many of the conservation NGOs discovered the oil industry for the first time with the construction of OCP, and though several of them wanted to be invited to the "party,"[69] they were not asking to join the mayor's party. "A major party has been organized," claimed an environmental director, "but only a few have been invited. Not many of us have seen the positive side of that process [of the oil industry]. We have only seen the negative side."[70] For those in the conservation community, the OCP pipeline represented their first occasion—via the multinationals, not the state—to enter into the nation's political oil economy. Never directly or personally impacted by the OCP project, these professional NGOs underwent a series of transitions from confrontation to negotiation, from elation to criticism, and from fatigue to recovery in an attempt to gain greater political and technical control over the environmental direction of the country. However, their inexperience in oil-environmental contact led them into an alliance with the industry and international NGOs, at the expense of former and potential ties with affected communities and grassroots ecologists along OCP's route.

Unlike the oil-impacted communities at the receiving and shipping end of the pipeline, these urban-based organizations represented the environmental elite of Ecuador and mimicked the organizational path of their more privileged Northern partners. In this case, the midlevel, domestic NGOs had their feet planted precariously between their international and Northern partners and the affected communities where they carry out their research and conservation projects. On the one hand, these smaller domestic NGOs live and work in Ecuador and share land interests with neighboring communities. On the other hand, they are financially and perhaps technically dependent on their international partners and funders, whose headquarters had established links with corporations or had reputations of seeking corporate partnerships. To be sure, there are both first-tier domestic and international environmental NGOs, as well as second-tier domestic and international NGOs. The relative financial strength, staff size, and project portfolio differentiate first-tier from second-tier organizations. First-tier organizations include the largest U.S.-based environmental organizations with corporate partnerships, extensive financial and project portfolios, and a broad geographical range. Ecuador had first-tier domestic organizations as well, which were strongly affiliated with their Northern partners. Likewise, second-tier or midlevel domestic and international NGOs existed with smaller portfolios and lesser name recognition.

With the announcement of OCP, these Ecuadorian organizations, which had been ignored by the state, turned to their international partners to pressure the oil consortium to reroute the pipeline, to improve its environmental impact assessment (EIA), and then eventually to meet for direct negotiations for an environmental compensation fund. International partners served as leverage, a point made first by Margaret Keck and Kathryn Sikkink, and then by Alison Brysk in her study of Indigenous movements in Ecuador.[71]

Keck and Sikkink's boomerang model, however, can be extended to account for a more layered degree of support or impediment experienced by the NGO community. Environmental NGOs ignored by the state may turn to their international partners to pressure oil multinationals for direct negotiations. This act may also be juxtaposed by similar boomerang actions by multinational corporations. In this case, oil corporations turned to their international conservation partners, with whom they had already established a working relationship, in order to request that their international NGO associates provide a framework of oil-NGO relations for the domestic groups. Both actions, the NGO boomerang effort and the corporate boomerang effort,[72] pressured and influenced the Ecuadorian debate on the feasibility of an extractive economy coexisting with environmental protection initiatives. These efforts converted into a double burden on domestic NGOs, which witnessed a decline in community alliances and perhaps a decline in their ability to advocate for the country's natural environment after increasing contact with the oil industry.

This chapter is organized to reflect the evolving responses and adaptations of Ecuador's NGO community—particularly the midsize domestic groups—to the OCP pipeline project and to their relationships with affected communities, each other, their international partners, and the consortium companies. Though long-running oil contention in Lago Agrio culminated in a transformative event, or the take of oil facilities alongside strengthened ties between the town's mayor and the community, the NGOs in Quito—without a firm or historical stance on the oil industry—experienced bursts of agendas and positions one after another as they embarked upon a transnational campaign to influence the oil sector. Yet their transitions may have had greater impact on the organizations themselves than on the country's environmental policies and practices. Certainly neither Quito's nor Lago Agrio's mobilization efforts hampered the political and economic might of the petroleum sector in Ecuador nor did they lessen the damage an oil spill might incur.

STAKEHOLDERS: CONSERVATION NGOS DISCOVER OIL

Once the environmental NGOs in the capital were alerted to the pipeline project, their agendas and actions were not particular to the metropolitan area or to OCP's direct impacts on the capital. Instead, organized opposition by a small contingent of professional NGOs occurred after the announcement of OCP's route through the Mindo-Nambillo and Chocó-Andean protected reserves,[73] which were identified as previously unstained by the oil industry. To be sure, the majority of environmental NGOs in Ecuador had remained indifferent to the oil industry despite its contentious history in the Amazon. "The environmental community didn't engage at all here [on the expansion of the oil industry], which is amazing," acknowledged one NGO spokesperson. "It had been an issue for a long time, and there had been a little bit of sniping from the side, but nobody really recognized the magnitude of the issue."[74]

Organizations including first- and second-tier, domestic and international NGOs, which wanted to protect their conservation work, to expand Ecuador's conservation efforts, or to insert themselves into Ecuador's oil economy,[75] found the construction of OCP as an opportunity to do so. Over the course of construction, at least five types of Quito-based organizations responded to the pipeline, as shown in table 3.1. They could also be categorized as (1) early resisters and negotiation launchers, (2) nonresisters and negotiation joiners, (3) constant and active oil resisters, (4) nonresisters, and (5) uncertains.

In the first category, the regional office of U.K.-based BirdLife International, which was based in Quito, BirdLife's local partner CECIA (Corporación Ornitológica de Ecuador), and Fundación Maquipucuna constituted the first responders to OCP, the first resisters, and the first to introduce collective bargaining for environmental compensation.[76] In mid-2000, these three had already begun a strong resistance campaign against the "northern" route followed by a campaign against OCP's EIA in 2001. In both efforts, they were joined by expert grassroots ecologists, in many ways their conservation

Table 3.1. Quito-Based Organizations

Domestic/International Radical Ecologists	Domestic			International	
	Second-Tier Conservation	First-Tier Conservation	Second-Tier Social and Environmental Justice, Legal and Human Rights	Second-Tier Conservation	First-Tier Conservation
Acción Ecológica (3)	Ambiente y Sociedad (2)[a]	FFLA[c]	CDES	BirdLife (1)[ab]	CI[d]
Oil Watch (3)	CECIA (1)[ab]	Natura (2)[a]	CEDA (2)[a]	WCS	TNC[e]
	CEDENMA		CEDHU		
	EcoCiencia (2)[a]		INREDH		
	Jatun Sacha		Pachamama		
	Maquipucuna (1)[ab]		SERPAJ		
	Pro Ruta[b]		Truth Commission		

Note: Many of these organizations conduct critical research in their fields of expertise.

(1) Early resisters and negotiation launchers; (2) Nonresisters and negotiation joiners; (3) Active oil resisters

[a] Participants of the environmental fund negotiations.

[b] Original group opposing OCP's northern route near Mindo before initiating fund talks.

[c] FFLA works on environmental conflict management and prevention and sustainable development, not conservation per se. FFLA is categorized under conservation for this table as its director served as the mediator of ecofund talks.

[d] CI acted as an informal consultant to some of the NGOs participating in the environmental fund.

[e] One of TNC's Quito-based representatives sat in on environmental fund discussions as an adviser and an observer, not as an official TNC spokesperson.

Abbreviations:

CDES, Centro de Derechos Economicos y Sociales (Center of Economic and Social Rights)

CECIA, Corporación Ornitologica de Ecuador

CEDA, Centro de Derecho Ambiental (Environmental Rights Center)

CEDENMA, Comite Ecuatoriano para la Defesna de la Naturaleza y el Medio Ambiente

CEDHU, Comision Ecumenica de Derechos Humanos (Ecumenical Commission on Human Rights)

CI, Conservation International

FFLA, Fundación Futuro Latinoamericano

INREDH, Fundación Regional de Asesoria de Derechos Humanos (Regional Foundation of Human Rights)

SERPAJ, Servicio Paz y Justicia (Peace and Justice Services)

TNC, The Nature Conservancy

Truth Commission, Comision de Veeduria Socio Ambiental del OCP (OCP Truth Commission)

WCS, Wildlife Conservation Society

equals, in the affected Andean region of Mindo and Tandayapa. The president of CEDENMA, Ecuador's umbrella environmental organization,[77] was also aligned with this group, which at the time was calling itself the Comité Pro Ruta de Menor Impacto, or the Committee for the Route of Least Impact.[78] The Comité also launched initial links to the financiers and to EnCana, the largest shareholder of the OCP consortium. In addition, BirdLife would also join with the expert grassroots ecologists and ornithologists of the Mindo area to form the Mindo Working Group to prepare an alternative EIA for the Mindo Important Bird Area (IBA).[79]

Once BirdLife, CECIA, and Maquipucuna determined that the route of the pipeline project was nonnegotiable, they collaborated—at the exclusion of the grassroots ecologists in Comité Pro Ruta and the Mindo Working Group—to initiate ecofund talks with the consortium. At this time, CECIA, which was established in 1986, would also receive three contracts from OCP: (1) to minimize impact in the Mindo IBA; (2) to determine microvariations in the route in five areas in the Mindo IBA; and (3) to map, monitor, and protect the black-breasted pufffeg hummingbird (*Eriocnemis nigrivestis*). OCP provided US$166,121, US$9,389, and $65,747 for each project respectively.[80]

In June 2002, these three organizations were eventually joined by Fundación Natura in their discussions for an environmental fund.[81] Fundación Natura is the largest domestic NGO in Ecuador and is partnered with TNC and WWF. For additional clarification, Natura initially joined the others in rejecting the route, but then split temporarily from them when Natura's then director engaged in talks directly with OCP without organizational approval and without other NGO participation.[82] This director was replaced in April 2002, and Natura rejoined the other three organizations in ecofund talks in June 2002.

Among the other second-tier domestic environmental NGOs, EcoCiencia and Fundación Ambiente y Sociedad may have opposed the Northern route and the process's lack of transparency and public consultations, but they were not active or visible resisters to the pipeline project before or after it was approved by the government. Both NGOs joined environmental fund discussions only after talks had been ongoing for nearly one year. Fundación Ambiente y Sociedad, for example, advocated for greater transparency and participation; however, it suspended its own participation in debates on the OCP project after the pipeline's EIA met official approval and the project was awarded its environmental license. In addition, Ambiente y Sociedad, which was founded in 2000 by some of the most well-established members of Ecuador's environmental circle, received funds from OCP to monitor part of the project, so they initially determined that participating in environmental fund negotiations would be a point of conflict as well.[83] EcoCiencia, founded in 1989, acknowledged the importance of oil exploitation to Ecuador's economy and with Ambiente y Sociedad participated in meetings with the Ministries of Environment and Energy and Mines to revise the EIA.[84] As an older research organization, EcoCiencia may have also had the most experience with oil projects in the Amazon. In addition, Centro de Derecho Ambiental, or CEDA, which was founded in 1996 to specialize in environmental legal rights, was also perhaps reluctant to join in the fund discussions, but did so in 2002.

At the time of OCP's construction there were sixty-eight active environmental NGOs in Ecuador under the umbrella organization CEDENMA. Of these sixty-eight NGOs, six participated in environmental fund negotiations with the OCP consortium during and after the pipeline's construction. The six were Ambiente y Sociedad, CECIA,[85] CEDA, EcoCiencia, Maquipucuna, and Natura.[86]

The Quito offices of the international NGOs BirdLife and TNC also participated in the fund, but were not members of the national organization CEDENMA.[87] BirdLife's Quito office was the regional office for the U.K. group, but its staff was engaged from the beginning on challenging the pipeline project through BirdLife-designated IBAs. TNC, which did not take a position on the pipeline project, served as an unofficial adviser and observer to environmental negotiations, while CI, particularly its Center for Environmental Leadership in Business, served as an informal consultant to the NGOs in the early stages of the negotiation. At the time, CI did not have a Quito office, though in the past and after the pipeline's project it would have one. In addition, two academic groups were also included in negotiations: Universidad San Francisco de Quito and Comité Ecológico del Escuela Polytecnica Litoral, a school on the coast that had been hired by OCP for some of the monitoring responsibility.[88]

After BirdLife, CECIA, Maquipucuna, and Natura failed to come to an agreement with OCP in mid-2002, the oil consortium hired Yolanda Kakabadse, an influential environmentalist in Ecuador, to facilitate and mediate talks between the NGOs and the private sector and to invite more NGOs to the table. This mediator was known as "one of the most prominent environmentalists in the country," noted one NGO,[89] and in this case prominent meant that Kakabadse had served as former environment minister, former head of the World Conservation Union (IUCN), former Ford Foundation board member, former executive president of Fundación Natura, former board member of World Wildlife Fund, and the then executive president of Fundación Futuro Latinoamericano (FFLA), an organization based in Quito that works on sustainable development projects and managing and/or preventing environmental conflict.[90] It should also be noted that the IUCN, like the other large NGOs, had also been charged with having contentious relationships with communities impacted by other large-scale projects. Michael Goldman, for example, details how the IUCN prevented the publication of reports that questioned the impacts of a World Bank dam project on neighboring communities in Southeast Asia.[91] In addition, EnCana's then-president and CEO identified this established professional as an environmental authority in Ecuador who endorsed EnCana's operations after touring their facilities with the comments: "I returned with a very favorable impression of the efforts being undertaken to go beyond environmental laws and regulations. Your enthusiasm and conviction are key elements for success. Congratulations!"[92]

In Ecuador, this mediator was a mentor for many, having hired many in the environmental field, and thereby creating dense ties with the directors of the large conservation organizations. When OCP hired the facilitator, Ambiente y Sociedad, CEDA, EcoCiencia, and the director of TNC's Quito office joined talks as well. To be sure, in a nation the physical size of Nevada and with a population of approximately thirteen million, the environmental class is a scaled-down version of "interlocking directorates," which occur when the corporate elite serve on multiple boards to influence macroeconomic and political concerns.[93] In this case, the interlocking environmental elite within Ecuador with extensive international experience served as a source of collaboration between leadership in the ministry and many of the Quito-based NGOs. At the same time, there was an informal expatriate network among nonnational NGO leadership, embassies representatives, oil executives, and nonnational chambers of commerce operating as well.

CI, TNC, WWF, and BirdLife were directly or indirectly active in Ecuador at this time. Though not direct participants in negotiations in Ecuador, the indirect involvement of these international NGOs was actively political and influential in outcome as a neutral or nonpolitical position is very much a political one, supporting directly or indirectly one side over the other. As an example, the political nature of conservation was indicated in a 2004 magazine article by TNC, which described Ecuador as relying on oil revenues "just to scrape by" and the construction of OCP "was like winning the jackpot for a nation where half the population was earning less than $2 a day."[94] This sentiment validates the petroleum industry as a singular option to elevate the nation out of its poverty. However, and as noted in previous chapters, there is a tremendous amount of research that indicates otherwise. Reliance on petroleum revenues is often an affliction for a nation's poor and the health and viability of its natural environment. State support of economic alternatives to the land-intensive, large-scale oil projects is frequently diminished, while debt access tied to the industry is accompanied by stipulations that weaken social support systems.

In Quito, other NGOs refused or were not invited to join ecofund negotiations. "The other NGOs didn't want to join this proposal, this initiative. They were reluctant. They were saying that given that OCP is creating so much damage it was unethical to try to get some money out of them for conservation,"[95] noted one participant. CEDENMA and Fundación Arco Iris in Loja were invited, but declined. CEDENMA was "completely against the idea" and Arco Iris was "reluctant to participate because they felt [there were] ethical issues going on and they don't think it's feasible to negotiate with OCP, given that much damage they are already causing," remembered one.[96]

Among the conservation NGOs, Fundación Jatun Sacha did not challenge the route or the EIA, nor did it collaborate on a fund. Instead, Jatun Sacha elected to confer directly with OCP for an independent contract to replant impacted flora along the pipeline's right-of-way. The project costing approximately US$564,000 included two stages over a three-year period.[97] The first stage involved the revegetation along the impacted area, and the second phase included subsequent monitoring of regrowth and controlling invasive species.

At the other extreme of the conservation NGOs were the more radical, anti-oil groups, including a large and mobile contingent of university youth, whose antiglobalization and anti-oil rhetoric often failed to resonate with many affected communities. The radical ecologist organizations included the internationally well-known and well-connected Acción Ecológica and its international sister organization Oilwatch. Together, they rejected the pipeline, rejected increased exploration, and eventually called for an oil moratorium in the country. Acción Ecológica served as a local broker for international activist organizations to partner with grassroots community groups, and in this regard Acción Ecológica was the initial key to organizing a transnational network of opposition. Acción Ecológica was also prolific in preparing environmental reports for affected communities.[98]

In the middle, serving as moderating and bridging voices, were the social justice organizations that embodied the primary principles of an environmental justice movement within a multinational context. These middle-ground justice groups, some with extensive international ties and others with only limited ones, targeted the state for greater transparency and a more inclusive and decisive role in the country's political economy. Included in this category were CEDA, which join OCP talks; CDES (Centro de Derechos Economicos y Sociales or Center of Economic and Social Rights); Comisión de Veeduria Socio Ambiental del OCP, or the OCP Truth Commission, which formed as a much smaller group after the demise of Comité Pro Ruta; and Pachamama, a local organization with strong international affiliation.[99] Human rights organizations in Quito were also a part of the second-tier justice bracket, though their focus was not exclusive to socioenvironmental concerns. The three human rights organizations included CEDHU (Comision Ecumenica de Derechos Humanos, or Ecumenical Commission on Human Rights); INREDH (Fundación Regional de Asesoria de Derechos Humanos, or Regional Foundation of Human Rights); and SERPAJ (Servicio Paz y Justicia, or Peace and Justice Services).[100]

These ecojustice and human rights organizations may have best represented civil society's interests, though they were not the groups that gained international media attention or extensive international platforms on OCP, even though most were supported by international allies. These were groups designed to realize justice for Ecuador, within Ecuador, through Ecuadorian law, and in collaboration with Ecuadorian communities. These middle-ground human rights and justice organizations opposed the process but accepted the pipeline's construction as an unmovable decision based on their perceptions of the nation's economic development strategy plans.[101] Some of them were also more committed to supporting long-running disputes between oil-affected communities in the Amazon and the state or individual oil companies than the cross-country pipeline project.

ORGANIZATIONAL AND ENVIRONMENTAL IMPACTS OF CONFRONTATION AND NEGOTIATION

In parallel with the pipeline's construction, the environmental NGOs transitioned from resistance to negotiation and accommodation, from decline to recovery, and from the national to the international and back again. Along the way they built and damaged bonds, and began again the rebuilding process with affected communities and the NGO community. Among the communities analyzed, this one formed a transnational campaign of negotiation—rather than resistance—with the OCP consortium, and by doing so established or strengthened ties with Northern NGOs, oil consultants, oil entities, and other international bodies. To better explain the overhauls and transformations that they experienced, this section is divided into four phases as a tool to organize their shifting positions, demands, and experiences. (For an overview, see table 3.2.) Though this book is grounded in the paradigms of environmental justice and political economy, a mesolevel analysis of the organizations as they undergo oil discovery is a significant step toward understanding how and why national and international NGOs impede or facilitate the petroleum industry's global environmental practices and how and why national and international NGOs hinder or assist low-income nations in governing industries and a nation's natural resources.

Stage 1: Community-NGO Collaboration

Prior to the government's announcement of OCP, the vast majority of conservation NGOs—if not all of them—accepted oil extraction as a necessary driver of the country's economy. Indeed in 2001 and 2002, several NGOs actively framed themselves as "non-activists" and "non-political," due to their conservation-only mandates and what would appear to them to be the pipeline's very political nature. "We believe that the oil industry is not bad per se," said one NGO spokesperson in 2001, encapsulating the conservation community's position. "But the oil industry should apply all the procedures, all the processes needed in order to extract and sell the oil that the country needs to sell, to export, but in a way that does not affect the environment."[102]

Table 3.2. Overview of Quito-Based NGO Response to OCP

	Targets[a]				Demands				Organizational Change in Position
	2001	2002	2003	2007–2009	2001	2002[b]	2003[b]	2007–2009[b]	
Conservation[c]	State	OCP	OCP	Ministries, Oil Operators	• EIA and Route Participation • Transparency • Rerouting • Monitoring Role	• • • Monitoring Role • Environmental Care • Ecofund	• • • Environmental Care • Ecofund	• • • • Protect Yasuní • Policy Role	• Oil Discovery • Challenge OCPˣ • Negotiations • Gain and Loss of Agency • Lack of Transparency • Community and NGO Conflict • Changing Policy
Environmental and Social Justice[d]	State	State OCP	State OCP	Ministries, Oil Operators	• Political Participation • Transparency • Accountability	• Political Participation • Transparency • Accountability • Ecofund	• Political Participation • Transparency • Accountability • Ecofund	• Political Participation • Transparency • Accountability • Stronger Laws	• Similar to Above
Radical Ecology	State OCP	OCP State	OCP State	Private MNCs, State	• Reject OCP • Reject MNCs	• Reject OCP • Reject MNCs • Moratorium	• Reject OCP • Reject MNCs • Moratorium	• Reject OCP • Reject MNCs • Moratorium • Protect Yasuní	• No Change: Ending Oil Exploration by MNCs Primarily

Note: MNCs = multinational corporations

[a]The targets are ranked. Some organizations targeted the state primarily, and then switched to targeting OCP primarily.

[b]A blank bullet point denotes that the request is no longer demanded.

[c]Some conservation NGOs ignored the OCP pipeline project until environmental fund negotiations had begun.

[d]This is only assessing the environmental and social justice organizations that participated in the environmental fund talks, not those that did not.

For some, the oil industry crossed this tolerable threshold of coexistence when OCP announced plans to route the pipeline across an area designated by the conservation community as one of ecological importance. At this point and as noted earlier, a core group of midlevel domestic NGOs with assistance from the regional Quito office of BirdLife joined with grassroots ecologists in the Mindo region to challenge both the route in the Mindo-Nambillo area and OCP's EIA. Questioning the industry's impacts and demanding a greater and more meaningful degree of participation and transparency, participation in the route selection, and official EIA became a critical point of debate between the NGOs and the state at this early stage before construction began.

Contesting the Route and EIA

In particular, the first point of conflict was the selected route. Three oil groups offered bids along three different routes in 2000. One route tracked near the Colombian border, the second patterned SOTE with a split near the southern tip of Quito's metropolitan area, which activist-ecologists and the conservation NGOs labeled the "southern route." The third route was OCP's bid, which cut through new territory north of the capital, and was referred to as the "northern route." No organization or community group was permitted to participate in the route or consortium selection, despite the number and expertise of Ecuadorian environmental, human rights and social justice NGOs.

When OCP's "northern route" was revealed in 2000,[103] a loose coalition formed between Quito's professional NGOs and people of the affected Andean region near the towns of Mindo and Tandayapa. The Quito-based NGOs included BirdLife's regional office, BirdLife's local partner CECIA, and Maquipucuna, while the grassroots ecologists included national and international landowners, hotel and resort operators, and knowledgeable community ecologists and ornithologists in the affected Andean region. CECIA and Maquipucuna managed reserves and conducted research and conservation projects in the protected cloud forest reserves of Mindo-Nambillo, Cuenca Alta del Rio Guayllabamba, and the Chocó-Andean Conservation Corridor. Along the route, this alliance between the professional NGOs and the grassroots ecologists represented Ecuador's environmental elite and the environmentally employed. Their mobilization efforts also represented the first collective Andean campaign against the oil sector in Ecuador.

When they first joined together, they called themselves the Committee for the Route of Least Impact. This loose coalition petitioned the state of Ecuador to alter the route away from the ecologically sensitive and internationally designated IBA and habitat of the black-breasted puffleg hummingbird and the umbrella-bird in particular, as well as other endangered and endemic species in the Mindo-Nambillo and Chocó-Andean regions.[104] Representing the general sentiment at the time, one coalition member said, "Very simply, we were against the northern route. We thought that initially a better analysis should be done of all the routes. And it wasn't. And that the northern route was preselected, if you will. And so, of course, we were against the process."[105]

The public review process was a particular point of dispute given that the public and the NGOs were burdened by limited time and limited access. The review process was closed after two weeks, and in some cases in rural areas, the ability to review the document was made available only by computer, which many rural residents had never used. Rural residents were inundated with words and technology that put a veneer on OCP's expertise, while blocking their participation.

A second point of contention was the official EIA, a 1,500-page document prepared by the Quito office of the Houston-based environmental consultant Entrix for OCP. The NGOs demanded a more visible role in providing their expertise in impact assessments and in monitoring the construction process with the intent of demonstrating the southern route to be a better one. At this time, their demands supported a growing and global recognition that EIA comprehensiveness and just outcomes require public participation and deliberation.[106] To the government, "the environmental impact study was just a requirement, not a key issue," declared a spokesperson for one NGO.[107] Yet on the contrary, it became a very critical issue to the NGO community.

After OCP presented its EIA to the Ministry of Energy and Mines in April 2001, NGOs had only one month to tender a reply. In May 2001, the Ministries of Environment and Energy and Mines invited eleven mayors along the right-of-way and two representatives from the NGO bloc, one from Comité Pro Ruta and one from CEDENMA, to offer comments on the EIA.[108] Pro Ruta's inclusion here speaks volumes to the importance that this alliance of grassroots ecologists and Quito-based NGOs garnered after their fight to reroute the pipeline. Nonetheless, by June 2001, the Environment Ministry had approved the project's environmental license.

At this time and for a second time, the professional NGOs and knowledgeable ecologists and ornithologists united under a new name, the Mindo Working Group, to address the Mindo-Nambillo and Chocó-Andean regions. BirdLife led the group, which was given US$16,000 by OCP to complete the assessment.[109] In the working group, some of the local ecologists and ornithologists held PhDs, were well published in their field, and/or were expert birding guides. Specifically, they sought to protect a 200,000-hectare area near the active Pichincha volcano, recognized internationally by BirdLife, CI, the World Bank, and WWF as a critically threatened ecosystem.[110] Together, they wrote their own alternative EIA, stressing their local knowledge of the flora and fauna and the economic use of the environment in their regions of expertise. These features were absent in the industry assessment.[111] Their report objected to the lack of transparency in route selection, the absence of alternative route analyses and community consultations, and the adverse ecological and potential health impacts, the economic costs, and prohibited participation. This report also identified five critical habitats, which support globally threatened bird species, including the black-breasted puffleg, whose world population is estimated to be 250 individuals, and which became a conservation icon for the organizations in the area. The report also objected to the location of OCP's Chiquilpe Reduction Station in the critical habitat of the puffleg, as well as the risk of access roads increasing human settlement and timber and wildlife extraction in the protected zones.

Given the limited frame of the participation and amount of information, only the Quito NGOs and grassroots experts of Mindo and Tandayapa responded officially and some of their comments were added to the official EIA.[112] "Some of the recommendations were included in the EIA and some weren't. But in the end, the government took the decision to go through the Mindo IBA, and at that point, the various groups went different ways," claimed one of the participants.[113] "[The government is] very closed-minded. And the people in the ministries were very closed, not aggressive, but they didn't want to talk with the NGOs," added another NGO representative.[114]

At this time, at least three other national groups evaluated the official EIA independent of the community-based working group.[115] One temporary bloc of NGOs, including Natura, Ambiente y Sociedad, CECIA, EcoCiencia, and Maquipucuna, asserted in a press release after the environmental license was granted that the window for feedback was only two weeks and that the ministries' review of their comments was less than two days. Both of these conditions, they argued, indicated that the ministry's decision was hasty and not based on sound technical assessments.[116] The NGOs charged the ministries with reaching a nonparticipatory and nontransparent decision,[117] while acknowledging their inability to influence the state's oil commitments. In their official report, which was supported by WWF, they ground their analysis of OCP's EIA on the impacts of the country's first trans-Andean pipeline completed in 1972.[118] They identified the past experience of fragmentation and loss of natural habitat due to access roads that led to settlements, deforestation, and increased hunting. They also expressed concern that the northern route was selected by OCP because it was forty kilometers shorter than the southern route, which would save the company in terms of construction costs. To the state, this bloc advised:

> The National Government ought to guarantee to the country that the selected variant is the best in reducing risk and social and environmental impacts, and that this decision was taken from comparative studies that clearly presented the risks, the costs, the impacts and mitigation alternatives, not only during the stage of construction but also during the period of operation.[119]

Acción Ecológica, the more radical of Quito's NGOs, offered a forty-page assessment of the EIA as well, and in its conclusions cited an incomplete EIA, inadequate methodology, and a project of high risk as being sufficient to warrant the cancelation of the project.[120] The report also identified that the national body with the authority to approve the EIA was the Environment

Ministry rather than the Ministry of Energy and Mines, and that the residents of Quito should be included in public consultations as their water sources will be affected. The report then identified sixteen high-risk areas.

In November 2001, six months after the EIA review process closed, Maquipucuna wrote a compliance analysis and an environmental risk assessment, based on the World Bank's *Environmental Hazard and Risk Assessment Sourcebook*.[121] The Maquipucuna report recommended an independent review of the EIA, a systematic comparison of alternative routes, and periodic public consultations. It also recommended environmental monitoring, full disclosure of OCP reports, control of erosion and landslides, as well as an oil spill contingency plan. The report requested control of the right-of-way and decommissioning access roads. On risk assessment, Maquipucuna advised the determination of habitat destruction due to landslides and the determination of sedimentation and oil spill impact on Mindo and Tandayapa's water supply.

In eighteen recommendations, ecological compensation was recommended four times, setting the stage for more formalized negotiations. In their early calls for compensation, Maquipucuna was supported by the World Bank's wildlands policy, which requires "compensatory preservation of comparable ecosystems when important wildlands" are impacted by World Bank–funded projects—even though OCP was not a World Bank project.[122] By this time, Maquipucuna, along with BirdLife and CECIA, had already been actively inserting the idea of ecological compensation into discussions with the OCP consortium along with calls for greater national participation and guaranteed contingency plans.

Connecting OCP to the World Bank

At this early juncture, the NGO community succeeded in one area: linking the World Bank to the OCP project by utilizing many of the bank's preceding practices and policies and social and environmental guidelines. Since 1989, when such assessments became mandatory on projects funded or sponsored by the World Bank, they have served as an international gauge for acceptable standards.[123] The World Bank claims and promotes its leadership in environmentally sustainable development projects and trains leaders of developing places in such projects.[124] Indeed, such self-promotion has cemented the bank's authority on industry standards in the loan-dependent South in particular. Affected communities would certainly set different and perhaps higher criteria than the World Bank, but the bank, rather than the affected communities, is the one that has succeeded in influencing global standards.

Secondly, WestLB, the primary financier of the OCP project, required World Bank standards, while thirdly the OCP consortium even promoted itself as adhering to them. The consortium's assertion courted criticism, and invigorated the NGO community to demonstrate OCP's failure to achieve its own self-promoted measurements. Finally, and to marshal international support, Fundación Maquipucuna sought to appeal to the World Bank directly given that the OCP project posed a risk to the Chocó-Andean Conservation Corridor, one of the bank's Global Environmental Facility (GEF) projects managed by the NGO.

Their success in connecting the OCP project to the World Bank fueled their conservation allies as well as the more activist-oriented NGOs, including Environmental Defense Fund in D.C., Amazon Watch in California, Greenpeace Germany, Rettet den Regenwald and Urgewald of Germany, and Friends of the Earth Germany. Their combined campaigns forced a response from the headquarters of the World Bank and the project's oil and financial companies.

"The World Bank became involved in the pipeline issue. . . . Although they wanted to stay away from it, they were dragged into it," recalled one NGO representative. "At one point, the World Bank sent a note, a memo, suggesting strongly that OCP support conservation activities in sensitive areas along the pipeline, and in fact even suggested strongly that they support the World Bank–funded project of Maquipucuna."[125]

One of the first meetings between the World Bank and Ecuador's environmental community occurred in December 2001 when the then CECIA director traveled to Washington D.C. to discuss the idea of an environmental fund with the bank, TNC, WWF, and CI.[126] According to one of the NGO representatives who chose not to attend this meeting:

The whole thing was that we had to be ready to take our proposal to Washington, to kind of have a validation from the international environmental NGOs. So the idea was to present it to CI, World Wildlife Fund, Nature Conservancy and to the World Bank. I mean that was the plan that OCP made for us; they set the date; they set everything. We said, "No way. You are rushing us. We are not ready. . . . Look, under these conditions we are not going."[127]

Among the invited NGOs, only CECIA's director attended. This director would later be dismissed, or would leave voluntarily, due in part to this contact and subsequent handling of the OCP project. Despite rejecting the international meeting, the NGO community, particularly BirdLife, CECIA, and Maquipucuna, continued to link the project to the World Bank and continued to demand compensation. Eventually, the World Bank responded.

In December 2001, Ian Johnson and David de Ferranti of the World Bank wrote to Hernán Lara, then executive president of OCP Ecuador. In addition to expressing their "deep concern about the impact," they wrote, "We would like to recommend that OCP provide specific, independent verification of compliance with World Bank standards or, alternatively, refrain from claiming such compliance."[128]

Assessing the bank's involvement in OCP, one international advocate claimed, "For the World Bank, it was virtually unthinkable. I can't think of a single case before [in which] they have written to criticize a project that they themselves, where, you know, there is actually no involvement."[129]

On another front, the NGO community also contacted their partner organizations and allies to pressure the individual oil companies in the United States, Canada, Italy, Spain, and Argentina, as well as the financer's offices in Germany. This effort could be seen as a transnational campaign of opposition or resistance initiated by Quito's professional NGOs and Mindo's grassroots ecologists—except for the eventual switch to negotiate with the oil consortium for environmental compensation. At the time, the NGO effort in Germany was accompanied by a large save-the-rainforest effort, which also included activists from Mindo and Lago Agrio traveling to Germany to present their claims. The actions of Acción Ecológica and the grassroots activists, who opposed the pipeline or the manner in which it was being constructed, and the NGOs' calls for a conservation fund led to a meeting in January 2002 in Germany with representatives of the state of North Rhine-Westphalia, which was 43 percent owner of WestLB.

After the meeting in Germany, German parliamentarians Ute Koczy and Bernhard von Grunberg of the state of North Rhine-Westphalia traveled to Ecuador in April 2002 for an inspection visit and to meet with others in the Ecuadorian NGO community. "That was an interesting and pivotal meeting in terms of pressuring OCP to come to the table on the ecotrust," said one participant.[130] At this time, seven Quito-based NGOs wrote a joint declaration.[131] Of the seven, six would eventually form the network of negotiation; the seventh was the umbrella environmental NGO, CEDENMA.[132]

The nine-point declaration opened with a supportive claim that OCP was an important national project for the economy of Ecuador. The declaration then stated that local communities and institutions should be participants in environmental and risk evaluations and that the pipeline's construction was an opportunity for both WestLB and OCP to demonstrate the application of a best practices approach. Framing their presentation in terms of the inevitability of the project, the conservation NGOs took a moderate tack by stating the importance of oil exploitation for Ecuador, while simultaneously stating that OCP and in particular the Argentinean contractor Techint were not complying with World Bank standards.[133] "We felt that if WestLB bank was not allowed to give the loan, any other bank would do it," recalled one participant. "And at least through the German government, we have a chance of improving standards, rather than if we go, let's say to an American bank or a Caribbean bank."[134]

At this time, the midlevel domestic organizations were actively challenging the consortium, its financing sources, and the international institutions with interests in Ecuador to guarantee best practices and highest environmental standards. During this stage, their organized campaign reached beyond the state to present their primary concerns and to lobby for the environment's protection at international bodies.

It is also important to note that their campaign to target World Bank standards initiated at least three outside experts to reevaluate the OCP project using such standards in 2002. The findings of one outside expert bolstered the claims of the domestic NGOs, while the other two failed to support their position. According to an external review of the EIA by Robert Goodland, a former World Bank environmental standards adviser who was hired by the international opposition network, OCP's EIA failed to comply with four of the World Bank's social and environmental policies. OCP failed to demonstrate that the least impact route was selected, failed to consult adequately with affected communities, failed to address resettlement plans, and failed to analyze the impacts on particularly vulnerable communities, including Indigenous communities in the Amazon and Ecuadorian communities of African descent on the coast.[135]

Another influential report, prepared by the Monitoring and Assessment of Biodiversity Program (MAB) of the U.S.-based Smithsonian Institution, supported the northern route as the route with the least number of negative impacts. Commissioned by the Environmental Protection Subsecretariat of Ecuador's Energy and Mines Ministry, this analysis noted the degree of contention between the anti-northern-route campaign and OCP and concluded with a breakdown of the advantages and disadvantages of both routes.[136] In the Smithsonian's estimation, the southern route had fewer advantages and more disadvantages than the northern route. The disadvantages of the southern route included its location of twenty and thirty kilometers south of Mindo, its passage through Antisana Ecological Reserve, archeological sensitivity, high effect on existing infrastructure, and its location in Quito's more densely populated southern tip.

A third report was prepared by Stone & Webster Consultants on behalf of the senior lender WestLB to determine whether the project met bank standards.[137] Stone & Webster found that "OCP has committed to undertake all reasonable, practicable measures to mitigate the impact of the Project" in the Mindo Cloud Forest.[138] Likewise, Stone & Webster supported the Smithsonian assessment of least impact along the northern route, and noted that "certain hard-line NGO's [sic] want to stop the construction of the pipeline to prevent the further exploitation of Amazonia. The Project is essential to the monetization of the Amazonia hydrocarbon reserves."[139]

Embraced within this final assessment, whereby entities with vested interests in the success of the oil industry are commissioned to assess the oil industry, is an unwavering commitment to oil production as a means toward economic development and a staunch orientation to viewing those who question the rights and means of the petroleum sector as hard-line extremists or radicals.

This stage marked a time of far-reaching collaboration and network building between the professionals in Quito and the residents in the greater Mindo region and their combined success at forcing the World Bank and the OCP consortium to respond to their efforts. Yet they were unable to change the route. In acknowledgment, the professional NGOs stopped challenging the project and started negotiating with the OCP consortium for environmental funds. This flip-flop, unexpected by the grassroots ecologists, instigated an immediate split between the two sides. This turnaround also revealed the organizational agility and elasticity required of midlevel domestic NGOs, which divided their time between field projects in important ecosystems inhabited by rural communities and their international contacts, including their Northern allies with Northern-inspired and/or Northern-funded initiatives and agendas. On the one hand, initial ties with Mindo's influential birders, ecologists, and activists lent the professional NGOs a degree of local and grassroots credibility and expanded their international reach on this count. On the other hand, this grassroots solidarity was short-lived. After foraying briefly into such activism and alignments, the NGOs chose to work more closely with the private sector rather than the affected residents, thus returning to the more formalized, closed-door meetings—more typical of the larger international NGOs—and impairing future alliances with the grassroots ecologists.

Stage 2: Evolution to Funds, Nonparticipant Contempt

Once Quito's NGO community concluded that the pipeline's route was a de facto state decision without sufficient public debate, they exchanged their position of confrontation with the state for one of negotiation with the oil consortium for microvariants, for paid assessment projects, and for environmental funds. Noting their inability to influence the state, one NGO director described the decision to negotiate as the final option to remain engaged in the country's oil economy for environmental gains:

> You can spend years talking to your government and see no results because they don't hear. We don't have a participatory and access-to-information culture in this country. . . . So, dealing with the government is not, at this moment, a good strategy. . . . We did not approve the way it [the pipeline project] was done. It was obscure and non-transparent. . . . So the ecofund sounded like the only way out to at least get some compensation for the terrible decision that they made going through a national, or a pristine site.[140]

Even though early international efforts to reroute the pipeline failed, transnational ties were discovered to be more influential on the individual oil multinationals, before and during environmental fund negotiations, than on the state. "The fact that we have a very weak institution for the environment" makes us think that unless there is this responsibility among the different investors of committing to the best practices and committing to the precautionary principle, in terms of causing the less [*sic*] damage, nothing can be achieved, or barely looked to be achieved, through the authority of the Ministry of the Environment," noted the same director.[141] "So this is sort of an exercise as well, not only a claim for justice, but an exercise in terms of inviting the rest of the new companies to come to implement different strategies to compensate for the damage the investment could cause to the communities and to the environment."[142]

Operating within these restricted parameters, the NGOs chose to work for change through the private sector, rather than the potentially slower process of challenging or enforcing Ecuador's environmental laws alongside affected residents.[143] "We have to turn to the voluntary basis and dialogues, when you cannot enforce law because there's not the political will to do it," lamented the same representative.[144] Reflecting in 2007 on the decision, another added, "Probably all the organizations were dealing with these confrontations of 'to be or not to be.' So against our will, negotiate or not to negotiate, it was a very key turning point for our [Ecuadorian] organizations."[145]

These organizations, which wanted to protect their conservation work, to expand Ecuador's conservation efforts, and to insert themselves into the nation's oil influence and revenue stream, made the strategic identification of OCP as their means to do so. By first lobbying their international partners to pressure the individual oil multinationals, they then began to negotiate their own conservation funds with the oil consortium. "We entered into a negotiation with OCP deciding that if indeed they were going to go through ecologically sensitive areas than we wanted them to set aside a significant amount of resources that could be used to either manage, conserve, or undertake investigations in sensitive areas, that would be conserved for all time," noted one.[146]

Clarifying this point, the NGO representative continued:

> When the decision was made, we sat back and reflected a little bit on the process. . . . [OCP] did some clearing along the route, particularly in a sensitive area. And we decided we needed to act. And the way that we acted was to try and engage [OCP] in a way that we could either suggest alternative routes, micro-variants, or different practices, which would minimize the impacts of the construction on the species. So we took a middle road, if you will. . . . I'd say it was more of an evolution towards trying to do something constructive.[147]

Through OCP, these organizations became "policy entrepreneurs"[148] by connecting oil extraction to conservation and scientific research removed from the state's influence. Yet there were at least two penalties for this entry—a consequence that has become an increasingly common practice: payment for impact and for payment, a loss of potential allies. Negotiations, collaboration, cooperation, and compromise displace arguments for the precautionary principle or for alternative energy developments, and invariably lead to accepting monetary compensation for future and given, known, and impending damages. Yet given the economic dominance of oil in Ecuadorian politics, the advancement of any agenda, whether for conservation or community projects, may be realized if the oil sector is part of the negotiations (in the Quito case) or part of the leverage (in the case of Lago Agrio). Pragmatically, oil gets some conservation done; unwisely, oil-NGO unions also split landscapes into conserved or polluted territories even when the two reside one on top of the other.

Mechanisms of an Environmental Fund

For their efforts, the environmental NGOs of Quito realized a twenty-year US$16.9 million environmental fund. Their achievement was not trivial. With negotiations enduring for more than three years, demands ranged from US$1 million for a particular zone to US$20 million along the right-of-way to a dream high of US$35 million, according to participants.

The first team of four, BirdLife, CECIA, Maquipucuna, and Natura rejected OCP's offer in June 2002 of US$1 million up front, followed by $100,000 annually for ten years.[149] "We felt that we'd be selling our souls if we tried to get an ecofund for about $2 million," noted one negotiator.[150] Then after the facilitator joined and brought with her others, including Ambiente y Sociedad, CEDA, EcoCiencia, two university groups, and a representative of TNC's Quito office, all parties settled at US$16.9 million. Distribution of funds began in 2005.

Though the dollar amount may appear impressive to some or not so note-worthy to others, depending on an NGO's budget and impact assessments, the process of negotiation is informative for organizations wishing to engage multinationals as well as for those resisting collaboration or fearing co-option once at the table. At this point, it is important to restate that the NGO community had adopted, perhaps with reservation, perhaps without question, a capitalist and development worldview that then restricted the choices before them.

EnCana Corporation, the lead oil operator in the consortium, anchored the meetings and patterned the fund after other NGO-oil collaborations in North America, including the Canadian Alberta Ecotrust Foundation.[151] The Alberta Ecotrust is a fund with Canadian environmental organizations, including Canadian Nature Federation, which is also a BirdLife partner. In 2004, the Alberta Ecotrust granted from Can$3,300 to Can$20,000 to such projects as a web-based land use simulator for educational purposes, an assessment project to learn how to disseminate information to individuals on environmentally sustainable practices, and the development of a web-based tool to promote online debate on the boreal forest.[152] The latter is particularly incongruent given Canada's large-scale development of its oil sands, or tar sands, in Alberta Province, which have been presented as destroying Canada's unique boreal forest.[153] Local projects in Canada also included a paper-recycling project and a primary school butterfly garden.[154]

Clearly, these projects fail to address the environmental, social, economic, and physical impacts of oil. They are soft, diversionary projects that target the individual for changing his or her behavior (recycling and sustainable practices) and shift attention away from the impacts of the industry to the visually attractive (butterfly garden). Indeed, using the Alberta Ecotrust as a provisional guide for the Ecuadorian talks mitigated organic frames of dialogue, tempered national insights and contributions, and may bode poorly for conservation outcomes in the Andean-Amazonian nation.

For the Ecuadorian fund, EnCana committed US$7.4 million as the largest owner of the pipeline project, while the other oil companies in the consortium contributed the remainder.[155] In March 2005, a year and a half after the pipeline began operation, EnCana and OCP announced in a low-publicity press release that an agreement had been reached.[156] In this account, the EcoFondo as it is called in Ecuador was framed as a project of OCP Ecuador S.A. and EnCana Corporation, rather than a conservation and research fund demanded and achieved by the NGO community.

The press release announced that OCP and EnCana created the EcoFund Foundation Ecuador to support and supervise environmental projects. Then, the EcoFund Foundation created the EcoFondo Ecuador Trust to disburse and manage OCP's ecocontributions. Both were designed to transfer funds periodically to Ecuador's National Environmental Fund, the Fondo Ambiental Nacional (FAN), a semipublic, semiprivate Ecuadorian entity that was to be responsible for administering the funds for five years and for announcing how to submit proposals. The five-year arrangement, which may be extended, marked OCP's concern of FAN's capacity, accountability, and transparency to dispense the funds. However, FAN's initial involvement was a victory for the large conservation organizations with strong ties to its establishment. Initially, TNC, CI-Ecuador, and IUCN had provided "significant contributions" to FAN along with European and U.S. government agencies, so each of the environmental NGOs would arguably have a vested interest in FAN's success and role in fund distributions.[157] Two debt-for-nature swaps with the German government and a World Bank GEF grant were also critical to launching the first phase of FAN's operations prior to the OCP fund.[158]

Throughout the OCP negotiations, there was a great deal of wrangling over the role of FAN, a public-private nonprofit hybrid, in which the environment minister and a CEDENMA representative automatically sit. The larger NGOs advocated for FAN's ultimate authority and independence, while the oil representatives worked to ensure that they governed FAN by requiring periodic reports and direct accountability to an international board. Even though FAN was formed in 1994, it did not become an active institution in managing environmental donations until 2000.[159] The oil sector's concern was based on skepticism that FAN may change its public-private nature, becoming a more public, state-influenced body, or fold altogether. For this concern, the oil sector sought assurances that annual transfers to FAN would be spent once received, rather than accumulating over time.

In these negotiations, the oil negotiators were forcing greater transparency and accountability among the NGOs and FAN, more than the NGO community or the oil sector expected of itself. It is also likely that guaranteeing funds to be distributed through FAN may consolidate the interconnecting ties and environmental influence among a few, including FFLA, TNC, FAN, and Fundación Natura. Among these, none was critical of the pipeline, nor were they the ones to initiate the environmental fund talks.

In the Ecuadorian case, the EcoFondo was not designed to remediate oil effects or to protect the impacted environment should a break occur. The fund was designed to finance conservation projects, build capacity, and conduct research in three geographical zones, including (1) areas along the pipeline's right-of-way, or OCP's "area of influence," (2) areas within the oil-producing region of the Amazon, and (3) national priority areas.[160]

Area One, which is earmarked for 60 percent of the funds, encompasses six kilometers on each side of the OCP pipeline, plus a number of nature reserves and protected forests through which the pipeline intersects. The designated areas include the IBA of Mindo and Cuenca Alta de Río Guayllabama II, as well as nature reserves, including Cayambe-Coca, Antisana, Pululahua, and the protected forests of San Francisco, Milpe Pachijal, and Cumandá.

Area Two, for which 30 percent of the funds are targeted, includes sites of oil production in the Amazon, plus protected areas within the zone of production including the Cuyabeno Reserve, the Limoncocha Reserve, and Yasuní National Park.

Area Three is to receive 10 percent of the funds annually for areas designated as national priorities that are not included in the previous two zones, but could include dry forests, wetlands, and the *páramo*, a landscape in the Ecuadorian Andes that is above the timberline and marked by low-lying vegetation.

Eligible recipients include Ecuadorian NGOs, community organizations with discernible ability to manage fiscal responsibility, local governments if paired with NGOs, and research and educational institutions. A looming and expected hierarchy among potential applicants and recipients is evident. Even though the professional NGOs, which participated in forming the EcoFondo, would not be involved in administering the fund, they may be best qualified in writing conservation proposals that fit the guidelines that they assisted in writing.

The multinationals also blocked the state from benefiting directly by excluding national parks. In this way, the oil sector manipulated and continues to manipulate through the fund's duration an image of itself as better than the state in supporting Ecuador's conservation and research initiatives. This dubious manifestation of benevolence resembled the oil industry's promotion of its "development" projects in the Amazon, which are exhibited as reminders of their community engagement to the community, to other oil companies, and to outside visitors.

In this instance, even some of the NGOs supported OCP's reluctance to work with state officials. "I would say that having worked in this country, they are right," noted one representative. "If the people, let's say in any town in the area, wanted drinking water, they [OCP] built the drinking water system. They didn't give money to the mayor."[161] Yet were these NGOs making considerable achievements in conservation and in their own participation in the nation's oil economy or were they enabling the oil consortium to protect its image without advancing conservation practices or policies, while undermining the role and perhaps obligation of the state in protecting the nation's natural resources and undermining the more inclusive, economic, and social calls being heard among the affected communities?

Transnational Agents: Manipulating the Local and Global

During this second phase, the midtier NGOs, which initiated talks, honed their negotiating skills and increased their monetary demands "for national conservation priorities," yet remained silent publicly on the potential environmental and social impacts of the pipeline. Despite these omissions, they were jubilant, initially, in advancing their environmental agendas and demonstrating to themselves and to the private sector their competence, proficiency, and aptitude in conservation and policy making. Once negotiations were under way, they perceived that their transnational efforts had brought the multinationals to the negotiating table, hosted by the domestic NGOs. They appeared to be empowered transnational agents, harnessing the ongoing anti-oil campaigns of other NGOs and grassroots ecologists for their own benefit, while orchestrating their international partners to pressure the OCP consortium for, and then to maintain, talks on the ecofund.

At the national level, these NGOs constructed themselves as critical, but moderate, stakeholders. However, no one denied the importance of the most extreme groups in continuing to contest the project, which also spurred talks to begin. "[The radical organizations] have a very strong role, and if it wasn't for them we would not be able to push OCP as strongly as we could," claimed one of the participants.[162] According to another, "For example, in Germany, they are aware [of this issue] because, and I have to give that point to Acción Ecológica, because [Acción Ecológica] moves a lot of strings also at the international level."[163]

These second-tier NGOs were also invigorated by their ability to both mobilize and restrain their international partners. "We convinced them [our international partners] to let us negotiate without putting a lot of pressure [on the bank], and they *can* put a lot of pressure," said one participant.[164] "The fact that we can make it very difficult for them in Italy, in the United States, in Germany, just by picking up the phone and sending a press release off, because in each one of these countries the issue of rainforest protection is huge, so we just play on that," added another NGO representative.[165] Although some international partners may have been displeased with an Ecuadorian request to remain silent, the on-site organizations maintained control over their national agenda in the early phases of the negotiation process, energizing their confidence in their position in this new global arena. "So far we have been successful in keeping our international allies quiet, because after all this is an Ecuadorian matter," noted one in 2002.[166]

An additional cause for celebration was the belief that the ecofund would be the first in Latin America established through organized pressure that eventually led to negotiations with the private oil sector in terms of monetary value and breadth of oil-NGO collaboration, even though others had been established with governments and the World Bank GEF program.[167] According to one participant, "The whole process leading up to the signing of the eco-trust will be a first for the Andean countries, if not for Latin America—in this respect, the way that it was done."[168]

The OCP project also presented them an occasion to challenge North-South double standards in environmental practices and conservation debates. "What worries me most, in some cases, is the application of double standards," challenged one director. "Some of the companies in their home offices, or their homeland, they apply certain standards because they do have a lot of regulations, a lot of enforcement. But [when] they go abroad, they apply half of those, or they apply none of those, or they dump."[169] "Dumping" is in reference to the practice of importing old and inferior equipment, which is then used and discarded in Ecuador without penalty or enforcement of proper disposal. Likewise, the Ecuadorian NGOs used their newfound role as impetus to demand that Northern NGOs be accountable to the local NGO community as well. "Partners in the South are saying, 'Okay, are you [Northern partners] going to give us the money to conserve *our* bio-diversity. Not yours, *ours*. And we have more than you,'" claimed one NGO delegate.[170]

Analyzed collectively, these sentiments reveal how the midlevel NGOs were feeling empowered by their ability to pressure OCP as well as the international environmental community. In this, OCP instigated local NGOs to openly question and advocate for a higher position of influence within global conservation debates. Yet even with this newfound authority, there was at least one grassroots check upon their enthusiasm. The switch to negotiations ignited a chain of animosity between the urban-based, professional NGOs and the increasingly alienated community-based, grassroots ecologists closer to the affected areas of Mindo. More activist-leaning international groups aligned with the Mindo community and formed a transnational campaign of resistance or opposition that disfavored collaboration with the industry, and together they vehemently rejected the Quito NGOs that negotiated the fund.

Elation or Ecocrumbs?

Despite generating monetary means for conservation, oil-NGO negotiations also engendered a tremendous amount of misunderstanding and mistrust, which was never alleviated due in part to the closed process of the ecofund talks. In particular, Acción Ecológica in Quito, former members of Pro Ruta and the Mindo Working Group, and other community-based ecologists in Mindo called the evolution toward monetary compensation unethical and distanced or severed ties with the conservation NGOs.[171]

Some of the NGOs that had previously maintained working relations with landowners, naturalist guides, and ecotourism operations in the Andes realized the domestic pitfall of negotiating with the private sector, yet accepted the trade-off. "Other NGOs, even the more, the not so radical NGOs, . . . they also were kind of angry with us because we started working with OCP," recalled one NGO.[172] "We lost image because in the beginning we were fighting against the OCP completely, and then we started working with OCP. . . . People from [one NGO] have come to me and said, 'You betrayed us. [Your organization] just betrayed us. We are not working together anymore.' Something like we sold ourselves to the company, things like that."[173] A year later, the same person continued to reflect on the impact of this decision:

> People started to perceive us as the NGO that sold itself to OCP. In the people's mind, it is like OCP is paying us for not saying anything. So there was a huge cost. At the beginning, I was against the idea. Because I knew it was going to be a huge cost for our organization in terms of our image. But to tell you the truth, after these two years, I'm really happy that we made this decision. I'm really glad, because we have made very positive things for Mindo, while if we weren't there, it would not have happened.[174]

Expectedly, the participating NGOs, which were aware of the rancor toward them, viewed the ecofund negotiations differently than the grassroots ecologists. One NGO spokesperson noted that the fund was perceived to be a legal obligation according to the pipeline's contract. This person stated, "We are not asking for money as beggars, but we are working together in order to accomplish some regulations that OCP needs to accomplish and as NGOs we want to accomplish in the best way."[175] Another added:

> We made that very clear at the beginning of the [ecofund] process that to be part of this process does not mean to any extent that we are endorsing or with our participation approving the ways in which this process [bidding and route selection] took place. . . . So with that disclaimer, we participated.[176]

Still another NGO participant offered:

> We even had an encounter with [one group] because they had spread rumors in the whole Mindo area and everything that [we and others] had received money from OCP. They knew it wasn't true because . . . we talked to them and they knew exactly our position. And yet they came and they spread rumors, which made our life really difficult when we go to the Mindo area and everything. These people don't trust us anymore, eco-money and everything. . . . They are philosophically against oil exploration.[177]

In a study on South Africa, Derick Fay writes that "an NGO which prematurely promotes a 'win-win' scenario is likely to see its initiative backfire, leading to mistrust and the loss of community support. But more importantly, a mutual gains approach may undermine the bargaining position of communities."[178] In the Ecuadorian case, not only were the bargaining chips of the communities affected, it was also clear that corporate-NGO negotiations undermined the collaboration and bargaining position of the participating NGOs themselves with affected residents. After the completion of the pipeline and the ecofund negotiations, an NGO director with projects in the greater Mindo region claimed relationships with the Mindo-based activists were still difficult, hampering conservation and dialogue in the area. In further reflection, another NGO participant stressed the number and scale of the NGOs at the negotiating table also alienated the grassroots ecologists of Mindo. "[The negotiations] successfully brought together many of the stakeholders who hadn't been engaged . . . [before], which again I think alienated a lot of people because [the negotiations] brought in people who are bigger NGOs here, the bigger players here in conservation to the table to talk about that," the participant said. "Again, I think the Mindo community felt isolated, alienated, because they were not represented at that table or in those discussions."[179]

Mindo's activists who rejected compensation and negotiation with the oil sector were personally hurt and angry by the professional NGOs, while the international NGOs, which did not participate in the fund, were not individually offended; they were however professionally annoyed. Admonishing the negotiating NGOs, members of the transnational network of opposition claimed the conservation groups joined talks from a position of weakness and likened the fund to "dining with the devil"[180] for "a couple of crumbs."[181] According to one international organizer:

> The only thing [OCP was] willing to negotiate was about this ecofund, and it was clear, anyway, it was mainly a PR thing. Yeah, I wonder about the Ecuadorian NGOs that bought into that thing, because in my view or in my experience, you, as an NGO, if you negotiate, you negotiate from the position of power, because that's the only way you are really going to get some place. . . . If somebody is coming and offering you a couple of crumbs, then [you do not negotiate]. And that's the way I see the ecofund. I see it as a couple of crumbs and the possibility for a few NGOs to make some money. But it's pretty clear to me that it's not going to help people, and it's most probably not going to help the environment very much. It's more an alibi action than anything else, just to be able to say they are doing something.[182]

Four years after the international organizer spoke, at a time when OCP was completed and the ecofund was beginning to be dispensed, at least one grassroots ecologist in the greater Mindo region was coming to a very similar conclusion. Not only was this activist questioning the use of the ecofund; this activist had also identified how conservation projects in general were selected for funding for intentionally weak results. Importantly, it was the OCP project that brought about this reckoning.

I don't think that they [OCP, World Bank, and other funders] want to build up and strengthen organizations that could eventually be against them. . . . Because I do know a lot of pretty crummy projects that are getting financed . . . , and I sort of draw, dot to dot, and I come up with sort of the same results. It is better to finance projects that are not really going to go very far because you don't really want to strengthen possible groups of organizations that could actually do damage in the long run to you—to where the money is coming from.[183]

Despite these domestic frustrations, it was also a time of jubilation for the midlevel NGOs who initiated the fund and who were beginning to see themselves as important players in directing Ecuador's position on oil extraction and environmental conservation. Their triumph, however, was short-lived. OCP's defensive position and the NGOs' empowering one were brief interludes before their roles would be reversed.

Stage 3: Oil Greened, NGOs Tarred

A third phase experienced by the conservation NGOs during the end of the negotiations revealed four experiences. One was a less-than-beneficial relationship built on patronage between OCP (the patron) and the NGOs (the clients).[184] OCP needed local NGO cooperation, or reciprocity, to green its image internationally and to lessen international attention on the affected communities, which were clamoring for much more than conservation funds. In this, the negotiations resembled a "mutually binding obligation," which required mutual accountability to achieve.[185] At least two objectives were to green the project and to silence protest in exchange for conservation projects. In contrast, while the conservation NGOs were entering into a new relationship of patronage with the oil companies, the oil-affected communities in the Amazon were challenging a history of paternalism in which the benefactor is not accountable and goods given may be useless and determined solely by the benefactor.[186]

Not to quip, yet given the political influence and economic power of the petroleum industry in Ecuador relative to civil society and even some ministries, it would appear then that both the NGOs in Quito and the affected residents of Lago Agrio were—at this time—on the same humble playing field, relegated to the cold room in the house or the back room at the party, mobilizing on the fringes of the political oil economy for nominal contributions—though the conservation community may be loath to identify itself as such.

Tensions due to the power disparities between the North and the South and between corporations and NGOs led to other hardships for the domestic NGOs. It was not a win-win for all, though some benefit (a second experience realized) was achieved. For example, the NGOs gained working experience with private companies, and the environment was better protected in certain areas during the construction process. However, the toll of the fund's realization shrunk the sense of proficiency among the midlevel NGOs as they began to support and defer to the oil industry while the larger NGOs gained greater control over ecofund deliberations, marking a third series of experiences. The manner in which the talks were constructed also exposed how collaboration with the petroleum sector diminishes transparency of operations and withholds on-site and perhaps pertinent information from affected communities, a fourth realization of cooperation.

Green-Coating OCP?

In the 1980s, industry efforts to green corporations and to co-opt environmental organizations began in the United States as a backlash to some of the successes of the environmental movement.[187] Begun as an orchestrated retaliation against environmental regulation, "greening" is a tactic used by corporations to appropriate the environmental discourse for its own benefit and for its own image.[188] In Ecuador, the concept of greening was used with contempt by Mindo's activist community to depict the ecofund NGOs as facilitating OCP's environmental image. "They are painting them [OCP] green," declared a Mindo activist, who later added: "They [OCP] must pay to be painted."[189]

Even though Ecuador gained short-term conservation initiatives, the political impetus and strength of the global environmental movement may be less powerful today than it was in the 1970s in the United States. To be sure, it is some of the legacies of the environmental movement in the North that may have diluted the environmental influence, effort, and alliances of Southern NGOs. In contrast, it is the potential of blue-green, labor-environmental alliances in Latin America that may be much more successful in protecting the environment. Such alliances may also form more easily in Latin America given that several towns in Ecuador, and none in the United States, are led by leftist, labor party representatives. However, much of the environmental ideology in Ecuador is adopted from the North, and the most influential voices in Ecuador—BirdLife, CI, TNC, and WWF—are certainly not embedded in deep blue-green networks in either the North or the South. So instead of Ecuadorian NGOs leading here, as they could have by developing domestic alliances of their own initiative, they found themselves stalled, waiting to learn from the North rather than leading the North. Had the environmental NGOs in Ecuador identified points of solidarity with the laboring poor of Lago Agrio, rather than the conservation NGOs of the North, their impact and import may have been strengthened rather than diminished.

Over time, the corporate strategy in the North enabled industry to present itself as the "true environmentalists" or environmental stewards in contrast to the radical or "extreme" environmentalists, who were constructed as more destructive to society than the corporations themselves.[190] Recall Stone & Webster's reference to "hard-line" environmental NGOs in Ecuador. Corporations also constructed themselves as promoters of sustainable development to developing nations,[191] even though technology transfers, environmental safeguards, and just working conditions remain limited in the developing world and in low-income nations. These tactics have also been used by the World Bank,[192] and when combined have cultivated a dominant and corporate worldview that disables Southern and Northern societies from demanding, with legitimate authority, a transparent account of how natural resource extraction burdens communities and ecosystems for the benefit of an elite few.

To the oil consortium, the ecofund represented what others have called an "elegant solution."[193] Part of the sophistication of the conservation-corporation agreement was its exclusion of grassroots communities and their multifaceted concerns, unpredictable patterns of confronting extractive industries, and unwillingness to relocate compensation away from the ecosystems and communities most directly impacted. If cultivated, these variables could have become the NGO community's homegrown advantage. However, negotiations served the industry by isolating the conservation NGOs from affected communities and by introducing them to corporate-led negotiation processes and corporate-supported research projects already accepted by Northern NGOs.

Moreover, the consortium companies manipulated an image of themselves as more committed to Ecuador's environmental future than the state itself, which should certainly hold a much stronger allegiance to the country's ecosystems, even though this may not be commonly known among state officials. To this, both the ecofund and the community projects in the Amazon are exhibited by the oil companies to remind the NGOs, affected residents, and international audiences of the industry's "engagement" with and generosity toward the communities and environments of the Southern class.

The ecofund also appears an attempt to enhance OCP and particularly EnCana's conservation status among the international environmental community and EnCana's shareholders, not necessarily to achieve long-lasting conservation goals in Ecuador. Though Joseph Galaskiewicz suggests that corporate contributions to charity were supported for social currency and status among elite business corporations, rather than for marketing, public relations, enlightened self-interest, or tax strategy,[194] this analysis would suggest that environmental donations from industries that have been documented and perceived as potentially polluting the environment may engage in conservation donations as a means to improve their image or silence their objectors. In a press release on the ecofund, OCP and EnCana wrote, "This unprecedented investment in Latin America constitutes fundamental support to the people whose security and future depend on the integrity and good handling of the ecosystems."[195] As noted previously, the participating NGOs, which had expended four years on these negotiations, were relegated to a brief clause in this press release: "Several Ecuadorian environmental organizations participated in the preparation of the agreements."[196] Even from this press release, it appeared that the environmental fund was designed to benefit OCP's international image and international relations, rather than its domestic ones—though given the reputational risk of aligning with the oil sector, the NGOs may have chosen that their names not be associated with the fund.

In both the Ecuadorian and the Alberta funds, the grant distribution formula favored small, short-term, low-cost projects, which may have only limited and temporary impact. Even while the Ecuadorian fund was still being finalized, the Alberta Ecotrust had acknowledged limitations in the original distribution formula. At the time, the Alberta Ecotrust conducted a study of academia, industry, government, and NGOs, which argued that to "maximize effectiveness" grant caps should be extended beyond the Can$20,000 earmark.[197] Yet Ecuadorian negotiations were unable to capitalize on this argument.

In addition, while the OCP consortium and its individual oil companies were actively presenting themselves as environmental custodians, the participating NGOs were beginning to vocally support and defer to the oil industry. To be sure, the NGOs were constrained by global and national, political and economic systems that led to a state decision to build a second pipeline in order to double export capacity. As in most oil-driven economies, state officials were also prone to endorsing oil projects with minimal input from civil society. Given these restrictions, the NGO community was itself limited in influencing the pipeline project and making considerable contributions to conservation or their own participation in the country's oil-led environmental politics. So they swung between praising the OCP consortium companies—excluding the Argentine constructor—and lamenting the damages to the Mindo area, and between decrying the perceived weaknesses of the state and favoring the private sector's greater and more immediate responses to their claims. For instance, one NGO representative after early contact with OCP suggested that "sometimes they can, sometimes they can't" heed the advice of the ecologists and conservationists on important habitats. "I think it's worth saying that the technology they are using is state of the art now. And again they have shown a willingness to take our recommendations within a certain limits . . . because you know, Mindo is a very hilly area and a difficult one," stated this conservationist. "So within certain limits, they have shown real commitment to do so."[198]

Another NGO offered a similar, balanced interpretation that at once complimented OCP's construction commitment, while stressing the potential impact of a break:

> What we have seen through the monitoring project in Mindo is that in these areas which are critical for biodiversity, OCP is doing an excellent job. They are really being very careful, about the construction and the construction techniques. And the environmental department of OCP is very open-minded. They are open to negotiate many things. But the problem is that the impact anyway is going to be huge. It doesn't matter how careful they are. And there are places in which, okay, they are constructing with all these techniques and everything, but in the event that the pipeline breaks, for, let's say, an earthquake, it's going to be a huge impact over there. . . . All the major drinking water sources are going to be contaminated, polluted with oil.[199]

According to another NGO participant in the ecofund talks:

> This is the first time we have had this kind of experience working with the industry, with the private sector, and it has really been a great experience. We have

learned a lot. Of course, we think of some of the limitations provided by their background and their interests, because of course they have an economic interest, but OCP as a consortium has a good deal of interest in the environment.[200]

For clarification, that interest is relative to the perceived commitments of the state and other oil companies to the environment.

At the negotiating table there were two factions: the one side who actively and initially opposed the route through the Mindo area and the other that waited to take a position once ecofund talks were started. The previous quotes were from those who resisted the route, while the following one is from someone who joined the talks later. This comment, made in 2001, reflects an orientation toward supporting the oil sector or weighing an individual's daily behaviors and consumption pattern as on par with the impacts of the petroleum industry. Capturing the sentiment of some NGOs even before negotiations began, this person claimed:

We are not confrontational with the productive sector. We think that we have to have allies everywhere for conservation. . . . Each individual has a level of responsibility. Even the most pure conservatives are having an impact by solid wastes, by energy consumption, by the use of clothing, the use of many things.[201]

Stressing a similarity between individual human behavior and the extraction and production of fossil fuels appears to be an unreasonable effort by some environmental groups to deflect criticism away from the environmental and community injuries experienced after a spill, leak, or disaster.

Not only were ecofund participants supporting the environmental commitment of OCP and minimizing differences between individual and industrial activities, but some of the nation's environmental experts also began deferring to the oil experts and emphasizing the difficulties faced by the industry. "Yes, there has been possibilities of changing the route, but according to OCP's team of experts, they say that the construction is impossible on financial grounds," according to one NGO interviewed in 2002. "It would be a lot of money to divert, or in some cases on geological grounds. So, but [we are] no expert in those areas. We wouldn't like to say, 'They are right or wrong.'"[202]

These endorsements expose how corporate-NGO associations may dilute the NGOs' environmental agenda, as well as reveal the subordinate negotiating position and subordinate material and monetary power of the NGO community vis-à-vis oil multinationals. Their reflections also disclose a perceptual encroachment among the organizations that they were viewing themselves as negotiating from a position inferior to that of the industry—whether that inferiority arose from scientific expertise, monetary and material resources, and/or influential contacts. A large body of literature would indicate that these NGOs were being brought into the fold of the private sector to enable or participate in their own marginalization.[203] Not only were they acquiescing to the industry, and perhaps most importantly, the ecofund negotiations effectively quieted the NGOs' initial transnational campaign against the route, the EIA, the manner of construction, and the risk associated with oil transportation by land and by sea.

Grit and Gains

Nevertheless, the organizations and the environment benefited somewhat from their involvement in the pipeline project. Some upsides included steady access to OCP personnel, which created a role for the NGO community and their environmental contributions. They were pivotal in suggesting microvariants, monitoring one section of the pipeline, minimizing impacts on threatened species in one area, and designating critical areas for protection. Access to OCP personnel enabled the NGOs to ensure that native species were replanted along the right-of-way and to encourage the use of handheld equipment and an aerial cable system for transporting the pipes in the Mindo region. Alongside Mindo's activist-ecologists, they also succeeded in narrowing the width of the right-of-way in areas in the Andes designated as important even though OCP's environmental consultants claimed that a narrower right-of-way on a narrow ridge would actually make the pipeline less stable since the pipeline could not be laid as deep. As first-time participants in the nation's oil economy, the domestic NGOs certainly gained experience on a large-scale project and established a working relationship with the individual companies of the private oil sector.

Though environmental fund negotiations and on-site environmental efforts were separate entities, direct talks with OCP representatives facilitated controlled access along the right-of-way. Likewise, the NGOs that conducted OCP-funded water quality tests, species count and habitat research, noise impact tests, and revegetation projects were pleased with their ability to work at the perceived international level that the multinational consortium required. CECIA, in particular, published a report on preliminary results on the impacts of the pipeline's construction, including a decline in abundance of two bird types, though noise during construction was a confounding factor.[204]

Though several NGOs sought individual contracts to monitor the pipeline's construction, the Ministry of the Environment was the sole entity responsible for officially monitoring or contracting the monitoring along the entire right-of-way.[205] According to one landowner in the Mindo region, "I'm sure they [the Quito-based organization] made mistakes, but this was notably, literally monitoring directly on the spot, and checking that there was minimal amount of damage."[206] For the NGOs and the natural environment, these were conservation and organizational gains that may not have been achieved through confrontations with the state or continued opposition to the pipeline.

So were these NGOs active participants as they claimed in 2002 or did they become consenting employees? At this time, I walked a fine line between thinking these mainstream organizations had been co-opted completely by the oil industry, as a large body of literature would indicate, and co-opted by the larger

NGOs as this research would indicate, but also cheering for the underdog—my fingers crossed that the Ecuadorian NGOs, especially the midlevel ones that initially resisted the pipeline's EIA and route, would get the better of the multinationals. This bias bordered on college sports mania, when many outsiders want the short, slow, unknown team to win. They never do. They can win one or two games, and it feels like a miracle to them and to their audience, but they never win the tournament. They lack the depth, the experience, the recruiting, the staff, the bench, and the legs to do so, though an entire arena and television audience may be cheering for them. In 2002, when I was meeting with the NGOs negotiating "ecological compensation," I was also inspired, caught up in their enthusiasm and my own naiveté that they could negotiate as equal partners with the oil sector.

Likewise and as expressed previously, these NGOs also admired and silently applauded the activist groups in the greater Mindo area, and even Acción Ecológica, which remained committed to resisting the pipeline. These two points—their underdog stature, while they were simultaneously rooting for an even weaker group (the affected residents in Mindo)—are powerful testaments to the dexterity and spirit of the domestic, midlevel NGOs. Forced to navigate between confrontations with Mindo's activists where they had conservation projects and disputes with the oil sector for a compensation fund, at a level not experienced by them previously, speak to their spirit and determination. They worked to reduce impact along the right-of-way in the Mindo area, to improve the country's environmental standards and conditions, to enhance their own organization's reputations as expert environmentalists within the oil industry, and to test their individual abilities to meet the expectations of the competitive and international oil industry—though they sacrificed ties with those who opposed their actions.

Deactivation in a Transnational Context

For all of their fortitude, when compensation agreements had not been reached in late 2003, it became apparent that the smaller and inexperienced NGOs lacked the depth of staff for the duration and stamina required of negotiating with the oil multinationals. Being outsized was particularly apparent given the extensive negotiation portfolios of the multinationals and the institutional dominance of the largest NGOs. In this third stage, the oil industry's initial defensive position and the midlevel NGOs' empowering one were revealed to be brief interludes before these roles were reversed. Likewise, old resentments and distrust between the NGOs that initially confronted the pipeline project and the larger apolitical-political NGOs that joined discussions later slightly undermined NGO solidarity in these negotiations. Indeed, relations between them became increasingly "corrosive," much like the findings of a "corrosive community" following a technical environmental disaster.[207] Exposing a rift between these two contingents, one of the first resisters to the pipeline noted, "It kind of annoyed us a little bit that these large NGOs entered this issue when they saw there [was], apparently, funding."[208] Over time, these two factions formed a closed yet conflicted network with the oil consortium, while the conservation heavyweights commandeered negotiations. Despite the midlevel NGOs' willful purpose, this phase revealed an erosion of organizational agency, a slippage in controlling their agenda, and further estrangement from domestic networks.

"You tend to get tarred, if you will, as an organization that's willing to work with the private sector," lamented one participant several years after the negotiations ended.[209] This descent occurred after OCP brought in an environmental mediator with a history of industry-conservation collaboration, who in turn invited other organizations to participate in the negotiations. The inclusion of an environmental facilitator and a wider body of NGOs with greater international and corporate experience effectively dismantled the organizational agency of the second-tier NGOs. Even though these established and politically influential organizations had not launched discussions, nor had they actively or publicly challenged the pipeline's construction, they dominated the negotiation process, thereby weakening the standing of the original contesters.

To this, Mac Chapin has presented how "two layers of control" operate on domestic NGOs.[210] One layer consists of the bilateral and multilateral donors, such as the World Bank and the bank's GEF projects, while the second comprises the large international NGOs, which regrant or serve as gatekeepers to international funds. In this manner, the midlevel NGOs experienced a second weight of co-option by the NGO community itself. First, their environmental role was diminished by the oil companies, and then their influence was weakened by the more influential environmental leaders in Ecuador. Indeed, the "non-political" NGOs, who did not resist the pipeline project, were arguably master political organizations in their domination of the conservation side of the negotiations and in the brokering of regrants.

Simultaneously, the environmental talks lent the petrochemical industry an international image as being committed to Southern environments, while quieting the NGOs' discontent over the pipeline project and diluting the more progressive agenda of the second-tier organizations that initially sought greater transparency, access to OCP reports, a monitoring role, community participation, and mitigation. In 2002, for example, a spokesperson for one of the smaller domestic NGOs presented their earliest and most universal of demands:

> To make an environmental showcase of best environmental practices [of the behavior of OCP in this region]—that was our proposal. We said transparency, available information, the best technology, the best information, the best willingness to communicate with people to make them understand what you are doing because we saw [this] as a great possibility to create that as a great precedent of what should be the future behavior of petroleum companies in the Amazon. So we presented the proposal to them. . . . But we haven't gotten a response from them.[211]

Once ecofund negotiations were under way, NGO effort was directed toward preparing the mechanisms of grant distribution and a framework for the application process.

OCP's ability to eliminate discussions of transparency and open communication was facilitated or seconded by the international conservation NGOs with whom oil companies had a history of partnering. To be clear, the domestic NGOs had national and international partners before negotiations began. But the oil companies had their own corporate-friendly, internationally connected partners within the conservation community as well. The boomerang actions of the environmental organizations were overlaid by similar boomerang actions of the multinationals. Environmental organizations ignored by the state turned to their international partners to pressure oil multinationals for direct negotiations. Likewise, oil multinationals turned to international organizations, with which they had already established a working relationship, to request the international NGOs guide or demonstrate to their Ecuadorian colleagues a procedural context of oil-NGO relations. Through this process, the domestic NGOs experienced the burden of a ricocheting effect and a gradual marginalization of their initial concerns and demands. Essentially, the transnational nature of the negotiations escalated the level of negotiations from the more confrontational second-tier NGOs and toward the multinationals and the more business-friendly international NGO (INGO) community.

Even though OCP required the cooperation of domestic NGO to greenwash its image internationally, negotiations were largely legitimated and owned among international participants, not domestic ones. To be sure, the ecofund negotiations protected the global image of the individual oil companies, while simultaneously and secondarily greenwashing the five-hundred-kilometer-long pipeline. According to one NGO participant,

> I got the feeling that, of course, they want to raise their profile, OCP, and this is most internationally with the international profile, because I don't really think they care about our opinion. It's more about these other companies that formed the consortium, they are all international companies, like Alberta Energy company, . . . or Agip and they have a lot of environmental pressure in their own countries because, you know, there is more environmental awareness in Europe or Canada. So they have a lot of pressure from within their countries. So they want to raise the international profile of OCP by creating the eco-trust. So they are really concerned about the international image. So what is the best way for doing this? So it's creating the eco-trust. Of course, they have to negotiate with us because we are the local parties and we know what is going on.[212]

Still another NGO said:

> [The oil companies] know that they have a lot to lose if they don't work with NGOs. So they need to keep this green image alive. . . . And they would not like to present this kind of idea—of working alone—to other parts of the world. They

are six oil companies. So it's important for them to present this kind of image that they work with the government and not only with the government, but with some NGOs.[213]

That it was the Northern multinationals that were receptive to oil fund negotiations, and not the state or the state-owned PetroEcuador, was apparent to the NGO community as well. "I would like to stress that *some* companies fear that their image could be distorted if they do not comply with the different, legitimate petitions of civil society," commented one participant. "And to see that some companies are sensible to that, and can foresee what could happen in the future if they do not commit to the best practices, that's something good."[214]

In addition to globally greenwashing the project, the ecofund negotiations lent greater international legitimacy to the domestic conservationists than they had previously constructed for themselves before OCP's arrival. However, this trade-off became their own weakened capacity to build legitimacy *within* oil-impacted areas, to convert it into contingency plans and permanent monitoring mechanisms, to mitigate impacts along the route, to influence the design of alternative economies and energy sources for the nation, to include affected communities, and to maintain collaborative ties with community-based groups. These costs for the NGOs may have been the oil consortium's goal all along.

For the domestic NGOs, the impacts of negotiations lingered for years after the ecofund was finalized. "I'd say that a smaller NGO . . . could (be) put out of business completely," complained one of the participants.[215] During the interview, this person said that NGOs may experience a temporary decline in fundraising, as a result of negative charges against them, though substantiated evidence of this drop in funding was not obtained.

> On the fundraising side, it had quite a significant impact for the organization[s] because there are . . . a number of outspoken foreigners that live in Mindo . . . and they are extremely well connected internationally, and they were also very much against the OCP pipeline, and again very much against [our] decision to work with the private sector and the government on this.[216]

"We were heavily, heavily criticized for that, for taking a stand (for negotiating the ecofund)," recalled one participant.[217]

Even the EcoFondo itself was "tarred." According to one participant in 2007, "There's stigma. Several of the NGOs are reluctant to apply for the ecofund funding."[218] According to an anti-OCP grassroots ecologist, "We don't really want to take money from the OCP if that's going to bring resentment from the other groups. We are just better off doing it other ways, and making sure and being very proud of the fact that we can do it without them."[219]

In this case, as the NGO community became tarred domestically and internally, the image of the oil multinationals became greener—at least among the nonimpacted, Northern-centric conservation community. However, in this use, "green" refers to the oil sector's monetary maintenance of conservation projects for conservation NGOs, rather than a demonstration of environmental protection or blue-green justice. Throughout negotiations, the oil consortium contained the parameters of the ecofund, effectively manipulated the NGOs, defined compensation, and diverted NGO calls for greater participation and transparency from the state and oil sector onto the NGO community itself. Acknowledging the NGO quagmire, one said, "They don't care if we the local NGOs keep talking about all the things that they are doing wrong, as long as the ecotrust is created, with nothing to blur this image."[220] In essence, the oil multinationals molded the industry's environmental image internationally, while temporarily corroding the efficacy of the domestic NGOs during the pipeline's construction.

Transparency Trap

Once ensconced in corporate meetings, the conservation NGOs also fell into a transparency trap of their own. In this way, they actually failed to deliberate with the oil industry in a transparent manner, a process they had once demanded of the industry and the state. Not only were the NGOs demanding clarity from the state initially, and then the oil industry, they were also grappling with how to participate in the country's oil economy for the first time and in a transparent manner. More or less, their calls for greater and more meaningful degrees of participation and inclusion in the country's oil politics failed, while they themselves became burdened by the fund's own lack of openness. First, the negotiations were conducted privately in spaces without community or state involvement, and without public announcements. At this time, the assembly of largely non-member-based and foreign-funded NGOs bore little resemblance to their earlier demands for an expanded role of civil society as they were becoming increasingly more exclusive. "We tried inviting other NGOs, but I think there were perceptions that maybe this was not a clear process," recalled one participant. "So these other NGOs said, 'No, it's not ethical because OCP did not do a correct environmental assessment and are not complying with the World Bank standards.' . . . But we still invited them to participate."[221]

Secondly, the midtier NGOs, which initially felt empowered in launching the talks, were prevented from critiquing the construction process and were becoming trained in oil-designed environmental standards, rather than the environmental justice concerns of oil-impacted communities and non-oil experts. Scientific information and general observations that were gathered by participating NGOs and NGOs with projects near the right-of-way were prohibited from being released to the public. During construction, data were routed through OCP for review, approval, and ownership. OCP-funded or OCP-approved research along the right-of-way was reported to OCP, which then presented reports to the Environment Ministry, where prohibitive procedures made retrieving the reports daunting.[222]

Acknowledging this dilemma, one NGO representative said, "One of the things we are not happy with is that there are all of these groups doing the monitoring, and so on and so forth, but none of the information is readily available. All of the information is filtered through OCP. . . . But the only thing that's public is what OCP says can be public."[223] Substantiating this experience, another person corroborated how the conservation community struggled with this situation: "It is difficult to maintain that line between what we can go public with and what we cannot go public with."[224]

To nonparticipating NGOs and community groups with no official access, these NGOs appeared as nontransparent and nonparticipatory as the state and oil sector. Community groups interpreted Quito-based NGOs as working alongside OCP near their community, and demanded information and informal observations of the construction process, which they themselves could not access legally. The pipeline's right-of-way was heavily guarded in high activist zones, effectively blocking on-site inspection by community groups and, at times, leading to physical confrontations and arrests in the Mindo region. According to one Quito-based conservationist familiar with the Mindo community:

> What we did was to stop having a relationship with them, because they were always very aggressive against us. They were all the time trying to push us to get information. We can release scientific information. We cannot release any other kind of information because any other kind of information is private to the company, and we have this confidentially clause. . . . So we had a lot of pressure from these activists for us to share this kind of information, and we couldn't, we shouldn't. . . . And now they kind of complain that we haven't involved them in the monitoring process.[225]

At the same time, some of the participating organizations, including the original core that opposed the route and that received monitoring roles at certain points along the route, appeared to regret the direction of the negotiations and the realization that their high level of influence in the negotiation process had been a mirage. "It was a learning process for all of us, all the campaign against OCP and all the things that happened afterward. I think we were quite naive before," acknowledged one participant.[226] Another added: "To be quite honest, if I were to do it again, I think I would be much stronger on opposing OCP and would have had a much heavier hand in bringing to light the issues to the international community."[227] Still further, another admitted: "We were very, very slow. And we didn't see in advance what would happen in the future with the OCP. And of course, OCP was thinking about the construction of the pipeline much, much earlier than three years ago."[228] Remarking on a more private level, the participant added,

"So it's a pity, but as a conservation movement in Ecuador we are worried more with small parts of the conservation problem and we are very slow with the big issues."[229]

Ecuador is not alone. The small parts have successfully bogged down the environmental movement in the United States as well, which has contributed to the industry's deep-seated entrenchment and the public's ignorance, apathy, and underorganized potential to block ecologically taxing practices. One of the more proactive and increasingly political organizations, which chose to negotiate with OCP, also noted the NGOs' dilemma:

> First, and it's probably a good lesson, but it's too late, is awareness and being more insistent and stronger and more determined to act before things are done. We are patient, and we believe in dialogue. But, of course, sometimes we are naive and we were left behind. When things are already done, we are then taken into consideration. That's a lesson to learn: the capability of reacting and proposing new things instead of commenting [on what] has already been set up by the government.[230]

In short, the cost of these negotiations may be reduced cohesion, trust, and collaboration between NGOs and between NGOs and communities in future oil debates. Moreover, whether these realizations of regret translated into a discontinuation of contact with or reorientation to the oil sector remains uncertain. Indeed, collaboration, cooperation, and negotiation may be perpetuated in future oil-NGO contact in the Amazon, though it is uncertain whether such an alliance between the individual oil companies and the conservation community would continue in the absence of Northern oil companies, Northern financiers, and Northern NGOs. This final point may be of pressing concern given that some Northern companies are being replaced in oil blocks by state-owned oil companies from South America and Asia, which may have fewer pressure points to meet NGO- and community-demanded standards and to protect or compensate affected communities.

Stage 4: Realizing the Ecofund; A Critical Eye toward Oil Extraction

The fourth and final phase reveals how the pipeline project and subsequent ecofund negotiations were pivotal events in the operations and activities of the Ecuadorian NGOs despite the hardship, exhaustion, and doubt experienced during the final phase of ecofund negotiations. In this final evolution, two outcomes are particularly notable. First, their work produced a twenty-year US$16.9 million fund that will provide much-needed support to the country's important biodiversity and landscape. Second, the NGOs themselves discovered an interest in and a capacity for interjecting their expertise in oil debates—to strengthen the anemic Environment Ministry, to support civil society, to cultivate greater environmental appreciation at the Ministry of Energy and Mines, and to monitor oil exploration in the Amazon. They established themselves as a more experienced and perhaps more potent force in influencing the oil industry than they had been before the pipeline.

Distributing the Fund

The first funds were distributed in 2005 to six NGOs and two university groups, out of 45 applicants, for projects ranging from one to three years in duration. In 2006 FAN received 36 applications, and funded seven projects. In 2007, 106 applications were received. For the first four-year period of 2005–2008, twenty-nine projects had been funded in the three designated areas. These include fifteen in Area One, the area along the pipeline's right-of-way, eight in Area Two, in the region of oil production in the Amazon, and six in Area Three, which includes national priority areas outside of the oil production and transportation sites.

Among the NGOs that participated in fund negotiations during the first four years of its operation, CECIA received two of the twenty-nine grants for projects in the IBAs, including one for research in the Mindo IBA and another to support local groups near three IBAs in protecting the area's biodiversity.[231] EcoCiencia also received a grant for the El Chaco area, and the Universidad San Francisco de Quito received one to produce a guide of the nation's parks and reserves. Other internationally known groups that received funds included Wildlife Conservation Society (WCS) for a project in Yasuní National Park and CI-Ecuador for a project on Isla de la Plata, a protected bird sanctuary approximately ten miles offshore. The range of recipients included local and regional NGOs, colleges and universities as well as groups with ties to Indigenous organizations or communities in the Amazon. The Organización Indígena Secoya del Ecuador (OISE) and the Fundación Sobrevivencia Cofan (FSC) each received a grant, and four other organizations with projects with Indigenous communities, including Kichwa in Yasuni, Kichwa in Napo, and the Cofan, also received support.

Despite these projects, there were lingering tensions surrounding the negotiations, distribution, and limitations of it. For instance, some of the participating NGOs claimed that the amount of nearly $17 million was too small and its funding of projects of one to three years in duration was too shortsighted to have an impact on conservation. "The ecofund, of course, is not entirely satisfactory for any of the parties," observed one participant at the end of negotiations. "I think OCP made a good deal. The money is less than half of what we estimated it could take for the monitoring and prevention in the future. So actually we were faced with the decision of getting something or nothing."[232]

Some also suggested that instead of negotiating a terminal fund, they should have negotiated an endowment instead. "It should [have been] like a revolving fund, not a sinking fund, but a revolving fund or an endowment fund. Something like that, you know, that generates money [all the] time to fund changing necessities, or needs, or projects."[233]

Petitioning for funds also became an ethical barometer. Those who did were suspect or viewed as ecologically bankrupt by some of the Mindo activists, who adamantly refused to request conservation funds. For example, a group of landowners in the Mindo region with a lawsuit against OCP's route said they would continue to reject any of OCP's monetary offers to settle the lawsuit "because that would mean that they would buy us like all the others."[234] This position may be purely posturing, but according to the same community activist, seeking funds from the ecofund was never a consideration: "There was never a temptation for that."[235] Another landowning activist, who also refused to petition for ecofunds, clarified the sentiment of many antipipeline organizations in the greater Mindo region:

> This is our own philosophy. We don't believe that you can condone bad actions by just putting money out. They [OCP] should have done the *right* thing, then you put money out, and then everybody would have taken it, and then everybody would have gone forward for the better good. But to do all of the wrong things, and then to say, "Oh here is the money, and this is going to make up for it." That's not the way I do things, and I know other organizations feel the same. . . . I feel that we can get, it may not be easy, but I feel that we can get clean money.[236]

In contrast, others in the Mindo area approached the fund as a means to complete community and conservations projects, though they too were reluctant to be seen publicly as endorsing the project. It was a difficult dilemma given the need alongside the prolonged animosity in the Mindo area toward anyone aligning with OCP. "We have already voted in [a] previous time *against* accepting that money as being from the OCP," recalled one community member. "But the question was directly put to the OCP as to whether we were obliged to stick [the name] OCP on all the things that we do. And for help, [for another collaborative project], we actually turned it down for that reason. And I think that was possibly a mistake now [because of the community's need]."[237] In further reflection on accepting tainted and stigmatized money, the same person added, "Maybe you could say the ecofund helped partly, in monies derived from the ecofund, but you wouldn't have to say that it was OCP. . . . The idea is that the money actually does then go toward useful things in the region."[238]

Another point of concern was the selection process. "Is the OCP just trying to benefit by saying that if it wasn't for them, then all these wonderful things wouldn't be happening [through the ecofund]?" asked a grassroots ecologist. "Or are they actually giving the important money to the important projects. . . . I do believe that very, very good, hands-on solid projects are probably not getting financed by them."[239] After the establishment of this hard-fought fund, the NGO participants joined others in a varied assessment and receipt of funds, including the critique of its monetary value and its distribution.

There were other limitations to the fund. The fund failed to address remediation or the environmental or social impacts of the oil process in the most oil-saturated regions, and failed to mitigate impacts, to monitor impacts, or to develop and test contingency plans. These failures resemble how corporations argued that the North American Free Trade Agreement (NAFTA) should not include environmental considerations, while simultaneously suggesting that NAFTA is already the most environmentally friendly trade agreement.[240] In this case, the corporate side of negotiations in Ecuador made the ecofund independent of the pipeline's potentially harmful social and environmental impacts, while also implying that OCP was a critical protector of Ecuador's natural environment. Hidden in the mechanisms of the fund is that the NGOs' primary leverage to force negotiations was the explicit and demonstrable impacts of the industry in the Amazon region. If the industry's environmental damages were not known and were not certain, there would not have been a channel to link the pipeline to an environmental fund.

In an analysis on environmental aid, Tammy Lewis finds that aid is distributed according to international donor interest in protecting "unused natural resources, a global resource" rather than local environmental need, and in "supporting the protection of 'pristine' nations (those with high biodiversity and undeveloped areas) rather than nations that are already polluted (those with poor water quality)."[241] Lewis identifies how aid flows to low-income nations that have closer political and economic ties to donor nations, than to areas of greatest need.[242] In the environmental fund negotiations in Ecuador, we see that even within one nation, the private oil companies, very much a component of the political-economic matrix, favor organizations with strong ties to the international environmental community and international organizations, rather than grassroots ecological groups or affected communities. This position leads to funds being available for conservation projects and research rather than environmental health projects and environmental health research in communities most impacted by the oil industry. In addition, these conservation efforts fail to raise the political participation of rural Ecuadorians in determining how the country's oil revenues are to be spent, or whether additional oil blocks will be leased, or whether taxes on the industry be imposed to develop clean, renewable energy for the nation's post-fossil-fuel future. This work builds on Lewis's findings by suggesting that areas or regions within an oil-dependent nation also become designated as either pristine, and therefore worthy of conservation, or polluted, rather than challenging contamination universally and promoting alternative energy globally.

Claiming a National Role

A second postfund transition for the NGOs was the realization of a role and a responsibility to improve the nation's political and legal environmental mechanisms. To be sure, some had regrets: what they could have done or should have done when they first learned of the OCP project. But through their efforts of opposition and then negotiation, some identified additional tasks for themselves within Ecuador.

At the beginning of their campaign, one could interpret the NGO community's decision to switch from challenging the state to negotiating with multinationals as costing it dearly in terms of long-term conservation. Indeed, one of the most secure actors in oil policies is the state, which in this case owns all subsurface material, controls the military, and remains a sovereign entity capable of evicting oil multinationals and nonnational guests. So by relieving the state from greater accountability and transparency during the construction process, conservation initiatives may have been diminished in the long term. Yet this tentative assertion has been moderately countered by the NGOs more recent post-OCP efforts to remain engaged in oil issues and to shift back toward targeting state bodies—a testament to their resiliency and skill and their commitment to Ecuador as well as to the industry's transient business ethos.

Even before the completion of the ecofund talks, NGOs had identified a duty to strengthen the Environment Ministry given that state-directed and state-enforced biodiversity protection may have more lasting impact than the short-term ecological compensation agreements of a few receptive multinationals. What they evoked unknowingly perhaps was that it was the global environmental movement in general that created many of the environment ministries or government agencies that many nations have today. For the *idea of* the potential of government bodies to govern industries for the good of a nation's ecosystems and people, they committed (or recommitted in some cases) to reinforcing government agencies to regulate industry.

OCP served as an impetus in this direction and as a conduit between the NGOs, which had been working on their individual projects removed from the state, and the state, which determines through policy or force the direction of the country's petroleum industry. To be certain, while some of the environmental NGOs discovered the oil industry, they also discovered weaknesses in the country's environmental laws and sought after the pipeline's completion to correct for this. In light of this, one NGO acknowledged:

And that means that we need to invest, as Ecuadorians, in all the mitigation, in all the impact assessment that we need to do and in all the environmental action plans in order to confront the possible and the probable impacts of whatever project. However, without supporting legislation, future participation is not guaranteed.[243]

Through earlier efforts at contesting the EIA and the route, and with the OCP behind them, another NGO spokesperson identified that their future work lay in the country's legal system:

We have a very strange legal framework. . . . It is very advanced conceptually, but not with the resources. And now, for example, the judges, they don't even know how to deal with environmental terms or for example, there is "acción popular," a class action is what the U.S. says. It was very similar to here, but not known before, not used, so people were talking about very new things in a traditional law, so it was very, very, very difficult to explore and to make a case of that. . . . Here it was dealing with a *potential* issue and how to measure potential things.[244]

Even while negotiating the ecofund, another also identified the critical role of the national government in making lasting change:

> If you have the opportunity to work with the multinational companies, I think it would be very important. But I think they have their own agenda, and probably they don't want to work with you. . . . And with the local, the national companies, [they] are very difficult to work with. For example, with PetroEcuador, it's very, very difficult to influence their decisions. This is the problem for us. But if you go through the government, if you go through the Ministry of the Environment or through the Ministry or the Minister of Energy, you can influence, as well, PetroEcuador.[245]

Concurring, another NGO representative added in 2007, "[The government] they just have to insert the environmental variable and the private companies have to comply with them, so the way we see it, we have to go with the government."[246] These comments speak to the fluidity of the NGO community and the irony of conservation concerns. Recall that many of the country's leading environmental NGOs targeted the state initially to influence the EIA and to reroute the pipeline. It was after their failure with the state that they turned to the private sector. Yet even while exhausting their time, energy, and resources on private-NGO negotiations, the NGOs identified the state as the most critical, or ultimate actor in protecting the country's biodiversity.

From this identification, a remarkable incongruity also arose. That is, in 2007, a conservation organization was laying out a framework to raise funds for technical environmental training for members of the Ministry of Energy and Mines, perhaps one of the more influential ministries in the oil-driven, low-income nation. Yet this is a reoccurring theme in oil disasters, including the more recent BP oil spill in the Gulf of Mexico. Entities that grant permits and inspect industrial operations may lack the skill, capacity, technology, authority, independence, and/or will to monitor the industry, to determine risk and impact, and to shut down operations when risk to human life, wildlife, and the environment exceed short-term production and short-term profits for a few. It begs the oil justice question relative to the demands originating in the Amazon: should independent monitoring capacities be a requirement before extractive industries begin operations? It is not known whether the NGO effort to train the Ministry of Energy and Mines was achieved, but it was being discussed. Many communities that reside near oil facilities would possibly suggest raising oil rents or implementing an environmental impact surcharge on the profitable industry to strengthen the government's (and community's) role in environmental inspection, monitoring, and capacity rather than seeking money elsewhere.

The NGOs, which had become accustomed to meeting on a fairly regular basis, also identified a future role for themselves in the Amazon as environmental experts on the oil industry. In particular, some participants joined with nonparticipating NGOs to collaborate against oil expansion in Yasuní National Park in the Amazon. With the assistance of the Environment Ministry, this NGO alliance blocked the construction of a road by the Brazilian oil firm Petrobras, also a member of the OCP consortium, in Yasuní through direct dialogue with the oil company. They were also organizing to keep Petrobras's Central Production Facility outside of Yasuní National Park. "We were aware that we have to be watching out over these projects developing in the Amazon because at any point they were going to cross into a national park given that the oil blocks are overlapped with the national protected areas," recognized one member of the ecofund, who now sat on a Yasuní committee. "And I think that in general the OCP and ecofund process made us very aware or even more aware than in the past that we have to keep an eye on these developments."[247]

An environmental consultant for the oil industry also acknowledged the more vital role and effective impact of the NGO community in the Amazon as well as a more forceful Environment Ministry, when asked about a change in environmental standards since OCP's construction.

Basically, you have got a whole group of NGOs who have been working out there [in the Amazon], they have worked in the government, they are friends with the government, and they all communicate, so you come to some kind of detente basically with all of those stakeholders. . . . And if you don't understand that delicate balance and you try to save some money or time [in environmental standards or safeguards], things can shut down. The NGOs, especially with the Ministry of Environment, are very well connected. . . . They'll just shut the project down, especially if it's an international oil company.[248]

For the NGOs, the benefits of negotiating the fund included a channel of communication with the oil sector, greater government awareness and recognition of them and their conservation initiatives,[249] greater access to government officials at the ministerial level, greater (though inconsistent) influence at the Environment Ministry, as well as the formulation of a model for future dialogue with the private sector or challenges against other oil entities in the Amazon. Again, the pipeline project served to link the NGOs to the industry and to the state, which may prove decisive given that oil multinationals are mobile entities searching the world for "optimal" working conditions.

Nationally and internationally, their achievements and knowledge may serve as a template for future agreements, and the individual participants may find a role for themselves as consultants in compensatory deliberations between NGOs and the fossil fuel industry in Latin America as well. Such a shift would strengthen Southern-to-Southern dialogue, commitments, and collaboration. Certainly, their international image has been enhanced among some for achieving an environmental fund in a volatile, oil-dependent, low-income country. It remains uncertain, however, whether this experience, or exercise, will translate into a permanent and exacting presence in oil debates in the Amazon.

In addition, the engaged, and increasingly political, NGOs also identified a new role in strengthening the ministries of the environment and energy after the pipeline's construction and after their ecofund negotiations. As oil operations transition in the Amazon from one oil company to another, NGOs could have greater leverage in protecting the environment and pressuring all oil entities, rather than Northern multinationals alone, if operating in conjunction with impacted residents and directly on the oil companies as well as on the state's environmental agencies. The NGOs have long identified this. Yet they still need to achieve it; and whether their commitment to these goals is temporary or long-lasting remains uncertain.

In sum, through their own frustration, jubilation, and reflection, we witness how a few midlevel conservation NGOs experienced the construction of the OCP pipeline. Simply put, if success was defined as rerouting the pipeline away from ecologically sensitive areas—as it was defined by some of these organizations in 2001—it was not achieved. Materially, an environmental fund was established, though it may best be quantified as conservation "crumbs" by nonparticipants as well as by some participants, to whom the fund was less than optimal. Politically, they found a voice and place within official and oil circles, and rediscovered the crucial state function of regulating all oil operators, not just Northern ones.

Along the way, their words conveyed the tightrope these NGOs walked. The expression of regret in 2003 and again in 2007 was not indicative of a narrative of tragedy. Rather it was a reflection on the organizational compromises and internal struggles inherent among NGOs when negotiating with entities with much greater resources, political influence, and global power than their own. In particular, it was the midlevel domestic organizations, which intercept and reflect the demands and positions of community groups as well as the international NGOs, whose constraints and dynamism are most easily captured in a longitudinal study. Straddling multiple and competing worldviews, their transition to a transnational campaign of negotiation and their recovery from it were rapid and vigorous—reflecting their limited practice in oil conflicts as well as the strength, determination, facility, proficiency, and hope of the midlevel NGOs.

In many ways, the postfund period marked a time of revitalization: a revival from the process, a renewal of their own conservation direction and agendas, and perhaps a recovery of their organizational prestige, especially for the smaller, domestic groups. While recuperating, some sought to repair relationships within the NGO community as well as among the community-based activist-ecologists. However, internal doubts and tensions impeded full camaraderie between the two blocs of the nation's most passionate environmental caretakers—the midlevel NGOs and Mindo's activist-ecologists. If the two sides could collaborate in the future, for Ecuador's natural heritage and biodiversity and undeterred by their ideologically polar positions on OCP, they could become a formidable force, perhaps even the offense that leads the nation's environmental future.

Oil contamination in the Amazon is not a news breaking disaster, like an offshore oil explosion or a tanker collision. Here, oil is an unending contaminant, found as small oil lakes, oil ponds, oil depressions, and oil-peat, a boggy mix of oil and decaying leaf and grass matter. This photograph was taken in October 2003.

An environmental justice activist placing an anti-Texaco sticker on an accessible oil facility in the Amazon. Anti-oil activists lead observational, fact-finding missions to easily reached sites to demonstrate the industry's ordinary presence, routine leaks, and common pathway exposures of neighboring and affected communities.

To bid farewell to the grievances and injustices of a passing year, Quito residents hold a New Year's Eve demonstration and parade. In 2003, oil contamination as experienced by Indigenous communities in the Amazon was a frequent theme. Here, the sign reads "Without oil we were born, with oil we die. We live and fight in dignity."

The Texaco lawsuit, OCP, and the environmental impacts of oil industry in the Amazon featured prominently at the New Year's Eve parade in Quito in 2003.

In the Andean cloud forest in the greater Mindo region, the buried pipeline's right-of-way was planted with native and nonnative plant species. The route will always be cleared of trees to avoid stressing the underground pipeline. At the time, tour operators suggested converting the cleared path into a walking and monitoring trail. This proposal was not adopted by OCP. This photo was taken in 2003.

Police and OCP security guards prevent Mindo's activists from walking further along the pipeline's right-of-way. Many of the activists would establish an overnight camp in the cloud forest as part of a symbolic encampment. Earlier in 2002, some of them had maintained a campsite along the ridgeline for nearly three months. (The photograph was first published in Widener 2007b: 100.)

In Mindo town, and as part of Fundación Puntos Verdes's educational campaign, a notice in 2002 greets visitors: "I want Mindo clean and pretty. Don't throw trash on the ground or in the rivers."

Ernesto Estupinán, the mayor of Esmeraldas in 2003, calls for residents to maintain the city's beaches as part of his campaign to get them more actively involved in their community: "Yes, it's possible to change Esmeraldas. . . . Las Palmas is your beach, maintain it cleanly."

4

Mindo

Oil and Tourism May Mix

The rural and nature-based community of Mindo represented a conceptual bridge between the working poor of Lago Agrio who lived adjacent to the oil industry and the urban and educated conservation professionals in the capital. Mindo was a community of small business owners, ecotourism operators, and ecologists staking their modest livelihoods on their natural surroundings. The town supported a cottage industry of nature treks, river tubing, bird watching, and butterfly and orchid farms, while the greater Mindo region also supported trout and cattle farming, timber extraction, and the cultivation of bananas, yucca, sugar cane, and guayabas.[1] The Mindo region was already internationally recognized for its conservation efforts and nature-based tourism when the OCP pipeline project was announced.

Nearby, the protected forests of Cuenca Alta del Río Guayllabamba and Mindo-Nambillo were home to more than 450 bird species, forty-six of which were threatened with extinction at the time of the OCP pipeline. The latter site was declared a protected forest in 1988, but among international birders, the region's position was not officially launched until 1996 when Mindo joined the International Bird Count held annually in December.[2] A year later it was affirmed when BirdLife International designated Mindo an Important Bird Area (IBA).[3] Then in 2002, *National Geographic* listed the Chocó-Darién region of western Ecuador, near the Mindo area, as one of the world's twenty-five "hotspots," or sites "conservation biologists define as natural environments containing exceptionally large numbers of endangered species found nowhere else."[4]

Mindo's ecologists had already spent fifteen years cultivating the area as a small-scale tourism destination, rich in biodiversity and birdlife when the pipeline project was announced.[5] With its announcement, they advanced their ecological and small-business commitment and sought to raise the community's environmental awareness and the region's ecological profile to counter the oil project specifically and the country's oil dependency more broadly.

The greater Mindo community—especially its tourism providers—worked, lived, and protested along the turbulent line between environmental justice and conservation. Major tenets of the EJ movement include greater economic and environmental security alongside greater community participation in resource decisions that affect households and places of work and play. Rural communities may be particularly vulnerable to environmental injustice given that their households, places of play, and work are at times one and the same. In Mindo, for example, café owners may live upstairs or in adjoining rooms, while guesthouse owners live on-site and their children may work on school projects where visitors dine.

Mindo represented a nature-based or ecotourism community trying to commit to sustainable practices. Though tourists and tour operators may interchange the definitions and expected practices of nature-based, eco- and sustainable tourism, they are theoretically distinct. Nature-based tourism involves traveling to nature for its beauty, for the image of clean air and open spaces, and/or for physical activity. Scale up the physical activity and the risk of such travels and you shift into adventure tourism or even extreme adventure tourism. Ecotourism, on the other hand, requires a responsibility and commitment on the part of the traveler to be environmentally, eco-nomically, and socially aware and responsible with regard to supporting a local community's ecological and economic efforts, learning environmental and social issues important to the community, and leaving the culture and ecosystem intact.[6] Sustainable tourism, much like ecotourism, is generally presented as a sustainable balance of local economies, cultures, communi-ties, and environments.

Each one is commonly supported by government agencies, the private sector, conservation NGOs, and local communities as a means to develop an area economically as well as to conserve an area's natural environment.[7] International lenders have also supported ecotourism in particular as a means to assist low-income nations,[8] as well as to conserve the environment,[9] while conservation NGOs may also utilize a place, ecosystem, and wildlife for the economic development of a community.[10] In addition, rainforest preserves that have been opened to tourism and recreational use may generate enough revenue for greater land acquisition for the protection of biological diversity, the collection of renewable harvests, and scientific research.[11] Successful col-laboration between conservation organizations and tourism-affected commu-nities for the benefit of both parties and the natural environment is possible, yet its success is relatively new.

Previously, efforts to form national parks or preserves for tourism especially in low-income areas led to the displacement of communities already margin-alized due to their ethnicity or status, which further led to their exclusion from the economic benefits associated with tourism.[12] In a chapter entitled "Purity and Pollution," Jake Kosek identifies "environmentalism's troubled (and troubling) 'heart of whiteness.'"[13] In his analysis, the origins of the American environmental movement was an effort for both racial and environmental purity; in other words, to cleanse pristine landscapes from nonwhite or polluted races, which included pushing Native Americans from their land to create national parks and segregating recent immigrants to restrict contact between races at the end of the eighteenth century and through the first quarter of the nineteenth. Though the past is Kosek's backdrop, his actual study is based on current tensions between white conservationists and Hispano residents with regards to using, guarding, and redefining public space in the forests of northern New Mexico. In a similar case, the Chicanos of New Mexico lost not only their land to the National Park Service, but also became poorly paid, part-time, and seasonal service workers for the tourism industry.[14] Much like many others who suffer from rapid changes brought on by tourism, the Chicano community was also unable to afford to live in the communities where they worked due to the elevated cost of living in tourism towns.[15]

Each one—nature-, eco-, and sustainable tourism—is also advertised as avoiding the negative impacts associated more commonly with mass and resort tourism. Commercial and affluent tourism have been charged with re-mastering local environments for foreign tourists,[16] extracting an area's natural resources *from* the local community, while narrowing the community's economic opportunities to tourism alone.[17] Indeed, some local communities—self-sufficient prior to the arrival of the tourist trade—are at risk of morphing into a more culturally and economically vulnerable "consumer-oriented and dependent society."[18] Some host communities especially in low-income or developing places have also begun to view their own way of life as inferior or a reflection of their poverty relative to the tourists. This perception then drives in part the existence of a global "consumer monoculture," in which everyone wants to consume the same mass-produced items or to practice the same mass-viewed behaviors.[19] It may also lead to begging.[20]

Tourism destinations in the Caribbean, for example, experienced employment opportunities, alongside a reduction in community access to natural resources, a degraded environment, inflated land prices and increased land use struggles among displaced farmers.[21] Given that the tourism industry serves nonlocals and nonlocal interests, residents have felt limited ownership or responsibility to protect the resources that they could neither use nor enjoy,[22] and some have felt that foreign-owned operations received preferential political protection.[23] Indeed, the hotels, cruise ships, and tour operations are frequently foreign owned, thereby undermining local efforts and limiting the economic advancement opportunities of locals,[24] which may further escalate tensions between local and foreign residents.[25] Tourism initiatives, especially those backed by Northern interests in low-income destinations, are susceptible to fiscal "leakage" as well. Such leakage includes revenues from tourism that leave the country to pay for imported goods, to pay foreign owners of in-country tourism services (such as hotels) and of out-of-country services (such as air travel), to repay the nation's external debt, or that is remitted by foreign workers back to their home country.[26] On the one hand, foreign residents and owners of tourism facilities may deem themselves as contributing to a community's environmental awareness and protection, especially in regions where locals are perceived to exhibit ecologically destructive practices.[27] On the other hand, local or native residents may perceive foreign residents and tourism operators as exhibiting a "carelessness and general disrespect for the environment."[28]

These inequities are experienced by marginalized communities worldwide. In one harrowing case, 250 Filipino villagers were removed from their lakeside community for ecotourism development,[29] though their experience was not an isolated case.[30] In another example, the Gwich'in people of Alaska have persistently resisted nonlocal tourists as well as hunters and the oil industry with only limited success.[31]

What appears absent in the literature and perhaps among the Northern economic-residents of the South is a strong critique that their lifestyle and what they have achieved may not have been possible had they not left their home countries. Instead of being economic refugees rejected at the border, they are economic-residents enjoying a lifestyle and opportunities that would be impossible for them in their Northern birthplaces.

For the most part, much of the tourism literature is of Western or Northern tourists visiting and impacting places in developing or low-income countries. It is this North-South East-West dynamic that has served to "reshape" local environments to fit Western expectations of natural and societal relationships as well as to introduce or reinforce a capitalist orientation to the cultural exchange and natural experience expected from ecotourism.[32] Ecotourists of the North arrive wanting an "authentic" experience, and by authentic they desire to see "exotic" people and lands before civilization or globalization or others like them arrive destroying both the culture and the landscape that they so desire to experience.[33] In other words, these tourists are paying to see a people and a place untouched by them and untainted by the capitalistic relationship between people and nature. But their arrival and their demands actually introduce or reinforce what it is that they are trying to escape. Environmental managers in Jamaica, for instance, have been forced "to embrace ecotourism and to do so in a way that expresses and tends to reproduce specific Western understandings of that environment."[34] Likewise, communities in Papua New Guinea adopted capitalist values and a capitalist orientation to tourism *after* the arrival of foreign visitors, Northern conservation NGOs, and international agencies.[35] In this case, local leaders and residents spent two years carefully negotiating the location of a foreign-funded tourism facility that was acceptable to the majority of local people. The site, however, was rejected within hours by a nonnational NGO representative of the funding agencies, who sought to accommodate foreign tourists rather than to support the democratic decision-making processes of the community. In addition, a two-month-long process to decide on how to distribute and rotate work opportunities among the tribes was also rejected by the nonnationals, who endorsed a permanent placement structure that limited jobs to only a few.[36] That government aid agencies and international NGOs and lenders promote and finance ecotourism ventures that are not necessarily desired by ecotourists or by local communities speak volumes to the autocratic, top-down nature of some ecotourism ventures that aggravate inequalities and communal tensions.[37]

As for the tourists, their desire to see a people and a place left "primitive" and untouched by other tourists is "a new twist to the institutionalisation of racism" and serves to link today's tourist to their colonial past, in what has been referred to as neocolonial tourism.[38] The sun, sea, and sand experience, as Ian Munt argues, may be more aptly reconfigured as a demand for "subjugation, subservience and servitude."[39] One of several examples Munt cites for this interpretation of ecotourism was found in a tourism brochure for a safari in Africa that depicted thirty-five porters carrying the supplies of six tourists.[40] The product was not only wildlife viewing, but it was also the opportunity to walk in the shoes of former colonial masters. Deborah McLaren also identifies tourism brochures that describe a happy, unthreatening, and servile local population as promoting "glib, racist caricatures,"[41] rather than promoting individual connections and cultural exchanges. Indeed, some tourists, expecting the "royal treatment" or "a charming plantation" experience as promoted by tour operators, "expect that goods and services—even human ones—are available for a nominal price."[42] Too often, it appears that the construction of difference,[43] or otherness, divides the middle-aged tourists and tourism providers who have more in common than they may want to acknowledge: economic worries, children joys, and physical ailments.

Physically, tourism affects the landscape, including the air, the land, the view, and the area's water quality. Airports produce air and noise pollution, tourists consume more packaged items than local residents, and cruise ships have dumped human waste and postconsumer plastics at sea.[44] In the Caribbean and elsewhere, markets have been constructed, accommodations built, roads expanded to accommodate buses, and tunnels carved into mountainsides to facilitate travel.[45] In natural areas, the flora and fauna have been disturbed by the presence of human and pet traffic and off-road vehicles[46] and the introduction of nonnative species.[47] Some tourism facilities, such as marine mammal parks, have been rejected as "contrary to the spirit of ecotourism" and harmful to the wildlife by local residents and even some tourism providers.[48]

"Greenwashing" occurs in the tourism industry as well, much like corporate campaigns that present highly pollutant industries as environmentally friendly.[49] Large hotels and resorts for example label themselves as green for their recycling efforts, while consuming disproportionate amounts of energy and using chemicals in the landscaping.[50] Travel trade organizations also encourage green behavior of travelers (don't damage the coral), while failing to effectively monitor the facilities that espouse ecotourism practices. This practice has been called "ecotourism lite" for the masses.[51]

An alternative perspective identifies the economic, social, and environmental benefits associated with nature-based, eco- or sustainable tourism. Importantly, studies that identify the success of ecotourism identify the critical role of the local community in determining and developing sustainable businesses to which they benefit economically and to which the natural environment is protected and perhaps to which it even thrives. In Latin America, ecotourism initiatives have succeeded when an integrated and engaged community commit to an equal share in managing and owning tourism facilities and participating in development plans,[52] while community cooperatives operate well when they reach consensus in profit-sharing arrangements.[53] This was attempted by the local leaders of Papua New Guinea but was circumvented by more influential international interests.

Rural communities in particular may succeed if they maintain local control over decisions and operations, resist being overtaken by nonlocal companies, and use local resources, residents, and organizations.[54] In some cases, a supportive local government is also beneficial.[55] In the Ecuadorian Amazon, for example, the Indigenous Cofan community initiated the development of a "forest protection strategy" through tourism to counter oil extraction.[56] Other Indigenous communities in the Amazon also increased their commitment to forest conservation due to successful tourism operations, which in turn reduced their available time for hunting.[57] In Indonesia, budget or backpacker tourism, which has been ignored or discouraged by many governments or tourism ministries, changed a community's self-perception from one of slum dwellers to an international urban neighborhood.[58] They identified their individual and collective efforts, initiatives, and abilities to remake their guest houses, shops, and restaurants in a manner appealing to the travelers that they welcomed as part of their growing pride in their community.[59] In Mark Hampton's analysis, budget travelers represented bottom-up or "pro-poor tourism" in that they stayed in low-income communities and ate and shopped in locally owned places, all of which were started with minimal investment by low-income households.[60] Likewise in China, the efforts of a village to stop the dumping of wastewater from a fertilizer plant led the affected community to reposition itself as a domestic tourism destination for urban nationals seeking a fishing and nature-based experience—rather than as a town associated with an industrial waste dump.[61]

Reversing out-migration and generating income opportunities for women and young people are also important concerns for rural communities. In Greece, a rural mountainous community achieved both by adopting ecotourism as a conservation and economic initiative.[62] The success of the Greek ecotourism enterprise was achieved due to a balance of ecological and small-scale economic initiatives, as well as broad support from local residents, the European Union (EU), conservation organizations, and

Greek officials.[63] In addition, they also protected an important habitat area for threatened or endangered species and educated visiting schoolchildren on the ecology of the area. Unlike the Papua New Guinea case, the Greek one demonstrated the potential success when external actors listen and collaborate with local ones, while respecting local knowledge and valuing local insights and rights. Success in ecotourism development in mountainous areas may also require a strategic development plan that identifies the importance of gradual development and oversight so as to avoid the known dangers and mishaps with the adoption of rapid tourism expansion for rapid economic growth.[64]

The introduction of tourism into a community may be particularly rewarding for women for both the increased economic opportunities that it may provide as well as the enhanced self-esteem. Similar to the Greek case, tourism initiatives in the interior cloud forest region of Monte Verde, Costa Rica, enabled creative business opportunities among women, who became skilled artisans and contributors to the household's budget.[65] In Monte Verde, tourism also converted the male population from former hunters into knowledgeable birdwatchers and camera-toting tourists within their own community,[66] much like the case in the Ecuadorian Amazon. Even though tourism came more slowly to a small fishing village in Costa Rica, the local women persisted in forming an association in order to learn new crafts, to meet and collaborate with each other, and to market their products—despite criticism from their partners and their community.[67] In another case in a rural mountainous community of Mexico, Indigenous women formed a cooperative and developed a successful ecotourism hotel, which contributed to their collective women *and* Indigenous voices being spoken and heard.[68]

Trust within a community or between community members and outsiders is an important determinant of success as well. One study in Peru found that a community's degree of heterogeneity and distrust and history of regional terrorism impeded consensus on tourism-related management and planning issues, while a second community's greater homogeneity and integration raised local awareness and local reliance to develop tourism.[69] In Honduras, historical distrust between the local Garifuna population, an Afro-Indigenous group, and Honduran business leaders and international conservation groups threatened to undermine collaboration and endorsement of marine protected areas.[70] Distrust was sharpened further when restrictions on traditional practices and uses of the marine environment without economic assistance or compensation for the community's loss were put into practice.[71] But a history of mistrust is also not insurmountable. In South Africa, collaborative tourism initiatives were assessed as building trust between black and white communities with a long history of discrimination and prejudice.[72] Leaders of both communities worked together to develop tourism as a development plan for a seaside resort town as well as to address high unemployment rates in the black township.[73] However, and this occurs anywhere in the world, any community designations or demarcations due to race or ethnicity signal separate and unequal.

Indeed, and despite the identified economic, cultural, and environmental strengths of eco- or nature-based tourism, until the tour guides, restaurant workers, and guesthouse owners of developing places or marginalized communities are able to travel freely across borders as tourists with cash in their pockets it remains a highly unequal and servant-like affair. I would also suggest that until ecotourism fulfills this obligation of an equal exchange of experiences it is not a just enterprise. Likewise and under this scrutiny, the practice of sustainable tourism is impossible. If all of the world's tourism suppliers also became global tourists we would need another planet or two to accommodate them.

Until space travel becomes readily available, there are still many other varieties of tourism. There are, for example, dark tours to death camps, war sights, and places of assassinations,[74] and to premeditated and intentional disasters, including the bombing of a federal building in Oklahoma City in 1995 and the attacks on New York City's World Trade Center in 2001.[75] In Bali, deeply private and religious cremation ceremonies are viewed by vanloads of tourists arriving in beach attire.[76] There are also postdisaster historical tours, such as "flood tourism" following Hurricane Katrina in New Orleans,[77] and human misery tours, including "poverty tourism" to the *favelas* of Brazil and the townships of South Africa,[78] slum tours to Mumbai,[79] or even "toxic tours" to oil-contaminated places in the Amazon.[80] These types of tours are likely to be part of a roster of planned events that include nature treks, seaside vacations, resort meals, and a robust nightlife to wipe away the sense of hopelessness and to relieve the anxiety of viewing the social and environmental wreckage of our world. It is also clear from these diverse examples that people tour social and ecological disasters, and from these disasters spring tourism destinations.[81]

This chapter is an attempt to shed some light on the creation of a tourism destination arising from within a local community as well as to explore the impacts of tourism on the tourists themselves. The introduction of the OCP pipeline generated a response among grassroots activists—aided by international allies—that strengthened their commitment to ecotourism, environmental justice, and conservation. Likewise, the arrival of new domestic tourists—made aware of the Mindo region due to the town's anti-OCP activism—increased the environmental education opportunities for Ecuadorians, while risking the pristine back-to-nature image of the town itself. In a comprehensive literature review, Amanda Stronza identifies an emphasis on the origins of tourism as lying with Western or Northern tourists and the impacts of tourism as being experienced by local communities in economically underdeveloped nations.[82] From this assessment, Stronza argues that the incentives and impacts of tourism need to be analyzed for both the tourist and the host community for a more complete understanding of how the four intersect and how they could lead to positive experiences for all parties.[83] In the Mindo case however, the impacts and the experiences are owned by Ecuadorians.

In this analysis, tourism *and* the petroleum industry do converge. For one, the former is dependent on the latter at least until buses, trains, cars, and airplanes run on something other than fossil fuels. In addition, "tourism vied with oil as the world's largest legitimate business"—at least at the beginning of the 1990s.[84] Sometimes the two intersect directly, when, for example, fishing charters operate alongside the offshore oil rigs in the Gulf of Mexico or when former or existing oil towns build oil museums to honor the industry's economic importance to the region.[85] In the Ecuadorian Amazon, Ken Gould argues that "tactical tourism" emerged "as a form of local resistance" by an Indigenous community against the state-supported oil industry.[86] Gould's case also speaks to Stronza's concern that more attention needs to be devoted to the activism of communities to determine and generate tourism for their own interests. Other similarities include the extraction and supply of a resource (oil) or an experience (tourism) to nonlocal consumers, who enjoy the benefits of both industries, without the social, economic, and environmental burdens associated with residing alongside either one. Though some tourists complain, and at times they experience a disproportionate amount of hardship when, for example, they are robbed, their flights are delayed, and a new cuisine leaves them ill or homesick, for the most part the travel experience is rewarding. To the impacts of tourism on the host community and the traveler, this chapter contributes an analysis of the convergence of oil and tourism. It explores how the construction of an oil pipeline, perceived by some to be an environmentally destructive event, created conditions for the tourism industry, which may lead to more subtle, yet damaging, ecological changes and social conflict.

A TRANQUIL, TURNED RADICAL, DESTINATION

Mindo was a rustic, Andean, one-street town of approximately 2,000–2,500 people in 2001,[87] slightly more than two hours by road west of Quito. From the main highway, a road approximately three miles long descended into the town, and stopped. This single artery ran through the village, with shops, restaurants, and guesthouses lining the paved road, while dirt roads splintered off to connect homes and a few additional shops and guesthouses. While local activists estimated that between 75 and 80 percent of the population lived off of tourism,[88] to an outsider in 2001, Mindo appeared more hopeful of tourism, rather than an active and established destination.[89] Several guesthouses and cafés were closed, and those opened always had vacancies. Mindo's tourism torpor, however, would end when the local grassroots ecologists mobilized an impassioned resistance campaign against the pipeline project. Yet, to be clear, the pipeline was never planned to pass through or even near the town of Mindo. It passed north of the community through the Mindo-Nambillo Protected Forest, which the activists were attempting to protect.

In brief, and unlike the populist politics found in the petroleum hub of Lago Agrio or the monetary negotiations achieved by the conservation NGOs in Quito, Mindo's landowners, youth, and nature-based business owners opposed OCP's entry into their neighboring cloud forest reserves and their own budding tourism destination. Initially resembling "not in my back yard," or "not in my—very broad—backyard," activists,[90] they demanded the relocation of the pipeline. However, over time, they broadened their position to challenge the state's narrow support of an oil economy and neglect of alternative, locally owned and environmentally and economically sustainable businesses.[91] Unlike the other affected communities and organizations along the route, Mindo's activists targeted international NGOs and international audiences to pressure the project's financiers while also pushing other Mindo residents to adopt environmentally sustainable economic practices. In the process, they attracted national attention and became Ecuador's vanguard of an environmental age, even though they failed to reroute the pipeline or stop its construction or use.

Among the sites analyzed, Mindo's activists resembled the Quito-based NGOs, in terms of their inexperience with the oil industry, their strong international ties, their representation of Ecuador's environmental elite, as well as a tremendous transformation of strategy over the course of the pipeline's construction. In quick succession, the Mindo community discovered the oil industry, established an anti-oil campaign, demanded the pipeline's rerouting, became increasingly radical in their actions, collaborated with international advocates, and transformed the town into a global beacon for anti-oil activism, capitalizing well on the area's *environmental currency*, which others along the route lacked. In this sense, Mindo possessed protected forests, international status as an Important Bird Area, unique biodiversity, endemic species, an activist-oriented outlook, ecotourism opportunities, and receptivity to international visitors and support.[92] They also experienced the erosion of national and local ties, acquired land through international funds, generated tremendous media attention, became an environmental icon for the nation, witnessed a rise in visitors that was accompanied by greater local environmental stress than the pipeline itself, campaigned for the local adoption of an ecological commitment, and may be the site of the country's first organic environmental generation. This rapid chain of events demonstrates the extent of upheaval that a small, but active grassroots campaign may experience and may impose upon others in the community when confronted by an entity much larger and much more cohesive and powerful than the community itself.

The community's uniqueness structures this chapter into sections on their international, national, and local development in order to better demonstrate how Mindo's activists advanced multiple frames for multiple audiences, which were coupled with contradictory outcomes. To wit, the establishment of extensive international attention on Mindo led to national-level burdens, including greater environmental care in the Mindo area at the expense of other sensitive ecosystems along the route as well as an international neglect of other communities fighting against social and economic injustices rather than environmental protection alone. Second, while seeking greater affirmation from their international partners, they also damaged existing, and marginalized potential, national and local support networks. Third, their activism attracted so many new domestic tourists to the area that the area's ecosystems and environmental resources were strained beyond, debatably, the pipeline's construction impacts. This chapter also speaks to a rural community's long-term resiliency, vibrancy, and buoyancy even when confronted with community tension induced by oil conflict and community fears of a looming oil disaster.

GRASSROOTS ACTIVISTS: CLAIMING "MINDO"

At first introduction, Mindo's rural charm was enchanting for international activists, visitors, and researchers alike. Mindo appeared an idyllic respite from oil intrusion and urban life, where international advocates often work and international travelers often live. In the early morning, fish were delivered on horseback when the fish courier, an aging woman with long loosely braided hair and knee-high rubber boots, rode into town, selling farmed trout from two mud-caked plastic pails. In 2001, Mindo offered no public Internet service, no photocopy machine, and no newspaper service. To make photocopies, a person had to take a forty-minute bus ride from Mindo to Los Bancos, a bus ride that left three times daily; and for those people wishing to read a newspaper, they also had to travel to Los Bancos or hope visitors left their papers behind. The absence of technology and communications at the time would hinder local activists' correspondence with their international supporters, while the ease of time and limited alternatives would supply an ample number of young activists.

Mindo was also a place where foreign travelers from Europe and the Americas wandered through, and then stayed to buy land, marry, and build ecotourism businesses. Indeed, Mindo was composed of national and nonnational farmers, landowners, and ecotourism operators and was unique along the pipeline's route for its number of international residents involved in land preservation and ecotourism businesses. Yet Mindo was also a corrosive and combative community, whose members used the surrounding environment in a multitude of conflicting and competing ways.

Though the pipeline passed north of the Mindo town, landowners and activists in the greater Mindo area, including landowners, lodge owners, and tour operators outside of the town proper, mobilized early and strong resistance to the construction of OCP near the Mindo-Nambillo cloud forest reserve and the area's three river systems, Cinto, Mindo, and Blanco.[93] In truth, however, the first "Mindo" campaign arose among national and international landowners and conservationists outside of the valley town, some of whom lived along Rio Alambi, near the town of Tandayapa, or who spent the workweek in Quito; yet they presented themselves as being part of the greater Mindo area and defenders of the region's biodiversity.[94] "Mindo," in other words, included the small, rural town of Mindo as well as the Quito-based conservation projects in the greater Mindo-Nambillo area and the homes, lodges, and resorts of the area, some of which overlooked Mindo town. In the initial stage of activism, both the truly local and the nonlocal mobilized together to defend the greater Mindo-Nambillo area. As it happened, it was the Quito office of U.K.-based BirdLife International that generated some of the first international media attention on the OCP pipeline and in particular its impacts in Mindo-Nambillo.[95] However, collaborations splintered over the course of the pipeline's construction, while articulations of "Mindo" by Quito-based activists and conservation NGOs fueled tensions and distinctions between the truly local and the nonlocal or part-time local.

Ecoactivists and Grassroots Ecologists: Active, Idle, and Dissolved

Four groups formed when news spread that an oil pipeline would be constructed through the region, while two environmental organizations were already established in the Mindo area, another resurfaced after the completion of OCP, and still another formed independently of OCP but with key leaders in the initial anti-OCP-route movement. These groups included Pro Ruta de Menor Impacto, the Truth Commission, the Mindo Working Group, Acción por la Vida, Fundación Puntos Verdes, Amigos de la Naturaleza de Mindo, Fundación Pacaso y Pacaso, and the Mindo Cloudforest Foundation (MCF).

Comité Pro Ruta de Menor Impacto, or Committee for the Route of Least Impact, was the quintessential NIMBY organization that formed in October 2000 with twenty-two representatives of NGOs and grassroots groups.[96] It comprised relatively wealthy and educated, national and international private landowners and environmentalists with peripheral ties to the small town of Mindo. Other Pro Ruta participants included members of Fundación Puntos Verdes, as well as individual environmentalists in the Quito office of BirdLife and Quito-based conservation organizations, including Fundación Maquipucuna and CECIA, which have conservation and research projects in the region. To be clear, the majority of the most active members of Pro Ruta were not living in Mindo town. Nevertheless, they were established conservationists and/ or influential landowners in the region who were able to meet with the Ministry of Energy and Mines, the Ministry of the Environment, OCP personnel, and officials at the American and Canadian embassies. In contrast, Mindo's local activists would never achieve this access during their prolonged anti-OCP campaign after Pro Ruta dissolved.

Initially, Pro Ruta led the area's campaign, even coining for the nation the designations of routes: the "northern route" (near Mindo) and the "southern route" (considerably south of Mindo and south of the ecotourism businesses, private property, and conservation projects in the greater Mindo area). Pro Ruta supported the pipeline running along the southern route, a route proposed by Houston-based Williams Company, even offering the campaign slogan: "Oleoducto Si, Por Mindo, NO!" (The Pipeline Yes, Through Mindo, NO!). Months later, a condensed slogan advocated: "The Pipeline through Mindo, No!"

At its peak, Pro Ruta gathered fifteen hundred names to protest the northern route that led the Ministry of Energy and Mines to send an inspection commission along the southern route.[97] A map prepared by Entrix, the primary environmental consultant for OCP, to chart the southern and northern routes indicated that both routes had highly sensitive and/or risky areas through BirdLife's IBA, with the northern or Mindo path running 3.5 kilometers long and the southern section at 6 kilometers in length. In addition, Entrix's assessment of the two routes indicated that the southern route crossed through 30 kilometers of the IBA and the northern route crossed through only 20 kilometers of the IBA.[98] "It's rather inconceivable that we would select something that would become a cause for contention if we honestly believe that there was a viable alternative," noted one oil representative in Ecuador. "The southern route is not a viable alternative. . . . Take a drive down the SOTE, look at the number of houses, look at the number of people, look at the actual area that would have to be cleared. The northern route is the route of least impact."[99]

In neither support nor opposition, five Quito-based NGOs with support from the World Wildlife Fund concluded that greater analysis of the impacts and management plans were required before proceeding with construction and that data provided in the official EIA were insufficient to determine whether the northern or southern route would be of least impact.[100] After a hurried assessment of the official EIA due to its release and allocated time to reply, the NGOs advised the government "to adopt adequate measures that would guarantee that the selected routes and procedures would be the best in minimizing environmental and social impacts."[101] In total, there were seventy-two objections to the EIA submitted in May 2001.[102]

Indicative of Pro Ruta's mobilization strength as a mix of educated national and international landowners, and despite Entrix's support of the northern route and the NGOs' indeterminate assessment of the two routes, OCP launched a rapid media response of its own in 2001. OCP's public relations campaign declared: "We are the correct route. The northern route is the best for least impact."[103] The OCP ad further stated that the southern route would affect 260,000 people, and the northern one would affect no one essentially.[104] In clarification, Entrix actually estimated that there were 222,755 people along the southern route and 101,341 people along the northern one.[105]

Given the number of advertisements placed by OCP at this time, it appeared clear that the private consortium was concerned that Pro Ruta's campaign could tarnish the project's image. Nevertheless, Mindo's activists believed that they were not provided equal opportunity to be represented in the media since they were unable to buy advertising space.[106] In contrast to the activists' interpretations, the Ecuadorian oil industry dismissed OCP's media rebuttal and the multinationals' efforts to respond to community protesters as pandering to civil society's quest for monetary compensation.[107] According to one oil spokesperson in 2001:

> All these advertisements have really riled up the people, opened their eyes on how good business could be. They [OCP] should have done it quietly, and got it done. I mean it is ridiculous the amount of money spent [on the media advertisements]. And all it did is open the eyes of everybody: "Boy, there's a chance for money here." They should never have done that advertisement the way they did it. And we told them from the beginning, "[Construct] it, [and] shut up."[108]

In this case, the differences between OCP's handling of the conflict with Pro Ruta in particular and a national interpretation of OCP's response supports assessments that Northern multinational corporations (MNCs) play a role in exporting environmental consideration to Southern companies,[109] and perhaps even participatory space—though not one Mindo activist would agree with this assessment.

In spite of Pro Ruta's strength in 2001, it disbanded shortly after construction began. Some landowning members leased access to the right-of-way, while others determined it was too late to change the pipeline's course.[110] "What changed for me was when the government would not move, when the president said, 'We are not going to allow it to be stopped. . . . And these four people that are trying to stop this, we are not going to listen to it,'" recalled one member of Pro Ruta. "So, at that point, we decided it was either now or carry on for another year, and then probably in the end have the land expropriated by the government because it was considered a national priority, and therefore in the end, one did not have the right to stop it."[111]

After Pro Ruta disbanded, a small splinter group based in Quito formed the *Truth Commission*, a public committee under the auspices of the state's Anti-Corruption Commission to monitor and inspect the pipeline's construction, but without the legal authority and/or government support to do so. This organization sought to achieve greater transparency and greater public participation on national and multinational projects, including the pipeline; however, the Truth Commission was never given access rights to monitor or to obtain official documents on OCP, which were held at the ministries. Nevertheless, it served as an open storehouse for any material gathered and organized a public forum on OCP in Quito in August 2002. It also speaks to the democratic practices and political spaces for civil society at this time, relative to many other oil economies in other Southern places.

The *Mindo Working Group*, also presented in the previous chapter, was a loose group of nineteen ecologists; geologists; ornithologists; locally known bird, amphibian, and orchid experts; and Quito-based NGOs and nonnationals with interests or ties to the area. It also included members of Pro Ruta. After individual members offered OCP their regional expertise to reassess impact in the protected forests, the Working Group wrote a counter–environmental impact assessment, specifically for the Mindo region, at the request and support of OCP.[112] The oil consortium gave the Working Group eight days to design an assessment plan, gather baseline data on the flora and fauna, and write a report. However, instead of implementing their recommendations as the Working Group had expected, OCP attached the report as an addendum to the official EIA with no major change to the route, except for microvariants and to recommend that particular care be taken in this area during the construction process.

Pro Ruta and the Mindo Working Group are noted here to establish how these two short-lived groups launched a national and international focus on Mindo, framing Mindo as an ecologically sensitive environment of extreme biodiversity for Ecuador, and perhaps more importantly for the world's diminishing habitats and wildlife species. Over time, however, Quito-based conservation groups as well as Mindo-based Acción por la Vida would capitalize on the early efforts of Pro Ruta and the Working Group in seemingly contradictory ways.

Acción por la Vida, or Action for Life, was a grassroots community group that formed in 2001 as a truly local Mindo organization after the formation of Pro Ruta.[113] In interviews, Pro Ruta members claimed that the community of Mindo, including members of Acción por la Vida, demonstrated little interest in challenging OCP in 2000 and early 2001 when the project was announced. As claimed by one Pro Ruta member, "We got to the stage where we were on the television a lot, fighting it, talking about it, getting interests going. [We] got the interests going in Mindo."[114] But when Acción por la Vida eventually formed, it woke up with a vengeance. It protested the route, established international ties, dropped contact with the early activists, and remained active throughout the construction process. Once construction was completed, Acción por la Vida's exposure to oil impacts in the Amazon led its leadership to campaign locally for the establishment of greater ecological awareness in Mindo and to establish contacts with groups in the Amazon to support other grassroots challenges to increased oil production. Moreover, Acción's core group of activists became increasingly politicized, learning their rights as citizens and landowners and learning the environmental laws of the country.

Acción also comprised some of the most radical and committed individuals along the pipeline, as well as many un- or underemployed youth. The youth found perks in activism, including free transport out of town when active in regional campaigns. The more committed members were landowners, conservationists, grassroots ecologists, and small business owners, including many without land along the right-of-way. Their commitment was based on a belief that it was unjust and unethical to impose an oil pipeline on the cloud forest reserves and near their small businesses. Their vision was militant: "Activism is the soul of our organization; it's being alert, not sleepy; it's justice, not violation; it's transparency, not corruption," wrote Acción in 2004.[115]

Acción por la Vida was also the most visible and active organization in the area. Assisted by several national and international organizations, Acción members launched their dispute with the pipeline project in a much more informal and threatening setting than the Quito-based conservationists. Acción por la Vida met with OCP personnel in open-air and standing-room-only spaces on dusty lanes and steep Andean slopes, while being observed by armed guards. More formally and with the support of Fundación Puntos Verdes, Acción sent local representatives to Germany to present their position to the German Parliament of the state of Westphalia and to the lead financier, WestLB. Acción also welcomed German and Italian organizations and parliamentarians to Mindo.

Significantly, Rettet den Regenwald of Germany held a donation drive in Germany in order to buy 2,150 acres up to Guarumos, a ridgeline in the Mindo-Nambillo cloud forest, including three kilometers along the OCP right-of-way, which they donated to Acción por la Vida.[116] Land ownership enabled Acción members to monitor the construction process and to initiate a lawsuit against OCP.[117] Along the route, Acción por la Vida and Puntos Verdes represented the most internationally integrated activist groups responding to the construction of OCP. Together, these two organizations transitioned from rejecting the proposed route, to rejecting the entire pipeline, to rejecting the state's support of an oil economy and neglect of small business interests. They also became more organized on local ecological and political issues.

Fundación Puntos Verdes was located outside of Mindo town. It was founded in the 1990s, by an Ecuadorian-German couple with former ties to the local NGO Amigos de la Naturaleza, to conduct scientific research and reforestation, to increase conservation efforts, and to raise the ecological knowledge of the youth in the greater Mindo region. This organization was known locally for its youth-centered environmental education and community-centered trash disposal campaigns.[118] With German ties, Puntos Verdes was pivotal in raising German awareness against the German financier WestLB, raising funds to buy land for conservation in the area, and establishing ties between Acción por la Vida and German advocacy organizations.

Another preexisting group was *Amigos de la Natureleza de Mindo* (Friends of Nature of Mindo). Amigos was an environmental NGO founded in 1986 to manage and monitor the protected forests, including Mindo-Nambillo. In the 1990s, Amigos had shifted primarily to tourism activities and was viewed by the community "as opportunists reluctant to share the benefits of their success" and benefiting from their contact with international groups and financiers.[119] During the time of OCP, this organization had ties with the Environment Ministry and ran a rustic lodge and camping ground primarily for the education of Ecuadorian children and adolescents. Since Amigos remained silent on the pipeline, some members of Acción por la Vida referred to this long-standing organization as "enemigos de la naturaleza," or enemies of nature. In response, Amigos argued that their goal was to educate, rather than to fight political battles. When it first opened, this NGO had financial assistance from groups in Germany, Switzerland, the United States, and Canada,[120] but at this time it was operating with limited assistance from the Environment Ministry and revenues from school group tours. In 2003, Amigos appeared comparable to some government bodies in Quito: a team of individuals who lacked the resources, networks, and foresight to make headway in a campaign to protect the environment or to provide environmental education. This organization prepared sporadic monitoring reports for the Environment Ministry, received no response, but continued filing one-page denouncements of illegal logging and hunting operations in the area it oversaw.[121] It was an organization in inertia, waiting for more funding, leadership, and direction. On one afternoon, it resembled a poorly organized day care program, centered on a television set showing wildlife programs. Amigos is mentioned here to underscore that there was an environmental organization in Mindo that chose not to mobilize against OCP, as there were also tour operators, ecolodge owners and landowners that rejected the activists' antipipeline position.

Fundación Pacaso y Pacaso formed in the 1990s as a hiking guide group from breakaway members of Amigos de la Naturaleza,[122] but it was not functioning as an organization during the construction of OCP. Therefore, many individual members joined Acción por la Vida. It was not until after the pipeline's construction that this organization reemerged to organize the First Ecuadorian Environmental Congress in order to gather provincial leaders from across the country to discuss how to make environmental protection economically viable, sustainable, and locally governed. It was held in Mindo in June 2007, nearly four years after the pipeline's completion.

The final organization is *Mindo Cloudforest Foundation*, which was formed in 2001.[123] Many of its key members were established ecologists, birding guides, and ornithologists. They were published birding authorities on the greater Mindo region, some of whom initially supported Pro Ruta and who were influential authors in the Mindo Working Group assessments. They were not members of Acción por la Vida, and after the conservation NGOs began negotiating funds, members of this foundation returned to their birding tours and lodges and to developing reserves and ecoscenic routes in the greater Mindo area.

Some of the residents of Mindo resembled William Freudenburg and Robert Gramling's portrait of the residents of northern California in their adamant opposition to the introduction of oil development in their region and their high value on the area's biophysical environment.[124] In northern California, there appeared to be no silent majority: northern Californians were united in their opposition to offshore oil development. However, in Mindo tourism operators, ecolodges, environmental organizations such as Amigos, landowners, town council members, and many residents were silent or indifferent to the pipeline, supportive of it for its short-term employment opportunities, or opposed to the activists personally or due to their radical tactics. Likewise, these unvoiced residents, including farmers, hunters, loggers, and the un- or underemployed, also viewed the same environment as having economic value other than tourism or conservation.[125] Yet they were largely overshadowed by the international publicity and advocacy networks of the early groups, Pro Ruta and the Mindo Working Group, and the later emergence of Acción por la Vida.

Pointing to residents who sat on the fence or who supported the trickle-down employment opportunities that the pipeline project presented, an oil spokesperson accurately assessed the impact of oil money flowing into poor communities as a deterrent to opposition along the route:

> Once you have five different areas in which you are starting on the pipeline and the people in these areas start getting jobs or things like that, nobody is going to stop that pipeline. And then they [OCP employees] are going to buy bread for breakfast, and they are going to buy lunch here and there. Along the route, people are going to do business, small business, but they are going to do business. I'd like to see anybody get involved in trying to stop that pipeline. But it needs to get started.[126]

In the greater Mindo area, oil revenue entered the community through employment, leasing of land, and small business arrangements such as feeding and housing construction workers. In Ecuador, as with oil-dependent economies, a constant intermingling existed between laborers, families, small businesses, and the oil sector.[127] For example, when then-mayor Marco Calle of the municipality of Los Bancos agreed to the pipeline in 2001, he negotiated two hundred job slots for local residents.[128] In this case, approximately fifty men in Mindo received temporary employment in construction or guarding services along the route. Those fifty men most likely supported an extensive family network and may have received enough surplus money to start small tourism businesses when they finished their OCP work.

In a petroleum nation where oil's influence and wealth are unmatched, oil money is able to silence critics or promote supporters whether in the oil town of Lago Agrio, among Quito's conservation NGOs, or within the ecotourism town of Mindo. This monetary interdependency was exhibited in Mindo when El Monte Sustainable Lodge, an ecolodge in Mindo, was hired by Occidental Petroleum, one of OCP's partners, to manage the customer service and hospitality of Sani Lodge in the Amazon. Sani Lodge was started in December 2002 in Occidental's oil block 15.[129] Was the timing of collaboration coincidental? The lodge was owned by the Sani Quichuan community but was designed and constructed by Occidental, a California-based oil company, in exchange for a secondary pipeline right-of-way and drilling rights.[130] El Monte in Mindo assisted the Indigenous owners in their initial start-up, and was not publicly opposed to the OCP project. It is mentioned here as an example of the crosscutting exchanges between oil and small businesses in an oil-dominated economy where many people, public services, private businesses, and the tourism trade are shaped or silenced by the petroleum industry.

Acción Ecológica: An Activist Broker

Acción Ecológica is a Quito-based, militant, ecofeminist organization with extensive national and international networks and funders that proved instrumental to linking Mindo to external allies. During the construction of OCP, Acción Ecológica was often described by other Quito-based conservation NGOs as not always accurate in their environmental assessments but as critical in their commitment, fervor, radicalism, and capacity to mobilize youth and to implement media-generating action, which were unprecedented among environmental organizations in Ecuador. Acción Ecológica also had a reputation as being one of the most difficult organizations to work with among other NGOs and impacted communities.[131]

In this case, Acción Ecológica served a central role in temporarily bridging the gap between the demise of Pro Ruta and the Mindo Working Group and the rise of Acción por la Vida. Acción Ecológica also established Mindo's ties to international networks, including California-based Amazon Watch, which staged a demonstration in California alongside a representative of Mindo, and communities in the Amazon. Summing up Acción Ecológica's role in Mindo, one ecologist observed that "most people think they are crazy, that they are fanatics and whatever. But . . . I felt when nobody else was doing stuff, they were. And so when everyone else fell apart in Mindo, they started this whole thing themselves."[132]

Acción Ecológica was also unique in that it had been unwaveringly opposed to the pipeline and to the oil industry since its inception, even calling for a moratorium in 2003. In one of several green action alerts, Acción Ecológica wrote that "the OCP is a project of destruction to the environment, of corruption, of dependence, of violation to national sovereignty."[133] Though Mindo was against the route, and not the oil industry initially, Acción Ecológica saw the potential for victories against the oil industry in Mindo, especially given Mindo's international and environmental appeal. According to the same activist, Acción Ecológica "realized that if they got some kind of victories in Mindo, it could mean bigger victories somewhere else. So they actually started pushing and started talking to the community in Mindo."[134]

At the time, Acción Ecológica was a significant activist broker in Ecuador, connecting international organizations with affected communities. Many transnational actions would have been impossible without the contacts and logistical support of this organization, which organized toxic tours to the Amazon and town hall meetings and tours along OCP's route. Acción Ecológica's Quito office also served as a meeting house and comfort zone for international advocates when in-country and a vital rest stop and shelter for community organizers and activists seeking a hot cup of coffee; bus fare to attend actions; and access to newspapers, telephones, fax, and photocopy machines when in the capital. Acción por la Vida's core leadership, however, sought to distinguish itself from Acción Ecológica by establishing their own agenda to maintain local control over its campaign, preparing their own press releases, building direct ties with international advocates to receive support directly, and marginalizing contact with Acción Ecológica.[135] Acción por la Vida not only rejected the conservation organizations due to their limited activism and acceptance of the pipeline project; it also rejected Acción Ecológica for its prominence in anti-oil activism in Ecuador.

Trout Farmers and Nontourism Interests

There were many in the area who would be affected by the pipeline's construction or a spill and yet who failed to respond, as there were also many who engaged in utilizing the area's resources for economic activities contrary to the efforts of the activist community and their image of sustainability. In one early effort of collaboration, farmers, cattle breeders, and ecologists submitted a legal petition to stay construction.[136] However, this alliance proved temporary, and only the grassroots ecologists and ecotourism businesses persisted in resisting the pipeline. Indeed, one of the greatest paradoxes is that it was the woman riding into Mindo to deliver fish on horseback who would experience the greatest threat to her way of life if the pipeline broke near the Rio Alambi area. But the trout, cattle, and agricultural farmers of the area failed to organize a sustained response against the pipeline, even though many knew that the farming settlement of Alaspungo could be "seriously affected" if an oil spill occurred.[137] To be sure, a landslide or oil spill would expose numerous communities along the route to damaged or contaminated water sources, jeopardizing a family's livelihood and threatening a household's food security. Another local and only minimally contested impact in the Andean region included the influx of fourteen hundred temporary OCP workers to Nono, a town of three thousand, which actually overwhelmed the community's services and resources.[138] Finally, there was a significant number of un- or underemployed men with a history of confronting the environmentalists and exploiting the natural environment through logging, charcoal production, hunting, and cattle farming.[139] "People make charcoal day and night during the summer in this region, where now they are talking about [birds]," noted one Quito-based conservationist, ". . . but activists are not doing anything about that because that's not big propaganda. That's not, you know, a cause for advertisement."[140] These tensions in uses and interpretations of the environment proved relentless throughout the construction process.

Free Riders or Future Leaders?

Another contingent was Mindo's youth, who were a strength and a weakness. For the most part, Acción por la Vida's campaign comprised a few committed adult leaders who worked to direct the youths' activism. Some of the young people were extremely dedicated, camping for weeks in the trees and willing to be arrested during protests, and thereby generating national and international media attention through their risk taking. And it is Mindo's youth who may best guarantee the town's future as a nature-based tourism destination. Unlike their counterparts in Lago Agrio and Quito, Mindo's youth have been exposed to nature-seeking tourists, international environmental groups, and adult ecologists for much of their lifetime. Even years after the anti-OCP campaign, the adult efforts continued to foster a climate of engaged citizenship among Mindo's youth, which may prove more durable than a pipeline transporting a finite fuel. During Acción's campaign, however, the inconsistent commitment of the area's youth tested the group's internal trust and cohesion.[141] Indeed, one activist described Mindo's youth as willing to participate in actions only if it included travel that was paid for by others.[142] An audience and notoriety were also inducements,[143] which is more of an assessment of youth worldwide than a criticism of the young people of Mindo. Perhaps more importantly, anti-OCP activism inspired and managed by the adult leaders of the community—even if the youth contingent was somewhat unreliable—served to teach them notions of civic engagement and the right and the need to fight for healthy ecosystems and sustainable local economies now and in the future.

A "Rave" against OCP: Local Challenges for Nonlocal Activists

One early event warrants mention here as it revealed the energy and capacity of a small community to contain outside influence and to maintain local control over its resources and its youth. In July 2001 before pipeline construction began, Quito-based youth activists organized a weekend demonstration against OCP—in Mindo. The youth-oriented events were to include a Saturday night antipipeline fundraiser and "rave," while street demonstrations and an educational fair on Sunday were designed to raise awareness of the region's biodiversity.

One week before the scheduled events,[144] many Mindo residents were uncertain of the weekend activities. A youth volunteer at the Mindo tourism booth described it as a dance event with wealthy Quito youth and foreign tourists traveling to Mindo. She was very excited about it. A guesthouse employee described it as a rock concert, a demonstration, and an informational fair. Guesthouse owners questioned why it was not being held at a larger venue in Quito. Middle-aged resident-activists claimed a dance party for the expected three thousand visitors would overwhelm the town's water, trash, and housing capacity, causing minor ecological damage of its own. One hotel owner, who was concerned about excessive alcohol and drug use, believed the out-of-town activists were going to tarnish Mindo's commitment to ecological sustainability and to fighting the proposed OCP route on their terms.

Buried in the promotional hype was the fundraising effort to charge US$5–6 per person, a prohibitive cost for most locals. It was also unclear which organizations would control the funds and how the funds would be used. While rumors spread, the town council and private school officials met and warned parents that their children would be expelled if they participated in any events that would bring drugs and alcohol to Mindo.[145] At one town hall meeting, an attendee listened as "several people started to talk about the danger of Satan and the danger of rock music. I couldn't believe my ears."[146] The threat of drugs, alcohol, Satan, and rock music may seem dramatic, but in a rural environment, it worked.[147]

On the weekend of the proposed event, the town of two thousand shut off contact to the outside world. A steel pole was laid across the single road that descended into Mindo, behind which stood a human barricade of police and residents, barring entry of all bus, automobile, bicycle, and foot traffic to Mindo. A sign read "No concert in Mindo," while the roadblock forced traffic to turn east to Quito or west to Los Bancos.[148]

On the one hand, this failed event revealed the deep distrust of this small community for outsiders and how this rural community could mobilize effectively to resist outside influence. It also demonstrated how steep the obstacles were for the antipipeline activists to organize locally and exposed how the broader community determined nonlocal youth to be more harmful to their way of life than an oil pipeline. On the other hand, it illustrated the persuasive power of oil-funded projects on a rural community, as the school, police department, and town council would benefit materially from the oil consortium. At the time of this event, Acción por la Vida had yet to establish itself as the definitive voice of an anti-OCP position in Mindo, but it would begin to do so after the failed rave.

A DETERMINED DEMAND: "THE PIPELINE YES, THROUGH MINDO, NO!"

In 2001, the Mindo Working Group and Pro Ruta de Menor Impacto demanded the rerouting of the pipeline south of the area's cloud forest. In 2002, Acción por la Vida doggedly called for a variant in the route off the mountain ridge, especially the narrow and controversial ridgeline called La Cuchilla (The Knife) and down to the valley floor. Then in 2003, Acción por la Vida initiated a lawsuit to stop the pipeline's use in order to prevent an ecological disaster. See table 4.1.

Removal and Recognition

Mindo's grassroots activists and ecologists demanded the relocation of the pipeline and national recognition of their efforts to fashion Mindo into an ecotourism destination without state assistance or oil revenue support. They feared that the construction of the pipeline would lead to soil erosion, landslides, land settlement, polluted water sources, impacted vegetation, damaged

Table 4.1. Overview of Mindo's Grassroots Response to OCP

	Targets[a]			Demands				Organizational Change in Position
2001	2002	2003	2007–2009	2001	2002[b]	2003[b]	2007–2009[b]	
OCP	OCP, WestLB, International Audience, Local Residents, Quito-based NGOs	OCP, WestLB, International Audience, Local Residents, Quito-based NGOs	Local Residents, National Audience	• EIA and route participation • Rerouting • State Support of (or No Harm to) Nature-based Economic Efforts[c]	• • Rerouting • State Support of (or No Harm to) Nature-based Economic Efforts • Stop Construction	• • • State Support of (or No Harm to) Nature-based Economic Efforts • Stop Construction • Rejection of Oil • Rejection of Mayor/Town Council	• • • State Support of (or No Harm to) Nature-based Economic Efforts • • • • Nationwide Community-based Ecological and Economic Sustainability	• Oil Discovery • Challenge OCP • Increased Politicization • Community and NGO Conflict • Oil Tourism • Ecological Consciousness of Ecuador

[a]The targets are ranked.
[b]A blank bullet point denotes that the request was no longer demanded.
[c]This demand was not presented to the state directly but was articulated in interviews and prepared position papers. They were not calling for direct state assistance; instead they were calling for no harm caused by state decisions.

primary and secondary forests, and habitat loss of threatened species, which in addition would affect their nature-based businesses. In addition, activists argued that roads built to construct the pipeline would enable farmers, cattle grazers, illegal timber operators, and charcoal producers easier access into remote areas as had been experienced in the Amazon. Activists also believed that volcanic activity from the nearby Pichincha volcano guaranteed an eventual break in the pipeline, and that the construction process and/or a pipeline break would damage the nearby river systems.[149] In identifying the regional risks, one activist said:

> They [OCP] also got their environmental license taken away in that area for a poorly made service road.[150] It is just that in the winter we have so many landslides because the earth is so unstable, and you start cutting away trees and everything, all the plants and everything that gives it stability and you know it all just comes tumbling down. And that is what was happening to the service road. And that is what will happen to everything that gets built up there.[151]

In contrast to Mindo's local assessment and lived experiences, OCP and an environmental consultant for the oil industry offered alternative perspectives. On the suspension of its environmental license, OCP identified vandalism on the pipeline's erosion protection devices as explanation.[152] As for the route's selection, a consultant claimed that the northern route was the least impactful given the pipeline's need to cross the Andes Mountains and to reach the Pacific Coast.

> The Mindo ridge is very difficult to construct, and it was very difficult from the socio-economic standpoint, but it is a very short section that you have problems and then you end up going down this alluvial fan, a dissected alluvial fan all the way to the coast where there really aren't very many problems. If you went south, there are a series of ridges that you would need to cross.[153]

A second proposal by Mindo's grassroots ecologists advocated for the relocation of the pipeline from the ridge to the valley floor. For instance, one activist argued, "It would affect less primary forest. . . . It would affect fewer water sources because it would be on the north side of the mountain range instead of on the south side. Or at least fewer water sources that would affect the Mindo, the greater Mindo area."[154] As noted earlier, an assessment of the official EIA by Quito-based NGOs failed to identify the northern route as being more damaging than the southern one.

Beyond the tangible rerouting demands that were never achieved, the activists also presented a moral claim to preserve the country's natural heritage against the injustices of the state and the petroleum industry. To this end, a public release claimed that Mindo's ongoing opposition to the pipeline was for the nation's future: "Nature is our principal resource. It is the responsibility of everyone to well protect this patrimony for current and future generations."[155] In a subsequent proposal, Acción por la Vida clarified their position:

> The mission of Acción por la Vida is to defend the conservation of the Mindo area to protect the threatened fauna and flora, while also defending the dignity of all humans. The goal is to provide opportunities for residents that are environmentally sustainable, while taking direct action to protect the natural areas.[156]

The small business owners were expressing frustration by their lack of participatory capital with the state, relative to the nonnational oil companies; and they were doing so from a patriotic position. They viewed their work as offering the nation an alternative to oil dependency and an environmental model for other communities, and by doing so they sought recognition of the value of "sustainable development" through small business entrepreneurship. Sustainable and development are sometimes contradictory campaigns. In some ways Mindo was economically and materially underdeveloped compared to other ecotourism destinations worldwide, but Mindo also had greater economic and material resources than many others along the route. Sustainability is also a nebulous notion. Local sustainability would indicate the needs of the community could be met locally or regionally without ever undermining or overusing the natural resources that meet those needs. However, the energy resources required to transport Northern travelers to Mindo and to transport Mindo travelers to the North—on multiple trips over a lifecourse—are not sustainable uses of the world's natural resources. Otherwise, sustainable development means a highly uneven trade-off: foregoing traveling yourself so as to allow and cater to the travel of others.

In spite of this contradiction, Mindo's activists believed that the pipeline would destroy the area's tourism, reforestation efforts, and environmental education campaigns, and reacted strongly against the government's endorsement of the oil industry without equitable support of their life's work and their ecological commitment. "All of the initiatives of civil society are not appreciated, are rejected by the government," claimed one Mindo activist.[157] Another activist-ecologist worried about their future inability to teach the value of environmental awareness and sustainability to the region's youth if they failed in their power struggle to divert the pipeline.[158]

Though the grassroots activists demanded intractably the rerouting of the pipeline, in the end, the pipeline was built according to OCP's original proposal with only minimal microvariants. And even though the activists sought validation on the environment's primacy and fragility, OCP provided incidental concessions relative to their requests.[159] As negotiated by the local authorities, OCP supplied a computer and printer for the local government and police department, upgraded the sewage and potable water systems, financed mechanisms to increase water flow for the water system, supplied

150 chickens to a cooperative, bought twenty sports uniforms, funded civic events, and supported educational activities and sanitation facilities at the local school.[160] The town's sports stadium was upgraded and fenced off, while men received temporary construction work and guard positions along the right-of-way. Additionally, the public swimming pool was retiled and reopened, though at its official reopening a scuffle occurred between the activists and OCP personnel,[161] and for the next eight days Mindo experienced a heavy police presence.

Those in tourism or with desires to work in tourism received workshops on hotel management, tourism service, food service, hygiene, and sanitation. Quito-based CECIA, a participant in the environmental fund negotiations, was contracted to provide courses for naturalist guides and to map the habitat of the black-breasted puffleg hummingbird. Extrapolating from a report on the importance of the Quetzal bird to tourism in Costa Rica,[162] oil-funded research on and promotion of this hummingbird could inspire similar quests for locals and visitors to view, to protect, and to consume products made in its image.

There were no public consultations on what all community members demanded, needed, or wanted,[162] and given the amount of media attention Mindo generated from the efforts of Pro Ruta, the Mindo Working Group, Acción por la Vida, and Fundación Puntos Verdes, the town certainly could have received much more. According to one town council member in 2003, "There are people that are not content, but they also do not dialogue, so this is not the way to reach a solution. I want better presentations, plans for proposals for prevention, care, permanent monitoring, all of this is necessary."[164] An oil expert concurred:

> Make sure that the best technology is utilized to minimize the damage. And that is where ecologists could help. But I do not hear them proposing anything. . . . Give us advice at what is the best way not to damage the environment besides not building it. Be productive. Be proactive. Tell the world how we can minimize damage. They have not given one advice other than, "Don't build it." And that's not possible. This country needs it. Twelve and a half million Ecuadorians need it.[165]

All sides called for greater participation of civil society. However, the government and OCP permitted microsuggestions and compensatory requests, while the activists were in essence calling for a participatory democracy, or the opportunity to vote on the pipeline project itself.

In recognition of their local actions, and coupled with pressure placed by the Quito NGOs, special environmental care was achieved in the region. OCP moved pipes by mules and aerial cable-car systems, rather than building access roads as they had in other areas. OCP also used handheld equipment rather than heavy machinery in the areas designated ecologically sensitive, and reduced the right-of-way—only in this area—to 4 meters, rather than a standard of 9–15 meters and up to 30 meters in some areas. "If you go to Guarumos, they are opening the trail by hand. . . . They could have done that, they *would* have done that by bulldozers, but they are doing it by hand," acknowledged one Quito-based NGO.[166]

This degree of environmental awareness and protection was not realized, or demanded, along other segments of the pipeline, so its achievement could be considered a minor triumph given the disparity between the oil objections of the multinationals and state and the limited influence of affected communities. It is also possible that the particular topography of the area, its steepness and narrowness, forced such care, which then was promoted as the consortium's concession to environmental demands. In addition, Mindo's activism also enabled the mayor of San Miguel de los Bancos to negotiate for more projects and nearly twice the amount of monetary compensation than what was received by two neighboring municipalities, Puerto Quito and Pedro Vincente Maldonado.[167]

Globally Resonant Actions

In this case, Mindo's opposition and activism were symbolically ecological and global, which attracted international advocates who were ideologically opposed to multinationals trampling the rights of local communities and environments worldwide.[168] In particular, Acción por la Vida enacted what global ecoactivists are increasingly expected to do, and they did so in an increasingly vitriolic manner. A timeline of their activities, for example, reveals that they camped in treetops, deflated truck tires, blocked road traffic, and got arrested. Each public act would have been known to be particularly resonant for media selection processes and significant to confrontational NGOs in the North.

In 2001, when OCP was to hold one of its public consultations in a neighboring community, activists from Mindo and Quito disrupted the forum by heckling the OCP speakers and pouring oil in their water glasses. Though this action effectively canceled the meeting for those attendees who wanted to hear from OCP, their actions inspired one attendee to comment: "One was heady to see the opposition—that we were actually getting somewhere. But it was really only a small pocket of opposition."[169]

A few months after the disrupted public meeting, construction began at multiple points along the route, including Mindo. Construction also put activists and OCP workers in contact, which heighten the tension in the area. At the peak of Mindo's activism, local and international activists maintained tree camps along Guarumos, a cloud forest ridgeline, to raise awareness and to impede construction.[170] This camp was maintained for nearly three months, from 2 January–25 March 2002,[171] enabled by community donations as well as provisions given by U.S.-based Amazon Watch, which included "sleeping bags, mats, a digital video camera for the camp, tarps and a cash donation for provisions" and "logistical support and transportation to and from the area of the camp," which was supplied by Quito-based Acción Ecológica.[172] One activist captured the enthusiasm and commitment of the Mindo community to their antipipeline campaign, while conveying the national reach of Mindo's activism to school groups in the capital:

> We basically started with nothing, just a couple of people from Mindo went up, and started camping up there. [OCP] had suspended construction in the area [for about four months] because of the weather. . . . We started just a few guys up there camping out. And we started getting organized, taking donations for food, for money, for equipment. Sure enough the word got out. We were working with [international organizations]. They sent down donations, a lot of donations for basic equipment, climbing equipment, as well as camping equipment. We were rounding up donations for food around here. They put up eight platforms in the trees, and were occupying that area. There were whole classes of students going up there to receive the environmental talks from the protesters. There were international news reports, national news reporters. I mean it was just more than we had ever even hoped exposure-wise for the issue. . . . Sometimes there were 40 to 50 people up there. Not all the time, but at any one time, mostly on the weekends.[173]

In February and March 2002, international groups that hiked to Guarumos to interview activists included Amazon Watch, Greenpeace Germany, Italian Campaign for World Bank Reform as well as a Bolivian NGO working against Spanish-owned Repsol and groups from Chile, Argentina, and Peru.[174] With Greenpeace Germany there was a particular solidarity, as it had demonstrated against the German financier WestLB in 2002, while Mindo activists were in the treetops; and in 2003, Greenpeace Germany laid out a red carpet with oil stains and oil drums in front of WestLB's headquarters.[175] Despite these joint actions, Acción por la Vida sent out an uncertain memo following Greenpeace Germany's 2002 visit:

> Although Acción Por La Vida did not get concrete answers regarding funding and direct support for our camp up in Guarumos, we all agreed that the meeting was successful in the sense that the more we are connected with concerned international groups, especially those that carry such political weight as GreenPeace, the better chance we have of victory, whether it be the total closure of the project, or negotiating a microvariant in the OCP route.[176]

In March 2002, after activists had maintained a presence in the treetops for more than fifty days,[177] the national police raided the camp and arrested nineteen activists, including five Ecuadorians and fourteen international demonstrators from France, Ireland, Sweden, Germany, Colombia, Italy, and the United States.[178] After the arrests, the main highway was blocked for more than six hours by local protesters, and two trailers carrying OCP pipes were redirected into Mindo valley, where their tires were deflated. When the tires were repaired, it was said that local women laid themselves along the single bridge to block the only exit out of Mindo. The Ecuadorian activists were eventually released, and the foreign activists, who outnumbered locals by nearly three to one, were deported. At nearly three nonnationals arrested to every one local tree sitter, the detainment appeared to present a greater commitment or lesser fears of reprisals by international visitors than local residents to protect Ecuador's cloud forest from oil. To be sure, the oil sector and the state attempted to portray the commitment as not representative of Ecuadorian sentiment. According to one oil spokesperson in an interview:

> You cannot count 10 people against it [the pipeline], though the hotels in Mindo are against it because of their business of tourism. I only hear foreigners complaining in Mindo: Greenpeace, Germans and Colombians and Chileans. Ecuadorians are not complaining. They can leave Ecuador and get out. If I laid down in the U.S., I would go to jail. It is not principles there [in Mindo], but business interests.[179]

The press also reported President Gustavo Noboa as mocking the international ecologists:

> We Ecuadorians are the ones who decided policies. Let four or five little Germans from Greenpeace come and tell us, "die of hunger because you have to die of hunger since you live in a Third World country, while us First Worlders, let's go to the Third World sunburned and well-fed."[180]

Despite or due to international support for antipipeline activists, Noboa's comments may have stoked a simmering antiforeign sentiment and national reality, belief, or suspicion that Ecuadorian poverty and marginalized development were induced by international entities, in this case foreign activists rather than foreign oil entities. The government claimed nonnational activists were insolent to challenge a national pipeline, while international advocates claimed their right to challenge oil companies and oil-project financiers, which are based in the activists' home countries but work on oil projects in Ecuador.

In an additional act in July 2002, a few months after the tree camp and arrests, Julia "Butterfly" Hill, a North American activist who spent 738 days in a redwood tree in northern California in the late 1990s,[181] arrived to support Mindo. Her presence brought a professional media event to the area and further encapsulated Mindo's position along the route as the site to protest the OCP pipeline.[182] When Hill and Amazon Watch arrived in Mindo, approximately forty-five people gathered to voice their concerns and to listen to how she would support them.[183] She told them she could "bear witness," that "personal testimony is powerful," and that she would return to the United States and tell others what she had heard and witnessed along the route. She spoke in American-style sound bites about "greenwashing," "giving voice," "bearing witness," and "testimony." The meaning of these words was not significant or part of the repertoire among local residents before OCP, but they had become part of an increasingly common and meaningful language among the most committed activists during the course of their anti-OCP campaign.

In Mindo, local activists were desperate for international publicity. During the meeting, their hopes to save the mountain ridge, but more importantly to be heard, hinged on her presence and her possible arrest, which had been implied, and at times perhaps touted, by some of the local, national, and international activists. The day before the proposed and symbolic "take back the land" hike with Hill, an international journalist appraised the proposed action as a "complete media event," while waiting to submit the article's lead paragraph: Julia Butterfly was arrested in Ecuador today protesting an oil pipeline.[184]

On the day of the hike, the diversity of ages ranged from the teens to the low seventies, and roles ranged from mothers to sons, from small business owners to a German television crew.[185] At the first trailhead, OCP guards blocked access, supported by the local Nono police who said they could not interfere in a "public-private conflict."[186] To the activists, distinctions between public and private lands remained an ambiguous feature throughout the construction process. OCP was privately owned and privately financed; however, the pipeline was of national importance for the national economy. Likewise, in this region a historic and public walking trail was bisected by an OCP service road, presenting a continuous juncture of conflict between the activists on the public road and the OCP guards on the private one. Summarizing the frustration over the private-public nature of this particular intersection, one international advocate for Mindo's campaign said:

> Ecuador seems not to be a sovereign country anymore since OCP, because not the local authorities, not the Ministry of the Environment, [not the] Ministry of Energy and Mining are deciding who is entering which area, but OCP. They decide who is allowed to use this public road leading to [the activists'] property. And they are supported by the police.[187]

After beginning the hike from the second trailhead and crossing this public-private road, the group topped a crest to Guarumos and was met by additional OCP guards, local police, and an OCP official. Each side demanded proof of land ownership, with Acción por la Vida only recently acquiring land in the region through fundraising efforts by Rettet den Regenwald. According to Acción por la Vida:

> Our group took over two and half hours to reach the top and once we arrived the confrontation with police began. They were blocking the way up to where our original tree-sit camp had been. They claimed to have an order from the Superintendent of Police (which they could not produce) not to let anyone pass, not even the legitimate land owners. We were armed with our land deed and the property plan that shows that Guarumos is inside our property line. They refused to let us through, claiming that the issue needs to be taken up in court.[188]

After being prevented from progressing further, some of the activists set up camp farther down the ridge away from the right-of-way, while others descended to Mindo to prepare for a second day of actions in Quito. The next day, the Mindo activists were joined by others along the route to stage a protest in front of the Quito office of Occidental Petroleum (Oxy).[189] Oxy was targeted rather than the OCP headquarters because the lead international team was from California, where Oxy is headquartered.[190] Julia Hill claimed to have a scheduled appointment with Oxy, but she was prevented from entering the building when she arrived with approximately fifty activists from along the route.[191] While Mindo's youth blocked a busy street, chanted in front of Oxy's doors, tried to enter the building, and pushed for their own arrests, the older social and economic justice activists along the route waited outside Oxy's building for a meeting to present their grievances.

After a couple of hours, the police, who had been monitoring the demonstrations, arrested eight activists, including Julia Hill.[192] In a documentary filmed before Hill's arrest and deportation from Ecuador,[193] Hill said into the camera, "I'm here in solidarity. If foreign corporations can come in and destroy this land and people, then foreign activists can come in here and stop it." Stirring national sentiment, President Noboa offered a different interpretation. With his characteristic flourish to diminish the activists, Noboa was quoted as saying, "The little gringos have been arrested, including the old cockatoo who climbs trees."[194] Oil indeed breeds confidence and condescension among some elected leaders.

Eventually, a group of five, including Amazon Watch and an Ecuadorian contingent of representatives of different communities along the route, held an after-hours meeting with Oxy representatives. According to Efrain Toapanta, a representative of Acción por la Vida, the activists presented their demands and complaints, which depended on their position along the route, and Oxy offered no resolution. Toapanta was quoted in an Acción por la Vida report as saying: "The meeting was disappointing. . . . They easily wash their hands of all responsibility for the destruction they cause here in Ecuador by stating over and over again that they are obeying Ecuadorian laws so therefore they are doing nothing wrong."[195]

In 2002, the Ecuadorian activists earned tremendous national and international press coverage from their tree camp, their Guarumos hike, and their protests outside of Oxy's Quito offices. However, media coverage failed to convert into meeting immediate or tangible local goals. Though Amazon Watch served notice that it would continue to monitor and pursue Oxy wherever it operated, it was the Ecuadorian state, ironically, that eventually stopped Occidental's oil extraction in the Amazon. In 2006, the Ecuadorian government seized Oxy's operations, citing operational irregularities, and handed over its operations to the state-owned PetroEcuador, which one could argue was one of the country's worst environmental offenders in the oil fields.

During these international efforts in 2002, the international makeup of Mindo's campaigns made it not only susceptible to charges of being led by nonnationals, but also made the local groups vulnerable to losing direct control over their demands, campaigns, and grassroots effectiveness. In Mindo in particular, charges that international residents, international landowners, and international advocates drove the campaign, rather than local residents, were so convincing that local grassroots leaders and their international advocates were forced to act in order to reverse these perceptions. For an awareness-raising caravan along the pipeline's route, Acción por la Vida was asked to send an Ecuadorian, not a non-Ecuadorian resident, to be representative of Mindo. In another case, when Julia Hill was to be deported, local activists were advised to send Ecuadorians not just international supporters to the detention center to support her.

Absent in the government and oil portraits of international activists were the real threats, intimidation, and fears experienced among local activists. Local activists in Mindo and the greater Mindo area told me that their homes were videotaped, their telephones were tapped, threatening phone calls were received, and security guards without clear identification cards showed up on their property.[196] Activists also reported to me that they believed that bolts were loosened on car tires and that tires were deflated. When they traveled to Quito, they feared being taken off the streets, and they also feared for the safety of their families and homes in Mindo when they were away.

These accounts were the grounded reality and everyday risk of their struggles— unlike the Quito-based organizations, who negotiated during the workweek in boardrooms, and unlike international advocates, whose families and homes were safely elsewhere and who traveled to and from Ecuador at their own discretion. At the peak of protests, their concerns were very real. "There are risks definitely," claimed one activist. "We do not know if today we will be living and tomorrow we will be dead. We never know. This is clear."[197] Furthering the activists' commitments, this one added, "But even for this, we are not going to close our mouths. We are not going to stop protesting. . . . The majority of Mindo do not accept OCP. It is only that there is a majority that is afraid of OCP. This is the difference."[198]

Compared to other communities along the route, Mindo was an ideal site for international advocacy organizations. Acción por la Vida was a recently organized group in a community somewhat dependent on tourists, with members willing to be arrested protecting a region of high biodiversity. Lago Agrio experienced arrests as well, with much more severe state repression, curfews, tear gas, firearms, and perhaps loss of life. Yet Lago Agrio accepted the pipeline and the oil industry rather early in arbitration. Although Lago Agrio initially mobilized for the rerouting of the storage and pumping facilities away from the town, arguing on the grounds of security and health safety, they did so through an activist mayor rather than a transnational network. Mindo was also the only community actively continuing to oppose the route in 2002,

which garnered international appeal and sustained international commitment to this community. Within Ecuador, Mindo's confrontational stance also
made it environmentally relevant, or at least noteworthy, to many educated,
middle-income Ecuadorians.

TRANSFORMING A TOURISM TOWN

Mindo's activists and their anti-OCP campaign never succeeded in rerouting
or blocking the pipeline project. However, their activities resounded across
borders and impacted the nation and the community itself. First, Mindo's
activists identified an international audience as being critical to their campaign, and by doing so constructed themselves as the singular antipipeline
community along the route. Through their efforts, Mindo became the Ecuadorian center of a transnational network of opposition to the pipeline.
Second, and toward the end of Mindo's antipipeline campaign, activists
became the national voice and inspiration for eco-economic and ecopolitical
rights. By expressing demands for greater local control over environmental
decisions and by supporting local efforts to build environmentally healthy
communities and environmentally sustainable economies, Mindo's activists
inserted the idea of ecological democracy into national discussions.[199] Additionally, at the national level, Mindo's campaigns stimulated a discovery
of Mindo as a nature-based destination, for which local and international
activists were willing to be arrested. Finally, Mindo's environmental activism
shifted onto the community itself, germinating the country's first organic
environmental generation. With a heightened sense of environmental commitment and awareness relative to others in the nation, Mindo's activists
sought to become the nation's environmental vanguards. In doing so, and
in order to do so, they shifted their energies onto constructing the town as a
model for others and as the national authority on sustainable, nature-based
economic development. In short, the town itself epitomized an unparalleled
social and economic conversion, and conversation, along the route, due in
large part to the community's inexperience with the oil industry. However,
the residue of these rapid changes, including a rise in domestic tourists,
may leave a greater and more lasting impact on the community's natural
resources than the pipeline project itself.

Targeting an International Audience: A "Best Fit" for Rainforest Protection

While Lago Agrio targeted the state and the Quito-based NGOs negotiated
in boardrooms with the oil consortium, Mindo's grassroots activists lacked a
local target. They, therefore, capitalized on what they had in abundance and
what others along the route lacked: their environmental currency. Such currency included threatened and unique habitat and wildlife, as well as their

social capital, including nonnational residents, a trickle of international travelers, an ecotourism mind-set, and a contingent of activist-minded youth. To attract international support, Mindo's activists cultivated an image of grassroots protection of a cloud forest untarnished by oil intrusion and unsullied by negotiations with multinationals. This image was contrasted against the *contaminated other*, including the oil-impacted communities of the Amazon, Quito's conservation professionals who negotiated with the oil industry, and the state's oil dependency in general.

In their singular and marketed position, Mindo became the international icon of antipipeline activism in Ecuador and a specific case for international campaigns against "Big Oil." Initially, however, they promoted their fight as for all Ecuadorians, claiming in one brochure that "if we preserve this region, all Ecuadorians win—forever!"[200] Shortly there afterward, Acción por la Vida identified the critical role of international groups to their campaign, and actively shifted their motivational frame as an international and moral one. Through a series of demonstrations and commentaries, Acción por la Vida linked its local fight to global environmental struggles, in contrast to others along the route, and by doing so demonstrated that one important target in their campaign was an international audience and international NGOs.

During the peak of their 2002 campaign, for example, one local tree sitter claimed, "It's important to remember that 'la pelea no es sola para nosotros sino para todo el planeta' (the fight isn't just for us, but for the whole planet)."[201] In an undated pamphlet, Acción por la Vida promoted the community with these words: "Mindo carries out a noble fight for the defense of its eco-system, but also in defense of all human beings."[202] By 2003, Acción por la Vida had installed a banner near the entrance to Mindo, which read "The World Is Not for Sale." This new sentiment marked a dramatic departure from Pro Ruta's earlier campaign slogan, "A Pipeline Yes, Through Mindo, NO!"

Mindo's claims were inspired by and resonated with international advocates, including anti-oil, World Bank reform, antiglobalization, and rainforest protection groups, and fit with the international NGOs' global campaigns to improve the environmental standards of public and private lenders, as well as to hold multinationals accountable to Northern standards. Once established, international networks carried Mindo's campaign to the doors of the World Bank, the offices of European financiers, and the headquarters and shareholder meetings of the European and North American oil companies. However, the split between Mindo's immediate need and the international advocates' nonlocal campaigns exposed the local risk and global benefit of transnational alliances.

Emulating the boomerang model that local activism generates international pressure, which leads to national-level changes,[203] Acción por la Vida wrote, "In collaboration with [international] groups, our aim is to generate international press attention to expose the environmental threat of the OCP to such a degree that the Ecuadorian government would be forced to withdraw from the expropriation process."[204]

However, Acción por la Vida overestimated the impact of transnational campaigns against oil projects and the national government in general. Given that some of the Quito NGOs had greater national and international experience, one offered one reason why the Ecuadorian government was little affected by international sentiment. "It is worse to put activists in jail, I think, for the international image. But for the local and national image, it is better because it shows authority," claimed one NGO representative. "Governments, here in this country, are used to working like they were hacienda owners. [They say,] 'It is going to be done my way, not your way. I say that this project is going to be built, so it is going to be built.'"[205]

Mindo's global rhetoric was also indicative of its lowly position among national priorities and its lack of a local target. To the state, the capacity of the oil towns to stop production warranted greater concern and required a much heavier-handed response than was necessary to control tree-sitting ecoactivists and their international supporters. Within the context of a nation with prohibitive debt, local and international activism failed to influence the government, which portrayed international activism as interference in the country's economic development, or at least its debt repayment. In addition, local and international activists never succeeded in demonstrating the incongruity of a national project being constructed and owned by multinationals despite Ecuador's thirty years of oil experience. Even though this point was a primary concern of Ecuador's oil union, Mindo's ecoactivists and the country's oil workers never partnered on it.

In contrast to the state's marginalization of Mindo's protests, international scrutiny[206] and the demands of the Quito-based conservation groups pressured the multinationals to respond. Indeed, international environmental activism promoted greater care and improved construction technique, such as manual digging, controlled access along the right-of-way, and aerial cable systems to transport pipes in the greater Mindo region.[207] Such attention focused on areas designated environmentally important to Northern advocates and nationals with international ties—at the expense of other regions, topographies, and communities along the route. In this, the environmental elite class of both Quito and Mindo served to protect an area previously uncontaminated by oil, which may have fostered an environmental neglect in the other affected regions. Acknowledging the inequities in environmental attention along the route, one Mindo activist claimed, "At least, in the Guarumos part, they worked very hard trying to avoid greater damages because the international focus was always on Guarumos more than any other part on the line."[208]

Needless to say, Mindo's staunch antipipeline position served in tandem with the landowners and conservation groups to increase environmental care in the area. Interestingly, it was the landowners who sold the right-of-way and who were ostracized by Mindo's activists for doing so, who remained influential in containing impact, such as blocking the construction of access roads, demanding the removal of trash and cleanup of small diesel spills, and promoting careful construction practices. Likewise, Quito-based conservation organizations that worked in the area minimized impact through one-on-one interaction with the construction teams, while Fundación Maquipucuna's Global Environmental Facility project with the World Bank provided international leverage to achieve higher environmental standards in the area as well. Conversely, efforts by both the landowners and conservation organization were sustained indirectly by the media attention generated by Mindo's extreme activism. Had these three forces collaborated, their achievements may have been even greater.

The dominance of international attention held by the environmental radicals and moderates within Ecuador transpired into an environmental disregard of the other ecosystems, communities, land-owning campesinos, and labor groups along the route. First, what could have become a transnational campaign along the route against environmental, social, and economic injustices became simplified for an international audience through the international network of opposition as one primarily for environmental protection in the Mindo area.

To illustrate this absence in other affected areas, there was no orchestrated activism around the construction of OCP near the Papallacta River, even though it was one of Quito's water sources. Early attention was warranted as the movement of OCP's heavy equipment in the area may have led to structural insecurities in the older SOTE pipeline, which broke in 2003, spilling oil into the river. In a second case, the volcano Reventador near Lago Agrio erupted in November 2002, scouring out the buried OCP pipeline and moving it several feet. Canadian advocates documented how residents near the volcano charged OCP with polluting and blocking the community's water supply,[209] while an environmental specialist for Acción Ecológica reported on volcanic risks for communities and ecosystems in an unpublished document.[210] Otherwise, international activism in both the Papallacta and Reventador areas was never sustained.

Nevertheless, events such as the volcanic eruption were employed by OCP's environmental consultants, who were able to argue for greater reinforcement and deeper burial in that specific area.[211] OCP's environmental consultants also believed Mindo's successful campaign to narrow the right-of-way may have actually weakened the security of the pipeline in the Mindo-Nambillo cloud forest. According to one consultant:

> A lot of [people] in Mindo were very concerned about the total right-of-way width. They wanted to minimize that. And it is a real trade-off, because if you minimize your width, there is less earthwork that you can do and geo-technical work to stabilize the area for the long term. So yes, you are cutting down fewer trees, but trees grow back. The real concern is the stability of the pipeline. You don't want it to break, because an oil spill is a much bigger impact than cutting a few extra meters of trees, which you can reforest pretty easily. And so, I have al-

ways argued we should really be giving the constructors the right-of-way that they need in order to put in a stable pipeline, and also to put in the erosion control and slope stability control that they need in order that the impacts long term, the risk long term, is minimized.[212]

In short, Mindo's international social capital, and its global and environmental currencies, generated an international response to save the cloud forests, while the oil consortium responded to national and international pressure by using greater environmental care in the construction process in this region. However, extra care in the Mindo area created inattention to other areas along the route and may have led to a less secure burial even in Mindo's cloud forests. A comparison of sites also indicates how international advocates are organized to respond quickly to save rainforests, rather than to assist poor farmers or oil towns. Adult poverty and working-class injustices are not easily condensed into visuals or media icons that provoke and inspire international attention and assistance. Temporal limitations existed as well for international networks against the experienced environmental injustices. OCP's construction was completed in two years, with a three-month window between the announcement of the EIA and the beginning of construction. This limitation may be one reason rainforest protection networks launched more quickly in Mindo than support for protracted antipoverty campaigns in the Amazon or on the Pacific Coast.[213] Indeed state and industry time lines to produce, rather than to discuss, impede environmental and community protections.

Not the Contaminated or Negotiating Others

To strengthen international commitment to the area and to reinforce local cohesion, Mindo activists set themselves and the Andean cloud forests apart from the oil-saturated communities of the Amazon, or the contaminated other, and apart from the professional conservation NGOs in Quito, or what could also be called the negotiating other. After Acción Ecológica used toxic tours to expose Mindo's leaders to the environmental and social impacts of oil production in the Amazon, activist leaders returned adamant that the greater Mindo area would not become a polluted environment. Cynically, their livelihoods depended on it. But more importantly, their way of life and sense of well-being did so as well.

One Mindo activist acknowledged holding a "softer" opinion of the oil industry before the OCP project. But after inspecting oil impacts in the Amazon, for the first time, this grassroots ecologist began to question the country's oil policy:

> They [the government] always say that when they go to build the pipeline it [will] bring prosperity to the country, to the people. . . . But during the last thirty years you do not see prosperity in the country. You know, the poverty of the people is increasing, and so I am asking, what really is the benefit of exploiting oil for the people? You know, all the villages, the cities in the Oriente, are really not villages you would like to visit.[214]

Another landowning activist in the Mindo region elaborated:

It is in those cities that you can see the reality of what an oil pipeline really brings
to a country. Coca and Lago Agrio are some of the worse cities in the country for
hospitals, schools, clean water, decent sewage systems, anything. They are hell-
holes. And yet, they are the axis for the production of what is the biggest producer
of money in the country, which is why the whole propaganda [of the benefits of
OCP and the oil industry] was a lie.[215]

Not only did Mindo activists construct the difference, international
activist-organizers also contrasted Mindo with the Amazon. "[The people of
Mindo] have made a strategic choice as a community to be really pursuing
alternative ways of developing their community that were more sustainable," noted one international advocate. "I mean you go into the Amazon
and anywhere else along the route and all that area is totally deforested.
And to have something so close to Quito and all that's still preserved, that
comes from the people of Mindo."[216] The international community's selection of Mindo also underscored how international campaigns seek strategic
alliances with anti-oil or antimultinational activists, or in this case one of
the environmental elite communities of Ecuador, as a specific and contemporary case for their long-running global arguments against the extensive
and indiscriminate environmental destruction of Northern entities operating worldwide. By actively framing Mindo as retaining a fifteen-year commitment to ecological protection in contrast to the Amazonian communities,
which had accepted the oil industry, Mindo's activist community localized
international attention on their "uncontaminated" environment, despite a
history of timber extraction, hunting, farming, and charcoal production, and
over time used this frame to unite like-minded locals against becoming a contaminated place like the Amazon.

Not negotiating with the oil industry was a second mark of distinction cultivated by Mindo's activists, who identified land leases in the area and Quito's
environmental fund as personal betrayals to their anti-OCP campaign. For
landowners who leased land for the pipeline's right-of-way, Mindo's distain
was palpable. According to one landowner who initially resisted the pipeline, "They think we negotiated behind their backs. So they say we are guilty
for the construction."[217] Yet criticism may have come easy because the most
extreme activists were not landowners along the right-of-way, until land was
purchased for them through a fundraising campaign in Germany. According
to one landowner,

A lot of the people in Mindo who were in conflict [or were fighting] do not have
land along the route. So it is very easy for them to be against the pipeline. But at
the moment it passes through your land, at that point you have to make some
compromises or accept that they take the land anyway.[218]

In addition to land agreements, Mindo's activists were incensed by the NGOs in Quito that negotiated an environmental fund, but especially by CECIA and Fundación Maquipucuna, which maintained conservation projects in the Mindo area. In an assertion directed at the conservation NGOs, Acción por la Vida declared: "We risked our lives to protect the forest in the past, so we can also assure to fight on basis of principles (and not wages) for the future of the forest."[219] In a further testament to Mindo's position as nonnegotiating locals, one activist said, "We've basically said, 'No [to a Quito NGO]. We do not want you to use our name. We do not want you to put in a brochure that you are helping the community of Mindo, the affected people of Mindo.'"[220]

As further demonstration, in a letter to the heads of the World Bank and the financier WestLB to stop the pipeline's construction and to present themselves as the only organization representing Mindo, Acción por la Vida named CECIA, Maquipucuna, and Fundación Natura as presenting themselves as representatives of Mindo's environment when it was Acción por la Vida that worked to defend "life" without economic interests.[221] Years after the pipeline's construction, some of the Quito-based NGOs said community relations with Mindo were still tense. "I still think there is quite a bit of resentment towards them from certain sectors, particularly in Mindo," noted one in 2007.[222] "So to continue to work in that area, . . . it is very difficult right now because people question [our] ethics and the decisions that we [as the NGO community] made."[223]

Even though Mindo initially represented a NIMBY community and had limited national influence, Mindo exemplified a "best fit" for international advocates opposed to the oil industry and the pipeline's construction. International advocates with a history of challenging multinationals and international institutions in global oil struggles acknowledged the flexibility required in linking with a NIMBY organization, while maintaining an international objection to the entire pipeline and to other oil projects in general. Such elasticity counters and supports Clifford Bob's work on how local campaigns market themselves to appeal to international support networks.[224] On the one hand, Mindo's activists were offering a local interpretation to the pipeline to offset an international one, while also constructing and promoting themselves as the only community in Ecuador that mobilized for the environment. Despite such nuances, Bob's argument holds: affected people and NGOs in the Global South are forced to actively market and alter their agendas and demands to gather attention and to reach international media.[225]

Mindo's core activists harnessed their network capital and environmental currency to identify and to promote the weaknesses of other communities along OCP's route in order to attract international attention as well as to strengthen the community's local commitment. They built their own reputation as the only community in Ecuador rejecting the encroachment of the oil industry, which in the process weakened the veracity of other perspectives and delineated the other ecosystems along the route. Yet after the pipeline's construction, Mindo's activists sought ways to prolong their anti-oil and international interconnectedness.

Defenders of the Amazon?

In a short-lived effort, Acción por la Vida sought to bridge its anti-oil position in Mindo into the Amazon, which they had earlier constructed as a bastion of oil contamination. In 2004, after the pipeline's completion, Acción por la Vida pressed for international funds to defend the Amazon, suggesting that the local inhabitants appeared unable to do so and appeared prone to accepting the oil industry rather than challenging it like themselves. Unstated was that such assistance would funnel funds from affected Indigenous and non-Indigenous communities to a grassroots group, culturally and geographically removed from the Amazon. Furthermore, their attempted insertion into another community's oil position was precisely what Acción por la Vida had fought against when the Quito-based organizations tried to speak for the Mindo region.[226]

There are a few ways to interpret Acción por la Vida's attempted transition from a grassroots, locally oriented organization to a national one. On the one hand, this change revealed greater national-level interest in challenging the state and the oil industry regardless of locale and an orchestrated effort to enhance the quality of life of oil-impacted communities, to protect threatened ecosystems, and to demonstrate their model of development to communities in the Amazon. On the other hand, this transition appeared to be an entrepreneurial move to expand or to save the organization, which would seem problematic on several fronts.

First, as a grassroots organization, this departure to a national, anti-oil organization with interests in environmental protection could overextend the group itself, as key members of Acción por la Vida were still engaged in a land dispute with OCP, and all members were volunteers. Second, this move would have Acción por la Vida potentially competing rather than collaborating with professional, internationally funded Quito-based NGOs in directing conservation and ecotourism projects in the Amazon or challenging oil expansion altogether. When Acción por la Vida formed, it sought direct ties with international advocates, excluding Quito intermediaries, to direct local campaigns and access international funds for local initiatives. At the time, Mindo's activists portrayed the Quito-based organizations working in the greater Mindo area as outsider organizations and nonrepresentative of the local perspective. Indeed, Mindo had constructed a negative image of the NGOs to generate international support for them alone and to strengthen local cohesion for their antipipeline campaign.

Like Quito-based Acción Ecológica, Acción por la Vida ran the risk of re-peating cycles of being accepted and then rejected by affected communities due to their tactics and agendas. Though it is uncertain, Mindo's national outlook appeared to be inspired by access to international contacts, a re-cent discovery of international funds for environmental campaigns, and a moral commitment to confronting the oil industry and the nation's oil dependence.

In spite of their strong ecological commitment, this outward initiative was short-lived—perhaps due to their failure to generate international funds to save the Amazon. Mindo's activists were able to capitalize on the area's high biodiversity, sustainable tourism efforts, and radical tactics for an international audience for their own impacted region. However, they overestimated their international prominence and overreached their area of expertise as identified by the lack of potential supporters for their Amazon campaign. Nevertheless, their activism still generated a long-term outcome beyond the OCP project: national name recognition of their tiny Andean town.

Stewarding National Environmental Awareness

While contesting the pipeline project, Mindo's grassroots ecologists became galvanized to transform Mindo into an Ecuadorian model of low-impact de-velopment and cloud forest protection through ecotourism. In particular, they offered their ecotourism efforts as a counter model to the state-supported ex-tractive and resource-intensive industries. Indicating presciently their national aspirations as early as 2002, Acción por la Vida claimed Mindo a model for the nation:

> The Mindo example will be used to demonstrate to other Ecuadorian commu-nities, the possibilities of investing in a situation where residents work in an environmentally sustainable fashion. Through these activities the protection of Ecuador's natural areas will become a more important national priority with grass-roots support.[227]

Many activists and small business owners expressed a similar sentiment that tourism in Mindo, which still needed protection and support from the greater community, could become a viable economic model for other communities. "This whole area is so great for tourism," claimed one activist. "It really has the potential to do wonders for the country. Because, obviously the country has ignored tourism, like it has ignored everything else, except for petroleum."[228] Emphasizing the local role in developing tourism, another activist organizer asserted: "We are volunteer activists, wanting to protect our natural environ-ment. We have worked seventeen years in environment conservation and preservation and we are looking for sustainable activities for this town."[229]

Still another, interviewed on the same day in 2002, contributed, "The people here have been conscious for a long time about preserving the area, and about how valuable this place is, and how we need to keep [it], you know, we need to conserve it as well as we can."[230]

Identifying themselves as being, and priding themselves on being, the ecological capital of Ecuador, these activists sought international support to expand their local efforts once confronted with the pipeline. "[Mindo] knew environmentally it was going to be a disaster," recalled one international advocate. "I think they knew that economically that ecotourists are not going to come, are not going to raft down the rivers when they are full of crude, and they are not going to come when the trees are felled and there are no birds."[231]

These long-held sentiments, as well as international support of them, are noted here to emphasize the potential injurious ironies of grassroots activism and local tourism endeavors. As a caveat, this book challenges suggestions that oil presence is beneficial to local communities and ecosystems. Nevertheless and quite unexpectedly, and perhaps even destructively, middle-class Ecuadorians began to visit Mindo in unprecedented numbers—due to the activists' anti-OCP campaigns.

Connecting a Disaster and a Destination

Oil tourism, as identified in this case, may occur when an area promoted to be environmentally unspoiled is perceived to be damaged or threatened by an oil project.[232] In Mindo, it developed through three stages. First, the pipeline's siting near a promising tourism destination, constructed as rich in biodiversity, triggered anti-oil activism, which then generated national media attention. Media coverage, a second requisite of oil tourism, crafted the Mindo region as a singular environment threatened by oil.[233] Though not an immediate disaster such as an oil spill, OCP's siting was perceived to be a disaster event, and forerunner of a more potent catastrophe. In Mindo in particular, the grassroots activist-oriented campaign, tree camps, informational fairs, and confrontations with oil personnel garnered enough media attention to contrast a pristine visual image of Mindo against the constructed image of the pipeline's potential to destroy the cloud forests.

Though Mindo's activists portrayed the pipeline's construction as having the potential to ruin their nascent destination, oil and money flowed together from multiple sectors, the third factor in oil tourism, to support tourism.[234] Indeed the introduction of the pipeline near this ecotourism destination ignited a commitment to expanding tourism activities and services,[235] though not necessarily environmentally sustainable ones, across a broad spectrum of groups including local officials, OCP, and activist and nonactivist residents.

To be sure, the oil industry had a vested interest in funding soft tourism projects. Such investments mute potential critics, increase the sale of gasoline, and detract from the harmful impacts of the industry, including degraded ecosystems and elevated health risks.[236] But international NGOs, the nonactivist Mindo community, the activists, existing tourism and hotel operators, new and nonlocal tourism and hotel interests, and local government officials were also awakened by OCP's arrival to invest in tourism as well. Each converged to support nature-based tourism through monetary investments and communal commitments to building or renovating tourism services and opportunities.

Landowners along the pipeline's right-of-way used their revenues from land leases to OCP to buy additional land for conservation, while others promoted the conversion of unpaved roads to bird-watching scenic routes or "ecoroutes." The idea would include households along the ecoroutes providing refreshments, lodging, or small attractions. Concurrently, the Mindo Cloudforest Foundation (MCF) opened the Milpe Bird Sanctuary in 2004 and the Rio Silanche Bird Sanctuary in 2005. Then in 2006, MCF collaborated with the Ministry of Tourism to publish a national strategy plan for identifying and developing ecoscenic routes in Ecuador for sustainable bird-watching tourism, or "aviturismo."[237]

Rettet den Regenwald of Germany supported Acción por la Vida's anti-OCP campaign by purchasing more than two thousand acres of primary and secondary cloud forest in the affected area.[238] While this purchase enabled Mindo's activists to stage "take back the land" actions on their land and to initiate a land-use lawsuit against OCP, it also represented a potential tourism opportunity not available prior to the pipeline's arrival.[239] Though ethical purists could argue international funds to buy cloud forest property constituted compensation for their activism, an activist leader classified their receipt of funds in terms of the provider. "Some environmental organizations asked for money, and are receiving money from the oil companies, and that is very dirty. We cannot receive this kind of money. We want clean money," noted the activist, while faulting the Quito-based NGOs for negotiating with the OCP consortium for environmental funds and revegetation contracts along the route.[240] On the other hand, the town of Mindo—not the activists directly—received "dirty" money when the oil consortium funded training courses on hotel management, tourism, and food service, and indirectly supported tourism by funding the improvement of the sewage and potable water systems, community swimming pool, and soccer field.[241]

"If the pipeline, in a sense, brought it together, well that would not be so bad," claimed one activist, presciently in 2002. "But obviously, the existence of the pipeline is a big threat over our heads."[242] A subsecretary of the environment ministry also foretold that tourism would increase due to the attention generated in Mindo.[243] Incorrectly, the government official predicted a rise in German tourists due to the media attention and activism in Germany.[244] In actuality, urban middle-class Ecuadorians discovered an "unspoiled" and "natural" environment only a short drive away and, surprising even the local activists, flocked to Mindo on the weekends.[245]

Before OCP's construction, Mindo attracted approximately five thousand tourists a year according to activist assessments,[246] the majority of whom were international birders, international nature enthusiasts, and international independent travelers. However, the makeup of Mindo's visitors had begun to change as early as 2002 alongside the activists' sit-ins and protests. "From a place that nobody had even heard about, now Mindo is one of the most talked about places in Ecuador," said an activist in 2002. "A lot of Quito people have been going to Mindo on the weekends, like never before. . . . I even have friends who do not know anything about birds, who have gone [to Mindo], supposedly bird watching."[247]

Expressing early reservations about Ecuadorian day-trippers in 2003, one grassroots ecologist conveyed a local worry:

> These are tourists which do not behave as we would like tourists to behave. So, the waste problem has increased definitely during the weekend. And these are people who do not come to Mindo especially for nature, because they are happy to just stroll along in the town, eat there. And most of them do not even eat there. . . . A lot of people are coming to Mindo, but they are taking along their own food . . . and then they leave the rubbish.[248]

Unexpected tourist arrivals in 2002 and 2003 served as a harbinger for changes to come.[249] Indeed, it was the rise in the number of tourists and tourism-related services that revealed the underlying irrationalities and accompanying burdens of many economic initiatives, whether large or small, when seized by business interests for nearsighted profits. By 2007, nearly four years after the pipeline's completion, the numbers of tourists had grown even further, especially among visitors who were seeking a nature-based experience, not necessarily an ecological or sustainable one. "People from Quito are going down on the weekend and it is getting filled with people," said one activist against the pipeline. "And everywhere in Ecuador they talk about Mindo. . . . I do believe that the pipeline thing, this whole OCP thing, brought that together."[250]

Yet local and nonlocal investment in the Mindo valley challenged the original idea of protecting the cloud forest against the oil industry and protecting Mindo as an ecotourism destination. Post-OCP developments, which provided weekend work and income for local residents, included restaurants, street-side food vendors, bars, resorts, residential courtyards to observe hummingbirds and orchids, horseback riding, cable cars, canopy zip lines, dirt bike rentals, private truck services to carry tourists to the waterfalls, and a growth in the number of rafting tours. Several of these new ventures were generated by local residents with old (or recycled) resources. New hummingbird viewing sites were formerly front yards, backyards, or side yards, while a "night sounds frog concert" would have formerly been known as a pond. Each, however, represents little capital investment and supplemental cash income. The single road to the waterfalls was also widened to accommodate trucks and buses, which induced traffic jams and increased air pollution on busy weekends.

"Most people, unless they are young students, are going to be shocked [by the changes]," said one longtime tourism operator in the area.[251] But the emphasis on young visitors also points to the opportunity for young locals to find work. Mindo's post-OCP investment in nature-based tourism or weekend recreational activities may represent an economically viable alternative, such as becoming rafting guides, to outbound economic migration.

However, each new expansion represented the potential rise in the negative effects of tourism as well, including deforestation, inflated land prices, insertion of nonlocal interests, and increased competition.[252] "One of the problems with Mindo is that the tourism is a little bit unfocused, and so there's some good and some bad tourism," noted one tourism service provider.[253] "Mindo is suffering from poor planning. It's not sustainable, and in the long run they are going to run into real problems. They already are."[254]

An environmental director in Quito expressed a similar concern: "It's waste and water. Solid waste management is one of the problems, and liquid wastes in the water. [The] water is being polluted."[255] Continuing, the conservationist added, "Now a massive amount [of people] are going to Mindo, and they don't have, they never developed a tourism plan."[256] As for conservation in particular, one natural resource coordinator for EcoCiencia, a Quito-based NGO that participated in the environmental fund, suggested that poorly practiced ecotourism in general, and if enacted around the world, may have impacts on conservation projects that are comparable to oil extraction.[257]

In Mindo, these new visitors were welcomed primarily by residents and nonresidents who had not mobilized against the pipeline but who were able to capitalize upon the image of Mindo as a nature-based retreat to generate their own economic opportunities. This adaptation to the activists' tourism model included more residents to tourism's economic benefits, which had been identified as lacking in Mindo since the mid-1980s.[258] Others have also identified the importance of complete community collaboration, discussion, participation, and benefit for successful tourism initiatives, and perhaps particularly for successful eco- and sustainable tourism. Interestingly, Acción por la Vida even identified one of its missions as providing "opportunities for residents that are environmentally sustainable."[259] In reality, they actually motivated a range of economic opportunities, though they were still grappling with the concept of sustainability.[260]

Given the local and long-term animosity among community members and their differing interpretations of natural resource uses, a rise in Ecuadorian tourists and tourism initiatives only heightened community tensions. Consequently, the distinction began to widen between the residents of Mindo town, who were now catering to young, adventure-seeking Ecuadorians, and the activist-ecologists, reserve owners, and resort operators in the greater Mindo region, who continued to attract wealthier Ecuadorian and international travelers. Even though some of the town residents were the most extreme anti-OCP activists and even though some of the early anti-OCP campaigns linked the communities of Mindo, Nambillo, Tandayapa, and Bellavista,[261] by 2007 many residents and activists living outside of the town acknowledged a reluctance to visit the town on weekends and were considering publicizing the differences between the wildlife and natural experiences found in the reserves and trails above and beyond Mindo and the more raucous, recreational experiences found in the town of Mindo itself.

Be forewarned if you are a grassroots activist just starting your campaign: depicting other communities in a negative light may come back to haunt you. Though with humility, most of us know this to be the case even if we are not grassroots activists or work for NGOs. In essence, a geographically and economically elevated branch of environmental elitism began to divide the greater Mindo area into the activists and new business interests in Mindo and those in the reserves above and beyond—even though each party extracted economic value from the region's biophysical surroundings.

This paradox evolved over time. By 2007, the reserve owners, even those who leased land to the pipeline, began to identify their own efforts as protecting the area's biodiversity, while the low-lying Mindo residents, including some former activists, were depicted as exploiting their environment, as being unable to control or influence development in the valley, or as benefiting from these new, and designated unfavorable, tourists.

Undaunted by a rise in the number of tourists, by the strains between residents of Mindo town and the greater region, and by the lingering resentments between community members who supported or were indifferent to the OCP project and who were now capitalizing on the tourism environment, Mindo's activist community persevered. Post-OCP, they launched a national educational campaign, further revealing the agency of these committed activists and ecologists and further illuminating the dynamism of small towns.

Ecological Redemption: The Ecological Consciousness of Ecuador?

Despite the ups and downs, core activists laid the foundation for the country's first community-based environmental movement and initiated a national discussion on ecological democracy. For them, educational activism became a determined attitude as they sought to foster greater ecological awareness and commitment both locally and nationally. "Sustainable development in a holistic sense doesn't only include environmental protection, but also good education and a society which is socially right, politically democratic and transparent," wrote Acción por la Vida in 2004.[262] Elaborating further, they wrote, "The target groups are the citizens themselves, but also international tourists and mainly national tourists. Mindo can and must become the ecological consciousness of Ecuador."

In this case, Mindo's grassroots efforts of ecological conversion reflected Richard Hofrichter's "cultural activism," a strategy for social change that incorporates new meaning, constructs unity, and raises a community's awareness.[263] Their failure to influence corporate activity and political decisions was moderated by their ability to construct new meaning and unity within a hostile community that was almost as challenging as rerouting a pipeline, but not nearly as impossible.

It was unclear whether the activists launched a local awareness campaign due to their inability to influence the construction of OCP or due to a perception of empowerment following their international campaign. Degrees of each may have converged to set the stage for this development, and if this suggestion is accurate a larger ecomorality campaign by core activists may endure beyond the pipeline's use. Unfortunately for Mindo's activists and perhaps for the physical environs, they were not able to guide the proliferation of small tourism businesses before the proliferation occurred.

A more immediate and visible education campaign targeted the new urban visitors. Signs were posted to assist visitors in distinguishing between and disposing of organic and inorganic trash, and to remind visitors to turn off idling cars to reduce air pollution and to turn down car radios to lessen noise pollution. Long before the tourism boom and at the height of their antipipeline activities, activists had converted the tourism office, staffed mostly by Mindo's youth, into a news and oil information depot for both local residents and national and international visitors. A photo chart of oil spills in the Amazon, maps of the northern route, and news articles on OCP in Spanish and German were hung on the wall. The tourism booth continued to be a place of ecological information in 2007, though by then it was fielding many more tourism-related questions from weekend visitors.

Mindo's OCP and post-OCP educational activities and antipipeline reputation may be more influential in generating a normative experience among Mindo's rural youth as well as among Mindo's urban visitors, even though conservation NGOs have been operating in Ecuador since the 1980s. Ecuador's professional environmental NGOs are not member based and remain primarily dependent on international funds for their activities. In contrast, Mindo is a site adept at attracting teenage groups, young families, and school groups who live, work, study, and play in Quito or the neighboring towns, and who are motivated to experience a new environment and to learn a little weekend ecology. Mindo offered a lived and inclusive environmental education that the Quito-based NGOs could not provide. Neighboring schools were capitalizing on the destination as well by bringing groups to the area for hands-on learning and play.

"In general you'll start to get this feeling that they are talking about biodiversity now, they're talking about the environment. I mean that never happened before," observed one activist in 2007. "People aren't as complacent as they were about the environment. It's just becoming more and more common dialogue."[264] For instance, and after the pipeline's construction, the greater Mindo region rejected an initiative to develop a series of small hydroelectric projects in the Tandayapa Valley and along Rio Alambia due in part to an absence of environmental impact studies. "When the OCP came through, they didn't want to fight anything, now they want to fight everything," commented one activist. "The forest has value now, which it didn't before. We fought all seven [hydroelectric] projects. We were able to just knock them all off."[265]

Following the pipeline's construction, Fundación Pacaso y Pacaso also re-emerged as an important ecopolitical group, demanding the localization of environmental authority across Ecuador despite its own failure to mobilize against OCP. Seeking to build on Acción por la Vida' struggle, Pacaso y Pacaso cultivated a national-level role by promoting healthy ecosystems and healthy economic systems as alternatives to intensive resource extraction and authoritarian and oil-dependent political policies. To this end, Pacaso y Pacaso launched the First Ecuadorian Environmental Congress in Mindo in 2007 to discuss local environmental rights, local environmental initiatives, and the decentralization of environmental control.[266] Community leaders in potential nature-based destinations across Ecuador attended this weekend event to learn how to utilize their natural surroundings for tourism, to cultivate locally based environmental and economic opportunities, and to learn their environmental rights to contest or to counter state policies. Together, they finalized their congress in a memo from the participants to the government requesting a moratorium on timber extraction, a declaration that all natural forests in Ecuador be designated as untouchable, a guarantee that water is recognized as a human right accessible to all, and a commitment to teaching environmental education in primary and secondary schools.[267] If sustained, this congress may have a longer-lasting impact than the microvariants and special care achieved by landowners, activists, and NGOs in the greater Mindo area. Teaching environmental education, in particular, would potentially alter the nation's politics and its economy in a generation.

The congress also speaks to Mindo's position linking conservation and environmental justice in Ecuador. On the latter point, Mindo offered other rural communities an alternative economic model that had not been cultivated by state agencies. To this suggestion, Mindo's activism may have been a factor that invigorated (or reinvigorated) the nation's Tourism Ministry to identify the importance of sustainable practices and rural Andean places for international visitors. In 2006, the Tourism Ministry, with assistance from the Inter-American Development Bank, formulated the nation's Development of Sustainable Tourism Strategy Plan 2020, shortened to Plandetur 2020. The plan prioritizes some of Mindo's arguments: to promote the economic viability of tourism, to promote certified sustainable tourism operators, and to improve tourism conditions. "There has been a realization since then, [since the OCP], that government support for tourism needs to be more real," claimed one tourism operator in 2007.[268] In this instance, if OCP provoked Mindo's ire, and if Mindo's ire instigated the arrival of domestic tourists, which energized the national government's commitment to support "sustainable tourism" conditions, well then everyone may have won something, except perhaps for the environment.

Stronza has argued that the incentives and impacts of tourism need to be analyzed for both the tourist and the host community to better realize positive experiences for all parties. This section has been an attempt to do just that: to explore the creation of a tourism destination as well as to identify the educational impacts of nature-based tourism on the tourists themselves.[269] At the national level, Mindo's response to the pipeline was an impetus for other events and reactions. For one, it is learned that tourism may be generated from a combination of internal and external factors that are not related to nature-based tourism, including in this case anti-oil responses to a pipeline project. Tourism may also be socially, economically, and ecologically beneficial or burdensome, but this case demonstrates that each one is prioritized by someone even in "ecotourism" destinations. The grassroots activists prioritized the ecological advantages of sustainable tourism, while those formerly excluded from tourism revenues prioritized the economic value of new Ecuadorian arrivals. Given these two competing commitments, social well-being, including local unity and trust, had remained elusive. Nature-based tourism that expanded on the back of resistance to the petroleum industry created a more environmentally aware population, whose first experience with "nature" followed vigorous anti-oil efforts, but whose prolonged exposure to the idea of healthy ecologies may invigorate their own participation in questioning, debating, and perhaps challenging the nation's oil commitments in the future. Local governments neighboring Mindo discovered tourism, while the national tourism ministry awoke, or was reawakened, to the importance that some communities place on tourism sustaining their communities, economies, and environments.

Finally, the domestic visitors may be the most significant ones. Like the pro-poor backpack travelers who may spend less per day than resort travelers but who buy local and stay for longer, domestic visitors may also spend less per visit but visit more frequently. School groups in particular may be a fairly budget, but steady, supply which represents a nation's future. Frequent visitors may also commit to taking care of a place, and the petroleum consumed to get there is much less than international flights.

Local Animosity, Local Recovery

Over time, this case revealed how an outside force could both strain and mend a small town's social and economic cohesion. For more than a decade, communal discord, historical distrust, and community misgivings had been palpable in

Mindo. Thomas Perreault, who studied Mindo in the early 1990s, describes the town of approximately seventeen hundred as "factionalized" due to land-use conflicts and the "authoritarian approach" of Amigos de la Naturaleza in managing and protecting the Mindo-Nambillo Protected Forest.[270] In the early 1990s, Amigos was seen as benefiting monetarily from the protected area and their tourism initiatives that resembled a monopoly, while others in the community were excluded from using the land and the area's resources. These local disagreements culminated in 1993 when thirty community members "occupied" the protected forest until they were evicted by the military.[271]

Locally, the pipeline project brought contentious factions and combative residents, who had differing interpretations of the natural environment's value, back into the ring after a decade's hiatus. Undaunted and perhaps even buoyed by these frictions, Mindo's activists attempted to lead reluctant residents toward an ecological consciousness and a sustainable economic path. At the peak of OCP activities, Mindo's primary activists were not only fighting OCP for cloud forest protection, they were fighting or rejecting potential advocates in Quito, landowners who accepted the pipeline along the right-of-way, Quito-based organizations that negotiated an environmental fund, early activists who formed Pro Ruta and the Mindo Working Group, the town council, Amigo de la Naturaleza, and nonactive or OCP-supporting residents. A low point during the heat of confrontations with OCP occurred when activists accused nonactivists of feeding OCP personnel in their restaurants.

Even among themselves, apprehension and skepticism lingered and flared when some activists charged other activists with lacking a genuine commitment. One activist claimed another activist had joked years ago about profiting off international travelers who came to Mindo to bird watch; and another was said to have hunted until only a few years ago. Some activists were believed to support the campaign only as a new way to make money, a sentiment that was supported by Fenna Snater's findings.[272] These types of economic transitions, from hunter to birding guide, were also identified in a study in Costa Rica,[273] but they probably speak less to moral trickery as espoused by some community members in Mindo and more to changing environmental values due to exposure and economic opportunity.

Members of Acción por la Vida also exhibited fallibility in their own environmental commitment. When a landowner, who accepted the pipeline's right-of-way, went to the activists for help in blocking the construction of an access road, the group, as one member recounted, said they would mobilize if the landowner paid for the costs of the mobilization, including food and transportation. The landowner left without their assistance. But their decision to support the landowner only if paid begs two questions: Were they economic opportunists, as suggested by some of their own members, or did they forego an opportunity to minimize impact due to communal animosity or an unwillingness to cooperate with affected landowners who consented to the right-of-way?

In another assessment of challenges in developing and maintaining community commitment and solidarity to each other and to the campaign, one community activist, who opposed the pipeline from the start, stated:

> At the beginning, everyone thought we'd win or gain something or whatever. It's going to be easy and will last only a few months. But when they got aware that it was not so easy, it was hard for most of us who were really invested in this way that most of the people were only lip-saying that. They were actually not one hundred percent behind the case, you know. This provided a lot of ruptures as well which was the sad side.[274]

In another telling example of Mindo's self-imposed isolation due in part to their narrow criteria of solidarity, they rejected a Quito-based activist when the potential advocate failed to attract media attention to an early demonstration in Mindo. "Nobody in the news was interested and they did not go. So then we get this call from Mindo saying that, 'You people have abandoned us,'" recalled the spurned supporter.[275] According to another activist, some of their animosity toward others had become "ridiculous" at the height of tensions because the activists of Mindo themselves were slow to respond to OCP. "There was no interest whatsoever in Mindo. It took a long time for any interest to be mobilized, because they did not see it as affecting them. Because it does not affect them really," claimed the resident-activist. "It affects the forest. It affects the village socially because of the same divisions that I am talking about with some taking work and others being against them for taking work. It did not actually, physically, affect the village."[276]

At the peak of antipipeline activism, criticisms that would appear trivial to an outsider—and sound trivial here—divided neighbors from neighbors, and activists from activists. Even noting their petty disdains for each other may appear insignificant or even mean-spirited. However, it is through their comments that the activists' environmental pretense (or recent awareness), favored campaigns (or strategic ones), and preference for conflict (or uncompromising stance) are revealed. Indeed, as the construction of the pipeline advanced, Mindo became an increasingly "corrosive community," a term used by Steve Kroll-Smith and Stephen Couch, based on their observations of the "social hatred" and "the way people responded to one another that constituted the most profound disaster" in a community affected by an environmental disaster.[277]

These microconflicts speak to the powerful role of small groups in small places. Some have even argued that "tiny publics" are indicative of a healthy democracy and a participatory society, suggesting that a consequence of small groups is the growth of more small groups.[278] However, a proliferation of small groups *in small towns* may also be a consequence of long-running exclusionary and antagonistic practices. Indeed, a high number of small groups may indicate a robust democracy or community antipathy toward each other.[279] The former may be more constructive, while the latter's primary goal may be to counter or to diminish the strength and/or success of the former.

Despite generating national attention and international alliances, community cohesion had proven to be perhaps one of the most daunting and most significant challenges for the activist-ecologists. Even at the beginning of construction, activists interpreted their inability to stop or divert the pipeline as diminishing their influence in a reluctant and guarded community. "If we cannot change the route, our work will become really difficult. . . . If people see we have been defeated, that we could not reach our aim, they will come to the conclusion that whatever we do, they [the government and extractive industries] are going to beat us," worried one grassroots ecologist in 2001. "So all the years of work, perhaps, we will have to start at point zero again."[280]

Activist fatigue after the pipeline's construction was understandable. "One day we said enough. We want to retire. We want to go from the front line to the back line," recollected one activist in 2007. "What was really frustrating was all our efforts against OCP. What we would have really liked to have achieved, we couldn't achieve. Yeah, it was very, very frustrating."[281]

At the same time, another former activist was developing a plan to gain community access to the pipeline's right-of-way. "Of course, this is the only way that we are actually going to be able to defend ourselves or actually be able to be aware if there are problems on these routes is to actually have people who care on them," strategized the former, or renewed, activist.[282] "If there's an oil spill, those guys will just shut it up, quiet the whole thing down, make believe it didn't happen, blame it on someone else."[283]

Likewise, the nonactivists of Mindo were never exhausted. Even if they were tired of the activists' tactics and wary of persistent communal conflict, they were not too exhausted to ignore or to misidentify that these new economic prospects depended on a healthy environment. Indeed, an environmental consciousness may have developed among residents, including nonactivists as well as activists whose environmental commitment or understanding had been questioned. However, instead of an environmental commitment presenting the community with an economic alternative to natural-resource extraction as advocated by the activists, new economic avenues and opportunities available to the community may lead them to protect their environment. Commenting six years after first mobilizing against OCP, one former activist said in 2007, "You can notice a change, in their [Mindo's] environmental, something like a change in their consciousness. . . . Their environment consciousness has risen in total, I would say, compared to what it was before and it is still on the rising side."[284]

A community-wide ecological dialogue and commitment to sustainable livelihoods may have proven more daunting for Acción por la Vida and Puntos Verdes than attracting international support and a national tourism base. But once the pipeline was completed, a lull in activity, activists' weariness, the emerging tourism aspirations of the community, and the heightened exposure to national and international visitors inspired a collective focus on tourism as an additional or alternative economic prospect.

In sum, Mindo's legacy may be the inspiration of an environmental generation, despite the activists' foibles and their fights. First, they raised local consciousness, and second, they stirred national ecological interest. To clarify, this assessment is not saying that at the local level communal trust had been restored, nor is it to say that everyone in Mindo would agree on or support sustainable, ecological practices. But the economic opportunities available from an intact and healthy ecosystem were identified by many residents. Even though the core activists, who exhibited lofty ecological goals relative to the community's ambitions, appeared frustrated by the pipeline's construction, disillusioned in their setbacks, and disappointed in the community, their anti-OCP efforts may have left a positive impact on the community's future. Mindo's youth in particular may have been motivated by the adults' campaigns and inclusion of them in meetings and strategy planning sessions to commit wholeheartedly to ecological sustainability and to become the region's future environmental leaders. In addition, the entire community may be much more resilient than the idealistic activists ever realized, and in this sense anti-OCP activism may have laid the groundwork for Mindo to become Ecuador's cloud forest reserve known among nature-based travelers of North America, Europe, and South America, and perhaps most importantly among Ecuadorians.

Second, Quito's conservation organizations had established environmental awareness and Lago Agrio's communities had been contesting environmental damages by the oil industry for more than a decade, but Mindo's anti-OCP campaign came at the right time to capture the imaginations of Ecuadorians who wanted to visit a place that Ecuadorians and their international allies were willing to fight the state and the oil industry to protect. Through tourism and educational tours, Mindo was the center of a domestic and grassroots environmental movement. However, their localized efforts marginalized other ecologically important or environmentally risky sites along the route, while their efforts also revealed a myopic local focus and a weakness of anti-oil campaigns to achieve site-specific and minuscule environmental modifications, rather than large-scale changes to oil dominance. This is the bind and challenge for Mindo's ecoactivists: to make national what may become an Andean environmental movement that emphasizes Andean landscapes and topographies at the expense of ones that Andean travelers do not visit, including parts of the Amazon and the Pacific Coast.

5

Esmeraldas

Finding Dignity

The fourth case study in this analysis is the industrial port town and coastal community of Esmeraldas, which represented a unique position along Ecuador's extract-to-export supply chain. Spatially, Esmeraldas was of critical importance to domestic refining, the shipping of crude oil, and the placing of OCP's output terminal and storage tanks. Esmeraldas was a community primarily of African descent with a historical and contemporary status of profound social, economic, and political marginalization.[1] Living and working and playing on the coast, the people of Esmeraldas had been nearly voiceless and invisible in their poverty and minority position long before the announcement of the pipeline project. Like many of the oil towns, they embodied the structural suffering that is associated with living near the petrochemical industry,[2] as well as the "localized effects" of global environmental politics.[3] Unlike others along the route, they were also saddled with the additional burden of national as well as global environmental racism.[4]

Environmental racism occurs when racial minorities in places such as the United States or Ecuador experience environmental injustice or environmental contamination due to their race or ethnicity. Environmental racism also occurs when the majority of people are people of color who hold minority political and economic status. Though majority populations experienced, overtly and explicitly, environmental racism during the time of colonialism, nations (and regions) of color continue to experience ecological racism in relation to others in this increasingly global and interconnected world.[5] Environmentally racist practices, policies, and decision-making processes are perpetuated within and between communities and nations. Once relegated, they experience disproportionate exposure to chemical toxins, or what could be called a targeted injustice, where they live, work, study, and play. They also receive disproportionately slower responses by government and industry to clean up known toxic sites, or what appears to be premeditated delay.[6] In other words, national and global practices of environmental racism infect the decisions, precaution, and policies with regard to the production and location of known toxins, while potentially impeding the rapid and complete cleanup and restitution of acute and chronic environmental disasters thereby further undermining recovery.

For the impacted community, environmental racism snowballs. People of color are relegated to unused or unwanted land spaces.[7] Political influence, economic opportunities, and social services such as education, housing, and health care are then systematically withheld from them over long periods of time. Then, and this is a very simplistic portrait, unwanted factories or facilities are placed in these same communities. They are known to be toxic, perceived to smell, believed to be unsightly, or sensed to be too loud. But what they produce is determined to be necessary—in the "treadmill of production" and the "polluter industrial complex"—by someone, including workers, consumers, elected or unelected leaders, and industry.[8] Once established, others follow suit instituting a chemical alley or toxic corridor. Sometimes the first one arrives out of geographical necessity: water, a river, a port, or a buried cache. But they keep coming.

Resistance is found in those same foundational factors: political, economic, social, historical, and geographical. But oppositional coalitions and networks remain marred in histories of racial tensions, mistrust, and misunderstandings. These racial strains exist within and between communities, nations, and potential international allies. Racism has proven to be persistent. If human rights or moral considerations are not powerful enough to eradicate it, perhaps explicit demonstrations of how racist behaviors, actions, or policies harm the racist network, nation, or regional bloc may be successful in thwarting such practices. But too few of these accounts have been documented or popularized.

Timmons Roberts and Bradley Parks offer one of the more thoughtful and contemporary examples of such payback. They found that in climate change policy debates, developing nations stalled or obstructed negotiations and/or agreements due to persistent (and intended) inequalities between the have and the have-not nations and due to profound (and warranted) mistrust of the developed nations. But in physically based struggles, the possible retaliation of an injustice for an experienced injustice is currently too diffuse to ensure lay awareness of the linkages. The rewards associated with the injustice may also be perceived (or learned) as too good to decline. For example, the host community of Esmeraldas supplies gasoline for Ecuador's commercial and personal needs and enables the country to export crude oil for low-cost consumption in North America, and in China as well. In this case, the community's international oil importance is more of an affliction than a privilege.

At the time of OCP's construction, Esmeraldas already suffered greater environmental and social hardship relative to many others along the route. The poverty rate for Ecuadorians of African descent, for example, was 48.7 percent, compared with 34.6 percent for mestizos and 33.2 percent for whites.[9] Only Indigenous people, especially those in the Amazon, lived a more precarious existence, with 70 percent experiencing poverty, or what may be considered deep and prolonged poverty.[10] In terms of education, Ecuadorians of African descent averaged 6.3 years of school and 10 percent of the population was considered illiterate, while the national average was 7.3 years with a 9 percent illiteracy rate, both of which are underestimates for the mestizo population due to the inclusion of Indigenous people, who averaged 3.3 years of school and a 28.2 percent illiteracy rate.[11]

In a few ways this community resembled the town of Lago Agrio with its thirty-year oil history. Like Lago Agrio, Esmeraldas was connected by road to the capital only in the early 1970s after the nation's oil discovery.[12] Like Lago Agrio, Esmeraldas was critical to the country's oil revenue stream. In Esmeraldas Province, the OCP project represented a storage tank farm at Balao Terminal on the coast and south of the city center, as well as passage of the pipeline to the terminal and to offshore loading facilities. Esmeraldas also hosted the country's first and aging oil pipeline, the SOTE. Unlike Lago Agrio, Esmeraldas also represented the country's largest oil refinery for domestic consumption.[13]

Like Lago Agrio, the people of Esmeraldas had access to and knowledge of the industry's vital pressure points. Shutdowns in the refinery's production led to transportation slowdowns for the country. And like Lago Agrio, Esmeraldas was removed from state-level decision making, isolated from distributive benefit, and becoming increasingly resistant to being ignored by the state's centralized authority, which was led by too few with personal ties to the province. Along the pipeline's route, Esmeraldas resembled Lago Agrio in making claims for community projects and employment at just wages, rather than environmental protection alone. Despite these similarities, there was at least one distinction. In contrast to Lago Agrio's familiarity in negotiating with oil multinationals for compensation packages, reparations, and community projects, Esmeraldas had been laden with a state oil refinery, owned by PetroIndustrial (an affiliate of PetroEcuador), and the state-owned pipeline SOTE—neither of which had demonstrated receptivity to negotiating or making concessions with affected communities, especially the community of Esmeraldas.

Given their history of oil burden, the OCP project provided the town's mayor, the first mayor of African descent, with a platform to direct deliberations for public good. Mayor Ernesto Estupinán, of the Popular Democratic Movement Party, the same party as Lago Agrio's mayor but not the party of national leaders, led the people of Esmeraldas in finding dignity and respect in themselves, their city, and their province through direct negotiations with OCP. Mayor Estupinán also acquired many community projects, which were presented as community-determined projects not just token gifts as received in the past. "Compensation is not the solution, but it is something," said one development director. "The city received support from the mayor who has a different vision, who believes in good investment."[14]

The northwest province had long been toiled for timber, shrimp, agriculture, and cattle. Its port was lined with tankers and fishing boats; its land was crisscrossed with oil and gas lines; and its air was polluted from the refinery. If forced to prioritize their most pressing oil concern, most residents would have identified the state-owned refinery rather than the OCP pipeline. At the Cathedral of Esmeraldas, where the well-liked Monsieur Eugenio Arellano received human rights complaints, not one complaint had been filed against OCP by late 2003, though several citizens had filed complaints against the refinery.[15] When a visiting ecologist surveyed high school students on urgent environmental issues, all of them identified the refinery. We were "asking them to think about the five most environmental problems which produce the biggest impacts and all of them mentioned the refinery—sixteen, seventeen, and eighteen year olds," recalled the ecologist in surprise.[16] The ecologist's shock also speaks to how we teach environmental injustice to those who have never experienced it. Those who have lived it discern it intimately, while their young learn of it at the kitchen table and in the neighborhood.

In comparison to the country's political leaders and the state-owned refinery, the OCP consortium was perceived to have met with the leftist mayor, to have heard community demands through him, and to have responded with the level of compensation, employment, and public projects that the community commanded and badly needed. This is not to say that OCP was well received in all quarters of Esmeraldas. It was not. The oil project was acknowledged for what it was: a nonnegotiable state directive that may serve the community in obtaining necessary reparations from longer-running complaints. In summing up community sentiment, one director of a development organization said, "I repeat that people are not content to the maximum, for certain, but the support from OCP has been significant for Esmeraldas."[17] The people of Esmeraldas were not content with the poor environmental health record of the oil industry in general, with their limited economic opportunities, cultural invisibility, and political exclusion. But given the town's past, OCP was perceived to be more amenable to community deliberation than state entities had been, and this became a key step for the province to revive an awareness of its own value and importance.

Likewise, acceptance of the pipeline is not meant to imply that the community was so well informed on the social, economic, and environmental impacts of OCP as to come to a well-advised understanding of what OCP meant to the nation and to the impacted communities. Like other public consultations along the route, meetings were not venues to air community concerns, to receive unbiased information, to make informed decisions, or to influence the construction process. Public consultations were largely a setting for OCP and the state to explain, from their perspective, how a second oil pipeline would benefit the country and the residents of each affected location. Nevertheless, six hundred people turned out for three different meetings.[18]

SETTING: CHANGING THE POSSIBILITIES

Since the mayor's election in 2000, the community had been undergoing a campaign of self-determination, self-affirmation, and local organization for the improvement of their daily lives. Speaking to the need to see themselves as agents of change, Mayor Estupinán's political and inspirational slogan read "Yes, it's possible to change, Esmeraldas."[19] After his election, the OCP project served as a catalyst to demonstrate this change.

Mayor Estupinán was a charismatic leader who wore blue jeans and work shirts when marching in street demonstrations against the national government, linked arm-in-arm with religious and union leaders of the community. His election and subsequent negotiations with OCP were steps in a larger effort to convince the population that they were deserving of a life of dignity and that they were equal among Ecuadorians in defining and resolving their unmet needs. In appraising his efforts in the city, years after the completion of OCP, Mayor Estupinán identified the citizens of Esmeraldas as the "key actors of change" alongside a community and political commitment to "the re-valuation of local culture and affirmation of local identity."[20]

To be sure, local black culture, identity, and empowerment had long been discounted, undervalued, and subverted in the country, even though Ecuadorians of African descent made up about 70 percent of the province and 5–10 percent of the national population.[21] In the early twenty-first century, they acknowledged attempts to "whiten" their children through marriage with lighter-skinned people for greater social mobility.[22] In a study on race and education in Esmeraldas, Ethan Johnson also found that high school students identified discrimination in the classroom,[23] and that high school social science textbooks hid the presence of the Afro-Ecuadorian community.[24] In three textbooks, published in 2000 and 2001, Johnson found only three references to the Afro-Ecuadorian community and the grade 11 social science textbook had no reference at all to this population.[25] Officially, the existence of people of African descent was not formally recognized until constitutional amendments in 1996 and 1998.[26]

To Be of African Descent

Historically, the social, political, and economic life of Ecuadorians of African descent along the Pacific Coast was one of subjugation, subordination, discrimination, and invisibility. In residence, employment, political aspirations, and education, they were kept separate and treated unequally. In an assessment of their lived experiences between the 1960s and 1980s, Norman Whitten writes that they "live a subsistence existence at the bottom of national class hierarchies."[27] For instance, as Esmeraldas became more urbanized, labor unions formed among lighter-skinned residents, while darker-skinned residents became concentrated on the city's outskirts between rural and urban settlements and were discouraged, disabled, or excluded from participating in government and business.[28] As Esmeraldas became an increasingly important export center for the nation, distinctions sharpened between local labor, who were more likely to be darker-skinned, and lighter-skinned, nonlocal managers.[29] Religious leaders of the time also discouraged political aspirations and participation among black residents except through the conservative party.[30]

"We see one clear case of *black disenfranchisement as a concomitant of economy growth and development*," wrote Whitten in 1986 from fieldwork in the 1960s.[31] In a brutal example of disenfranchisement, Jaime Hurtado, the first Afro-Ecuadorian congressperson and deputy for the Popular Democratic Movement Party was assassinated in 1999 near the Supreme Court House in Quito.[32] After Hurtado's assassination along with his nephew and bodyguard, Whitten understated: "To be black in modern Ecuador can also be dangerous."[33] In assessing the degree of neglect and erasure of black Ecuadorians within a national context, Adam Halpern and France Twine conclude that "in addition to white/*mestizo* political hegemony, white/*mestizo* control over the economics of visibility is evident both in the absence of Black Ecuadorian professionals and college graduates, and in the prevalence of the common perceptions of Blacks as maids and lazy thieves."[34] To this, a 2010 United Nations report on racism and human rights in Ecuador identified "negative representation" of Ecuadorians of African descent in the media as a persistent legacy of past discrimination, while also underscoring that the country's 2008 Constitution, in particular the Law on Collective Rights, recognized the rights and protection of vulnerable groups including people of African descent, which was assessed as a positive attempt to combat the population's disenfranchisement.[35]

Despite Esmeraldas's importance to the oil industry, despite electing a populist black mayor and strong attendance at OCP consultations, national stereotypes and derogatory perceptions persisted about the residents. Along the pipeline's route, the people of Esmeraldas were depicted as a downtrodden population, incapable of challenging the oil project, and for this they were either excluded from or marginalized within national and international environmental networks. That is, national racism may have infected potential domestic environmental networks, which diminished the ability of the province to attract international support; however, like Lago Agrio, they looked inward, rather than outward, for strength and direction on the OCP dispute.[36]

No Nature to Preserve

A second distinction and disservice was the community's image of being without a "natural" environment to protect, even though many from Quito traveled to the beaches south of Esmeraldas for holiday. While Esmeraldas resembled Lago Agrio in prioritizing public compensation and employment and in loathing the national government's uneven distribution of oil funds, it differed dramatically from Quito's and Mindo's conservation campaigns.

Exotic flowers and birds, which gave Mindo its national and international repute, were considered to be scarce in the coastal lowlands and particularly sparse in the urban area of Esmeraldas town.[37] It was accepted that the dominance of oil, fishing, timber, shrimp farming, shipping, and agriculture, including banana, coffee, and cocoa, and the historical boom and bust cycles of gold, ivory nut, and rubber had depleted the region's natural resources.[38] As further reflection of the region's poverty, subsistence lifestyles, and ecological inattentiveness, the collection of bird and turtle eggs for consumption and for sale continued at least through the 1960s.[39] These communities were not just accustomed to depleted resources, but they participated in exhausting and overworking their own resources.

However, the links between land-use activities, poverty, external pressures, and how others benefited from these dynamics were too often ignored. Indeed, they had lived sustainably along the region's rivers, in its forests, and near its mangroves, before outside exploitation changed their relationship to their land. Without thought to resource management plans, the externally driven economic booms and busts particular to the province created "social, cultural, and ecological crises,"[40] while producing a people who sought to "maximize the advantages and minimize the disadvantages" for themselves of the intensive extraction practices conducted by and for the benefit of others.[41] Furthering their hardship, traditional landowners in the northwestern province also lost their land or the use of it to outside developers and settlers when they failed to provide proper land titles.[42] For some traditional landowners, land title concerns created "incentives to exploit them for their present day value."[43] Daniel Faber shrewdly refers to the overexploitation of one's own resources as the "survival strategies by the popular classes."[44] The rural communities in Esmeraldas Province—not the town itself—were existing on this edge when OCP was announced.

As for the environmental NGOs, there were a few organizations working along the coastline though not along the pipeline corridor or directly with the people in Esmeraldas affected by the refinery or oil terminals. They were primarily engaged in protecting the primary forest in the northwest corner of the province against increased settlement, shrimp farms, and residential and industrial deforestation. Since the mid to late 1990s, for example, CARE and its Ecuadorian partners EcoCiencia and Jatun Sacha have used USAID funds to assist landowners in establishing land rights and developing sustainable economic forestry practices in the province.[45]

Yet for both the urban dwellers of Esmeraldas town and the rural people of Esmeraldas Province, even local organizations perpetuated outsider claims that the people of Esmeraldas were not concerned with local ecosystems. One development spokesperson in Esmeraldas claimed in an interview that "there doesn't exist an environmental movement or ecologist movement here in Esmeraldas. . . . The people are much more preoccupied with the day-to-day. . . . The people are worried about things much more concrete. . . . The issue of food; the issue of security."[46]

But these external, and even internal, assessments may be measured as ecological betrayals, or untruths, intentionally or unintentionally promoted about the residents of the province. These judgments ignore that the people were concerned for the environment even as they participated in destroying it in the rural areas and because they were suffering from it in the urban ones. They were just less concerned for a protected nature reserve identified by professional organizations, supported by international bodies, or lamented by grassroots ecologists or nature-based tour operators—unless they participated in benefiting economically, politically, and socially from it. And those in the more urban area or on the fringe of Esmeraldas town where oil facilities were placed lacked access to adequate green space for play and socializing, which they prioritized, alongside clean air and water. These dynamics, interpretations, and misinterpretations represented the quintessential conflict between the more grassroots and urban environmental justice movement and the increasingly employee-led and rural conservation one. In Ecuador, it is not necessarily an urban-suburban tension; it is an urban-rural one, where staff members of conservation organizations in isolated areas may work oil-like schedules: stretches of fieldwork, stretches of urban office work, and stretches of vacation.[47]

Back in the field and on the coast, landowners and fishermen feared a pipeline break would pollute their water and land, harm their family's health, and destroy their livelihood. Residents also feared that a break in any line could cause a domino-effect catastrophe given the multiple oil and gas pipelines crossing the province. Their grounded concerns resonated along the right-of-way, exemplifying a pervasive laboring-class attitude that sought to balance use of natural resources with economic security and healthy living and working spaces.

The region also had a long record of environmental protection. In the 1930s, there was an Afro-Ecuadorian grassroots organization in the province call Amigos de Bosque, Friends of the Forest,[48] and even as recently as the mid-1990s, local residents had begun to identify sustainable forestry, ecotourism, and collective bargaining with outside buyers as alternatives to resource depletion.[49] In the 1990s, there was one important government body in the area, the Instituto Ecuatoriano Forestal y Areas Naturales (IEFAN), which managed the mangroves in Cayapas-Mataje Reserve and managed and collected taxes on the logs carried out of Cotacachi-Cayapas Reserve from the coast to the Andes.[50] In some cases, IEFAN provided public space for direct negotiation between the local communities and external exploiters to create "workable plans of sustainable development," which led to the use of new technologies and local coalitions for marketing products.[51]

Clarifying the region's historical environmental awareness, encouraging its revival, and stressing the urban-rural linkages in the region, Mayor Estupinán advocated that "since the concept of 'waste' was almost non-existent in our local culture, we needed to go back to our roots to solve our waste problems, i.e., respecting the natural environment and not using our city as a waste dump."[52] In his efforts to change the city, its citizens, and their self-perceptions, Estupinán elected to turn "to the real 'experts on the city,' the citizens themselves. We wanted the people to be accountable and to be in charge of the changes" with regard to their environmental concerns.[53] From a series of meetings, "action projects" were determined, including reforestation, public green spaces, and improved urban sanitation. Calls for nature-based tourism initiatives were also made and were eventually formalized in 2003 in a national campaign "Equatorial Paradise: The Pacific Coast." The plan was to invest in and to promote tourism to the province, which offers a coastline interspersed with mangroves and sandy beaches as well as tropical forests.[54] Like Lago Agrio on the edge of one of the world's most attractive ecosystems, Esmeraldas was also a gateway community to the province's coastline and tropical rainforests, some of which remain intact of endemic species.[55]

To this, we see how Estupinán was articulating and supporting a return to a time when the people of Esmeraldas governed themselves and their natural resources, before both their labor and their resources were overexploited for the benefit of others. In this case, Esmeraldas could improve upon Mindo's successes and learn from Mindo's mistakes: when locals are denied or fail to receive economic benefit from accessing their surrounding environment, they fail to protect and to invest in their natural environment.[56] In places where nature-based or ecotourism is identified as possible and where local residents collectively plan and benefit from such enterprises, environmentally sustainable and economically important initiatives may arise.

AFFECTED RESIDENTS: POOR, YES; DISORGANIZED AND APATHETIC, NO

The residents of Esmeraldas were not passive or resigned to the oil industry as some outside groups claimed them to be. The affected and mobilized included local government, local development and social justice organizations, religious groups, as well as landowners and those seeking employment. They offered a list of demands, met most of them, and then continued contesting what they had determined to be bigger problems for their community: the state's desertion of the province, the state's indifference to the refinery's pollution, and the state's unwillingness to distribute more of the nation's resources and services to the province.

An Activist Mayor

It is worth mentioning Mayor Estupinán again—given that everyone in Esmeraldas spoke so highly of him. Even a United Nations report, in a resounding compliment two years after his election, described Esmeraldas under his leadership as having an "active volunteer movement and highly motivated mayor." [57] He was praised for one of his projects, the formation of a "citizen's assembly" that met twice a year to evaluate and to monitor whether the city's citizen-driven action plan for urban improvement was being implemented and successful.[58]

But he also demanded something personal from the residents. From the community, he demanded that they have pride in themselves and their city. To assist them, he commissioned a number of murals and statues of black leaders and contributors, or what Johnson calls the "first celebrations of Blackness."[59] These citywide images, according to Johnson, were in stark contrast to former murals and statues that depicted the men of Esmeraldas as "pushing a boat, wearing no shirts and ragged hats."[60]

For the port town, Mayor Estupinán identified OCP as a fortuitous event, and sought financial compensation, employment, and improved infrastructure throughout the city. In particular, he argued for, but failed in achieving, a percentage of OCP operations rather than a one-time payment, demonstrating an effort, along with other mayors, to seek greater autonomy from the state via continuous and direct oil rents.[61] In a speech after the pipeline's completion, the mayor also identified that one of the factors that impeded Esmeraldas's sustainable development in general was the "corruption of political parties and their paternalism and political clientelism."[62] To these charges, OCP represented an occasion for the mayor to rectify how state-promoted projects had only benefited a few, and not the majority, and most definitely not the most burdened.

From the pipeline project, he also massaged the idea of greater participatory spaces, of dignity-in-life realizations, and of higher self-esteem among the area's residents. Even though community consultations resembled one-way promotional informationals everywhere along OCP's route, the community expressed a sense of participation in the decision-making process via their elected mayor. They were being respected enough to be informed, and that was a significant step—not in terms of OCP alone, but in terms of the community's place in the nation. According to one representative of a development organization, Esmeraldas for the first time received compensation after being excluded from oil wealth for thirty years. "There has been a tremendous investment into the country, yet there was nothing given to Esmeraldas. The new mayor has a different vision, a vision for change and he has succeeded in [receiving] investment from OCP."[63]

Community Organizations: Addressing Poverty and the Refinery

Esmeraldas was a semi-urban environment with a host of professional and grassroots groups addressing the material needs of and providing collective spaces for its residents. Like the Indigenous of the Amazon, they too wished for egalitarian citizenship. And like residents of the Amazon and NGOs in

Lago Agrio, they too were fighting against other prolonged injustices commonly found where oil and communities coexist. Though promoted conveniently or dismissively by outsiders as disorganized, apathetic, or indifferent, they were not. They were just too consumed by other campaigns, especially against the state-owned refinery, when OCP was announced. Oil communities in Ecuador, unlike Quito and Mindo, which only recently discovered the industry and had never been directly impacted by it, were disputing the oil industry and oil politics on multiple fronts, and had been doing so for years. Comparatively, the OCP pipeline project was a less urgent issue than others at the time.

For one, the Codesa neighborhood group Unidos Somos Más de Codesa, or United We Are More, was an active grassroots organization challenging the air and water pollution of the refinery. In addition, Comité Delfina Torres de Concha del Barrio La Propicia Uno was also a community group that organized for environmental health protection and filed a lawsuit against the refinery.[64] Likewise in 2004, La Asociación de Negros del Ecuador (ASONE), or the Association of Black People of Ecuador, sought assistance from the Center for International Human Rights of the University of Denver in a lawsuit against the refinery.[65]

There were also socioeconomic and development organizations, such as the Development Project of Indigenous and Black Communities of Ecuador (PRODEPINE) and the national organization Fondo Ecuatoriano Populorum Progressio (FEPP), which had offices throughout the country. With support from the United Nations, the World Bank, and the International Fund for Agricultural Development (IFAD), PRODEPINE's campaigns included food security, natural resource management, local capacity building, and rural development, with specific projects including provisions of solar energy panels, support of the construction of a preschool, and establishment of radio access in rural communities.[66] FEPP, which also receives assistance from IFAD and the World Bank, supported microeconomic and rural development projects throughout the country. Both organizations acknowledged the potential impacts of the pipeline, while accepting OCP with a degree of relief, for it provided temporary employment for the city's underemployed and much-needed community projects. Their weakness is that many of these land rights and economic development organizations were supported by the World Bank, which propagates market-based and extractive industries to wed people to capitalism's use of land, labor, and resources.[67]

Local organizations also had projects with UNESCO and other international development groups. For example, in 2005 UNESCO facilitated an international meeting to discuss the creation of an International Center of Esmeraldas for Afro-Indo-American Cultural Diversity and Human Development. Specific projects for the center included a literacy campaign as well as the formation of a Center of Resistance and Afro-Indo-American Dialogue and an Afro-Indo-Americas Culture Museum.[68]

Afro-Ecuadorian and Indigenous organizations and communities had also worked together against the state and against national perceptions of themselves as second-class citizens.[69] Though Indigenous organizations by population were much larger and better known internationally, Ecuadorians of African descent mobilized against similar injustices. In 1997, for example, Indigenous and Afro-Ecuadorian people joined to oust then-president Abdalá Bucaram Ortiz.[70] It could also be argued that in 1999, the third Indigenous uprising included working-class demands for economic reform that encompassed Afro-Ecuadorian issues and people as well.[71] In earlier chapters, the environmental professionals of Quito and the ecoactivists of Mindo discerned the means and opportunities to contest national policy and multinational practices through political and economic openings that were first identified and utilized by the Indigenous movement. Likewise, the people of Esmeraldas learned from the Indigenous and contributed to their movements as well.[72]

Relief for Landowners

Along the pipeline's right-of-way, many poor landowning farmers, some of whom lacked running water, electricity, health centers, or educational facilities, were affected. Many of these small farmers had also suffered greatly years before when the country addressed inflation by converting its currency to the U.S. dollar, pricing many of them out of the cheapest produce market. So when OCP sought to lease a portion of their land in 2001, many of these farmers were more desperate than others for cash. Believing that the land would be expropriated anyway—a view also held by much wealthier landowners in the forests near Mindo—they accepted.

In this province, OCP paid approximately US$1.26 per square meter, according to one assessor, with prices varying from US$0.14 to US$3.00 per square meter.[73] Depending on use and negotiations, landowners in Esmeraldas received less than the average in Lago Agrio ($1.59 per square meter) and more than the average in Nono ($0.79), a small community near Mindo, while the range in the Mindo region was between $0.25 and $1.80 per square meter.

"If five thousand or ten thousand dollars, or even less, or more, is given, it is money that is going to lift them from the economic problems that they have," said one community organizer, reminiscent of similar words spoken in Lago Agrio. In an attempt to summarize landowner sentiment, the organizer continued, "So there were people that didn't put up resistance to the work. I think there were not any worries about ecological problems or of landslides or of environmental contamination."[74]

Outside of the province, others viewed them as having leased their land for less than they could have received if they had joined together. "I think they have just resigned," commented one activist in Mindo. "They have become indifferent during [this period] because they were living already with the SOTE.

And they have experienced that they do not have any rights, or the rights that they have, they cannot really claim."[75]

Being long overdue for greater compensation may have been an accurate assessment; however, these landowners were not uninterested. Like other landowners, they too experienced construction debris scattered on their land, destruction of property, and latent feelings of unjust compensation. Among fifteen landowners interviewed in the area, 87 percent feared that the construction or operation of OCP would destroy or contaminate their water sources, 87 percent were affected by the noise, and 60 percent were affected by the dust during construction, according to one report.[76] They were dissatisfied landowners, who were just not plugged into, and perhaps not trusting of, national networks to support a national claim against the pipeline's construction practices.

Organized against the State Refinery

While fears of OCP's impacts were real, the Esmeraldas Refinery was considered a greater, more constant and looming danger to their health, their water sources, and even the communities themselves. For years, residents had been demanding a state response to the adverse health impacts they suffered from living and working near the country's largest, state-owned oil refinery.[77] Like the Amazon, communities near the refinery were immersed in oil daily. By-product waste ponds were scattered near the refinery and near the settler community that followed the refinery road. Smoke billowed, contaminating the air; and persistent leaks and untreated wastewater polluted the rivers.

For the neighboring communities, a turning point occurred in 1998 when an explosion at the refinery killed eighteen people and wounded a hundred more. Breaks in the refinery's pipelines caused oil and gas to run into the Tea-one and Esmeraldas Rivers, creating oil and fire landslides that burned down the community of La Propicia Uno. People died as a direct result of the fire and as a result of drowning in the river when trying to escape.[78] Afterward, the community continued to experience skin sores, burns or lesions, and sore throats from the contaminated river water that was still being used for cleaning and bathing.[79] Fish loss was an additional hardship for the community, and at this time, community efforts against the refinery were supported by Acción Ecológica.[80]

Two years later, in 2000, three oil spills occurred at the refinery, polluting nearby rivers, causing acute illnesses, and reviving memories of the 1998 accident.[81] Then in June 2002, two recovered sulfur pumps were damaged, causing the release of toxic gases into the air, affecting seven neighborhoods, totaling approximately fifteen thousand people.[82] Residents complained of the smell of sulfur and of fever, headaches, dizziness, and stomach problems. Community residents claimed untreated water from the refinery was being dumped in local water systems. Strikes, protests, roadblocks, and bonfires in the streets began. As had become increasingly common in oil disputes, the military and local police were brought in to guard the refinery facilities. In addition to demanding a temporary shutdown, the community of Codesa, united under the cooperative United We Are Better, joined the long-running demands for wastewater treatment and a burn unit.[83] The burn unit had been a constant request since the 1998 refinery explosion, even though the publicly owned refinery refused, claiming a burn unit to be the responsibility of the Public Health Ministry. With community pressure for and state rejection of a burn unit, Mayor Estupinán linked OCP to its realization, and OCP agreed to conduct a study on how to support the implementation of a burn unit.

Before, during, and after the construction of OCP, ASONE and Comité Delfina challenged the refinery. Both organizations had lawsuits pending for damages and loss of life following the refinery fire, as well as for ongoing water and air pollution and illness associated with its operations.[84] The primary difference between the Esmeraldas lawsuit and the one against Texaco in the Amazon was that Esmeraldas was waging one against a state-owned company, and the Amazon's lawsuit was against a U.S. multinational. A secondary difference was that the community of Esmeraldas needed to mobilize twice as loudly for the same amount of national and international attention. The noise in the Amazon and the silence on the coast revealed how environmental isolation and persistent, institutional discrimination raised the burden on some groups, while privileging others.

Despite these hurdles, the community of Propicia Uno was awarded US$11 million in 2002 against the Esmeraldas Refinery for fire damage and for a past record of carelessness and contamination experienced by the community of approximately 250 households, or about fifteen hundred inhabitants.[85] The court decision mandated that the money be used for community projects, not individual payments. Two years later, in December 2004, the realization of any project had yet to occur, returning the community and Mayor Estupinán to the streets. They blocked two roads to the refinery for a day demanding that the money be used and be used at the community's determination.[86] A national newspaper argued that the court's decision favored contractors, consultants, and public officials, rather than the affected community, and earned the mayor's attention because the municipality's budget is only US$5 million, less than the award settlement.[87] One could also argue that a paternalistic court assessed the affected residents as unqualified to determine their own need and to wisely allocate oil money. Similar accusations have been made against Indigenous communities by the country's environmental and economic stewards and against the political leaders of developing nations by international lenders. Esmeraldas is just one of those endpoints in a long line of stepping on the backs of others to distinguish oneself without crediting the aid, or worse, blaming them for the widening gap.

After the 2004 demonstrations and before compensatory projects would begin, the refinery announced that it would use 109 of its 169 hectares as a forest buffer between its industrial complex and the city.[88] Over the past ten years, the city's inhabitants had moved increasingly closer to the refinery, as demonstrated by Propicia Uno's loss. For these reasons, the refinery began a concerted effort to buy up and reforest adjacent lands with more fire-resistant trees as a cushion between the complex and the community.[89] It was not clear, however, whether PetroIndustrial was attempting to achieve this transformation with settlement money. In addition, a Quito-based environmental assessment stressed in 2000 the need to modernize the nation's three refineries for greater efficiency and higher environmental standards if the state were to achieve a balance between oil dependency and environmental protection.[90] At this point, it is unclear whether the company is improving its in-house standards or whether it has opted only to physically distance itself from neighboring communities with a green buffer.

Organized for La Concordia

In July 2002 and still in the middle of OCP construction, workers at the refinery joined a citywide demonstration to shut down traffic in and out of the city and to stall production at the refinery.[91] Through joint actions, the port, airport, and primary roads were taken, paralyzing the province's key industries, including fishing, palm oil, timber, refined oil, and small commerce.[92] National press reports expressed a fear of a disrupted domestic gas supply,[93] worries that were grounded in real shortages in 1999, following a temporary closure of the refinery for repairs. The refinery's national importance also became apparent at that time when the energy minister and president of PetroEcuador resigned after failing to end the two-week oil shortage.[94]

This time, and even though OCP workers from Esmeraldas also stopped work in solidarity,[95] oil was not the focal point of these actions. The demonstrations were in response to a territorial dispute with neighboring Pichincha Province, which included the capital Quito.[96] Both the provinces of Esmeraldas and Pichincha claimed the community of La Concordia, an important agricultural producer that was founded in 1959.[97] The leaders of Esmeraldas claimed historical and legal precedence of La Concordia as the eighth canton of Esmeraldas Province.

Though La Concordia did not represent a sustained campaign, the demonstration was evidence of the capacity of a united community to cripple the state on an issue designated important to their leaders, without national or international support. It is presented here as a point of contrast, and to demonstrate how news of the territorial dispute reached the capital via fears of a domestic oil and gas shortage and via reaffirmed distinctions between the Andes, including Quito and Mindo, and the coast.

Esmeraldas did not mobilize as a united force against OCP; rather they united with the local government to seek compensation. This is not to say that all the residents were supportive of OCP, but the events noted in this section were indication of how OCP ranked low in a long list of grievances against the national government primarily, but also against national sentiment and treatment that the communities and province were inconsequential to the nation.

DEMANDS: BENEFITS AND DIGNITY THROUGH OCP

Through 2001 and 2003, street beggars and casual acquaintances were commonly heard in the city streets and rural pathways of Ecuador asking others, "Give me a little gift." This little request was also a reminder of a colonial past. Scaled up, this microinteraction resembled the political and economic elites handing out *regalitos* at their discretion and preference to the provinces. Indeed, Esmeraldas was a city bestowed with "little gifts" from the state. Like candy and toy donations, state aid failed to adequately address the structural inequities experienced in and between the provinces; instead, it maintained a national hierarchy of resources and opportunities.

This belittling dynamic was altered with the arrival of OCP, according to the people of Esmeraldas. From the mayor's demands, the community received "with dignity" better roads, water and sewage systems, and ambulance services. Residents determined that Esmeraldas was not receiving "gifts" from OCP and other outsiders, but that "now there is investment in what the people prefer."[98] Argued one community worker, "Before, the community didn't have the opportunity for living [decently]. For many years—'oh, they are only blacks'—we didn't have the opportunity to live with dignity. This is what was reclaimed."[99] A radio broadcaster also announced at this time that "the most significant result is that in this latest period we have restored self-esteem to the population" from their direct negotiations with OCP.[100]

For and Beyond the Basics

Esmeraldas and the smaller communities along the right-of-way negotiated development projects and short-term funds for civic projects and were pleased—not fully, but more or less mollified—with the outcome. Much of the significance beyond the tangible was the awareness of their competence through elected leadership to participate in decisions and agreements for personal and community enhancement. OCP provided them with the expansion, improvement, and pavement of roads, more than two hundred latrines, the construction or improvement of potable water, sewage and waste management systems, remodeling and equipment for a dispensary, an ambulance, and school building improvements, including concrete block classrooms and school desks.[101] Each one is arguably the responsibility of the national government if they cannot be fulfilled by local or provincial funds.[102] In the absence of state support for these basic social needs, the arrival of a team of multinationals willing to subsidize these projects was perceived as a windfall of justice and respect for the people of the region.

Some communities also received specific compensation, such as nine reinforced concrete posts for their neighborhood or the construction of a stoop. The OCP project completion report failed to identify the use of these concrete posts, and they are only noted here to call attention to the simplicity of need. It was also not clear whether in the past these communities had been requesting local and state officials to provide these projects, but what is important in this analysis is that when OCP materialized, communities seized the opportunity to meet previously unmet needs at their determination, and they felt validated by their achievements.

Most importantly perhaps in OCP-community relations was the consortium's contributions to assessing plans for the construction of a burn unit. The burn unit was to be housed in Hospital Delfina Torres de Esmeraldas and was to be completed by PetroEcuador with the support of the Public Health Ministry and the municipality of Esmeraldas.[103] After conducting a feasibility study of the burn unit, OCP served as an impetus to push the community's long-running demand—since the 1998 refinery explosion—further along. Even though an agreement was signed to provide a burn unit and intensive therapy center in November 2001, as of July 2004 the fifteen-bed unit had not been completed. The refinery claimed that revenue deficiencies and cost overruns impaired its completion.[104]

This list of OCP projects is also not meant to support such projects. Indeed, many of the projects were not development projects designed to improve the living conditions of residents. Roads, for example, are particularly deceptive projects. Roads are both required for and destroyed by the oil industry transporting heavy equipment and pipes,[105] and oil companies do not volunteer in protecting, sustaining, and repairing these projects. Even though OCP signaled it would invest in conserving the state of the roads, at least one community spokesperson along the route accused OCP of repairing roads to transport their equipment and then failing to repair them after they were damaged by the transportation of their equipment. Once the pipeline was laid, road maintenance was no longer required to support the industry, except in the oil-producing areas. And in most cases, it was the municipality that requested guarantees that the roads would be improved and that damages from transporting the equipment would be corrected.

OCP, as is perhaps common with oil projects, also dispersed petrodollars across the route to assure consent, or at least to minimize disputes. Incidental projects for lesser-known groups included one-time support for civic events along the right-of-way, radio announcements for Esmeraldas, the 2002 Esmeraldas Carnival, and a special publication in the June 2002 issue of the popular national magazine *Vistazo*.[106] OCP also provided the Association of Professionals for the Construction of OCP with a computer, table, and chair; the Municipal Band with provisions for instruments; and the Association of Northern Residents of Esmeraldas with support for an international festival with Afro-Ecuadorian musicians. OCP supported the Cacao Corporation of Social Investigation, the Association of Muralist Painters of Esmeraldas, and the Red Cross. To an outsider, it seems easy to discredit the efforts of Esmeraldas when organizations accept nominal gestures rather than large-scale development projects. Funds for civic parties and musical instruments for the municipality's band seem frivolous by many standards, given the great social need of the region. But if these funds were used to bolster pride in local and indigenous music and art, then it supported the province's more recent efforts to validate their own culture and customs that had historically been disregarded or derided.

More importantly, the negotiations were not only about receiving projects. To the community, *who* determined these projects mattered. From Mayor Estupinán's campaign, he was there to change the realities of the community, and OCP served him in this purpose. OCP represented an early step in a process to discover the community's ability, via its mayor, to make demands and to be a participant in determining its future direction. As presented earlier, Mindo also received what could be perceived as token gifts: daylong courses on tourism and hospitality and a refurbished public swimming pool. This final point serves as a reminder of the similarities along the route and the acceptance of OCP projects.

Organized against OCP

Even though the vast majority of people in Esmeraldas rallied behind their mayor, sporadic protests against OCP occurred in the province. "There is awareness, there is contamination, but there's not a . . . systematic movement," explained one NGO spokesperson.[107] Nonetheless, affected residents organized against local councils whose negotiations with OCP did not meet community-determined need and construction workers went on strike for higher wages, and in solidarity with general strikes in Esmeraldas. In February 2002, for example, approximately seven hundred construction workers went on strike, the third time since construction began, to demand higher wages, hazard pay, and job security.[108] A subsequent report claimed:

> Hundreds of manual laborers who have been laid off, promised false wages and treated poorly are now on strike (in Esmeraldas). Before the strike these workers were getting paid $3.14 a day for 12 hours of work six days a week and only one meal per day. Many have complained of the poor treatment from the supervisors and of the dangerous nature of the work. They are now asking for higher wages, life insurance, and injury insurance. Construction in that area has been halted while the workers meet with Techint [the Argentine constructor].[109]

Life and injury insurance speaks volumes on the working conditions of the laboring class.

A few months later in June 2002, armed with machetes and sticks, the community of Quinindé, outside of Esmeraldas town, detained two OCP engineers to leverage the "donation" of a truck driver, machines, and equipment, including two tractors, two bulldozers, and two small trucks—to repair damaged roads.[110] When OCP and local municipality representatives arrived, the community wanted to negotiate directly with OCP, not through the municipality. In the news report, OCP claimed it had already compensated the municipality of Quinindé and would not give in to any additional grassroots demands.[111]

In another incident, in December 2003, months after the construction had been completed, a man from Esmeraldas said on a popular radio program that he represented approximately seven landowners who received unfair compensation or were dissatisfied with their settlement and negotiations with OCP. Though seven landowners do not qualify as a high or low indicator of mobilization, landowners west of the Andes would and could organize to seek redress or justice. Certainly, the size of mobilization efforts varied across a range of issues, such as the refinery, border disputes with a neighboring province, road work, and land-use compensation. In this province, the range represented a progressively engaged, diverse, and mobilized civil society—more so than the singular agendas of and limited numbers found in Quito and Mindo. The move to detain two oil engineers in particular spoke to their spirit and their frustration.

In this way, OCP served as an occasion for the mayor's campaign to radically inspire the people of Esmeraldas and to provide them an opportunity to demonstrate to themselves and the nation how Esmeraldas was changing. Esmeraldas was finding its voice in directing compensation rather than accepting projects at the option of the elite and lighter classes. The process of demanding projects from OCP became another step in Esmeraldas's self-determination, not only from the state, but also from the initiatives of outside organizations. Yet, the defining moments for Esmeraldas to mobilize were not mobilizing points for national or international networks opposing or negotiating with the OCP consortium.

ENVIRONMENTAL RACISM WITHIN NETWORKS

Even if Esmeraldas was considered a backwater by others in the nation, its importance in linking Ecuador to global markets was uncontested. Ever since exploitation of the region's resources began, it was the people and local organizations that had remained active participants in, responders to, and sufferers of the increasingly global world economy. Simultaneously, and ironically enough, they were also being kept from national politics and national and international environmental assistance relative to others. In Esmeraldas, community groups and professional NGOs were balancing the local and lived experiences of the coastal city with the global opportunities and obstacles that accompanied their location as a supply and transit point of raw materials. In acknowledging these binds, Whitten describes the community as "active, organized people who move according to *their own* strategies and rules in response to inevitable external pressures."[112] In addition to their local needs and global importance, the degree and longevity of national exclusion promoted local organizing and racial solidarity among trusted networks. The cohesiveness and solidarity of such bonds served to identify and to address the collective and immediate needs of the community given the limited resources and opportunities available to them.

Though environmental ties failed to materialize, there was justification for a strong environmental movement against the pipeline project along the Pacific Coast. OCP ran under the ocean seafloor for offshore tanker loading, and was buried and secured with concrete or rock blankets to protect against ship collisions. An OCP break or tanker collision could be on the scale of the 1989 *Exxon Valdez* oil spill, or the other and numerous offshore and near-shore oil disasters. It would not be like the 2010 offshore explosion and continuous spill of BP oil in the Gulf of Mexico as tankers contain a specific volume and transportation pipelines are equipped with stop valves.

On shore, the cliffs and hillside of Esmeraldas and the northwest coastline in general were particularly unstable and prone to landslides and erosion. *El Niño* events, which are coupled with a rising sea level, and the decimation of mangroves for shrimp farming tanks have led to "a very severe process of rapid erosion."[113] The roots of the mangroves collect sediment and stabilize the shoreline; however, shrimp exports, which replace mangroves with farms, follow behind only oil and banana in terms of importance to the nation's economy.[114] Here, healthy ecosystems and export-led economies collide once again.

A study conducted between 1989 and 1999 estimated that the cliff's edge along the coast was retreating approximately one meter per year due primarily to *El Niño*, sea level rise, and shrimp farming practices.[115] Furthermore, Stone & Webster Consultants identified construction of the terminal "atop a seismically active escarpment," or cliff, to be one of the five most significant challenges for the OCP project.[116] For these known instabilities and to compensate for the shoreline erosion, special attention was given to the oil tank farm on the shoreline's southern hill and the pipeline was buried on the beach and cut deeply into the cliffs.[117] However, these responses were only technical measures to reduce the risk of impact, not infallible measures to eliminate risk altogether. Pipeline breaks, leaks, and spills are an inherent risk and expected event of the oil industry.

Despite these concerns articulated by the industry's consultants, environmental support networks failed to identify a shared agenda with this coastal community or coastal environment due in part to the community's focus on state-level injustices and its hard-won appeasement through the mayor's negotiations with OCP. In addition, the prominent environmental NGOs with a marine focus favored the renowned Galapagos Islands.

This study then suggests that environmental racism played three roles.[118] One, the region was poor due to deliberate and long-running political neglect and institutional racism. Two, the region failed to establish strong environmental ties due to the privilege among urban and educated whites and mestizos, including those who formed an environmental elite class in the Andes. And due to their position they were able to select among a range of environmental disputes. Three, generations of discrimination may have also led the marginalized of Esmeraldas to eventually reach the point of rejecting assistance from external groups or institutions, particularly as strong local leadership existed at the time. Not only was Esmeraldas excluded from national networks, but the community was also actively seeking to consolidate power and instill confidence among themselves and their local leaders.

In this case, environmental NGOs of resistance (Mindo) and cooperation (Quito) established ties with like-minded community members and groups, rather than the affected communities of Esmeraldas and Lago Agrio, which were also battling environmental contamination but which were more inward-looking for sustenance and confirmation. This is not to say that anyone or any community would want an environmental agenda imposed upon them. It is noted here to acknowledge mutual hesitancy or distancing influenced by a history of exclusion, mistrust, and discrimination. Community initiatives to take back representative power had already begun when the OCP project was announced, which reaffirmed that part of the divisions between local, national, and international ties was due to the community's increased self-sufficiency, local consciousness, and internal (and previously underappreciated) capacities.

In contrast, national activists opposed to OCP minimized, deprecated, or discredited the importance of the mayor's negotiations for the people of Esmeraldas. Outsiders suggested that Esmeraldas could have and should have negotiated for more due to its critical port. According to one activist in Quito, "You've got the mayor from Esmeraldas who took quite a while before he signed (an agreement with OCP). He has quite a strong position so he got quite a lot of money for the city to do things. And well now he's really positive for OCP. But I think, in my opinion, he's really the one who could get more money and more things for the city," summing up a perspective held by others along the route.[119]

National Perspective: Apathy for an Affected People

Most national Quito-based organizations failed to support Esmeraldas on their demands against OCP. Even though a few NGOs had projects in the northwest province, others would identify conservation and development projects only after OCP's completion. Before and during OCP, U.S.-based CARE and Quito-based Fundación Alternativa para el Desarrollo Sostenible en el Trópico (ALTROPICO) worked to conserve and promote sustainable use and development in the northern portion of the province—but did not take a public position on OCP. In addition, Fundación Natura, the largest national organization, worked on the impacts of landslides and erosion in the region, which were not related to the pipeline project, while Acción Ecológica had an active campaign challenging the impacts of shrimp farming practices on the coastline's mangroves. In 2003, some Quito-based conservation organizations initiated a campaign to address the national timber and African palm oil industries in the northern zone under the umbrella organization CEDENMA. In addition, Fundación Maquipucuna, with funding from the U.S. Fish and Wildlife Services and MacArthur Foundation in 2007 and in collaboration with the Northern Esmeraldas Cocoa Producer's Association (APROCANE), secured land titles for local inhabitants for a cocoa cultivation project in Esmeraldas Province.[120]

Despite these rural projects, which may even risk subverting local initiatives and control, commentary by outside organizations that responded to the OCP project was tinged with the sentiment that local organizers and urban and rural residents of Esmeraldas were wanting. According to one activist leader in Quito:

> Contacts in Esmeraldas are difficult. . . . For me, it is usually the weakest point along the route. And it is terrible because the conditions in Esmeraldas are terrible. You have got Lago Agrio where the people are really well organized, and really willing to move, and you do not have the same energy and organization in Esmeraldas.[121]

A human rights leader in Quito also summed up a national-level perspective on the differences among the communities along the route when claiming:

> In the Lago area, people are organized. There is some kind of organization there. You have the church that has been there for years, organizing the people. So there is a sense of an organization there and the people, they will organize and try to do something. Mindo is a little different because of the whole ecological area. It really would be terrible to have that area destroyed, so you did get a lot of effort there. . . . We do not have information on that area [on Esmeraldas], but what I would say would be the lack of information and that they are more isolated. I mean, if you have one finca [plot of land] way off and a company goes and they said, "Look we are going through anyway." You kind of take what you can get. . . . There has not been that much of an issue, the OCP [in Esmeraldas].[122]

The perspective of an activist in the Mindo region was even more disparaging:

> Esmeraldas is one of the most depressed areas of the country in many ways. I think one of the realities of this kind of thing is that you can get a lot of people motivated, "Okay, we'll go out and shout." But understanding? You need a leader, someone who understands and can talk a little bit about [needs] with a language that is understood by the OCP people as well.[123]

These depictions were also shared by some in the oil industry—though not an OCP employee—as demonstrated by the statement: "Esmeraldas is cheap to buy."[124]

Organizations in Esmeraldas were not necessarily eager for external support either. They too acknowledged that there was no shared identity, cause, or culture between themselves and the established groups in the capital. For instance, when Quito-based activists and ecologists traveled to Esmeraldas, they spoke an uncommon language disassociated from the day-to-day and local experiences of the people. Esmeraldas was not disorganized, but an anti-globalization, antimultinational, anti-oil rhetoric failed to resonate with their worldview, even though (or because) their position in the global supply of oil was critical and of much greater consequence than the position of the organizations challenging or partnering with the Northern oil industry.

In contrast to the nonlocal NGO community, which offered little in terms of viable economic and social securities, residents of Esmeraldas said the government and OCP spoke in quantified clarity: money distributed locally and number of jobs. In the words of one director in Esmeraldas:

> The ecological and environmental groups know [the problem with the country's current development path] more or less. The problem with them is in the communication. . . . They are [portrayed in the media] as worried about the little birds, worried about the trees, which is almost ridiculous. And also they do not know how to communicate with the rural communities. They do not use clear, simple, direct language. . . . [The government and OCP] are simple; they are direct. They speak a clear and direct language [of jobs and money].[125]

This divide is not only experienced in the United States between low-income communities and educated professionals; it is a rift and distinction shared among "southern" communities and secured "northern" communities, organizations, industries, and political parties within the same nation.

Environmental and ecological networks failed as well in their inability to offer Esmeraldas an alternative development or security model. This limitation had also been articulated by local groups in Lago Agrio when they criticized nonlocal organizations. For a community laden with a history of discrimination, advocacy networks had to offer them an immediate answer to their existing state of poverty, neglect, and exclusion, rather than additional controls. In this case, they failed to do so. It was also a misconception, perhaps even disingenuous, for outsiders to assess Esmeraldas as submissive, inactive, and dejected in response to OCP, as some portrayed it to be.[126]

But perhaps more importantly, the manner of discounting the people and organizations of Esmeraldas may have been an expression of hidden fear and veiled uncertainty of their own position if (and when) the province becomes more powerful. Esmeraldas had begun to show discontent of its own for the national (Andean) status quo, for the disproportionate extraction of provincial resources for the economic gain of others in the country, for the political encroachment on their border, and for the compulsory use of their port for the export and import of goods that failed to benefit them explicitly. As one Quito-based activist said, Esmeraldas did have more muscle than they have ever used.[127] And if (and when) used, many of the Andean region, where the Andean culture, NGOs, and privilege are based, may lose some ground.

International Networks: Limited by National Bias

Not only were there biases and mistrust between organizations and communities within Ecuador, but such national misgivings detracted from potential ties and solidarities between Esmeraldas and the transnational networks that responded to OCP. Ecuador is not alone in these race- and class-based reservations. Directors, staff, and volunteers of environmental organizations in North America and Europe are primarily not of African descent or from working-class backgrounds either.

In reference to the absence of international support for Ecuadorians of African descent, Halpern and Twine argue that "neglect by NGOs is somewhat surprising," given the extensive ties between environmental and human rights groups in the North with affected communities in the South in general.[128] Halpern and Twine contend that such neglect further "contributes to the already daunting challenges facing Ecuadorians of African descent."[129] But they were not evaluating the OCP project. They were assessing the reception of five Black-Latino leaders among hundreds of delegates at the Summit of the Peoples of the Americas, which was a counter to the heads of state Summit of the Americas in Santiago in 1998. This is not to say that racism is found only in South America; of course, it is found worldwide. But contention and mobilization campaigns with regard to OCP indicated that national racism and Esmeraldas's minority status jeopardized potential North-South ties to the region.

In the case of OCP, international organizations,[130] directly and through national ties, established advocacy connections along the right-of-way with community groups receptive and accustomed to international contact. For instance, international environmental networks found resonance with Mindo's antipipeline position and environmental currency, which echoed their own agendas, audiences, and concerns. This propensity resembled how environmental organizations are prone to enter countries receptive to them, unlike human rights groups who force their entry into unreceptive nations.[131]

International NGOs were also restricted in advocating for Esmeraldas on at least two other important counts: Esmeraldas's more primary contention with the state and its subordinate position in the nation. First, the community's larger fight was against the state refinery and the national government that redirects resources from the coast to the Andean capital without beneficiary return. Second, Esmeraldas was burdened with an enduring second-class status and national economic and political system that redirected attention away from the coastal community. Though some have argued that "international NGOs participate in the political, economic and geographic erasures that have plagued Blacks since European colonisation,"[132] this case demonstrates that race-based biases and neglect (whether intended or not) existed first in national networks, and were then transferred or perpetuated in transnational collaboration campaigns.[133]

Within Ecuador, domestic contacts, whether established through professional organizations in Quito, nonnational residents in Mindo, or older solidarity campaigns in the Amazon, guided international advocates in campaign and site selection. And with only limited contact with Esmeraldas, national groups misconstrued, perhaps unknowingly, the community's power to mobilize and to challenge environmental burdens. Even though national and international advocacy campaigns utilized the oil images of Esmeraldas—they toured Esmeraldas, went on fact-finding tours to breathe refinery emissions, and met with dissatisfied landowners and residents through Acción Ecológica—they never staged or supported demonstrations *in* Esmeraldas or facilitated community-led actions or lawsuits against the state oil refinery.[134]

Along the route, there was no national or international campaign to assist landowners along the right-of-way in negotiating higher pay, in achieving greater environmental care during construction, and in guaranteeing revegetation efforts postconstruction. There was no national or international campaign to support the establishment of a community-led oversight committee to monitor the state refinery's air emissions and to routinely inspect OCP's tank farms and buried pipeline. There was no national or international campaign to support community-led initiatives to limit environmental damage and to supervise environmental health risk. At this time, there was no national or international campaign for OCP's laboring poor to get better wages, to get technical training, to get insurance, or to obtain more permanent work. And there was also no national or international campaign to negotiate a continuous dividend share of oil profits for affected communities. All of which were issues important to the people of Esmeraldas.

Indeed, residents of Esmeraldas were likely to request assistance in monitoring and demanding road repairs, but such a need may be too prosaic to attract sustained national and international advocates, though this may be supported in general by development aid agencies. Not only were national cases against global injustice competing against other developing, low-income, or Third World nations for international support, resources, and media attention, but communities within this affected nation were competing against each other for the same.[135] There are more global conflicts than global advocates, and those struggling (or benefiting) are inhibited in their day-to-day fight (or pleasures) from linking their conflict (or lifestyles) to hardships endured elsewhere.

From the many global campaigns vying for policy-changing publicity, national and international advocates of environmental and social justice organizations were forced to select communities that best represented and articulated a palatable position for international audiences. Routinely, the laboring poor fail to cut the grade. In this case, Esmeraldas represented a community of limited international appeal. Like Lago Agrio, they represented a poor, non-Indigenous community seeking just employment and community projects within an extractive economy to which they benefited very little but of which they were relatively quite important at least for Ecuador. It was not a community challenging multinational presence or safeguarding primary rainforests. Esmeraldas was alone in its fight against state injustice, and in its unaided attainment of dignity in deliberations with the multinationals.

Outsiders in this study assessed the people of Esmeraldas as "resigned," "indifferent," "abandoned," "difficult," "weak," and "depressed," while other researchers have identified Ecuadorians as portraying the people from the coast as "unprogressive and primitive,"[136] and those from the rural parts of the northwest province as having "no manners."[137] However, these portrayals were deceiving. It was accurate that relative to other communities along the pipeline's route, Esmeraldas was a city suffering from extreme poverty, national neglect, and limited oil benefit. But it was this relative experience of poverty and second-class status compared with the industry, the state, and other communities along the route that unified the community while limiting its access to outside support systems.

Unaccustomed to receiving compensation from the oil sector and united behind their activist mayor, the people of Esmeraldas found dignity—the word they most commonly used to describe their experience—through direct negotiations with the oil consortium for community service projects. They did so without national or international assistance or state-level intervening. Seemingly for the first time, the OCP project served as an opportunity for the mayor to foster community awareness of their own high regard, importance, and capacity to advance their living conditions, and as an occasion for the city to determine fair compensation, rather than to be the mere recipients of projects at the discretion of others.

In reality, Esmeraldas could and did mobilize against environmental contamination from the state-owned oil refinery, against unjust wages on the OCP construction site, and with local leadership in a border dispute. They had the faculty to stop domestic oil and gas production, and they did so when community leaders determined it necessary to gain national-level attention. Yet these defining moments for Esmeraldas were not marshaling points for national or international networks challenging the construction of OCP and the country's oil dependence. Indeed, when Esmeraldas mobilized, the nation feared shortages imposed upon it. Neither is this to say that the community and landowners of Esmeraldas were seeking national and international advocates to voice, mediate, determine, or meet their demands. Despite, or due to, the community's local cohesion, environmental justice position, self-esteem-building initiatives, and prolonged disputes with the state and its refinery, outside organizations were restricted from sustained contact with the town's affected residents, landowners, and community organizers.

Significantly, Esmeraldas represented a unique position along Ecuador's extract-to-export supply chain. The geographical positioning of Esmeraldas was crucial to exporting and storing for-export oil extracted from the Amazon. Ships arrived near the port, and filled up. Imported equipment for the pipeline's construction and for the industry in general arrived at the port as well. Esmeraldas had also been Ecuador's gateway to oil consumers in the United States since the

1970s and more recently has become the gateway to Chinese consumers and industries as well. Yet Esmeraldas, due in large part to exclusionary practices, held weak ties with national environmental organizations and even weaker ones with international NGOs. The sustained opposition and negotiation campaigns that rose from within Ecuador and that then formed transnational ties were established in the Andes, a region of lesser importance to the overall supply of oil, but of greater social, economic, and political privilege relative to the coastal community.

To appreciate Esmeraldas's limited environmental justice networks and to reveal the politics of global environmental coalitions requires an examination of the advanced conservation networks that the Andean environmental groups of Mindo and Quito were able to achieve. In this case, global oil importance and global environmental networks were polarized forces. Esmeraldas—of crucial importance to the supply of oil—experienced limited environmental ties, while communities and organizations in Mindo and Quito, which would experience minimal impact, relative to the input and output terminal towns, generated tremendous transnational ties with international NGOs as well as international institutions and multinational corporations to either resist the project or to negotiate with it for conservation and research funds. The distinction was aggravated by a vocalized Andean perspective that Esmeraldas was too poor to be active or organized, which masked Andean apprehension of an economically and politically active and organized province, which Esmeraldas was certainly becoming. Disproportionately, Esmeraldas had been making sacrifices for the nation, in particular for Quito and Guayaquil—the political and economic cores of the country—for years with only minimal returns. A new leader and a "yes we can" population were attempting to correct these historical patterns and had found the construction of OCP as an opportune moment to realize a sense of dignity for themselves and their community. Their local efforts and achievements let the nation know that they were not only a facilitator of the nation's oil dependency, but expected to be a beneficiary as well. Some residences garnered paved roads and some individuals received musical instruments, but the collective in Esmeraldas stood alone and achieved a pride in governing their own self-subscribed economic and community development.

6

Transnational Responses

Evidence for a Southern-Led Global Democracy

From the preceding four chapters, we have seen eclectic and electrified societies forcing their way into oil debates via street demonstrations, tree camps, state agencies, and boardroom negotiations. At times, they were alongside leftist mayors and/or international advocates. Throughout, they expressed a discontent for the political, economic, and environmental decisions and events taking place without their consent both within and outside of Ecuador. For those in Lago Agrio and Esmeraldas, it was a pervasive bitterness given three decades of embodying the impacts of the country's oil economy without enjoying the benefits. For others, including those in Mindo and Quito, it was a newfound disenchantment with the state-backed oil industry, and what they had been led to believe was the country's lifeline to modernization and development.

At one time, approaches to understanding social movements had been designated into two camps: old social movements and new social movements. Old social movements focused on instrumental class struggles against the state, including resource mobilization,[1] political opportunities, and/or political processes.[2] New social movements emphasized more expressive, culture- and value-based contention across multiple points of target. This distinction established movements-in-conflict, or "false dichotomies," according to Marjorie Mayo, who adds that "the 'new' may not be so 'new' in practice, or the 'old' so 'old', whether nationally or internationally."[3] Donatella Della Porta and Mario Diani also argue that social movements are a more "fluid phenomena" than early theorists permitted,[4] while there have also been calls for greater integration of the two approaches.[5]

Studying domestic and transnational oil conflict across multiple sites in Ecuador contributes to analyzing the integration of these two approaches within a transnational context. For example, we see how the labor and oil communities of Lago Agrio and Esmeraldas differed markedly from the environmental organizations and community groups represented by Quito and Mindo. In this case, the oil towns may better resemble the typecast of an old social movement, advancing an oil struggle discourse against the state to address environmental justice, economic opportunity, and poverty reduction. On the other hand, the nonimpacted or lesser impacted communities better represented a new social movement in being based on environmental values and perceptions and expressive in terms of organizing tree camps in protest.

This work adds that when transnational advocates and international venues were available they combined to emphasize environmental values over class struggles. Yet domestically, both were operating in full force in what could be called an oil justice movement as very few were universally against oil exploration. The "old" agenda did not disappear, though increased global interconnectedness may have marginalized or subverted it. To study only one community, the grassroots ecologists in Mindo for example, would have meant missing the nuances and complexities of positions, demands, and adversarial identification along the OCP corridor. Comparing these cases further would also suggest that—and as I have presented them here—Lago Agrio and Esmeraldas represented on-again, off-again campaigns against the state, though the two were not well aligned, which has remained a weakness of the environmental justice movement. The groups in Quito and Mindo, on the other hand, were part of a larger and transnational environmental movement, though their activities were so particular to the OCP pipeline as to also suggest that they were campaigns inspired by a movement, but short-term campaigns nevertheless.

This chapter adds the role of transnational actors to the expected and unexpected dynamics and strains between OCP's oil multinationals, the Ecuadorian state, and civil society, while incorporating an analysis of the micro- and mesolevel nuances within and between the different domestic sites of conflict. In this chapter, transnational engagements, including the involvement of advocates, Northern NGOs, and international institutions, will be examined along two dimensions of oil contention. One encompasses a concern for environmental degradation due to the petrochemical industry,[6] which was well articulated along the pipeline's route. The other considers problems of global economic inequalities due to external debt obligations, privatization drives, and capital support for extractive, export-oriented industries. Economic insecurities and inequities were voiced in the oil-important communities, while environmental concerns were voiced more singly by Ecuador's professional conservation NGOs and grassroots ecologists. To be sure, environmental justice struggles, including public participation and deliberations, are increasingly transnational in nature, especially where neoliberal policies and the rights of humans, environments, and communities collide.[7] But when placed in competition with environmental issues, including conservation management plans and species and habitat protection and research, these ecojustice struggles risk becoming overshadowed within national networks and diluted in international campaigns. It is an understatement to say that they are too messy and that their very complexity relegates solutions toward short-term, piecemeal projects rather than holistic and just endeavors.

By selecting four sites within one nation, this study sought to understand how the embodied environments of organizations and communities generated divergent responses to local and global oil processes within both a national as well as an international context. Throughout, I have sought to understand how Ecuadorian communities at different points in the petrochemical process responded to the OCP project given that they were weighted by a political economic system that condoned Northern and neoliberal nepotism at the expense of healthy ecosystems, "participatory publics,"[8] and just socioeconomic initiatives. When and how NGOs and community groups countered or sustained such conditions demonstrate that place matters in the externalities of and distributive struggles with the oil-industrial core, or the industry's processes and practices and its power and politics.

In this case, transnational campaigns incorporated national-level distinctions, which demonstrated how location matters just as much in mobile transnational struggles as they do in the physical or grounded landscape of such disputes. But the place-based connection may not be easily apparent. That is to say, the communities most critical to the global supply of oil and most directly impacted by the industry—such as Lago Agrio and Esmeraldas—were least tied to transnational support systems. When confronting a truly transnational project—a project that was owned and/or financed by several multinational corporations—transnational campaigns selected among multiple impacted communities and were selected by the communities and NGOs with greater international experience and environmental currency. The selection and attraction process was uneven, but given that transnational support led to benefit and to harm for domestic groups and their agendas, the exclusion of the oil-important communities may not be such a burden after all.

This chapter analyzes the dynamics and relationships between communities and NGOs in the Global South and support and advocacy networks in the North. First, this chapter investigates the advantages and disadvantages of international collaboration on Ecuador's national organizations and grassroots community groups. Second, this chapter examines the intersections of global oil disputes and the material flow of oil to reveal how the regions that are most impacted directly by oil fail to transport their demands where oil is consumed and were oil decisions are made. To be sure, a trail of conservancy, exposure, and siting disputes has followed the material flow of oil around the world, but the claims of affected residents have followed oil flows outside of Ecuador discriminately.[9] Moreover, Northern groups have maintained a privileged position as experts—outside experts really, as compared to the inside expertise of the people who embody the impacts of working, playing, and residing in and near oil towns.[10]

From these two points, the ongoing frictions between Northern and/or elite conservation efforts and the global environmental justice claims of the South's subaltern are further demonstrated. The former emphasized the pipeline's impacts on nationally threatened and endemic species and habitats, while the latter focused on local contamination and environmental health concerns, alongside the persistence of global social and economic inequalities and the demand for more secure employment and greater inclusion in domestic and international decisions that impact their locally lived lives. These North-South tensions occurred between domestic campaigns with place-based demands tilting toward one side or the other, between domestic groups and potential Northern supporters, and between affected communities and Northern corporations, entities, and institutions. Oil-driven economies, and their host of international boosters, which expands on Daniel Faber's polluter-industrial complex,[11] favor site-specific conservation initiatives over local and global, social and environmental justice. As pointed out by Gay Seidman, corporate codes of conduct, which have been advocated by international groups, have actually led (or enabled) companies to favor simple, short-term community projects that quickly generate favorable points on international social responsibility scales.[12] For the oil industry, its support of conservation initiatives is also indicative of how oil economies—unless redirected by the state and governed by the people—may lessen what Leonardo Avritzer calls "deliberative, problem-solving publics,"[13] and may diminish what one Indigenous advocate in Ecuador has called a "constructive, long-term, locally driven development process."[14]

When combined, these experiences establish an argument for a Southern-led ecological and participatory democracy.[15] Such a call was made by affected communities, but failed to transpire into a global demand. A democratic process of this scale would enable political, economic, and ecological deliberations to arise from any quarter, including the fields and alleys, and to include, and to be decided by, informed communities and citizens with the rights and opportunities to determine, govern, accept, reject, and monitor any invasive, impactful, or extractive project where they live, work, study, and play. To globalize an old adage, the people of Ecuador, representing many in the Global South, were calling for a vote on oil impact and oil benefit, per each local body, not per each global dollar.[16]

FOUR COMMUNITIES AND TWO
TRANSNATIONAL CAMPAIGNS

Before analyzing (1) the benefits and burdens of transnational ties, (2) the inverted flows of oil impact and international advocacy, and (3) the calls for oil justice and an ecoparticipatory democracy, this section presents and clarifies the distinctions between two "transnational environmental regimes" that formed in response to OCP's construction.[17] Due to the pipeline's multinational ownership and private financing, contention had the potential to spread to eight nations—Argentina, Brazil, Canada, Germany, France, Italy, Spain, and the United States. In this case, the two campaigns that formed spread from Ecuador to Europe and North America with additional ties between organizations on the two Northern continents being established for the first time or existing ones strengthened.

One environmental bloc formed a transnational campaign of opposition to the pipeline, which was linked most substantively and tactically to the community groups of the greater Mindo region, while Quito-based Acción Ecológica served as a pivotal broker in establishing initial contact between the international groups and the local ones. At the height of anti-OCP rhetoric, this coalition included U.S.-based Amazon Watch and Environmental Defense, Urgewald and Rettet den Regenwald of Germany, GlobalAware Canada, Greenpeace Germany, Attac Italy, Friends of the Earth Italy, and the Campaign for World Bank Reform in Italy.[18] Many others with lesser supporting roles joined this campaign, including twenty-three organizations from ten nations that signed a joint letter to the World Bank in 2001.[19]

The other coalition, as presented in chapter 3, formed a transnational campaign of negotiation aligned most closely with the professional environmental and conservation NGOs in the capital Quito. This bloc negotiated an environmental fund, and included the representatives of the international NGOs BirdLife International, Conservation International, The Nature Conservancy, and the IUCN—each with an office or representative in Quito. These international NGOs, which had not mobilized a unified response to Ecuador's oil industry prior to OCP's construction, maintained their conservation-only mandates with some acknowledging the damaging impacts of oil in the Amazon. This network framed its position in terms of seeking conservation atonement for the expected environmental impacts of the pipeline project and based its argument for funds on former corporate-conservation partnerships in the North. As indicated in chapter 3, the midtier domestic NGOs were squeezed between the affected communities of Ecuador and the international NGOs and institutions. Likewise, the transnational campaign of negotiation was wedged between the oil industry and the worldwide community of environmental NGOs, whose members were not clearly opposed to or whose members were in support of corporate-led economic globalization.

Using Jackie Smith's analysis of two "rival transnational networks," which include the NGO-led democratic globalization network and the corporate-led neoliberal globalization network, this study suggests that the campaign of negotiation in the Ecuadorian context transitioned from being a technical rival to a technical ally of the neoliberal network by supplying an environmental endorsement and a technical role to the pipeline's operations without challenging the rationale for its construction. When an oil disaster occurs, such as the BP Deepwater Horizon oil flow in the Gulf of Mexico, we see the deeper problems associated with these ties. BP, for example, is a corporate partner of TNC, which if well known may have provoked a backlash among fee-paying TNC members with anti-oil-pollution ideals.[20] Such partnerships also served—before the spill—to greenwash the oil company and to bifurcate land- and seascapes to either the conserved or the polluted.

For additional clarification on the two OCP campaigns, the campaign of negotiation included boardroom "stake-asserting NGOs," as coined by Jagdish Bhagwati, while the campaign of opposition comprised visible, street savvy "stake-wielders," including some stake-asserting NGOs with long histories in confronting the World Bank on its practices and policies.[21] However, despite these differences, both campaigns mimicked each other in focusing on the environment, targeting international entities, reinforcing Northern standards, representing the educated and middle class of Ecuador, and protecting land, habitat, and species of the Andean mountains. Both coalitions also inadvertently softened calls for global inclusion for Southern societies and NGOs in general, which had initially emanated from the domestic environmental NGOs and grassroots groups in Mindo and Quito. If Quito and Mindo were the only cases studied, Mindo's claims could have been distinguished as more economically based and perhaps affiliated with common environmental justice struggles: grassroots and residential mobilization against potential community contamination. But when the oil towns are inserted into the comparison, Mindo's claims resemble a hybrid of conservation and relative justice. Mindo's bridging nature is also apt given that tourism towns are at times hybrids of local and global experiences, cultures, dialogues, and economies.

In action and over time, only the Andean-based environmental elites,[22] originating either in Mindo or Quito, received sustained international access with regard to OCP contention. Both sites and types of organizations perceived the route as having a detrimental impact on sensitive Andean ecosystems and endangering local species and habitats, which had not been touched previously by the oil industry. For the environmental elite, a label of elitism may be either a compliment or a criticism given that their elite stature is a qualified and relative assessment. These groups were not elite in terms of political or economic power. But compared to the farmers, landowners, and general populace in the oil communities, they were of a higher socioeconomic status and could claim important network resources, most notably their access to influential contacts, including the World Bank, European banks, and European parliamentarians, and greater ease, comfort, and experience at international venues. Many of their local leaders or directors had traveled, lived, worked, or studied abroad.

As noted in previous chapters, links between the campaigns of opposition and negotiation began early when Quito-based CECIA and Fundación Macquipucuna first mobilized to resist OCP's route through the Mindo-Nambillo Cloud Forest, thus aligning temporarily with others in the Mindo region. However, once the professional NGOs accepted the pipeline and its route as a state directive, they launched talks with the OCP consortium and were joined or supported by national as well as international environmental NGOs. At the same time, the Mindo-based opposition grew locally and became more radical in their action, which attracted more activist-oriented international NGOs to their side.

These two environmental campaigns were in stark contrast to the populist, environmental justice demands originating in Lago Agrio and Esmeraldas. For one, the oil communities continued to demand greater national inclusion as a priority in their long-running disputes with the state and had only peripheral ties with national and international organizations in challenging the OCP pipeline. Yet even between them, a hierarchy of sorts had been established long ago. Lago Agrio's leaders and Indigenous leaders of the Amazon had traveled to North America and Europe to present arguments against individual oil operators before shareholders meetings and international bodies—even before the OCP project and even though they had yet to be included as equal citizens in national politics. To be clear, the Indigenous communities and organizations in the Amazon and Lago Agrio's well-known Frente de Defensa de la Amazonia,[23] which supports Indigenous and non-Indigenous communities and organizations of the Amazon, had extensive transnational connections. Amazon Watch, Center for Economic and Social Rights (CDES), Earth Rights International, Friends of the Earth International (FOEI), Oxfam International, Pachamama Alliance, and Rainforest Action Network—to name a few—have supported many Indigenous communities and organizations in the Ecuadorian Amazon where oil is extracted.[24] However, during OCP's construction, the Indigenous people of the Amazon elected not to mobilize and Frente was engaged in a protracted lawsuit against Texaco, supported substantively by many American NGOs and advocates.[25] Esmeraldas, on the other hand, a community that experienced greater degrees of poverty and racism along the route, held the least in terms of global aspirations or contacts—despite (or due to) being a port town and a significant gateway to the country's imports and exports.

Without a doubt, international advocates were aware of oil's direct impacts in the Amazon and on the Pacific Coast. They had written numerous reports and press releases on the oil industry's social and environmental impacts. Several have sections of their websites devoted to oil awareness campaigns. On OCP alone, they interviewed affected residents and documented the pipeline's impacts. Caravans of American, Canadian, German, and Italian activists traveled the pipeline's route. One Canadian filmmaker and activist in particular generated a great deal of media and shareholder attention on EnCana's work in the Amazon, and may have been instrumental in EnCana's exit from Ecuador in 2005. Other NGOs created media attention in their home countries and repeatedly updated their websites with action and news alerts. In addition, they invited oil-impacted citizens from the Amazon to present their experiences at company offices and international venues in Europe and North America in what one international advocate called their "speaking truth to power strategy."[26] Numerous international organizations linked thirty years of oil injustices in the Ecuadorian Amazon to the pipeline project as exemplified in a sixteen-signatory letter to the lead financiers of the OCP project:

Ecuador is experiencing the highest rate of deforestation in the Amazon Basin. What steps are your institutions taking to ensure the same environmental and social devastation that the past 30 years of oil development has inflicted on the Ecuadorian Amazon will not be repeated over the next twenty years? . . . The Ecuadorian government and the OCP Ltd Consortium have not considered or disclosed the medium and long-term impacts of the new pipeline on ecologically and culturally sensitive areas in the Amazon region.[27]

Yet despite these broad assessments and durable concerns, the transnational campaigns failed to sustain long-term ties with affected community groups in the Amazon,[28] while documentaries were not made and constant support or frequent meetings were not established with the people of Esmeraldas, who had a longer history with the state oil refinery rather than multinational oil extractors. The lack of transnational ties was due in part to the communities' demands (redistribution of oil wealth, investment in community projects, a role in oil budgets, just and permanent employment), their target (the state primarily), their own inward orientation and internal capacity to address community problems alongside like-minded mayors, and the industry speed in completing the pipeline project. It could also be argued that strengthening these communities may have posed a challenge to the conservation efforts of the professional NGOs, which would have been known to them and which may have dissuaded collaboration or resource sharing.

In these cases, Lago Agrio and Esmeraldas resembled the "instrumental, self-help, stand-alone activism" exhibited by an oil town in Scotland when the operations of the petrochemical industry tipped from enabling an economic "boom town" to producing an environmental "danger dump."[29] At that point, affected residents and workers in Scotland became "self-help" activists with an environmental bent that rejected traditional environmental organizations. Likewise, the oil-important communities in Ecuador stood unaided in articulating their determination of *oil justice.*

To clarify, oil justice is not an endorsement of oil-dependent economies, oil industry practices, or fossil fuel dependency. As used here and learned from and advocated by the oil communities, oil justice is compulsory community-led deliberation on the social, economic, and environmental impacts of each step in the production and supply of petrochemicals, enforced by a guaranteed role in influencing and in monitoring industry actions and state oil revenue spending, in the ability to accept or reject oil projects based on community-determined assessments and appropriations of the costs and benefits and in receiving and determining the use of oil royalties. One of the most important components of oil justice is a state commitment and enforcement of ending oil dependencies by developing alternative energy sources that lead to the healing of oil-contaminated places and to healthy and respectable workplaces. Oil justice was sought in the most affected oil towns, while it was not sought by the Quito organizations and Mindo, which developed a more NIMBY-esque version of it.

This comparison also indicates how environmental empathy continues to best economic empathy among Northern NGOs and international institutions when in direct competition. Issues of local poverty, community compensation, and deliberative and participatory democracies slipped through the gap in NGO narrative-to-action plans, especially when conservation issues are more readily funneled, or fast-tracked, by the multinationals, lending entities, and international institutions themselves and when the state serves as an enforcer of oil projects rather than as a supporter of the people. Oil workers and oil communities demanding oil work in particular were not easily identified as bound to Ken Gould and Allan Schnaiberg's "treadmill of production," and therefore they were constructed as being part of the problem.[30] In contrast, the larger conservation groups appeared to be fringe insiders, but insiders relatively speaking, in the oil-industrial complex without any repercussion for the association (except for Mindo's ire).

In the end, both transnational campaigns, one of opposition and one of negotiation, consolidated around the organized, environmental elite of Ecuador with specific demands: the removal of the pipeline in Mindo and a cessation to the pipeline's private financing for the campaign of opposition, and conservation research, project, and protection funds for the campaign of negotiation. The first two demands were not realized; the latter one was.

OPPORTUNITIES AND OBSTACLES OF TRANSNATIONAL SUPPORT

Transnational campaigns to support organizations and community groups in the Global South have become increasingly common with the increasing ease and speed of global communication, of human travel, and of product mobility, and given the global "need" of the world's natural and national resources.[31] That Ecuador has failed to raise itself beyond its peripheral status despite the touted promises of an oil-led economy only fuels the mobilization of international advocates who reject in rhetoric Northern political and economic dominance in natural resource decisions and uses. Yet it is also Ecuador's very position in the global political economy that invites, enables, and solidifies the role of Northern NGOs in meeting and advising affected communities and domestic NGOs.

Though increased global interconnectedness and governance may sound appealing to domestic activists prevented from participating in the decision making of their nation-state and/or the oil-industrial core,[32] international linkages are not without negative consequence. Transnational advocacy networks (TANs) may engage in long-term single-issue campaign coalitions, form only short-term event-based coalitions, provide occasional instrumental support, or reach near-permanent partnerships.[33] TANs often assist domestic activists by exchanging information on shared resistance,[34] lobbying international bodies,[35] working with intergovernmental institutions,[36] and offering monetary and tactical support.[37] TANs also hire international experts, organize boycotts of services or products, disrupt shareholder meetings,[38] present persuasive images to international audiences, and train affected communities on their national and international rights. In addition, TANs coordinate letter-writing campaigns, mobilize joint international actions,[39] target ethical investment firms, and subvert corporate advertising campaigns with their own anticorporate campaigns.[40] In building transnational coalitions, Sidney Tarrow argues that "mobilization on the ground was the necessary springboard of the campaign, but [transnational] coalition formation was a distinct process that gave it 'legs'" to reach international audiences and venues.[41] But TANs are not transnational movements; they are networks or long-term or short-term linkages of members, some of whom may be connected to a movement.

Transnational movements, as defined by Tarrow, are "mobilized groups recruiting across borders engaged in sustained contentious interaction with powerholders in which at least one state is either a target or a participant."[42] In an earlier work, Tarrow describes a transnational social movement as characterized by (1) transnational political opportunity, (2) greater access to transnational resources, (3) a state's weakened capacity to constrain local movements, and (4) future development of a "transnational civil society."[43] The transnational campaign of opposition could be considered a single campaign in a transnational anti-oil movement; however, only the domestic organizations Acción Ecológica in Quito and Frente de Defensa in Coca and Lago Agrio could be considered part of a transnational movement against oil injustice. The political opportunity and access to resources was available to some, though the Mindo contingent was focused primarily on local concerns and Esmeraldas and Lago Agrio were, more broadly speaking, waging only national campaigns. The unrestricted corporeal flow of human bodies would also be integral to the ideal of a transnational civil society—and as yet Southern civil society remains physically blocked at state borders by immigration policies, while the links between immigration advocates and transnational environmental campaigns are minimal if even existent.

Transnational advocacy networks do pressure corporations, raise awareness, and keep calls for change on the table. In the OCP case and against individual OCP companies, TANs pressed the consortium, the individual companies as well as the financiers, and stimulated Northern awareness of the case. After presenting at an oil company's shareholders meeting, one international advocate recalled the success of the meeting on behalf of Ecuadorian activists: "I was expecting the worst because a lot of people who go to shareholder meetings get booed out of there."[44] But after presenting on the financial impacts if the company continued with the OCP project, "I had people come up to me afterward and say, 'Oh, good points, good points.'"[45] According to another international advocate, "It's gotten to the point where you ask common people on the street [in Germany], you say 'WestLB,' and they say, 'Oh, that's the bank that's financing that really nasty oil pipeline in Ecuador.' That's the first thing that comes to mind."[46]

International NGOs were also critical to establishing allies within companies or banks in their home countries to gather information and to influence internal industry debates. "Part of the dialogue strategy is not just dialoguing with the top," noted one international activist. "But all the way. [We are] trying to dialogue with very different parts of the institution, also to create more tension within and to find allies, who can argue from within."[47] In other words, some NGOs try to find the corporate accountant, consultant, engineer, or environmentalist to pressure from within by keeping the issue on the table and having someone on the inside as moderator between their demands and corporate resistance. The strategy is supported by the literature, which indicates that there are "subcultures" within companies that shape a company's response or actions to environmental concerns and that those subcultures compete to have their strategies or solutions adopted.[48]

Affected residents in the Global South, however, cannot attend annual shareholder meetings, cannot generate public awareness in the North, and cannot infiltrate internal discussions in corporate headquarters without Northern allies. Even beyond discourse and in the more grounded realities of a domestic campaign, Southern groups rely on Northern ones for basic material assistance. Mindo-based Acción por la Vida, for example, expressed gratitude to Amazon Watch of California for providing "sleeping bags, mats, a digital video camera for the camp, tarps and a cash donation for provisions" and to Quito-based Acción Ecológica—which is funded by Northern grants and entities—for providing "logistical support and transportation to and from the area of the camp."[49] In Ecuador, international efforts ranged from material support (buying land and seeking financial aid) to advocacy support (pressuring oil and bank headquarters), and from an instrumental role (conducting interviews with the international media and launching an online listserv of OCP news) to a moral and morale-building one (on-site visits, off-site invitations, and steady communication).

From the transnational campaign of opposition, two critical functions emerged. One, transnational advocates or partners verified and marketed local claims, and two, they influenced the financing of future large-scale projects by prompting the realization of voluntary lending guidelines. Yet nested within or between the positive functions were crosscutting contradictions and unintended consequences.[50] The documented risks found in other North-South campaigns have included dependence, stratification, and co-optation,[51] misrepresentation and limited accountability,[52] identity conflicts,[53] disenfranchisement through loss of control and representation,[54] and change in community membership.[55] In Northern transnational movements between North America and Europe, hazards included increased policing or militarization,[56] and a degree of decentralization that led to incoherence and leadership by the most engaged who were actually few in number.[57] In this case, the costs of association were reinforced by the campaign of negotiation, and as a consequence included (1) emphasizing and confirming conservation and World Bank standards at the expense of local dignity-in-life claims, and (2) marginalizing national avenues and contacts, including the role of the state and domestic networking building.[58]

Building on the works of transnational researchers and theorists,[59] this section offers one overarching theme, or broad interpretation of events. In short, each positive and negative action culminated into the ongoing maintenance of Northern expertise, experts, and agendas. The disparities in need,[60] the inequities in accessing resources,[61] the selection of domestic contention and Northern mechanisms that sustain a Northern-centric capitalist worldview perpetuated an insipid environmental agenda and maintained unequal relationships rather than building egalitarian ones. The transnational campaigns hinged on the OCP pipeline project—as I have presented throughout this book—but the two domestic campaigns in Lago Agrio and Esmeraldas were not only about the pipeline. The pipeline project served as a domestic *opportunity*—especially for the greater Lago Agrio community—in another round of their "cycle of protest" against the state,[62] which excluded direct participation of the Northern advocates or organizations.

Again, and to reiterate, abbreviated campaigns when rushed, perhaps intentionally by state and oil decisions and production schedules, are unable to invest in hearing all the demands and requests of impacted communities and incorporating those demands and requests into a campaign or a larger and stronger transnational movement. "You define what you think is the best way for that campaign to work, and then you start telling the [local people], 'We think this is the best way to do it.' And a lot of times the agendas can get really mixed up," acknowledged one international advocate on the general weaknesses of North-South relations. "And [local people and] organizations aren't given space to be making decisions. . . . And respecting that space, it's something that's pretty hard to maintain."[63]

This North-South bind was well known and treated with trepidation by the Northern activists in the campaign of opposition, even though they were unable to resolve the dilemma. Summing up the sentiment of several Northern advocates, one acknowledged:

> I felt very nervous about [meeting with one of the companies] for two main reasons. One, because there is no consensus here [in Ecuador]. So if we tried to channel demands from Ecuador to [the North], it would basically mean that some groups' demands might be met, while others would be compromised. And I didn't feel prepared to make that decision for groups. I don't feel like that's my role. . . . I shouldn't have as strong a voice as Ecuadorian stakeholders, because it's really them that are affected on a day-to-day basis. And I wanted to be careful that my voice never became larger than theirs, and never deviated from what they were trying to say.[64]

Northern and Southern apprehension, the dominance and pervasiveness of a Northern worldview, persistent and interrelated inequities, and the environmental schism between the North and the South raise legitimate concerns for the viability of a transnational environmental justice campaign, let alone a transnational movement. For a global environmental justice and ecodemocracy movement to be launched and sustained, this study suggests that such a movement needs to be directed and managed by affected Southern communities and laborers, which have much more to gain than to lose by overhauling the global political economic system. A movement is also made of perceived peers, and in this case, the two largest communities in terms of numbers were not a connected part of the transnational campaigns. Again, Lago Agrio is unique. Lago Agrio's most established organization, Frente de Defensa, has, I would suggest, stronger international ties than national ones, though in this case the community's national demands removed them from establishing firm international ties. The insertion of Southern deliberation and Southern identification of unmet needs into transnational campaigns could perhaps reduce the inequities between local and global economic opportunities and political participation. It could also bridge the divide between local workers and communities that facilitate a global political economy and the natural environment, which is increasingly constructed as a global treasure or resource rather than a local home, setting, or location. But their inclusion is not necessarily theirs to determine: economic realities and state policies restrict access, or human flows, to Northern sites, forcing Northern NGOs who are attempting to resist such patterns to invite or to sponsor their Southern comrades. The global structure restricts the responses of the most impacted people who are resisting prolonged local and global injustices. So though this chapter is written to better understand the two transnational campaigns that consolidated around the Quito NGOs to negotiate and the Mindo grassroots ecologists to resist the pipeline project, it analyzes the absence of the two oil-important regions and the impacts their absence would have on the pipeline project.

Up One: Verifying and Marketing Local Claims

Since the late 1990s, documentaries and handheld videos by local and international activists in Ecuador have captured a disturbing image of industry practices and of the prolonged conflicts between the state, the oil industry, and affected residents.[65] Their images and sounds depict oil ponds, gas flares, sickened fish and cattle, Indigenous protestors, and children with rashes walking barefoot on oil-sprayed roads. In one documentary on EnCana and the OCP project, a campesina or rural woman was shown trying to enter a government office with an OCP executive inside. She was blocked by young guards, who looked on uncomfortably as she shouted at the closed door, "I've been left without water! Why are you hiding? Why doesn't he receive us? . . . You destroyed my farm, you ruined the fish farm of my children. You caused the suffering of my family."[66] Activists in film also attempt to link Northern consumption with Southern hardship: "I think about people in America saying, 'But it's my right to drive an SUV,'" states Julia Hill in *Amazon Oil Pipeline*. "What about the rights of the people here? What about the rights for them to be able to bear healthy children?"[67]

This is what transnational advocates do well: capture resident anger and injustice in photography and film; and then to generate Northern awareness and indignation, to change Northern consumption habits, and to pressure corporate headquarters, they make them available to international audiences on their websites, by direct presentations to shareholders, and at small screenings at independent theaters and university campuses. University libraries serve as an important warehouse for these films, while the website youtube .com spreads awareness by making amateur or lay footage easily available.

In addition to visual verification of environmental injustices, transnational advocates also provide expert authentication of domestic claims. In this case the environmental elite of Quito and Mindo gathered baseline data, conducted analyses, and determined potential impacts, while strengthening ties to Northern contacts. Their early efforts both support and counter findings that suggest expert knowledge flows from North to South.[68] Initial investigations arose within Ecuador by Ecuadorians and non-Ecuadorian residents with extensive Northern contacts and work-related experiences. To claim that knowledge still flows from the North to the South ignores the two decades of learning and collaborating within the transnational NGO community. Nevertheless, what could be claimed in this case is that knowledge was *forced* to flow from the North to South, and back to the North by Northern experts and institutions, though knowledge originated in the places of impact.

International knowledge brokers and observers were called in to legitimate and substantiate the claims of local experts. In particular, transnational opposition organizations from the United States, Germany, and Italy hired a former World Bank adviser to assess whether OCP's construction practices met World Bank environmental and social standards. According to the report, OCP procedures failed to meet World Bank standards.[69] Amazon Watch also hired a former representative of World Wildlife Fund to determine whether OCP met World Bank natural habitat and environmental assessment policies. The report provided seven objections, including that OCP's assessment was too narrow in time and space to provide an accurate impact assessment, that mitigation measures were inadequate, that the impacts of expansion plans in the Amazon to feed the pipeline were not analyzed, that there was no alternative comparison of the costs and/or benefits of not constructing the pipeline, and that there were insufficient community consultations.[70] Urgewald of Germany and Environmental Defense of the United States commissioned a paper on the project's financing.[71] And at the invitation of Acción Ecológica, a three-member international mission from Argentina, Costa Rica, and Spain also rejected the project after conducting preconstruction observations.[72]

Some international advocates knew both the power and influence of their access as well as the risks and limitations of "speaking for" affected residents. "I really didn't feel like I was in a position to speak on behalf of Ecuadorian people, and negotiate on behalf of Ecuadorian people," claimed one international advocate after meeting with an oil company's representatives. At this meeting, "in not so many words, they said, 'What do you want? What is it going to take for you to shut up?' Basically. And I told them, 'Listen, I'm not going to make a list of demands, because that's not my place, but you have to talk to Ecuadorians, and you have to talk to Ecuadorian groups to see what they want.'"[73]

While revealing the care and caution of international advocates when operating in Ecuador, this passage also discloses industrial and institutional strategies to establish North-to-North deliberations and expertise that some Northern NGOs are unable to resist. The establishment of OCP's conservation fund also demonstrated a Northern-bias given that most participating NGOs had strong ties to North America or Europe and that the fund was modeled on existing Northern agreements. Likewise, the lead financier Westdeutsche Landesbank (WestLB) commissioned U.S.–based Stone & Webster, Ecuador's Energy Ministry commissioned the Washington D.C.-based Smithsonian, and EnCana and OCP commissioned another outside consultant to reassess impact and OCP's original EIA.[74] The first two international assessments supported the pipeline's route and impact assessments, while the consultant's assessment was designed to identify how to bridge communications between OCP personnel and the activists and communities of the Mindo-Nambillo region.

These multiple and rival assessments made impotent the lay expertise of affected residents, while shifting the debate to experts at international sites. In this way, the scientific and lay contributions of domestic groups became triggers and vignettes for international reports that invigorated an international commitment to pressuring the pipeline project to meet impersonal Northern standards, rather than the more exacting Southern ones. And even though the initial domestic complaints were invaluable to drawing attention to the project, they rarely received the validation or authority as expert Southern NGOs, lay experts, or "specialized citizens."[75]

In addition to the visual, spoken, and written verification of domestic claims, transnational networks also marketed local assertions by importing Ecuadorian residents and NGOs to Northern sites to represent the environmental and/or the people's position on OCP. Access included local activists and NGO professionals traveling to North America and Europe to attend meetings, conferences, and demonstrations. Collaborative actions ranged from protests in front of the lead financier to meeting with the North-Rhine Westphalia parliament, to meeting in Washington D.C. with the World Bank and in New York with Standard & Poor's, a credit rating agency for investors.

For instance, after Moody's Investors Service, an insurance and credit rating agency, downgraded their evaluation of the OCP project, the campaign of opposition determined to focus their efforts there. But before a meeting in May 2003 with Moody's in New York, Moody's stopped rating OCP altogether for lack of transparency, according to one activist. "So I went to try and push a little on Standard and Poor's," acknowledged the activist in Quito. "We hoped that we could drill a hole there. But in fact we didn't succeed. . . . But it was very interesting because I think it's not usual that ecologists are meeting financiers to try to work on that level."[76]

Ecuadorians also traveled to Canada to raise awareness on EnCana Corporation's operations, to California to speak against California-based Occidental Petroleum Corporation, to Italy to generate support against the Italian oil company ENI-Agip and the Italian bank Banca Nazionale del Lavoro (BNL), and to Spain to lobby against the oil company Repsol-YPF and the Spanish banks Caja de Madrid and Banco Bilbao Vizcaya Argentaria. "It is our right to criticize nationally," claimed one Ecuadorian community leader. "But if there is not an outlet, we have to look elsewhere."[77] For domestic groups, such actions confirmed their local efforts, boosted their morale, expanded their strategies, and generated international and domestic recognition of their campaigns.

Over the course of three years, the transnational campaign of opposition verified and marketed domestic claims against the pipeline project in Ecuador, North America, and Europe. At times, the breadth and vitality of campaign efforts were inspirational for domestic stakeholders ignored or mocked by national leaders. Indeed, the community leaders and NGO directors in Ecuador were presented to international audiences and were able to express their fears, worries, and anger at international venues. Many were possibly under the impression that given how national and international decisions launched the pipeline project in the first place, perhaps international actions could block it as well.

Up Two: Targeting International Financing, Creating the Equator Principles

With the seven-member OCP consortium, there were no shareholder meetings, no international name recognition, no product, and no international office at which to launch a campaign. With these deficits, the campaign of negotiation targeted the World Bank and EnCana, the largest shareholder of the OCP consortium and also the oil company with a history of funding conservation projects. While the campaign of opposition also targeted the World Bank,[78] it focused primarily on the financiers and pressured the individual oil companies as a sidebar to the larger financing campaign.

To assess the strengths and limitations of the campaigns of opposition and negotiation, Emily McAteer and Simone Pulver's analysis of shareholder advocacy campaigns provides a useful tool. They identify three levels of goal achievement, which include generating internal corporate discussion on an issue, changing policy, and then changing practices in the field.[79] In application, both OCP campaigns realized each level of goal achievement—though with each step the achievement grew weaker.

Transnational pressure generated internal dialogue within the OCP consortium, the individual oil companies, the Italian and German financiers, as well as the World Bank (which is not directly affiliated with the pipeline project). Internal discussions have been acknowledged in interviews with environmental consultants within OCP, in OCP's media advertisements launched after Mindo's resistance campaign began, as well as in a letter to the editor written by EnCana's CEO challenging an earlier report on EnCana's operations in Ecuador.[80] The World Bank also corresponded with OCP on the activists' claims, and the additional assessments requested by oil and government bodies attest to NGO pressure. It is clear that the international entities involved in the pipeline's construction heard the complaints of Ecuadorian and Northern NGOs and activists in Quito and Mindo primarily.

In changing policy, the second step, the campaign of opposition proved most successful in influencing future banking policies, even though it was not able to stop the Ecuadorian project. First, and for a German audience, Rettet den Regenwald successfully linked Ecuador's pipeline to Germany by renaming OCP the "WestLB-Pipeline in Ecuador."[81] Then by using an image of oil damage in the Amazon and the natural beauty and threatened habitats of the Andes and by grounding their arguments in inadequate impact assessments and inconsistencies, a German-led coalition succeeded in pressuring WestLB to initiate the Equator Principles.[82]

The Equator Principles is a voluntary agreement among banks to finance only socially and environmentally responsible projects that is based on the guidelines of the World Bank and its private-sector investment division. Established in June 2003, before OCP's completion, the principles include concerns for natural habitat protection, indigenous populations, involuntary resettlement, and child and forced labor. As of late 2009, the principles had nearly seventy banking members.

Even though the principles' website fails to acknowledge the role of grassroots activists and their international allies,[83] early demonstrations against the OCP project in Ecuador launched international awareness campaigns that provided momentum for the banks to seek more stringent regulations of their projects. The principles are also only voluntary. Without independent monitoring and mandated targets, the principles are likely to resemble other global environmental mechanisms that fall far short of their goals, and far short of community demands, when large-scale projects are developed in the Global South. The principles are also not informed or monitored by affected laborers and communities. Corroborating this interpretation, Rainforest Action Network (RAN) claimed that the principles failed to "address the core issue: whether or not banks invest in projects that destroy endangered ecosystems and native communities."[84] Earlier in 2003, activist NGOs had presented the more stringent Collevecchio Declaration calling for private banks to commit to six principles: sustainability, do no harm, responsibility, accountability, transparency, and sustainable markets and governance.[85] However, these were not adopted in the Equator Principles.

Despite legitimate concerns for its effectiveness in reducing social and environmental injustices, the Equator Principles are an acknowledgment that banks share some role and responsibility in the social and environmental impacts of projects that they finance. The principles originating in Ecuadorian struggles are also a truly remarkable feat that should not be diminished by this chapter's critical analysis of Northern biases in transnational campaigns. The principles may also serve as a more formalized tool or guideline for banks and constructors to meet voluntary benchmarks, and perhaps more importantly, to which local and global inspectors may be able to hold them accountable. Overall, the Equator Principles were both a success as well as a weakness for the campaign of opposition. As noted in one press release, "The irony [is] that the Principles would still have allowed the banks to finance the infamous OCP oil pipeline."[86]

Expressing local defeat and international victory, one European activist claimed, "There is frustration that we could not build on this campaign, but on the other end from this experience we have a new campaign on private banks. This was a precedent case. It was not a loss."[87] Another lamented emphatically the limited role of Northern campaigns:

> We lost a very important battle. OCP is finished and WestLB is still in the boat. As a German NGO we lost this battle, because for us it's not only interesting the OCP, but also what WestLB is doing. But we are going to win the game, in a way, concerning the banks. But that's very bitter for the people in Ecuador that are affected by OCP. Because they have nothing, I mean, it's nothing for them that we will probably win the campaign in three to five to ten years. But it might help the next generation in Ecuador, in Venezuela, in Russia, wherever. . . . But as I said before, it's very bitter for the people living in the Amazon here, or living close to the OCP right-of-way. It doesn't help them.[88]

A third European campaigner also expressed how bitter affected communities must feel given the campaign's failure to actually stop the pipeline.

> I always find it bitter for a community, which has really been fighting for a long struggle because often with that project you can't stop it. If you come in too late for a project and the financing is already arranged and the whole project has achieved a certain amount of momentum. For people who were fighting very hard, often it doesn't lead to the project being stopped. But it does lead those players, like the banks, which have been involved in the OCP case, to really think twice about funding another project of this type.[89]

Several activists regretted the time it took to launch a campaign against the financiers. While citing discussions with other colleagues on the failure of the campaign to block the pipeline's financing, one activist said, "We stopped so many projects before with so much less effort. We can't believe that with this much effort, and with so many, you know, with so much controversy that we've raised, we haven't been able to stop this damn pipeline." The first-time advocate in Ecuador continued, "If they had been able to come together like they did before the loan agreement was signed with WestLB, I think they would have had it."[90]

If the analysis of transnational ties stops at the Equator Principles, international supporters appear to be assisting affected grassroots group and professional NGOs elsewhere in transporting local contention to international venues and in achieving another layer of enforcement and/or regulation on the practices of multinational corporations beyond this case via financing restrictions and regulations. Yet compliance reports on international principles or global codes of conduct are usually provided by the corporations themselves, and therefore may be less than straightforward. Additionally, "global" codes or principles are based on generic Northern standards rather than originating within a local context where the impacts are most felt.[91] If community projects or investments are also part of these requirements, rarely are their impacts monitored or assessed.[92] Oftentimes, when the NGO community achieves corporate policy changes, it is the NGO community that is left to assess the impacts of such changes, while still having only limited recourse to address them.

Transnational advocacy has additional limitations as well. On the one hand, the advocates held an accurate perception of local demands and needs as well as the weaknesses of international campaigns. They were well aware of the petroleum-generated injustices experienced in Ecuador. "There's no way this [OCP] project should go forward," noted one international advocate. "The consortium didn't comply with any of the basic things that they were supposed to—like consulting the people, dealing with the long-term impacts of the project in the Amazon."[93] Yet despite these understandings, for international audiences and institutions, Northern networks framed local conflict with tangible and marketable images of cloud forest and rainforest protection to create a persuasive and compelling environmental campaign against international targets for greater global gain rather than local goal achievements.[94]

In practice, changes with the OCP pipeline were also project specific. Improvements were not necessarily industry-wide or even realized in the oil fields where the oil companies operated. For example, additional environmental care and microvariants were taken in certain areas particularly in the Andes after domestic NGOs mobilized and established international support networks. But the extra care and species-protecting variants near the greater Mindo region were fractional concessions, identified in a very limited area and seen as a lackluster achievement by many. This care was also achieved along the line rather than at the input and output terminals where the oil industry held sway not only in decisions but in expanding their presence. Here we see how when goals shifted from dialogue to policy, and then from policy to practice in the field, the rigor and scale of attainment withered and narrowed with each step.

An international focus on the banks also became a hindrance for sustained ties with the Ecuadorian organizations fighting against a pattern of oil injustices in general, which were then exacerbated by the second cross-country pipeline. "In the second phase, we looked for legitimacy from Ecuador [to follow through on these other initiatives], and didn't get it once the pipeline was completed or near completion," recalled one international NGO. "In Ecuador, they were shifting toward not expanding the oil frontier, but that has nothing to do with the banks,"[95] which were the only ties that bound some of the European activists to Ecuador.

In this case, community demands were "enunciated," as pointed out by Maren Klawiter, by transnational actors, but what was "enacted" in the field was land conservation initiatives and minor habitat species protection, reflecting the concerns of international audiences and the Ecuadorian environmental elite.[96] The result is the step-by-step reduction of achievements. Despite good intentions, the achievements are often not on changing corporate practices, eradicating poverty, enacting global environmental justice, meeting a community's unmet needs, or alleviating the working conditions of the laboring poor. After the construction of OCP, those needs still included sustainable community projects, improved environmental health standards, increased community and worker safety, more economic opportunities, greater global inclusion, and expanded deliberative power in oil decisions and oil revenue spending. Inadvertently, international involvement weakened the multifaceted domestic concerns, inflated calls for conservation (which resonated with soft Northern interpretations of global problems), perpetuated a Northern worldview, and sustained a role for the international community in future oil-related projects.

Down One: Supporting Conservation and World Bank Standards

Linking economic security, community rights, and healthy ecosystems has remained particularly challenging for transnational advocacy networks. Global environmental justice—perhaps a bridging ideology between the South and the North—encompasses environmental, social, and economic equality; precaution; the absence of environmental risk (or at the minimum an equal distribution of environmental risk); revisiting the precautionary rule again; sustainable development; and the participation of diverse and affected communities in determining environmental, political, and economic initiatives, setting policies, and monitoring practices.[97] Yet Northern environmental justice activists have yet to establish strong ties with affected communities and the laboring poor of the South, while they have also failed to frame shared struggles that resonate in both places.[98] A strong transnational EJ movement is weakened by its very members, who are Southern and marginalized where they reside and who are primarily community members beleaguered by their own local struggles. When connections have been established, the North may be represented by professional advocacy groups that replace the more stringent Southern demands for Northern ones that are based on their limited experience with extreme global injustice.

For example, Seidman found that labor groups in South Africa may be better served by the state's ability to regulate corporations, rather than international corporate codes of conduct that are voluntary and guided by Northern pressure groups,[99] while Jay Mandle also found that the student-based antisweatshop movement emphasized the use of codes of conduct, rather than strengthening workers' rights and the International Labor Organization.[100] Environmental injustice has multiple meanings in the United States, and range from Native American land rights to campaigns against toxic toys. Add the community and working experiences of those in semiperipheral and peripheral nations, and the points of understanding fragment further. While depictions of the living and working conditions in the Global South may attract the attention and energy of student groups, the EJ movement in the United States is primarily not a movement of university students; and those who are fighting EJ struggles in the United States may have limited time and energy to devote to others' disputes. The increasingly more professional nature of environmental justice organizations in the United States has also led to a weakening of demands and a reduction in the movement's more radical foundation.[101] The movement is increasingly less about radically altering the relationship between the capitalist system, government agencies, and a town's, a nation's, or the world's population.

In Ecuador, the two transnational campaigns were essentially environmental campaigns, while the demands in the oil towns resembled more typical EJ struggles—yet each site fit within the country's oil-dependency structure. Mindo sought a rerouting; Quito sought a rerouting and then conservation and research funds from the industry; while the oil-important communities sought greater participation in the system, including local employment and deliberation, and also demanded compensation given the realized and potential impacts of the industry. As asserted by Robert Benford and supported by Faber,[102] environmental justice groups and their demands are increasingly bound within a capitalistic political system, in this case a global one, where community activists seek local, distributive change, rather than attempting to defeat a disabling and unequal system. International advocates reinforce this constraining arrangement, while also undermining the demands and bargaining power of the most affected in the South.

When leaders of oil-saturated communities in Ecuador and transnational advocates colluded, there was a tendency for the immediate, multifaceted, yet pragmatic claims of local leaders to become marginalized at international venues. Dignity-in-life claims appeared both too byzantine as well as too localized to garner sustained international attention. But the latter is a double bind. Dignity-in-life claims were too "local" in the sense that Northern audiences and entities were unable to relate for longer than a promotional minute, while such claims were also too painfully "global." That is to suggest, dignity-in-life claims originating in the oil towns of Esmeraldas and Lago Agrio were too interwoven with Northern privilege, luxuries, and lifestyles—a mingling so intimate, so personal, and so complex as to negate a discussion of it. This is not to say that international NGOs were indifferent or unaware; they were not. International advocacy worked against global injustices and spoke out on the interconnectedness between the North's lifestyles and luxuries and the South's poverty and hardships. But in a global, capitalist world system, they compartmentalized their own enunciations to suit the vanities and sensibilities of Northern institutions, Northern lenders, multinational corporations, and Northern audiences.

"One thing that struck me is that OCP is like a model case of everything that is going wrong about globalization, right now," declared one international activist.[103] "It's these international financial institutions that are writing the economic prescriptions for the country of Ecuador. This pipeline was mandated by the IMF that a second pipeline be built, that it be a privately run oil pipeline and they are demanding that 80 percent of the revenues from it go to paying down their external debt, which is owed to the IMF," vented another.[104] "Yeah, it has everything to do with these international institutions that have this kind of economic stranglehold on the country of Ecuador, and who are promoting these kinds of privatization and extractive resource policies that so clearly have failed all over the world."[105]

In a meeting—the 2nd International Workshop against OCP held in Lago Agrio in October 2003—they made it abundantly clear that they formed a campaign against the OCP project to support the affected communities and landowners along the entire right-of-way. At this roundtable, fourteen Ecuadorians and fourteen international representatives signed a declaration that identified human rights violations during OCP's construction, including the arrest of seventy-three people, an increase in the country's external debt, and the number of poor after thirty years of oil exploration as justification for reconsidering the project's proposed benefits. The declaration then presented nine demands, including that the consortium compensate people for damages to their private and collective properties, remediate environmental damages along the route, and complete its promises to communities and individuals. The document also requested that the Ecuadorian government protect the rights of the Indigenous communities in the Amazon and declare an oil moratorium—a request that had been demanded earlier in the year by Oilwatch International, Acción Ecológica, and Pachamama Alliance.[106]

Despites these articulations, the short-term campaign appeared disconnected from the global causes and local demands of affected residents, who were seeking the intangible, such as dignity, alongside the tangible, such as greater electrical supply. One example is particularly informative of the detachment between the anti-oil global narrative and the more sweeping local one. In 2004, I had the opportunity to accompany a community leader from the Amazon to an ethical investors' meeting in the North. The grassroots leader was invited by a Northern advocate, whose position was to demand that one particular oil company open communication channels with affected residents and address the social and environmental impacts of its operations in Ecuador. Yet the community leader's demands were anchored in the community's needs, including oil employment, local purchasing,[107] paved roads, and public transportation.

In a follow-up interview, the grassroots leader said that community members also advocated for the local production of worker uniforms, rather than the importation of such basic supplies, and added that clean water, clean air, better environmental protection, and safeguards for a healthy environment were just as important to this community as they were to Northern support groups. But when forced to prioritize community need, however, he pressed for economic justice and a community-driven development path.

This example is also illustrative of the "unpredictable" nature of affected residents. Affected communities will talk with transnational advocates, and researchers, about the contaminated environment and the poor health of their children, their community, and their domestic animals. But when given an opportunity to present demands, which they think may be realized by a corporate audience, they will, as demonstrated in this case, prioritize the economic need of the subaltern.

This is the plight of the Southern poor: not expecting egalitarian treatment, they are forced to rank their basic and unmet needs, including economic security against human, environmental, and community rights. Worldwide, it is known that a paved road is much easier and cheaper to realize than universal education, equal representation, just economies, and healthy environments, so requests for paved roads float to the top by the laboring poor themselves. Yet listening to the communities of Esmeraldas and Lago Agrio would also indicate that a paved road is not just concrete or asphalt. A paved road may be an immediate and visible symbol of a community's realized dignity and esteem—realized through hard-fought cycles of resistance to the status quo.

The dignity-in-life claims voiced by the two oil-impacted communities—employment, community-determined concessions, just wages, economic compensation, paved roads, healthy environments, a monitoring role, locally controlled rents or royalties, and global and local mechanisms to guarantee community input on oil decisions—surpassed international standards.[108] Nevertheless, the two Northern campaigns consolidated around two leading themes: conservation, which was achieved through the ecofund and land purchases in Mindo, and adherence to Northern or World Bank standards for the OCP project and for future international financing agreements, both of which represented a lateral shift rather than a progressive one directed by the South.

That both transnational coalitions targeted the World Bank for greater input in the OCP project further endorsed the bank's standards as acceptable ones even though individual advocates in the campaign of opposition were against the bank's policies and practices. "We know that World Bank environmental guidelines are minimal and weak, and so to even meet those is definitely not acceptable," maintained one international activist.[109]

Calling OCP a "disastrous project" that "should not be built," the Northern campaigner also noted that the organization was "respecting the rights of these communities to decide and to demand what it is that they feel that they want. . . . But at the same time doing work to support communities like Mindo, who seem to be pushing toward a change in the route as opposed to stopping the whole pipeline."[110]

Several international activists also identified joining the campaign of opposition as a way to avert a disaster not only with regard to the pipeline's construction but how it will enable oil exploration further in the Amazon even if local communities were not really pressing claims on future impacts. According to one,

> I think it's been proven from time and time again these companies are allowed maximum privilege and minimal accountability. And we really could see that was building up, you know, the big disaster that was building. The long-term impacts, the route of the pipeline, the companies involved, some of the same usual suspects that have horrible environmental and human rights track records in other countries. All these forces were combining, plus pressure from financial institutions, like IMF, and the World Bank, and plus the government, who thinks that oil is going to be the panacea for this country. All these things were building to what we could really see was going to be a giant disaster.[111]

Over and over again, the Northern advocates were pointing to what Faber has written as the "dissonance between the promises" and "the actual results of neoliberal policies" that is creating a "deep crisis of legitimacy" for international institutions including the World Bank.[112] To be certain, the bank has installed itself as arbitrator of world standards, especially when Northern entities are involved in the Global South. To many scholars, activists, and scholar-activists, World Bank standards favor and enable extractive economies, fail to address the social and economic inequalities realized locally through the processing of a region's natural and national resources, perpetuate global inequalities, and establish low thresholds for affected communities and ecosystems.[113] Indeed, World Bank standards are especially feeble when compared to the demands for the holistic, global, and deliberative ecodemocracy arising in the oil centers.

It would appear that basing the site-specific OCP practices and the more universal Equator Principles on World Bank standards only represented the deepening institutionalization of Northern values rather than the inclusion of more comprehensive local concerns of affected communities. Others argue this point much more strongly. Michael Goldman cautions that international regulatory regimes exhibit a hegemonic practice of "green neoliberalism,"[114] while Vandana Shiva presents the global environment as a persistent system of apartheid, in which the South becomes increasingly governed by nondemocratic international bodies.[115] That it was domestic environmental NGOs in the campaign of negotiation and international advocates in the campaign of opposition that initially drew the World Bank into the OCP debate, which strengthened the bank's international role as standard-bearer, is particularly incongruent, especially when given the robust calls for greater global justice and participation emanating from within the oil towns. While adherence to bank standards came to dominate OCP claims and the counterclaims of the environmental elite and their international supporters, they were actually punitive thresholds for affected communities and ecosystems.

During the OCP campaign, early calls for a monitoring role by affected communities, Quito-based conservation NGOs, and international supporters were another telling example of how significant local requests became obstructed unintentionally by Northern discussions. It was not that demands for independent, NGO, or community-based monitors became lost in the litany of complaints from multiple quarters, it was that the request was discarded once national and international NGOs sat down with the oil consortium, the World Bank, and the European financiers.

In Italy, for example, nine NGOs organized the "Italian Campaign against the OCP," which targeted the Italian partners of OCP, including the oil company ENI-Agip and the banks Banca Nazionale del Lavoro (BNL), Unicredito, and Banca Intesa. The campaign included letter writing, press conferences, demonstrations outside the banks, and meetings with the president of BNL, the largest financer in Italy.[116] This campaign against the Italian financiers was also supported by four bank-worker unions—Italian General Confederation of Labor (CGIL), Italian Confederation of Workers' Trade Union, (CISL), Italian Workers Union (UIL), and Autonomous Federation of Italian Bank Workers (FABI). They sought greater environmental and social responsibility by bank management and included independent monitoring as a requisite to financing. The request for a monitoring panel had originally been proposed in Robert Goodland's 2002 report to WestLB. The Italian campaign also presented a similar request to BNL, calling for a panel to monitor "environmental damages, human rights violations, the use of royalties made by the Ecuadorian government and the strategic environmental impact assessments on the whole Ecuadorian Amazon."[117] Such a panel would probably have reduced the harmful impacts of oil operations in Ecuador. But it was never realized.

"We made the request to the [BNL] bank to monitor the pipeline, but the request collapsed because we were the only national campaign that asked for it. The bank president promised to follow through on it, but he did not," claimed one advocate.[118] After working on the OCP campaign in Italy for sixteen months, "we closed the OCP campaign when OCP construction was complete and its use started. BNL was only a small contributor to the financing, so without all the banks involved we couldn't only hold them to monitoring the pipeline. . . . In Ecuador and among the INGOs there was no effort to make it [monitoring] a bigger demand."[119] The call for monitoring was made along the route, but linking the particular communities to the INGOs in the Italian contingent was lacking.

Another international activist interpreted a future role in monitoring, not through on-site inspections but through newsworthy events or disasters. "Part of our strategy is to make these kinds of experiences as painful as possible, and as publicly painful as possible for those banks," claimed the advocate. "So, I'm quite serious when I say to WestLB: look, loan repayment is going to take sixteen years, we are going to keep monitoring this project for the next sixteen years. Everything that goes wrong about it, your name is going to be in the papers, time and time and time again."[120] These are the crucial contributions of transnational campaigns to keep international bodies guarded and working to minimize negative impacts, but a monitoring role guaranteed for affected community members is not consistently and systematically commanded and rarely is it realized.

At this time, the World Bank also entered discussions on how to better monitor extractive projects in the Global South. In 2003, the Extractive Industries Review was conducted to assess the impacts of the bank's policies of financing extractive industries in developing nations and to offer recommendations for the bank to improve the conditions of people and ecosystems in the impacted regions. In response, the World Bank wrote, "We will establish independent monitoring mechanisms in our largest projects, and encourage the development of capacity in communities to monitor projects that affect them."[121]

That a review was commissioned and that the World Bank responded to it are indicative of the strengths of transnational networks that have confronted the World Bank and the IMF repeatedly on their policies and projects. It was not the laudable challenges against OCP that launched the Extractive Industries Review. It was, however, the hundreds of confrontations worldwide between affected communities, mobilized networks, and extractive industries that finally drove this introspection.

Whether this is a creditable achievement remains to be seen. There were too many loopholes in the summary and too long a history of disempowered people and sullied ecosystems for affected communities to become too optimistic. Independent inspections, for example, may just increase the number of Northern consultants rather than build and enable community-led monitoring teams of the South in the South. In the executive summary, the word "encourage" also avoids a deadline for achievement. "When requested" and "developing-country capacity" may actually shift responsibility onto the Southern states to govern or monitor international decisions and actions. Designations, such as "for significant projects" and "our largest projects," may limit applicability, while the words "first step" and "we strongly support the principle" may actually limit significant changes. Indeed, the alteration of World Bank policies may be a minute modification relative to the tremendous need for change in the relationship and power differentials between the South and the North.

Communities and NGOs had several avenues to pursue a guaranteed role in the monitoring of OCP and future projects in the Ecuadorian Amazon or anywhere oil is processed. However, a monitoring role was not guaranteed in the Equator Principles, nor was it achieved in the ecofund talks, nor was it mandated by the World Bank in this case, nor was it broached by Ecuador's government officials. In this, the above cases and examples share one thing in common: the marginalization of affected communities in the Global South to realize and participate in local- and national-level monitoring systems on corporate and state practices.

With the OCP project, transnational advocates slipped into a Northern-biased entrapment. The campaign of negotiation as noted earlier prioritized conservation and succeeded in garnering research and project funds. In contrast, the campaign of opposition endorsed in principle permanent community participation, permanent community monitoring, state-backed environmental health regulations, and more just national-level oil redistribution schemes. Yet, in practice, they reaffirmed their position in influencing national outcomes and reaffirmed a Northern bias for Northern standards (backed by the efforts of the conservation groups), while failing to correct South-North imbalances and failing to achieve greater Southern empowerment of community and state leaders.

Down Two: Marginalizing State Function and Domestic Networks

In addition, a Northern slant also strengthened global perceptions or stereotypes of ineffective states, while a Northern presence weakened domestic networking building. These two points may augur poorly for Southern societies seeking a permanent role in debating and influencing the economic and political outcomes and operations of extractive industries, as both may be vital sources of strength for empowering Southern places to seek global restitution and an equal voice in global decisions, policies, and practices. The contestation of international institutions served as a prominent reminder that state agencies were, at times, on the sidelines of their own oil-driven economy and at other times more aligned with industry than civilian interests. This chapter is not suggesting that the oil-industrial core is state driven.[122] It is not necessarily. The obscure industry is a dominant global actor, but in specific sites at specific times the state shifts from being an appendage to actually governing site-specific oil entities for the betterment or detriment of citizens and ecosystems. Certainly, professional NGOs and organized civil society are many paces removed from the oil complex and, more frequently than not, a few steps beneath the state.

Secondly, the presence of international allies oriented domestic groups Northward, rather than toward building stronger local and national ties. These outward functions, however, may be only short-term expressions realized at the height of anti-OCP sentiment. It is possible, though not determined, that once international focus shifted off Ecuador and the pipeline project, domestic stakeholders would turn within to establish denser local and national ties in order to seek consistent attention and permanent redress among the deeper and more comprehensive complaints. This analysis is examining a project-specific campaign, which for the oil-important communities was just one in a long series of oil struggles, but which for the conservation groups and grassroots ecologists was a first experience mobilizing in response to oil activities.

This transnational analysis reminds us that state leaders and state agencies remain critical to the development and empowerment of the Global South. At times, however, this statement needs repeating especially when the strengths of transnational advocacy networks are overemphasized. In many developing nations, oil is a nationally owned resource, and not only do states force the flow of oil, elected officials also champion impacted communities. At this fulcrum between growing numbers of affected people and disgruntled organizations on one side and the oil operators and their international boosters who are few in number on the other side, sits the state and elected and unelected government officials. For the most part, the nation-state remains the final protector and guarantor of citizen rights, labor rights, human rights, and environmental rights within their boundaries. To meet this obligation, community-based activism, rather than professional international networks, not only pushes state agencies to respond, a mobilized civil society serves as a constant monitor that state regulations are being advanced, upheld, and enforced.[123]

In addition, petrostates in particular are also becoming more experienced in negotiating contracts with the industry.[124] Optimistically, improved state-level negotiating skills may increase oil rents, which, if coupled with public reports on oil revenues and citizen participation, may endorse a social justice development path that emphasizes sound national attention on equal education, improved health attainment, sustainable economic security, and healthy ecosystems, communities, and workplaces. As a reminder to corporate-led neoliberal advocates who suggest that an economic world order operates beyond state borders: It is the Ecuadorian state that calls for bids and leases oil production rights. It was the Ecuadorian state that in 2006 evicted California-based Occidental Petroleum for irregularities of operations and sales.[125] And it was the Ecuadorian state within the past decade that began courting Chinese investment.

In several studies, the state has been found to buffer communities from the most egregious corporate actions—though not yet in Ecuador.[126] On Indigenous participation in environmental management decisions and activities, for example, researchers found that Australian laws in 1989 and 1996 increased the bargaining power of Indigenous communities and enabled Indigenous communities to offer suggestions and to participate in joint decisions with industry operating in their territories.[127] When transnational activism failed to support workers in American companies during South Africa's apartheid, Seidman argues that one solution would have been for local activists to influence and enforce state laws and to strengthen the regulatory and monitoring capacity of developing nations.[128] In Vietnam, Dara O'Rourke finds that communities influenced a polluting entity directly or indirectly by first pressuring the state to intercede.[129] Fred Buttel has also argued that environmental activism directs state reform better than state regulation alone, which remains critical.[130] Martin Janicke finds that the state remains crucial in curbing the nonlocal interests of multinationals,[131] and in Latin America, David Kaimowitz also finds that environmental protection is successful only when endorsed and legitimized by the state.[132] Finally, Smith argues that social change activists should focus on the state in part because influencing the state has been one of the most successful achievements of the corporate-led neoliberal globalization network.[133] It has been argued that state leaders adopted corporate-led neoliberal policies because they were not being pressured by democracy-supporting advocates or networks to do otherwise.[134] To be certain, several nonlocal entities would benefit from a weak rather than a strong state in national and international negotiations. The World Bank, for example, would stand to lose its influence over "development" schemes in Southern nations if states and affected communities were negotiating with the private sector and international institutions as equal stakeholders collaborating on an alternative development model.

However, Northern NGOs with no direct leverage over Southern states oftentimes ignore and are ignored by the state. In Ecuador to be sure, international NGOs were on the margins of state politics. The oil-important Ecuadorian communities knew it; and the state certainly knew it. Recall how then-president Gustavo Noboa ridiculed members of Greenpeace Germany as "sunburned and well-fed,"[135] and the activist Julia Hill of California as the "old cockatoo who climbs trees."[136] He was mocking the international activists for a nationalistic audience. It was also the environmental elite groups in Quito and Mindo with no leverage on the state or the sites of oil production or shipping that sought and received international attention.

The Ecuadorian president's banter with international environmentalists was as playful as he got during his tenure during OCP's construction. In the Amazon, he and other state leaders were known to use force to drive the oil process. In the case of OCP, demonstrations, arrests, tear gas, and a state of emergency situation in the Amazon supports empirically Shiva's assessment that globalization may increase a state's policing role of its citizens to protect the interests of multinationals.[137] Even though the Ecuadorian government had used heavy-handed measures to ensure the flow of oil exports, it never—at least to my knowledge—publicly jeered labor and community calls from the oil hubs. The globally important oil town of Lago Agrio and port town of Esmeraldas, which targeted the state for reparation and a change in policies and practices, garnered the full attention of the state each time they mobilized—due to their critical locations in the oil process.

In addition and on environmental issues alone, a domestic orientation toward international bodies may actually harm long-term environmental and conservation goals as current agreements have been struck with impermanent Northern entities. The constant reconfigurations of oil operators in the Amazon, from North America, Latin America, Europe, and Asia, mean less Northern influence on non-Northern operators. The state and the state's legal system are much more permanent fixtures in oil debates and environmental governance. Indeed, state-supported biodiversity protection measures may actually have more durable impact than short-term ecological compensation packages and/or environmental protection agreements from a few receptive, but impermanent, multinationals and financiers.

In the revised 1998 constitution, the government actually supported affected communities by guaranteeing—at least in name—public consultations on oil projects.[138] In particular, article 88 obliged the state and oil companies to consult with communities if a project potentially threatened the environment or the local population.[139] Though in practice these consultations appeared designed to pacify the public with oil presentations rather than community deliberation, in attitude and in inspiration these state-mandated public meetings promoted affected communities and local governments to demand greater access, greater accountability, and greater transparency from both the state and the multinationals.

Indeed, guaranteed public consultations on oil projects would be tested for the first time on a national scale with the construction of OCP. In practice, article 88's national debut resembled an obligatory checklist of multinational outreach. Moreover, the potency of this guarantee would be undermined by the state itself, when Ecuador's National Congress passed a new framework for the "modernization" of the country, known as the Trole II law. Enacted before the construction of OCP, this law took the capacity and competency of reviewing and accepting environmental impact of investment activities from the Environment Ministry and moved it to the Ministry of Energy and Mines.[140] The ambiguity with respect to the actual environmental authority in the country generated conflicts and distrust between environmental departments and undermined environmental controls.[141] A hierarchy existed, such that the environmental subsection within the Ministry of Energy and Mines often superseded the Environment Ministry itself. Though hydrocarbon laws oftentimes override environmental ones worldwide, oil-community meetings may in the future inspire more community pressure on the state (any and all states) and state-owned companies.

It is reasonable that international NGOs and Northern entities fail to work closely with affected residents and state agencies because both are so baffling to the Northern outsider. In the South, they may say one thing, and then they do another. But are they really that puzzling? Or is it that they cannot afford the luxury of straight, singular goals and objectives. Their primary goal—shared by both state leaders and residents of the Global South—is most possibly an end to South-North and East-West inequities in their social, economic, environmental, and political realities. The goal is not—and their achievement of it will not be—a linear process easily written down in a boardroom or government office.

But until this is achieved, Northern entities should expect residents of the South to say that they want a toxin-free environment on Monday, paved roads and electricity on Tuesday, twelve years of free education on Wednesday, and the right to vote on global decisions on Thursday. Given the perceived political and economic arrogance of Northern entities and consumption patterns of Northern lifestyles—on the backs of Southern laborers, communities, and ecosystems—it should be a Southern right to be "unpredictable" at least until their securities and dignities meet those of the North.

A second weakness of international collaboration was the unintended diminishing of domestic ties. Even though grassroots groups have been found to build important lateral networks, while simultaneously establishing or maintaining global-local linkages,[142] this case analysis indicates that local-to-global linkages may moderate efforts to establish and maintain domestic connections at least in the initial mobilization efforts and during the height of conflict. Coalitions risked not only consolidating rather than diversifying organizational makeup,[143] their presence may have discouraged local and national network building. For example, at the height of opposition, Mindo's grassroots ecologists rejected the professional Quito-based NGOs, while also rejecting local residents, the town council, and landowners along the right-of-way—each of whom shared common interests. In addition, the conservation NGOs that negotiated environmental funds directly with OCP excluded grassroots groups and affected residents from participating in such negotiations. It could be argued that had the material and moral support of international collaborators not been available, the Ecuadorian environmental blocs would have sought greater ties with each other, and perhaps with the more oil-important communities and organizations.

In short, domestic NGOs and community groups that formed international ties achieved global gains from domestic hardships, which may be particular to challenging projects of short duration and networking with newly formed groups and contacts. A campaign of longer duration may first initiate environmental considerations in order to then incorporate dignity-in-life claims later on, though at least one evaluation of the institutionalization of environmental action supports the finding of environmental dominance, regardless of campaign duration.[144] Likewise, Southern groups with an established agenda before international assistance may reassert greater control over their campaigns than groups that have recently formed, in the case of Mindo, or are taking on a new issue, in the case of Quito. For the German and Italian finance campaigns, this campaign was the first for them in Ecuador as well.

As for the oil towns, they may have deemed international advocates as temporary interlopers, with whom collaboration endangered their long-standing contention with the state for greater participatory spaces and greater economic redistribution. Thirty years of oil experience may have made them skeptical of the impact of international advocacy, even though they would have been aware of the significant lawsuit against Texaco waged by a powerful South-North coalition and of the tremendous capacity of Indigenous organizations and communities in part due to the assistance of Northern networks.

Finally, two important global achievements were made, and should not be diminished as both originated in Ecuador through the initial efforts of Ecuadorians. The Equator Principles is a significant international tool or standard that could be used by international NGOs to pressure lending institutions to meet their own voluntary requirements worldwide. Yet due to the degree of "professionalism" that Northern entities require in environmental governance deliberations, the most immediate beneficiaries of the Equator Principles may be the Northern NGOs, which may have created an advisory or monitoring role for themselves in the financial sector on future projects in other developing nations.

Additionally, pressure on the European banks introduced European activists to the banks, and vice versa. According to one European activist, the OCP case is still a reference case in Italy. The banks remember the campaign. The OCP campaign was also the first time to meet with the banks, and the first time for these groups to work together.[145]

Another European activist concurred.

> For two and a half years they [WestLB] refused to talk with us. Not only with our NGO, but with all the NGOs that are involved with the campaign in Germany. They refused it. . . . And ten days ago [October 2003], there was a big One World conference in Germany. . . . And the motto was 'Alternative World Economies Is Possible.' Something like that. There, for the first time, [was] a WestLB manager. . . . And we had a chance to ask questions and to give our comments and so it was the first time that they really started a dialogue with civil society, and with politicians and affected people, OCP-affected people [who were in attendance].[146]

Still another European activist noted the importance of their campaign on other banks. "People from other large private banks in Germany have told me repeatedly, like from the environmental departments, they've said, 'You know, when bad projects come up now in our bank and I want to make sure that our bank doesn't fund them, all I have to do is say, 'You know this could get us in the shoes of the WestLB's project. Look what happened to them with OCP,'" cited the activist. "So I recognized the strategic importance of the campaign."[147]

For some of the domestic NGOs and community groups that aligned with international partners, and for the communities and ecosystems for which they fought, the gains were tempered by the losses. Mindo's grassroots groups received land for conservation, achieved special environmental treatment and conservation in the region designated important to them, realized a tourism boom, and is perhaps becoming home to the nation's first environmental generation. Quito's professional organizations negotiated a multimillion-dollar conservation fund for the nation, polished their boardroom negotiating skills, and are poised to become consultants for future NGO-corporate negotiations. Both sides presented their environmental agendas on international stages and were heard by members of the World Bank and German parliamentarians as well as additional points of influence in the United States, Spain, and Italy. The pipeline was built, however, along its original route, and its completion is driving oil expansion across the Amazon. Likewise, Ecuador remains a marginalized voice in global oil politics even though oil exports steer its economy, shape its politics, impact its people, and alter its ecosystems.

OIL IMPACT AND ADVOCACY FLOW INVERSIONS

This comparative case study also indicates how the spatial and temporal locations along oil's extract-to-export chain give rise to discrete exposures, process-specific injustices, and varied conflicts.[148] The place-bounded distinctions, as identified in the previous four chapters, also influence network formation, points of leverage, and target selections (the state, the oil industry, and/or international bodies). By charting the material flow of oil and the nonmaterial flow of environmental advocacy and deliberations in Ecuador, this comparison advances the "environmental flow" perspective of Arthur Mol and others,[149] while maintaining a lens on the state,[150] and an awareness of the extreme differences in global influence.[151]

By overlaying oil flows with issue flows during the construction of this highly contested project, I found, unexpectedly perhaps, that place-based oil conflicts may vary inversely in their integration within the global supply chain and within global networks. Lago Agrio and Esmeraldas, which were linked to global oil markets and of critical importance to Ecuador's production and exportation of oil, were locally bounded and least incorporated in transnational networks at the time of OCP's construction. In contrast, the environmental communities of Quito and Mindo, which were of nominal value to the production and transportation of oil and which were removed from oil-related environmental and health burden, established denser international ties and experienced the scaling up of their conservation and environmental concerns from the local to the international. The links between impact and resistance are upturned in some cases if you had presumed that the places of most oil impact would experience the greatest degree of global solidarity and resistance.

It is important to note—as I have done throughout—that the Amazon region had generated tremendous Northern support, until it was competing with the environmental elite groups in Quito and Mindo.[152] When communities outside of the Amazon are inserted into the analysis as they are in a study of the country's second cross-country pipeline, Lago Agrio's state-targeted demands earned less direct Northern support than the Quito- and Mindo-based groups.

In this case, the disparities between bottom-up marketing and top-down selection processes across nations, as depicted by Clifford Bob,[153] are also experienced within a single nation and between campaigns confronting the same large-scale project. According to one campaign organizer in North America, "There is a lot of outrage about the project all along the pipeline route. . . . But the Mindo people seemed to be the only ones that did not have a specific demand. Their demands were sort of moral or environmental, and not that they get better roads or that they get something from the company."[154] This clarification demonstrates both the Northern selection process as well as the domestic marketing efforts. With a decade of experience in Ecuador, the international advocate continued, "It seemed like the strongest, [most] determined and focused concern and resistance to the pipeline was coming from Mindo."[155]

Another international advocate acknowledged a similar commitment by Mindo's tight activist community: "There were six or seven people sitting in front of me, and they all said, 'I swear to you, I would never ever give up the fight for some millions.' . . . They all said, 'They can give us $100 million, we'll never, never in our lives accept it for the price of stopping our protest or our campaign against OCP.'"[156] This intensity sustained international attention on Ecuador as well. To be sure, international advocates, who frequently receive "urgent calls from different places all over the world," have to determine the ones that are genuinely committed to what could be a prolonged campaign.[157] "It was really good, a good experience for me," noted one international activist, "because I was a little bit afraid" that the degree of local perseverance was lacking. In explanation, the activist continued, "Most of the people are very poor, that are fighting against OCP in Mindo. Not poor-poor, they are not starving of hunger, but they are not rich people."[158] Yet poverty and commitment are relative variables. The two poorest communities in terms of greater need and fewer social services, which had also demonstrated more than a decade of experiencing and resisting the oil industry, were no longer assessed as committed once they reached concessions or agreements with the state and/ or OCP consortium.

Put another way, this analysis suggests that the demands of the environmental groups were limited, focusing on conservation and rerouting alone, yet widespread, flowing to the World Bank, the international financiers, as well as the headquarters of the oil companies. In contrast, the demands of the oil towns were extensive, yet abbreviated, flowing between the communities and the national government primarily and between the communities and the OCP oil companies secondarily. And even though the oil-impacted communities never entered into sustained national or international networks—they were not sought by, nor did they seek dense ties to, transnational actors—it was their images, experiences, and histories that were utilized in international campaigns. Yet their realities were transported to serve as a backdrop for the pristine Andean cloud forest.

By adopting an environmental flow perspective, this analysis identified how issues became simpler when complex, on-the-ground demands shifted in scale from local campaigns to global ones. But the simplification process was not a straightforward one either. The tactics of the two oil-important cases, for instance, were *more* radical in confronting global discriminatory practices than the actions of international advocates. They blocked roads, shut down airports and oil facilities, and provoked a state of emergency. Yet their calls for immediate concessions, electricity, roads, and sewage systems, were more pragmatic in the short term than the anti-oil, antiglobalization rhetoric of some nonlocal actors. To be clear, the antiglobalization narrative is based on a commitment to "cooperation and inclusion rather than economic competition," though this distinction risks being overlooked,[159] and is oftentimes difficult to achieve even within antineoliberal campaigns.

In the long term, and despite, *or due to*, their limited international ties, the oil communities sought a much more progressive standard of economic justice and poverty reduction by incorporating people-centered deliberations in oil revenue spending and oil decision making.[160] In brief, the oil-important communities with least international connections were more radical in action, more practical in short-term concessions, yet more revolutionary in the long-term goal of establishing an equal and voting voice on national and global decisions that impact their communities than the grassroots ecologists and professional environmentalists and their international supporters.

In this case, international NGOs limited their support of community-demanded democracy when it also meant including them in oil negotiations and/or targeting the state for environmental and global justice. In general, these findings speak to other assessments of how labor in a global context may lead to a democratic movement beyond the scope of the prodemocracy elite class, rather than a race to the bottom in labor wages and conditions.[161] Indeed, dependence on international agendas may further undermine challenges against global economic inequalities and injustices that are most compelling to local communities, which suggests that in some cases a lack of international resonance may not be entirely a negative attribute for affected groups of the Southern subaltern class.

International Symbols and Icons: Crossing Your Fingers for a Spill

In a competitive global environment with more conflicts than advocacy groups, Southern activists and organizations are forced to sell themselves and alter their collective presentation to appeal to Northern advocates.[162] When transported or articulated by international supporters, their grounded and dynamic dignity-in-life claims, which integrate healthy ecosystems with improved infrastructure, community and human rights with global participation, and social concerns with economic ones, are compressed into provocative images alongside contemporary illustrations. "As you know, the media always needs something dramatic to happen," observed one international advocate. "And so it's terrible that you are crossing your fingers for an oil spill."[163] Said seven years before the BP disaster in the Gulf of Mexico, this sentiment acknowledges that ecological disasters launch national, and perhaps international, discussions on oil regulation, oversight, dependency, and projects.

During the time of OCP, global flashpoints included environmental degradation, human rights abuses, and Indigenous injustices.[164] In the absence of the latter one with regards to OCP, transnational advocates touched upon human rights abuses especially in 2001 and 2002, but emphasized environmental concerns over the course of the pipeline's construction. As noted earlier and not to downplay what transpired in Ecuador, human rights violations did occur and areas were militarized. Along the route, more than sixty people were detained for challenging the pipeline project. The majority were detained for one day though one was detained for approximately six weeks.[165] Though the majority of conflicts, arrests, and detentions occurred in or near Lago Agrio in Sucumbios Province, twenty-eight people were also detained in Mindo and eight were detained in Quito. In Sucumbios Province, private landowners and community activists were beaten by the military and national police, exposed to tear gas, arrested, and detained.[166] Frequently, landowners in Sucumbios Province were mobilizing not to block the project permanently, but for "better indemnities and more respect to their properties and rights."[167] For example, one sixty-year-old landowner was held for more than a month for allegedly assaulting a police officer who was on his land. He denied the allegations, but while he was in jail, the pipeline was laid on his property.[168] In another landowner dispute that was captured on film, one woman said, "The OCP came and asked us permission [to build on our land], but offered us a very low price. And because I wouldn't let them pass, they beat me, they arrested me, and brought me to jail in Lago Agrio." In the documentary, the producer asks, "Who beat you?" "The military and police, who were guarding the company," replied the landowner, who was also unable to stop the pipeline's construction on her land.[169]

But given the gravity of human rights abuses worldwide relative to the Ecuadorian cases,[170] the human rights angle failed to generate sustained concern. In a last-minute attempt to raise human rights considerations, twelve NGOs, including six from Canada, sent a letter to Canadian-based EnCana, the largest owner of OCP. In the letter, they wrote that "OCP has employed Ecuadorian National Police during the construction of the pipeline who have subjected landowners and those opposed to the pipeline to intimidation, harassment, assault, and illegal imprisonment."[171] The letter then identified one reason why charges of human rights violations failed to gain traction. "Neither EnCana nor the OCP has taken these allegations of human rights violations seriously."[172] Such a statement nearly concedes that the network of opposition was unable to make human rights violations the key point of contestation.

Given the unsavory distinction of human rights abuses where oil is found, oil companies in Ecuador may have been fairly confident that a tabulation of such abuses would have ranked the OCP pipeline quite low on a scale among industrial practices. At one shareholders' meeting, for example, when asked if the company "would be willing to arrange for a third party investigation into human rights violations, accusations of human rights violations against OCP," a spokesperson for the company "said that in a country like Ecuador, Ecuador is a democracy, and so in a democracy you don't have problems of human rights violations," which muted further discussion.[173] Certainly, Northern oil companies have a vested interest in discussing environmental protections rather than human rights violations, but perhaps Northern consumers are also comforted by such diversions as well. To be sure, the oil consortium succeeded in evading a human rights campaign against the pipeline.

An Economic Empathy Gap

Eurocentric oversimplification continues to operate when images, people, and sounds from the South are imported to the North. Even when not held by any individual in the campaigns, discriminatory biases permeated the Northern collectives nonetheless. Northern advocates chance adopting a singular focus on charismatic groups such as Indigenous communities, much like they do charismatic megafauna, rather than poor populations, such as the rural poor of developing and developed places, including those communities within their own nations. This streamlining of issues depicts a worldwide economic empathy gap among Northern bodies, through which slip issues of poverty, workplace grievances, daily community grievances, and global economic justice. In the United States, there is a great deal of sociological work on how Americans identify individual explanations and solutions for a person's poverty rather than structural factors and resolutions.[174] In a network comparison, and though the ill impacts of the industry were well known, able-bodied working adult poverty was somewhat of a curse in itself.

For instance, Northern interests in general have emphasized improving the global environment,[175] over equalizing community deliberations that would work toward ending relative poverty. They do so through the use of Northern standards that fail to invite the South in as equal partners and especially not as the more dominant one. In 2000, for example, researchers found that 26 percent of the transnational social movement organizations formed for human rights and 17 percent for the environment, respectively, while only 10 percent focused on development and empowerment.[176] As noted earlier, international advocates were aware of the extensive environmental and economic injustices perpetrated by Northern entities and experienced among affected communities and ecosystems in Ecuador. Some had even participated in other social and environmental justice campaigns or coalitions in Ecuador. "It's not that people are very happy and welcoming of this project because they love it," advised one international activist with extensive experience in Ecuador. "It's that they are in a position now, and that they are using this as an opportunity to get some basic things from this company that the government and [the companies] should have been giving them all along, like potable water, basic, basic health services and things like that. I could see and respect [that]."[177]

Yet for international audiences and institutions during a short-run, project-specific campaign, the multifaceted domestic concerns slipped into compartmentalized icons of Northern naiveté. For a public accustomed to manageable treatments of social problems,[178] international NGOs erased the disquieting imagery of laboring poor adults with the beauty of rainforests. With the poor's removal, Northern entities and institutions, including the Northern financiers, the World Bank, and the Northern oil multinationals, were again the ones served. They became the beneficiaries of weakened standards more easily solved by environmental impact assessments, conservation funds, cost-benefit analyses, and green propaganda.

In the transition from the local to the global, there is still no broad-based international antipoverty movement, unless visual images of hungry children can be telecast into Northern homes and offices. Poor, but working adults, who are angry and opinionated, and dressed in standardized attire, whether ripped or frayed, threaten middle-class audiences and elite international institutions. They are articulating redistributive, class-based struggles not only against the state, but against global institutional practices and against the lifestyles of Northern households.

From these accounts, it could be argued that their marginalization occurs because a mobilized population of the global working poor appears menacing and endangers the standards of Northern living. Their demands may also serve as inspiration for the working poor of the North. Said more eloquently by Ethel Brooks in a study halfway around the world, "In the case of child garment workers, we [Northern consumers and NGOs] would protect them from the evils of exploitation until they reach the age of 'consent' to sell the products of their labor."[179] Ending child labor in the garment industry in Bangladesh is certainly commendable. Nevertheless, as Brooks argues, the singular focus of the campaign on child labor in one export-oriented industry served the conscious of Northern consumers while failing to address the working conditions in the factories, failing to achieve livable wages for working adults in the country, and failing to provide educational security for all Bangladeshi children.

During anti-apartheid campaigns linking U.S. corporations with South African practices in the 1980s, Seidman also found that racial oppression resembled human rights abuses, which resonated with academic- and church-based institutional investors.[180] Fair wages and just working conditions, however, were morally ambiguous issues that were intentionally overlooked.

Seidman in the transnational anti-apartheid movement and Brooks in the transnational anti-child-labor movement identified what I am calling a persistent *economic empathy gap*, which was found in both transnational campaigns in Ecuador. Even though the advocates in the North were aware of the economic and political hardships experienced by Ecuadorians due to North-South power structures, the actual campaigns failed to promote this awareness worldwide or to alter such dimensions and experiences.

From this investigation, it appears that when a capitalist economic and political orientation has been adopted or endorsed universally, the laboring poor resonate with no one, nowhere. The injustices of the laboring poor's living and working conditions are too ambiguous to generate, and perhaps too necessary to sustain, moral outrage. Not only is the economic and political influence of the North at risk, but the individual psyche of Northerners may also be in jeopardy, especially among those who are comforted in the belief that they are more skilled, more intelligent, harder working, and perhaps even more moral than the poor, including the people of the South.[181]

With deep histories of social, economic, and political marginalization, representatives of Lago Agrio and Esmeraldas sought dignity through direct, self-determined negotiations with OCP—not just token gifts delivered at the discretion of state leaders and oil companies. In contrast, stakeholders in Quito and Mindo, who perceived the impacts of the oil industry to be environmental ones, had only recently discovered the oil industry and represented Ecuador's environmentally employed. Those in the Andes initiated and enabled international discourses on environmental management, environmental funds, nature-based tourism alternatives, environmental research, and environmental impact assessments. Each is important, and this assessment is not meant to devalue these hard-won achievements. But singly or collectively, these foci fail to end the oil-industrial complex, fail to alter the North's position in the world system, and fail to eradicate extreme systemic inequities and global disadvantages.

Judging impact to be the persistent and inseparable risk of oil contamination and nonlocal monetary benefit, community groups with the backing of elected local officials organized for localized democracy and self-rule in determining the redistribution of oil wealth and oil investment practices, while advocating for community-determined projects, community-directed oil spending, and greater local oil employment. Unlike the sites inexperienced in the oil industry, the oil-impacted communities incorporated contention against the pipeline into their long-running struggles against the state, including the perceived mismanagement of their natural resources in Lago Agrio and the state refinery in Esmeraldas, the inferior provisions of services given the regions' oil worth, as well as the inequitable distribution of oil revenues given thirty years of monetary outflow. What is the visual icon and arresting image for these realities?

Given the breadth and depth of global injustices, the global poor are relegated behind the environment when it comes to oil flows. In this way, Northern organizations, audiences, and institutions lack economic understanding of the world's laboring poor. Even though international "emergency action alerts" accurately claimed Lago Agrio's residents were demanding basic health services, including roads, potable water, and greater electricity, as well as farm subsidies and support, they reframed the image of the oil provinces as "once pristine rainforest" destroyed by the oil industry.

Non-Indigenous Ecuadorian communities in and along the Amazon rarely if ever refer to the Oriente as a "pristine rainforest." It was a land that the state encouraged them to settle in order to log, hunt, produce coffee, start trout farms, raise farm animals, and grow crops. They live and work the land, much like European settlers in North America, who moved across the land in a pattern of deforestation, the destruction of Native people and cultures, wildlife overkill, population growth, and pavement, aspiring for greater development, modernization, and consumption and supported by state leaders to do so.[182]

This comparative analysis also found that international networks and coalitions may practice frame relocation, or utilizing one site of contention or impact for the benefit of another, while neglecting the demands of the former.[183] David Snow and colleagues present how through "frame extension" stakeholders expand their frame boundaries to reach interests, or interest groups, that are not primary or core to the social movement,[184] and how through "frame transformation" global interpretive frames were constructed to convert or displace one frame for another. This study of multiple sites of conflict and transnational engagement exposes how domestic images of oil contamination in the Amazon may be manipulated to appeal to international audiences and in the process may then be refocused, relocated, or retooled to benefit less impacted areas, such as the Andean Mindo-Nambillo Cloud Forest, or other international concerns, including environmental protection.

For example, in describing the international campaign of opposition, one activist said, "We made a lot of actions in front of these banks. . . . [We were] always trying to inform the clients. 'Did you ever expect that your bank is part of or is involved in destroying the Amazon in Ecuador?'" According to the activist, the public responded, "'I don't want my bank destroying the Amazon.'"[185] Nevertheless, the immediate and greater land gains were experienced in the less well-known Andean cloud forests, many miles from the sites of oil production in the Amazon.

The more established international NGOs, however, cautioned newer ones from perpetuating this type of risk especially when forming coalitions or networks. In this way, NGOs with greater experience in the South, or in Ecuador in this case, educated newer ones on how to avoid manipulating local experiences for their own gains.

> Often there's a tension, like some Northern groups will use case studies from the South, but really they are just instrumentalizing, because they are just using it. They'll have an institutional reform agenda, and then they'll use a case. I don't know a dam project in India or an oil pipeline, but they are just using it to illustrate. And, then often in effect that means if the project is not popular with the

press anymore, or if they have lost, they'll go on and look for a new, sexier project, to use as an example for whatever they are trying to prove or show.[186]

In contrast, "we think it's totally disempowering to local struggles if for a little while, there's all this attention, and then everybody just goes off and does other things. You know, if they are dropped like that, it could have a really bad effect," acknowledged an INGO spokesperson.[187]

"A real understanding, a mutual understanding, is needed, and mutually defined, or shared values or principles, to really have an effective alliance, I think. And I think most people don't have enough time for that. Time or money. You've got this: 'Run, run, run. We've got to fight the oil companies,'" commented another one. "There's not enough reflection, not enough sitting down and saying, 'Okay, what's going on? Are we really better off now? Is this campaign effective? How do we decide what effective is? Is effective impacting the company? Or is effective improving the lives of the communities?'"[188] This is the hectic nature of transnational activism. Transnational advocates understand local conditions and are committed to assisting affected local populations; however, the frantic pace of their efforts are not set by them, but by the oil-industrial core.

In sum, as both campaigns originating in Quito and Mindo transitioned from the local to the global, the oil communities of Lago Agrio and Esmeraldas were both visible and invisible. Although oil-impacted communities provided the authenticity of oil contamination and oil poverty, images that were critical to the campaigns of nonimpacted communities, it was the nonimpacted communities that captured the attention of international collaboration. In this case, the dialectical flows between the communities integrated in the global oil economy (Lago Agrio and Esmeraldas) and the environmental communities integrated in global advocacy (Mindo) and global conservation efforts (Quito) perpetuated impact and advocacy disparities. The oil-important community of Esmeraldas also missed out on establishing initial ties with the strongest and most committed among the international NGOs, especially the ones that link themselves enduringly to a community. Yet despite these handicaps, the isolation of the oil towns in particular may have enabled them to press their homegrown demands against the state, which would have otherwise risked being weakened from Southern to Northern concerns, and being shifted from the state to international bodies.

DEMANDING GLOBAL INCLUSION AND AN ECOLOGICAL AND PARTICIPATORY DEMOCRACY

The distribution of oil benefit and burden has been depicted as one of the bleakest and most inequitable faces of globalization and one of the most blatant abuses of Southern resources for Northern consumption. As demonstrated, community location in oil's supply chain leads to site-specific disputes and varied impacts—and points to the necessary inclusion of Southern voices in each link to rectify such disparities. Community insertion, as called for by affected peoples, would include community deliberation, community monitoring, and the ability of communities to accept, reject, or alter the conditions under which oil exploration, production, and transportation occur. Each step would have to be mandated and protected by the state to be ensured, while state guarantees would be required to prevent involuntary relocations in an effort to silence potential objectors. But it is possible, and it may be one of the most important avenues to correcting the historical power imbalances that have occurred since natural resources, and fossil fuels in particular, became privately or nationally owned commodities.

In Ecuador, calls for oil justice, or mandatory and protected community deliberation at each point in the petrochemical process and community oversight of the government's use of oil revenues, were growing louder. Their calls were ignited and inspired by the thousands of micro- and megademonstrations and campaigns of community- and labor-based organizations, Indigenous and advocacy groups, environmental justice and global justice networks, and conservation NGOs worldwide. National and international discontent buoyed Ecuadorians' engagement in the extractive industry and pushed for the expansion of dialogue, whether in the streets, government buildings, or boardrooms, to multiple stakeholders and multiple users of the country's natural resources. "The people in the South are saying, 'Enough is enough. This needs to stop,'" declared an activist in the campaign of opposition. "And the people in the North need to hear that and change."[189]

Ecuadorians all along the right-of-way, and perhaps in particular the most oil-exposed communities, were calling for global representation, given the uneven allocation of Northern and global benefit alongside local and Southern burden. To demonstrate this point, an international advocate, an oil spokesperson, a government official, and a researcher—this is not a joke—may hear only requests for paved roads, a health clinic, or a potable water system, or they may hear only calls for environmental protection or environmental management, or they may hear only demands for employment in the oil fields. But the material is a Southern euphemism for global representation, made globally palatable for what would otherwise be quite alarming to Northern sensitivities. Southern communities still lack the economic and political authority to bait and switch, which they may rightly deserve a go at, but they are mobilizing for greater and more meaningful degrees of local *and global* participation, transparency, and accountability.

Their target is not only the "North" or the oil-industrial core. In democratically dynamic places in Latin America, "affected" and marginalized people are "affected" and marginalized by state actions and inactions as well. To be sure, Southern states have hampered the democratic rights of civil society, while also being hindered by their position in the global political economy. So if state entities have lost their ability or commitment to represent their citizens, civil society is demanding to speak for itself locally, nationally, and globally.

There are examples, in what Avritzer has called "participatory publics" and "political public space," of citizen groups in Argentina, Brazil, and Mexico being incorporated into local and national decisions.[190] Brazil, Mexico, and Argentina, three of Latin America's more robust semiperipheral nations, provide situations where "public space" is negotiated for local or national issues including "participatory budgeting" in two Brazilian towns, local and national election monitors in Mexico, and an accounting of human rights violations by the Argentine state.[191]

In contrast, Ecuadorians were seeking to be political and economic participants in national *and global* spaces. In the OCP dispute, Ecuador represented approximately thirteen million people, some of whom rejected being marginalized and disempowered. Their call for an ecological and participatory democracy with regard to the oil sector was not only a local or national demand; it was a global one. The demand was justifiably global—given that they were struggling against the state as well as against corporations and institutions, which were themselves not bounded by borders and were even protected for, and by, being borderless.

In theory, Avritzer's "participatory publics" would have analyzed oil alternatives, determined oil impacts, accepted or rejected oil projects, and if accepted, they would have monitored each link in the extract-to-export resource chain. Inserting community deliberations, community power to accept, reject, or alter projects, and community-based monitors and regulators along oil's material flow may be imperative to holding states and extractive industries answerable to affected communities and ecosystems. Faber argues that communities most exposed to unhealthy environments due to corporate contamination are really calling for "economic democracy,"[192] which clarifies his earlier call for "ecological democracy."[193] The working poor are seeking at least equal, if not greater, participation in the social, economic, political, and ecological decisions that are made in local, national, and global places and that affect, as environmental justice activists suggest, where they live, work, study, and play. Indeed, the uneven impacts of oil and advocacy flows present an argument for a Southern-led, community-driven global justice founded in an ecological and participatory democracy. And research in Ecuador points to the capacity of and need for communities commanding a critical space at each stage of the decision-making process.

By examining oil, oil-resistance, and oil-deliberation flows, we witness how the arrival of a pipeline led to the sharpening of democratic demand in the national and global governance structures of oil among a wide and increasingly critical and exacting audience. The insertion of community-led deliberation and the role of the state to endorse and enforce equal economic opportunities and environmental safeguards are revealed to be critical, perhaps particularly when the commodity of conflict is globally mobile, but state owned, and where the impacts are locally experienced. Identifying and supporting the mechanisms to insert and maintain community-level supervision appear crucial and call for bottom-up, race-to-the-top oil regulations and standards until the production and use of petroleum ceases. The greater goal is the eventual end of fossil fuel use.

However, expanding rightful participatory spaces for affected communities in extractive economies has proven challenging worldwide. For states and communities stalled at this juncture, Avritzer offers four elements to creating participatory publics or deliberative democracies.[194] The response by Ecuadorians during the construction of OCP met the first two. Indeed, OCP represented one conflict in a series of former and future struggles that can be expected in Ecuador until participatory publics and a deliberative democracy are installed not only within Ecuador, but between Ecuador and the North, including its multinationals, lenders, consumers, and institutions. The first two of the elements included public mechanisms and spaces for voluntary, face-to-face public deliberation on contentious issues. The second two steps institutionalize public deliberation as part of, or incorporated into, state-level deliberations. The first two steps create informal opportunities for civil society to discuss, debate, and offer solutions to local problems, while the latter two steps transform informal (street-side) deliberation into formal, state-side provisions for community-guided decision making and problem solving. Such deliberation would be guaranteed, endorsed, incorporated, and legitimated by the state.

In Ecuador, a critical outcome of the announcement of the OCP was the broad street-side and informal engagement of a diverse spectrum of citizens, who varied in their oil histories and oil conflict experiences and who mobilized to contest the policies, actions, and inactions of the state and the oil industry. "The pipeline and all the reaction to the construction is a good indicator of the people of this country being more aware of their environmental needs and rights," noted the director of one NGO in 2002. "I think the process itself was a good precedent in the country, . . . it was a very good learning process for everybody."[195] Five years later, an activist recalled that "the OCP thing was one of the first times that people actually responded, you know, maybe not properly, but people were asked to think about it [the oil industry]."[196] In the United States, an EJ activist can only hope the BP disaster does the same.

With the construction of OCP, oil contention in Ecuador was no longer isolated among Indigenous communities in the Ecuadorian Amazon. Bottom-up participatory demands reverberated locally, nationally, and globally, even though affected societies have yet to receive a state invitation to become state-side deliberators. That said, the Ecuadorian government may become more receptive to participatory spaces when it realizes that several grassroots and professional actors actually supported building state mechanisms to control and to influence multinational operations. Several groups were not against the state. They were for a more inclusive and democratic state that had the political will and social commitment to govern the oil sector and to influence the global political economy for the betterment of the people's daily lives and for the protection of the country's natural heritage.

Grassroots leaders pointed to their role in pushing local authorities and civil society to respond to the pipeline project. "Local authorities, I think, will be much more rigorous than they have been in the past. And I think that's our far greater success," noted one activist, before adding another achievement. "I think a secondary success, not with the same level of intensity, is I think public opinion realized the power that they have. And that individual citizens can complain, and that individual citizens have a right to be heard and that individual citizens' rights need to be defended." Elaborating further, the activist added, "And I think we taught a lesson also to the NGOs who were becoming a bit complacent."[197]

Learning to force their national and international participatory legitimacy and authority was also shared among the conservation NGOs. "I don't think a second OCP would take place in the same way, for example, because we've learned what to do and what not to do at the international level in this particular case," recalled one conservation director. "So next time we hear about a project—and I say we, the conservation community—we would put pressure that the EIS [environmental impact study] would be done beforehand, according to the law."[198] Again, the Ecuadorian law is noted as a critical component toward achieving and sustaining environmental protection.

Collectively, affected communities and organizations inserted themselves in advancing greater public participation toward altering the prevalent trickle-down, oil-led development practices that have failed to meet the needs of communities and ecosystems. Additional insight on creating spaces for affected people is found in the work of researchers in Australia, who have developed a six-point scale to measure and to advance a community's role in mitigating social, cultural, and environmental impacts with regard to resource extraction.[199] Though based on Indigenous participation in environmental management decisions in Australia, it is applicable to resource contention worldwide. The scale begins with a basic corporate commitment to comply with the state's environmental legislations, followed by company consultations with affected people. The third step accounts for Indigenous access to and evaluation of industry information on environmental issues, while the fourth step includes guaranteed rights for Indigenous people to suggest improvements to the management system. The fifth denotes joint or collaborative decision making between affected people and the company, while the final criterion protects the right of Indigenous people to act unilaterally to address their environmental concerns, which may mean suspending operations.

Though the steps are not mutually exclusive nor are they achieved in order, they offer a guideline or barometer for advancing community inclusion into the decision-making processes of extractive industries. With the case of OCP, for example, we see that the mobilized groups of Mindo and Quito achieved the fourth step, that is, they were able to make slight suggestions that led to additional care in particular zones designated important to them. They accomplished this achievement due to their own fortitude, rather than state guarantees. They were, however, unable to achieve the third step: access of company information and independent evaluation or monitoring of the construction process. The more significant aspiration, the final criterion or the authority to unilaterally suspend or cancel a project that they determine to be detrimental to areas of social, cultural, or environmental importance, was never realized. In Australia, the researchers also found that communities that achieved a higher standard of inclusion also achieved other benefits, such as employment or training.[200] Their cases demonstrated that environmental participation was not traded for other benefits, and that the two actually dovetailed in many cases.[201]

In Ecuador, the trajectory of democratic participation in oil decisions remains uncertain. On the one hand, oil presence provokes calls for greater deliberation among affected communities and their support networks. Through their opposition to state and industry practices, "organizations in most parts have grown stronger," acknowledged one activist.[202] Yet, on the other hand, oil presence consumes the time, resources, and energy of many community leaders who are then unable to invest in constructive, long-term, locally driven development and participatory processes, as noted by the same Quito-based activist. "I think the organizations haven't been able to dedicate themselves to proactive work on behalf of their communities because they are so busy reacting and trying to defend their territories and their way of life against the threat of imposed, government-imposed oil exploration and exploitation."[203]

Returning to Avritzer's seminal work, if Ecuadorians were empowered to participate as equal members in oil deliberations, how would they have responded to a proposal to build a second cross-country pipeline in order to expand the country's oil production capabilities? In all likelihood, the public would have supported the pipeline project.[204] Many along the route had accepted, not necessarily wholeheartedly, the view that an oil-led economy will—eventually—lead to development and modernization. But we know that a people's pipeline would have looked quite different.

Here's the gist of what a Southern-led, people's pipeline project may have looked like: Construction would have started after affected publics were consulted, provided input, altered, and then accepted independent social, environmental, and economic impact assessments that answered the specific questions posed by affected communities. It would have been constructed by local workers at just, family-supporting wages, with greater worker safety and postconstruction training to transition into permanent oil work. It would have been publicly owned. Citizen collectives would have monitored—with the right to intercede—each leg of the construction process and inspected it throughout its use. Many towns and communities would have moved the terminals, pump stations, and pipeline much farther from their town centers, their communities, and their water sources. Ecosystems and cultural sites designated as critical, endangered, threatened, or important would have been spared—though the environment would have ceded to community concerns. Much more money would have been invested in the communities along the route, and the residents, communities, towns, and/or provinces would have received annual royalties. Additional royalties would have been deposited into a national fund—overseen by civil society—to promote small businesses and energy and economic alternatives for a time when oil is depleted from Ecuador's fields or is a banned substance. Circling back to some of the national and international critiques of the OCP pipeline project, we see how an ecological and participatory democracy may have resolved some of the objections. For the oil industry and the state, the project would have been delayed and there would have been no corporate profits, but it most likely would have been built.

Conflicts between oil industry boosters and oil industry objectors will persist until a more ecological and participatory global democracy is realized. In Ecuador, their fundamental ideology—which the OCP project forced them to articulate—was global, political, ecological, and economic inclusivity for themselves and for their Southern nation. As Smith argues, and this analysis supports, Southern states are seeking democratic relationships between states, while social movements are demanding and supporting democratic practices within as well as between states.[205] In Ecuador, electricity and conservation funds were merely local and instrumental manifestations for deeper and richer calls for a more democratic and participatory world system.

A CAUTIONARY LESSON AND A CALL FOR GLOBAL ENVIRONMENTAL JUSTICE

When confronted with the OCP project, community groups and professional NGOs mobilized along its zone of impact to demand material compensation and a greater role for themselves in influencing the direction, impacts, and benefits of the country's oil-led economy. Their responses to the quick-to-construct project, operated by seven multinational corporations and financed by even more private and public banks, galvanized an international reaction. Yet the moral and material strengths of transnational collaboration were mitigated slightly by domestic consequences. Even though transnational advocates held personal and professional commitments to global justice and a global democracy, their networks elevated Northern standards over the more challenging Southern ones, and emphasized environmental concerns over the Southern-led dignity-in-life ones. In part, their more progressive efforts were stalled by global mechanisms that primarily protect international capital and industries and respond to the calls of the Southern subaltern at a glacial pace.[206]

For example, long-term gains in establishing the Equator Principles will serve other developing places, not necessarily Ecuador, and will serve to meet Northern standards that are beneath the more comprehensive, resourceful, and democratic demands arising from the oil hubs of Ecuador. In addition, an international attempt to meet World Bank standards, for instance, endorses the bank as a global authority on environmental and social standards, while undermining the economic initiatives and grassroots authority of affected communities. The participation of international NGOs and their Northern focus also diverted domestic efforts from the state, an entity with a much longer-term commitment to Ecuadorian communities, and from national network building, which inflated inadvertently the role, importance, and hierarchy of Northern entities. In particular, this case study reaffirms that Southern societies, most encumbered by the externalities of oil processes, have remained excluded from full participation in global discourses despite, or due to, being vital to the supply of provisions to North.

This chapter is not arguing that these local groups would have been better off with or without international support. International support makes multinationals more responsive, accountable, and accessible, primarily when international advocacy groups target influential shareholders or successfully boycott a product. We see this when multinationals are arguably more responsive than are state oil companies, such as PetroEcuador, to environmental protection and social programs. International support has also provided much-needed resources and morale, and has facilitated participatory spaces for affected residents and local NGOs. Furthermore, if international networks remain intact or transition deeper into a global environmental justice movement, they could become formidable forces in future challenges to oil expansion in the Amazon—regardless of the origins of the oil operator and consumer. But until this occurs, domestic stakeholders still demand change today at sites of contention and under conditions that address their basic needs—not all of which were achieved. As a local leader acknowledged after the pipeline's completion, "Yes, they [the residents] think and feel ecologically, but first is the need of the poor. This is how it is."[207]

Given the economic and political ties and dependencies between the petroleum industry and oil-producing nations, affected communities and concerned organizations mobilized, contested, responded, debated, and negotiated in the marginal spaces allotted to them by the oil-industrial core and the state's oil economy. To this, the pessimist-activist-scholar sees secondary spaces and trivial tokens granted reluctantly to mollify civil society, until another, and perhaps a more powerful, round is triggered.

An environmental flow perspective inserted into this transnational analysis indicated how issues became simpler when complex demands shifted from the local to the global. But the simplification process was not straightforward. The tactics of the oil-important communities were *more* radical than the environmental groups and their international allies in confronting global discriminatory practices, while their calls for immediate concessions were more practical in the short term than the anti-oil, anti-Northern rhetoric of some of the local and nonlocal actors. The communities of Lago Agrio and Esmeraldas were temporarily assuaged by the concessions that they attained. Yet in the long term, the oil communities sought a much more progressive and revolutionary standard of economic justice and poverty reduction by incorporating community-based oil deliberations in state and international decisions and actions.[208]

Primarily, affected people of the Global South want equal input into local, national, and global decisions that impact their daily lives. In this case, the integration of community-based deliberation into the environmental flow of oil would not necessarily halt oil production. Many communities would probably have accepted oil extraction, production, and transportation for the prospect of global inclusion in economic and political systems. Pragmatically, increased local, national, and international deliberation would build local capacity, provide greater community knowledge of the industry, and potentially reduce petroleum's impacts. As noted, each stage along oil's supply chain threatens the environment and health of communities and workers.[209] If each leg of oil work is informed, influenced, and monitored by local residents, who have a vested interest in checking and upgrading technology and protecting communities and natural environments, we could witness higher standards and less damage worldwide—without even undermining the oil industry—until global oil dependency is replaced.

Ideally, such deliberations would not only influence global and national decisions, they would bolster the status of low-income nation-states in global economic and political circles. Leaders of the developing South would be carrying their citizens as the public would be holding up their developing nation-states as equal and essential voices in global decisions on the global production, supply, and consumption of oil. To be sure, affected communities in the South are calling for a Southern-led, community-driven global justice founded in an ecological and participatory democracy with origins in the South but with impacts also felt in the North. And certainly, Southern people have much more to gain by overhauling the current political and economic system. Ideally, environmental, economic, and social wrongs will be righted, and a people-centered, community-led order will be achieved justly and without displacing harms onto other communities.

7

Post-OCP

Governing and Contesting Correa and China in the Amazon

This book was never about Ecuador alone, even though Ecuadorians provided the grit of a contemporary oil experience. This book is about global oil injustice and the global practices of the oil industry, including petroleum corporations, petrostates, and petro-endorsing institutions, that favor extractive practices over the rights and well-being of communities and ecosystems. Such an arrangement has persisted due in part to the absence of people-centered and ecocentered state policies and global practices. Likewise, the OCP project was never just about a single oil pipeline. OCP enabled the doubling of production, which drove oil expansion throughout the Amazon. In addition, and due to this drive, community-oil conflict remained as persistent as it had been during OCP's construction, while Ecuador's political system remained just as turbulent. The Northern-led oil industry also remained just as secure in Ecuador; that was until 2005.

During OCP's route proposal and construction process, three oil companies were sold, merged, or abandoned the project. These are not uncommon changes within the petroleum industry. After OCP's construction, oil operations were also bought and sold and new blocks were tendered, which are also expected practices. Activities of more geopolitical interest occurred when the Ecuadorian state seized the operations of two private companies, one from the United States and the other from France, and when China became a dominant player in the Amazon's oil fields. This chapter is an effort to address these petropolitical transitions.

TRANSITIONS IN THE AMAZON

Rafael Correa's election in late 2006 initiated a leftist shift in Ecuadorian politics that included preferential treatment of state-owned oil companies, greater state oversight of Northern oil entities, and direct challenges to Northern neo-liberal influences, as well as the state's escalating authority over oil contracts and revenue redistribution schemes. Among OCP's six original operators, three left the country. EnCana sold its operations to a Chinese consortium be-fore Correa's election; while the Ecuadorian government seized the operations of Occidental (also before Correa) and Perenco (during Correa's administra-tion). Later, Petrobras was encouraged by the Correa government to concede some fields to PetroEcuador, the state-owned oil company. Combined, these changes shifted the majority ownership of the OCP pipeline, meant to be held in private hands for twenty years, into the hands of state-owned Chi-nese and Ecuadorian oil companies. Ironically, in 2000 when the Ecuadorian government was promoting private oil investment, the then energy minister was quoted as saying that Ecuador has a "good track record" in not breaking contracts and not nationalizing the industry.[1]

Initiating the cascade in 2005, EnCana, the major partner in the OCP con-sortium, willingly sold all of its Ecuadorian assets to Andes Petroleum, which included China National Petroleum Corporation (CNPC) and China Petro-chemical Corporation (or Sinopec).[2] Specific reasons for EnCana's retraction were unclear; however, pressure from Canadian NGOs,[3] community protests, socially conscious shareholders, and politically unstable governments in Ec-uador may be a few.

Then in 2006, the Ecuadorian government led by Alfredo Palacio seized U.S.-based Occidental's operations, citing irregular operational practices in the past when Oxy sold a percentage of its operations to EnCana without state au-thorization.[4] The state handed Oxy's oil fields and equipment over to PetroEc-uador, before launching a new state-run company, PetroAmazonas, to manage Oxy's former fields under PetroEcuador's expanding umbrella.[5] (In late 2009, there was indication that Ecuador may be seeking a partnership with PdVSA, Venezuela's state-owned oil company, to operate Oxy's former blocks.[6])

This seizure was followed three years later, in 2009, by the state's takeover of the French company Perenco's Blocks 7 and 21.[7] It is believed that the state commandeered Perenco's workers to keep oil flowing before completely confiscating Perenco's operations. At the time, Perenco had threatened to stop production temporarily due to a tax dispute with the state. Perenco's announcement was used as justification for the state to intercede so as to maintain the flow of oil.

Additionally, though less dramatically, Petrobras, or Petróleo Brasileiro, and City Oriente handed some or all of their operations over to PetroEcuador in 2008 after being prompted by the state. City Oriente, a much smaller oil entity based in Panama but owned by U.S. investors, ended its contract with Ecuador thirteen years prematurely when it agreed to hand over its operations to PetroEcuador or one of its subsidiaries.[8] Petrobras had already been put on alert when officials in the Energy Ministry declared in 2007 that Petrobras may be a company non grata in an oil consortium because of its "mixed" status as a state company with private leanings.[9] Petrobras offered shares in Brazilian and U.S. markets. Petrobras, which environmental NGOs had also taken to court in April 2008 over its environmental license, acquiesced to Ecuadorian pressure, transferring one of its blocks, Block 31, to the state in October 2008, while retaining its other operations.[10]

Block 31 is particularly noteworthy. Block 31 is situated in Yasuní National Park, a highly contentious, partially protected, human inhabited, and oil-rich national park. Though environmental groups and CONAIE, the nation's leading Indigenous organization, had wanted Petrobras out of Block 31, they were not necessarily expecting oil operations to be transferred to PetroEcuador.[11] Though CONAIE claimed it would hold the Ecuadorian state as responsible as foreign entities, it is not certain whether the Indigenous and environmental groups will apply the same pressure on PetroEcuador as they had done on Petrobras. The weakness of both the Indigenous and environmental positions is that it is not clear who or what can intercede in the government's oil-driven nationalism and the government's limited or low priority orientation to the health of the nation's ecosystems and inhabitants.

As for the OCP pipeline, these ownership changes meant that the formerly privately owned pipeline was increasingly becoming a state-owned project, shared between China and Ecuador. Among the six petroleum corporations that built the OCP pipeline, only ENI-Agip of Italy, Repsol-YPF of Spain and Argentina, and Petrobras, Brazil's national oil and gas company, remained in Ecuador. China's Andes Petroleum owned EnCana's operations; Ecuador's PetroAmazonas owned Oxy's operations; and PetroEcuador operated Perenco's facilities.

Repsol, like Petrobras, had also been put on notice after experiencing an oil spill of approximately one hundred barrels in Block 16 on the border of Yasuní National Park.[12] Given the spills perpetrated by PetroEcuador, this spill in 2008 would be considered a minor one. However, Correa's government took a hard line against nonnational and private oil companies, so this single spill, which Repsol reported as having cleaned up, put Repsol on watch and on the defensive.

Each change has shaken Northern investors as well, while each transition has also revealed to students of transnational movements the folly of ignoring the state and the limited, short-term impact of targeting multinationals, which possess a transitory presence given a nation's precarious policies—and a rising leftist tide in Latin America. Each transition has also pointed to the potentially more sustained impact of empowering civil society and concentrating on the state in Southern and Northern places to meet the economic, social, and environmental demands of affected and engaged people, who are much less mobile than capital, investors, international banks, corporations, and transnational advocates.

If these changes in Ecuador sound familiar, they appeared patterned off Hugo Chávez's petroleum and socialist policies in Venezuela. In Ecuador, the political climate took a dramatic shift at the end of 2006, when the Ecuadorian people elected Correa, an economist and leftist leader and an ally of Chávez. Correa was then reelected in 2009, reinforcing his march leftward. Correa's brand of new socialism and his campaign for social and economic equality through a "Citizen's Revolution" strengthened a renewed socialist bloc in Latin America between Venezuela, Bolivia, Ecuador, Cuba, and more recently Nicaragua,[13] that staunchly rejected U.S. hegemony in the region. To further demonstrate this solidarity, the nations of the Bolivarian Alternative of the Americas (ALBA) announced plans to implement an electronic or virtual currency, the sucre, to facilitate trade between member nations, which include Bolivia, Cuba, Ecuador, Nicaragua, and Venezuela.[14] These alliances were also sympathetic with current political leadership in Brazil and Argentina.[15] Additionally and of equal significance, Ecuador rejoined OPEC (Organization of the Petroleum Exporting Countries) as the smallest oil producer among them, after a fifteen-year hiatus between 1992 and 2007.

Two of the leftist nations in South America, Venezuela and Ecuador, are oil economies that openly acknowledged the role of oil in financing their social programs. Among his Latin American peers, Correa resembled Chávez as an oil-funded socialist whose programs were tethered to the country's oil fields. Correa was also confined by his inheritance. Correa governed an oil-dependent nation that had failed for three decades to balance oil extraction with other sustainable endeavors. Ecuador was a nation that had adopted neoliberal restructuring policies, that had acquiesced to debt payment schedules, and that had severely neglected the economic and social needs of Ecuadorians. Given this scorecard and still early in his tenure, Correa promised to favor the domestic social debt owed to Ecuadorians over the external monetary debt, which he referred to as illegal anyway.[16] Correa also focused on changing relations and agreements between the oil sector and the state. One of his first commitments as president was to revise and/or renegotiate oil contracts with all of the foreign, private, and state-owned oil companies. For his efforts, editors of the *Latin Business Chronicle* labeled him "the angry leftist who runs Ecuador."[17]

In 2006, when oil prices were high, the Palacio government, which was in power for less than two years, set a 50 percent "surplus" or "windfall" tax on the difference between the monthly anticipated or average price of oil and the unexpectedly high prices of the time. The difference represents a sudden "extraordinary income" for the operators, which the Ecuadorian state had not accounted for in its original agreements.[18] So in 2006, the Palacio administration instituted Law 42 of the Hydrocarbon Law, or a means to acquire 50 percent of the unpredicted and "extraordinary" oil revenues. When Correa came into office in 2007, he changed the windfall tax to 99 percent of the difference between the projected monthly average price and the realized peak prices, payable to the state. He later rescinded the tax to 70 percent.

This change aggravated oil-state relations and preceded several of the changes in the oil blocks. Correa's repeated commentaries on North-South relations further exacerbated an already tense situation. In 2008 for example, the daily national newspaper *El Comercio* wrote that Correa advised transnational companies to "understand that the Banana Republic is over. Here conditions will not be set by the companies but by the country."[19] It is one thing when an academic, which he was, says these things, and it is quite another when a nation's leader makes these comments to companies with investments in the country.

Correa continued his stance in a media address in early 2009 identifying the French company Perenco as well as the Spanish-Argentinean company Repsol-YPF as trying to treat Ecuador "like a colony" for not wanting to pay the windfall tax.[20] By the middle of 2009, Correa had seized Perenco's operations, and by the end of 2009, he had announced in a town hall meeting that oil companies "will invest or leave the country."[21] Repsol and China's Andes Petroleum heeded his threats, and renegotiated their contracts.[22]

Like Venezuela, Ecuador's socialist drive was an oil-financed one. Correa's new socialism used oil monies to support social programs for the benefit of the country's poor and to demonstrate Ecuador's leadership in rejecting the neoliberal policies that consolidated national priorities on paying its debt and privatizing its industry rather than meeting basic humanitarian needs and assuring a life led in dignity for the majority. However, in redress, the private oil companies began taking their claims against the Ecuadorian state, and at times against PetroEcuador—but in impact perhaps against the Ecuadorian people—to the International Centre for Settlement of Investment Disputes (ICSID), an arm of the World Bank.

Beginning in 2001 and until the end of 2009, there had been thirteen arbitration cases filed against Ecuador through the ICSID, of which eight were related to hydrocarbon concessions, oil exploration, and/or oil refining.[23] In comparison, zero cases had been filed against the government of Colombia and Brazil; one each against Mexico, Nicaragua, and Panama; three against Bolivia; five against Peru; nine against Argentina; and thirteen against Venezuela.[24] In 2008 for example, Perenco sought arbitration with the ICSID, which determined in favor of the oil company in May 2009. Seeking to push the court's findings, Perenco threatened to halt production, which facilitated Correa's appropriation of its operations, as noted earlier. It was clear that the private companies were not abandoning their investments without a fight for compensation or legal support of their claims, but Correa was not altering his agenda either.

Then in late 2009, Correa announced plans to renegotiate each company's oil contracts to shift from a production model to a service provider contract. Under a service model contract, the oil would be state owned and private companies would be paid a service or production fee by the state for their investment and extraction services.[25] Correa also announced plans to renegotiate the OCP pipeline's agreement with the state, which he referred to in one of his weekly national addresses as an arrangement equivalent to "stealing" from the Ecuadorian state.[26] By early 2010, Won Loon, current president of

OCP Ecuador and indicative of Andes Petroleum prominence in the consortium, expressed a commitment to working with Correa's administration in a transparent manner.[27]

Correa had also spoken of a future in which the oil sector is held by joint ventures between PetroEcuador and other state-run oil companies with PetroEcuador being the largest shareholder. Nikolas Kozloff reports that Ecuador would like "energy integration" with Venezuela,[28] which began with plans for PdVSA and PetroEcuador to build an oil refinery, Refineria del Pacifico or Pacific Refinery, in Manabi, south of Esmeraldas.

Like Chávez's policies, each shift was a move toward greater resource or energy nationalism,[29] and independence of Northern influences. Each modification also left international investors hesitant to invest, and those already committed cautious with their operations. Initially, organizations with nationalistic leanings and brewing frustration over the power of private companies favored these rapid changes. These shifts and demands "pleased a big portion of the environmental movement," noted the head of an environmental NGO.[30] Yet such early optimism may have been premature. Communities and ecosystems continued to be threatened, endangered, and ultimately sacrificed.

COMMUNITIES AND ECOSYSTEMS UNDER CORREA'S NEW SOCIALISM

Clearly the exasperatingly unequal distribution of power and wealth enabled by the policies and practices of the Northern capitalist model, the national elites, and the oil-industrial complex needed to be shaken up (or to implode)—and the raucous democracy of Ecuador proved to be fertile ground. Indeed, Correa's "new socialism" and his "Citizen's Revolution" appealed to advocates of national sovereignty and social justice, including the most disenfranchised members of Ecuadorian society, who genuinely expected social and economic retribution from the populist leader.[31]

Yet Correa's calls for both sovereignty and justice were sufficiently ambiguous. And over time, Indigenous, human rights, and environmental organizations that favored leftist rhetoric began to disfavor leftist action and inaction. They supported and were motivated by Correa's ideology. But they worried over his enforcement, and some even learned firsthand the heavy-handedness of this particular leftist regime. Like Chávez's campaign, the implementation of Correa's social and economic justice initiatives had been developed on the back of oil and mining royalties, both of which remain hotly contested industries in the Amazon. Yet unlike Chávez, who welcomed community initiatives and alternative bottom-up power-sharing structures, Marc Becker argues that Correa was less secure and was less comfortable with national or community participation if it meant dissent.[32] Such an assessment may have spoken more to the relative newness of his position than a character trait, though some of

Correa's policies and actions were vexing to analysts, media, academics, and even his allies.[33]

Relying on the country's oil supply to finance his socialist initiatives, one of Correa's visions of oil-enabled twenty-first-century socialism included dictating the tempo and the agendas of the country's social movements. In practice, Correa's reaction to the nation's robust and organized grassroots groups and special interest NGOs became one of suppression either by co-option, coercion, domination, or exclusion. For example, the Indigenous movement, led by CONAIE and the political party Pachakutik, was too savvy, or too wary, to be co-opted and too influential to be coerced. So it was silenced. In the past, the Indigenous movement had been prominent in forcing two presidential terminations (too savvy and too influential), and had learned in their misguided alliance with the Gutierrez government to be wary.[34] With Correa, divisions began as early as 2005, Becker argues, when Correa was launching his campaign for presidency and the Indigenous camp was also positioning their own candidate.[35] Then after his election, Correa failed to bring Indigenous leaders and their long-running issues for a plurinational state, including Indigenous territory, Indigenous education, Indigenous legal proceedings, and Indigenous medicine, into his administration.[36] This slight was interpreted as intentional.

Even after appointing a Kichwa woman to be his communications secretary, Correa's rapport with Indigenous leaders remained fractured. As a side note that reaffirms distinctions between the political struggles of the Indigenous populations and the community of African descent, Correa's appointment of an Afro-Ecuadorian man from Esmeraldas to head the Culture Ministry, marking the first time that an Ecuadorian of African descent had been appointed a cabinet position,[37] was received with greater enthusiasm within the Afro-Ecuadorian communities than the Indigenous appointment received among Indigenous leaders, who wanted more. Calls for political and social dignity made in Esmeraldas during the time of OCP were being advanced under Correa's leadership—perhaps because the requests were minor and nonthreatening, relative to the more strident demands and population numbers of the Indigenous communities.

Once in office, Correa also requested a constituent assembly to rewrite the nation's constitution and invited several environmental professionals to participate and to advise the government directly or indirectly. Less than two years after he came into office, the nation accepted the new constitution, which some argue is the most progressive in Latin America on environmental issues.[38] For example, clean drinking water and healthy communities became a right. Yet the new constitution also enabled greater mining extraction in the Andean highlands, which was likely to lead to the expropriation of Indigenous lands.[39] The nation had never been a mining one, argued Latin American analyst Raúl Zibechi, but these changes in the constitution were enabling it to become one,[40] while restricting Indigenous and landowner participation to consultations rather than the right to determine such land impacts.[41] In collective protest, Indigenous, community, and ecological groups mobilized roadblocks and demonstrations across the nation in January 2009, and were labeled "childish" by Correa for their efforts.[42]

On the environmental side alone, Correa practiced a carrot-and-stick, rhetoric-and-reality strategy, swinging between co-option and coercion. "[Correa and Chávez] are leftists," acknowledged one international advocate, "but it doesn't mean that they are environmentalists."[43] An environmental oil consultant added that Correa had "streamlined" or fast-tracked the permit procedures and requirements for oil companies to begin exploration, by reducing, for example, the number of public meetings from two to one for the environmental impact assessment alone. "Things are going through quicker," claimed the consultant. "I don't think he has much patience for protests."[44] Such changes may intensify environmental risk as well as environmental demonstrations.

Interestingly and demonstrative of Correa's social justice leanings, the Environment Ministry became an environmental justice ministry when it assumed more responsibility for social issues, including shelter, clean water, health, and economic security that intersected with environmental considerations. To this, Northern nations should be humbled by Ecuador's shift to environmental justice at the national level, while conservation-only NGOs may also need to reconsider their mandate. In 2009 for example, the Environment Ministry began investing in houses for families severely affected by oil contamination.[45] The ministry was also assigned the role of supplying or monitoring the supply of clean water to the communities, and took upon itself a program to initiate a "micro-network" of physicians in the Amazon to respond to emergencies along vía Auca, from the oil town of Coca, east into the Amazon. Importantly, the addition of a social component to its portfolio, including the supply of uncontaminated shelters and water, converts the ministry to an environmental justice one, though its name has yet to be changed. These projects were enabled through an oil revenue sharing agreement that was initially launched when Correa was Ecuador's economic minister in 2005.

"We cannot conserve or practice conservation, until the people have a certain standard of living," suggested a newcomer to the Environment Ministry, who linked the limited economic alternatives in the Amazon for individuals to pay for health care, for example, as environmentally damaging. To generate cash to pay for basic health services, this government representative identified two possibilities for locals: cutting down trees or working for the oil industry. "If the people don't have things they need, we cannot conserve the land," claimed the official. "If the people don't have access to basic services that they need, conservation is not possible."[46]

Building on this awareness and designed to address the environmental needs of the nation and monetary needs of its citizens, the government offered individual landowners monetary compensation per hectare per year if they conserve land that was designated as ecologically sensitive, important, or vulnerable. This change supported Article 71 of the new constitution, which identified the role of the state to provide incentives for environmental protection.[47]

Perhaps due to the expanded role of the Environment Ministry, the environmental NGOs wanted greater influence at the political level as well. Many of them had supported Correa's run with this expectation in mind. Yet in the first few years of his administration, so many changes were afoot that they watched and waited, while some even participated in formulating the new constitution. The more radical ones would have celebrated when the oil multinationals departed or were forced to pay higher taxes for oil access, while nationalistic pride or fervor would have overridden any creeping environmental and community concerns. For a brief time, the expectations of change far exceeded the more mundane antirevolutionary reality of oil rent dependencies.

Correa's Citizens' Revolution and his invitations for Ecuador's environmental professionals to join his administration succeeded in keeping critics at bay, initially, while rallying many professional and community leaders to support his people-centered agenda. Nevertheless, professional NGOs were becoming increasingly worried. "They [the government] are always talking about higher values, like social justice," brooded one environmental director. "And if you are talking about that who will not sympathize with you. . . . Even the pressure that was always placed on the Environment Ministry, all the time, 24 [hour] press, disappeared."[48] Further lamenting the rapid changes, the environmentalist continued: "All the NGOs that have that role to denounce publicly, to make a fuss out of things, to create media pressure, they just joined 'The Project' [Correa's agenda]. . . . So there is a big hole now. Who will be carrying claims or the worries in the public eye?"[49]

As their original demands had yet to be met, there are a few possible explanations, though not an exhaustive list, for their hesitancy to confront Correa's stance. For one, Ecuadorian NGOs may be quite weak in the absence of international allies. For another, the more radical ones had actually hidden an overriding prosocialism or antiforeign sentiment—despite a reliance on international supporters—over a commitment to the environment. Or their professional status oriented them toward a capitalist utilization of the environment, regardless of whether that political support came from the right, the center, or the left. Or they were returning to small piecemeal campaigns. Or finally, the sheer number of environmental challenges needing to be confronted remained so overwhelming that they were merely taking a breather and determining the best strategy under this new regime.

It was, however, Correa's actions that revived the political activism in the environmental movement. The gravity of Correa's intent to diminish objectors was underscored when Acción Ecológica, arguably the nation's most vocal environmental activist organization and probable Correa supporter, lost its non-profit status temporarily under his administration.[50] This radical organization had hounded the Ecuadorian government, multinational corporations, international agencies, local communities, and other environmental NGOs since its founding in 1986—without losing its license, though some members and followers had a history and notoriety of arrests. It had been both admired and ridiculed, but it was perhaps the only environmental organization in Ecuador that could consistently mobilize a contingent of urban, educated youth and committed activists for a street demonstration against environmental destruction in the Amazon. Though its status was reinstated eventually, the act was chilling. The NGOs perceived the move as a threat to their role of placing demands on the government and supporting local communities and environments.[51]

Many environmental experts also began to fear that Correa's new extractive socialist agenda was a further burden on the nation's ecosystems. According to one, his policies toward the oil sector in particular were detrimental "because the accountability of public enterprises is very poor in the region. So if you shift the production of natural resource operations into their hands, you are just assuring less capacity to the environment. . . . [State-owned companies] don't need transparency. They don't need to follow procedures or standards if they are a state-owned company."[52]

The professional environmentalist cited PetroEcuador and its oil-related companies including Petroproduction as some of the nation's worst offenders. For instance, the Esmeraldas refinery was state owned when the explosion occurred, while the oil fields of Texaco, which was battling a lawsuit by community residents, had been operated by PetroEcuador since 1992.[53] These fields had yet to meet the standards called for by neighboring communities and environmental networks. It was not that all state-owned oil companies failed to meet international or Northern standards or community expectations. Simone Pulver demonstrates how Pemex, Mexico's state oil company, actively imported "climate protection norms and practices" from private oil industry networks, rather than civil society and environmental pressure groups,[54] while Dara O'Rourke found that in Vietnam the most effective form of environmental regulations was "community-driven regulation," or community pressure on state agencies, which in turn pressured state and joint venture companies.[55] In Ecuador even, the new national company PetroAmazonas was reputed to model the best of the private oil operators in its adoption of higher environmental standards than its older counterpart PetroEcuador.[56]

Corporate claims also gave pause to accepting Ecuador's commitment to environmental considerations. For instance, Chevron Corporation filed an international arbitration claim through the Permanent Court of Arbitration at The Hague arguing that when Texaco left Ecuador in 1992 it had met its obligations and remediation claims under Ecuadorian law. The press release stated:

> In 1998, after the requisite remediation work was performed and independently validated, Ecuador and PetroEcuador released Texaco Petroleum and its affiliates from further liability. Ecuador assumed responsibility for any remaining impact caused by the consortium's pre-1992 activities as well as any future impact caused by PetroEcuador's own ongoing operations in the former concession area. Since Texaco Petroleum's departure, PetroEcuador has drilled over 400 new wells in the concession area, compared to the 321 wells that were drilled during the consortium. Compounding the situation, PetroEcuador's environmental record as an operator has been notoriously poor, with more than 1,400 oil spills since 2000 alone.[57]

Corroborating Chevron's claims, one environmentalist in Ecuador noted the weakness of the country's environmental NGOs in holding Ecuador's state-owned company accountable.

[The country's most radical ecologists] have never been able to denounce once what PetroEcuador was doing in the Oriente. What PetroEcuador has done in the Oriente with their operations to me is horrible. But that's not a problem, because that's not a private corporation. The standards of private corporations here are well above the standards of PetroEcuador. You can see that easily, visiting the operations, but of course that doesn't sell.[58]

Both comments are included here not to minimize Texaco's actions in the Amazon during the 1970s and 1980s, but to indicate that Ecuador had operated those fields for years with minimal introspection and minimal attention to cleaning them up. The point is that state-owned companies and a nationalistic passion do not necessarily diminish oil contamination and may worsen them. With state backing, such corporations may be even more recalcitrant to community demands and environmental rights. PetroEcuador was also one of the most cash strapped of oil operators in the Ecuadorian Amazon, as its revenues returned first to the state, which explained in part why it may have invested so little in environmental safeguards. National oil companies need to maximize profits for investment in their own operations, while also maximizing rents for state use, argues Bernard Mommer, while this constrains and forces compromises that are not applicable to private companies that operate under a more singular direction: maximize profits and minimize rents.[59]

Though funded by Northern grants to end oil injustice, oil injustices by national companies, which weather political instability and social unrest better than private Northern firms, may be more palatable for some NGOs. On the other hand, their recent hesitancy may speak more to limited national opportunity and an indeterminate target. When international advocates were available to support local campaigns, those campaigns targeted international entities. Now in the absence of Northern targets and allies, Southern spaces for NGO voices appeared greatly curtailed. Indicative of the movement's more recent hesitancy to speak out against certain environmental risks, NGOs were assessed as mum when Venezuela's state-owned company PdVSA announced plans in 2009 to construct an oil refinery in Manabí on the Pacific Coast. According to one environmental spokesperson in Quito, Manabí is a unique and fragile ecosystem, though "nothing was said about it. Everybody that tried to say something was censored. Right away the President himself said we were extremists, said they [we] were against change, against the government."[60]

Perhaps Ecuador was not quite ready to transition to state-owned companies that lacked external pressure points. Socialist policies in general have marginalized the environment, and state-owned oil operations in Latin America may be weak entities to launch ecosocialism, or an ecological and environmentally sustainable socialist campaign.[61] Then, and now, the Ecuadorian state lacked the environmental authority, controls, incentives, and punishments to regulate and monitor the industry's impacts. For example, the OCP pipeline experienced its first break in early 2009, which dumped approximately fourteen thousand gallons of oil in the Santa Rosa River, a water source for numerous Indigenous and settler communities, farmers, and ranchers.[62] A one-year anniversary assessment indicated that river waters were still contaminated and that agreements between OCP and affected landowners and communities had yet to be realized.[63] Noting the inadequacies of oversight and regulation, one international advocate said, "You can have a great environmental impact assessment on paper, but what happens out in the field is often very different. And the government doesn't have a lot of capacity or sometimes a lot of political will to go in there, and actually monitor what companies are doing and to hold them to any kind of standards."[64]

At least in the short term, Correa's primary commitment supported oil and mining revenues before a healthy environment. But he was not alone. In the first decade of the twenty-first century, the majority of world leaders whose countries were endowed with natural resources such as oil and gold elected to exploit them at the expense of neighboring communities and ecosystems. These leaders are in the Global North and the Global South, reside in democracies and dictatorships, and are capitalists and socialists. However, unlike previous Ecuadorian leaders, Correa appeared committed to redistributing some of the nation's oil royalties for national and social needs, which for the majority of poor was perhaps a welcomed respite and which for a few of the wealthy was an antithetical assault on their accustomed privilege.

An Oil-Driven Militarized Socialism

For that wealth, however, someone and some place had to be sacrificed. And that had always been the complaints out of the oil-important centers. For four decades now, the Indigenous communities of the Amazon and the non-Indigenous border hubs of Lago Agrio and Coca had made communal and ecological sacrifices for the nation's oil-led "development." Correa's administration was asking for the same sacrifice, with a hint of hopefulness that this time more of the country's social and economic needs would be met, including those of the most oil-important regions.[65]

Yet community sacrifices remained coupled with state repression. The Dayuma case of November 2007 was a case in point and a clarifying moment on Correa's position on the nation's oil supply. To be clear, petroleum was not negotiable during the time of OCP, and it was not negotiable almost a decade later.[66] If anything, the success of the pipeline project committed the nation deeper into a petropolitical economy, while the new constitution was also making Ecuador a mining nation as well. In Dayuma, the community had organized for a paved road that had been promised by the state, but which had yet to be received. Though some sources indicated it was yet another oil conflict in the Amazon, it was not. The original complaint, which was supported by local government officials, came after a road asphalting company ceased operations in July 2007 due to nonpayment by the central government. In November, the community blocked the road with rocks and dirt, demanding that the central government, Correa's government, pay the company so that it would complete the asphalting job. The community also expanded their demands to include other services such as water, electricity, and local employment, and an end to the oil industry's discharges of oil wastewater or by-products. The following day a smaller contingent of protesters seized the closest oil facilities of Petroproduction, an arm of PetroEcuador, halting production. At this point, the central government responded.

The government declared a state of emergency, sent in the military, labeled the protestors "terrorists," and escalated tension in the community that led to direct conflict between the community and the military. On November 30, twenty-five people were arrested, followed by twenty-two more residents and local officials a week later. All would be released by March 2008, except for one. Guadalupe Llori, the prefect or governor of Orellana Province and member of the Indigenous Pachakutik Party, would remain in detention, charged with terrorism and sabotage, until September 2008.[67] She was reelected governor in April 2009.[68]

The Dayuma conflict resembled many other oil-related conflicts in the Amazon as presented previously. The site of oil production and/or facilities continued to serve as a leverage point for residents to resist state or industry practices, actions, or inactions regardless of whether contention was directly related to the oil industry or not. "Petroleum has become the body through which state and citizen meet, contest, and legitimize each other," argues Gabriela Valdivia in an assessment of Ecuadorian oil conflicts.[69] The actual facilities of the oil industry as well as the spatial representation of the oil industry contextualized a space and a cause for communities, state bodies, and industry operators to convene—forced by oil presence, state absence, and community vigor. Yet oil had enabled the state to ignore communities as well. Thomas Friedman in his analysis and coinage of the "first law of petropolitics" argues that increases in the price and demand of oil facilitated less democratic openings and more authoritarian leadership worldwide.[70]

In this milieu, Correa's twenty-first-century socialism united the country when he presented his plans to correct the legacy of chronic, Northern-induced inequities in the country. Yet to achieve this vision, communities rich in fossil fuels and minerals remained the historical and contemporary fatalities. In acknowledgment of their relentless sacrifices, one government representative said that "these sectors invest very little because the people [of these regions] don't represent much to the people [of influence] and to the government, not like Guayaquil, Quito or Cuenca. Lago Agrio represents oil workers and people that don't have money or education, and [others don't hold] a good public opinion [of them] in general."[71] These are the types of people to be sacrificed.

It is not then too critical to label this manner of governing as oil-driven militarized socialism. The oil economy and the militarization of the oil communities have been intertwined since oil discovery in the late 1960s. Initially, it was governed by the military, then by elected elite probusiness leaders, and now by an elected leftist. Before and during Correa's administration, landowners and oil-affected communities could influence the oil industry. For example, they could influence which side of their house that an oil pipeline would run. But then, and now, they could not determine whether a pipeline would be laid. And this narrow definition of participation or consultation has not been expanded under Correa.

To be certain, the similarities of demands between Dayuma and the oil towns of Lago Agrio and Esmeraldas during OCP's construction were nearly identical: roads, water, electricity, employment, and an end to oil by-product dumping. In these cases, local officials and community members supported each other in contesting the actions and inactions of the central government. The tactics were similar as well: if the state failed to hear your demands for basic material well-being and dignity through that realization, seize the closest oil installation. At this point, the government responded in much the same way: declared a state of emergency, militarized the area, and arrested people who mobilized initially for something as easy and as essential as asphalt.[72]

Given Correa's petroleum position, it would appear that in the oil-producing region, he was an economic leftist who favored the nationalization of the country's natural resources, rather than a populist who supported the exploited. Oil towns and oil communities have consistently remained marginal political players. Before the Dayuma case and before Correa's terms, the oil towns of Lago Agrio in Sucumbios Province and Coca in Orellana Province had been traditionally and particularly volatile; community activists had been systematically harassed, and some had even been assassinated. Ángel Shingre was shot to death in Coca in November 2003. He was the coordinator of the Environmental Rights Office that assisted affected residents and communities in documenting and contesting oil injustices on their land. Then in 2005 Andrés Arroyo Segura, a community activist fighting against the construction of a dam also in Orellana Province, was found dumped in a river. Segura was a member of the National Network of Popular Ecologists for the Protection of Nature, Life and Dignity (Red Nacional de Ecologistas Populares en Defensa de la Naturaleza, Vida y Dignidad—REDIVINA).[73] In another incident, the president of CONAIE, Leonidas Iza, escaped an assassination attempt in 2004 after returning to Quito following a meeting against the Free Trade Area of the Americas (FTAA) in Cuba.[74] Three family members were injured.

Many individuals and communities have made tremendous sacrifices for environmental justice in the Ecuadorian Amazon. Correa was asking them and the Amazon to make more. "The new government said we had to change our economic model, to invest in other sectors. But for this investment, there are going to be great sacrifices, and when he [Correa] talks of great sacrifices, he is probably referring to ITT [Ishpingo-Tambococha-Tiputini] or Pañacocha or the oil camps in the South that have not yet been explored," said one government employee in Quito.[75] Pañacocha is a biological corridor and protected forest in the central region of the Amazon between Cuyabeno Wildlife Reserve and Yasuní National Park.[76]

The new government, while perpetuating oil dependency, had also indicated that it was committed to "clean oil," to not exhausting the nation's natural resources, and to defeating oil injustices in the Amazon. To achieve these commitments, the government began to increase the power, resources, and capacity of the Environment Ministry, and to commit both the energy and environmental ministries to maintaining the oil industry, while cleaning it up. "This is about the future," claimed an official of the Environment Ministry. "We are in the process of empowering the ministry. . . . We are waiting [to know]. We are waiting [to see what happens]. [There are other] influences on this project: the world, the world economy, oil, the price of oil, oil revenues, the world crisis, various factors."[77] Yet, even if Correa takes credit for adopting "clean oil" policies, it was still the country's radical and conservative environmental NGOs and grassroots community groups that had been demanding them for years and had become particularly vocal and organized during OCP's construction.

To Save Yasuní: The Sale of Carbon Credits?

In truth, Correa may have underestimated the strength and stamina of Ecuador's professional organizations and grassroots campaigns. They were not so easily co-opted, and they truly wanted tangible change in the Amazon, not just antineoliberal speeches. Over time, the NGO communities and grassroots organizers identified that Correa's support was not necessarily guaranteed, and when they did, they began to fight back, recalling old demands that had yet to be realized under new leadership.

Earlier, in 2003, several anti-oil groups had requested a moratorium on new oil developments to provide both the communities and the environment a reprieve. Recalling their efforts, one activist claimed, "We think it makes a lot of sense for the government to hold off on exploration in the southern Oriente, and say, you know, we owe it to ourselves to look into the other options. And we think a real concrete proposal to do that is to set aside these five million or more acres of pristine rainforest that's Indigenous territory, avoid social conflict, sort of invest in a sustainable society in both an environmental [way] and economic and social justice terms."[78]

The activist also offered how even if oil was adopted after a reprieve, it would be on different terms for the most affected.

> We know that after three years, in the worst-case scenario, everybody gets a lot more informed about what's going on, and we really realize that oil is more

beneficial in financial terms or something. But the Indigenous organizations also grow and strengthen and can then be part of a really more constructive process; if they do decide they do want oil or either (a) have to deal with government-imposed oil, or (b) decide that the Indigenous organizations want to work with oil companies, they are going to be stronger and in a better position to negotiate and get better benefits, and to also be part of a real [process].[79]

They were ignored.

So when Correa came into office, perhaps with an eagerness to mock Northern commitments to Southern environments, he made an offer. In 2007, Correa began promoting his own carbon credit plan whereby oil exploration would be prohibited in ITT, at the eastern edge of Yasuní National Park, if the Global North would pay for its protection at the price of the lost petroleum.[80] Though some environmentalists greeted this announcement as heralding a postpetroleum economy, first published by Acción Ecológica in 2000,[81] few believed that the proposal was genuine, and still others believed that the Global North would not support the idea. So in lieu of the uncertainty, oil companies and even the Correa government continued simultaneously to promote and to prepare for oil expansion in Yasuní and into ITT. To this, China's state oil company Sinopec, Chile's state oil company ENAP, PdVSA of Venezuela, and Petrobras of Brazil founded a consortium in 2008 to bid for future development rights.[82] Given the state's demands for greater joint ventures, PetroEcuador later joined the consortium.[83] In identifying Petrobras and Andes Petroleum of China in particular, one international activist wrote, "These newcomers are less concerned about their reputations and are less susceptible to indigenous and environmentalist campaign pressure."[84]

But the offer suggested that perhaps it was never the petroleum that was nonnegotiable in Ecuador but the money that petroleum generates that had been nonnegotiable. For his carbon credit exchange, Correa selected a team of four, including the foreign minister and Yolanda Kakabadse, who was influential in designing the OCP-financed environmental fund, to develop a framework. This model, which became known as the Yasuní-ITT Initiative, would allow Northern governments and industries primarily in the United States and Europe to exceed their industrial carbon dioxide (CO_2) output or part of their greenhouse gas emissions in exchange for paying Ecuador to not exploit oil in ITT.[85] *El Comercio*, the nation's business daily, reported that the proposal could "prevent the emission of 410 million metric tons of CO_2," and the retention of 850 to 960 million barrels of crude oil (depending on the source), while generating nearly US$350 million per year for Ecuador or US$3.5 billion in ten years.[86]

In May and June 2008, the four-member delegation traveled to the United States and to Europe to promote the initiative, which was perhaps the only one of its kind. At the time, Spain, France, and Italy agreed to cancel or renegotiate Ecuador's debt, while Germany pledged US$50 million per year for thirteen years.[87] However, by January 2010, the foreign minister had resigned after failing to secure firm monetary commitments from the European nations.[88] At the same time, Correa, after a series of threats throughout the year, announced plans to begin developing ITT in June 2010 if foreign funds were not in the bank. Block 31, which was already under development, shared a border with ITT.

Yet given Correa's previous actions with regard to the oil industry, it is little wonder that Northern companies and government agencies were wary of an agreement with Ecuador that may have lacked specificity, external controls, and transparency. Indeed, activists attributed the international community's lukewarm reception to the mixed signals emanating from the Ecuadorian government, which led them to discount the seriousness of the ITT proposal,[89] while the *Economist* suggested the offer would allow Correa to blame the international community for being "stingy" if it failed.[90] Likewise, it was not clear whether the country under new leadership would cancel agreements and begin exploration. If so, Ecuador would benefit monetarily from not exploring and deforesting the area for exploration, only to develop the oil fields after a certain number of years if more money was not forthcoming, even though the initial proposal called for a permanent fund that would continue to generate money for the nation after the first ten years. A "draft certificate" provided by Oilwatch as a template stipulated that if the agreement was altered or overturned, and oil extraction was begun in ITT, the Ecuadorian state would reimburse investors the amount paid plus interest.[91]

Immediately after Correa declared plans to begin developing ITT, Acción Ecológica and Oilwatch, an international oil watchdog group based in Quito, declared that such exploration would violate the nation's new constitution. In particular, oil exploration in ITT would violate Article 407, which prohibited oil exploration and extraction in protected lands and Article 57, which banned extractive activities near communities in voluntary isolation in the Amazon.[92] According to one government representative, the new constitution recognized the people in voluntary isolation in the Amazon as "people of Ecuador" and recognized the land as an intangible.[93] Some in the ministry and the movement were inspired to document the existence of these people, which would automatically prohibit oil exploration according to the new constitution.

Initially, Oilwatch's technical team, including support from Edgar Itsch, a former environment minister for a brief stint during the time of OCP, prepared an ITT proposal. Supporting arguments for the proposal included Ecuador's contribution to reducing carbon dioxide emission, protecting the area's biodiversity, developing an alternative economy, and protecting the Huaorani communities as well as three relatively unknown Indigenous communities, Tagaeri, Taromenani, and Onamenane, who have chosen voluntary isolation and who reside in Yasuní and ITT.[94] With each claim, the Oilwatch technical team identified economic and food sovereignties as part of the beneficial bundle.[95]

A more nuanced support of, and perhaps impetus for, the proposal was prepared by a team of researchers, including academics, a former government official, and an activist.[96] Their report, while overall supporting the initiative, was also a reflection of how concerned and engaged individuals who hold divergent views may collaborate and achieve a level of consensus for perhaps the good of an affected area and population.[97] In particular, they identified how two components of the country's new constitution—the rights of nature and a development model for the achievement of "good living" among its residents—supported the defense of the ITT initiative, while the plan also dovetailed with an inevitable post-oil reality.

At this time, the ITT proposal was a test case for many. The success or failure of the initiative may be more indicative of Correa's commitment to economic alternatives and to the persuasion of Ecuador's Indigenous and environmental movements, than the commitments of Northern governments and industries to reducing greenhouse gas emissions. Correa's erratic stance on his own ITT initiative, however, begged the question: what president would allow several oil companies, including his or her own state company, to line up at the door of a promising oil field and not open it? The ITT initiative, or talk of the initiative, is noted here as a debate to watch. Not only will its outcome determine the development or protection of the ITT area, international discussion on the Ecuadorian offer opens a new round for global climate justice initiatives and climate accountability claims between nations.

However, if achieved, there are concerns that such an agreement would mimic debt-for-nature swaps managed by conservation NGOs. When critically examined, debt-for-nature trades benefited commercial banks rather than indebted nations, their national parks, and their landless. Ecuador, for example, was one of the first low-income, developing nations to enter into a debt-for-nature swap. In 1987, World Wildlife Fund (WWF) purchased a land allotment via debt payment and in 1989, WWF, The Nature Conservancy, and the Missouri Botanical Gardens expanded upon this initial effort.[98] However, Ecuador remained in debt and its land remained threatened by illegal loggers, legal oil companies, and landless settlers years after those agreements. Subsequently, a 1992 report by the Brazilian Institute for Economic and Social Analysis (IBASE) identified that debt-for-nature swaps in Latin America failed to develop or strengthen complimentary environmental policies and failed to include community participation, while legitimating a debt that many nations, including their more democratic leaders, have argued was obtained illegally.[99] These failures are identified here as notes of caution: North-South agreements have a pattern of misleading promises and uneven gain. The inequities are so great, however, that lower-status places are forced to keep initiating or consenting to newfound North-South agreements, relationships, and arrangements that strengthen dependencies rather than charter new paths.

Legal Securities

After the Dayuma case and the government's threat to enter ITT despite the presence of communities in voluntary isolation, some NGOs identified that the state-run petroleum industry would continue unrestrained, unless there were greater transparency, greater independence, and greater capacity in the local and national courts to rule against the state and state-owned companies and to adhere to the new constitution. There are two legal cases in Ecuador that indicate Ecuadorian courts will—at times—support communities and ecosystems against state-owned oil.

One community in Esmeraldas was awarded US$11 million in 2002 against the state-owned Esmeraldas Refinery, held by PetroEcuador, for fire damage and for a past record of carelessness and contamination experienced by the community.[100] "That is a good precedent, but that is the only one," acknowledged an environmentalist.[101] In addition, an Ecuadorian court in 2002 ordered a U.K. insurer to pay more than US$10 million to the Galapagos Island National Park for damages due to an oil spill by *Jessica*, an Ecuadorian tanker in 2001.[102] The tanker was carrying PetroEcuador's oil to a local island.[103]

Internationally, Ecuadorians could also take the state to the Inter-American Court of Human Rights (IACHR) in Costa Rica, a branch of the Organization of American States (OAS). In Ecuador, the only celebrated case was the Indigenous community of Sarayaku, which went to the IACHR, and so far has successfully resisted oil exploration in their territory. Their success may be at risk, however, if Ecuador and Venezuela back out of OAS, after determining it to be an arm of the United States.[104] As for pressuring Chinese-owned oil companies, legal avenues have not been tested, but they are of particular concern given the absence of direct pressures from Northern NGOs and Northern courts, such as in the case of EnCana and Texaco respectively, on China's overseas operations.

HOLDING CHINESE OPERATORS ACCOUNTABLE

After Correa's election, the second most important transition following the completion of OCP was arguably the expansion of Chinese oil operators throughout the Ecuadorian Amazon.[105] In addition to Andes Petroleum's purchase of EnCana's oil fields and share in OCP, other Chinese oil entities under the umbrella of Sinopec, CNOOC, or support companies also began operating in the Amazon and on the coast where smaller oil reserves are found. In July 2009, China signed a US$1 billion "loan-for-oil deal" whereby Ecuador agreed to a two-year commitment to export approximately three million barrels of oil per month to China.[106] Then in January 2010, the Ecuadorian government announced an agreement with the Chinese company Sinohydro to construct a hydroelectric dam in the Amazon, with the bulk of the financing coming from China's Export-Import Bank.[107] To a lesser degree, the state was also encouraging China to invest in or to bid for an oil refinery on the Pacific Coast, an airstrip in the Amazon, and an airbase on the coast that had formerly been leased by the U.S. military—though these discussions were not realized.[108] And on the Pacific Coast in Guayas Province, the technology, equipment, and services company BGP China National Petroleum was conducting seismic testing that provoked the Indigenous Nationalities of the Ecuadorian Coast (CONAICE), a member of CONAIE, to call for a suspension of activities.[109]

"They are another player that has come in and they are totally out of anybody's accountability or control," remarked one international environmentalist in 2004.[110] Five years later another international advocate with a history of work in South America added: "We've had this conversation at [our organization] and with many NGOs. Everyone's like gasp [sucks in breath], 'Chinese companies, what do we do?'"[111]

Much like the OCP project, activists had identified two focal points for their campaigns. One was the actual operations, and the other was the lending practices. China's position as both a loan recipient as well as a loan provider to lesser developing or peripheral nations was unprecedented in scale. This type of lending arrangement was also both a bind as well as an opportunity among national and international environmental groups with a history of targeting campaigns against public and private lenders.

"In theory I think the idea of the World Bank and IMF being sort of losing favor among countries, I think, is great," acknowledged an international environmentalist, who had spent more than a decade contesting oil multinationals and international institutions in the Amazon.[112] "I don't know if that's the best solution, you know, the Chinese government stepping up and just bankrolling all the infrastructure that needs to happen."[113] Five years earlier, another international advocate acknowledged the primacy of addressing the nation's debt before ending the injuries associated with oil production. "The threats that are created to [our partner's] territory by oil, government-mandated oil exploration, and exploitation, is the foreign debt issue," noted the activist. "Basically you are not going to solve the oil problems without addressing the debt issue."[114]

The shift from private Northern operations to Chinese state operators may also aggravate human rights abuses, labor injustices, and ecological destruction. Yet to be fair, there was currently no internationally enforceable code with regards to human rights,[115] for relatively new state-owned companies to follow, while international standards on labor and the environment remained inadequate and unjust in most places where oil was found. These obstacles were also coupled with the practices of the current Correa administration. Correa's team had appeared more focused on reducing the monetary benefits of the oil sector between the nonnational oil operators and the Ecuadorian state, rather than correcting previous community and environmental hardships due to the industry. It is not to say that the Correa administration will never address these ongoing problems, but given Ecuador's debt and national anger over neoliberal policies, the Correa administration prioritized efforts toward greater social and economic redistribution for the country's total poor, rather than the nation's most oil-impacted communities.

Standards and Expectations

If some view China's involvement as a race to the bottom, they may be mistaken. A downward shift may not actually occur unless Ecuadorians permit it. Even as the Northern corporations depart, Ecuador's active community groups, grassroots ecologists, and professional NGOs are likely to retain their skills, capacities, and commitment to pressuring the industry and confronting the Correa government. Finding examples of their mobilization capacity is not difficult. In 2006, for instance, Ecuadorian protestors seized the facilities of Chinese-owned Andes Petroleum, taking more than forty workers hostage, and temporarily shutting down production in their ongoing demands for employment and social services from the state and oil industry.[116] Until their social and environmental demands are met, oil entities, including Chinese state-owned enterprises, can expect prolonged tension surrounding their operations, especially among affected workers and communities most wed to the industry.

However, Chinese state-owned oil operations resembled yet differed from private, Northern companies in terms of their own technical knowledge and community experience.[117] On the one hand, China's engineers and technocrats were increasingly equipped with the technology and skills to meet Northern standards, or even improve upon them, if those standards were demanded. China's government invested in research and development, opened its doors to international consultants, required foreign investors to transfer research and technological knowledge in exchange for market access, and created joint ventures with the world's leading oil companies to produce competitive petroleum companies.[118] In addition, China's domestic environmental reforms and political environmental awareness had been building, supported in part by market checks or incentives.[119] In the absence of urgent profit pressures and the presence of strong petroleum need, China's technocrats may also invest in and even develop advanced and less damaging technology, including the production of hybrid and fuel-efficient cars.[120] Again, Pulver's work on Pemex, Mexico's national petroleum company, is informative. Industry peers and leaders, such as BP, were more influential in directing Pemex's climate and environmental policies than civil society's direct action.[121] Yet Pemex and Mexico are established oil producers, and that assessment was before the BP disaster in the United States.

China's economy, on the other hand, requires unprecedented amounts of oil that had in the past propelled many nations to go through a range of measures and maneuvers to acquire them, much like China is doing today. For oil access in low-income nations, China often offered low-interest, easy payment loans without regulatory stipulations, bid the lowest or the highest, forgave debt, provided bilateral trade agreements, and built schools, hospitals, railroads, bridges, and dams.[122] Yet it remained unclear whether the seemingly benevolent offers of assistance mimic Northern offers that failed to alleviate poverty or to meet the catholic demands of affected communities,[123] or whether

China's aid actually met community need. Given that China also imported its own labor, used its own supplies, and hired its own service companies when operating oil fields overseas, there was greater indication that Chinese interests were met first, followed by local interests, if at all.[124] In China, the socialist importance on community is in relation to the motherland and the state; it is not necessarily directed toward a global civil society or to nonlocal, non-Chinese, and nonsocialist communities, where China seeks petroleum.

Tied with Correa's fast track for increased oil production, environmental safeguards and community considerations may not be keeping pace with China's national drive and its need for fossil fuel. Despite the welcome mat, as a newcomer China was also aware of Correa's determination to regulate foreign firms. When Ecuador expelled Occidental for irregular practices, the Chinese venture Andes Petroleum experienced its own field losses, as it held a 40 percent interest in one of Oxy's oil blocks. China was also amenable to renegotiating oil terms with Correa's government to maintain oil supply;[125] however, this agreement may have facilitated China's entry into Yasuní and perhaps into ITT in the near future.

In addition to the state and civil society setting the pace of China's operations, Northern multinationals had also established protocol when operating first or in adjacent fields. In Ecuador, for example, there was initial indication that when the Chinese oil consortium Andes Petroleum obtained EnCana's block,[126] it adopted EnCana's community and environmental standards. An oil consultant, who had worked for North American and Chinese companies in Ecuador, observed that for the Chinese company, Ecuador "is a test case on how to become an international player, how to become a major, big oil company."[127] Pointing to China's commitment to identify and to meet global environmental norms, the same consultant added, "With the Chinese, [their environmental awareness is] more of a reaction to what they perceive as to what they need to do to operate internationally in an international world."[128]

But by 2009, four years after the takeover and two years of Correa streamlining oil bids and favoring state-owned oil companies, the fallout had begun. The first- and second-tier managers at Andes Petroleum had left their posts to third-tier managers with limited skill and vision, relative to their predecessors and to the requirements of the position. According to one professional oil worker, more than half of the managers left the company immediately when EnCana sold its operations.[129] The second-tier managers were prepared to succeed them and were able to maintain national legal requirements of operations for some time. They were motivated by the opportunity to lead and to meet national standards. A year or two later, however, the second-tier managers had moved on and were replaced by the third tier, who lacked the training, capacity, and skill to meet national standards, let alone move the company's technical, environmental, and community relations fields forward. Some of these transitions are expected given any corporate restructuring or change of ownership and/or management.

In contrast, the oil employee suggested, the larger private companies typically exceeded national legal requirements. Even though Andes Petroleum succumbed to operating below national standards for a time, the worker acknowledged that this would be corrected soon so as to maintain good relations with the state. From this assessment, the Northern oil companies imported standards and conditions that exceeded national requirements, while Chinese, and perhaps other state-owned companies, set targets at national standards, whereby state policy and regulations dictate the social and environmental conditions experienced in the oil blocks.[130] Those interviewees claimed that one of the critical differences was how large private companies invest in preventing problems in the field, whether technically, environmentally, or socially, before they arrive, while the Chinese, and perhaps state-owned operators in general, have adopted a firefighting, short-term mentality, of putting out the conflicts or problems as they arise. This anecdotal assessment warrants additional investigation from social scientists as private to state-run transitions in oil fields may be on the rise worldwide.

Contributing an additional workplace insight, one added that "the managers of these [private multinational] companies come out of a new generation, an environmental generation of the 1970s and 1980s, so they either genuinely care about the environment . . . or they have to in order to be in the position that they are in."[131] In contrast, the directors or managers of South American and Asian companies may lack this perspective. Indeed, China's limited value for or appreciation of the environment and limited understanding of environmental justice may generate even more substandard practices if permitted by national leaders where China's oil companies operate. To this, the consultant added, "So there's no peer pressure, basically to do the right thing."[132] At the time, there was also insufficient national and public pressure to correct for a peer deficiency.

Yet environmental activists and affected communities in the Amazon would probably caution us to be wary of a pro-Northern tendency among professional oil workers and researchers when comparing national oil standards. "I have yet to see an example of responsible oil drilling in the Amazon. Not a single one," declared one activist. "So I think 'best practices' are sort of a myth, when you are talking about such a fragile ecosystem, like the Amazon, and a place where the people depend on the resources of the forest and they depend on clean water. I just think they cannot coexist."[133]

According to another activist in the Andean region, who ran into "two or three people from old EnCana" by coincidence, "They sort of talked to me like we were all old buddies and stuff. . . . They were saying, [well] there were a couple of comments, but similar things like, 'Too bad the really good people are gone from the project.' And as far as we were concerned nobody was ever good."[134]

In 2003, toward the end of the anti-OCP campaign, another activist who had grown increasingly wary of multinational goodwill said, "I'm getting the feeling that a lot of these corporations have a checklist of what they need, what criteria they need in order to be considered socially and environmentally responsible. . . . But when you examine what meaning lies behind that checkmark, it's very shallow."[135] This activist's interpretation of oil operations may be fairly accurate. But given changes in the oil industry, what may be important is the checklist, and whether private oil companies have a different checklist from state-owned companies of South America and Asia.

Two years before EnCana's departure, a campaigner against its operations in Ecuador and against the OCP pipeline project reflected on whether success would be achieved if EnCana left Ecuador and on its meaning to neighboring residents. According to this advocate:

> It's very hard, personally, for me to define what success is. My success depends on what Ecuadorian groups want success to be. I've often asked myself the question all the time. Well, do you want to try to get EnCana out of there or not? And it's a really, really huge question. Because let's say that this campaign gets EnCana out. That's great. EnCana has been taught a lesson, and they are going to think so much harder the next time before they go into a controversial area. But at the same time, another company is going to replace them. And EnCana's argument, and the argument of a lot of other companies, is well, "We are doing it better than a lot of other companies, so it better be us than somebody else." . . . My response is "Yeah, but you're still not good enough."[136]

This activist's prescience is admirable given what had transpired in Ecuador after EnCana's departure and OCP's completion. It also lends a note of caution to first-time transnational campaigners. Global advocacy is two steps forward, one and three-quarters steps back. But they appear to keep working and to keep recruiting activists for that one-quarter achieved per decade. NGOs are outnumbered by corporate interests in terms of capital, resources, political influence, networks, and sheer number of adherents. Returning to China, China was not doing anything worse than or much different from Northern oil practices in Ecuador. For more than a decade, community demands for employment, healthy environments, and global justice have been presented to Northern multinationals and state leaders with only limited, and rarely just, remedy. Moreover, it was the practices of Northern multinationals and the policies, austerity measurements, privatization demands, exclusionary practices, and entrenched inequities of the Global North that led Ecuador to court Chinese businesses.

That said, China's interpretation of environmental norms and human rights may be the most problematic, and it warrants careful consideration. If China's officials and its citizens have an anemic barometer on these issues or have a high tolerance for civic abuse for themselves, they may have higher tolerance for greater injustice for others. In China, arrests of political activists, inadequate labor safeguards, inequitable distribution of resources between rural and urban populations,[137] and a legacy of environmental negligence, including toxic spills and air pollution, paint a dismal picture especially if these practices and policies are transported overseas.[138] China's operations in Sudan and Burma were particularly alarming. China had been criticized for neocolonial practices;[139] for exploring and extracting oil in Burma, which in a climate of political suppression had led to land seizures, local economic destabilization, and polluted rivers;[140] for arming Sudan, heightening internal displacement there and underwriting Sudan's human rights abuses;[141] and for also swaying other oil-needy nations, such as India, to disregard international standards when acquiring oil overseas.[142] Beyond the specific harms, Vaclav Smil suggests that China's history of drastic policy instability, or "abrupt lurches from one extreme to another," will continue to be experienced, thereby maintaining a cycle of economic and societal hardship.[143] Now, such hardship may be distributed beyond China's borders.

In Ecuador, these practices had yet to materialize, though China may practice less transparency and accountability than its predecessors.[144] "With regards to social and environmental issues, the company is not one that is manifesting much transparency," noted a government representative in reference to Chinese oil operators in general. "For example, with regards to oil spills, we [just] don't know."[145]

But if you expect China's standards to be worse overseas than in China, an analysis of Chinese practices may disappoint you. In this situation, China represents an anomaly. In some places, China's global operations may be governed by a social and environmental commitment and standard that is greater than even their domestic practices, unlike Northern corporations whose practices slide downward when operating abroad.[146] China's oil operations can and will meet the standards expected of them, even if those standards are higher than Chinese ones.

Curbed by NGOs and INGOs?

In the past, international NGOs have been successful in pressuring oil companies to alter their practices by utilizing a formulaic response. Identify the victim and the corporate culprit, as well as the lender. Build a negative publicity campaign in a company's home and host countries, and around any retail operations. Tarnish their image among shareholders, especially those with social responsibility obligations. Become relentless with mass mailings, media coverage, street-side demonstrations, and disruption of shareholders' meetings. However, with China's state-owned oil operators, leverage or pressure points remain challenging to identify. The Chinese oil companies lack name recognition, have no retail outlets in the North or even in Ecuador, are self-financing, and lack an international image worthy of protection. "It's definitely an uphill battle and there's probably, in general, less avenues of pressure, which I think in turn just creates less transparency, and less accountability in general, but I'm not ready to cede and say well they are Chinese companies and we cannot do anything," said one international advocate in 2009.[147]

But to the Chinese companies operating in the Amazon, it appeared that the Ecuadorian government was the singular stakeholder, which would correspond with Beijing's dominant presence and far-reaching control over all of China, including Tibet and the Uighur people's region. In China, political leaders determine the country's environmental awareness, environmental reform, and sustainable practices. In Ecuador, Chinese businesses also "figure the government will deal with all the other stakeholders in the country," noted one oil professional.[148] However, in Ecuador, community and professional groups are active political participants, whether welcomed or not, and can destabilize a project with local strikes or blocking rights with legal or government assistance. Including multiple stakeholders in meetings is a model—demanded by organized civil society—that had yet to be adopted by Chinese companies in Ecuador, given their own less than democratic practices at home.

Even though Southern-to-Southern and state-to-state agreements as experienced between Ecuador and China undermine the traction and relevance of North-South transnational campaigns, Northern NGOs have expressed a commitment to stand alongside their community partners. "We have partnerships with these communities and we are there to help defend their rights," noted one. "And if they are saying that 'we do not want this company.' To us it doesn't really matter who that company is."[149]

Despite robust activism and professionalism in Ecuador and the country's new constitution that represents a legal tool, there are at least two weaknesses to challenging Chinese oil operations in the Amazon. First, Ecuador's recent commitment to a new kind of resource-driven, twenty-first-century socialism may further marginalize impacted communities and ecosystems. Second, there are no Chinese watchdogs overseas to monitor the activities of Chinese companies. Currently, Chinese companies operate without the co-presence of independent Chinese activists, NGOs, scholars, and journalists to inform, monitor, and question the former's practices.[150]

China's overseas operations—despite their own advocacy vacuum—point to the indirect pressure and success of Northern NGOs, which have demanded higher standards among Northern entities, which have then been adopted by Chinese entities. Consider, for example, China's 2007 efforts to incorporate social and environmental considerations into its lending policies, based on the Equator Principles. These principles are a voluntary agreement among a group of banks to finance socially and environmentally responsible projects that were inspired by the transnational campaign of opposition to the OCP pipeline. Sinopec Corp., PetroChina Co. Ltd., and CNOOC, like Petrobras, are each publicly traded entities, a position that the INGOs see as one possible avenue to influence the companies' environmental practices. "We've had conversations with a couple of shareholder groups—basically around this issue," claimed one environmental activist in Ecuador. "But at the time, we were talking more about Petrobras, which is also just expanding everywhere. And there are a lot of U.S. shareholders that have shares in Petrobras."[151] As to what is possible, Fidelity Investments dropped its PetroChina shares and other shareholders are being pressured to do so by a human rights campaign against PetroChina's operations in Sudan.[152] In addition, the West-East gas line linking Burma and China generated enough international pressure that BP withdrew its support.[153]

In another example of transnational pressure on state-run companies originating in the South, activists from Ecuador, Costa Rica, Paraguay, and Mexico held
a panel at the 2009 World Social Forum in Belem, Brazil, to raise awareness and
to form greater Southern ties on the petroleum, hydroelectric power, and biofuel
practices of Brazilian transnationals in the region. Even though the panel was
sponsored by Rosa Luxemburg Foundation, a German-based foundation for
political education, this panel demonstrated an increasingly empowered Southern network that was beginning to contest the impacts of extractive practices in
general, not just Northern practices due to the support of Northern advocates.
The direction of Southern-owned operations in the Amazon is not certain. But
it is not predetermined either. Ecuador's civil society is likely to press for greater
accountability and transparency through enforced legal mechanisms, boardroom
negotiations, and/or street-side demonstrations until economic, social, and environmental justice is realized in and near the sites impacted by the oil industry.

OCP-INSPIRED LEARNING

At the time of OCP's construction, Ecuador was a dynamic democracy with
a domestically mobilized military.[154] Political leaders were routinely ousted,
while unions and disgruntled communities regularly took to the streets for a
variety of perceived state offenses. Community consultations granted by the
state to oil-impacted communities fostered demands for even greater and
more meaningful degrees of civic participation on national and international
decisions. Indeed Lago Agrio—and the second oil town of Coca—appeared
best suited and well positioned to influence and negotiate with *any* oil operator. They were on the verge of achieving greater local authority and autonomy
in monitoring oil processes, participating in oil management plans and decision making, and locally delegating the distribution of oil wealth. Rather than
oil multinationals bringing democratic processes to Ecuador and oil-affected
communities, Lago Agrio represented a site where an organized community
seized an opportunity to introduce democratic and participatory practices to
both the state and the oil-industrial core. To be sure, the multinationals would
not have responded and the international advocacy groups would not have arrived without local mobilization efforts that were indicative of a forceful and
engaged civil society.

This potent analysis, written immediately after the OCP construction, collapsed during the time of Correa. Correa's commitment to oil-fueled socialism, rather than green- or ecosocialism, required the continued sacrifice of
communities and ecosystems sitting above the Amazon's oil reserves. The
slipperiness of Ecuadorian politics and China's epic quest for oil worldwide
pinpointed the importance of civil society as educators, monitors, and enforc-
ers of environmental, social, and economic justice despite newfound political
and global obstacles. Indeed, the insertion of Chinese oil companies and

state-owned oil operators in the Amazon tests Ecuador's NGOs and communities to challenge oil contamination, regardless of a company's place of origin, and without the influence of Northern networks. But under Correa's citizens' revolution, the country's environmental and participatory standards may drop while its societal principles, including laudable poverty reduction measures, rise. The more insidious threat to Ecuador's civic mobilization and participation realized in the countryside is not coming from the outside but may now be coming from within.

Despite this rather formidable note and the advancement of oil exploration and extraction across the Amazon, the numerous grassroots and professional campaigns formalized to counter the OCP pipeline proved advantageous. The community that resisted EnCana near Lago Agrio continued to defy Andes Petroleum. Some of the Quito-based professional NGOs, which negotiated the environmental fund with OCP, were crucial in formulating and initiating a discussion on a postpetroleum economy and expanded conservation plans, including the Yasuní-ITT Initiative to reduce greenhouse gas emissions and to keep Ecuador's oil in the ground. In Mindo, the grassroots ecologists persisted in building themselves as a national model of ecological consciousness—at least to receptive communities—by implementing small-scale, locally controlled economic opportunities and linkages through sustainable resource use and local initiatives. They were actively presenting their alternative ideas and ideals, even though they still struggled to meet them themselves. In Esmeraldas, the city continued to mobilize for just and equitable recognition of its vital location near the port and as site for one of the nation's most important refineries.

Three lessons emerged when comparing OCP campaigns with post-OCP activities in Ecuador. First, neither a capitalist democracy nor a socialist democracy succeeds in including those who have been traditionally excluded in an oil economy: the most affected and impacted communities. Therefore, how to effectively include the excluded in project decisions (including the ability to reject projects deemed too damaging or costly by the people most affected) before a project receives government approval and begins construction remains a pressing concern. A mandated inclusion of affected people needs to be incorporated into both models until a sustainable and ecologically just economic model is adopted that is governed by affected people for communities and ecosystems rather than for the current political economic system.

Second, the oil industrial base appears more inclusive in terms of spreading power and influence to new overseas oil producers and extractors than the political systems of some nations in spreading power and influence to communities and other nations. Petroleum companies of semiperipheral nations, especially China, are sitting on the edge of the oil-industrial core and are perhaps gaining entry to it, via their Southern-to-Southern influences and operations.

When coupled, the first and second lessons beg for the third. The final impression is that Southern-led initiatives by the most-affected and most-impacted people remain paramount in countering an ever-expanding global and unequal marketplace of visible and invisible suppliers, including the hidden yet most damaged ecosystems and people, and the least harmed consumers.

Two patterns that speak to the global political economy are also identified. Oil and impact flows and advocacy flows remain marred and disconnected from each other. This pattern persists and is perhaps aggravated by the rise of Southern socialism influences, or Correa's policies and China's practices in particular. From Ecuadorian fields, crude oil and power are flowing to China and to South American nations, yet impact remains localized at the site of production, transportation, and refining. Advocacy networks, however, remain obstructed. Nationally, Correa is blocking arguments by grassroots and professional dissenters against his administration's policies. Globally, China is hindering opposition by disabling China's own civil responsiveness to its national struggles let alone becoming aware of China's harmful overseas practices. Elsewhere I suggested that China's national pride—like America's—may prevent it from either identifying the injuries that it causes worldwide or may identify them and elect to ignore them.[155] The second pattern reveals how transnational advocacy networks sustain selected campaigns, as in the case of OCP, but have little direct leverage over states and operators where they do not reside. Their indirect influence in altering Northern practices is then adopted through corporate peer learning and competition. But such adoption also needs constant reinforcement from a vigilant society and a government that is fully committed to the rights and well-being of human beings and ecosystems.

To generalize from the changes and impacts brought on by the Correa administration and China, the importance of a community's history with the oil sector and locale in the oil process, and the importance of a nation's global position and social commitment to the most excluded and most affected, cannot be understated. Left unchecked or unmonitored by affected people and concerned advocates, democratic, socialist, or capitalist leadership and for-profit or for-state oil extractors operate with impunity, thereby pressuring downward environmental, community, and worker standards, provisions, safeguards, and protections. For a global environmental justice movement to occur and for a global ecological and participatory democracy to be launched and sustained, this study supports a Southern-led initiative by the most-affected communities of current political and economic systems, who are also most tied to their local ecosystems, to formulate a new economic model. A people's just and sustainable economic system in a democratic and participatory political sphere is not beyond them, above them, or beneath them. It would be by them and for them, theoretically and materially. It would be people putting people and the natural resources necessary for life first. If not, then climate change, to which the processing and use of petroleum is a significant contributor, may prompt a people (or an elite) movement toward systems that are small and just (or exceedingly exploitive and unequal), and that build dignity and sustainability (or shame, excessive hoarding, and uninhabitable environments).

Appendix

Data Collection and Researcher Participation

The parameters of this book were established by my preliminary research questions on the efficacy and impacts of transnational advocacy that were grounded in a contemporary event: the local, national, and transnational mobilization of environmental organizations and affected community groups in response to the construction of an oil pipeline, the Oleoducto de Crudos Pesados or OCP, in Ecuador. The research process incorporated an inductive, flexible, and reflexive design in line with the qualitative research processes of grounded theory and rhythm analysis.[1] The inductive and emergent process enabled the research questions to inform the data, as the data informed the questions.[2]

CASE SELECTION

For this mesolevel analysis, I conducted an ethnographic, comparative case study using a longitudinal research design. Rather than comparing transnational campaigns across countries, this research project examined the diversity in domestic and transnational ties across four sites in a single low-income or developing country over nine years (2001–2009) and at three periods in the construction process (preconstruction, during construction, and postconstruction).

Each case was selected to illustrate and analyze the distinctions and nuances of local, national, and transnational networks, and each was notable in its oil history with the state and the industry and its position in the petrochemical process. As noted in chapter 1, Lago Agrio was a frontier town on the edge of the Amazon and a site of oil exploring, storing, and receiving. The capital Quito headquartered government bodies, professional environmental NGOs, and oil companies. Mindo was a nature-based, ecotourism community, previously inexperienced in the oil industry. The fourth site was Esmeraldas, a community on the Pacific Coast with a history of oil refining, storing, and exporting, and the location of the pipeline's output terminal. At each site, grassroots community groups, established NGOs, and/or activist mayors mobilized a response to the announcement of the pipeline project.

In addition, two other cases were examined briefly for greater insight into the four primary ones. These included the town of Coca, an oil community on the edge of the Amazon that mobilized at times alongside Lago Agrio to challenge the state's use of oil resources, and the Indigenous communities of the Amazon, represented by national and local Indigenous organizations. Unlike other works on Ecuador, this research was not specific to Indigenous populations.

For this study, the unit of analysis was the organization or group. Organizations represented professional nongovernmental organizations established prior to the construction of OCP that focused on environmental rights, environmental law, environmental conservation, environmental scientific study; the protection of Indigenous, social, and/or human rights; or were anti-oil, antiglobalization, antineoliberalism, and/or antiprivatization. The majority of national organizations were not member based but instead relied on international support.

Community groups represented the mobilization of lay activists in response to OCP. In the case of Mindo and Lago Agrio, a community group included town residents, as well as landowners, lodge owners, or tour operators outside of the town proper. In the case of Mindo, some landowners of tourism operations and ecological reserves were physically closer to the towns of Los Bancos or Tandayapa but marketed themselves as being affiliated with the town of Mindo. In particular, this community represented landowners, hostel and lodge owners, and tour operators near the greater Mindo-Nambillo Cloud Forest Reserve. Likewise, outside of the town of Lago Agrio were landowners and colonists, or settlers, who moved into the area when the oil industry first built access roads. The town of Lago Agrio served as a focal point for rural landowners to shop, to conduct business, and to meet.

One limitation to this research was a nonexhaustive selection of cases. I narrowed my cases to four on the basis of each one's historical, geographical, and political position in the country's oil economy. However, there were other communities along the route that protested the pipeline or negotiated agreements with OCP that I did not select for analysis. For instance, the people of San Vicente de Andoas, a town of 1,500, stopped OCP construction in 2002 by staging a roadblock. Within a week, this community reached an agreement with OCP to fix four kilometers of highway between Andoas and El Cisne.[3] There were other communities like this one that initiated fairly quick campaigns until they received assurances that their minimal demands would be met by OCP or the Ecuadorian government. In another case, the town of Nono, which is only four kilometers from the pipeline's route, swelled by 1,400 people to 4,400 due to OCP's construction.[4] In 2003, the community denounced OCP workers for throwing their trash in the Pichán River. Another type of impact occurred in Manta,[5] a port town south of Esmeraldas. Though not along the pipeline's right-of-way, heavy equipment for the pipeline's construction was brought into Ecuador via three ports, Esmeraldas, Manta, and Guayaquil, which created a temporary wave of economic activity and employment in these locales. In general, these smaller communities resembled the Esmeraldas case in that they exhibited appeasement once a demand or need was met or a quiet displeasure if the demand or need went unmet.

CONTACT SELECTION

Without prior experience or contacts in Ecuador, I initially drew up a contact list by gathering the names of the most established organizations in Ecuador, including affiliates or partners of U.S.-based conservation organizations and those with links to U.S. networks, such as Amazon Watch, Rainforest Action Network, and Amazon Alliance. Organizations were further identified through a broad reading on environmental, social rights, and Indigenous issues in Ecuador. Once in Ecuador, additional contacts were discovered from roundtable discussions and seminars on OCP and the oil industry. These events included a roundtable at Facultad Latinoamericana de Ciencias Sociales (FLACSO) and the International Congress on Petroleum, the Environment and Development in 2001, and the OCP Truth Commission conference in 2002. Contacts were then asked to identify others, including national and international partners or advocates, for potential participation.

INTERVIEWS

I conducted open-ended, semistructured interviews with grassroots community leaders, directors of national and international environmental, development and human rights organizations, local government officials, white-collar workers in the oil sector, and environmental consultants. Fieldwork occurred during three time periods in the construction process. Preliminary fieldwork in 2001 represented preconstruction mobilization and responses, fieldwork in 2002 occurred at the peak of construction and community/NGO contention, fieldwork in 2003 and 2004 was immediately postconstruction, and fieldwork in 2007 and 2009 represented a distant temporal point from immediate construction impact, negotiation, and conflict. Participants came from nine countries in South America, North America, and Europe.

In Ecuador, I conducted 14 interviews with 17 people in 2001, 23 interviews with 27 people in 2002, 49 interviews with 53 people in 2003, 12 interviews with 13 people in 2004, 15 interviews with 16 people in 2007, and 12 interviews with 13 people in 2009. The majority of interviews were conducted in person in Ecuador, though a few were conducted in person in Washington D.C. and Montreal, Canada, in 2004, and two were conducted by phone in 2004. In total, I conducted 125 interviews with 139 people. Most people were between

Table A.1. Interviews Conducted

	2001	2002	2003	2004	2007	2009	Total
Grassroots Group	7	9	8	1	5	0	30
Domestic NGO	4	7	21	2[a]	3	4	41
INGO w/ Quito Office	1	5	5	3	3	2	19
INGO	0	1	4	6	0	0	11
Oil Industry or Consultant	5	4	8	0	1	4	22
Government Agency	0	0	5	0	2	2	9
Other[b]	0	1	2	1	2	1	7
Interview Encounters	14	23	49	12	15	12	125
People Interviewed	17	27	53	13	16	13	139

[a]One director of an NGO in Quito was interviewed by telephone in 2005, but I am counting that interview as occurring in 2004 in this table.
[b]Other includes international institutions or affiliates as well as tour operators and landowners not affiliated with an organization.

thirty and fifty-five years old, and 95 were men and 44 women. Of the people and organizations interviewed, several were interviewed twice, a few were interviewed three to four times, and one was interviewed five times over the years.

Interviews were conducted in English or Spanish, and sometimes both languages were used. When their English was better than my Spanish, I asked them if they would speak in English. Some agreed, while others spoke to me only in Spanish. Interviews were tape-recorded, if permitted, and transcribed. A few times a translator was present; at other times, a translator assisted in transcribing the tapes. Interviews lasted from thirty minutes to nearly two hours.

From the beginning, the line of questioning resembled a continuous design described by Herbert Rubin and Irene Rubin as reevaluating and redesigning future interview questions, based on the discovery in previous interviews.[6] Initial questions in 2001 were broad in order to discover the organization and its initial orientation to the OCP pipeline and its existing networks. In 2002, at the peak of construction and contention or negotiation, questions focused on the evolution of the organization in terms of its position, networks, and access to external agencies. By 2003, I designed both follow-up and reflective questions. In 2007, I focused on the environmental fund initiated by the Quito-based organizations and Mindo's efforts in establishing itself as a national example of ecotourism. In 2009, I focused on the NGOs responses to the Correa administration and a replacement of private Northern oil operators with Southern state-owned ones.

PARTICIPANT OBSERVATION

In addition, I observed activist campaigns as well as routine organizational activities. I observed some of their mobilization efforts, internal meetings, and press conferences. See textbox A.1. Though I had approached my research with the intent of only observing the different activist campaigns and NGO meetings, I became a participant-observer among the actions organized in Mindo, Quito, Lago Agrio, Tena, and smaller villages in the Amazon. Regardless of my intent, my presence at some grassroots meetings or actions was perceived as supportive. It was not my perception of my work, but their perception of my presence that determined I was a participant-observer. I believe I was seen as an international body aligned with their campaign, and a body to boost the numbers participating in their actions, which they hoped would receive national and international media coverage and affect local change. As they told me later, those who did not know me often assumed, or possibly hoped, that I was a foreign journalist, which was understandable given their desire for media coverage.[7] Though national and international journalists were at the various actions, I was also there with camera and pen and paper. While I was seeing them as "participants" in my research, I believe that their perception of my presence influenced their actions especially when confronting the police. At least once, an activist looked in my camera with a defiance that appeared constructed for the front page of a newspaper.

In many cases, the lives of the person interviewed and the setting of the interview commingled. Interviews in Mindo were often conducted on porches, in kitchens, and at dining tables; and oftentimes they were conducted with two activists at a time, such that one picked up the theme or thread of thought of the other. Scheduling appointments was haphazard; oftentimes I just showed up or stopped by on several occasions before we both had available time to meet. In Esmeraldas and Lago Agrio, the interviews were conducted in sparse offices, and at times they were conducted outdoors. Interviews with Quito's professional NGOs were more formal: they were arranged by assistants or by e-mail, and scheduled appointments were always kept. Interviews with public officials resembled Quito's professional arrangements in the capital and small-town informality outside of the capital. Everyone was busy. Their OCP campaigns were added onto their other campaigns or their day job. Of course, I remain extremely grateful for everyone who took time out of their campaigns and work, and after-work schedules, to give me access to what they were thinking, interpreting, and assessing with regard to the pipeline project.

Meeting oil representatives and employees of international bodies in their Quito-based offices was a different experience. When I entered some of these offices, I passed through a metal detector, had my bag searched, and was required to leave photo identification and my cell phone and tape recorder at the guard's desk, unless I received authorization to enter the interior with a recorder. I would then be escorted to the appointed place. Once, I received a visitor's badge and a written guide in both Spanish and English on the rules of conduct while in the building. Needless to say, the experience between interviewing a grassroots activist at his or her home, and sharing a meal together afterward, was completely different from interviewing a representative of an oil company or an international agency in his or her office. The view of a snow-capped volcano from some offices was breathtaking though. It was also noted

---

TEXTBOX A.1. ORGANIZED EVENTS ATTENDED

2001

- Roundtable discussion, "Ecuador Post-Petrolero vx. Construccion del OCP" (Post-Oil Ecuador vs. OCP Construction), Facultad Latinoamericana de Ciencias Sociales (FLACSO), Quito, 20 June.
- Congreso Internacional Petroleo, Ambiente y Desarrollo (International Congress on Petroleum, Environment and Development), Hilton Colón, Quito, 9–11 July.

2002

- International inspection-action-hike to Cerro Guarumos with Julia Hill and media, Mindo, 15 July.
- Action-demonstration in front of Occidental Petroleum, Quito, 16 July.
- OCP Truth Commission conference, Quito, 14 August.

2003

- Demonstration and presentation regarding a secondary Perenco pipeline, Tena, 3 August.
- Action in front of police headquarters to request the deportation of International Monetary Fund officials for misconduct, Quito, 4 September.
- FLACSO-Petroecuador conference, Quito, 12 September.
- Talk on Texaco trial, sponsored by Amazon Watch and Acción Ecológica with Bianca Jagger, Quito, 10 October.
- Toxic tour with Quito and Cofan youth groups, Lago Agrio and Amazon, 11 October.
- Community meeting of Kichwa, Huaorani, and Acción Ecológica, San Carlos, 12 October.
- International inspection meeting, Borja, 21 October.
- International inspection tour of OCP route, Quito–Lago, 21 and 25 October.
- International inspection of Papallacta oil spill, Papallacta, 21 October.
- 2nd International Workshop Against OCP, Lago Agrio, 22–23 October.
- International forum on OCP, Quito, 27 October.
- International press conference on OCP, Quito, 27 October.
- Court proceedings of Texaco trial, Lago Agrio, 28 October.
- Sarayacu demonstration outside of Argentina embassy, Quito, 27 November.
- Youth demonstration against Texaco, Quito, 29 November.
- Sarayacu rally and protest march, Puyo, 5–6 December.
- Tribunal hearing on OCP, Quito, 10 December.
- Teacher union's protest, Quito, 10 December.

2004

- Press interview on EnCana's operations in Ecuador, Montreal, Canada, 17 March.
- Speaking tour by GlobalAware Canada "Rude Oil: Canadian Involvement in the Amazon," Montreal, Canada, 17 March.
- Special screening of *Trinkets and Beads*, followed by a discussion on oil exploration in Yasuní National Park, Quito, 3 June.

2007

- General meeting on Acción Ecológica's Yasuní Campaign, Quito, 18 May.
- 1er Congreso Ambiental Ecuatoriano en Mindo (First Ecuadorian Environmental Congress in Mindo), Mindo, 2–3 June.

2009

- World Social Forum, Belem, Brazil, February.

that one of the buildings for an oil company had energy saving devices (such as motion sensors for light in the hallways) that were probably adopted due to energy saving commitments, a green quotient checklist, or environmentally friendly and sustainable requirements.

I include a description of these interviews in my discussion of observations as the process served as a secondary source of observational material. Indeed, interviews gathered both the spoken word of the participants as well as observational data of a participant's workaday landscape, whether that is a living room or an office tower.

The two extremes of oil and grassroots, with mainstream organizations and environmental consultants at the fulcrum, served to balance interpretations of events, sift inconsistencies, and countercheck my observations and experiences between the divergent participants. For example, on a "toxic tour" in the Amazon, I inspected oil pools, poked at fresh oil pockets emerging from the soil, talked to landowners, and observed their young children with skin rashes that they believed are caused by oil-contaminated water. The group then gathered the next day at a Kichwa village to drink chicha, a drink of yucca and plantain that is left to ferment before drinking, and to inspect and record the oil ponds in their community. The heat of the oil burn-off, the strong stench of oil pools, and the skin rashes of the children were disturbing. People's fear that they would not be able to stop the current oil practices in their community was palpable and thoroughly disheartening. And then when I returned to the capital after the toxic tour, I met with an oil spokesperson for an imported meal.

After two days of boiled chicken, rice, and plantains in the Oriente, the chance to bathe with lukewarm water to clean the dirt from under my nails, and then that evening to have imported wine with my meal was as proportionately pleasurable as it was disquieting. I hope neither experience co-opted my perception. Rather, I believe the research process and my perspective became clearer as the polar disparities served to ground the realities and contexts of the different groups. The experience also located me between the two: renting a modest, shared apartment and routinely dining somewhere between boiled plantains and imported salmon.

DOCUMENTS

Many of the organizations and networks had prepared public position papers, proposals for the media, meeting notes, online correspondence, and alternative environmental and social impact studies of the pipeline construction. Documents provided the focus and point of persuasion of the organizations and were particularly important in analyzing how domestic stakeholders framed and claimed a position and demands in relation to OCP, how international advocates then reframed and reclaimed local position and demand, and how both of these dynamics varied over time.

The more professional organizations also prepared reports or hired consultants to report on the existing or potential environmental and social impacts caused by the pipeline construction. For prepared assessments see the Mindo Working Group (2001), Fundación Maquipucuna (2001), Fundación Natura et al (2001), Acción Ecológica bulletins in 2001 and 2003, Weemaels (2002), Frente de Defensa de la Amazonia and Instituto de Ciencias y Estudios Interdisciplinarios (2001), and Amazon Watch (Caffrey 2001; 2002). Visiting experts, including the Smithsonian Institution (2001), Goodland (2002), van Gelder (2003), Snater (2002), and Stone & Webster (2002), were additional sources of information. Acción Ecológica and Oilwatch are particularly prolific on the oil industry in Ecuador.

Documents also included videos, including *Risky Business: EnCana and the OCP in Ecuador* (2003) produced by Nadja Drost for GlobalAware Canada; *Between Midnight and the Rooster's Crow* (2005) directed by Nadja Drost and produced by Rocinante Productions; *Amazon Oil Pipeline—Pollution, Corruption and Poverty* (2002) produced by Juan Pablo Barragán and Ivonne Ramos and distributed by Rainforest Information Centre of Australia; and *Trinkets and Beads* (1996) directed by Christopher Walker and distributed by First Run/ Icarus Films of Brooklyn, New York. A more recent film is *CRUDE: The Real Price of Oil*, by Joe Berlinger (2009).

I did not conduct a systematic sampling of documents prepared on OCP and documents gathered were not from an exhaustive list. I collected for primary analysis the reports prepared by a range of organizations. Most of the reports I collected directly from the organization, though I received additional reports through secondary sources. For secondary analysis, I also gathered news media reports from general, environmental, and oil news sources, as well as World Bank discussion papers on Ecuador and the oil sector.

TRIANGULATION AND COMPARISON

Two strengths of this research were found in its triangulation of data and its constant comparison between cases. The triangulation of data, including interviews, observations, and documents, and the triangulation of contacts, including national and international organizations and oil entities, served as a constant and ongoing reliability check. The comparison of domestic and international organizations and community groups between four site-specific cases and over multiple time periods, holding constant a single petroleum project that was enabled by multinational corporations and external debt, enabled a more thorough analysis of transnational advocacy and localized community campaigns.

I clustered my data by case to find similarity and patterns among organizations within a single case (such as Lago Agrio), and then expanded my analysis to explore commonality and diversity between sites (such as between Lago Agrio and Esmeraldas). I began in chronological order with the data I had gathered from organizations and news accounts of Lago Agrio. I then expanded this analysis to incorporate national data gathered outside of Lago Agrio, but in regards to Lago Agrio to better inform my analysis of this case. I then included data from international sources for an informed analysis of Lago Agrio's position in transnational networks. Next I returned to the national-level data to compare across locations, such as between Quito and Mindo, or Lago Agrio and Esmeraldas.

Though one could argue that by examining cases within a single country, I was controlling for cultural context in transnational campaigns, this study demonstrates case-by-case differences in responding to OCP and to outside organizations. The marginalized community of Esmeraldas better resembled the marginalized people of the world than the mainstream conservation organizations in Quito. Likewise, the internationally educated directors of Quito's largest NGOs better resembled their Northern counterparts than affected oil communities in the Amazon.

RESEARCHER ACCESS AND BIAS

Phil Brown suggested that in-depth interviews make for "a more charged situation" and construct the research process as "a negotiated interaction."[8] For such research, initial and continuing access is critical. I gained and built access to the divergent participants through a varied approach of personal characteristics and repeated contact. However, "negotiating entry,"[9] and I would add reentry, varied over time and by the participant's role in the very contentious OCP oil project. I was always an outsider.

As I was unfamiliar with Ecuador and with Ecuadorian organizations in 2001 and to facilitate access, I first met with a few spokespersons of the different organizations to introduce myself and to explain my research, before requesting a more formal interview. These initial meetings were not tallied in the interview count, though they provided me a broad understanding of the early issues and enabled the participants to reflect on my questions and their answers before our next meeting. For those individuals and their organizations that were recommended to me by others, I did not begin with an introductory meeting.

My American nationality served as both a point of access, as well as a barrier. In 2001, some Ecuadorian directors of NGOs, who had studied in the United States, were open to receiving me without prior introductions. Others who worked within a U.S. network or were from North America or Europe were also open to me as one foreign person to another. On the other hand, some groups were also aware that oil companies in developing places hire social scientists to facilitate community acceptance of oil presence. I myself was witness to one oil consultant offering a contract to a local social scientist. For those groups uncomfortable with, or untrusting of, my nationality and/ or occupation, I gained access over time and through my appearance at their actions or in their offices, restaurants, and communities and by my constant reiteration that I was meeting with different pockets of affected people, professional organizations, and oil representatives. My source of funding to conduct my research was a point of concern with some of the smaller organizations, as they believed initially that I had received funding from oil companies. They also probably believed that my research funds would have been better spent supporting their campaigns. It is a luxury to be able to travel worldwide to conduct research and to talk with people. Recommendations and introductions by other stakeholders helped as well. Individual oil companies or organizations verified my credentials, and some were open to meeting with me.

By 2002, NGOs and community groups had taken a particularly strong and active position on the OCP project and were energized, mobilized, and willing to spend a great deal of time talking about their roles in the process. Those I did not meet with in 2001 were receptive to meeting with me after I explained my ongoing investigation and demonstrated my knowledge of the OCP project. One activist quizzed me on the oil companies composing the OCP consortium to test my knowledge, claiming that even some activists did not know which companies they were protesting.

On the other hand, oil representatives, consultants, and the OCP consortium in particular had retracted and had taken a position of extreme caution when meeting with me. In 2001, oil representatives and their consultants were more open to meeting with me than they were in 2002. For example, in the second year, one did not permit the interview to be tape-recorded, though I was permitted to do so in 2001. During this same interview, a third party at the participant's request was present to take notes during the interview. A third refused to meet with me, even though we had met the previous year.

By 2003, the positions of the grassroots groups and oil representatives had flipped. In 2001, NGOs, grassroots groups, and oil representatives were receptive to meeting with me. By 2002, NGOs and grassroots groups were very receptive, while the oil entities were less so. However, by 2003 that dynamic would be reversed among a few. Overall, Quito-based NGOs remained accessible, while some grassroots leaders were recuperating alone, perhaps demoralized and exhausted from their extensive efforts with little impact. Oil representatives, on the other hand, had seen the completion of their project and the initial oil flow from Lago Agrio to the tanks waiting on the Pacific. Some had completed their term in Ecuador and were leaving soon and were willing to meet. These observations in changing access warrant additional investigation that is not fully addressed here.

Sponsorship or alignment with one organization is also a critical consideration for research. Prior to traveling to Ecuador, I had anticipated some type of local alignment. However, once I was in Ecuador, I realized that an introduction or sponsorship of my research by a local NGO would have impaired my ability to meet with other competing stakeholders, particularly among established organizations and community groups. Given the polemical relations not only between OCP and civil society, but also between the organizations in Ecuador that compete for international funds and for national prominence, I chose the slower process in 2001 of introducing myself to the various stakeholders.

Throughout the research process, I sought a researcher's role of being both embedded and autonomous of the mobilized communities.[10] That is, I sought to establish linkages that did not lead to co-option. This idea of an embedded and autonomous researcher originates in Peter Evans's "embedded autonomy," or ideal model of a state's economic role in development.[11] Successful state intervention involved a balance of the state being both closely engaged in the process of industrialization, as well as sufficiently removed as to govern business. Degrees of both also served as a foundation for conducting fieldwork, to be closely engaged with the organizations, as well as to be sufficiently removed as to offer independent assessment and interpretation.

I believe that many participants either initially or after a few contacts or a background search among mutual contacts felt that I was sincerely "trying to tell their story in a supportive fashion," identified by Brown as an important component in community research.[12] Nevertheless, as the process was negotiated, participants had questions of their own, including the one on funding already addressed. Other common questions included (1) Why did you select Ecuador? (2) What do you really think of OCP? (3) Who have you been talking to and what did they say? In 2001, I was a first-time field researcher and stumbled through and struggled with my responses. By 2003, they knew me and I could clearly respond to these same questions.

As for the first question, I felt initially that some oil representatives thought I selected Ecuador and the OCP project from the standpoint of a personal grievance against particular North American multinationals—that I had selected OCP to attack the individual companies. Some held this view particularly in the second year. To prove otherwise, I spent a great amount of time explaining my research, my qualifications, providing the general guiding research question of my work, expressing my desire to learn and discover from them. On the other side, some of the grassroots activists thought, or wanted to believe, I selected Ecuador because of a love of the country. The country of Ecuador is beautiful. Its natural diversity includes the Amazon jungle, the Galapagos Islands, and the Andes Mountains. But certainly and sincerely, I knew nothing of Ecuador and the specific oil companies when I began this research. My primary quest was an understanding of how transnational networks work to hold any oil multinational operating in any developing country accountable for its impacts on natural and community resources and how its presence or absence supports and/or hinders local campaigns. Ecuador was selected because of the timing of the OCP pipeline project and because of the access between Ecuador and the United States.

As for the second question, I described my own efforts to approach this with an open mind and without preestablished opinion. What I did not mention was that when I left the office of an oil representative or environmental consultant, I left hopeful that contingency plans had been implemented and precautions had been taken to safeguard against any spills. But then when I left the offices of NGOs and the homes of community groups, I also felt either their desire to recuperate resources for the protection of other sites or their panic over the potential change in their environments and lifestyles. At other times, I was angered by the extreme inequities between the various "stakeholders" and appalled by my own privileged position when speaking to some and my own disadvantage when speaking to others. Their points of view were so varied, litigious, and passionate as to skew my perception of the construction process toward the middle even though I understand that oil spills are toxic and cause short-term and long-term, ecological, community, and individual harm and damage.

And as for the third question, the seemingly most pressing question for many participants particularly at the height of conflict, I explained in general terms that I was meeting with various representatives and that I could not and would not share what was told to me by any participant, and that as with them the interviews were confidential. Several of the affected people as opposed to the more professional organizations seemed set in persuading me of the correctness, truth, and accuracy of their position. At times, they appeared to seek international acceptance of their position through international advocacy groups as well as through nonnational researchers.

Despite achieving a balance in data collection and assessment, I nevertheless attempted to conduct my research in the service of community groups, activists, and mainstream NGOs in developing places, which were confronting the resources and power of multinational corporations much greater than their own. I also felt deep empathy and respect for the community groups and more activist-minded NGOs that expressed a level of commitment against seemingly strong obstacles. I am also uneasy with multinationals from the United States operating in developing places at a standard below those in the United States, which is an inadequate standard for communities and ecosystems. I also see a role for organizations in the United States holding U.S.-based multinationals accountable for their actions at home and overseas. On the other hand, my educational training had constructed me to be moderately comfortable with the language of oil consultants and oil spokespersons as well as members of the environmental conservation movement. This style of talk seemed solid and concrete, and there was comfort in the numbers and the detailed language of technicians, whereas days of activist-speak became exhausting and frustrating, especially when it became antiforeign. Nevertheless, as I conducted this research, I tried to remain open to discovering the events and experiences of the multiple participants.

RESEARCHER INFLUENCE

To Brown, research of this kind is "tinged with a pro-community ethos," and the researcher in the field of environmental sociology, environmental health, development, or globalization may "feel a responsibility to balance the re-source inequity by allying with affected people."[13] Moreover, Jackie Smith said it well when she wrote, "Given the enormous inequalities of our day, I find it hard to even fathom the notion that any scholar might want to remain a neutral analyst of social reality, even if this were possible."[14] I would like to think my work sits in this realm.

I influenced the process inherently by being there among the stakeholders, and concretely, at times to my discomfort. I met with one grassroots activist who was very active in 2001, had ceased activity against the pipeline in 2002, and then we met in 2003. We met on three different occasions that year, and at the end of each occasion, he thanked me for my visit and for renewing his interest in the potential impacts of the construction. He expressed a strong and active desire to return to the fold of OCP negotiations and environmental land protection, after a year of ignoring the construction going on around him. In another case, an activist presented me as a student who supported and ac-companied the group on its actions. I smiled a tight line across my face at the grieved landowners, who were looking at me for support, while I was wonder-ing in shock: Is that me? Is that what I do?

I also made tangible contributions to the operations of various grassroots groups. For example, I made photocopies of public documents for groups with limited Internet access and photocopy funds. I carried videos from the United States from one advocate to a local organization to reduce their postage costs and to increase the likelihood of receipt. I stood beside them at actions. I took photographs during their protests and gave them duplicate copies as they did not have cameras. Perhaps if asked, I would have downloaded and photo-copied articles for the OCP member companies, but they never requested or needed such assistance from a graduate student. Indeed when a community schoolteacher wrote a glowing testimonial of how a multinational oil corpo-ration provided her school with US$1,000, I know that is pocket change for the corporation and a windfall for this school, just as I understood that my contributions to the grassroots groups were disproportionately important to them and of little effort by me, and that a $1,000 contribution to the school would have been disproportionately beneficial to them and inconsequential to an oil company.

Yet influence is also dualistic, and I was influenced greatly by them and the research process. Grassroots activists, operating out of their homes against multinationals, were a constant source of encouragement outside of the research process. One activist greeted me, after nine months out of town, with a smile and the words: "The fight continues." I know that rush of energy and excitement. I felt it while demonstrating in 2003 against then-president George Bush's war in Iraq, after learning from the Ecuadorians how to demonstrate publicly for what one believes. I was not a street-side activist in the United States until I observed activists in Ecuador. The point here is that the experience nurtured a hope for a semblance of humanity and decency that lives on in an increasingly doubtful mind.

As a final note, I would caution first-time field researchers because I went to the South and discovered the North. In this ever-increasingly interconnected and interdependent world, this finding is perhaps not so unexpected. For others, I would suggest that if we study low-income, developing, or Third World nations or communities anywhere in the world and ignore middle-to-high income, developed, or First World communities, entities, or nations nearby, we may have missed something critically important in our research. When we do this, we have spread the disadvantages of the poor and powerless by studying their deficiencies and have perpetuated elite advantages by privileging them with invisibility.

Notes

CHAPTER 1
OIL DISASTERS AND CONFLICTS

1. For assessments and comparisons of the different environmental movements in the United States as well as the origins of the discipline of environmental sociology, see Faber 2008: 1–6; Freudenburg 2008; Gottlieb 1993; and Hannigan 2006: 38.

2. North-South distinctions are not used here as geographical divisions; rather they denote the historical, political, economic, and social power of wealthier nations (the North, the First World, the core, and/or developed places) at the expense of poorer nations (the South, the Third World, the semiperiphery and periphery, and/or developing places). There are, for example, "Southern" pockets or communities in "Northern" nations or regions, and "Northern" enclaves in Southern places. The two extremes are linked, however, as one's position is realized due to the other's position.

3. On the environmental movement, see Gottlieb 1993, as well as the introductions of other recent works on environmental justice, including Faber 2008 and Pellow 2007.

4. On the racist practices and ideologies of environmentalism, or "environmentalism's troubled (and troubling) 'heart of whiteness,'" see Kosek 1996.

5. See Hannigan 2006: 77–78 on how "popularizers" translate science for lay or mass environmental understanding.

6. Carson 1962; Colborn, Dumanoski, and Myers 1997; and Steingraber 1997. The quote from *Living Downstream* by Sandra Steingraber is from the work's title.

7. See Brown 2007 on the environmental health movement; Brown 2002 on popular epidemiology; and Kroll-Smith, Brown, and Gunter 2000 on contested diseases.

8. Davis 2002: 143.

9. Davis 2002: 143.

10. Davis 2002: 143.

11. Brown 1995; Bullard 1993, 1994; and Pastor Jr., Sadd, and Hipp 2001. Researchers cite the grassroots EJ movement as emerging from Lois Gibbs's fight against the toxic contaminants at Love Canal, and the environmental racism movement as rising from the 1982 African American struggle in Warren County, North Carolina, against a proposed PCB (polychlorinated biphenyl) landfill. Environmental racism, in particular, gained acceptance with the publication of *Toxic Wastes and Race in the United States* in 1987 by the United Church of Christ.

12. Principles of Environmental Justice, 1991, http://www.ejnet.org/ej/principles.html. Environmental justice is increasingly used in decision making and policy implementation of resource use and industry, and in citing agreements between communities, government, and industry in the United States. For example, then-president Bill Clinton, in response to community concerns, issued an executive order for federal agencies to prioritize the identification and assessment of environmental health risks of children (Gibbs 2002: 108). In 1997 the U.S. Environmental Protection Agency selected the construction of a Shintech polyvinyl chloride plant in Louisiana as its first environmental justice test case (Roberts and Toffolon-Weiss 2001). Activists have also succeeded in the passage of the Superfund and the right-to-know legislation (Gibbs 2002). In California, activism spurred a requirement that the location of new school building construction pass a state environmental review (Morello-Frosch, Pastor Jr., and Sadd 2002: 59). In Louisiana, a request by Louisiana Energy Services to site a uranium facility was the first ruling in which a federal agency, the Nuclear Regulatory Commission, cited environmental justice concerns as substantial reason to rule against it (Roberts and Toffolon-Weiss 2001).

13. For contaminated communities, see Edelstein 1988. For toxic struggles, see the edited volume by Hofrichter (1993). For collective trauma and loss of communality, see Erikson 1976. On racism as practiced in the capitalist economic system, see Pellow 2007.

14. Gottlieb 1993: 304. Labor and environmental concerns coincided temporarily and then dissolved after disputes between employment versus the environment were fueled by corporate slogans and economic hardships during the 1970s and 1980s (Faber and O'Connor 1993; Rowell 1996). Along with subverting a potential labor-environmental bond in the 1980s, industry reorganized, reframed, and recast the debate on the environment in a process to "greenwash" their practices (Rowell 1996: 128). Nevertheless, evidence of industry deception and government bias toward industry grew. For example, leading industries, including asbestos, tobacco, lead, and vinyl "knew of dangers from their products but chose to ignore or conceal them," while the U.S. government presented a double face by forming regulatory bodies while failing to create them with sufficient regulatory power over the entities they were designed to govern so as to govern in the interest of communities and workers (Markowitz and Rosner 2002: 300–301). See Obach 2004 on several state-level case studies of environmental groups and labor union collaboration from the 1970s to early 1990s.

15. Gottlieb 1993: 304.

16. On environmental racism and the ties between historical and current racism, see Bullard 1993, 1994; Cole and Foster 2001; Lerner 2005; Pellow 2007; Pulido 1996; and Westra and Lawson 2001.

17. Bullard 1993: 200.

18. Pellow's (2007: 234) work on the global toxic trade emphasizes the role of historical and contemporary racism in government, cultural, social, and market practices and configurations, while also identifying deep mistrust between people of color and whites within environmental justice networks in the United States. Faber (2008: 239), while emphasizing class solidarity over racial distinctions, also identifies weaknesses in the American EJ movement due to limited efforts in overcoming racial tensions within the networks.

19. Faber (2008: 239, italics in the original) refers to environmental justice struggles as a "*politics of the minority*" in the United States and as a "*politics of the majority*" in the developing world. See also Tilly (1998), who studies inequalities through the relational differences between categorical pairs (women-men, black-white, high income–low income) across time and place. Tilly's longitudinal and cross-national focus builds bridges between subjugated peoples and communities in pockets of North and South America, Europe, Africa, and Asia—and offers insight, though not explicitly, into how the environmental justice movement may establish diverse networks to span beyond the United States.

20. See Cantzler's (2007) work on using social movements and the environmental justice paradigm to understand the traditional and cultural commitment to whaling by the Makah Indian Tribe as opposed to the moral and wildlife protection efforts of environmental activists. Both value and protect whales in vastly different and conflicted ways.

21. Environmental Justice Principles 1991.

22. See Pellow 2007.

23. See Pellow 2007: 2–3.

24. See Faber 2008 and Pellow 2007 on how successful environmental struggles in some communities have promoted the relocation of factories, industry, and waste to other communities.

25. Rowell 1996.

26. Pellow (2007, chap. 5) presents how developing nations adopted the Green Revolution through international loans and now require further loans to either clean up the chemical pollution or accept incineration projects to clean up others' waste products.

27. Pellow (2007) charts how communities and transnational networks have resisted the dumping of toxic wastes in the South through successful "return to sender" campaigns.

28. Roberts and Toffolon-Weiss 2001: 18. See Speth 2008: 58 on the need for greater government and consumer regulation and penalties to rein in capitalism's overuse and pollution of the environment.

29. Faber 2008.

30. Schnaiberg 1980; Gould, Schnaiberg, and Weinberg 1996; and Gould, Pellow, and Schnaiberg 2008.

31. Faber 2008: 8–9.

32. See Schnaiberg 1980; Gould, Schnaiberg, and Weinberg 1996; and Gould, Pellow, and Schnaiberg 2008. For other interpretations and uses of Schnaiberg's treadmill of production, see Hannigan 2006: 20; and Pellow 2007.

33. Gould, Schnaiberg, and Weinberg 1996.

34. Pellow 2007 contributes the perspective of racism to the global capitalist system.

35. See Williams 1980 on "empire as a way of life." Colony as a way of life, as informed by the works of Kloby 2004, Rodney 1972, and Rothenberg 2005, would be the political, economic, and social adoption of one's colonized and subservient position postcolonialism.

36. For an important and alternative view of global civil society, see Smith et al.'s (2008) assessments of the World Social Forums, which gather global activists who are resisting current political and economic arrangements.

37. On the political ecology perspective, see Peet and Watts 2004; and Rocheleau, Thomas-Slayter, and Wangari 1996.

38. On "transboundary problems" and "communities of fate," see Held et al. 1999: 445. On "circles of poison," see Pellow 2007: 30.

39. Pellow 2007.

40. Faber 2008: 223.

41. Hofrichter 1993: 9.

42. Bullard 1993.

43. Szasz 1994: 81.

44. Markowitz and Rosner 2002: 232–33.

45. Faber 1998a: 50.

46. Pellow, citing the comments of Southern activists, identifies how the South credits the United States with founding the EJ movement, but attests through example that the United States should listen and learn from Southern EJ practitioners, who have succeed in stopping or returning toxic waste back to the sites of origins.

47. Roberts and Parks 2007.

48. See Bandy and Smith 2005a; Khagram 2004; Pellow 2007; and Tarrow 2005.

49. See Bullard 1993; Bullard 2005a on "politics of pollution"; Bullard 2005b: 13 on "sacrifice zones"; Bullard, Johnson, and Torres 2005 on human rights and environmental injustice; Adeola 2000 on human rights and extractive economies and toxic waste; and Gruskin et al. 2005 on human rights and health, violence, and development.

50. United Nations Universal Declaration of Human Rights, written in 1948, http://www.un.org/en/documents/udhr/, downloaded 28 October 2010.

51. United Nations Declaration on Social Progress and Development, written in 1969, http://www2.ohchr.org/english/law/progress.htm, downloaded 28 October 2010.

52. Umlas 2009: 13 and 23. In this report (p. 23), a BP joint venture in Brazil was identified as using forced labor in its sugar cane and ethanol refinery.

53. Watts 1996: 279–80.

54. Tarrow 1994.

55. Manby 1999; Okonta and Douglas 2001; Watts 2004.

56. See Imle (1999), then vice chairman of California-based Unocal Corporation.

57. By "kept," I am referring to Jonathan Kozol's (1991, 2005) assessment of the American educational system. Are students educated to be engaged participants in a robust democracy or are they kept until low-skill work requires their service? Kept students are produced to be uncritical and unchallenging and perhaps supportive of a system that has withheld advantages and opportunities from them.

58. See Engler 1961, 1977; Sampson 1975.

59. For the U.S. import market, Ecuador ranked thirtieth in 2002. Yet the disparity in supply between first-ranked Saudi Arabia and Ecuador was the difference between 554 million barrels and 37 million barrels in 2002 (U.S. Energy 2003).

60. Though Ecuador refined some oil for domestic consumption, Ecuador was an exporter of unrefined oil and an importer of refined oil at this time.

61. See Mol and Spaargaren 2003 and Spaargaren, Mol, and Bruyninckx 2006 on "environmental flows."

62. See the appendix on data collection.

63. For Indigenous-oil conflict in Ecuador, see Brysk 2000; Finer et al. 2008; Gedicks 1993, 2001; Gerlach 2003; Kane 1995; Kimerling 1991; Sawyer 2004; Smith 1996; Tidwell 1996; Yashar 2005.

64. Estimates of the population of Indigenous people range from 12–45 percent. CONAIE, the Confederation of Indigenous Nationalities of Ecuador and the leading Indigenous organization, estimates the Indigenous population to be 45 percent (www.conaie.nativeweb.org). Schodt (1987) estimates the population to be 40 percent Indigenous, 40 mestizo, 10–15 percent white, and 5–10 percent black; Corkill and Cubitt (1988) concur with the Indigenous and mestizo percentages, though they claim 15 percent white, and 5 percent black. Gerlach (2003) suggests an unattributed estimation of the Indigenous population to be 25 percent. Pallares (2002: 6) believes that the lowest percentage, depending on the calculation, is 12 percent, based on self-reporting of native languages in the census taken in 1990.

65. See CIA World Factbook for basic national assessments.

66. Conaghan and Malloy 1994: 111.

67. Barthélémy 2003: 7.

68. Abuse of oil wealth is not exclusive to low-income developing nations. In 2006, the U.S. federal government was deciding whether to relinquish US$7 billion in state royalty payments over a five-year period to oil and gas companies extracting in federal territories; see Andrews 2006. Likewise, oil development in Louisiana, which was orchestrated by a few political and economic elites of the state, offered limited external regulations and generous tax relief (Allen 2003: 11–13). Communities most adjacent to petrochemical processes in Louisiana lived a rural life of poverty, unemployment, poor health, illiteracy, and inferior skills relative to the employment demands of the industry, though corporations and state officials persisted in framing oil works as a marker for the state's economic prosperity (Allen 2003). In one instance in Louisiana, a chemical factory's expansion created seven hundred to eight hundred temporary construction jobs and twenty permanent jobs for the highly trained (Allen 2003: 74–75). As is often the case in developing places, the petroleum jobs were too skilled and too technical for local people kept undereducated.

69. From 1847 to 1950, cacao, or cocoa bean, was Ecuador's principal export; banana then dominated in 1960 and 1970, to be surpassed by oil by the mid-1970s (Schodt 1987: 13). In percentage of total value of exports, cacao peaked at 71.3 percent in 1920; banana represented

60.8 percent in 1960 and 46.8 percent in 1970. By 1980, oil accounted for 62.1 percent of total value of exports, followed by banana (9.4 percent), cacao (8.4 percent), and coffee (5.2 percent; Schodt 1987).

70. *New York Time*'s op-ed columnist Paul Krugman. See Krugman 2000.

71. See Gerlach's (2003) work on Ecuador's recent history of Indigenous uprisings and shuffling presidencies between 1997 and 2000. For an earlier work on Ecuador's political and economic systems see Conaghan and Malloy (1994).

72. Freire (2002) identifies specific causes that would deem Ecuador's debt as illegitimate: if acquired under a military dictatorship, when the bulk of the state budget goes to debt payment (for example 65.2 percent of the budget in 1999 and 54 percent in 2000), and when repayment is more than triple the original debt. On the latter point, Freire (2002: 23–24) cites an initial loan of US$13.5 million that was then totaling $50 million, despite the state having already paid $14 million on it. See Perkins (2006: xiii and 20–21) on Ecuadorian debt and the role of external debt in general.

73. See Benford 2005.

74. In 1990, environmental justice activist Dana Alston wrote that people were being affected where they "live, work and play," and it is now one of the movement's most popular organizing demands.

75. Renner 2002.

76. Karl 1997, 1999.

77. Kashi and Watts 2008.

78. Karl 1997, 1999.

79. Ross 2001.

80. Renner 2002.

81. Ecuador joined OPEC in 1973, suspended its membership in 1992, and rejoined in 2007.

82. Karl 1997, 1999.

83. Dréze and Sen 1989. For example, Kuwait and Qatar used oil revenues in the 1970s and 1980s to fuel welfare systems and distribute material benefit to civil society (Crystal 1989). In addition, Norway is the world's third largest oil exporter and in 2005, for the fifth straight year, received "best country to live in" status from a United Nations assessment (Reuters 2005a). Norway's high marks were due to its social health, generous welfare system, and egalitarian salaries. Oil deposits below the North Sea subsidize Norway's comfort.

84. Crow 2000.

85. The absence of linkages is due in part to higher import tariffs placed by industrialized nations on value-added, processed goods, such as polyethylene for grocery bags or shampoo bottles, than on unprocessed goods, such as crude (Oxfam 2001: 10).

86. United Nations 2004.

87. World Bank 2004.

88. World Bank 2004.

89. For a critical analysis of the distribution of oil impacts at different points in the supply chain, see the work of O'Rourke and Connolly 2003.

90. Berry 1975. Currently an oil pipeline network, including the Keystone and Alberta Clipper pipeline systems, is being constructed or proposed across the North American continent from the tar or oil sands of Alberta, Canada, through the American Midwest to the Gulf of Mexico. Much of this research is based on the oil production in Alberta rather than the expanded pipeline and refinery systems. See Israelson 2008 on the air and water impacts.

91. Absolute poverty is being used at the individual level as material deprivation, including inadequate food supply, limited clean water access, unsafe or insecure shelter, clothing deficiencies, and utility shortages.

92. Kimerling 1991: ix.

93. Acción Ecológica 2001a, 2001c. An oil disaster's predictability is further underscored by the twentieth anniversary of the International Oil Spill Conference on Prevention, Preparedness, Response and Restoration, which was held in 2008.

94. *El Universo*, "Cada tres días hay un derrame, admite Petroecuador," 12 July 2001: 11.

95. In the United States, where Texaco was headquartered at the time, the Federal Water Pollution Control Act was created in 1948 to prohibit the unauthorized discharge of industrial waste into waterways (Beamish 2002: 159). Likewise, the injection of hazardous waste into underground wells, or closed containment systems, began in the 1960s in the United States before Texaco began extracting oil from the Amazon. Despite the Northern awareness of the potential health risks, in Ecuador Texaco appears to have continued to operate without precautionary measures.

96. Recent studies indicate that benzene, which causes leukemia and toxicity to bone marrow, has an adverse health impact at exposure levels below 1 part per million (ppm), which is currently the U.S. occupational standard (Lan et al. 2004; Stokstad 2004.) On the other hand, Wong and Raabe (2000: 78) found that "there was no increased mortality from digestive cancers (stomach, large intestine, liver, or pancreas), lung cancer, bladder cancer, kidney cancer, or brain cancer" among petroleum workers when Raabe was employed by Mobil Business Resources Corporation. Such findings can lead to the burden of proof being placed on the worker rather than the corporation, industry practices, or government regulation and oversight. Davis (2007: 34) also identifies the health risks associated with benzene.

97. San Sebastian et al. 2001; Hurtig and San Sebastian 2002; Instituto 2000.

98. Hurtig and San Sebastian 2004.

99. San Sebastian et al. 2002.

100. San Sebastian et al. 2001. Elevated cancers in the community included stomach, larynx, liver, cervix, melanoma, and leukemia.

101. Hurtig and San Sebastian 2002. They found significantly elevated risk for cancer of the stomach, rectum, skin, soft tissue, and kidney in men, and cervix and lymph nodes in women. Their report, and cancer research in developing countries in general, was challenged by Siemiatycki (2002: 1028), who argued that design limitations, including limited use for replication and limited verifiable diagnosis of cancer due to prohibitive medical cost in developing places, diluted the study to "no more than a hint that there may be a cancer problem in the area around oil fields." However, technical challenges to environmental health research in developing places ignore why communities in oil-rich regions are underdeveloped and unable to access reliable medical care and early diagnosis in the first place. These types of technological challenges place the burden of proof on the oil-poor and the oil-sick, rather than on the likely perpetrators.

102. Kimerling 1991: 71.

103. On October 11, 2003, I participated in and observed a toxic tour of Texaco's former oil fields, including a visit to a health clinic where we met with one of the clinic's physicians. The trip was organized by Acción Ecológica for Quito, Mindo, and Cofan youth activists. Ineke Lock, at the time a graduate student at the University of Alberta, Calgary, and I "toured" an oil camp and its community projects in 2003 with the community relations director. One stop during the daylong tour was an oil-funded health clinic. When we arrived the physician greeted us, and left a patient waiting in his office while he attended to us: we shared the feeling that his attendance to us was obligatory. As the clinic was still under construction and not supplied with air conditioning, we were led into the home of the oil physicians. The clinic is staffed by two physicians who rotate their schedules, much like an oil worker: fourteen days in the field, fourteen days off, when they would return to their families, usually in Quito. In this physician's on-site home, the community director appeared to both of us to be more "at-home," providing us drinks, settling us in, than the physician, who appeared as much a guest in his home as we were. As we sat with our icy cold drinks, the physician changed from his button-down shirt to an oil-branded short-sleeve pullover. And at the end of the eight-hour tour, Ineke Lock suggested we condense our respective research projects to the simplicity of one question: why did the physician change his shirt?

104. In the United States, there has been a history of occupational physicians serving industrial practices by focusing on individual responsibility and lifestyle choices, rather than protecting workers in toxic environments (Walsh 1987; Brodeur 1973; Bowker 2003). Corporate physicians, or "corporate medical directors," straddle management and health care, and refer to themselves as doctors in corporations, doctors of corporations, and vice presidents of corporations (Walsh 1987: vii, 63, 136). Today in developing places, multinationals support community physicians,

who mimic occupational physicians by selecting individual and behavioral patterns as causes of poor health, rather than industrial pollution. The simplistic placation is that some health care is better than no health care.

105. Caldwell 1986: 172.

106. Caldwell 1986.

107. Shiva 2000.

108. Dreze and Sen 1989.

109. Farmer 2003; Sen 1999.

110. See Faber 2008: 178 on the more general "dissonance between the promises of globalization and free trade and the actual results of neoliberal policies."

111. It has been common for me to present this research and then to be asked about the "Indigenous position." The pipeline did not pass through Indigenous territory, and Indigenous communities and organizations did not mobilize in response to it.

112. Ecuador's constitution since 1988 requires that the state seek public consultation and participation in decisions that may impact a local community's environment. This law was followed by an official recognition in 1992 of Indigenous territories in the Amazon, giving Indigenous communities much greater negotiating power and national legitimacy. That said, land titles to Indigenous people could be revoked if communities impede or block oil or mining work, though Indigenous communities in the Amazon have the legal right to demand compliance with environmental and community protection laws (Kimerling 1995: 358).

113. For a thorough account of the Yasuní Biosphere Reserve, see Finer et al. (2009).

114. Whitten Jr. (2003b: 63) counted five Indigenous uprisings from 1990 to 2001, and notes that the fifth uprising included in its list of twenty-three demands a reduction in gas prices and stabilization of diesel and oil prices. I have firsthand observations of two of the campaigns, the Sarayacu campaign and the Texaco trial, supplemented by prepared community documents, advocacy reports, and newspaper accounts. For the Achuar and Shuar case, I relied primarily on reports from U.S.-based advocacy groups and Quito-based newspapers.

115. The Kichwa people reside in both the highland Andean region and the lowland Amazonian region of Ecuador. They are the largest group of Indigenous people in Ecuador. Kichwa is also, and frequently, spelled Quichua or Quechua. For a more detailed examination of the Sarayacu community, see Sawyer 2004.

116. Information on the government's threats to militarize the Sarayacu territory, the community's declaration of a state of emergency, and the ongoing conflicts between these two stakeholders was taken from the daily Quito-based newspaper *El Comercio*: "Oposición a Militares en Zona de Sarayaku," 10 October 2003; "En Canelos No Detuvieron la Marcha Indígena," 8 December 2003; "En Sarayaku Estan Listos para Levantarse," 18 December 2003; "The Sarayaku Community Declares Itself in Territorial Emergency," 25 January 2004; "El Discurso de Romero Preocupa en Sarayaku," 6 April 2004: D3; as well as the Inter Press Service News Agency report "Indigenous Community Brings Its Struggle to Argentina," filed 9 November 2004, by Marcela Valente. Sarayacu's declaration of a state of emergency and trip to Argentina were filed as a community press release to national and international media and national and international advocacy groups. To a lesser degree, the Sarayacu community has utilized the Mexican Zapatistas' Internet communication strategy to reach supporters and the media. Journalist Juan Forero (*New York Times*, "Seeking Balance: Growth vs. Culture in Amazon," 10 December 2003) wrote that the Sarayacu community hired a New York–based public relations firm to contact the media. For information on Sarayacu, in Spanish and English, see their website www.sarayacu.com.

117. I observed a Sarayacu demonstration outside of the Argentina embassy in Quito on 27 November 2003 and a weekend rally and protest march in Puyo, 5–6 December 2003.

118. Though this research examines oil contention in Ecuador, laws in the United States are increasingly important for transnational networks. International advocates are examining how to use U.S. law to assist people in developing places, particularly when the offenders are multinationals and international financiers. For example, Burmese victims of forced labor sued Unocal in U.S. courts on human rights violations perpetrated by the Burmese state for the oil company's construction project.

119. In 2001 Texaco and Chevron merged and was renamed ChevronTexaco. The company then changed its name again to Chevron Corporation, perhaps in part due to an international campaign against Texaco's former operations in Ecuador; see http://www.texacotoxico.com. In 1999, Chevron also purchased interest in an exploration block in Ecuador.

120. On 29 October 2003, I observed the legal proceedings of Texaco's trial in Lago Agrio.

121. For more on this case, see Kimerling 2007.

122. Much of the information on the legal case *Maria Aguinda v. ChevronTexaco* was provided in media packets prepared by AMC Public Relations team for the plaintiffs' legal team. Media packets were obtained in Lago Agrio, Ecuador, in October 2003, at the start of the trial. See the works of Rogge (2001), Kalas (2000), and Kimerling (2007, 1995) in law journals as well as the 2009 documentary *Crude: The Real Price of Oil*, a film by Joe Berlinger, produced by Red Envelope Entertainment. The website of Amazon Watch, www.amazonwatch.org, provides extensive and up-to-date accounts of this case.

123. For organizing this legal campaign, two Ecuadorian men, Luis Yanza, cofounder of Frente de Defensa, and lawyer Pablo Fajardo Mendoza, received the Goldman Environmental Prize in 2008, an award of $150,000 each, for their class action lawsuit against Texaco. See http://www.goldmanprize.org.

124. See Simon Romero and Clifford Krauss, 2011, "Chevron Is Ordered to Pay $9 Billion by Ecuador Judge," *New York Times*, 15 February: A4; John Schwartz, and Dave Itzkoff, 2011, "Scenes Cut from Film Find New Role in Court," *New York Times*, 3 January: A13; and Environmental News Service (ENS), 2011, "Ecuador Court Fines Chevron $8.6 Billion for Rainforest Pollution," 14 February.

125. Much of the information I present on the Achuar and Shuar conflict with ARCO and Burlington Resources comes from two advocacy organizations, California-based Amazon Watch (www.amazonwatch.org) and Pachamama Alliance (www.pachamama.org), with offices in Quito and San Francisco. See also Perkins 2006.

126. As of 2009, ConocoPhillips owned Block 24, after acquiring Burlington Resources, and is joint owner of Block 23 with CGC, an Argentine producer.

See http://www.amazonwatch.org/amazon/EC/burling/index.php?page_number=99 (downloaded 3 September 2009).

127. Newspaper sources include "Shuar y Achuar Opuestos a Presencia de las Petroleras," 13 December 2004, *El Universo*; "Burlington Resources' Plans for Ecuador Run into Opposition," 22 April 2004, *New York Times*; Juan Forero's report in the *New York Times*, "Seeking Balance: Growth vs. Culture in Amazon," 10 December 2003; and Gorman (2002).

128. The Achuar people are represented by the Federación Interprovincial de la Nacionalidad Achuar del Ecuador (FINAE), while the Shuar people in Block 24 are represented by the Federación Interprovincial de Pueblos Shuar del Ecuador (FIPSE) and Federación Interprovincial de Centros Shuar (FICSH).

129. In a letter dated 14 May 2003 to the CEO of Burlington, the presidents of three Shuar and Achuar organizations wrote:

We wish to remind you that the territories of Blocks 23 and 24 are in fact the ancestral homelands of the Shuar, Achuar, Zapara and Kichwa peoples. The approximately 400,000 hectares that make up the two concession areas contain well-conserved and ecologically diverse primary rainforest. We do not wish to see the contamination, deforestation and cultural destruction that the northern part of the Ecuadorian Amazon has suffered. We believe that our country can develop without destroying our environment and culture, and that there are sustainable alternatives to oil exploitation for our development. We will do everything in our power to see that our rights and our territories are not sacrificed for the sake of paying off foreign debt through oil exports.

For more on Indigenous shareholder advocacy with regards to Burlington attempts to explore for oil, see McAteer and Pulver 2009.

130. A common point of reference for Indigenous rights precedent is the International Labor Organization (ILO) Convention No. 169. In 1989, the ILO adopted Convention 169 concerning

Indigenous and Tribal Peoples in Independent Countries. One section of the convention states that the ILO recognizes "the aspirations of these people to exercise control over their own institutions, ways of life and economic development and to maintain and develop their identities, languages and religions." See www.ilo.org, as well as Gorman 2002.

131. The United Nations passed the Declaration on Rights of Indigenous People in 2007 after two decades of debate. See http://www.un.org/esa/socdev/unpfii/en/declaration.html or http://www.un.org/esa/socdev/unpfii/documents/DRIPS_en.pdf.

132. From the literature, one would expect Indigenous mobilization, as the Indigenous people of Ecuador have been in conflict with the oil industry and the state since the late 1980s. However, in this case, Indigenous organizations and communities failed to respond to the OCP pipeline. It is plausible that their absence reflected their primary, identity-based demands for equal and special Indigenous rights and opportunities.

133. See Widener 2007b.

134. Ali 2000.

135. Carruthers (1996) refers to the alliance between environmental and Indigenous organizations as "Indigenous ecology." See Gedicks 2001 as well.

136. Newsome 1997.

137. It was explained to me in 2001 by an oil executive that for each barrel of crude the state earns 25 percent and the oil companies earn 75 percent, so that if a barrel's gross income is US$15, the state earns $3.75 and the collective oil companies $11.25. However, the net income for the state is $3.37 for a $15 barrel and $3.53 for the oil companies. The reduction from gross to net income includes transportation tariff, operating costs, and development costs. The oil companies also pay about US$0.50 per barrel to the government agency Eco-Rae, or Ecodesarrollo en la Región Amazónica Ecuatoriana, which is designed to develop or support ecological development in the Amazon through oil funds. In sum, the state earns approximately US$4 per barrel for every US$2 per barrel profit of the oil company based upon the agreements of 2001. There are forty-two gallons in a barrel of oil. But see Perkins (2006: xxiv), who calculates that for every $100 worth of oil extracted, Ecuadorian people see less than $3 while oil companies receive approximately $75. Most of the difference goes to debt payments.

138. In 2007, Ecuador paid off its debt to the IMF. Associated Press, "Ecuador Pays Off IMF Debt, Says Will Sever Ties with Institution," *International Herald Tribune*, Americas, 15 April 2007.

139. "Letter of Intent, Memorandum of Economic and Financial Policies, and Technical Memorandum of Understanding," signed by Mauricio Yepez Najas, president of Central Bank of Ecuador, and Mauricio Pozo, minister of economy and finance, on 10 February 2003 in Quito for the Ecuadorian government to the International Monetary Fund. http://www.imf.org/external/np/loi/2003/ecu/01/index.htm, downloaded 28 August 2008.

140. In 1987, for instance, an earthquake stopped oil transportation for six months, which can cripple an economic and political system dependent on a single, exported commodity. The state was also expected to lose approximately US$80 million per year in transport fees, which the private consortium companies had previously paid for using the state-owned SOTE.

141. Information on the proposed routes and bids were gathered from community groups and NGOs in 2001 and from oil industry journals, including *Platt's Oilgram News* ("Ecuador Selects Group to Build OCP Crude Export Pipeline," 16 November 1999) and *Oil & Gas Journal*. See Wyss 2001; Moss 2000; Fletcher and True 2000; and True 2001.

142. In 2007, President Rafael Correa divided the Ministry of Energy and Mines into the Ministry of Mines and Petroleum, and the Ministry of Electricity and Renewable Energy. See Silvia Santacruz, "Ecuador President Correa Divides MEM into Two Ministries, May Create Third," *Ecuador Mining News*, 27 July 2007.

143. Entrix 2001.

144. Entrix 2001.

145. Entrix 2001.

146. Despite these claims, in 2003 I witnessed the pipeline exposed on a private farm. The boggy soil on the eastern slope of the Andes depresses with body weight and washes away easily to reveal patches of the pipeline.

147. Oil multinationals and Ecuadorian tax agencies had been in conflict since August 2001 over eligibility of rebates on a value-added tax on imported items for export production. The amount in dispute totaled approximately US$200 million. California-based Occidental Petroleum (Oxy) had taken the dispute to international arbitration in U.S. courts. In addition, in 2002 the United States excluded Ecuador from the Andean Trade Preferences Pact (ATPA) until the tax dispute was resolved (see van Gelder 2003.) In 2004, the Ecuadorian state retaliated by charging that Oxy was company non grata. Ecuador's attorney general asked the Energy Ministry to terminate Oxy's operation contract, citing thirty-four violation of its contract ("Attorney General Targets Occidental," *Los Angeles Times*, 25 August 2004). Oxy began its operation in Block 15 in 1985, and was forced out in 2004.

148. Monetary resources from PetroEcuador's production are given to the state, which then dispenses the revenues with only a portion returning to the company. In one interview conducted by Leslie Jermyn for GlobalAware, Eduardo Naranjo, PetroEcuador's director of institutional relations, said that in the mid-1990s a law that had allowed 10 percent of PetroEcuador's earnings "to be reinvested in exploration and maintenance" had been rescinded and that currently, in 2002, approximately ninety wells required maintenance before operating again. See Jermyn (n.d.).

149. The pipeline companies include EnCana Corporation (formerly Alberta Energy of Canada or City Investing in Ecuador), 31.4 percent; Repsol-YPF of Spain, 25.6 percent; Pecom Energía of Argentina (former parent company was Perez Companc of Argentina, and since October 2002 has been Petrobras of Brazil), 15 percent; Occidental Petroleum of the United States, 12.2 percent; ENI-Agip, or Agip Oil Ecuador BV ENI, of Italy, 7.5 percent; Techint, 4.1 percent; and Perenco of France and Britain, but founded in Singapore with headquarters in Paris and London (formerly Kerr-McGee Corporation of the United States), 4 percent. The percentages indicate a company's ownership and oil transportation commitment. For example, EnCana, the largest owner, holds 31.4 percent of the pipeline and is committed to transport 31.4 percent of the pipeline's oil capacity. These individual oil companies are both owners of the pipeline as well as the clients, or shippers, of OCP Ltd.

150. Once the pipeline was constructed, executives of OCP became nearly invisible, with some community members and NGOs claiming that verbal agreements were left unfinished. Rodin and colleagues (1997) have identified how Exxon's practice of changing its on-site personnel following the *Exxon Valdez* oil spill impeded community relations as well.

151. See Khagram 2004 for how communities have mobilized against international lenders of dam projects.

152. Chase Manhattan (USA), OCP's financial adviser, arranged the financing, which was led by WestLB (van Gelder 2002). The financial consortium also included ABB Credit Company (Switerzland), now belonging to GE Commercial Finance (USA), Banca Nazionale del Lavoro (Italy), Banco Bilbao Vizcaya Argentaria (Spain), Banco Espirito Santo (Portugal), Bank of Scotland (Great Britain), Caja Madrid (Spain), and Unicredito Italiano (Italy). In addition, 43.2 percent of the shares of WestLB are owned by the State of North Rhine-Westphalia. The public status of WestLB was used by activists to hold the state government answerable as well. Seven insurance companies and pension funds were also part of the consortium, contributing a third, or US$310 million of the US$900 million line of credit. International groups considered the participation of insurance companies and pension funds as unusual. These included John Hancock, New York Life, and Provident (now part of Nationwide Financial), all of the United States. The time frame for credit payment was 17 years, 13.5 years among the bank credits, plus an additional 3.5 years among the insurance companies. Urgewald, a German activist organization and World Bank monitor, compiled this list of lending information; see van Gelder 2002. Risk to the financial institutions was particularly great as the lenders arranged guarantees of payment even if the pipeline was not completed, the companies went bankrupt, or the pipeline was nationalized. Particularly risky companies, such as Pecom Energía, required a letter of credit or guarantee of payment, arranged by Deutsche Bank (Germany) and Citibank (USA; van Gelder 2003).

153. On "ecological democracy," see Faber 1998b, 1998c.

154. Gustavo Noboa, whose administration approved the construction of OCP, was prolific and graphic with the media in his disdain for any national or international opposition to the project. Here, I am quoting from the *Economist*, "Oil and Cloud-Forests Don't Mix," 23 June 2001. The word Noboa used was *joder*. Noboa's descriptions of and challenges to the opposition were well publicized in national media, and were frequently cited among activists. See Acción Ecológica 2001d for other quotes.

155. In Ecuador, Ecuadorians of African descent or African-Ecuadorians are more commonly called Afro-Ecuadorians.

156. Ray 1999: 6, italics in the original.

157. See Bob 2005.

158. Freudenburg and Gramling's (1994) analysis of environmental perception in Louisiana and California provides a point of comparison. The oil industry entered the Amazon, and Louisiana, when environmental and social justice awareness was quite low. It became an established industry and economic indicator in both sites through gradual and persistent expansion. Freudenburg and Gramling (1994) contrast Louisiana's reception to oil with that of California's rejection as Californians value the image of a pristine environment untarnished by oil.

159. See Spaargaren, Mol and Bruyninckx 2006, 5.

160. See Spaargaren, Mol, and Bruyninckx 2006; Spaargaren, Mol and Buttel 2006; and Mol and Van den Burg 2004.

161. Mol and Spaargaren 2003 and Spaargaren, Mol, and Bruyninckx 2006.

162. Hopkins and Wallerstein 1986; Gereffi and Korzeniewicz 1990; and Gereffi 1994.

163. See Widener 2009a as well.

164. On old and new social movements, see Brown et al. 2004; Della Porta and Diani 1999; Mayo 2005; McAdam 1988, 1998; McAdam, McCarthy, and Zald 1996; McCarthy and Zald 1977; and Tarrow 1994.

165. In 2002 at the peak of pipeline construction and antipipeline mobilization, Transparency International ranked Ecuador 89th out of 102 countries worldwide supporting local challenges to the lack of transparency in government decision making with regards to the oil sector.

166. See Widener 2009b.

167. Benford 2005 notes how the environmental justice movement's radical focus has been diminished over time.

168. See Widener 2007a.

CHAPTER 2
LAGO AGRIO:
COMMUNITY-DRIVEN OIL JUSTICE

1. For "struggle for ecological democracy," see Faber 1998b, 1998c.

2. Castells 1997: 68–69; see Held et al. 1999 and Rothenberg 2005 as well.

3. Shiva 2000. See also Rothenberg 2005.

4. Avritzer 2002: 7. See also the informed community consensus committees on technological risk realized in Denmark and analyzed by Fischer 2000.

5. Habermas 1984.

6. O'Donnell and Schmitter 1986: 52, 53.

7. O'Donnell and Schmitter 1986: 53.

8. Gramsci 1971: 182.

9. Gramsci 1971: 244.

10. The state is but one actor, perhaps not even the authority or active participant, in global and/or corporate relations with local communities. For example, in Lesotho, the state watched the development industry and development aid agencies construct "least developed" status onto communities, which were indigenous and agricultural, and ignore the potential of public participation

to direct development monies and efforts. In a capital city, for example, the blueprints for a moderate project, a two-room school or clinic with adjacent toilet facility, may seem marginal. In a dirt road village of less than one hundred people, such a "development project" may loom large—its negative impacts and repercussions, such as imposition of hierarchy, greater inequality, and greater nonlocal control, unintended but substantial. In the end, the community in Lesotho lost and the development industry failed, while the state watched and waited as roads were built with development money into previously inaccessible areas, which then fell under the governance of the state and enabled the extension of the military. On Lesotho, see Ferguson 1994: 252–53. Scott (1998) also presents a horrific glimpse at state planning run amok, including routinized and monoculture of plant species that die in two to three generations, and land planning through grids on a map rather than on-site assessments and local knowledge, local management, and actual use and viability of the terrain.

11. Evans 1995.

12. Avritzer 2002; Baiocchi 2001.

13. Baiocchi 2001: 55. Though co-optation was thought to be a risk, years of experience in community participation influenced the degree of participation, rather than gender or educational level (52). For clarification, the participatory budgeting effort owed its existence to the electoral success of the Popular Front, aligned with the Worker's Party, which ran on democratizing and decentralizing the administration.

14. Pulido 1996.

15. Heller 1999, 2000.

16. Peet and Hartwick 1999: 205–6.

17. Tilly 1998.

18. Avritzer 2002; Tilly 1998.

19. Sen 1999.

20. Sen 1999.

21. Buttel 2003; O'Rourke 2004.

22. Kaimowitz 1996.

23. Nugent 1996.

24. Tarrow 1994.

25. Roberts and Parks 2007 and Farmer 2003 identify the importance of geography in terms of climate impacts for the former and structural and relational suffering for the latter.

26. On 30 July 2001, *El Comercio*, the national, Quito-based daily newspaper, reported there were thirty-two assassinations in Lago Agrio from January to July 2001, "Frontera: Desde enero hubo 32 asesinatos en Lago Agrio: Sucumbíos es tierra de nadie en las noches": A2. Also see *El Comercio*, "Los 11 incidentes de los armados en la frontera," 10 June 2001: C1; and *El Comercio*, "Las incursiones ponen en jaque a Ecuador," 10 June 2001: C1.

27. Landívar 2004. See also Vickers 2003 for a review of this time period.

28. Due to the increased tension and movement along the Colombian border, the Ecuadorian state had moved part of its military from along the Peruvian border in the south to Lago Agrio and Coca. See the *Economist*, "The Americas: Collateral Damage," 3 February 2001.

29. Colombians bore the brunt of finger pointing when anything went wrong in Lago Agrio in 2001–2003. Taxi drivers complained of being robbed of their money and sometimes their cars at gunpoint by Colombians, though many of the Colombians in the region appeared to be border traders.

30. When I first arrived in Ecuador in 2001 and told Ecuadorians that I planned to go to Lago Agrio everyone warned me not to go at all, and definitely not to go alone to a place where trust or casual conversation was limited. But from all of my travels in Ecuador, I was least hassled as a foreign woman traveling alone in Lago Agrio. I am sure sex industry experts would dispute this, but from my experience, when there is an open, formal, and professional sex industry, women who are not sex workers receive the least amount of negative and aggressive attention. I am not suggesting that the sex industry protects women not in the profession, but that sex workers take on the double burden of their profession and their gender, while temporarily relieving women not in the business of their gender.

To my account, Olien and Olien (1982: 87) would argue that I am sensationalizing the sex worker industry in oil towns. But Frente de Defensa's analysis of the environmental impact assessment (EIA) and environmental management plan (EMP) lists sex work, delinquency, poverty, vandalism, drug trafficking, and alcoholism as direct effects of migration due to oil exploration. In addition, a study by Lobao and Brown (1998) in the Ecuadorian Amazon indicates that a state-led policy to extract natural resources, alongside the promotion of "live-frontiers," led to higher fertility rates among women along the Amazon frontier. These women had higher fertility rates due in part to lower education, limited paid employment, a family-based economy, exclusion from oil employment, and early marriage.

31. See Olien and Olien 1982: 87.

32. Today, Lago Agrio's official name is Nueva Loja (New Loja), reflecting the transplanted settlers from the southern town and province of Loja. I will refer to the town as Lago Agrio, or Lago for short. On Texaco's changes, see Texaco's website http://www.texaco.com/texaco. Downloaded 5 October 2004. For an additional link between Texas and the Ecuadorian Amazon, see Reid 1995. Between March 1902, when oil was discovered in the swamps of Sour Lake, Texas, and June 1903 drillers put in approximately 450 wells (see Olien and Olien 2002: 43).

33. Isaacs 1993: 16.

34. Lynch 1987: 33.

35. Recorded 17 March 2004, Montreal, Canada, spoken in Spanish with English translation.

36. Olien and Olien 2002: 220–21.

37. Olien and Olien 2002: 162–63. It was the Big Lake discovery.

38. Olien and Olien 1982: 65.

39. Oil multinationals contribute to oil, chemical, and engineering departments at Quito universities. The oil sector also views their work as contributing to an educated middle class, who receive job placement and promotions within the industry based on merit and skill, rather than by family connections. Interview 15 November 2003, near Lago Agrio.

40. Jochnick and Garzón 2006: 189.

41. Too often international loan stipulations require a reduction in health, education, and public services to pay back national debt.

42. Olien and Olien 2002: 99.

43. United Nations reported an underemployment rate of 57 percent in Ecuador (United Nations 2004). *El Universo* newspaper reported that workers for Petroproducción received a monthly salary of $160; see José Olmos, "Trajabjores gana 160 dólares mesuales en petroleras: Hombre y petróleo explotados," *El Universo*, 12 July 2001: 11.

44. Freudenburg and Gramling 1994.

45. See Peter Baker and John M. Broder, "White House Lifts Ban on Deepwater Drilling," *New York Times*, 12 October 2010.

46. Ohler and Hall 2000.

47. *New York Times*, "7 Hostages Freed in Ecuador after Reported Ransom of $13 Million," 2 May 2001.

48. Okonta and Douglas 2001: 98.

49. See Gerlach 2003; Sawyer 2004.

50. See Gunter and Kroll-Smith (2007) on the historical harbingers of environmental conflict.

51. It is important to locate mass demonstrations in one region to discontent expressed in other regions as well. I have presented the ongoing tensions in the Lago Agrio area due to non-oil-related activities including Plan Colombia and a rash of assassinations in 1999. In February 2002, strikes in the oil provinces also paralleled in timing protests across the country, including Quito, Guayaquil, and the southern city of Cuenca, against a government plan to privatize power companies. See Reuters report, "Two Police Injured by Gunfire in Ecuador Protests," 20 February 2002.

52. Amazon Watch Ecuador, Emergency Action Alert, "OCP Protestors in Amazon Attached by Military!" 28 February 2002; Amazon Watch Action Alert, "Ecuador Update: State of Emergency Lifted While Heavy Military Presence and Media Blackout Continue," 6 March 2002; Amy Taxin for Reuters, "Ecuador Amazon Protests End; Army Control Lifted," 4 March 2002; Reuters, "Ecuador Jungle Provinces in Emergency over Protests," 26 February 2002; Reuters,

"Ecuador Oil Output Dented by Amazon Protests, 25 February 2002." See as well Lucas 2002 and Barthélémy 2003.

53. In addition to advocacy reports distributed in the United States through Amazon Watch, I refer to Reuters news service coverage of the demonstrations: Amy Taxin, "Ecuador Army Slaps Curfew on Oil Provinces," 27 February 2002; "One Dead in Ecuador Protests in Amazon Oil Area," 28 February 2002; and Amy Taxin, "Ecuador Amazon Protests End; Army Control Lifted," 4 March 2002. Whitten (2003a: 16) wrote that four adults were killed.

54. Valdivia 2008: 460.

55. In May 2001, then-president Gustavo Noboa, apparently under great pressure to start the construction of OCP, said, "Nadie va a joder al país, el OCP va, porque va." The national press reported it in headlines. The *Economist* (23 June 2001) reported it as: "'I'm not going to let anyone screw with the country,' he said. 'I'll give them war.'" National activists and the NGO community would refer to Noboa's choice of words throughout their campaign. His message was received with a mixture of disgust, shock, and youthful glee. But activists knew where they stood with this president.

56. The quote "trench by trench" or "trinchera por trinchera" was reported by Acción Ecológica, in its *Alerta Verde Boletín*, no. 112, June 2001.

57. Sawyer 2004.

58. Shiva 2000.

59. The source of these demands was provided by Prodhecu, on 21 February 2002, through the D.C.-based Amazon Alliance network.

60. Acción Ecológica 2001d: 5.

61. Sawyer 2004: 39–40.

62. Lucas 2002.

63. The region's primary focus on the state, rather than multinationals, was corroborated in February 2006, when both provinces staged similar strikes by first shutting down SOTE, the state-owned pipeline, rather than OCP (BBC 2006a, 2006b). A secondary strike against an OCP pumping station to demand roads, bridges, and an airport from the state occurred fifty-five miles east of Quito forcing a temporary stoppage (BBC 2006b). This strike was also indicative of the spreading and mobilized discontent beyond the historically oil-impacted communities with the state and its use of the nation's oil wealth.

64. McClearn 2003: 33.

65. OCP 2005b.

66. On the community's concerns over the location of the Amazonas Station, see Weemaels 2002. Weemaels (12) cites *La Hora* newspaper (20 July 2001) as reporting that 80 percent of the population rejected the location of this facility. On 1 March 2003, the station leaked approximately sixty barrels of oil, and despite claims that it was cleaned up, others speculated that heavy rains at the time may have carried the oil off-site. On this spill see the monitoring report by Nathalie Weemaels for Acción Ecológica, "Derrame en la Estación De Bombeo Amazonas," 8 March 2003.

67. *El Comercio*, "Petroleum: (Mayors) Ask for Financial Endorsement for Development Works. Mayors Support OCP," 15 June 2001: B2.

68. Roberts and Parks 2007.

69. Recorded 17 March 2004, Montreal, Canada, spoken in Spanish with English translation.

70. At large demonstrations, a leader will commonly call for a "roll call" of organizations present, and those present and endorsing the protest shout "Presente."

71. FEPP is a national and religious-based organization with offices across the country. FEPP works on economic development, access, and opportunities of campesinos and settlers. Its offices resemble community centers, where many of one's needs, from health to education, from droughts to a lack of shoes, can be expressed and perhaps alleviated. This network along with other campesino community groups responded to the oil impact on the communities, where residents lived, worked, and played. They organized against the state's lack of transparency in oil spending and decision making, and against the location of the OCP facilities. They organized for community-directed distribution of oil revenues.

72. Channel 4 television interview with Lago Agrio mayor Maximo Abad, aired 30 July 2001, Lago Agrio.

73. I was given a photocopy of the agreement "Acuerdo de Compensación Social a Efectuarse en el Canton Lago Agrio por el Consorcio OCP-Techint." It was signed by Jerry Free, OCP project director; Ignacio Viboud, Techint project director; and five council members: Alejandro Orellana, Pedro Montero, Freddy Vizueta, Alejandro Vargas, and Felipe Estrada. The date of the official stamp is illegible, and it is not clear whether one of the council members actually signed or not, though five were in attendance.

74. Observation and recording of a press interview, 17 March 2004.

75. Federación Nacional de Trabajadores Petroleros.

76. In addition, reports of the International Labor Organization (ILO) on Ecuador indicate that the ILO worked to reduce child labor in the agricultural sector, rather than to bolster the demands of oil laborers.

77. "Ecuador: Oleoducto de Crudos Pesados 503 kilómetros de humillación nacional," position paper prepared by Fernando Villavicencio Valencia, for FETRAPEC. The report is not dated.

78. FETRAPEC position paper provided in English and Spanish: "Gutierrez Government Persecutes Oil Workers" (Gobierno de Gutierrez persigue a trabajadores petroleros). This position paper is not dated, though it is addressed to President Lucio Gutiérrez, who was in office from January 2003 to April 2005, and to Carlos Arboleda, former minister of energy. I received a copy on 5 July 2004.

79. For a 1999 incident, see Bloomberg News, "Ecuadorean Oil Workers Demand Money for Sector," *Houston Chronicle*, 31 March 1999: B2.

80. Interviewed 24 July 2001, Quito.

81. Byrne and Hoffman (2002: 97) identify the "necessary sacrifice" forced upon Native Americans in the United States to accommodate the mining industry and the nation's pursuit of nuclear energy and industrialization.

82. Paraphrasing from a Channel 4 television interview with Mayor Máximo Abad, aired 30 July 2001, Lago Agrio.

83. Karl 1999: 37.

84. Karl 1997: 190.

85. Karl 1997: 189–90.

86. Interviewed 31 October 2003, Lago Agrio.

87. Interviewed 8 December 2003, Quito.

88. Interviewed 30 July 2001, Lago Agrio.

89. Many oil multinationals advertise their tax payments to local, regional, and state governments; and today some do so on their websites. In 2001, EnCana paid US$1.8 million in taxes to four municipalities, including Lago Agrio and Cuyabeno, which became a municipality of Sucumbios Province in 1999. This figure was obtained on EnCana's website, under the document title "EnCana in Ecuador," which was downloaded on 5 October 2003. In November 2003, I was also given photocopies of receipts and cashed checks from City Investing to the municipality of Cuyabeno by community leaders, who believed the bulk of the revenues were being mismanaged by local officials. Those receipts indicated that City Investing paid Cuyabeno municipality US$934,676 in 2001 and $791,918 in 2002. During OCP's construction, Cuyabeno's mayor was an oil mayor, never having known this public servant role without oil subsidy.

90. Recorded 17 March 2004, Montreal, Canada, spoken in Spanish with English translation.

91. Recorded 17 March 2004, Montreal, Canada, spoken in Spanish with English translation.

92. Jon Arruti, representative of the Office of Environmental Rights and the Network of Community Leaders based in Coca, speaking at EnCana's annual general meeting, 28 April 2004. An account of his statement was provided by GlobalAware Canada.

93. Interviewed 31 October 2003, Lago Agrio.

94. In other cases in the past for example, Indigenous communities in Ecuador, who have gained local government positions, were not driven by self-sufficiency or separatism, but were driven to develop relations with the state, on their *own* terms (Bebbington 1996). Their demands included access to modern technologies enjoyed by other citizens and the desire to control and administer resources within their communities (Bebbington 1996: 58).

95. Seidman (2005: 174–75) is the first that I have found to identify when and why multinational corporations began to invest in community projects. Seidman's work on Sullivan Principles founded during South African apartheid to force U.S. companies to be socially responsible led to a rating matrix that favored investment in community projects rather than ending or addressing desegregation and affirmative action.

96. GlobalAware Canada's speaking tour: "Rude Oil: Canadian Involvement in the Amazon," 17 March 2004, University of Montreal, Canada.

97. GlobalAware, "Rude Oil."

98. I toured these facilities in November 2003.

99. Ohler and Hall 2000.

100. For media accounts of landowner-state conflict, see *El Mercurio*, "OCP recupera varios equipos," 9 June 2002; *Financial Times*, "Ecuador-Pipeline Ecuador Police Uproot Amazon Farmers in Pipeline's Path," 7 June 2002; *El Comercio*, "Las compensaciones de OCP no satisfacen en Sucumbíos," 20 June 2002: B2; *El Comercio*, "Sucumbíos presiona sobre el OCP," 19 June 2002: B1; and *El Comercio*, "250 finqueros bloquean la obra del OCP," 18 June 2002: B1.

101. Contract dated 15 February 2001. Weemaels (2002: 15) reports that 23 percent did not sign a contract with OCP or OCP subcontractors.

102. Weemaels 2002: 16, translated from Spanish: "Más de la mitad de los encuestados han sido amenazados, 42 de ellos por militares o policies, 30 por representantes del consorcio OCP y 18 by por desconocidos. Para 73 percent de ellos, la construcción del oleoducto ha generado la militarización de su región."

103. Weemaels 2002: 15–16.

104. *El Comercio*, "El nuevo oleoducto otra vez en conflicto," 9 June 2002; *El Comercio*, "250 finqueros bloquean la obra del OCP," 19 June 2002: B1; *El Comercio*, "Sucumbíos presiona sobre el OCP," 19 June 2002: B1; *El Comercio*, "Las compensaciones de OCP no satisfacen en Sucumbíos," 20 June 2002: B2; *El Comercio*, "Contrapunto: La política contra el OCP," 21 June 2002: B1 (an interview with Pablo Terán, minister of energy and mines); and EFE News Services, "Ecuador-Pipeline: Ecuador Police Uproot Amazon Farmers in Pipeline's Path," 7 June 2002.

105. Weemaels 2002: 15.

106. Jon Arruti traveled to EnCana's annual general meeting (28 April 2004) to attest to this type of discrepancy. Here is the full statement Arruti made through a translator: "EnCana has put forth compensation offers that are discriminatory towards indigenous peoples. For example, when the company was starting their seismic testing project Papagayo 3D, they offered the indigenous community of Pompeya $11 USD per hectare; however, in previous seismic projects, they offered $20 to non-indigenous settlers." An account of this statement was provided by GlobalAware Canada.

107. Interviewed 7 November 2003, Quito.

108. Lawsuits first commonly exhaust all national venues before becoming international cases and gaining support of the Inter-American Human Rights Committee. In Lago Agrio, among this small landowner group, there was hope of circumventing the national bodies, which was inspired by a German lawyer's brief initiative to use U.S. state laws against OCP.

109. Position paper by Frente de Defensa de la Amazonia entitled "Observaciones generales al EIA (Estudio de Impacto Ambiental) y al PMS (Plan de Manejo Ambiental) para la Construccion y Operación del OCP." It is undated, though it references meetings and events held between 17 April 2001 and 11 May 2001. Frente, the single organization in the Lago Agrio area with an environmental agenda, is well known both nationally and internationally. Established in 1994 to coordinate community organizations with a focus on oil extraction, it has extensive links to Indigenous organizations in Ecuador, environmental groups in Quito, and Indigenous advocacy groups in the United States. Since OCP's construction began, this organization shifted toward organizing community-based environmental monitoring and training for increased community participation as well. It attempts to support the multiple and conflictive positions of the Indigenous and local communities, without having an agenda or position of its own. It was a vital local organization in the formation and maintenance of the community-based lawsuit against Texaco, as mentioned in chapter 1.

110. Interviewed 29 July 2002, Lago Agrio.

111. Interviewed 31 October 2003, Lago Agrio.
112. Interviewed 31 October 2003, Lago Agrio.
113. Interviewed 16 July 2001, Quito.
114. GlobalAware, "Rude Oil."
115. Arruti, with regard to EnCana's operations in the Ecuadorian Amazon at EnCana's annual general meeting, 28 April 2004. Statement provided by GlobalAware Canada.
116. Edelstein 1988.
117. Brown and Mikkelsen 1990: 65; see Brown 1992 as well.
118. Interviewed 31 July 2002, Lago Agrio.
119. Tilly 1998.
120. Patricia Trottier, wife of Gwyn Morgan, president and CEO of EnCana, Calgary, Canada, chaired Fundación NanPaz. Ms. Trottier worked with United Nations World Food Programme to support nutritional programs. [See Gwyn Morgan's letter to the editor in *Canadian Business*, "EnCana's Morgan Responds," 14 April 2003: 7.] The Ecuadorian-Canadian Development Fund (Fondo Ec-Canadienese por Desarollo), a state-run Canadian aid agency, also provided funds into the region through NanPaz.
121. See "EnCana Community Investment in Ecuador," an undated file on http://www.encana .com. On community complaints of NanPaz actions see Jermyn (n.d.).
122. Interviews and observations 15 November 2003, Lago Agrio area.
123. I toured these community relations projects on 15 November 2003 with Ineke Lock, who was at the University of Alberta, Canada, at the time.
124. In this subhead, I am referring to the absence and presence of Indigenous leadership with regards to the OCP pipeline project. However, the absence of Indigenous leadership in the Amazonian communities and presence of Indigenous leadership in the larger towns induce concern and unease among some NGOs that support Indigenous organization. Though perhaps not directly pertinent to an analysis of the OCP pipeline project, one interview in June 2004 was particularly telling of the complexity of oil imposition on Indigenous communities and the role of national and international NGOs. I include it here in length:

So we think, on the one hand, we see it as absolutely vital that these [Indigenous] organizations be able to have a center, to have an office, to have a phone line, to have a fax machine, to have a computer, to have an accountant. To be able to develop projects, capture funding, pressure, network both within the Indigenous movement and with national and international allies from civil society, from the NGO sector. To be able to demand and capture or control state resources for their basic needs. You know, for education and health. All of these things require for there to be an office. And we provide funding for that. We provide funding for overhead, for telephone, Internet costs, sometimes for office staff, like an accountant. And we also, some organizations provide funding for Indigenous leaders, who have to live in a city, recognizing that, yeah, they are in the city, it's not their community, and most of these, the people that we work with, don't have communities within traveling distance. So they just can't walk to their communities from [the town]. It would be several days, if not much longer. And yeah, they have to be able to survive as well. They have to be able to eat, have a place to sleep and all that. And that requires money. We provide grants with the long-term vision that these, that this will be funding that will be leveraged by the Indigenous organizations, because they are going to be able to take advantage of this to create new allies, to develop, to strengthen their institutions, to successfully capture more state funding for their basic needs, and also to develop larger vision projects for their sustainable development. And that will allow us to start withdrawing funding from that area.
   On the other hand, yes, we definitely also see serious problems from leaders living in the city. I mean, from the fact that there are influences from alcohol, the Mestizo mainstream culture, if you want to call it that. Just in terms of even the bureaucracy and corruption of the normal political system rubbing off on Indigenous leaders, as well. To health problems, changes in diet, for them and their entire families. A lot of times they will bring their entire families

with them, their children. And their wives are not used to administering a household in the city. They have a very different culture, a very different way of life in communities. And they are not prepared, and they don't know how to provide a healthy diet for their families outside of their communities. And why should they? There's no reason for them to, but it provides serious health problems. The leaders end up drinking too much. They have the culture in the communities where they drink chicha, and then they come to the city and start drinking beer or liquor in the same way they used to drink chicha. And it causes serious problems.

Also the children of leaders, who often become leaders as well, grow up outside of their communities sometimes because they are in the city with their parents, maybe they are outside the bilingual educational system. And just the general change in perspective caused by leaders living outside their territory, living in a different culture with access to funds. Maybe if they are leaders, according to society around them, they need to have a cell phone, they need to have a car, they need to have secretaries, maybe they need to have lovers. All of that rubs off, as it would on anybody, Indigenous or non-Indigenous. And yeah, it creates serious problems.

So we see it as really mixed. It's a really problematic situation, but one where we can't—it's not black or white. You can't say, "well, they should just all stay in the communities." Because a lot of things wouldn't happen.

125. Pallares 2002; see also Becker 2008; Zamosc 2007.

126. For individual agreements between a community and an oil company, see Jochnick and Garzón 2006.

127. See Acción Ecológica 2001d.

128. For the code of conduct negotiated between the Secoya community and U.S.-based Occidental Petroleum, see CDES 2000; Vickers 2003.

129. "City" is a reference to City Investing or Alberta Energy.

130. Interviewed 31 October 2003, Lago Agrio.

131. Interviewed 11 June 2004, Quito.

132. Jochnick and Garzón (2006: 192–93) contribute how the Organization of Indigenous Peoples of Pastaza (OPIP) succeeded in negotiating a role in environmental assessments and forming a technical team in 1994, which was then undermined by the oil company Arco.

133. Interviewed 11 June 2004, Quito.

134. In 2003, CONFENAIE was said to have held 97 percent of the shares of the company Amazonia Gas, which was a trial Indigenous-owned business that collected the burn-off gas, or gas by-product, of the oil industry for conversion into usable gas for homes. The company was said to be assisted by a Canadian partner, which was said to have eventually left the enterprise, and to have received early loans from the Canadian government and the Inter-American Development Bank. From a recent report, it appears as if the operation has shut down due to mismanagement. See the unpublished report "Conference on Indigenous Peoples in Latin America: The Challenge of Poverty Reduction, Land Rights and Natural Resource Control," by the Center for Latin American Studies, Edmund A. Walsh School of Foreign Service, Georgetown University, 3 December 2004. I have not been able to substantiate this report with others.

135. See Kane 1995.

136. *El Universo.* "Huaoranis y Petrobras Energia Firmaron un Convenio de Cooperacion," 12 April 2004.

137. See Ali 2000 and Redford and Stearman 1993 on environmental NGOs and conservation biologists, respectively. On Indigenous and environmental conflicts in Ecuador specifically, see the report by the Advocacy Project editors, "The Fight for the Amazon: Dining with the Devil: The Dilemmas of Negotiating with Oil Companies," *Amazon Oil* 16(6), 14 March 2002.

138. Gedicks 2001; Alexander 1996.

139. National and international environmental NGOs appeared eager to be linked with Indigenous organizations and issues, yet that eagerness was not necessarily or consistently reciprocated. Some Quito-based and international groups promoted the alliances to be much stronger than they actually were as a boost to their own legitimacy as spokespeople for the Oriente. Though

many international advocates with Indigenous acceptance do exist, not all national and international organizations that claim to know Indigenous concerns are actually accepted by the communities they said they represent.

140. Sawyer 2004: 96. For Ecuador's 1979 Hydrocarbons Policy, see Perkins (2006: 168–69).

141. Becker 2008.

142. Egan 1996.

143. Interviewed 11 June 2004, Quito.

144. Interviewed 2 August 2001, Quito.

145. Interviewed 2 August 2001, Quito.

146. See Scott 1998.

147. On road impacts, see Finer et al. 2008.

148. Due to contemporary exploitative pressures by foreign missionaries and oil incursion, several of the Indigenous communities have been splintered and reduced in number. For example, Cofan communities and families have split due to differing degrees of engagement with former missionaries and current oil companies (Tidwell 1996). In particular, the Huaoranis bear the brunt of discriminatory and poverty-induced jokes and humor. Local stories depict some male leaders as receiving cash from an oil company on their territory and spending it over a few days in Lago Agrio, or hiring taxis for the nine-hour drive to Quito. Conservation workers say they will be stopped in their cars by groups of lowland Indigenous people, who may ask for $5 or $1,000 on any given day to permit their passage on public roads in the Amazon interior (interviewed 2 December 2003, Quito). Another Quito-based activist described collaborations with Huaorani as completely unpredictable: one day a joint demonstration against an oil company will be arranged, and the next they'll be told the Indigenous community is "at war" with them. Jochnick and Garzón 2006: 192 identify one Huaorani organization as being started and funded by the oil company Maxus to facilitate access. For additional consideration of the Huaorani, see Kane 1995 and Toledo and Ponce 2001.

149. Chapin 2004: 26–27.

150. Interviewed 2 December 2003, Quito.

151. In 2009, I visited Sani Lodge in the Ecuadorian Amazon. This lodge was launched in December 2002 in Occidental's Block 15 after Kichwa leaders among the Sani community negotiated with the oil company for start-up funds and management/operation assistance—in exchange for drilling, which came up dry, and putting in a pipeline. Occidental also built three classrooms. The lodge is now managed exclusively by the community with profits returning to the community's school, school boat, residence for the community's older students to attend secondary school in Quito or Coca, as well as language and naturalist training in the United States. Personal visit in 2009, and e-mail correspondence 6 December 2003.

152. Interviewed 31 July 2002, Lago Agrio.

153. Interviewed 30 July 2001, Lago Agrio.

154. Interviewed 30 July 2001, Lago Agrio.

155. Interviewed 8 December 2003, Quito.

156. Della Porta and Diani 1999: 16.

157. Szasz 1994: 81.

158. Castells 1997: 112.

159. See Widener 2009b.

CHAPTER 3
QUITO'S NGOS:
REALIZING AN ENVIRONMENTAL FUND

1. Controlling media access and making invisible the spill is specifically referencing the BP Deepwater Horizon oil disaster in the Gulf of Mexico that began in April 2010.

2. World Wildlife Fund (WWF) is also known as World Wide Fund for Nature (WWF).

3. See the works of scholars Faber 2008; Gottlieb 1993; Hofrichter 1993; and Humphrey and Buttel 1982, and environmental journalists and writers Chapin 2004; Hari 2010; and MacDonald 2008.

4. According to Hari 2010: 11.

5. On this exchange, see Chapin 2004; Hari 2010; and MacDonald 2008. On how environmental science is silenced by "burying science-based environmentalism in return" for donations on climate change policies, see Hari 2010: 11.

6. See Rowell 1996: 126–30, as well Gottlieb 1993. The success of corporations and their lobbyists and think tanks to construct climate change doubt, denial, and skepticism in the minds of the American public are also well documented by Jacques, Dunlap, and Freeman 2008.

7. On how presenting "politically realistic" environmental goals and standards by environmental NGOs is weakening climate change policy in the United States, see Hari 2010: 14.

8. See Rundall 2000.

9. Domhoff 1967: 5.

10. Humphrey and Buttel 1982; Hofrichter 1993.

11. Shwom 2009: 280–81.

12. Shwom 2009: 286.

13. See Chapin 2004. Chapin's work appeared in the November/December 2004 *World Watch* magazine and was followed by numerous letters to the editor by readers and NGOs, including CI, TNC, and WWW, in the January/February 2005 issue. The article even generated a comment by the *Washington Post*; see "World Watch, Kicking Dirt on Three Big Greenies," by staff writer Peter Carlson, 23 November 2004.

14. Hofrichter 1993: 7.

15. Humphrey and Buttel 1982.

16. Markowitz and Rosner 2002: 232–33.

17. See Principles 1991; Bullard 1993; Gottlieb 1993; Hofrichter 1993; Rowell 1996; Faber 1998c; and Roberts and Toffolon-Weiss 2001.

18. Chapin 2004.

19. Walker et al. 2007: 438.

20. Walker et al. 2007: 438.

21. Walton 2007.

22. Arenas, Lozano, and Albareda 2009: 184.

23. Shellenberger and Nordhaus 2005.

24. See Chapin 2004; Hari 2010; MacDonald 2008; and Shellenberger and Nordhaus 2005.

25. The symposium was held in 2005 and responses were published in a 2006 issue of *Organization & Environment* 19(1).

26. Shellenberger and Nordhaus 2005: 20.

27. Cohen 2006: 75.

28. Zelezny and Bailey 2006.

29. Brulle and Jenkins 2006.

30. See Rundall 2000.

31. Rundall 2000.

32. Markowitz and Rosner 2002: 217; see Rowell 1996 as well.

33. Corburn 2002.

34. Corburn 2002.

35. Speth 2008: 69.

36. TNC, CI, International Union for Conservation of Nature (IUCN), and BirdLife have corporate partners, corporate supporters, or board members from within the petroleum industry at the NGOs' headquarters or local or national branches. CI and BirdLife have had corporate partnerships with BP, while CI has also collaborated with ChevronTexaco and Shell through a Bank of America working initiative; in addition, IUCN signed an agreement to collaborate with Shell International in 2007. Following the BP spill in the Gulf of Mexico in April 2010, TNC came under heated media attention for its acceptance of grants, land, and partnerships with BP. See Joe Stephens, "Nature

Conservancy Faces Potential Backlash from Ties with BP," *Washington Post*, 23 May 2010; Amy Ridenour and David Ridenour, "Ridenour: Return BP Cash: Environmentalists and Politicians Enjoyed BP Green," *Washington Times*, 14 June 2010. For more on TNC's International Leadership Council and partnership with BP, see http://www.nature.org/joinanddonate/corporatepartnerships/partnership/art16288.html or http://www.nature.org/joinanddonate/corporatepartnerships/leadership/, downloaded 3 July 2010. On BirdLife's collaboration with BP since 1985, see its Conservation Leadership Programme (formerly BP Conservation Programme), which joins BirdLife, CI, Fauna & Flora International, and Wildlife Conservation Society (WCS) with BP; see http://www.birdlife.org/action/business/cons_leadership/index.html, downloaded 3 July 2010.

37. Chapin 2004: 22, 25.

38. On Monsanto, see Robin 2010.

39. On IKEA and the World Wildlife Fund, see Hari 2010: 13.

40. See Linton 2005.

41. See Stephens, "Nature Conservancy Faces Potential Backlash; and Ridenour and Ridenour, "Ridenour: Return BP Cash."

42. See Holly Hall, "Telethon for Gulf Cleanup Generates Relatively Few Gifts," *Chronicle of Philanthropy*, 23 June 2010.

43. Hall, "Telethon for Gulf Cleanup." http://philanthropy.com/blogs/prospecting/telethon-for-gulf-cleanup-generates-relatively-few-gifts/25026, downloaded 15 December 2010.

44. I am quoting Speth 2008: 63, who was writing about some of the root causes of an overemphasis on and valuation of the economy at the expense of the environment. Speth was not speaking to the BP spill or to oil-environmental conflicts in particular, but his word choice substantiates the point that I was trying to make with regards to environmental NGO and corporate collaboration.

45. See Meyer 1997.

46. Turner and Benjamin 1995: 209 identify the WWF as proposing debt-for-nature swaps to developing nations in 1984 as a means to manage their external debt.

47. See Turner and Benjamin 1995: 209; Meyer 1997.

48. Turner and Benjamin 1995: 249–50.

49. Turner and Benjamin 1995: 250.

50. Turner and Benjamin 1995: 250.

51. Turner and Benjamin 1995: 251.

52. Turner and Benjamin 1995: 251, citing Instituto Brasileiro do Análises Sociais e Economicas (IBASE), *Debt Swaps, Development and Environment*, Rio de Janeiro: Instituto Brasileiro do Análises Sociais e Economicas, 1992: 19.

53. See Meyer 1997 on the National Environmental Funds or NEFs.

54. Bayon et al. 1999.

55. Cowell 1997. See as well, The World Bank Global Environmental Facility, *GEF Lessons Notes*, no. 5, January 1999.

56. Meyer 1997.

57. In a detailed assessment of national environmental funds, Meyer 1997 refers only to non-profits and governments as international donors.

58. See http://www.conservationfinance.org.

59. Cowell 1997.

60. Morris 2004: 36.

61. On those tensions, see Brown and Masterson-Allen 1994; Gottlieb 1993.

62. Tarrow 1999: 14.

63. Guerrón-Montero 2005.

64. Guha 1989.

65. Fay 2005.

66. Shiva 1998: 234.

67. See Buttel's (2003) critique of ecological modernization, in this case NGO-corporate collaboration, and support of environmental activism.

68. Business News Americas, "Ombudsman Questions OCP Environmental License," 29 June 2001; Reuters, "OCP Ecuador Wins Quito Okay for Pipeline Route," 3 October 2001; *Platt's Oilgram News*, 15 August 2001, News briefs 79(157): 6; EFE News Service, "Ecuador-Oil Quito City Council Gives Green Light for New Pipeline," 2 October 2001.

69. Interviewed 18 July 2001, Quito.

70. Interviewed 18 July 2001, Quito.

71. Keck and Sikkink 1998; Brysk 2000.

72. Keck and Sikkink 1998 conceptualized the "boomerang effect." McAteer and Pulver (2009) conceptualized the "corporate boomerang," in which transnational advocacy networks pressure corporations and their shareholders. My use of a corporate boomerang effort is quite different. In the Ecuadorian case, the oil corporations sought out their Northern environmental partners to demonstrate to Ecuadorian NGOs "how to" negotiate conservation agreements with the oil industry.

73. For more information on the Mindo-Nambillo protected area, see Perreault 1996.

74. Interviewed 15 August 2002, Quito.

75. For additional insight into the Ecuadorian government's commitment to oil, see Gould 1999.

76. On BirdLife's collaboration with BP since 1985, see its Conservation Leadership Programme (formerly BP Conservation Programme), which joins BirdLife, CI, Fauna & Flora International, and WCS with BP; see http://www.birdlife.org/action/business/cons_leadership/index .html, downloaded 3 July 2010. BirdLife's headquarters resembles TNC, CI, and WWF in having corporate partnerships.

77. CEDENMA is the Comité Ecuatoriana para la Defensa de la Natureleza y el Medio Ambiente, or the Ecuadorian Committee for the Defense of Nature and the Environment. It is commonly referred to as CEDENMA.

78. As demonstration of their influence at this time, nine of fifteen meetings between OCP and an NGO in Ecuador, between the dates of 19 August 1999 to 10 May 2001, included CECIA, Maquipucuna, or Pro Ruta. See Stone & Webster Consultants report *The OCP Pipeline Project Independent Technical Review Public Domain Report* "Section 6 Compliance with World Bank Guidelines," prepared 19 April 2002.

79. See Mindo Working Group 2001.

80. Futuro Latinoamericano 2002: 17.

81. Futuro Latinoamericano 2002: 19.

82. Futuro Latinoamericano 2002: 19.

83. Futuro Latinoamericano 2002: 13.

84. Futuro Latinoamericano 2002: 13–14.

85. CECIA, or Corporación Ornitológica del Ecuador, changed its name after OCP negotiations, and is now known as Aves y Conservación.

86. For a background on each participating NGO, see Futuro Latinoamericano 2002.

87. A member of TNC Ecuador attended the negotiations as a mediator or adviser, not as a TNC-designated participant in negotiations.

88. Except for the two university groups, I interviewed each of the NGOs that participated in the ecofund negotiations at least once.

89. Interviewed 7 August 2002, Quito.

90. Chapin 2004: 28, 30. Though it is not the intent of this work to single out individuals, this expert, along with another colleague, was believed to have orchestrated the silencing or "embargo" of a study on conservation issues in the Global South for the Ford Foundation.

91. Goldman 2005: 165.

92. Gwyn Morgan, "EnCana's Morgan Responds," *Canadian Business*, Letters section, 14 April 2003: 7. This was a letter to the editor written by Morgan, president and CEO of EnCana Corporation, in response to a report on EnCana's operations in Ecuador entitled "Down the Tube," 17 March 2003.

93. Domhoff 1967: 47; Useem 1984: 38.

94. Morris 2004: 36–37.

95. Interviewed 17 July 2002, Quito.

96. Interviewed 17 July 2002, Quito.

97. Futuro Latinoamericano 2002: 22.

98. For example, in 2002, Acción Ecológica had prepared a five-series how-to manual for community environmental monitoring (*Manuales de Monitoreo Ambiental Comunitario*). In 2010, they updated this report.

99. I interviewed each one of these organizations at least once.

100. I interviewed only one of the three human rights organizations.

101. The capital Quito debunks the belief that oil-led development trickles down to the underprivileged. In 2001 and 2002, Indigenous women with babies wrapped on their back approached cars in the street to sell packets of gum, while Indigenous children begged on the streets with cheeks scabby, red, and crusted from dehydration and the strong Andean sun; others were nearly bald with puffs of stringy, orange-tinted hair from chronic malnutrition. Packages of gum being sold by poor children on street corners, buses, and trolleys was a disturbing sight at the time. In Asia in the 1990s, adults sold homemade food, including roasted chicken legs, sticky rice, and deep-fried grasshoppers on the street and at bus stops and train stations, with most of the profits going to themselves and their families. Though I have not read a study on the sale of packets of gum, or *chiclet*, it strikes me as a street-level portrait of the economic development differences between South America and Asia. Though chewing gum seems a frivolous digression, it indicates external profit, external influence, and external control at a base or microlevel.

102. Interviewed 18 July 2001, Quito.

103. Seventy-two objections to the EIA were submitted to the Environment Ministry in May 2001, as reported in the *Financial Times*, EFE News Service (U.S.), "Ecuador-Oil Ecuador Faults OCP Environmental Impact Statement," 22 May 2001.

104. BirdLife advocated for a route change as early as November 2000.

105. Interviewed 14 August 2002, Quito.

106. Connelly and Richardson 2005: 397.

107. Interviewed 20 October 2003, Quito.

108. Futuro Latinoamericano 2002: 11.

109. Futuro Latinoamericano 2002: 16.

110. See Mindo Working Group's report, as well as two of BirdLife's international press releases: "Position Statement on Ecuador's Heavy Oil Pipeline Construction Project Financed by WestLB," released 14 January 2002, Quito, Ecuador; "Disastrous Decision for Protected Rainforest in Ecuador," released 17 November 2000, Cambridge, U.K. See also BirdLife's "Letter to President of Ecuador Gustavo Noboa," dated 13 November 2000.

111. Mindo Working Group 2001.

112. In total, there were seventy-two objections to the EIA submitted during May 2001. As reported in the *Financial Times*, "Ecuador-Oil Ecuador Faults OCP."

113. Interviewed 22 May 2007, Quito.

114. Interviewed 7 October 2003, Quito.

115. Fundación Natura et al. 2001; Fundación Maquipucuna 2001.

116. Press release by Fundación Natura, Ambientey y Sociedad, CECIA, EcoCiencia, and Maquipucuna titled "Autorización Ambiental Apresurada para la Construcción del OCP," dated 8 June 2001 and provided on Natura letterhead.

117. *El Comercio*, "OCP: los verdes condicionan," 9 June 2001: B5.

118. Fundación Natura et al. 2001; see also *El Comercio*, "OCP: los verdes condicionan."

119. Fundación Natura et al. 2001: 4, translated from the Spanish original by the author.

120. Acción Ecológica 2001a.

121. Fundación Maquipucuna 2001.

122. Goodland 1987.

123. Goodland 1991.

124. Goldman 2005.

125. Interviewed 15 August 2002, Quito.

126. Futuro Latinoamericano 2002: 18.

127. Interviewed 7 August 2002, Quito.

128. A faxed copy of the letter dated 19 December 2001 from the World Bank to the attention of Dr. Hernán Lara, executive president of OCP Ecuador. The letter was signed by Ian Johnson, vice president and head of Environmentally and Sociologically Sustainable Development, and David De Ferranti, vice president of Latin American and the Caribbean Regional Office. The letter was copied to the ministers of five Ecuadorian ministries, the U.S. ambassador, World Bank directors in Germany and Ecuador, an assistant to a state minister of North Rhine-Westpahlia and the WestLB New York representative.

129. Interviewed 27 October 2003, Quito.

130. Interviewed 15 August 2002, Quito.

131. Unpublished original document entitled "Declaración Conjunta," dated 9 April 2002, Quito. See also Futuro Latinoamericano 2002: 15.

132. Though Acción Ecológica attended the meetings, they refused to sign the declaration.

133. The Stone & Webster report notes that Techint was an "experienced" contractor with "expertise" in constructing fourteen pipelines across the Andean region. Stone & Webster 2002: see "Overall Assessment."

134. Interviewed 17 July 2002, Quito.

135. Goodland 2002.

136. Smithsonian 2001.

137. See Stone & Webster 2002: section 6.

138. See Stone & Webster 2002: 3 of "Overall Assessment."

139. Stone & Webster 2002: section 11, "Assessment of NGO Complaints."

140. Interviewed 20 October 2003, Quito.

141. Interviewed 20 October 2003, Quito.

142. Interviewed 20 October 2003, Quito.

143. Transparency International ranked Ecuador 139 out of 163 nations in terms of corruption and lack of transparency in their Corruption Perceptions Index (CPI) 2006.

144. Interviewed 20 October 2003, Quito.

145. Interviewed 21 May 2007, Quito.

146. Interviewed 15 August 2002, Quito.

147. Interviewed 15 August 2002, Quito.

148. Coury and Lucanin 1996; Kingdon 1984.

149. Futuro Latinoamericano 2002: 18.

150. Interviewed 22 May 2007, Quito.

151. Alberta Ecotrust Foundation, is an oil-funded nonprofit with environmental groups for small community and environmental development projects. See www.albertaecotrust.com. Additional sources: Canada NewsWire, EnCana press release, "EnCana Launches $10 Million Community Fund," 6 January 2003; EnCana press release, "An Ecological Fund without Precedent Created in Ecuador," 19 March 2005, http://www.encana.com/investor/news_releases/news_2005/.

152. Alberta 2004a.

153. On Canada's oil, or tar, sands, see Marsden 2008 and Nikiforuk 2009.

154. Alberta 2004a.

155. One undated press release on EnCana's website claims that the participating NGOs would commit 30 percent of the fund through fundraising campaigns. The final agreement does not appear to support this.

156. EnCana, "An Ecological Fund without Precedent Created in Ecuador."

157. See Fondo Ambiental Nacional's (FAN) promotional material, "Organizational Profile," 2nd ed., September 2006: 22. Printed with assistance from TNC and the U.S. Agency for International Development (USAID).

158. FAN, "Organizational Profile," 17.

159. FAN, "Organizational Profile," 4–5.

160. For more information, see http://www.fan.org.ec.

161. Interviewed 22 August 2003, Quito.

162. Interviewed 15 August 2002, Quito.

163. Interviewed 17 July 2002, Quito.

164. Interviewed 9 July 2002, Quito.

165. Interviewed 15 August 2002, Quito.

166. Interviewed 9 July 2002, Quito.

167. For example, the Mexican Nature Conservation Fund was established in 1994 with contributions from the Mexican government, United States Agency for International Development (USAID), and then three years later with funds from a World Bank GEF grant. See "GEF Lessons Notes #7," April 1999, World Bank Global Environmental Facility.

168. Interviewed 15 August 2002, Quito.

169. Interviewed 18 July 2001, Quito.

170. Interviewed 9 July 2002, Quito.

171. The oil consortium would argue that the ecofund is not compensation for environmental damage. However, I use "compensation" here to indicate how the fund was perceived by non-negotiators.

172. Interviewed 17 July 2002, Quito.

173. Interviewed 17 July 2002, Quito.

174. Interviewed 22 August 2003, Quito.

175. Interviewed 7 October 2003, Quito.

176. Interviewed 20 Octobert 2002, Quito.

177. Interviewed 7 August 2002, Quito.

178. Fay 2005: 23.

179. Interviewed 22 May 2007, Quito.

180. The Advocacy Project, "From the Editors: Dining with the Devil: The Dilemmas of Negotiating with Oil Companies," 14 March 2002, *Amazon Oil* 16(6). http://www.advocacynet.org/news_view/news_193.html, downloaded 24 May 2002.

181. Interviewed 27 October 2003, Quito.

182. Interviewed 27 October 2003, Quito.

183. Interviewed 22 May 2007, Quito.

184. See Goodell 1985 on the ideal type of patronage, and on patrons and clients.

185. Goodell 1985: 253.

186. Goodell 1985: 256.

187. Rowell 1996.

188. Rowell 1996.

189. Interviewed 27 June 2002, Mindo. The activist actually said, "They must pay to paint." But I understood the participant to mean either, "OCP must pay to be painted" or "The NGOs must be paid to paint."

190. Rowell 1996:126, 130.

191. Rowell 1996: 130,

192. Goldman 2005.

193. Ali 2000: 85, 90, citing and utilizing the model of Fisher 1983.

194. Galaskiewicz 1989.

195. A joint OCP, EcoFondo, and EnCana Corporation press release, "OCP Ecuador S.A. and EnCana Corporation Fund the Project: An Ecological Fund without Precedent Created in Ecuador," 2005: 1. http://www.encana.com/media/newsreleases/2005/pdfs/p002414.pdf, downloaded originally in 2005, and then again on 7 October 2009.

196. "OCP Ecuador S.A. and EnCana Corporation Fund the Project," 1.

197. Alberta 2004b.

198. Interviewed 9 July 2002, Quito.

199. Interviewed 17 July 2002, Quito.

200. Interviewed 22 August 2003, Quito.

201. Interviewed 18 July 2001, Quito.

202. Interviewed 9 July 2002, Quito.

203. See Markowitz and Rosner 2002; Humphrey and Buttel 1982; Hofrichter 1993.

204. See Tellkamp et al. 2004. Likewise, CECIA continued to study the pipeline's long-term impacts in this area.

205. The Ministry of Environment monitored the pipeline's construction; however, the reports were not made public and the wall of bounded reports at the Ministry of Environment, which I looked at in 2003, were largely construction progress reports. Breaks and landslides were reported; however, these reports were not easily accessible and not made public.

206. Interviewed 13–14 September 2003, Mindo.

207. See Couch and Kroll-Smith 1985; Freudenburg 1997; Kroll-Smith and Couch 1990.

208. Interviewed 7 August 2002, Quito.

209. Interviewed 22 May 2007, Quito.

210. Chapin 2004: 26.

211. Interviewed 7 August 2002, Quito.

212. Interviewed 17 July 2002, Quito.

213. Interviewed 7 October 2003, Quito.

214. Interviewed 20 October 2003, Quito.

215. Interviewed 22 May 2007, Quito.

216. Interviewed 22 May 2007, Quito.

217. Interviewed 22 May 2007, Quito.

218. Interviewed 23 May 2007, Quito.

219. Interviewed 22 May 2007, Quito.

220. Interviewed 17 July 2002, Quito.

221. Interviewed 7 August 2002, Quito.

222. See Drost 2005, as well.

223. Interviewed 7 August 2002, Quito.

224. Interviewed 15 August 2002, Quito.

225. Interviewed 22 August 2003, Quito.

226. Interviewed 23 May 2007, Quito.

227. Interviewed 15 August 2002, Quito.

228. Interviewed 7 October 2003, Quito.

229. Interviewed 7 October 2003, Quito.

230. Interviewed 20 October 2003, Quito.

231. See http://www.fan.org.ec.

232. Interviewed 20 October 2003, Quito.

233. Interviewed 21 May 2007, Quito.

234. Interviewed 24 May 2007, Mindo.

235. Interviewed 24 May 2007, Mindo.

236. Interviewed 22 May 2007, Quito.

237. Interviewed 1 June 2007, Mindo.

238. Interviewed 1 June 2007, Mindo.

239. Interviewed 22 May 2007, Quito.

240. Grossman 2000: 78.

241. Lewis 2003: 157.

242. Lewis 2003: 158. In an earlier analysis, Lewis's (2000) research found that transnational conservation organizations entered politically open nations with active domestic organizations, rather than closed nations with greater conservation needs. Incorporating the "openness" criteria in this case, it appears that domestic NGOs with strong international partnerships engage "open," and predominately Northern, multinationals with experience in NGO-oil collaborations, rather than "closed," and perhaps more environmentally destructive, oil companies, such as the state-owned PetroEcuador. Rather than ranking oil company performance on environmental safeguards, the inclusion of PetroEcuador here is meant to acknowledge that the conservation community has greater leverage on and access to nonnational oil entities, rather than state-protected ones.

243. Interviewed 18 July 2001, Quito.

244. Interviewed 21 May 2007, Quito.

245. Interviewed 7 October 2003, Quito.
246. Interviewed 21 May 2007, Quito.
247. Interviewed 23 May 2007, Quito.
248. Interviewed 22 May 2007, Quito.
249. For example, the method used by BirdLife International to identify important biodiversity areas was adopted by the Ecuadorian Environment Ministry.

CHAPTER 4
MINDO:
OIL AND TOURISM MAY MIX

1. See "Project Rescue Centre—Management of the Protected Forest Mindo-Nambillo," an unpublished report prepared by Acción por la Vida in October 2004.
2. The Audubon Society supports an annual Christmas Bird Count in December. For annual results by site, see http://www.audubon.org/.
3. BirdLife International designated Mindo an Important Bird Area in 1997, a distinction that advocates greater conservation need. Mindo was the first IBA in the Americas. See: http://www .birdlife.org.
4. Wilson 2002: 87.
5. See Acción por la Vida 2004.
6. See Honey 1999: 6–7 and 22–26 on ecotourism, and see West and Carrier 2004: 483–84 on ecotourism leading to at least one journal, academic center, advocacy and trade organization, and a U.N. "international year of" designation. Ecotourism should also support the "human rights and democratic movements" of local people by not financing "repressive and undemocratic states" through tourism (Honey 1999: 24.)
7. Duffy 2000: 549.
8. Mastny 2002: 96.
9. Honey 1999: 14.
10. Brondo and Woods 2007: 15.
11. Tobias and Mendelsohn 1991: 93, in a study of Costa Rica.
12. Honey 1999: 11–12.
13. Kosek 1996[2004]: 125.
14. Pena and Mondragon-Valdéz 1998.
15. Pena and Mondragon-Valdéz 1998.
16. See Duffy 2000: 561 on how a Belize island was perceived to be "totally remastered in the pursuit of tourism."
17. See Baver and Lynch 2006; Pattullo 2005.
18. McLaren 2003: 66.
19. McLaren 2003: 40 and 71–73 on the cultural impacts. In contrast, increased homogeneity or a learned preference for all things foreign may not necessarily occur with the influx of foreign travelers. Macleod (2004: 218) identified a community in the Canary Islands with a distinct history and shared communal identity that enabled them to retain and to become consciously aware and proud of their uniqueness even after the arrival of visitors. Even though Macleod (2004: 216, 218) acknowledges the rapid societal changes caused by an influx of foreign travelers, some of whom stay and marry within the local population, he argues that at least in the period that was studied, individuals changed their self-perception and their roles, from fisherman to tour guide, but their long-running communal links reaffirm their cultural ties and distinctions.
20. McLaren 2003: 78.
21. See Duffy 2000 on reduced beach and pier access among the people of Belize; Macleod 2004 on displaced farmers; McLaren 2003: 25; and Miller 2006.
22. Miller 2006.

23. Duffy 2000.
24. Pattullo 2005.
25. See Duffy 2000 on tensions between foreign and local residents in Belize.
26. Prosser 1992: 44. Also see McLaren 2003: 25.
27. See Vivanco 2001: 85 on outsiders' dismissal of local peoples' knowledge and use of the cloud forest of Monte Verde, Costa Rica.
28. See Duffy 2000: 558 on Belizean assessment of the practices of some foreign newcomers to the tourism industry.
29. Mastny 2002: 96.
30. See McLaren 2003: 69–70 for community displacement due to tourism in Kenya and Hawaii.
31. Standlea 2006.
32. West and Carrier 2004: 485.
33. West and Carrier 2004: 485.
34. West and Carrier 2004: 486.
35. West and Carrier 2004: 486.
36. West and Carrier 2004: 490.
37. West and Carrier 2004: 495.
38. Munt 1994: 53.
39. Munt 1994: 54.
40. Munt 1994: 55.
41. McLaren 2003: 22.
42. McLaren 2003: 24.
43. See Memmi 1968.
44. Tenenbaum 2000.
45. Macleod 2004.
46. See Buckley 2004; Monz and Twardock 2004; Tenebaum 2000.
47. Honey 1999: 54.
48. Duffy 2000: 561.
49. McLaren 2003: 27.
50. McLaren 2003: 28, 85.
51. Honey 1999: 50–51.
52. Mitchell 2001.
53. Roberts and Thanos 2003: 85.
54. Lewis 2001.
55. Mitchell 2001.
56. Gould 1999: 251; Tidwell 1996.
57. Wunder 1999.
58. Hampton 2003: 98.
59. Hampton 2003: 98.
60. Hampton 2003: 85, 97.
61. Economy 2004: 86–87.
62. Valaoras, Pistolas, and Sotiropoulou 2002.
63. Valaoras, Pistolas, and Sotiropoulou 2002.
64. See Nepal 2002 on the risks of developing mountain ecotourism in developing areas. Nepal calls for greater international involvement to establish ecotourism criteria and monitors in the mountainous regions of developing nations to reduce the negative impacts associated with rapid ecotourism development (108–9).
65. Vivanco 2001.
66. Vivanco 2001.
67. Garrett 2004/2005.
68. Greathouse-Amador 2005.
69. Mitchell 2001.

70. Brondo and Woods 2007: 14.
71. Brondo and Woods 2007: 14.
72. Binns and Nel 2002.
73. Binns and Nel 2002.
74. Lennon and Foley 2000: 3; McLaren 2003: 50.
75. Sturken 2007: 65.
76. McLaren 2003: 48–49.
77. See Washburn 2005 on "flood tourism," identified by Martha Ward, an anthropologist at the University of New Orleans, in reference to the influx of visitors to New Orleans after Hurricane Katrina in 2005. Gotham 2007 also notes the commodification of the Hurricane Katrina disaster, including the production of souvenirs and tours of flooded neighborhoods.
78. See Scheyuens 2001.
79. Lancaster 2007.
80. Toxic tours, as experienced in the Ecuadorian Amazon, include visits to oil ponds, oil-sprayed roads, abandoned oil equipment, affected communities, and clinics that assist people with oil-related symptoms. I was able to attend such a tour organized by Acción Ecológica in October 2003.
81. See Widener 2009b: 268 on "oil tourism" following the construction of OCP.
82. Stronza 2001: 261.
83. See Agarwal 2005: 366 who suggests that the coastal resort owners and resort towns in the United Kingdom, which experienced a decline in tourism due in part to the rise of new destinations that were easily accessible and easily affordable, were not "passive victims of exogenous forces," nor was future decline predetermined.
84. Honey 1999: 9.
85. Some of the oil museums in the United States are California Oil Museum, Kansas Oil Museum, East Texas Oil Museum, Central Texas Oil Museum, and the West Kern Oil Museum.
86. Gould 1999: 248; see Tidwell 1996 as well.
87. In October 2004, Acción por la Vida estimated almost 2,500 residents in an unpublished report "Context of Mindo and Project Rescue Center—Management of the Protected Forest Mindo-Nambillo" (Acción 2004). For a historical look at Mindo's population growth, see Perreault 1996.
88. The 75 percent estimate was presented by Acción por la Vida in a funding proposal, "Proposal for Land Acquisition of 2,150 Acres of Ecuador's Threatened Mindo Cloudforest" (2002a). The 80 percent estimate was presented by Acción por la Vida in a project proposal (Acción 2004). The estimates may be high. Though these accounts claim that these percentages of the population live directly off of tourism, it is more likely that tourism supplements other economic efforts, or that tourism provides a cash income to complement subsistence and informal trade activities.
89. This comment is from personal observations of Mindo in 2001, before witnessing a change in tourism in 2002 and 2003. I returned again in 2007.
90. See Freudenberg 1984.
91. Gottlieb (1993) and Szasz (1994) identify that NIMBY campaigns can evolve into more sophisticated and inclusive collective action.
92. Von Hagen (1940: 280–81) describes how in 1927 fifty Austrians settled in Mindo at the invitation of the government. They never received assistance as expected. Von Hagen writes that many died and others left Mindo.
93. Hans Thiel, subsecretary of natural resources in the Environment Ministry, claimed that OCP would cross 9.5 hectares of the Mindo-Nambillo Protected Forest, while the country loses approximately 150,000 hectares per year (*El Comercio*, "OCP: una afectación leve," 15 February 2002).
94. Undated and unsigned fact sheet, "Mindo–Nambillo–Tandayapa–Bellavista: Recurso Natural de Todos los Ecuatorianos," identifying the environmental value of the region. I attribute the document to early campaigns in 2001.
95. Brian Unwin, "Oil Pipe Extension Threatens Ecuadorian Birds," *Independent* (London), 29 January 2001: 11.

96. See Snater 2002: 5.

97. See Snater 2002: 5. Fueling the uncertainties, the then environment minister, Rodolfo Rendón, said that the ministry favored the southern route; see *El Comercio*, "La ruta norte del OCP no se despeja," 27 May 2001: C2. Rendón was replaced in May 2001 by Lourdes Luque.

98. Entrix map for OCP on an analysis of the two routes in the IBA of Mindo, Project 131104, Figure 3.2–2a. It was dated "04/05," perhaps indicative of 04 May 2001.

99. Interviewed 16 July 2001, Quito.

100. Fundación Natura et al. 2001. This community of NGOs received the official EIA on 30 April 2001 and had less than fifteen days to review it.

101. Fundación Natura et al. 2001: 5, translated into English from the original Spanish.

102. As reported in the *Financial Times*, EFE News Service (U.S.), "Ecuador-Oil Ecuador Faults OCP Environmental Impact Statement," 22 May 2001.

103. Full-page ad in *El Comercio*, 7 June 2001: A6. The Spanish version of my translation read: "Estamos en la ruta correcta. La ruta norte es la mejor por ser la de menor impacto." The ad further stated that the communities of La Ecuatoriana, Héroes de Paquisha, San Juan de Chillogallo, Sangolquí, Amaguana, Píntag, and Uyumbicho would be affected by the southern route. The ad also claimed that the northern route guaranteed the most stability and security to the pipeline. Though not an exhaustive list, other advertisement placements included *El Comercio*, 10 June 2001: A7; *El Comercio*, 13 June 2001: A6; and *Hoy*, 17 June 2001: 7A.

104. Full-page ad in *El Comercio*, 7 June 2001: A6. The Spanish version of my translation read: "La ruta Norte no afecta a poblaciones."

105. Entrix map for OCP, Project 131104, Figure 3.2–2a.

106. In one interview (3 July 2001, Mindo), an activist believed their campaign efforts were being silenced in the media: "Several journalists told us there existed a censorship [in 2001]. So the owners of the biggest newspapers in the country said to their own people, 'You are prohibited to publish anything against OCP until the treaty is signed.' So there wasn't any chance for us to publish our concerns."

107. Many Ecuadorian families have benefited from the country's oil economy.

108. Interviewed 2 August 2001, Quito.

109. See Garcia-Johnson 2000.

110. OCP paid approximately US$0.79 per square meter in Nono, one of the closest affected communities to Mindo, though compensation varied between US$0.25–1.80 per square meter (Weemaels 2002: 21).

111. Interviewed 13–14 September 2003, Mindo.

112. Though Snater (2002: 5) writes that the Mindo Working Group began in 1999, it was more firmly established in 2001.

113. Acción por la Vida became an officially recognized NGO in 2003.

114. Interviewed 13–14 September 2003, Mindo.

115. Acción por la Vida 2004: 2–3.

116. Acción por la Vida 2002a. OCP denied activists access to inspect the construction site (Snater 2002).

117. As of 2007, a few core members of Acción por la Vida continued working through the legal system of Ecuador to have the pipeline removed from their land.

118. In 2002, Fundación Puntos Verdes organized Mindo students to board buses filled with weekend travelers from Quito to hand out flyers on the difference between organic and inorganic trash and how to dispose of both while visiting Mindo. Puntos Verdes also placed organic and inorganic trash bins throughout the town as well, as part of their ongoing education and environmental campaigns. In a humorous way to get locals to participate, the trash bins were labeled "for tourist use."

119. Perreault 1996: 172. Perreault dates the formation of Amigos as 1984.

120. Perreault (1996: 171) identifies World Wildlife Fund and Quito-based Tierra Viva as the NGOs primary financiers when the group formed.

121. As described to me in an interview in Mindo, 10 November 2003.

122. Perreault 1996: 172.

123. See http://www.mindocloudforest.org.

124. Freudenburg and Gramling 1994.

125. The mayor of San Miguel de los Bancos, the municipality of Mindo, accepted the construction of OCP in October or November 2001 and was promised US$800,000 for a potable water project in the area. OCP also agreed to provide two hundred jobs for people from three municipalities in the region, including SM de los Bancos. See Weemaels 2002: 19–20.

126. Interviewed 2 August 2001, Quito.

127. I believe this interface is found in other oil-dependent economies. In Alaska, there's a generation of twenty- to thirty-year-olds raised by families that moved to Alaska to build the Trans-Alaskan Pipeline in the late 1970s. Though they may now study or work in other industries, such as the environment, tourism, or commerce, they were raised in an oil-supportive and oil-aware environment. In addition, Alaska residents receive an annual Permanent Dividend Fund payment from oil revenues that in 2005 totaled US$845.76 per resident. Other types of interface in oil economies include academics who receive research funds from the oil industry to study oil impact and universities operating with oil endowments.

128. See Weemaels 2002: 19–20.

129. Direct communication with stakeholders in December 2003. See as well http://www .sanilodge.com and http://www.oxy.com.

130. I visited Sani Lodge in 2009, after Occidental had left the country. The lodge was community owned and self-sustaining with profits going back into the community, especially for the health and education of its youth.

131. Several national and international organizations described ideological conflicts and personal tensions with Acción Ecológica members, a finding that has also been supported by McAteer and Pulver's 2009 research.

132. Interviewed 2 August 2002, Quito.

133. Acción Ecológica 2001b.

134. Interviewed 2 August 2002, Quito.

135. For example, in a press release prepared by Acción Ecológica, only Acción Ecológica was referenced and quoted; see *Financial Times Information*, EFE News Service, "Ecuador-Protest/Environmentalists Set Up Camp in Ecuador Jungle to Stop Pipeline," 7 January 2002.

136. See *Hoy*, "Legal Actions Persist against OCP," 18 June 2001: A5; *El Comercio*, "OCP and the Northern Route Questioned Again," 15 June 2001: A7.

137. See Snater 2002: 5.

138. See *El Comercio*, "La parroquia de Nono cambió con la llegada del oleoducto," 5 August 2003: B8. Berry (1975) demonstrates similar impacts during the construction of the Trans-Alaska Pipeline.

139. On confronting environmentalists, see Perreault 1996. On employment need, an employment scam in 2002 demonstrated the community's susceptibility. A research participant in Mindo reported that a man came to the town claiming to be an OCP representative offering work for US$15 per day. Those individuals interested had to travel to Quito for training and would stay at a five-star hotel. They were told they had to pay US$10 each to cover initial costs. They paid, but a bus never arrived to take them for training and jobs never materialized.

140. Interviewed 7 August 2002, Quito.

141. At another collective effort, each member of one organization agreed to gather signatures against the pipeline, according to an activist interviewed. The majority gathered few or no names. Interviewed 27 June 2002, Mindo.

142. The direct translation of the Spanish word *jovenes* is youth. But people designated young, or *jovenes*, in Ecuador, range in age from fifteen to their early thirtiess. They may have limited responsibility and are likely to live at home. Work per se may be at the direction of their family, or as required on their family's property.

143. For one example, a Mindo youth had been selected to tour the oil fields of the Amazon and the pipeline's route with an international caravan as the Mindo representative. However, on the way to meet the caravan, the youth abandoned the trip to vacation elsewhere with a friend. Interview 16 July 2002, Quito.

144. The weekend before the event, South American jugglers, musicians, and artists with Caravana Arcoiris por la Paz (Rainbow Caravan for Peace) were practicing their trade and designing tie-dyed T-shirts for sale under a white canvas tent. It sounded like a "dance-eco-info" party, leading to eventual exhaustion before the informational component of the event.

145. Interview 27 June 2002, Mindo.

146. Interview 27 June 2002, Mindo.

147. Quiroga (2003: 168) writes how common stories of devil possession are re-created in the popular media in Ecuador, including an article in the magazine *Vistazo*, dated 5 July 2001, that "discusses how rock concerts are related to beliefs in the devil, and thereby pose a threat to young people."

148. I was in Mindo the weekend before the failed "rave" and attempted (and failed) to enter Mindo on the weekend of the failed rave. The account that the school spoke with parents regarding the weekend's event was told to me after the canceled events.

149. See Acción por la Vida 2002a and Snater 2002: 5, respectively.

150. In March 2002, the Environment Ministry suspended OCP's construction license until damage done in Guarumos was repaired, citing natural habitat destruction in breach of the oil consortium's license (Reuters Wire Service, "Ecuador Environment Ministry Suspends OCP License," 6 March 2002; Nicholas Moss, "Enel Fills a Gap to Help Expand Brazilian Power," *Financial Times*, 6 March 2002: 14). The then environment minister, Lourdes Luque, was replaced in January 2003 by Edgar Isch, who after only two weeks in office also suspended construction temporarily for environmental concerns (see Latin Petroleum Analytics, Energy eMonthly, January 2003). Minister Isch served for six months from January to July 2003 before being replaced.

151. Interviewed 24 June 2002, Mindo.

152. Stone & Webster 2002: 2, of "Overall Assessment."

153. Interviewed 3 December 2003, Quito.

154. Interviewed 24 June 2002, Mindo.

155. This pamphlet or press release from Mindo was undated, but demanded the release of the arrested activists. I approximate the date to be March or April 2002.

156. Acción por la Vida 2002a.

157. Interviewed 3 July 2001, Mindo.

158. Interviewed 3 July 2001, Mindo.

159. Mindo is in the municipality of San Miguel de los Bancos, whose mayor signed agreements with OCP in October or November 2001.

160. OCP 2005a, 2005b.

161. As described to me by a Mindo activist in Mindo, 11 August 2002.

162. Vivanco 2001.

163. Snater 2002: 15.

164. Interviewed 23 November 2003, Mindo.

165. Interviewed 2 August 2001, Quito.

166. Interviewed 7 August 2002, Quito.

167. Interviewed 1 August 2002, Quito.

168. Their international connectedness does not imply constant success. Acción por la Vida also contacted *National Geographic,* Greenpeace Canada, the World Bank, the Inter-American Development Bank (IADB), and received no response.

169. Interviewed 13–14 September 2003, Mindo.

170. January through April are slow construction months in the Andes Mountains due to heavy rains.

171. Dates gathered from interviews and press releases in 2002 and 2003 with Acción por la Vida.

172. Acción por la Vida, Base Camp Report #3, 4 March 2002.

173. Interviewed 24 June 2002, Mindo.

174. One source for this information was Acción por la Vida, Base Camp Report #4, 16 March 2002.

175. See Greenpeace Germany: http://www.greenpeace.org/international/news/global-action-for-ancient-fore, retrieved 22 April 2009.

176. Acción por la Vida 2002b. As used in this document, "microvariant" meant moving the pipeline to the valley floor or one side of the mountain rather than the ridgeline. In other uses, microvariant means much smaller changes.

177. Construction had stopped during the rainy season.

178. *Financial Times Information*, Global News Wire, "Ecuador to Deport 14 Activists Protesting Pipeline," 28 March 2002; *New York Times*, Reuters Wire Service, "Ecuador Releases 5 Jailed a Week Ago," 2 April 2002: A6; *Irish Times*, "Activists Freed from Prison in Ecuador," 3 April 2002: 3; *St Petersburg Times*, byline Reese Erlich, "Pipeline Unearths Ecuadorian Fury," 26 April 2002: 2A.

179. Interviewed 10 July 2002, Quito.

180. *Financial Times Information*, Global News Wire, EFE News Service (U.S.), "Ecuador-Pipelines: Ecuadorian President Mocks Greenpeace Ecologists over Pipeline," 25 February 2002.

181. Hill 2001.

182. Julia Hill had become an international supporter of grassroots environmental struggles since her activities in California in the 1990s.

183. At this time, Julia Hill also traveled on an anti-oil fact-finding mission along the pipeline, including in the Amazon, with Quito-based Acción Ecológica and California-based Amazon Watch.

184. Tricia Sheehy Skeffington, a freelance journalist covering Hill's Mindo hike and Quito protest, contributed to an article for the *San Francisco Chronicle*, "Julia Butterfly in Ecuador Jail after Oil Protest: Pipeline Would Cut through Reserve," 18 July 2002: A12, written by Glen Martin.

185. National media coverage included *El Universo*, "Cerrado el paso del OCP," 16 July 2002: 4A; *El Universo*, "Peritos resolverán disputa entre ecologistas y OCP," 17 July 2002: 4A; *El Comercio*, "Una famosa ecologista estuvo en Guarumos," 17 July 2002: C1.

186. Mindo's activists expressed to me that they had informed the Nono town police of the planned hike and that they had paid the police to support them (or at least not to block them) on this day.

187. Interviewed 22 October 2003, Lago Agrio.

188. Acción por la Vida's report on Julia Butterfly Hill's visit, dated 23 July 2002.

189. Description of the hike and protest in Quito comes from my own observations, as well as press reports and Acción por la Vida's report on Julia Butterfly Hill's visit, dated 23 July 2002.

190. On 19 June 2002, Italian activists with local counterparts demonstrated in front of the Quito office of Italian oil company Agip, or ENI-Agip, an OCP consortium member. ENI stands for Ente Nazionale Idrocarburi. The activists called for the exit of Agip from the OCP consortium (*El Comercio*, "22 activistas italianos protestan contra el OCP," 20 June 2002: A6). Other campaigns included an Italian fashion advertisement with Mindo as its backdrop.

191. An Occidental spokesperson said Julia Hill had not acted in good faith when she arrived to a scheduled appointment with fifty activists, as reported by Glen Martin in the *San Francisco Chronicle*, "Julia Butterfly Hill Deported by Ecuador after Oil Confrontation," 19 July 2002: A14. In contrast, activists in Mindo and Quito told me on several occasions that at scheduled appointments with national government officials or embassy representatives, OCP personnel would attend at the invitation of the government or embassy, even though they were not expected by the activists (interview 2 August 2002, Quito).

192. See *El Universo*, "Ocho ecologistas presos piden habeas corpus," 18 July 2002: 10A; and *El Comercio*, "Butterfly fue expulsada," 19 July 2002: B7.

193. Barragán and Ramos 2002.

194. Glen Martin, "Julia Butterfly in Ecuador Jail after Oil Protest; Pipeline Would Cut Through Reserve," *San Francisco Chronicle*, 18 July 2002: A12.

195. Acción por la Vida Update, 23 July 2002, Mindo, unpublished report.

196. Interviews, and an undated release by Acción por la Vida, "Por el bienestar de Mindo." I estimate the date as 2002.

197. Interviewed 11 August 2002, Mindo.

198. Interviewed 11 August 2002, Mindo.

199. See Faber 1998c.

200. Undated and unsigned fact sheet, "Mindo–Nambillo–Tandayapa–Bellavista: Recurso Natural de Todos los Ecuatorianos," identifying the environmental value of the region.

201. Acción por la Vida 2002c.

202. Acción por la Vida, "For the Well-being of Mindo."

203. Keck and Sikkink 1998.

204. Acción por la Vida 2002a.

205. Interviewed 17 July 2002, Quito. As reported in the press, then-president Noboa actually said, "Nobody is going to screw with the country. The OCP is going [to happen] because it's going [to happen]." See Acción Ecológica 2001d.

206. On the international attention that determined the Mindo-Nambillo region to be a critical natural habitat, see also the reports of Stone & Webster 2002; Goodland 2002; and Caffrey 2001, 2002.

207. See Heaps 2003.

208. Interviewed 10 November 2003, Mindo.

209. See Drost 2003.

210. See Nathalie Weemaels, for Acción Ecológica, "Informe de Monitoreo: Erupción del Reventador Afecta al OCP" (Monitoring Report: The Eruption of Reventador Affects OCP), 20 November 2002; and "Informe de Monitoreo: Case el Reventador" (Monitoring Report: The Case of Reventador), 14 February 2003.

211. Interviewed 3 December 2003, Quito.

212. Interviewed 3 December 2003, Quito.

213. Canadian advocates, including a Canadian film crew, produced a documentary to highlight the poverty and contamination of communities affected by the oil operations of EnCana, a Canadian oil company. The documentary was entitled *Risky Business: EnCana and the OCP in Ecuador* (2003). Director Nadja Drost released a second documentary, *Between Midnight and the Rooster's Crow*, in 2005.

214. Interviewed 3 July 2001, Mindo.

215. Interviewed 13–14 September 2003, Mindo.

216. Interviewed 17 July 2002, Quito.

217. Interviewed 13–14 September 2003, Mindo.

218. Interviewed 13–14 September 2003, Mindo.

219. Acción por la Vida 2004.

220. Interviewed 24 June 2002, Mindo.

221. Letter dated 17 February 2002 and addressed to Wolfgang Clement, President of the State of Westphalia; James Wolfensohn, President of the World Bank; Enrique V. Iglesias, President of the Inter-American Development Bank; Ian Davison of BirdLife International; Michael Wilde and Hans Alberta of WestLB; and Luigi Abete and Davide Croff of Banca Nazionale del Lavoro.

222. Interviewed 22 May 2007, Quito.

223. Interviewed 22 May 2007, Quito.

224. See Bob 2005.

225. See Bob 2005.

226. Acción Ecológica and some of the Quito-based conservation NGOs had campaigns to stop oil exploration and extraction and the construction of roads into Yasuní National Park.

227. Acción por la Vida 2002a.

228. Interviewed 2 August 2002, Quito.

229. Interviewed 24 June 2002, Mindo.

230. Interviewed 24 June 2002, Mindo. Two different activists were interviewed on 24 June 2002. The previous quote is by one; this one is by the other.

231. Interviewed 17 July 2002, Quito.

232. See Widener 2009b on oil tourism.

233. "An online search of a leading national newspaper, *El Comercio* (http://www.elcomercio.com.ec), using the search terms "Mindo" and "OCP" yielded 81 articles from September 2001

to December 2005 (5 in 2001, 58 in 2002, 14 in 2003, 2 in 2004, and 2 in 2005). *El Comercio*'s search engine dated from September 2001. Headlines included: "La OCP Suspendió Los Trabajos En Guarumos" (OCP suspended work in Guarumos), January 8, 2002; and "Los Ecologistas Impiden Que El Oleoducto Avance en Mindo" (Ecologists impede the advancement of OCP in Mindo), January 31, 2002," footnoted in Widener 2009a.

234. This research fails to investigate the explanation for the availability of funds, but it suggests that each sector had an existing pool of funds or the ability to quickly raise funds for high-profile cases that would otherwise be ignored in the absence of an environmental disaster.

235. Other occasions dovetailed with the oil-funded and community-led initiatives to stimulate tourism. In 2002, the road from the main highway descending into the valley of Mindo was repaved with public money, facilitating access, while Ecuador's first bird field guide was produced (see Ridgely and Greenfield 2001). A Spanish language version was published in 2007 by Fundación Jocotoco, Quito, Ecuador.

236. USAID 2006 also indicates that international entities commonly support nature-based tourism.

237. It is believed that in Ecuador, the Mindo Cloudforest Foundation first began using and making popular the use of "aviturismo" or bird tourism.

238. Acción por la Vida 2002b.

239. As told to me in interviews in 2003, active members of Acción por la Vida were debating how to "use" the land. Some wanted to conserve it with no human intervention. Others wanted to construct a wildlife rehabilitation center, and still others wanted to develop trails and campsites or lodges. As of June 2007 the land had yet to be altered pending a lawsuit against OCP.

240. Interviewed 3 July 2001, Mindo.

241. See OCP 2005a, 2005b. This list of services is not provided to suggest that oil concessions compensate for the lack of a contingency plan or mitigate impacts on the environment, community, or tourism industry.

242. Interviewed 2 August 2002, Quito.

243. See an interview with Hans Thiel, a subsecretary in the environment ministry, in *El Comercio*, "OCP: una afectación leve," 15 February 2002.

244. Thiel, "OCP: una afectación leve."

245. This assessment is not to deny that Ecuadorians may be traveling more in general and may have greater disposable income. This analysis offers oil tourism as an additional explanation for the growth in the number of visitors to nature-based destinations that have been struck by an environmental disaster.

246. Provided by an undated leaflet by Acción por la Vida, "Unete a la Lucha: No a la Ruta Norte," or Unite to Fight: No to the Northern Route, that I estimate was printed in 2001 at the start of the campaign.

247. Interviewed 2 August 2002, Quito.

248. Interviewed 10 November 2003, Mindo.

249. In addition to reporting on Mindo's anti-OCP activism, the media also reported on Mindo's unique birdlife without referencing OCP. See *El Comercio*, "Mindo tiene más diversidad de aves," 28 June 2001: C9; and in 2003, *El Comercio* dedicated a full page in its Daily Living section to family vacations in Mindo and along the road to Puero Quito: see *El Comercio*, "El noroccidente ofrece descanso para la familia," 22 August 2003: D8.

250. Interviewed 22 May 2007, Quito.

251. Interviewed 1 June 2007, Quito.

252. See Widener 2009b.

253. Interviewed 22 May 2007, Quito.

254. Interviewed 22 May 2007, Quito.

255. Interviewed 23 May 2007, Quito.

256. Interviewed 23 May 2007, Quito.

257. Flores 2006: 39.

258. See Perreault 1996: 172.

259. Acción por la Vida 2002a.
260. Importantly, oil tourism provided viable, weekend employment for Mindo's adults as well as the community's younger residents, which may discourage outbound, economic migration.
261. "Mindo–Nambillo–Tandayapa–Bellavista: Recurso Natural de Todos los Ecuatorianos."
262. Acción por la Vida 2004: 3.
263. Hofrichter 1993: 90.
264. Interviewed 22 May 2007, Quito.
265. Interviewed 22 May 2007, Quito.
266. See *El Comercio*, "El control ambiental tiene más actors," 4 June 2007 (Ultima Hora): 16.
267. Unpublished one-page memo, titled "Carta de Mindo," dated 3 June 2007.
268. Interviewed 1 June 2007, Mindo.
269. Stronza 2001.
270. Perreault 1996: 172, 174.
271. Perreault 1996: 172.
272. Snater 2002: 13.
273. Vivanco 2001.
274. Interviewed 24 May 2007, Mindo.
275. Interviewed 2 August 2002, Quito.
276. Interviewed 13–14 September 2003, Mindo.
277. Kroll-Smith and Couch 1990: 158. On corrosive community, see also Freudenberg (1997: 27).
278. See Fine and Harrington 2004.
279. See Widener 2009b.
280. Interviewed 3 July 2001, Mindo.
281. Interviewed 24 May 2007, Mindo.
282. Interviewed 22 May 2007, Quito.
283. Interviewed 22 May 2007, Quito.
284. Interviewed 24 May 2007, Mindo.

CHAPTER 5
ESMERALDAS:
FINDING DIGNITY

1. In the Esmeraldas region during the colonial period, free or escaped Africans were living in independent communities. Many of the people of Esmeraldas are descendants of freed slaves, runaway slaves, or slave ship survivors of a 1650 wreck, at which time the slaves escaped the ship and regained their freedom (Belkin et al. 1993; Breslin 2007; Von Hagen 1940: 282; Whitten 1986: 197). Von Hagen (1940: 284) writes of his arrival to Esmeraldas in 1936: "If we had not known this was Ecuador we might have taken it for some little village on Africa's Gold Coast." Ecuadorians of African descent have been referred as Afro-Hispanics (Whitten 1986), black frontiersmen (Whitten 1986), Afro-Ecuadorians (Quiroga 2003; Whitten 2003a), and more recently Ecuadorians of African descent (Johnson 2007). Whitten (2003b: 58) describes the people of Esmeraldas as self-identifying as "negro/a" (black), "moreno/a" (dark), or "afroecuatoriano/a" (Afro-Ecuadorian).
2. On structural suffering and structural violence, see Farmer 2003.
3. See Newell 2005: 71 on the importance of understanding "important aspects of global structures in global environmental politics through their localized effects which render them visible."
4. "Ecuadorians and Colombians are, at the same time, tolerant of racial *variety* to a far greater degree than North Americans, provided that West African racial features are not directly associated with observable non-national cultural patterns" (Whitten 1986: 195, italics in the original). However, "blackness is cognitively relegated to the bottom of the economic and social hierarchy" (Whitten 1986: 199).
5. Newell 2005: 74; see Pellow 2007 as well.

6. On environmental racism and the ties between historical and current racism, see Bullard 1993, 1994; Cole and Foster 2001; Lerner 2005; Newell 2005; Pellow 2007; Pulido 1996; and Westra and Lawson 2001.

7. See Allen 2003 and Lerner 2005 on land distribution and settlement in Louisiana among African Americans after the abolishment of slavery.

8. See Schnaiberg 1980; Gould, Schnaiberg and Weinberg 1996; and Gould, Pellow and Schnaiberg 2008 for the treadmill of production and Faber 2008 for the polluter-industrial complex.

9. Inter-American Development Bank (IADB), *IDB Country Strategy with Ecuador (2008–2011)*, undated report, http://idbdocs.iadb.org/wsdocs/getdocument.aspx?docnum=1726069, downloaded 27 September 2009.

10. IADB, *IDB Country Strategy with Ecuador (2008–2011)*.

11. Torres 2005, citing others. The national average overestimates the illiteracy rate of mestizos as the Indigenous population, which has the highest illiteracy rate in the country, is included in the national average. There is no category for mestizo or white, the two most educated populations in the country.

12. Even into the mid-1990s, smaller communities in the province remained physically isolated and underserved by the state with limited trash collection and paved roads; see Halpern and Twine 2000: 23.

13. At the time of OCP's construction, the second oil refinery, Shushufindi Refinery, was in the Amazon, near the point of production, and the other, La Libertad Refinery, was outside the commercial center of Guayaquil on the coast.

14. Interviewed 15 December 2003, Esmeraldas.

15. Informal meeting December 2003, Esmeraldas.

16. Interviewed 24 May 2007, Mindo.

17. Interviewed 15 December 2003, Esmeraldas.

18. Weemaels 2002: 22.

19. Seen on a beach billboard and T-shirt in Esmeraldas in 2003.

20. Estupinán 2007: 62.

21. Schodt 1987; Corkill and Cubitt 1998.

22. Johnson 2009; Halpern and Twine 2000.

23. Johnson 2007, 2009.

24. Johnson 2007.

25. Johnson 2007: 57.

26. Halpern and Twine 2000.

27. Whitten 1986: 176.

28. Whitten 1986: 92, 183.

29. Whitten 1986.

30. Whitten 1986: 187.

31. Whitten 1986: 191, italics in the original.

32. Whitten 2003a; Johnson 2007: 68; Revolutionary Democracy 1999; and Halpern and Twine 2000, which cite the assassination as in 1998.

33. Whitten 2003a: 17

34. Halpern and Twine 2000: 22. By the turn of the twenty-first century, Ecuadorians of African descent in Esmeraldas served as the superintendent of schools and held high positions at the port authority and the court; see Johnson 2009: 567.

35. United Nations 2010.

36. This is not to say that the region had not received international assistance. Monetary support for greater political participation and community enhancement had been provided after 1998 by the World Bank, the U.S. State Department, and USAID; see Minorities at Risk Project 2006.

37. Whitten 1986: 23.

38. Whitten 1986. In another point of unequal hardship, during the boom and bust cycles of Esmeraldas Province, women were deprived of income as men's labor in shrimp and timber destroy the land use of women, while on the other hand "women—associated with use-value and subsistence production—rescue men from the fluctuations of the international markets" (Quiroga 2003: 167).

39. Whitten 1986: 68.
40. Quiroga 2003: 172.
41. Whitten 1986: 74.
42. Breslin 2007.
43. Rudel 2000: 79.
44. Faber 2008: 11.
45. According to a CARE website account, CARE's SUBIR (Sustainable Uses for Biological Resources) ten-year project with $20 million in assistance from donors, including USAID, has achieved the titling of two hundred thousand acres for the Chachi communities and Afro-Ecuadorian households in or near the Cotacachi Caypas Ecological Reserve, which was established as a national protected area in 1979. See https://www.care.org/vft/ecuador/env_bkg.asp, as well as the journal entries. Though the entries are not dated, the photographs are dated 2001; downloaded 30 November 2010.
46. Interviewed 17 December 2003, Esmeraldas.
47. According to a CARE website account, staff members work twenty-two days in the reserve with eight days off. See https://www.care.org/vft/ecuador/env_bkg.asp, as well as the journal entries.
48. Belkin et al. 1993: 3.
49. See Rudel 2000.
50. To protect the area's biodiversity, IEFAN had thirty-two agreements with international aid agencies in 1996; see Rudel 2000: 80.
51. Rudel 2000: 82.
52. Estupinán 2007: 62. Mayor Ernesto Estupinán spoke at "The Urban [F]actor: Challenges Facing Sustainable Urban Development" conference in Brussels, Belgium, 18–19 December 2007. His speech "Esmeraldas: A New City for New Citizens" was transcribed from the recording of 19 December 2007.
53. Estupinán 2007: 62.
54. See Acción Ecológica, "En Esmeraldas El Paraiso," *Alerta Verde: Boletín de Acción Ecológica*, No. 137, September 2004.
55. See Rudel 2000: 79.
56. See Mitchell 2001.
57. United Nations 2002. As an example of his leadership, the U.N. report acknowledged the mayor's successful effort in facilitating community-led reconstruction of school buildings.
58. Estupinán 2007: 62.
59. Johnson 2009: 575.
60. Johnson 2007: 52; see 53–55 for photographs of these murals.
61. *El Comercio*, "Petróleo: A cambio piden respaldo financiero para obras de desarrollo: Los alcaldes apoyan el OCP," 15 June 2001: B2.
62. Estupinán 2007: 62.
63. Interviewed 15 December 2003, Esmeraldas.
64. This committee was assisted briefly by California-based Global Community Monitors, and in 2005 and 2006, I served infrequently as a translator of e-communications between Global Community Monitor and Jose Luis Guebara, a leader of Propicio Uno.
65. Viorst 2004. ASONE was established in 1988 as a nonprofit organization to address multiple issues of community improvement and political and economic advancement (see Whitten 2003b: 59).
66. "Proyectos PRODEPINE—Ecuador, Desarrollo de capacidades locales: Un ejemplo de participación en proyectos de inversion," from the regional office of Food and Agriculture Organization of the United Nations, http://www.fao.org/Regional/LAmerica/ong/proyecto/desarural/propedine.htm, downloaded 12 December 2005. On PRODEPINE, see Bebbington (1996b: 404, 414) as well.
67. See Goldman 2005 and Rich 1994 on the World Bank.
68. Meeting report, "II Meeting of Experts for the Formation of the International Centre on Cultural Diversity." Held in Esmeraldas, Ecuador, 1–5 August 2005.

69. Halpern and Twine 2000.

70. Whitten 2003b: 67.

71. Whitten 2003b: 62.

72. See Halpern and Twine (2000: 25), who also identify a learning transfer from the Indigenous groups to the Black movement.

73. Weemaels 2002: 23.

74. Interviewed 17 December 2003, Esmeraldas.

75. Interviewed 10 November 2003, Mindo.

76. Weemaels 2002: 23.

77. The Esmeraldas refinery would not refine oil transported through OCP, all of which would be exported.

78. Manuel Toro, "Incendio cambió barrio en Esmeraldas hace siete anos," *El Universo*, 26 February 2005; *Hoy*, "Multa de $7 millones contra PetroEcuador," 3 September 2004. See as well Acción Ecológica, "Alerta N. 70: Justicia Ambiental?" October 1999, www.accioneco logica.org.

79. See a nine-minute documentary by Josh Holst, *Esmeraldas: Petroleum and Poverty*, 2003.

80. See Acción Ecológica's green alert on the Esmeraldas Refinery: "Colapso Total en la Refineria," *Alerta Verde, Boletín de Acción Ecológica*, No. 87, March 2000.

81. Acción Ecológica, "Colapso Total en la Refineria," 4–5.

82. *El Comercio*, "Las denuncias ambientales persisten en Esmeraldas," 13 June 2002: C1; *El Comercio*, "Refinería: los barrios dieron otro plazo," 17 June 2002: C4; *El Comercio*, "Marcha escolar contra la Refinería," 6 June 2002: C3.

83. *El Comercio*, "Refinería: los barrios dieron otro plazo," 17 June 2002: C4.

84. Over time, ASONE's lawsuit was dropped and was seen as being "hijacked by the town of Esmeraldas which was awarded monetary damages." E-mail correspondence 26 December 2005. In this use, Esmeraldas connotes the community Propicia Uno.

85. *El Universo*, "Incendio cambió barrio en Esmeraldas hace siete anos," 26 February 2005.

86. *El Universo*, "Habitantes de La Propicia cierran vías hacia Refinería de Esmeraldas," 2 December 2004; *Hoy*, "El barrio más rico del mundo está en Esmeraldas," 6 November 2004.

87. *Hoy*, "El barrio más rico del mundo está en Esmeraldas," 6 November 2004.

88. *El Universo*, "Refinería de Esmeraldas tendrá bosque protector," 16 December 2004.

89. *El Universo*, "Refinería de Esmeraldas tendrá bosque protector," 16 December 2004.

90. Albán 2000.

91. *El Universo*, "Esmeraldas frenó envío de gas," 17 July 2002: 2A; *El Universo*, "Todos plegaron en Esmeraldas," 18 July 2002: 2A; *El Comercio*, "Tres grupos dividen a La Concordia," 22 July 2002: A2; *El Comercio*, "Esmeraldas con sus reservas casi llenas," 19 July 2002: B2; *El Comercio*, "El bloqueo de Esmeraldas genera pérdidas millonarias," 19 July 2002: B1; *El Comercio*, "Esmeraldas, asfixiada por el roldosismo y el Gobierno," 29 July 2002: D1.

92. *El Comercio*, "La Refinería trabaja a medio gas," 18 July 2002: B1; *El Comercio*, "El bloqueo de Esmeraldas genera pérdidas millonarias"; Nicholas Moss, "Ecuador Crippled by Mass Strikes," *Financial Times* (London), 19 July 2002: 3.

93. *El Comercio*, "La Refinería no procesa gas desde la trade de ayer," 22 July 2002: A2.

94. *Financial Times* (London), "Energy Minister Resigns," 24 February 1999: 3.

95. *El Universo*, "Esmeraldas frenó envío de gas," 17 July 2002: 2A.

96. A photograph in the newspaper *El Universo* depicted a demonstration led by the mayor, the city's beauty queen, the well-respected bishop of the province, a taxi union representative, a priest, and a former government official. "Todos plegaron en Esmeraldas," 18 July 2002: 2A.

97. *El Comercio*, "La Concordia es un importante emporio agrícola y comercial," 29 July 2002: D1.

98. Interviewed 15 December 2003, Esmeraldas.

99. Interviewed 15 December 2003, Esmeraldas.

100. Barthélémy 2003: 6–7, quoting Lenin Plaza Castillo, broadcaster for Radio Antenna Libre.

101. OCP 2005a, 2005b.

102. In demonstration of such humanitarian neglect, there was frequently no running water, and therefore no toilet facilities, at the public high school from 1999 to 2003; see Johnson 2009: 571.

103. OCP 2005a.

104. *El Universo*, "Hospital de Esmeraldas, sin unidad de quemados," 12 July 2004.

105. *El Comercio*, "Esmeraldas captará mayor volume" and "Energía: Los puertos de Esmeraldas y Manta están preparados para recibirlas. OCP: 250 000 toneladas en camino," 8 June 2001: B1.

106. OCP 2005a.

107. Interviewed 17 December 2003, Esmeraldas.

108. Advocacy Project, "Ecuador's Troubled History: On the Record—The Fight for the Amazon" 16(2), 28 February 2002, http://www.advocacynet.org. [This report is incorrectly dated on its website as 28 February 2001.]

109. Acción por la Vida, Base Camp Report #1, dated 15 February 2002. I acknowledge the problem of citing an activist organization in Mindo on actions in Esmeraldas, and it is also indicative of how much stronger my ties were to Quito, Mindo, and Lago Agrio, than Esmeraldas.

110. *El Comercio*, "OCP: Quinindé opta por los raptos," 28 June 2002: B2.

111. I have been unable to follow up on this event.

112. Whitten 1986: 74, italics in the original.

113. Federici and Rodolfi 2001: 163.

114. Federici and Rodolfi 2001: 166.

115. Federici and Rodolfi 2001: 168.

116. Stone & Webster Consultants 2002: 2 of the overall assessment section.

117. Interviewed 3 December 2003, Quito.

118. See Sundberg 2008 on the relevance of race in environmental injustices in Latin America. In particular, she identifies, compiling the works of others, the distinction between deliberate racist action and unconscious white privilege.

119. Interviewed 1 August 2002, Quito.

120. See "Kids and Conservationists Unite in Ecuador and Georgia to Benefit Cultures, Farmers, Forests and Birds," produced by Fundación Maquipucuna, September 2007, http://.www .rainforest-alliance.org/neotropics/eco-exchange/2007/september_07_01.html, downloaded 16 September 2009.

121. Interviewed 1 August 2002, Quito.

122. Interviewed 8 December 2003, Quito.

123. Interviewed 13–14 September 2003, Mindo.

124. Interviewed 28 June 2001, Quito.

125. Interviewed 17 December 2003, Esmeraldas.

126. There were limited coordinated efforts along the route, primarily through Acción Ecológica. For example, a small group from Esmeraldas traveled to Quito to protest in front of Occidental and alongside the Mindo community, supported by Julia Hill and Amazon Watch, though the engagement was not sustained.

127. Interviewed 1 August 2002, Quito.

128. Halpern and Twine 2000: 29.

129. Halpern and Twine 2000: 29.

130. I was unable to find any alliances with the International Labor Organization (ILO) on the issue of OCP.

131. See Lewis 2000.

132. Halpern and Twine 2000: 20.

133. Initially, I failed to confront racial and class biases in my contact selection as well. Even though I selected Esmeraldas as a case in 2001 due to its importance in shipping and refining, I failed to travel there until 2003 due to the degree, ease, and facility of contact that I established in Quito and Mindo primarily and in Lago Agrio secondarily. I also sought national contacts to point

me to the international contacts with which they were working, and vice versa. For the most part, very few identified contact or ties with communities or organizations in Esmeraldas.

134. An online search of the International Labor Organization failed to locate any incidents or cases with regards to the OCP pipeline project or the Esmeraldas refinery. In addition, when Greenpeace International, led by German activists, met with residents of Esmeraldas, locals expressed concerns for their "fishing reserves" near the Bilbao terminal. See Advocacy Project, "Ecuador's Troubled History: On the Record—The Fight for the Amazon."

135. For an auxiliary look at how Esmeraldas was situated internationally I searched major newspapers in the United States and found six articles that addressed Esmeraldas and the OCP pipeline project. Three primarily addressed Mindo, including two on Julia Hill's deportation. A fourth report addressed the country's debt, and also included Hill's deportation. The fifth addressed Lago Agrio. And the final report addressed the irregular presence of Colombian guerrillas on Ecuador's northern border. In each, Esmeraldas was mentioned solely as the site of the export terminal on the coast. The absence of Esmeraldas in U.S. media revealed the selection process and importance of international advocacy groups in constructing a Northern view on global environmental conflicts. I used LexisNexis™ Academic, and searched under the terms "Esmeraldas," "pipeline," and "Ecuador" for the period 2000–2005.

136. Johnson 2009: 580.

137. Rahier 1999: 107.

CHAPTER 6
TRANSNATIONAL RESPONSES:
EVIDENCE FOR A SOUTHERN-LED
GLOBAL DEMOCRACY

1. McCarthy and Zald 1977.

2. McAdam 1988, 1998; Tarrow 1994.

3. Mayo 2005: 91 on "false dichotomies," p. 74 on old-new distinctions.

4. Della Porta and Diani 1999: 17.

5. Della Porta and Diani 1999; Brown et al. 2004; McAdam, McCarthy, and Zald 1996.

6. See O'Rourke and Connolly 2003; Picou et al. 1997; as well as chapter 1.

7. See Agbola and Alabi 2003; Bullard, Johnson, and Torres 2005; Faber 2008; Faber and McCarthy 2003; Gedicks 1993, 2001; Gerlach 2003; Iles 2004; Kane 1995; Kimerling 1991; McDonald 2005; Okonta and Douglas 2001; Sawyer 2004; Tidwell 1996; Widener 2007a; Yashar 2005.

8. See Avritzer 2002.

9. On environmental flows, see Spaargaren, Mol, and Bruyninckx 2006; Spaargaren, Mol, and Buttel 2006; and Mol and Van den Burg 2004.

10. See Fischer's 2000 account on the "politics of local knowledge" as noted in the title and "specialized citizens" (xiii), or the expert knowledge of local people.

11. Faber 2008.

12. Seidman 2005.

13. Avritzer 2002: 9.

14. Interviewed 11 June 2004, Quito.

15. See Faber 1998b, 1998c on "ecological democracy."

16. Voting on oil projects may, however, favor oil projects. In South Dakota, residents of Union County voted in 2008 on whether to rezone land for industrial use for a Canadian tar sands oil refinery in particular, and the county voted 58 percent in favor of the refinery; see Widener 2010.

17. See Khagram 2004: 17 on environmental regimes; see Widener 2009a as well.

18. In addition, nine Italian environmental and development NGOs formed a national alliance called the Italian Campaign against the OCP and included Amici della Terra (Friends of the

Earth Italy), Attac Italy, Campagna per la Riforma della Banca Mondiale, Centrol Nuovo Modello di Sviluppo, Cric-Centro Regionale D'Intervento per la Cooperazione, Dea-Donne & Ambiente, Greenpeace, Legambiente, and Terra Nuova.

19. "Joint Letter to the World Bank from International Organizations regarding the OCP Pipeline in Ecuador." Addressed to Mr. James D. Wolfensohn, president of the World Bank Group, dated 3 December 2001. The signees came from ten countries: the United States (8), Australia (5), Germany (3), Ecuador (1), Brazil (1), Czech Republic (1), India (1), Italy (1), New Zealand (1), and Poland (1). Friends of the Earth Italy along with the Italian Campaign to Reform the World Bank would build an Italian coalition of nine NGOs.

20. See Joe Stephens, "Nature Conservancy Faces Potential Backlash from Ties with BP," *Washington Post*, 23 May 2010.

21. Bhagwati 2004: 28.

22. Barry and Smith (2005: 252) have also referred to the mainstream environmental NGO community as elite.

23. Luis Yanza, cofounder of Frente de Defensa, and Ecuadorian lawyer Pablo Fajardo Mendoza won the Goldman Environmental Prize in 2008 for their class-action lawsuit against Texaco. See http://www.goldmanprize.org.

24. Both CDES and Pachamama had local offices in Quito during OCP's construction.

25. See http://chevrontoxico.org/ for more on this lawsuit.

26. Interviewed 27 October 2003, Quito.

27. "Joint Letter from International Organizations regarding the OCP Heavy Crude Pipeline in Ecuador," dated 11 May 2001, and addressed to J. Morgan Chase, Citigroup, and Deutsche Bank AG.

28. The transnational coalition of opposition also failed to support or to establish ties with one of the more active antipipeline groups, FETRAPEC, the oil union, which rejected the nonunion, nonnational OCP consortium companies.

29. Schulter, Phillimore, and Moffatt 2004: 730, 722.

30. Gould, Pellow, and Schnaiberg 2008; Gould, Schnaiberg, and Weinberg 1996.

31. See Castells 1997 and Held et al. 1999 on globalization and global networks.

32. See Bandy and Smith 2005a and Smith, Chatfield, and Pagnucco 1997 on transnational protest; Keck and Sikkink 1998 on the appeal of transnational advocacy for affected communities and organizations in the Global South; Tarrow 2005a on global framing and the typology of transnational coalitions; Tarrow 2005b on the difficulties for transnational social movements; Bob 2005 on how local groups reach out or market themselves to international audiences; and Widener 2007a on the benefits and burdens of transnational advocacy for domestic groups and impacted communities in Ecuador.

33. See Tarrow 2005a: 167 on the typology of transnational coalitions.

34. Keck and Sikkink 1998.

35. Reimann 2002.

36. Smith 2005.

37. Treakle 1998.

38. See McAteer and Pulver 2009 for an analysis of two campaigns in Ecuador that targeted corporate shareholders.

39. With regards to OCP, the transnational campaign of opposition organized international actions in twenty-four different cities around the world. Interviewed 17 July 2002, Quito.

40. An example would be Frente's campaign "ChevronToxico" against Texaco. See http://chevrontoxico.org.

41. Tarrow 2005a: 170.

42. Tarrow 1999: 4.

43. Tarrow 1998: 233–34.

44. Interviewed 8 October 2003, Quito.

45. Interviewed 8 October 2003, Quito.

46. Interviewed 27 October 2003, Quito.

47. Interviewed 27 October 2003, Quito.

48. See Howard-Grenville 2006, who studied how two internal subcultures (the manufacturing technology development division and a division designed to address environmental impact) moved their ideas and solutions forward within a computer chip manufacturer.

49. Acción por la Vida Base Camp Report #3, 4 March 2002.

50. See Bandy and Smith 2005a, 2005b on conflicts within transnational networks.

51. Stewart 2004.

52. Mayo 2005.

53. Bandy and Smith 2005b.

54. Castells 1997: 68–69.

55. In an analysis of the impacts of outside funding on community association membership in Kenya, Gugerty and Kremer 2008 found that international funding altered the makeup of a local organization by increasing the participation and leadership of younger, more educated women, outside members, and men, which led to the departure of older women, who were the poorest and most disadvantaged community members.

56. Tarrow 2005b: 63.

57. Tarrow 2005b: 59.

58. See Rodrigues 2004 on the neglect of building domestic technical capacity.

59. Bandy and Smith 2005a; Bob 2005; Held et al. 1999; Rodrigues 2004; Smith, Chatfield, and Pagnucco 1997; Smith and Johnston 2002; Tarrow 2001, 2005a, 2005b.

60. Bob 2005.

61. Wood 2005.

62. Tarrow 1994 (chap. 9: 153) defines a cycle of protest as "a phase of heightened conflict and contention . . . that includes: a rapid diffusion of collective action . . . a quickened pace of innovation . . . new or transformed collective action frames."

63. Interviewed 11 June 2004, Quito.

64. Interviewed 8 October 2003, Quito.

65. See *CRUDE* (2009), *Between Midnight and the Rooster's Crow* (2005), *Risky Business: EnCana and the OCP in Ecuador* (2003), *Amazon Oil Pipeline—Pollution, Corruption and Poverty* (2002), and *Trinkets and Beads* (1996).

66. Drost 2003. Nadja Drost produced two documentaries, *Between Midnight and the Rooster's Crow* (2005) and *Risky Business: EnCana and the OCP in Ecuador* (2003), on the oil region's campaign against EnCana Corporation's operations primarily, and secondarily against the OCP pipeline, of which EnCana was the lead company. To produce both films, Drost worked for the Toronto Environmental Alliance initially and then GlobalAware Canada.

67. *Amazon Oil Pipeline—Pollution, Corruption and Poverty* (2002), documentary produced by Juan Pablo Barragán and Ivonne Ramos.

68. See Caniglia 2002; Reimann 2002.

69. See Goodland 2002. This report was presented in greater detail in chapter 3.

70. Caffrey 2001.

71. See van Gelder 2003.

72. Unpublished report, "Conclusiones de la Misión Internacional de Observación de la Propuesta de Construcción del Oleoduct de Crudos Pesados-OCP," dated July 2001 and prepared by economist Joan Martínex-Alier of Spain, environmental lawyer Alicia Chalabe of Argentina, and Costa Rican biologist Gabriel Rivas-Ducca.

73. Interviewed 8 October 2003, Quito.

74. It is unclear which party, whether OCP or EnCana, commissioned the outside consultant Fenna Snater's report "Stakeholder Perception Assessment: An Assessment of the Perception of Local Stakeholders on OCP's Impact in the Mindo-Cuenca Alta del Rio Guayllabamba Region." See Snater 2002. It focused exclusively on the most volatile region along the route, the Mindo-Nambillo area.

75. For "specialized citizens," see Fischer 2000: xiii. For lay knowledge and expertise, see Gottlieb 1993.

76. Interviewed 5 September 2003, Quito.

77. Recorded at a private meeting 17 March 2004, Montreal, Canada. Spoken in Spanish with English translation.

78. In one interview in 2004, one member of the network of opposition had indicated that they were optimistic that the International Monetary Fund's requirement for an economic and environmental study of Ecuador's oil sector would enable the NGO community to press the Ecuadorian government for greater contingency and remediation plans and studies on the Indigenous and environmental impacts through oil expansion in the Amazon to fill the OCP pipeline through this fund requirement. However, the Ecuadorian government failed to implement the required study. It is possible that the study was delayed by the government as the IMF was also assessing future liabilities for private companies whose expansion or participation in Ecuador's state fields was being promoted by the IMF. See the IMF's "Ecuador—Letter of Intent, Supplement to the Memorandum of Economic Policies, and Technical Memorandum of Understanding," Quito, Ecuador, 23 July 2003, http://www.imf.org/external/np/loi/2003/ecu/03/.

79. McAteer and Pulver 2009: 7.

80. Interviews with an environmental consultant in Quito, and a letter to the editor of *Canadian Business* magazine written by Gywn Morgan, president and CEO of EnCana, dated 14 April 2003: 7. Morgan was responding to an article by Matthew McClearn, entitled "Down the Tube," published 17 March 2003 in *Canadian Business*.

81. See Regenwald Report 3, 2003, C 3661, Nr. 3/03 "WestLB-Pipeline ohne Öl?" p. 3.

82. See http://www.equator-principles.com.

83. A financial journalist cites the controversies over the OCP and the Three Gorges Dam as two cases that led to NGOs targeting the banks, and the banks responding with the Equator Principles. See Jane Monahan, "Principles in Question," *The Banker*, 7 March 2005.

84. Rainforest Action Network press release, dated 3 June 2003.

85. For the Collevecchio Declaration, see http://www.banktrack.org or http://www.banktrack .org/download/collevecchio_declaration_2/0_030401_collevecchio_declaration.pdf, downloaded 3 December 2009. In 2006, the Collevecchio Declaration was followed up by the report "The Do's and Don'ts of Sustainable Banking: A BankTrack Manual."

86. Rainforest Action Network press release, dated 3 June 2003, "World's Biggest Banks React to NGO Pressure."

87. Interviewed by phone, 15 July 2004. This is a paraphrase, rather than a direct quote.

88. Interviewed 22 October 2003, Lago Agrio.

89. Interviewed 27 October 2003, Quito.

90. Interviewed 8 October 2003, Quito.

91. Seidman (2005: 175) argues that the absence of local context in the anti-apartheid Sullivan Principles was one of its major weaknesses.

92. See Seidman 2005: 176.

93. Interviewed 17 July 2002, Quito.

94. See Bob 2005 on marketing.

95. Interviewed by phone, 15 July 2004.

96. See Klawiter 1999 on "enunciated" and "enacted."

97. Faber 2008; Principles 1991; Schlosberg 2004.

98. See Faber 2005, 2008.

99. Seidman 2005.

100. Mandle 2000. See Gereffi, Garcia-Johnson, and Sasser 2001 as well on the successes, limitations, and vast differences between industry- or NGO-led certification, international guidelines, or code of conduct, for a range of mass-produced products.

101. Benford 2005.

102. Benford 2005; Faber 2008.

103. Interviewed 27 October 2003, Quito.

104. Interviewed 17 July 2002, Quito.

105. Interviewed 17 July 2002, Quito.

106. See Acción Ecológica press bulletin "Por el dia del medio ambiente piden moratoria en petroleo y mineria," dated 28 May 2003.

107. Demands for local purchasing were requests among oil communities to have or to encourage oil personnel to shop locally rather than continue the oil practice of housing and

feeding oil personnel on-site in oil compounds. See Ohler and Hall 2000 on local purchasing as well.

108. Direct citizen and/or worker receipt of oil revenue, rents, or royalties is feasible. In 1976, Alaskans, for example, established the Permanent Fund that collects approximately 25 percent of the state's oil revenues, and from it the Permanent Fund Dividend that pays each citizen of Alaska an annual dividend from the earnings on the fund's principal.

109. Interviewed 17 July 2002, Quito.

110. Interviewed 17 July 2002, Quito.

111. Interviewed 17 July 2002, Quito.

112. Faber 2008: 178.

113. For a short list, see Goldman 2005 and Rich 1994.

114. Goldman 2001.

115. Shiva 1998: 234; 2000.

116. Press release signed by nine Italian NGOs, dated 24 April 2003, Rome.

117. E-mail correspondence, dated 17 April 2003.

118. Interviewed by phone, 15 July 2004.

119. Interviewed by phone, 15 July 2004.

120. Interviewed 27 October 2003, Quito.

121. "Striking a Better Balance—The World Bank Group and Extractive Industries: The Final Report of the Extractive Industries Review." Prepared by the World Bank Group Management Response, 17 September 2004. The quote is on page 5 of the seven-page executive summary. See http://www.ifc.org/ifcext/eir.nsf/AttachmentsByTitle/FinalMgtResponseExecSum/$FILE/finaleir managementresponseexecsum.pdf, downloaded 19 November 2009.

122. Any use of oil-industrial core or oil-industrial complex is an attempt to make Daniel Faber's (2008) "polluter-industrial complex" more specific to the oil industry in developing nations.

123. See Buttel 2003 and O'Rourke 2004.

124. Ali 2008.

125. See Reuters, "Ecuador Cancels an Oil Deal with Occidental Petroleum," 17 May 2006, published in the *New York Times*.

126. See Tarrow 2001 on the importance of the state in setting national policy.

127. O'Faircheallaigh and Corbett 2005.

128. Seidman 2005: 180.

129. O'Rourke 2004.

130. Buttel 2003.

131. Janicke 2006.

132. Kaimowitz 1996.

133. Smith 2008: 231.

134. Smith 2008.

135. Global News Wire, EFE News Service (U.S.), "Ecuador-Pipelines: Ecuadorian President Mocks Greenpeace Ecologists over Pipeline," 25 February 2002.

136. Glen Martin, "Julia Butterfly in Ecuador Jail after Oil Protest; Pipeline Would Cut through Reserve," *San Francisco Chronicle*, 18 July 2002: A12.

137. See Shiva 2000.

138. Moreira 2001.

139. Moreira 2001. Articles 80 and 81 acknowledged the people's right to science, technology, and communication, including the right to improved productivity and the meeting of basic needs, as well as sustainable management of the country's natural resources (168). Article 86 was a collective "right to live in a healthy and ecologically balanced environment on the basis of sustainable development" (171). Included in this article was the state's obligation to conserve nature.

140. See Acción Ecológica 2001d: 8.

141. Albán 2000: 38.

142. Subramaniam et al. 2003.

143. Murphy 2005.

144. See Murphy 2005.

145. Interviewed by phone, 15 July 2004. This is a paraphrase, rather than a direct quote.
146. Interviewed 22 October 2003, Lago Agrio.
147. Interviewed 27 October 2003, Quito.
148. For an earlier assessment of Arthur Mol's "environmental flows" with regard to the OCP project in Ecuador, see Widener 2009a.
149. See Spaargaren, Mol, and Bruyninckx 2006; Spaargaren, Mol, and Buttel 2006; and Mol and Van den Burg 2004.
150. Building on Janicke 2006.
151. Building on Gille 2006.
152. For example, a Canadian activist with Toronto Environmental Alliance and GlobalAware Canada produced two documentaries at this time to support the community of Tarapoa in the Amazon, which is not along the pipeline's right-of-way, against Canada's EnCana Corporation, which has since left Ecuador.
153. Bob 2005.
154. Interviewed 17 July 2002, Quito.
155. Interviewed 17 July 2002, Quito.
156. Interviewed 22 October 2003, Lago Agrio.
157. Interviewed 22 October 2003, Lago Agrio.
158. Interviewed 22 October 2003, Lago Agrio.
159. Smith 2008: 5.
160. See Widener 2009b as well.
161. Silver 2003, 168.
162. Bob 2005.
163. Interviewed 8 October 2003, Quito.
164. See Castells 1997; Held et al. 1999; Keck and Sikkink 1998; Khagram 2004; Tarrow 2002. Brysk 2000 also suggests that international-Indigenous alliances may be fostered in guilt and exoticism.
165. Acción Ecológica 2003.
166. Acción Ecológica 2003.
167. Action alert by Acción Ecológica, dated 29 August 2002.
168. Action alert, dated 29 August 2002.
169. See Drost 2003.
170. Acción Ecológica (2003) provided a "green alert" bulletin on human rights violations during OCP construction that documented detention and arrests of landowners and demonstrators along the right-of-way.
171. NGO letter to Gwyn Morgan, CEO of EnCana, dated 30 September 2003.
172. NGO letter to Gwyn Morgan.
173. Quotes taken from an interview, 8 October 2003, Quito.
174. See Royce 2009.
175. Najam 2005: 123.
176. Smith and Bandy 2005.
177. Interviewed 17 July 2002, Quito.
178. Szasz 1994.
179. Brooks 2005: 136.
180. Seidman 2005: 171.
181. As someone who has tried to teach "poverty and society" in the United States, I know how difficult it is to revise this view.
182. Rudel 2009 writes on the strategic role of states and development coalitions in generating suburban sprawl and deforesting tropical environments.
183. To demonstrate how international advocates and media outlets invert impact, one international advocacy group exchanged the strikes in the oil provinces of the Amazon with the tree sitters in the Mindo cloud forest, nearly 150 miles from the Amazon. The report claimed "the government is committed to doubling the production of oil, even at the cost of destroying the Amazon. . . . This has infuriated environmentalists on both sides of the Atlantic. In Ecuador,

greens have prevented the pipeline from entering the Mindo Cloud Reserve, which is one of the most fabled bird sanctuaries in the world." In 2002, when this report ran, grassroots organizations in Mindo, presented in chapter 4, were involved in campaigning to relocate the pipeline away from their community, not to stop the construction of it. See the Advocacy Project, "Ecuador's Troubled History," *On the Record: Ecuador—The Fight for the Amazon* 16(2): 28 February 2001, http://www.advocacynet.org/resource/427.

184. Snow et al. 1986: 472.

185. Interviewed 22 October 2003, Lago Agrio.

186. Interviewed 27 October 2003, Quito.

187. Interviewed 27 October 2003, Quito.

188. Interviewed 11 June 2004, Quito.

189. Interviewed 17 July 2002, Quito.

190. Avritzer 2002: 7, 6.

191. Fischer 2000 has also identified how community consensus committees in Denmark are designed, much like the American jury system, to inform selected citizens on technological risks of a proposed project for their input and deliberation.

192. Faber 2008: 24.

193. Faber 1998b: 9.

194. Avritzer 2002.

195. Interviewed 17 July 2002, Quito.

196. Interviewed 22 May 2007, Quito.

197. Interviewed 9 September 2003, Quito.

198. Interviewed 16 September 2003, Quito.

199. O'Faircheallaigh and Corbett 2005: 637–40.

200. O'Faircheallaigh and Corbett 2005: 644.

201. O'Faircheallaigh and Corbett 2005.

202. Interviewed 11 June 2004, Quito.

203. Interviewed 11 June 2004, Quito.

204. In 2008, residents of Union County, South Dakota, voted on whether to rezone agricultural land for an oil refinery and 58 percent of them voted in favor of the refinery.

205. Smith 2008: 14–15.

206. "At a glacial pace" signifies a pre-350 ppm CO_2 emission rate; see Bill McKibben 2010 on climate change and his 350 movement.

207. Interviewed 31 October 2003, Lago Agrio.

208. See Widener 2009a as well.

209. O'Rourke and Connolly 2003.

CHAPTER 7
POST-OCP:
GOVERNING AND CONTESTING
CORREA AND CHINA IN THE AMAZON

1. *LatinFinance*, "Pipe Dreams: Ecuador Is Hoping New Foreign Investment Will Boost Capacity and Get Oil Revenues Flowing," September 2000, Latin American Financial Publications.

2. In the bid, India's Oil and Natural Gas Corporation was a contender, a duel that underscores the current consumption trends and new oil interests in the Amazon.

3. See the documentaries by Drost 2003, 2005. Drost as representative of GlobalAware Canada also organized a speaking tour across Canada: "Rude Oil: Canadian Involvement in the Amazon." Jon Arruti, a representative of the office of environmental rights and network of community leaders of Coca, Ecuador, also spoke at EnCana's 2004 shareholder's meeting as the representative of communities in Blocks 14 and 17. On the efforts of environmental and human rights activists to disrupt EnCana's annual shareholder's meeting in 2004, see the following news reports: James Stevenson,

"EnCana Corp. First Quarter Profits Drop 65% Due to Hedge Accounting Changes," *Canadian Press,* 28 April 2004; Claudia Cattaneo, "NGO Attacks Overshadow EnCana Meeting," *National Post,* 29 April 2004; and Paul Haavardsrud, "Ecuador Issue Plagues EnCana," *Calgary Herald,* 29 April 2004.

4. E. Douglass, "Ecuador Seizes Oxy Operations," *Los Angeles Times,* 17 May 2006: C1.

5. PetroAmazonas is said to have control over its budget like a private firm, so it has been able to maintain investments in its fields—though this has not been confirmed.

6. See Kozloff 2008: 33.

7. Associated Press, "Petroleum: Ecuador President Urges Crackdown on Foreign Oil Companies," *Miami Herald,* 9 June 2009: A6.

8. Associated Press, "Ecuador Takes Over City Oriente Wells," 1 August 2008; Reuters, "PetroEcuador to Seek End of Deal with City Oriente," 8 November 2007; and Stephan Kueffner, for Bloomberg, "PetroEcuador Asks to Revoke City Oriente Contract," 8 November 2007.

9. Reuters, "Ecuador Says Petrobras Could Be Out of ITT Oil Bid," 27 March 2007, http://www.reuters.com/article/idUSN2721666920070327, downloaded January 2010. In addition, Ecuador also froze the assets of Odebrecht, a Brazilian construction company, in 2008 for inferior practices on a hydroelectric project.

10. For earlier conflicts between Petrobras and environmentalists, see Matt Finer, "Insights: Oil Companies Poised to Penetrate Ecuadorian Amazon," *Environmental News Services,* 28 April 2004; Andrew Revkin, "Biologists Oppose Road Planned by Oil Company in Ecuador Park," *New York Times,* 17 February 2005; Associated Press, "Ecuador OKs Oil Drilling in Amazon Reserve," 27 August 2004; and a letter from fifty-nine scientists of Scientists Concerned for Yasuní National Park to the presidents of Ecuador and Brazil, dated 25 November 2004.

11. *El Comercio,* "Gobierno dice que reversión voluntaria de Bloque 31 refuerza lazos con Brasil," 3 October 2008; *El Comercio,* "El TC dio paso a un recurso de amparo contra Petrobras," 14 April 2008; *El Comercio,* "La Conaie presenta amparo contra la licencia ambiental de Petrobrás," 1 November 2007; and *El Comercio,* "Indígenas amazónicos protestan contra Petrobrás," 31 October 2007. See more reports on Petrobras and Block 31 at http://www.saveamericasforests.org.

12. Reuters, "Repsol Contains Small Oil Spill Near Ecuador Park," 31 January 2008, http://www.alertnet.org/thenews/newsdesk/N31369935.htm, downloaded 19 January 2010.

13. Venezuela elected Hugo Chávez in 1998 and reelected him in 2006. Bolivia elected Evo Morales in 2005 and reelected him in 2009, while Nicaragua elected Daniel Ortega in 2007. At the World Social Forum of grassroots activists to end economic, social, and environmental injustice, Correa, Chávez, Morales, and Fernando Lugo of Paraguay held their own forum on leftist, antineoliberal policies to move socialism forward. The World Social Forum was held in Belem, Brazil, in 2009. See Marc Becker's report, "The World Social Forum Returns to Brazil," Upside Down World, 5 February 2009, http://upsidedownworld.org/main/content/view/1701/1/.

14. See Kozloff 2009a.

15. The Brazilian leader Luiz Inánio da Silva and Argentinean leader Néstor Kirchner are considered to be not antagonistic with the United States, but support, in ideology and action, social justice and the end of historical injustices. Chilean Sebastián Pinera, of a right-wing party, won the Chilean election in early January 2010. See Kozloff 2008 as well.

16. Daniel Denvir, "Ecuador Defaults on Foreign Debt," 12 December 2008, Upside Down World, http://www.upsidedownworld.org/.../ecuador.../1627-ecuador-defaults-on-foreign-debt.

17. *Latin Business Chronicle,* "A New Low for Rafael Correa," 31 August 2009, http://www.latinbusinesschronicle.com/app/article.aspx?id=3638, downloaded 30 December 2009.

18. For further detail on this law, see International Centre for Settlement of Investment Disputes (ICSID) proceedings *Perenco vs. Ecuador and PetroEcuador* (ICSID Case No. ARB/08/06). http://icsid.worldbank.org/ICSID/FrontServlet.

19. *El Comercio,* "Repsol operará bajo contrato de prestación de servicios en un ano," 6 November 2008.

20. On "like a colony," see Reuters, "Ecuador to Freeze Assets over Repsol, Perenco Debts," 14 February 2009, http://uk.reuters.com/article/idUKN1425528620090214, downloaded 31 December 2009. See also Naomi Mapstone, "France's Perenco Oil Company Leaves Ecuador

Amid Tax Dispute," 24 July 2009, http://www.americasquarterly.org/node/805/, downloaded 31 December 2009; Reuters, "Ecuador Mulls Legal Action over Perenco Oil Move," 21 July 2009, http://uk.reuters.com/article/idUKN2124979420090721, downloaded 31 December 2009; and Eduardo Garcia, for Reuters, "Perenco to Press Case versus Ecuador at World Bank," 17 July 2009, http://in.reuters.com/article/rbssEnergyNews/idINN1748204520090717, downloaded 31 December 2009.

21. Efrain Hernandez Jr., "Ecuador President Rafael Correa Presses for Greater Investments from Oil Companies," *Los Angeles Times*, 5 December 2009, http://latimesblogs.latimes.com/laplaza/2009/12/ecuador-president-rafael-correa-oil-companies-contract-opec.html, downloaded 31 December 2009.

22. See Alonso Soto, for Reuters, "Repsol, China's Andes Agree to New Ecuador Oil Deals," 8 August 2008, http://www.reuters.com/article/idUSN0847383520080808, downloaded 31 December 2009.

23. The oil companies included Perenco, Repsol-YPF (twice), City Oriente, Tecnicas Reunidas, Murphy, Burlington, and Occidental.

24. Online search, 4 January 2010.

25. Mercedes Alvaro, for Dow Jones, "Ecuador to Release Oil Service Contract Model Wednesday," 8 December 2009; Reuters, "Ecuador Starts Contract Talks with Oil Companies," 10 December 2009.

26. Reuters, "Ecuador Wants New Pipeline Deal with Foreign Firms," 11 July 2009, http://www.reuters.com/article/idUSN1174820090711, downloaded 8 March 2010.

27. Mercedes Alvaro, for Dow Jones, "OCP Ecuador President Confident of Government Deal," 22 January 2010.

28. Kozloff 2008: 15.

29. For resource nationalism see Kozloff 2008: 4; for energy nationalism see the comments of Carlos Alberto López, former energy secretary of Bolivia, in the *New York Times* article "Neighbors Challenge Energy Aims in Bolivia," by Simon Romero and Andrés Schipani, 9 January 2010.

30. Interviewed 5 June 2009, Quito.

31. Correa's plans included greater social and economic equality through increased taxes on luxury goods, increased oil revenues, and increased investments in health and education (see Becker 2009: 124).

32. Becker 2009: 118, 127.

33. See a *New York Times* article on a police uprising due to Correa's cuts in police benefits that were received well by some of the working class. The report captures how Correa's "supporters and detractors" are perplexed by some of his decisions and actions; Simon Romero, "Ecuador Leader Confounds Supporters and Detractors," *New York Times*, 9 October 2010.

34. See Becker 2009 on relations between the Gutierrez government and Ecuador's Indigenous leaders.

35. Becker 2009: 106–07.

36. See Becker 2009: 172.

37. Kozloff 2008: 113.

38. Dosh and Kligerman 2009.

39. See the analysis of Dosh and Kligerman (2009) and Zibechi (2009) on the new constitution.

40. See Zibechi 2009.

41. See Dosh and Kligerman 2009.

42. Zibechi 2009, source for the "childish" remark by Correa. See also Dosh and Kligerman 2009.

43. Interviewed 12 May 2009, Quito.

44. Interviewed 2 June 2009, Quito.

45. According to a government representative, communities need to demonstrate contamination and the inability to move and/or to construct another home on their own.

46. Interviewed 2 June 2009, Quito.

47. See Dosh and Kligerman 2009.

48. Interviewed 5 June 2009, Quito.

49. Interviewed 5 June 2009, Quito.

50. For more on this event, see an online report by Jennifer Moore, "Swinging from the Right: Correa and Social Movements in Ecuador," Upside Down World, 13 May 2009, http://upside downworld.org/main/content/view/1856/49/, downloaded 5 January 2010. Acción Ecológica's nonprofit status was rescinded on the grounds that it was granted through the Health Ministry, even though the Environment Ministry was not established in 1986 when the NGO was formed.

51. In addition, Correa's administration had also targeted the media, in particular Teleamazonas, for disseminating misinformation. See *El Comercio*, "Teleamazonas ahora se defiende," 1 June 2009: 4.

52. Interviewed 5 June 2009, Quito.

53. In February 2011, an Ecuadorian court ordered Chevron to pay almost $9 billion. The verdict is being appealed. For Chevron's account, see http://www.texaco.com/sitelets/ecuador/en/. For the account of Frente de Defensa de la Amazonia and Amazon Watch, see http://chevrontoxico.com/. For more on transnational campaigns targeting ChevronTexaco, see McAteer and Pulver 2009.

54. Pulver 2007: 252.

55. O'Rourke 2004: 228.

56. An interview with two oil consultants, 2 June 2009.

57. Chevron Corporation press release dated 23 September 2009 and titled "Chevron Files International Arbitration against the Government of Ecuador over Violations of the United States-Ecuador Bilateral Investment Treaty," http://www.chevron.com/news/Press/release/?id=2009-09-23, downloaded 31 December 2009.

58. Interviewed 5 June 2009, Quito.

59. Mommer 1994: 33.

60. Interviewed 5 June 2009, Quito.

61. On ecosocialism, see Faber and O'Connor 1993; Faber 1998c; and the Belém Ecosocialist Declaration, presented at the World Social Forum, Belém, Brazil, January 2009.

62. See Amazon Watch newsroom updates: "Ecuador Pipeline Suffers Major Oil Spill: Thousands of Gallons of Heavy Crude Flood River and Surrounding Ecosystems," 27 February 2009; and "Oil Spill Seriously Affects the Health of Indigenous Communities along the River Coca," 4 March 2009.

63. Almeida 2010.

64. Interviewed 12 May 2009, Quito.

65. In Brazil, state and centralized governments had taken a different tack with regard to oil royalties. In Ecuador, oil-important states had mobilized to increase their share of oil royalties given their experienced impacts. In Brazil, non-oil-producing states had initiated a bill to force the sharing of oil royalties evenly among the states. The Brazilian government was debating their bill in early 2010.

66. For greater detail on this case, see Aguirre 2008. The information provided here is from Aguirre's investigation into the "Dayuma case" for CICAME, an Ecuadorian publisher that specializes in environmental and social justice issues in the Amazon.

67. For international reports on Guadalupe Llori's arrest, see Human Rights Foundation, "Ecuador Denies Opposition Politician Her Freedom; Government Dealings with FARC Reveal Double Standard," 17 March 2008, http://www.thehrf.org/media/080317.html, downloaded 12 January 2010; and Amnesty International, "Ecuador: Possible Prisoner of Conscience/Legal Concern: Guadalupe Llori," 25 March 2008, http://www.amnesty.org/en/library/asset/AMR28/001/2008/en/2f9c370a-ff22-11dc-b092-bdb020617d3d/amr280012008eng.html, downloaded 12 January 2010.

68. The Ministry of Mines and Petroleum opened an environmental office in Orellana Province in March 2008. It is not clear whether this office serves to receive and to respond to community complaints or to monitor community action.

69. Valdivia 2008: 460.

70. Friedman 2006.

71. Interviewed 2 June 2009, Quito.

72. Unlike OCP conflicts in 2001 and 2002, however, the website http://www.youtube.com provided a visual outlet for disseminating the conflict and community requests for basic services, while capturing the routine poverty experienced in Dayuma, a nondescript village along just another oil road at the edge of the Amazon.

73. International Federation for Human Rights, *Observatory for the Protection of Human Rights Defenders Annual Report 2006—Ecuador*, 14 March 2007, http://www.unhcr.org/refworld/docid/48747cdc19.html, downloaded 12 January 2010.

74. See Amnesty International, Public AI Index: AMR 28/002/2004.

75. Interviewed 2 June 2009, Quito.

76. For efforts to protect the Pañacocha protected forest, see Ancient Forest International, http://www.ancientforests.org/ecuador/project.htm, downloaded 12 January 2010.

77. Interviewed 2 June 2009, Quito.

78. Interviewed 11 June 2004, Quito.

79. Interviewed 11 June 2004, Quito.

80. Yasuní Rainforest Campaign has provided a great deal of the material on Correa's carbon credit offer; see http://www.saveamericasforests.org. Also see Amazon Watch's website reports, including "Newsroom Update: Yasuni-ITT Proposal Update," 27 July 2008, at http://www.amazon watch.org.

81. See Acosta et al. 2000, an edited volume by Acción Ecológica on postpetroleum Ecuador.

82. A memorandum of understanding was signed in March 2007 with Sinopec, PetroEcuador, Petrobras, and ENAP. AFX Asia Focus, "China's Sinopec to Help Develop Ecuador ITT Oil Field—Report," 26 March 2007. AFX is an independent Asia-Pacific financial news service. See also Business News Americas, "Enap, PDVSA, Petrobras, Sinopec Join for ITT Bidding—Ecuador," 27 January 2008, www.bnamericas.com/.../oilandgas/Enap,_PDVSA,_Petrobras,_Sinopec_join_ for_ITT_bidding.

83. Interviewed 2 June 2009, Quito.

84. Koenig 2007.

85. *El Comercio*, "Las contradicciones minan la Iniciativa ITT," 14 January 2009.

86. See Gonzalo Ortiz, Inter Press Service News Agency, "Ecuador: Environmental Inspection in Yasuní Park," 28 April 2010; *El Comercio*, "Las contradicciones minan la Iniciativa ITT," 14 January 2009; *El Comercio*, "Correa insiste en corresponsabilidad internacional en caso ITT," 5 June 2008; *El Comercio*, "El Yasuni-ITT Llega a la Casa Blanca," 31 May 2009; and the *Economist*, "Ecuador: Having It Both Ways," 23 June 2007: 47.

87. See Kozloff 2009b.

88. See Simon Romero, "Ecuador: Foreign Minister Resigns," *New York Times*, 13 January 2010: A12.

89. See Kevin Koenig, "Yasuní-ITT: Chronicle of a Death Foretold?" in Amazon Watch's Newsroom Update, 19 January 2010, http://www.amazonwatch.org/newsroom/view_news.php?. id=1987; and *El Comercio*, "Las contradicciones minan la Iniciativa ITT," 14 January 2009.

90. *Economist*, "Ecuador: Having It Both Ways," 23 June 2007: 47.

91. Oilwatch Technical Team 2007: 30.

92. See "SOS Yasuni: A Terrible Threat Is Hanging over Ecuador's Yasuni National Park," 18 January 2010, www.sosyasuni.org.

93. Interviewed 2 June 2009, Quito.

94. Oilwatch Technical Team 2007.

95. If oil is extracted in this area, the Oilwatch Technical Team (2007) identified deforestation, water and soil contamination, loss of subsistence activities for Indigenous communities, increased conflicts between oil workers and communities, which would require state intervention as well as heightened border conflicts with Peru, and finally the social impacts and losses of traditional culture for resident communities of ITT. By now, these are standard and known impacts when oil is explored in remote environments.

96. See Acosta et al. 2009.

97. The authors acknowledge their own differences on the ITT initiative alongside their committed effort to promote, demonstrate, and engage in dialogue so as to keep the idea and perhaps implementation of the proposal alive.

98. Mahony 1992.

99. Brazilian Institute for Economic and Social Analysis (IBASE) 1992. See also Kiefer and Benjamin 2002.

100. *El Universo*, "Incendio cambió barrio en Esmeraldas hace siete anos," 26 February 2005.

101. Interviewed 5 June 2009, Quito.

102. See *Ecologist*, "Oil Pollution Victory," Dec 2002/Jan 2003, 32(10): 8, as well as Megan Murphy, "Galapagos Park Seeks $10 Million from Markel for Tanker Spill," Bloomberg, 14 September 2006, http://www.bloomberg.com/apps/news?pid=20601086&sid=aRD8gtKG1cdA&refer =latin_america#, downloaded 4 January 2010.

103. In October 2007, the San Cristobal Wind Project began operating a wind-diesel hybrid energy system for the Galapagos Islands (see http://www.galapagoswind.org). It is a collaborative project between Elecgalapagos (the public electricity company on the Galapagos Islands), United Nations Development Program (UNDP), the United Nations Foundation, and the E8, an organization of electrical companies based in the member countries of the G8 (see http:// www.e8.org).

104. Ecuador and Venezuela threatened to leave OAS after Colombia crossed into Ecuador seeking a FARC (Revolutionary Armed Forces of Colombia) camp.

105. See Lafargue 2006 and Kurlantzick 2006 on China's early investment in Ecuador, and see Widener (2011) on a comparison between China's operations in Africa, Asia, and Latin America. On this section, holding China accountable, see Widener (2011) as well.

106. Reuters, "Snubbed at Top Table, China Chases Oil M&A Crumbs," 23 October 2009; Reuters, "Ecuador Set to Receive $1 Billion Loan from China-Report," 17 August 2009; Reuters, "Ecuador Signs Contract to Export Oil to China," 23 July 2009.

107. See *El Comercio*, "Firma china construirá sola el Coca-Codo," 6 October 2009, as well as an undated report in the *Latin American Herald Tribune*, "Chinese Firm to Build Hydroelectric Dam in Ecuador," http://www.laht.com/article.asp?CategoryId=14089&ArticleID=345267, downloaded 1 February 2010.

108. See Alvaro 2007 on the refinery and airport offer. The refinery was eventually handed to Venezuela's PdVSA.

109. Press release by CONAIE, "CONAICE exige suspension de actividades de exploracion sismica en las comunidades indigenas wankavilkas," 1 February 2010.

110. Interviewed 22 April 2004, Washington DC.

111. Interviewed 12 May 2009, Quito.

112. Interviewed 12 May 2009, Quito.

113. Interviewed 12 May 2009, Quito.

114. Interviewed 11 June 2004, Quito.

115. Meintjes 2000: 94.

116. *China Daily*, "Ministries Concerned by Embassy Robbery," 14 November 2006; Dow Jones, "Chinese Oil Co Faces Resident Protests to Ecuador Pipeline," Dow Jones Chinese Financial Wire, 10 November 2006; Juliette Kerr, "Protests against Chinese Company's Oil Operations End in Ecuador," *Global Insight Daily Analysis*, 13 November 2006; and Hal Weitzman, "Protestors Pour Trouble on Ecuador's Oil Producers," *Financial Times*, 3 March 2006. Such actions, coupled with limited new projects, led to financial losses for Andes Petroleum in the first half of 2007; see Watkins 2007.

117. See Widener (2011).

118. Altenburg, Schmitz, and Stamm 2008; Zhang 2004.

119. For an assessment of China's recent economic transitions through the lens of ecological modernization, see Mol 2006.
120. Altenburg, Schmitz, and Stamm 2008.
121. Pulver 2007: 252.
122. Gu, Humphrey, and Messner 2008; Guttal 2008; Hanson 2008; Junger 2007; Manji and Marks 2007; Zweig and Jianhai 2005.
123. Widener 2007a.
124. On this section on China, see Widener (2011).
125. Spencer et al. 2007.
126. In 2005 EnCana sold its Ecuadorian operations to Andes Petroleum, which includes China National Petroleum Corporation and China Petrochemical Corporation; see Reuters 2005b.
127. Interviewed 22 May 2007, Quito.
128. Interviewed 22 May 2007, Quito.
129. Interviewed 15 May 2009, Quito.
130. See Garcia-Johnson 2000 on how U.S. multinationals export environmental standards to Brazil and Mexico.
131. Interviewed 2 June 2009, Quito.
132. Interviewed 2 June 2009, Quito.
133. Interviewed 12 May 2009, Quito.
134. Interviewed 22 May 2007, Quito.
135. Interviewed 8 October 2003, Quito.
136. Interviewed 8 October 2003, Quito.
137. See Lee 2007; Shirk 2007.
138. See Economy 2004; Fishman 2005.
139. Guttal 2008: 45, 18.
140. Arakan Oil Watch 2008. China's oil companies entered Burma in 2001.
141. Askouri 2007; Hurst 2006; Junger 2007; Zweig and Jianhai 2005.
142. Chen 2007.
143. Smil 2004: 209.
144. In contrast, in 2009 some of the Chinese oil companies paid local laborers more than the industry standard. For example, PetroOriente paid approximately US$25/day with lunch, while PetroAmazonas, the Ecuadorian company, in Block 15 paid about US$15/day without lunch, but the average in the Oriente for day labor (not related to oil work) was about US$5–6/day without lunch. This difference put the Chinese oil operators in conflict with other oil operators, which had an unspoken agreement to not compete on raising day labor wages. Source interviewed 2 June 2009, Quito.
145. Interviewed 2 June 2009, Quito.
146. See Widener (2011) on a comparison between China's overseas practices in Africa, Asia, and Latin America.
147. Interviewed 12 May 2009, Quito.
148. Interviewed 2 June 2009, Quito.
149. Interviewed 12 May 2009, Quito.
150. Widener (2011).
151. Interviewed 12 May 2009, Quito.
152. Lou and Zhu 2007; and Josh P. Hamilton, "Berkshire Reduces Holdings in PetroChina," *International Herald Tribune*, 11 October 2007.
153. Economy 2004: 208–9.
154. See Beltrán and Oldham (2005a, 2005b) on the agreements between the Ecuadorian Armed Forces and oil multinationals in the Amazon.
155. Widener (2011).

APPENDIX:
DATA COLLECTION AND
RESEARCHER PARTICIPATION

1. See Glaser and Strauss 1967; Lefebvre 2004.
2. See Glaser and Strauss 1967; Ragin 1994.
3. *El Comercio*, "Andoas ya no se opone a la OCP," 29 July 2002: D1.
4. *El Comercio*, "La parroquia de Nono cambió con la llegada del oleoducto," 5 August 2003: B8.
5. *El Comercio*, "Manta ya tuvo experiencia con el SOTE," 8 June 2001: B1; and "Energía: Los puertos de Esmeraldas y Manta están preparados para recibirlas. OCP: 250 000 toneladas en camino": B1.
6. See Rubin and Rubin 1995.
7. See Widener 2007b on my experience photographing the various actions in Ecuador.
8. Brown 2003.
9. See Marshall and Rossman 1999: 80.
10. Presented by Patrick Heller at a talk on public sociology, "Public Sociology and International Research: Overseas, Other Places & Others," Sociology Department, Brown University, Providence, Rhode Island, 13 April 2005.
11. Evans 1995.
12. Brown 2003.
13. Brown 2003.
14. Smith 2008: ix.

References

Acción Ecológica. 2001a. "Comentarios de Acción Ecológica a los estudios ambientales del OCP." *Alerta Verde: Boletin de Acción Ecológica*. No. 109, May.

———. 2001b. "Ruta del OCP: 'Trinchera por Trinchera.'" *Alerta Verde: Boletín de Acción Ecológica*. No. 112, June.

———. 2001c. "Cuidado con el OCP." *Alerta Verde: Boletín de Acción Ecológica*. No. 104, March.

———. 2001d. "No Es Lo Mismo: Estar Jodiendo que Estar Jodidos." *Alerta Verde: Boletín de Acción Ecológica*. No. 113, July.

———. 2003. "Violaciones de los derechos humanos en la construccion del OCP." *Alerta Verde: Boletín de Acción Ecológica*. No. 126, May.

Acción por la Vida. 2002a. "Proposal for Land Acquisition of 2,150 Acres of Ecuador's Threatened Mindo Cloudforest." Press release, June.

———. 2002b. Base Camp Report #2, 22 February.

———. 2002c. Base Camp Report #4, 16 March.

———. 2004. "Context of Mindo and Project Rescue Center—Management of the Protected Forest Mindo-Nambillo." Press release, October.

Acosta, Alberto, Alexandra Almeida, Milton Balseca, Elizabeth Brazo, Fernando Carrión, Judy Kimmerling, Carlos Larrea, Esperanza Martínez, Diego Puente, Ivonne Ramos, Catalina Sosa, and Carlos Viteri (eds.). 2000. *El Ecuador Post Petrolero*. Quito, Ecuador: Acción Ecológica.

Acosta, Alberto, Eduardo Gudynas, Esperanza Martínez, and Joseph H. Vogel. 2009. "Leaving Oil in the Ground: A Political, Economic and Ecological Initiative in the Ecuadorian Amazon." *Americas Program Special Report* for the Americas Policy Program, 13 August.

Adeola, Francis O. 2000. "Cross-National Environmental Injustice and Human Rights Issues." *American Behavioral Scientist* 43(4): 686–706.

Agarwal, Sheela. 2005. "Global-local Interactions in English Coastal Resorts." *Tourism Geographies* 7(4): 351–72.

Agbola, Tunde, and Moruf Alabi. 2003. "Political Economy of Petroleum Resources Development, Environmental Injustice and Selective Victimization: A Case Study of the Niger Delta Region of Nigeria." In *Just Sustainabilities: Development in an Unequal World*, eds. Julian Agyeman, Robert D. Bullard and Bob Evans, 269–88. Cambridge, MA: MIT Press.

Aguirre, Milagros. 2008. *Dayuma: Nunca Más!* Quito, Ecuador: Cicame.

Albán, Jorge. 2000. "Biodiversidad, energía, minería y vías." Unpublished report, prepared for Fundación Ambiente y Sociedad, August, Quito, Ecuador.

Alberta EcoTrust. 2004a. "Community Grants Program in November 2004." J:\fund development\reports\grant summary report Nov 2004.doc, downloaded May 2005.

——. 2004b. "Maximizing Effectiveness: An Assessment of Environmental Priorities and Voluntary Sector Capacity Needs in Alberta." Unpublished summary report for the Alberta EcoTrust Foundation, October, Alberta, Canada.

Alexander, Lucy. 1996. "Colombia's Pacific Plan: Indigenous and Afro-Colombian communities challenge developers." In *Green Guerrillas*, ed. Helen Collinson, 74–81. London: Latin American Bureau.

Ali, Saleem H. 2000. "Shades of Green NGO Coalitions, Mining Companies and the Pursuit of Negotiating Power." In *Terms for Endearment*, ed. Jem Bendell, 79–95. Sheffield, UK: Greenleaf.

——. 2008. "Oil and Turmoil." *Policy Innovations* 12 March.

Allen, Barbara L. 2003. *Uneasy Alchemy: Citizens and Experts in Louisiana's Chemical Corridor Disputes*. Cambridge, MA: MIT Press.

Almeida, Alexandra. 2010. "One Year Anniversary of Oil Spill in Ecuador's Amazon: Still No Progress for Residents." *Indigenous Peoples Issues & Resources*, 3 March.

Alston, Dana. 1990. *We Speak for Ourselves*. Washington, DC: Panos Institute.

Altenburg, Tilman, Hubert Schmitz, and Andreas Stamm. 2008. "Breakthrough? China's and India's Transition from Production to Innovation." *World Development* 36(2): 325–44.

Alvaro, Mercedes. 2007. "Ecuador's President Seeks Stronger Ties with China." *Dow Jones Emerging Markets Reports*, 29 March.

Andrews, Edmund L. 2006. "U.S. Royalty Plan to Give Windfall to Oil Companies." *New York Times*, 14 February, A1.

Arakan Oil Watch. 2008. "Blocking Freedom: A Case Study of China's Oil and Gas Investment in Burma." October. Chiang Mai, Thailand: Arakan Oil Watch.

Arenas, Daniel, Josep M. Lozano, and Laura Albareda. 2009. "The Role of NGOs in CSR: Mutual Perceptions among Stakeholders." *Journal of Business Ethics* 88: 175–97.

Askouri, Ali. 2007. "China's Investment in Sudan: Displacing Villages and Destroying Communities." In *African Perspectives on China in Africa*, eds. Firoze Manji and Stephen Marks, 71–86. Cape Town, South Africa: Fahamu.

Avritzer, Leonardo. 2002. *Democracy and the Public Space in Latin America*. Princeton, NJ: Princeton University Press.

Baiocchi, Gianpaolo. 2001. "Participation, Activism, and Politics: The Porto Alegre Experiment and Deliberative Democratic Theory." *Politics and Society* 29(1): 43–72.

Bandy, Joe, and Jackie Smith (eds.). 2005a. *Coalitions across Borders: Transnational Protest and the Neoliberal Order*. Lanham, MD: Rowman & Littlefield.

——. 2005b. "Factors Affecting Conflict and Cooperation in Transnational Movement Networks." In *Coalitions across Borders*, eds. J. Bandy and J. Smith, 231–52. Lanham, MD: Rowman & Littlefield.

Barragán, Juan Pablo, and Ivonne Ramos (directors). 2002. *Amazon Oil Pipeline—Pollution, Corruption and Poverty*. Lismore, Australia: Rainforest Information Centre.

Barry, John, and Graham Smith. 2005. "Green Political Economy and the Promise of the Social Economy." In *Handbook of Global Environmental Politics*, ed. Peter Dauvergne, 249–69. Cheltenham, UK: Edward Elgar.

Barthélémy, Francoise. 2003. "Can the New President Control the Oil Companies? Ecuador's Pipeline out of Debt." *Le Monde Diplomatique*, English edition (January).

Baver, Sherrie L., and Barbara Deutsch Lynch. 2006. *Beyond Sun and Sand: Caribbean Environmentalism*. New Brunswick, NJ: Rutgers University Press.

Bayon, Ricardo, Carolyn Deere, Ruth Norris, and Scott E. Smith. 1999. "Environmental Funds: Lessons Learned and Future Prospects." http://economics.iucn.org (issues-20-01), and http://www.conservationfinance.org/Africa_Conference/Documents/EF_lessons_iucn_topics-18-01.pdf.

BBC. 2006a. "Protests Hit Ecuador Oil Exports." BBC News, 21 February.

——. 2006b. "Ecuador Agreement in Oil Protests." BBC News, 23 February.

Beamish, Thomas D. 2002. *Silent Spill: The Organization of an Industrial Crisis*. Cambridge, MA: MIT Press.

Bebbington, Anthony. 1996a. "Debating 'Indigenous' Agricultural Development: Indian Organizations in the Central Andes of Ecuador." In *Green Guerrillas*, ed. H. Collinson, 51–60. London: Latin America Bureau.

———. 1996b. "Movements and Modernizations, Markets and Municipalities: Indigenous Federations in Rural Ecuador." In *Liberation Ecologies*, eds. R. Peet and M. Watts, 394–421. New York: Routledge.

Becker, Marc. 2008. *Indians and Leftists in the Making of Ecuador's Modern Indigenous Movements*. Durham, NC: Duke University Press.

———. 2009. *Pachakutik!* Unpublished book manuscript.

Belkin, Allen, Charles Kleymeyer, Kemba A. Maish, Roland Roebuck, and Juan García Salazar. 1993. *Collective Memory: The African Presence in Latin America. A Study Guide on the Maroon Community of Esmeraldas, Ecuador.* Washington, DC: Network of Educators on the Americas.

Beltrán, Bolívar, and Jim Oldham. 2005a. "Ecuador—Oil Companies' Links with Military Revealed." *Las Lianas Quarterly Update* (Spring): 1–2.

———. 2005b. "Oil Multinationals Privatize the Military in Ecuador." *Synthesis/Regeneration* 38 (Fall).

Benford, Robert. 2005. "The Half-Life of the Environmental Justice Frame: Innovation, Diffusion, and Stagnation." In *Power, Justice, and the Environment: A Critical Appraisal of the Environmental Justice Movement*, eds. David Naguib Pellow and Robert J. Brulle, 37–53. Cambridge, MA: MIT Press.

Berry, Mary Clay. 1975. *The Alaska Pipeline: The Politics of Oil and Native Land Claims.* Bloomington: Indiana University Press.

Bhagwati, Jagdish. 2004. *In Defense of Globalization.* Oxford: Oxford University Press.

Binns, Tony, and Etienne Nel. 2002. "Tourism as a Local Development Strategy in South Africa." *Geographical Journal* 168(3): 235–47.

Bob, Clifford. 2005. *The Marketing of Rebellion: Insurgents, Media, and International Activism.* New York: Cambridge University Press.

Bowker, Michael. 2003. *Fatal Deception: The Terrifying True Story of How Asbestos Is Killing America.* New York: Simon & Schuster.

Brazilian Institute for Economic and Social Analysis (IBASE). 1992. "Debt Swaps: A Southern View." *The Ecologist* 22(3): 100.

Breslin, Patrick. 2007. "Lessons of the Elders: Juan García and the Oral Tradition of Afro-Ecuador." *Grassroots Development Journal of the Inter-American Foundation* 28(1): 6–13.

Brodeur, Paul. 1973. *Expendable Americans.* New York: Viking Press.

Brondo, Keri Vacanti, and Laura Woods. 2007. "Garifuna Land Rights and Ecotourism as Economic Development in Honduras' Cayos Cochinos Marine Protected Area." *Ecological and Environmental Anthropology* 3(1): 2–18.

Brooks, Ethel. 2005. "Transnational Campaigns against Child Labor: The Garment Industry in Bangladesh." In *Coalitions across Borders: Transnational Protest and the Neoliberal Order*, eds. Joe Bandy and Jackie Smith, 121–39. Lanham, MD: Rowman & Littlefield.

Brown, Phil. 1992. "Popular Epidemiology and Toxic Waste Contamination: Lay and Professional Ways of Knowing." *Journal of Health & Social Behavior* 33(3): 267–81.

———. 1995. "Race, Class, and Environmental Health: A Review and Systematization of the Literature." *Environmental Research* 69: 15–30.

———. 2003. "Qualitative Methods in Environmental Health Research." *Environmental Health Perspectives* 111(14): 1789–98.

———. 2007. *Toxic Exposures: Contested Illnesses and the Environmental Health Movement.* New York: Columbia University Press.

Brown, Phil, and Susan Masterson-Allen. 1994. "The Toxic Waste Movement: A New Type of Activism." *Society and Natural Resources* 7: 269–87.

Brown, Phil, and Edwin J. Mikkelsen. 1990. *No Safe Place: Toxic Waste, Leukemia, and Community Action.* Berkeley: University of California Press.

Brown, Phil, Stephen Zavestoski, Sabrina McCormick, Brian Mayer, Rachel Morello-Frosch, and Rebecca Gasior Altman. 2004. "Embodied Health Movements: New Approaches to Social Movements in Health." *Sociology of Health and Illness* 26(1): 50–80.

Brulle, Robert J., and J. Craig Jenkins. 2006. "Spinning Our Way to Sustainability?" *Organization & Environment* 19(1): 82–87.

Brysk, Alison. 2000. *From Tribal Village to Global Village: Indian Rights and International Relations in Latin America.* Stanford, CA: Stanford University Press.

Buckley, Ralf, ed. 2004. *Environmental Impacts of Ecotourism*. Oxfordshire, UK: CABI Publishing.

Bullard, Robert D. (ed.). 1993. *Confronting Environmental Racism: Voice from the Grassroots*. Boston: South End Press.

———. (ed.). 1994. *Unequal Protection: Environmental Justice and Communities of Color*. San Francisco: Sierra Club Books.

———. 2005a. *The Quest for Environmental Justice: Human Rights and the Politics of Pollution*. San Francisco: Sierra Club Books.

———. 2005b. "Introduction." In *The Quest for Environmental Justice: Human Rights and the Politics of Pollution*, ed. Robert D. Bullard, 1–15. San Francisco: Sierra Club Books.

Bullard, Robert D., Glenn S. Johnson, and Angel O. Torres. 2005. "Addressing Global Poverty, Pollution, and Human Rights." In *The Quest for Environmental Justice: Human Rights and the Politics of Pollution*, ed. Robert D. Bullard, 279–97. San Francisco: Sierra Club Books.

Buttel, Frederick H. 2003. "Environmental Sociology and the Explanation of Environmental Reform." *Organization & Environment* 16(3): 306–44.

Byrne, John, and Steven M. Hoffman. 2002. "A 'Necessary Sacrifice': Industrialization and American Indian Lands." In *Environmental Justice: Discourses in International Political Economy*, eds. John Byrne, Leigh Glover, and Cecilia Martinez, 97–119. New Brunswick, NJ: Transaction Publishers.

Caffrey, Patricia B. 2001. "Analysis of Compliance Oleoducto de Crudos Pesados (OCP) Project and the World Bank Environmental Policies and Guidelines." Prepared for Amazon Watch, 20 November.

———. 2002. "Comments on Stone & Webster Report." Prepared for Amazon Watch, 21 May.

Caldwell, John C. 1986. "Routes to Low Mortality in Poor Countries." *Population and Development Review* 12(2): 171–220.

Calimag, Priscilla. 2007. "Eco-tourism: Preserving Our Natural Treasures." Presentation at the League of Corporate Foundations Corporation Social Responsibility Expo 2007, Manila, Philippines, 18 July.

Caniglia, Beth Schaefer. 2002. "Elite Alliances and Transnational Environmental Movement Organizations." In *Globalization and Resistance*, eds. Jackie Smith and Hank Johnston, 153–72. Lanham, MD: Rowman & Littlefield.

Cantzler, Julia Miller. 2007. "Environmental Justice and Social Power Rhetoric in the Moral Battle over Whaling." *Sociological Inquiry* 77(3): 483–512.

Carruthers, David V. 1996. "Indigenous Ecology and the Politics of Linkage in Mexican Social Movements." *Third World Quarterly* 17(5): 1007–28.

Carson, Rachel. 1962. *Silent Spring*. New York: Houghton Mifflin.

Castells, Manuel. 1997. *The Information Age: Economy, Society and Culture*. Volume II: *The Power of Identity*. Boston: Blackwell.

CDES. 2000. "Negociacion del codigo de conducta entre occidental (Oxy) y la Organizacion Indigena Secoya del Ecuador (OISE)." Unpublished document, March, Centro De Derechos Económicos y Sociales (CDES). Quito, Ecuador.

Chapin, Mac. 2004. "A Challenge to Conservationists." *World Watch*, November/December, 17–31.

Chen, Matthew E. 2007. "Chinese National Oil Companies and Human Rights." *Orbis* (Winter): 41–54.

Cohen, Maurie J. 2006. "'The Death of Environmentalism': Introduction to the Symposium." *Organization & Environment* 19(1): 74–81.

Colborn, Theo, Dianne Dumanoski, and John Peterson Myers. 1997. *Our Stolen Future: Are We Threatening Our Fertility, Intelligence, and Survival?* New York: Plume.

Cole, Luke W., and Sheila R. Foster. 2001. *From the Ground Up: Environmental Racism and the Rise of the Environmental Justice Movement*. New York: New York University Press.

Conaghan, Catherine M., and James M. Malloy. 1994. *Unsettling Statecraft: Democracy and Neoliberalism in the Central Andes*. Pittsburgh, PA: University of Pittsburgh Press.

Connelly, Stephen, and Tim Richardson. 2005. "Value-Driven SEA: Time for an Environmental Justice Perspective?" *Environmental Impact Assessment Review* 25: 391–409.

Corburn, Jason. 2002. "Combining Community-Based Research and Local Knowledge to Confront Asthma and Subsistence-Fishing Hazards in Greenpoint/Williamsburg, Brooklyn, New York." *Environmental Health Perspectives* 110(Supplement 2): 241–48.

Corkill, David, and David Cubitt. 1988. *Ecuador: Fragile Democracy*. London: Latin American Bureau.

Couch, Stephen R., and J. Stephen Kroll-Smith. 1985. "The Chronic Technological Disaster: Toward a Social-Scientific Perspective." *Social Science Quarterly* 66: 564–75.

Coury, Joanne M., and Jasminka Despot Lucanin. 1996. "Mending the Social Safety Net after State Socialism: 'Dobrobit'—One Nongovernmental Organization in Zagreb, Croatia." *Nonprofit and Voluntary Sector Quarterly* 25(3): 283–301.

Cowell, R. 1997. "Stretching the Limits: Environmental Compensation, Habitat Creation and Sustainable Development." *Transactions of the Institute of British Geographers*, New Series 22(3): 292–306.

Crow, Patrick. 2000. "Ecuador's Solutions." *Oil and Gas Journal*, 4 December, 30.

Crystal, Jill. 1989. "Coalitions in Oil Monarchies: Kuwait and Qatar." *Comparative Politics* 21(4): 427–43.

Davis, Devra. 2002. *When Smoke Ran Like Water: Tales of Environmental Deception and the Battle Against Pollution*. New York: Basic Books.

———. 2007. *The Secret History of the War on Cancer*. New York: Basic Books.

Della Porta, Donatella, and Mario Diani. 1999. *Social Movements: An Introduction*. Oxford: Blackwell Publishers.

Domhoff, G. William. 1967. *Who Rules America?* Englewood Cliffs, NJ: Prentice-Hall.

Dosh, Paul, and Nicole Kligerman. 2009. "Correa vs. Social Movements: Showdown in Ecuador." *North American Congress on Latin America* 42(5), https://nacla.org/node/6094, downloaded 15 May 2010.

Dréze, Jean, and Amartya Sen. 1989. *Hunger and Public Action*. Oxford: Clarendon Press.

Drost, Nadja (director). 2003. *Risky Business: EnCana and the OCP in Ecuador*. Toronto: Global Aware Canada.

———. 2005. *Between Midnight and the Rooster's Crow*. Los Angeles: Rocinante Productions.

Duffy, Rosaleen. 2000. "Shadow Players: Ecotourism Development, Corruption and State Politics in Belize." *Third World Quarterly* 21(3): 549–65.

Economy, Elizabeth C. 2004. *The River Runs Black: The Environmental Challenge to China's Future*. Ithaca, NY: Cornell University Press.

Edelstein, Michael R. 1988. *Contaminated Communities: The Social and Psychological Impacts of Residential Toxic Exposure*. Boulder, CO: Westview Press.

Egan, Kristina. 1996. "Forging New Alliances in Ecuador's Amazon." *SAIS Review* 16: 123–42.

Engler, Robert. 1961. *The Politics of Oil: A Study of Private Power and Democratic Directions*. New York: Macmillan.

———. 1977. *The Brotherhood of Oil: Energy Policy and the Public Interest*. New York: New American Library.

Entrix. 2001. Oleoducto de Crudos Pesados Environmental Studies Abstract, Project 131104. Prepared for OCP Ecuador S.A., June. Quito, Ecuador. http://www.ocpecuador/com/documents/ingles/resumen.doc.

Erikson, Kai T. 1976. *Everything in Its Path: Destruction of Community in the Buffalo Creek Flood*. New York: Simon and Schuster.

Estupinán, Ernesto. 2007. ""Esmeraldas: A New City for New Citizens." Paper presented at the Urban [F]actor: Challenges Facing Sustainable Urban Development conference, Brussels, Belgium, 18–19 December 2007: p. 62 of seminar proceedings. [His speech was transcribed from the recording of 19 December 2007.]

Evans, Peter. 1995. *Embedded Autonomy: States and Industrial Transformation*. Princeton, NJ: Princeton University Press.

Faber, Daniel. 1998a. "The Political Ecology of American Capitalism: New Challenges for the Environmental Justice Movement." In *The Struggle for Ecological Democracy: Environmental Justice Movements in the United States*, ed. D. Faber, 27–59. New York: Guilford Press.

———. 1998b. "The Struggle for Ecological Democracy and Environmental Justice." In *The Struggle for Ecological Democracy: Environmental Justice Movements in the United States*, ed. D. R. Faber, 1–26. New York: Guilford Press.

——— (ed.). 1998c. *The Struggle for Ecological Democracy: Environmental Justice Movements in the United States*. New York: Guilford Press.

———. 2005. "Building a Transnational Environmental Justice Movement: Obstacles and Opportunities in the Age of Globalization." In *Coalitions across Borders: Transnational Protest and the Neoliberal Order*, eds. Joe Bandy and Jackie Smith, 43–68. Lanham, MD: Rowman & Littlefield.

———. 2008. *Capitalizing on Environmental Injustice: The Polluter-Industrial Complex in the Age of Globalization*. Lanham, MD: Rowman & Littlefield.

Faber, Daniel R., and Deborah McCarthy. 2003. "Neo-liberalism, Globalization and the Struggle for Ecological Democracy: Linking Sustainability and Environmental Justice." In *Just Sustainabilities: Development in an Unequal World*, eds. Julian Agyeman, Robert D. Bullard, and Bob Evans, 38–63. Cambridge, MA: MIT Press.

Faber, Daniel R., and James O'Connor. 1993. "Capitalism and the Crisis of Environmentalism." In *Toxic Struggles: The Theory and Practice of Environmental Justice*, ed. R. Hofrichter, 12–24. Philadelphia: New Society.

Farmer, Paul. 2003. *Pathologies of Power: Health, Human Rights, and the New War on the Poor*. Berkeley: University of California Press.

Fay, Derick A. 2005. "'Mutual Gains' and 'Distributive' Ideologies in South Africa: Theorizing Negotiations between Communities and Protected Areas." Paper presented at the Society for Applied Anthropology Annual Meeting, April 2005, Santa Fe, New Mexico.

Federici, Paolo Roberto, and Giuliano Rodolfi. 2001. "Rapid Shoreline Retreat along the Esmeraldas Coast, Ecuador: Natural and Man-induced Processes." *Journal of Coastal Conservation* 7: 163–70.

Ferguson, James. 1994. *The Anti-Politics Machine*. Minneapolis: University of Minnesota Press.

Fine, Gary Alan, and Brooke Harrington. 2004. "Tiny Publics: Small Groups and Civil Society." *Sociological Theory* 22(3): 341–56.

Finer, Matt, Clinton N. Jenkins, Stuart L. Pimm, Brian Keane, and Carl Ross. 2008. "Oil and Gas Projects in the Western Amazon: Threats to Wilderness, Biodiversity, and Indigenous Peoples." *PLoS ONE* 3(8): e2932.

Finer, Matt, Varsha Vijay, Fernando Ponce, Clinton N. Jenkins, and Ted R. Kahn. 2009. "Ecuador's Yasuní Biosphere Reserve: A Brief Modern History and Conservation Challenges." *Environmental Research Letters* 4(034005): 1–15.

Fischer, Frank. 2000. *Citizens, Experts, and the Environment: The Politics of Local Knowledge*. Durham, NC: Duke University Press.

Fishman, Ted C. 2005. *China, Inc.: How the Rise of the Next Superpower Challenges America and the World*. New York: Scribner.

Fletcher, Sam, and Warren R. True. 2000. "New Ecuadorian Pipeline Plan Elicits Three Bids." *Oil & Gas Journal*, October 9: 58.

Flores, Saskia. 2006. "Ecoturismo: ¿Petróleo del Siglo XXI?" *Ecuador Terra Incognita* 43(Sept-Oct): 34–39.

Freire, Patricio Pazmino. 2002. "Illegitimate Debts, Debt Relief and Citizen Audits." In *Upheaval in the Back Yard: Illegitimate Debts and Human Rights: The Case of Ecuador-Norway*, 10–27. Centro de Derechos Económicos y Sociales, June.

Frente de Defensa de la Amazonia (FDA) and Instituto de Ciencias y Estudios Interdisciplinarios (ISIS). 2001. "Comentarios al 'acuerdo de compensación social' realizado entre el consorcio OCP-Techint y el concejo municipal de Lago Agrio" Unpublished document, prepared in Nueva Loja, Ecuador, December 2001.

Freudenberg, Nicholas. 1984. *Not in Our Backyards!: Community Action for Health and the Environment*. New York: Monthly Review Press.

Freudenburg, William R. 1997. "Contamination, Corrosion and the Social Order: An Overview." *Current Sociology* 45(3): 19–39.

———. 2008. "Thirty Years of Scholarship and Science on Environment-Society Relationships." *Organization & Environment* 21(4): 449–59.

Freudenburg, William R., and Robert Gramling. 1994. *Oil in Troubled Waters*. Albany: State University of New York Press.

Friedman, Thomas L. 2006. "The First Law of Petropolitics." *Foreign Policy* (May/June): 28–36.

Fundación Maquipucuna. 2001. "Analysis of the Compliance of the Oleoducto de Crudos Pesados (OCP) Project with World Bank Safeguard Policies or Good Practice Standards." Unpublished document, prepared December 2001, Quito, Ecuador.

Fundación Natura, Ambiente y Sociedad, CECIA, EcoCiencia, and Fundación Maquipucuna. 2001. "Observaciones a la evaluacion de impactos ambientales para el proyecto Oleoducto de Crudos Pesados" (Notes on the environmental impact assessment of the Heavy Crude Pipeline project). Unpublished document, May, Quito, Ecuador.

Futuro Latinoamericano. 2002. "Fondo para la Conservación (Documento Base): Antecedentes del proceso de creación del Fondo financiado por OCP." Unpublished report, August.

Galaskiewicz, Joseph. 1989. "Corporate Contributions to Charity: Nothing More Than a Marketing Strategy?" In *Philanthropic Giving: Studies in Varieties and Goals*, ed. Richard Magat, 246–60. New York: Oxford University Press.

Garcia-Johnson, Ronie. 2000. *Exporting Environmentalism: U.S. Multinational Chemical Corporations in Brazil and Mexico*. Cambridge, MA: MIT Press.

Garrett, Stephanie. 2004/2005. "Poppies and Mangoes: Women's Empowerment, Environmental Conservation, and Ecotourism in Costa Rica." *Women & Environments* (Fall/Winter): 23–25.

Gedicks, Al. 1993. *The New Resource Wars: Native and Environmental Struggles against Multinational Corporations*. Boston: South End Press.

———. 2001. *Resource Rebels: Native Challenges to Mining and Oil Corporations*. Cambridge, MA: South End Press.

Gereffi, Gary. 1994. "Capitalism, Development and Global Commodity Chains." In *Capitalism and Development*, ed. Leslie Sklair, 211–31. London: Routledge.

Gereffi, Gary, Ronie Garcia-Johnson, and Erika Sasser. 2001. "The NGO-Industrial Complex." *Foreign Policy* 125 (Jul-Aug): 56–65.

Gereffi, Gary, and Miguel Korzeniewicz. 1990. "Commodity Chains and Footwear Exports in the Semiperiphery." In *Semiperipheral States in the World-Economy*, ed. William G. Martin, 45–68. Westport, CT: Greenwood Press.

Gerlach, Allen. 2003. *Indians, Oil, and Politics: A Recent History of Ecuador*. Wilmington, DE: Scholarly Resources.

Gibbs, Lois. 2002. "Citizen Activism for Environmental Health: The Growth of a Powerful New Grassroots Health Movement." *Annals of the American Academy of Political and Social Science* 584(November): 97–109.

Gille, Zsuzsa. 2006. "Detached Flows or Grounded Place-Making Projects?" In *Governing Environmental Flows: Global Challenges to Social Theory*, eds. Gert Spaargaren, Arthur P. J. Mol, and Frederick H. Buttel, 137–56. Cambridge, MA: MIT Press.

Glaser, Barney, and Anselm Strauss. 1967. *The Discovery of Grounded Theory*. Chicago: Aldine.

Goldman, Michael. 2001. "Constructing an Environmental State: Eco-governmentality and Other Transnational Practices of a 'Green' World Bank." *Social Problems* 48(4): 499–523.

———. 2005. *Imperial Nature: The World Bank and Struggles for Social Justice in the Age of Globalization*. New Haven, CT: Yale University Press.

Goodell, Grace E. 1985. "Paternalism, Patronage, and Potlatch: The Dynamics of Giving and Being Given To." *Current Anthropology* 26(2): 247–66.

Goodland, R. J. A. 1987. "The World Bank's Wildlands Policy: A Major New Means of Financing Conservation." *Conservation Biology* 1(3): 210–13.

———. 1991. "The World Bank's Environmental Assessment Policy." *Hastings International and Comparative Law Review* 14(4): 811–30.

Goodland, Robert. 2002. "Independent Compliance Assessment of OCP with the World Bank's Environmental and Social Policies." Unpublished document, 9 September.

Gorman, Leo B. 2002. "Ecuadorian Shuar and Achuar Indians Say 'NO' to Burlington Oil Company." *The Touchstone* 12(3).

Gotham, Kevin Fox. 2007. "Critical Theory and Katrina: Disaster, Spectacle, and Immanent Critique." *City: An Analysis of Urban Trends, Culture, Theory, Policy, Action* 11(1): 81–99.

Gottlieb, Robert. 1993. *Forcing the Spring: The Transformation of the American Environmental Movement.* Washington, DC: Island Press.

Gould, Kenneth A. 1999. "Tactical Tourism: A Comparative Analysis of Rainforest Development in Ecuador and Belize." *Organization and Environment* 12(3): 245–62.

Gould, Kenneth A., David N. Pellow, and Allan Schnaiberg. 2008. *The Treadmill of Production: Injustice and Unsustainability in the Global Economy.* Boulder, CO: Paradigm.

Gould, Kenneth A., Allan Schnaiberg, and Adam S. Weinberg. 1996. *Local Environmental Struggles: Citizen Activism in the Treadmill of Production.* Cambridge: Cambridge University Press.

Gramsci, Antonio. 1971. *Selections from the Prison Notebooks of Antonio Gramsci.* New York: International Publisher.

Greathouse-Amador, Louisa M. 2005. "Tourism: A Facilitator of Social Awareness in an Indigenous Mexican Community?" *Review of Policy Research* 22(5): 709–20.

Grossman, P. 2000. "Corporate Interest and Trade Liberalization: The North American Free Trade Agreement and Environmental Protection." *Organization and Environment* 13(1): 61–85.

Gruskin, Sofia, Michael A. Grodin, George J. Annas, and Stephen P. Marks. 2005. *Perspectives on Health and Human Rights.* New York: Routledge.

Gu, Jing, John Humphrey, and Dirk Messner. 2008. "Global Governance and Developing Countries: The Implications of the Rise of China." *World Development* 36(2): 274–92.

Guerrón-Montero, C. 2005. "Marine Protected Areas in Panama: Grassroots Activism and Advocacy." *Human Organization* 64(4): 360–73.

Gugerty, Mary Kay, and Michael Kremer. 2008. "Outside Funding and the Dynamics of Outside Participation in Community Associations." *American Journal of Political Science* 52(3): 585–602.

Guha, Ramachandra. 1989. "Radical American Environmentalism and Wilderness Preservation: A Third World Critique." *Environmental Ethics* 11: 71–83.

Gunter, Valerie, and Steve Kroll-Smith. 2007. *Volatile Places: A Sociology of Communities and Environmental Controversies.* Thousand Oaks, CA: Pine Forge.

Guttal, Shalmali. 2008. "Client and Competitor: China and International Financial Institutions." In *China's New Role in Africa and the South,* eds. Dorothy-Grace Guerrero and Firoze Manji, 17–36. Nairobi: Fahamu and Focus on the Global South.

Habermas, Jurgen. 1981 (1984). *The Theory of Communicative Action.* Boston: Beacon Press.

Halpern, Adam, and France Winddance Twine. 2000. "Antiracist Activism in Ecuador: Black-Indian Community Alliances." *Race & Class* 42(2): 19–31.

Hampton, Mark P. 2003. "Entry Points for Local Tourism in Developing Countries: Evidence from Yogyakarta, Indonesia." *Geografiska Annaler,* Series B, Human Geography 85(2): 85–101.

Hannigan, John. 2006. *Environmental Sociology: A Social Constructionist Perspective,* 2nd ed. New York: Routledge.

Hanson, Stephanie. 2008. "China, Africa, and Oil." Council on Foreign Relations report. See http://www.cfr.org/publications/9557/, downloaded 12 November 2008.

Hari, Johann. 2010. "The Wrong Kind of Green: How Conservation Groups Are Bargaining Away Our Future." *The Nation,* March 22: 11–19.

Heaps, Toby A. A. 2003. "Tightrope Act: Will EnCana Face a Talisman-type Backlash for Their Presence in Ecuador?" http://www.corporateknights.ca/stories/ecuador.asp, downloaded July 28.

Held, David, Anthony McGrew, David Goldblatt, and Jonathan Perraton. 1999. *Global Transformations: Politics, Economics and Culture.* Stanford, CA: Stanford University Press.

Heller, Patrick. 1999. *The Labor of Development: Workers and the Transformation of Capitalism in Kerala, India.* Ithaca, NY: Cornell University Press.

———. 2000. "Social Capital and the Developmental State: Industrial Workers in Kerala." In *Kerala: The Development Experience,* ed. Govindan Parayil, 66–87. London: Zed Books.

Hill, Julia. 2001. *The Legacy of Luna: The Story of a Tree, a Woman and the Struggle to Save the Redwoods.* San Francisco: Harper.

Hofrichter, Richard (ed). 1993. *Toxic Struggles: The Theory and Practice of Environmental Justice.* Philadelphia: New Society.

Honey, Martha. 1999. *Ecotourism and Sustainable Development: Who Owns Paradise?* Washington, DC: Island Press.

Hopkins, Terence K., and Immanuel Wallerstein. 1986. "Commodity Chains in the World Economy Prior to 1800." *Review* 10(1): 157–70.

Howard-Grenville, Jennifer A. 2006. "Inside the 'Black Box': How Organizational Culture and Subcultures Inform Interpretations and Actions on Environmental Issues." *Organization & Environment* 19(1): 46–73.

Humphrey, Craig R., and Frederick R. Buttel. 1982. *Environment, Energy and Society.* Belmont, CA: Wadsworth Publishing Company.

Hurst, Cindy. 2006. "China's Oil Rush in Africa." Washington, DC: Institute for the Analysis of Global Security.

Hurtig, Anna-Karin, and Miguel San Sebastian. 2002. "Geographical Differences in Cancer Incidence in the Amazon Basin of Ecuador in Relation to Residence near Oil Fields." *International Journal of Epidemiology* 31: 1021–27.

———. 2004. "Incidence of Childhood Leukemia and Oil Exploitation in the Amazon Basin in Ecuador." *International Journal of Occupational and Environmental Health* 10(3): 245–50.

Iles, Alastair. 2004. "Mapping Environmental Justice in Technology Flows: Computer Waste Impacts in Asia." *Global Environmental Politics* 4(4): 76–107.

Imle, John F., Jr. 1999. "Multinationals and the New World of Energy Development: A Corporate Perspective." *Journal of International Affairs* 53 (1): 263–28.

Instituto de Epidemiología y Salud Comunitaria, and Manuel Amunárriz. 2000. *Informe Yana Curi: Impacto de la actividad petrolera en la salud de poblaciones rurales de la Amazonía ecuatoriana.* Coca, Ecuador: CICAME, Medicus Mundi Gipuzkoa.

Isaacs, Anita. 1993. *Military Rule and Transition in Ecuador, 1972–1992.* Pittsburgh, PA: University of Pittsburgh Press.

Israelson, David. 2008. "How the Oil Sands Got the Great Lakes Basin: Pipelines, Refineries and Emissions to Air and Water." Document prepared for the Program on Water Issues, Munk Centre for International Studies, University of Toronto. http://www.powi.ca/pdfs/events/2008-10-08-how_the_oil_sands.pdf.

Jacques, P. J., Riley. E. Dunlap, and M. Freeman. 2008. "The Organisation of Denial: Conservative Think Tanks and Environmental Scepticism." *Environmental Politics* 17(3): 349–85.

Janicke, Martin. 2006. "The Environmental State and Environmental Flows: The Need to Reinvent the Nation-State." In *Governing Environmental Flows: Global Challenges to Social Theory,* eds. Gert Spaargaren, Arthur P. J. Mol, and Frederick H. Buttel, 83–105. Cambridge, MA: MIT Press.

Jermyn, Leslie. n.d. "In Whose Interest? Canadian Interests and the OCP Crude Oil Pipeline in Ecuador." Dossier on the OCP pipeline in Ecuador: Essays and reports on a controversial pipeline to take crude oil from the Amazon to the Pacific Ocean, compiled for Global Aware Canada, http://www.globalaware.org/whoseinterest.htm, downloaded 4 March 2004. Material covered is until October 2002; publication date is approximately late 2002 or 2003.

Jochnick, Chris, and Paulina Garzón. 2006. "A Seat at the Table." In *Dispatches from Latin America: On the Frontlines against Neoliberalism,* eds. Vijay Prashad and Teo Ballvé, 183–97. Cambridge, MA: South End Press.

Johnson, Ethan. 2007. "Schooling, Blackness and National Identity in Esmeraldas, Ecuador." *Race Ethnicity and Education* 10(1): 47–70.

———. 2009. "Student and Teacher Negotiations of Racial Identify in an Afro-Ecuadorian Region." *International Journal of Qualitative Studies in Education* 22(5): 563–84.

Junger, Sebastian. 2007. "Enter China, the Giant." *Vanity Fair* (July): 126+.

Kaimowitz, David. 1996. "Social Pressure for Environmental Reform." In *Green Guerrillas,* ed. Helen Collinson, 20–32. Nottingham, England: Latin American Bureau.

Kalas, Peggy Rodgers. 2000. "The Implications of Jota v. Texaco and the Accountability of Transnational Corporations." *Pace International Law Review* (Spring).

Kane, Joe. 1995. *Savages.* New York: Knopf.

Karl, Terry Lynn. 1997. *The Paradox of Plenty: Oil Booms and Petro-States.* Berkeley: University of California Press.

———. 1999. "The Perils of the Petro-State: Reflections on the Paradox of Plenty." *Journal of International Affairs* 53(1): 31–48.

Kashi, Ed (photographer), and Michael Watts (ed.). 2008. *Curse of the Black Gold: 50 Years of Oil in the Niger Delta*. Brooklyn: powerHouse Books.

Keck, Margaret E., and Kathryn Sikkink. 1998. *Activists beyond Borders*. Ithaca, NY: Cornell University Press.

Khagram, Sanjeev. 2004. *Dams and Development: Transnational Struggles for Water and Power*. Ithaca, NY: Cornell University Press.

Kiefer, Chris, and Medea Benjamin. 2002. "Solidarity with the Third World: Building an International Environmental-Justice Movement." In *Toxic Struggles: The Theory and Practice of Environmental Justice*, 2nd ed., ed. Richard Hofrichter, 226–36. Salt Lake City: University of Utah Press.

Kimerling, Judith. 1991. *Amazon Crude*. Washington, DC: Natural Resources Defense Council.

———. 1995. "Rights, Responsibilities, and Realities: Environmental Protection Law in Ecuador's Amazon Oil Fields." *Southwestern Journal of Law and Trade in the Americas* 2: 293–384.

———. 2007. "Transnational Operations, Bi-National Injustice: ChevronTexaco and Indigenous Huaorani and Kichwa in the Amazon Rainforest of Ecuador." *American Indian Law Review* 31(2): 445–508.

Kingdon, J. 1984. *Agendas, Alternatives, and Public Policies*. Boston: Little, Brown.

Klawiter, Maren. 1999. "Racing for the Cure, Walking Women, and Toxic Touring: Mapping Cultures of Action within the Bay Area Terrain of Breast Cancer." *Social Problems* 46(1): 104–26.

Kloby, Jerry. 2004. *Inequality, Power and Development: Issues in Political Sociology*. Amherst, NY: Humanity Books.

Koenig, Kevin. 2007. "Ecuador's Oil Change: An Exporter's Historic Proposal." *Multinational Monitor* 29(4).

Kosek, Jake. 1996 (2004). "Purity and Pollution: Racial Degradation and Environmental Anxieties." In *Liberation Ecologies*, eds. Richard Peet and Michael Watts, 125–65. New York: Routledge.

Kozloff, Nikolas. 2008. *Revolution! South America and the Rise of the New Left*. New York: Palgrave Macmillan.

———. 2009a. "End of the Dollar Dictatorship? Hugo Chavez and Latin Leaders Hope to Bury the Greenback." *Huffington Post*, 23 October.

———. 2009b. "Ecuador's Rafael Correa: Copenhagen Climate Hero or Environmental Foe?" 14 December. http://news.mongabay.com/2009/1214-ecuador_kozloff.html, downloaded 20 January 2010.

Kozol, Jonathan. 1991. *Savage Inequalities: Children in America's Schools*. New York: Harper Perennial.

———. 2005. *The Shame of the Nation: The Restoration of Apartheid Schooling in America*. New York: Random House.

Kroll-Smith, J. Stephen, and Stephen Robert Couch. 1990. *The Real Disaster Is Above Ground: A Mine Fire and Social Conflict*. Lexington: The University Press of Kentucky.

Kroll-Smith, Steve, Phil Brown, and Valerie J. Gunter. 2000. *Illness and the Environment: A Reader in Contested Medicine*. New York: New York University Press.

Krugman, Paul. 2000. "Reckonings: Dollars and Desperation." *New York Times*, 19 January, A21.

Kurlantzick, Joshua. 2006. "China's Latin Leap Forward." *World Policy Journal* (Fall): 33–41.

Lafargue, Francois. 2006. "China's Strategies in Latin America." *Military Review* (May/June): 80–84.

Lan, Qing, Luoping Zhang, Guilan Li, Roel Vermeulen, Rona S. Weinberg, Mustafa Dosemeci, Stephen M. Rappaport, Min Shen, Blanche P. Alter, Yongji Wu, William Kopp, Suramya Waidyanatha, Charles Rabkin, Weihong Guo, Stephen Chanock, Richard B. Hayes, Martha Linet, Sungkyoon Kim, Songnian Yin, Nathaniel Rothman, and Martyn T. Smith. 2004. "Hematotoxicity in Workers Exposed to Low Levels of Benzene." *Science* 306: 1774–76.

Lancaster, John. 2007. "Next Stop, Squalor." *Smithsonian*, March: 96+.

Landívar, Natalia. 2004. "The Right to Adequate Food in Ecuador." Parallel report before the UN Committee on Economic, Social and Cultural Rights, produced/edited by FIAN International. Heidelberg, Germany: Food First Information and Action Network (FIAN) International.

Lee, Ching Kwan. 2007. *Against the Law: Labor Protests in China's Rustbelt and Sunbelt*. Berkeley: University of California Press.

LeFebvre, Henri. 2004. *Rhythmanalysis: Space, Time and Everyday Life*. Trans. Stuart Elden and Gerald Moore. London: Continuum.

Lennon, John, and Malcolm Foley. 2000. *Dark Tourism: The Attraction of Death and Disaster*. London: Continuum.

Lerner, Steve. 2005. *Diamond: A Struggle for Environmental Justice in Louisiana's Chemical Corridor*. Cambridge, MA: MIT Press.

Lewis, James B. 2001. "Self-Developed Rural Tourism: A Method of Sustainable Tourism Development." In *Tourism, Recreation and Sustainability: Linking Culture and the Environment*, eds. S. F. McCool and R. N. Moisey, 177–94. New York: CABI Publishing.

Lewis, Tammy L. 2000. "Transnational Conservation Movement Organizations: Shaping the Protected Area Systems of Less Developed Countries." *Mobilization: An International Journal* 5(1): 105–23.

———. 2003. "Environmental Aid: Driven by Recipient Need or Donor Interests?" *Social Science Quarterly* 84(1): 144–61.

Linton, April. 2005. "Partnering for Sustainability: Business-NGO Alliances in the Coffee Industry." *Development in Practice* 15(3/4): 600–614.

Lobao, Linda M., and Lawrence A. Brown. 1998. "Development Context, Regional Differences among Young Women, and Fertility: The Ecuadorean Amazon." *Social Forces* 76(3): 819–49.

Los Angeles Times. 2004. "Attorney General Targets Occidental," August 25.

Lou, Ying, and Winnie Zhu. 2007. "PetroChina Feels Sudan Heat as Fidelity Sells Shares." *International Herald Tribune*, 16 May. Bloomberg News.

Lucas, Kintto. 2002. "The North in Flames with Strikes and Repression." IPS news agency. Quito, 28 February.

Lynch, Gerald. 1987. *Roughnecks, Drillers, and Tool Pushers: Thirty-three Years in the Oil Fields*. Austin: University of Texas Press.

MacDonald, Christine. 2008. *Green, Inc: An Environmental Insider Reveals How a Good Cause Has Gone Bad*. Guilford, CT: Lyons Press.

Macleod, Donald V. L. 2004. *Tourism, Globalisation and Cultural Change: An Island Community Perspective*. Clevedon, England: Channel View Publications.

Mahony, Rhona. 1992. "Debt-for-Nature Swaps: Who Really Benefits?" *The Ecologist* 22(3): 97+.

Manby, Bronwen. 1999. "The Role and Responsibility of Oil Multinationals in Nigeria." *Journal of International Affairs* 53 (1): 281–301.

Mandle, Jay R. 2000. "The Student Anti-Sweatshop Movement: Limits and Potential." *Annals of the American Academy of Political and Social Sciences* 570: 92–103.

Manji, Firoze, and Stephen Marks (eds.). 2007. *African Perspectives on China in Africa*. Cape Town, South Africa: Fahamu.

Markowitz, Gerald, and David Rosner. 2002. *Deceit and Denial: The Deadly Politics of Industrial Pollution*. Berkeley: University of California Press.

Marsden, William. 2008. *Stupid to the Last Drop: How Alberta Is Bringing Environmental Armageddon to Canada*. Toronto: Vintage Canada.

Marshall, Catherine, and Gretchen B. Rossman. 1999. *Designing Qualitative Research*. Thousand Oaks, CA: Sage.

Mastny, Lisa. 2002. "Ecotourist Trap." *Foreign Policy* 133: 94–96.

Mayo, Marjorie. 2005. *Global Citizens: Social Movements and the Challenge of Globalization*. Toronto: Canadian Scholars' Press.

McAdam, Doug. 1988. *Freedom Summer*. New York: Oxford University Press.

———. 1998. "On the International Origins of Domestic Political Opportunities." In *Social Movements and American Political Institutions*, eds. Anee N.Costain and Andrew S. McFarland, 251–67. Lanham, MD: Rowman & Littlefield.

McAdam, Doug, John D. McCarthy, and Mayer N. Zald (eds.). 1996. *Comparative Perspectives on Social Movements: Political Opportunities, Mobilizing Structures, and Cultural Framings*. New York: Cambridge University Press.

McAteer, Emily, and Simone Pulver. 2009. "The Corporate Boomerang: Shareholder Transnational Advocacy Networks Targeting Oil Companies in the Ecuadorian Amazon." *Global Environmental Politics* 9(1): 1–30.

McCarthy, John D., and Mayer N. Zald. 1977. "Resource Mobilization and Social Movements: A Partial Theory." *American Journal of Sociology* 82(6): 1212–41.

McClearn, Matthew. 2003. "Down the Tube." *Canadian Business*, 17 March, 33.

McDonald, David A. 2005. "Environmental Racism and Neoliberal Disorder in South Africa." In *The Quest for Environmental Justice: Human Rights and the Politics of Pollution*, ed. Robert D. Bullard, 255–78. San Francisco: Sierra Club Books.

McElroy, Jerome L. 2003. "Tourism Development in Small Islands across the World." *Geografiska Annaler*, Series B, Human Geography 85(4): 231–42.

McKibben, Bill. 2010. *Eaarth*. New York: Henry Holt.

McLaren, Deborah. 2003. *Rethinking Tourism and Ecotravel*, 2nd ed. Bloomfield, CT: Kumarian Press.

Meintjes, Garth. 2000. "An International Human Rights Perspective on Corporate Codes." In *Global Codes of Conduct: An Idea Whose Time Has Come*, ed. Oliver F. Williams, 83–99. Notre Dame, IN: University of Notre Dame Press.

Memmi, Albert. 1968. *Dominated Man*. New York: Viking Penguin.

Meyer, Carrie A. 1997. "Public-Nonprofit Partnerships and North-South Green Finance." *Journal of Environment and Development* 6(2): 123–47.

Miller, Marian A. L. 2006. "Paradise Sold, Paradise Lost: Jamaica's Environment and Culture in the Tourism Marketplace." In *Beyond Sun and Sand: Caribbean Environmentalisms*, eds. S. L. Baver and B. D. Lynch, 35–43. New Brunswick, NJ: Rutgers University Press.

Mindo Working Group. 2001. "Rapid Ecological Assessment of the Proposed Northern Route of the Heavy Crude Pipeline." Unpublished document, prepared 10 April 2001, Quito, Ecuador.

Minorities at Risk Project. 2006. "Assessment for Blacks in Ecuador." Center for International Development and Conflict Management. 31 December. http://www.cidcm.umd.edu/mar/assessment.asp?groupId=13001, downloaded 30 November 2010.

Mitchell, Ross E. 2001. "Community Perspectives in Sustainable Tourism: Lessons from Peru." In *Tourism, Recreation and Sustainability: Linking Culture and the Environment*, eds. S. F. McCool and R. N. Moisey, 137–62. New York: CABI Publishing.

Mol, Arthur. 2006. "Environment and Modernity in Transitional China: Frontiers of Ecological Modernization." *Development and Change* 37(1): 29–56.

Mol, Arthur P. J., and Gert Spaargaren. 2003. "Towards a Sociology of Environmental Flows: A New Agenda for 21st Century Environmental Sociology." Paper presented for the International Conference on Governing Environmental Flows, June 13–14, Wageningen, The Netherlands.

Mol, Arthur P. J., and Sander Van den Burg. 2004. "Local Governance of Environmental Flows in Global Modernity." *Local Environment* 9(4): 317–24.

Mommer, Bernard. 1994. "The Political Role of National Oil Companies in Exporting Countries: The Venezuelan Case." Working paper number 18, Oxford Institute for Energy Studies, September.

Monz, Christopher A., and Paul Twardock. 2004. "Campsite Impacts in Prince William Sound, Alaska, USA." In *Environmental Impacts of Ecotourism*, ed. R. Buckley, 309–16. Oxfordshire, UK: CABI Publishing.

Moreira, María Elena. 2001. *Derechos Humanos en la Nueva Constitución Ecuatoriana*. Quito, Ecuador: Ediciones Abya-Yala.

Morello-Frosch, Rachel, Manuel Pastor Jr., and James Sadd. 2002. "Integrating Environmental Justice and the Precautionary Principle in Research and Policy Making: The Case of Ambient Air Toxics Exposures and Health Risks among Schoolchildren in Los Angeles." *Annals of the American Academy of Political and Social Science* 584(November): 47–68.

Morris, Ruth. 2004. "Refining the Search for Crude." *Nature Conservancy Magazine* 54(3): 34–43.

Moss, Nicholas. 2000. "Ecuador Mulls Pipeline Offers." *Financial Times*, 4 September, 2.

Munt, Ian. 1994. "Eco-tourism or Ego-tourism?" *Race & Class* 36(1): 49–60.

Murphy, Gillian. 2005. "Coalitions and the Development of the Global Environmental Movement: A Double-Edged Sword." *Mobilization* 10(2): 235–50.

Najam, Adil. 2005. "Why Environmental Politics Looks Different from the South." In *Handbook of Global Environmental Politics*, ed. Peter Dauvergne, 111–26. Cheltenham, UK: Edward Elgar.

Nepal, Sanjay K. 2002. "Mountain Ecotourism and Sustainable Development: Ecology, Economics, and Ethics." *Mountain Research and Development* 22(2): 104–9.

Newell, Peter. 2005. "Race, Class and the Global Politics of Environmental Inequality." *Global Environmental Politics* 5(3): 70–94.

Newsome, Justine. 1997. "Ecuador Call for Bids to Build Pipeline." *Financial Times*, 4 February: 4.

Nikiforuk, Andrew. 2009. *Tar Sands: Dirty Oil and the Future of a Continent*. Vancouver: Greystone Books.

Nugent, Stephen. 1996. "Amazonian Indians and peasants: coping in the age of development." In *Green Guerrillas*, ed. H. Collinson, 84–92. London: Latin America Bureau.

Obach, Brian K. 2004. *Labor and the Environmental Movement: The Quest for Common Ground*. Cambridge MA: MIT Press.

OCP. 2005a. "Proyectos y Apoyos para la Zona de Influencia del OCP en la Fase de Construccion." Prepared by Eduadro Terán S., 24 May, for OCP. Unpublished report.

———. 2005b. "Relaciones Comunitarias—Proyectos y Apoyos en la Ruta OCP. Presupuesto y Ejecucion Ano 2004 y 2005 (Operaciones)." Prepared by Eduadro Terán S., 6 May, for OCP.

O'Donnell, Guillermo, and Philippe C. Schmitter. 1986. *Transitions from Authoritarian Rule: Tentative Conclusions about Uncertain Democracies*. Baltimore: Johns Hopkins University Press.

O'Faircheallaigh, Ciaran, and Tony Corbett. 2005. "Indigenous Participation in Environmental Management of Mining Projects: The Role of Negotiated Agreements." *Environmental Politics* 14(5): 629–47.

Ohler, Shawn, and Vicki Hall. 2000. *100 Days in the Jungle*. Toronto: Key Porter Books.

Oilwatch Technical Team. 2007. "ITT Project Option 1: Conserving Crude Oil in the Subsoil." Unpublished report, 12 April. http://www.oilwatch.org.

Okonta, Ike, and Oronto Douglas. 2001. *Where Vultures Feast: Shell, Human Rights, and Oil in the Niger Delta*. San Francisco: Sierra Club Books.

Olien, Diana Davids, and Roger M. Olien. 2002. *Oil in Texas: The Gusher Age, 1895–1945*. Austin: University of Texas Press.

Olien, Roger M., and Diana Davids Olien. 1982. *Oil Booms: Social Change in Five Texas Towns*. Lincoln: University of Nebraska Press.

O'Rourke, Dara. 2004. *Community-Driven Regulation: Balancing Development and the Environmental in Vietnam*. Cambridge, MA: MIT Press.

O'Rourke, Dara, and Sarah Connolly. 2003. "Just Oil? The Distribution of Environmental and Social Impacts of Oil Production and Consumption." *Annual Review of Environment and Resources* 28: 587–617.

Oxfam America. 2001. "Extractive Sectors and the Poor." *An Oxfam American Report*, prepared by Michael Ross.

Pallares, Amalia. 2002. *From Peasant Struggles to Indian Resistance: The Ecuadorian Andes in the Late Twentieth Century*. Norman: University of Oklahoma Press.

Pastor, Manuel, Jr., Jim Sadd, and John Hipp. 2001. "Which Came First? Toxic Facilities, Minority-Move-in, and Environmental Justice." *Journal of Urban Affairs* 23(1): 1–21.

Pattullo, Polly. 2005. *Last Resorts: The Cost of Tourism in the Caribbean*. London: Latin American Bureau.

Peet, Richard, and Elaine Hartwick. 1999. *Theories of Development*. New York: Guilford Press.

Peet, Richard, and Michael Watts (eds.). 2004. *Liberation Ecologies: Environment, Development, Social Movements*, 2nd ed. New York: Routledge.

Pellow, David N. 2007. *Resisting Global Toxics: Transnational Movements for Environmental Justice*. Cambridge, MA: MIT Press.

Pena, Devon, and María Mondragon-Valdéz. 1998. "The 'Brown' and the 'Green' Revisited: Chicanos and Environmental Politics in the Upper Rio Grande." In *The Struggle for Ecological Democracy: Environmental Justice Movements in the United States*, ed. Daniel Faber, 312–48. New York: Guilford Press.

Perkins, John. 2006. *Confessions of an Economic Hit Man*. New York: Plume.

Perreault, Thomas. 1996. "Nature Preserves and Community Conflict: A Case Study in Highland Ecuador." *Mountain Research and Development* 16(2): 167–75.

Picou, J. Steven, Duane A. Gill, and Maurie J. Cohen (eds.). 1997. *The Exxon Valdez Disaster: Readings on a Modern Social Problem*. Dubuque, IA: Kendall/Hunt Publishing.

Principles of Environmental Justice. 1991. Adopted at the People of Color Conference on Environmental Justice, Washington, DC. http://www.ejrc.cau.edu/princej.html.

Prosser, Robert F. 1992. "The Ethics of Tourism." In *The Environment in Question: Ethics and Global Issues*, eds. David E. Cooper and Joy A. Palmer, 37–50. New York: Routledge.

Pulido, Laura. 1996. *Environmentalism and Economic Justice: Two Chicano Struggles in the Southwest*. Tucson: University of Arizona Press.

Pulver, Simone. 2007. "Importing Environmentalism: Explaining Petroleos Mexicanods' Cooperative Climate Policy." *Studies in Comparative International Development* 42: 233–55.

Purchase, Eric. 1999. *Out of Nowhere: Disaster and Tourism in the White Mountains*. Baltimore: Johns Hopkins University Press.

Quiroga, Diego. 2003. "The Devil and Development in Esmeraldas: Cosmology as a System of Critical Thought." In *Millennial Ecuador*, ed. Norman E. Whitten, Jr., 154–83.

Ragin, Charles C. 1994. *Constructing Social Research: The Unity and Diversity of Method*. Thousand Oaks, CA: Pine Forge Press.

Rahier, Jean Muteba. 1999. "Body Politics in Black and White: Senoras, Mujeres, Blanqueamineto and Miss Esmeraldas 1997–1998, Ecuador." *Women and Performance: A Journal of Feminist Theory* 11(1): 103–20.

Ray, Raka. 1999. *Fields of Protest: Women's Movements in India*. Minneapolis: University of Minnesota Press.

Redford, Kent H., and Allyn Maclean Stearman. 1993. "Forest-Dwelling Native Amazonians and the Conservation of Biodiversity: Interests in Common or in Collision?" *Conservation Biology* 7(2): 248–55.

Reid, Jan. 1995. "Crude Awakening." *Texas Monthly* (November): 140+.

Reimann, Kim D. 2002. "Building Networks from the Outside in: Japanese NGOs and the Kyoto Climate Change Conference." In *Globalization and Resistance*, eds. Jackie Smith and Hank Johnston, 173–87. Lanham, MD: Rowman & Littlefield.

Renner, Michael. 2002. "The Anatomy of Resource Wars." *Worldwatch Paper 162*.

Reuters. 2005a. "Best Place to Live in 2005? Norway," 26 August.

———. 2005b. "China Oil Firm Buys Encana Assets in Ecuador." *China Daily*, 15 September.

Revolutionary Democracy. 1999. "Ecuador: The Assassination of the Deputy Jaime Hurtado." 5(1), http://www.revolutionarydemocracy.org/, downloaded 25 September 2009.

Rich, Bruce. 1994. *Mortgaging the Earth: The World Bank, Environmental Impoverishment, and the Crisis of Development*. Boston: Beacon Press.

Ridgely, Robert S., and Paul J. Greenfield. 2001. *The Birds of Ecuador Field Guide*. Ithaca, NY: Cornell University Press.

Roberts, J. Timmons, and Bradley C. Parks. 2007. *A Climate of Injustice: Global Inequality, North-South Politics, and Climate Policy*. Cambridge, MA: MIT Press.

Roberts, J. Timmons, and Nikki Demetria Thanos. 2003. *Trouble in Paradise: Globalization and Environmental Crises in Latin America*. New York: Routledge.

Roberts, J. Timmons, and Melissa M. Toffolon-Weiss. 2001. *Chronicles from the Environmental Justice Frontline*. Cambridge: Cambridge University Press.

Robin, Marie-Monique. 2010. *The World According to Monsanto: Pollution, Corruption, and the Control of Our Food Supply*. New York: New Press.

Rocheleau, Dianne, Barbara Thomas-Slayter, and Esther Wangari. 1996. *Feminist Political Ecology: Global Issues and Local Experience*. New York: Routledge.

Rodin, Mari, Michael Downs, John Petterson, and John Russell. 1997. "Community Impacts of the Exxon Valdez Oil Spill." In *The Exxon Valdez Disaster: Readings on a Modern Social Problem*, eds. J. Steven Picou, Duane A. Gill, and Maurie J. Cohen, 193–210. Dubuque, IA: Kendall/Hunt.

Rodney, Walter. 1972. *How Europe Underdeveloped Africa*. Washington, DC: Howard University Press.

Rodrigues, Maria Guadalupe Moog. 2004. *Global Environmentalism and Local Politics: Transnational Advocacy Networks in Brazil, Ecuador, and India*. Albany: State University of New York Press.

Rogge, Malcolm J. 2001. "Towards Transnational Corporate Accountability in the Global Economy: Challenging the Doctrine of *Forum Non Conveniens* in *In Re*: Union Carbide, Alfaro, Sequihua, and Aguinda." *Texas International Law Journal* 26: 299–317.

Ross, Michael L. 2001. "Does Oil Hinder Democracy?" *World Politics* 53(3): 325–61.

Rothenberg, Paul S. 2005. *Beyond Borders: Thinking Critically about Global Issues*. New York: Worth Publishers.

Rowell, Andrew. 1996. *Green Backlash: Global Subversion of the Environmental Movement*. New York: Routledge.

Royce, Edward. 2009. *Poverty & Power: The Problem of Structural Inequality*. Lanham, MD: Rowman & Littlefield.

Rubin, Herbert J., and Irene S. Rubin. 1995. *Qualitative Interviewing: The Art of Hearing Data*. Thousand Oaks, CA: Sage.

Rudel, Thomas K. 2000. "Organizing for Sustainable Development: Conservation Organizations and the Struggle to Protect Tropical Rain Forests in Esmeraldas, Ecuador." *Ambio* 29(2): 78–82.

———. 2009. "How Do People Transform Landscapes? A Sociological Perspective on Suburban Sprawl and Tropical Deforestation." *American Journal of Sociology* 115(1): 129–54.

Rundall, Patti. 2000. "Commentary: The Perils of Partnership—An NGO Perspective." *Addiction* 95(10): 1501–04.

Sampson, Anthony. 1975. *The Seven Sisters: The Great Oil Companies and the World They Shaped*. New York: Bantam Books.

San Sebastian, M., B. Armstrong, J. A. Cordoba, and C. Stephens. 2001. "Exposures and Cancer Incidence near Oil Fields in the Amazon Basin in Ecuador." *Occupational and Environmental Medicine* 58: 517–22.

San Sebastian, M., B. Armstrong, and C. Stephens. 2002. "Outcomes of Pregnancy among Women Living in the Proximity of Oil Fields in the Amazon Basin in Ecuador." *International Journal of Occupational and Environmental Health*, 8(4): 312–19.

Sawyer, Suzana. 2004. *Crude Chronicles: Indigenous Politics, Multinational Oil, and Neoliberalism in Ecuador*. Durham, NC: Duke University Press.

Scheyvens, Regina. 2001. "Poverty Tourism." *Development Bulletin* 55 (July): 18–21.

Schlosberg, David. 2004. "Reconceiving Environmental Justice: Global Movements and Political Theories." *Environmental Politics* 13(3): 517–40.

Schluter, Achim, Peter Phillimore, and Suzanne Moffatt. 2004. "Enough Is Enough: Emerging 'Self-Help' Environmentalism in a Petrochemical Town." *Environmental Politics* 13(4): 715–33.

Schnaiberg, Allan. 1980. *The Environment: From Surplus to Scarcity*. New York: Oxford University Press.

Schodt, David W. 1987. *Ecuador: An Andean Enigma*. Boulder, CO: Westview Press.

Scott, James C. 1998. *Seeing Like a State: How Certain Schemes to Improve the Human Condition Have Failed*. New Haven, CT: Yale University Press.

Seidman, Gay W. 2005. "Monitoring Multinationals: Corporate Codes of Conduct." In *Coalitions across Borders: Transnational Protest and the Neoliberal Order*, eds. Joe Bandy and Jackie Smith, 163–83. Lanham, MD: Rowman & Littlefield.

Sen, Amartya. 1999. *Development as Freedom*. New York: Anchor Books.

Shellenberger, Michael, and Ted Nordhaus. 2005. "The Death of Environmentalism: Global Warming Politics in a Post-Environmental World." *Social Policy* 35(Spring): 19–30.

Shirk, Susan L. 2007. *China: Fragile Superpower*. New York: Oxford University Press.

Shiva, Vandana. 1998. "The Greening of Global Reach." In *The Geopolitics Reader*, eds. G. Ó. Tuathail, S. Dalby, and P. Routledge, 231–35. London: Routledge.

———. 2000. "Ecological Balance in an Era of Globalization." In *Principled World Politics*, eds. Paul Wapner and Lester Edwin J. Ruiz, 130–49. New York: Rowman & Littlefield.

Shwom, Rachael. 2009. "Strengthening Sociological Perspectives on Organizations and the Environment." *Organization & Environment* 22(3): 271–92.

Siemiatycki, Jack. 2002. "Commentary: Epidemiology on the Side of the Angels." *International Journal of Epidemiology* 31: 1027–29.

Silver, Beverly J. 2003. *Forces of Labor: Workers' Movements and Globalization since 1870*. New York: Cambridge University Press.

Smil, Vaclav. 2004. *China's Past, China's Future: Energy, Food, Environment*. New York: Routledge-Curzon.

Smith, Jackie. 2005. "Building Bridges or Building Walls? Explaining Regionalization among Transnational Social Movement Organizations." *Mobilization* 10(2): 251–69.

———. 2008. *Social Movements for Global Democracy*. Baltimore: Johns Hopkins University Press.

Smith, Jackie, and Joe Bandy. 2005. "Introduction: Cooperation and Conflict in Transnational Protest." In *Coalitions across Borders: Transnational Protest and the Neoliberal Order*, eds. Joe Bandy and Jackie Smith, 1–17. Lanham, MD: Rowman & Littlefield.

Smith, Jackie, Charles Chatfield, and Ron Pagnucco. 1997. *Transnational Social Movements and Global Politics: Solidarity beyond the State*. Syracuse, NY: Syracuse University Press.

Smith, Jackie, and Hank Johnston (eds.). 2002. *Globalization and Resistance: Transnational Dimensions of Social Movements*. Lanham, MD: Rowman & Littlefield.

Smith, Jackie, Marina Karides, Marc Becker, Dorval Brunelle, Christopher Chase-Dunn, Donatella della Porta, Rosalba Icaza Garza, Jeffrey S. Juris, Lorenzo Mosca, Ellen Reese, Peter (Jay) Smith, and Rolando Vázquez. 2008. *Global Democracy and the World Social Forums*. Boulder, CO: Paradigm.

Smith, Randy. 1996. *Crisis under the Canopy: Tourism and Other Problems Facing the Present Day Huaorani*. Quito, Ecuador: Abya-Yala.

Smithsonian Institution. 2001. "Reporte de la evaluacion del estudio de impacto amibental vinculado al tema biodiversidad para la construcción y operación del oleoducto de crudos pesados." Prepared by the Monitoring and Assessment of Biodiversity Program (MAB) of the Smithsonian Institution, June.

Snater, Fenna. 2002. "Stakeholder Perception Assessment: An Assessment of the Perception of Local Stakeholders on OCP's Impact in the Mindo-Cuenca Alta del Rio Guayllabamba Region." Unpublished report.

Snow, David A., E. Burke Rochford Jr., Steven K. Worden, and Robert D. Benford. 1986. "Frame Alignment Processes, Micromobilization, and Movement Participation." *American Sociological Review* 51(4): 464–81.

Spaargaren, Gert, Arthur P. J. Mol, and Hans Bruyninckx. 2006. "Introduction: Governing Environmental Flows in Global Modernity." In *Governing Environmental Flows: Global Challenges to Social Theory*, eds. Gert Spaargaren, Arthur P. J. Mol, and Frederick H. Buttel, 1–36. Cambridge, MA: MIT Press.

Spaargaren, Gert, Arthur P. J. Mol, and Frederick H. Buttel (eds.). 2006. *Governing Environmental Flows: Global Challenges to Social Theory*. Cambridge, MA: MIT Press.

Spencer, Starr, Carla Bass, Ronald Buchanan, Mary Powers, and Jens Gould. 2007. "Latin American Oil Nationalists May Turn Pragmatic." *Platts Oilgram News*, 85(4) [5 Jan.]: 1.

Speth, James Gustave. 2008. *The Bridge at the Edge of the World: Capitalism, the Environment, and Crossing from Crisis to Sustainability*. New Haven, CT: Yale University Press.

Sreekumar, T. T., and Govindan Parayil. 2002. "Contentions and Contradictions of Tourism as Development Option: The Case of Kerala, India." *Third World Quarterly* 23(3): 529–48.

Standlea, David M. 2006. *Oil, Globalization, and the War for the Arctic Refuge*. Albany: State University of New York Press.

Steingraber, Sandra. 1997. *Living Downstream*. New York: Vintage Books.

Stewart, Julie. 2004. "When Local Troubles Become Transnational: The Transformation of a Guatemalan Indigenous Rights Movement." *Mobilization* 9(3): 259–78.

Stokstad, Erik. 2004. "Factory Study Shows Low Levels of Benzene Reduce Blood Cell Counts." *Science* 306: 1665.

Stone & Webster Consultants. 2002. "The OCP Pipeline Project Independent Technical Review Public Domain Report." Prepared for The Lenders to the OCP Pipeline Project, 19 April.

Stronza, Amanda. 2001. "Anthropology of Tourism: Forging New Ground for Ecotourism and Other Alternatives." *Annual Review of Anthropology* 30: 261–83.

Sturken, Marita. 2007. *Tourists of History: Memory, Kitsch, and Consumerism from Oklahoma City to Ground Zero*. Durham, NC: Duke University Press.

Subramaniam, Mangala, Manjusha Gupte, and Debarashmi Mitra. 2003. "Local to Global: Transnational Networks and Indian Women's Grassroots Organizing." *Mobilization: An International Journal* 8(2): 335–52.

Sundberg, Juanita. 2008. "Tracing Race: Mapping Environmental Formations in Environmental Justice Research in Latin America." In *Environmental Justice in Latin America: Problems, Promise, and Practice*, ed. David V. Carruthers, 25–47. Cambridge, MA: MIT Press.

Szasz, Andrew. 1994. *Ecopopulism: Toxic Waste and the Movement for Environmental Justice*. Minneapolis: University of Minnesota Press.

Tarrow, Sidney. 1994. *Power in Movement: Social Movements, Collective Action, and Politics*. New York: Cambridge University Press.

———. 1998. "Fishnets, Internets, and Catnets: Globalization and Transnational Collective Action." In *Challenging Authority: The Historical Study of Contentious Politics*, eds. Michael P. Hanagan, Leslie Page Moch and Wayne Brake, 228–48. Minneapolis: University of Minnesota Press.

———. 1999. "Beyond Globalization: Why Creating Transnational Social Movements Is So Hard and When Is It Most Likely to Happen?" Paper presented to the Columbia University Workshop on Contentious Politics, 21 September.

———. 2001. "Transnational Politics: Contention and Institutions in International Politics." *Annual Review of Political Science* 4: 1–20.

———. 2002. "From Lumping to Splitting: Specifying Globalization and Resistance." In *Globalization and Resistance*, eds. Jackie Smith and Hank Johnston, 229–49. Lanham, MD: Rowman & Littlefield.

———. 2005a. *The New Transnational Activism*. New York: Cambridge University Press.

———. 2005b. "The Dualities of Transnational Contention: 'Two Activist Solitudes' or a New World Altogether?" *Mobilization: An International Journal* 10(1): 53–72.

Tellkamp, Markus P., Tatiana Santander, Irina Munoz, Fabián J. Cupuerán, Alexandra Onofa, and Fabián R. Granda. 2004. "Preliminary Results about the Short Term Impacts of the Construction of the Crude Oil Pipeline in Northwest Pichincha." *Lyonia: A Journal of Ecology and Application* 6(2): 97–125.

Tenenbaum, David J. 2000. "Trampling Paradise: Dream Vacation—Environmental Nightmare?" *Environmental Health Perspectives* 108(5): A214–A219.

Tidwell, Mike. 1996. *Amazon Stranger: A Rainforest Chief Battles Big Oil*. Guilford, CT: Lyons Press.

Tilly, Charles. 1998. *Durable Inequality*. Berkeley: University of California Press.

Tobias, Dave, and Robert Mendelsohn. 1991. "Valuing Ecotourism in a Tropical Rain-Forest Reserve." *Ambio* 20(2): 91–93.

Toledo, Alex Rivas, and Rommel Lara Ponce 2001. *Conservación y Petróleo en la Amazonia Ecuatoriana: Un acercamiento al caso Huaorani*. Quito, Ecuador: EcoCiencia/Abya-Yala.

Torres, Rosa María. 2005. "Illiteracy and Literacy Education in Ecuador: Options for Policy and Practice." Unpublished report prepared for UNESCO for inclusion in the 2006 Education for All Global Monitoring Report.

Treakle, Kay. 1998. "Ecuador: Structural Adjustment and Indigenous and Environmentalist Resistance." In *The Struggle for Accountability: The World Bank, NGOs, and Grassroots Movements*, eds. Jonathan A. Fox and L. David Brown, 219–64. Cambridge, MA: MIT Press.

True, Warren. 2001. "Environmentalism Transported." *Oil & Gas Journal*, 26 November, 19.

Turner, Terisa E., and Craig S. Benjamin. 1995. "Not in Our Nature: The Male Deal and Corporate Solutions to the Debt-Nature Crisis." *Review* 18(2): 209–58.

USAID. 2006. "Nature-Oriented Tourism in Ecuador: An Assessment Applying the Value Chain and Nature, Wealth and Power Frameworks." Washington, D.C.: United States Agency for International Development.

U.S. Energy. 2003. *Petroleum Supply Annual, Vol I*. U.S. Energy Information Administration.

Umlas, Elizabeth. 2009. "Corporate Human Rights Reporting: An Analysis of Current Trends." Report commissioned by Realizing Rights: The Ethical Globalization Initiative, The U.N. Global Compact and Global Reporting Initiative.

United Nations. 2002. *United Nations Volunteer Annual Report 2002.* http://www.unv.org.
———. 2004. "Committee on Economic, Social and Cultural Rights Reviews Second Periodic Report of Ecuador." Unpublished report, prepared 6 May.
———. 2010. "Human Rights Council Discusses Racism, Racial Discrimination, Xenophobia and Related Forms of Intolerance." Office of the High Commissioner of Human Rights, 23 March. http://www2.ohchr.org/english/, downloaded 30 November 2010.
Useem, Michael. 1984. *The Inner Circle: Large Corporations and the Rise of Business Political Activity in the U.S. and U.K.* New York: Oxford University Press.
Valaoras, Georgia, Kostas Pistolas, and Helen Yombre Sotiropoulou. 2002. "Ecotourism Revives Rural Communities: The Case of the Dadia Forest Reserve, Evros, Greece." *Mountain Research and Development* 22(2): 123–27.
Valdivia, Gabriela. 2008. "Governing Relations between People and Things: Citizenship, Territory, and the Political Economy of Petroleum in Ecuador." *Political Geography* 27: 456–77.
Van Gelder, Jan Willem. 2003. "The Financing of the OCP Pipeline in Ecuador." Research paper prepared for Urgewald and Environmental Defense, January, The Netherlands.
Vaughan, David. 2000. "Tourism and Biodiversity: A Convergence of Interests?" *International Affairs* 76(2): 283–97.
Vickers, William T. 2003. "The Modern Political Transformation of the Secoya." In *Millennial Ecuador: Critical Essays on Cultural Transformations and Social Dynamics,* ed. Norman E. Whitten, Jr., 46–74. Iowa City: University of Iowa Press.
Viorst, Tony. 2004. "Justice/Karma in Ecuador? Tony Viorst Heads to South America." *The Docket,* September. http://www.denbar.org.
Vivanco, Luis A. 2001. "Spectacular Quetzals, Ecotourism, and Environmental Futures in Monte Verde, Costa Rica." *Ethnology* 40(2): 79–92.
Von Hagen, Victor Wolfgang. 1940. *Ecuador the Unknown: Two and a Half Years' Travels in the Republic of Ecuador and Galapagos Islands.* New York: Oxford University Press.
Walker, David, John Paul Jones III, Susan M. Roberts, and Oliver R. Frohling. 2007. "When Participation Meets Empowerment: The WWF and the Politics of Invitation in the Chimalapas, Mexico." *Annals of the Association of American Geographers* 97(2): 423–44.
Walsh, Diana Chapman. 1987. *Corporate Physicians: Between Medicine and Management.* New Haven, CT: Yale University Press.
Walton, S. 2007. "Site the Mine in Our Backyard! Discursive Strategies of Community Stakeholders in an Environmental Conflict in New Zealand." *Organization & Environment* 20(2): 177–203.
Washburn, Mark. 2005. "New Orleans Celebrates Most Ghosts of Disasters." *Anchorage Daily News,* 31 October, A3. Wire source from Knight Ridder Newspapers.
Watkins, Eric. 2007. "Ecuador Taking Measures to Increase Oil Production." *Oil & Gas Journal,* 16 July, 31.
Watts, Michael. 1996. "Violent Environments: Petroleum Conflict and the Political Ecology of Rule in the Niger Delta, Nigeria." In *Liberation Ecologies,* eds. R. Peet and M. Watts, 273–98. New York: Routledge.
———. 2004. "Violent Environments: Petroleum Conflict and the Political Ecology of Rule in the Niger Delta, Nigeria." In *Liberation Ecologies,* eds. Richard Peet and Michael Watts, 273–98. New York: Routledge.
Weemaels, Nathalie. 2002. "Environmental Impacts of OCP Pipeline Construction." "Impactos de la Construcción del Oleoducto de Crudos Pesados." Unpublished report prepared for Accion Ecologica, May, Quito, Ecuador.
West, Paige, and James G. Carrier. 2004. "Ecotourism and Authenticity: Getting Away from It All?" *Current Anthropology* 45(4): 483–98.
Westra, Laura, and Bill E. Lawson (eds.). 2001. *Faces of Environmental Racism: Confronting Issues of Global Justice.* Lanham, MD: Rowman & Littlefield.
Whitten, Norman E., Jr. 1986. *Black Frontiersmen: Afro-Hispanic Culture of Ecuador and Colombia.* Prospect Heights, IL: Waveland Press.

———. 2003a. "Introduction." In *Millennial Ecuador: Critical Essays on Cultural Transformations and Social Dynamics*, ed. Norman E. Whitten Jr., 1–45. Iowa City: University of Iowa Press.

———. 2003b. "Symbolic Inversion, the Topology of *El Mestizaje*, and the Spaces of *Las Razas* in Ecuador." *Journal of Latin American Anthropology* 8(1): 52–85.

Widener, Patricia. 2007a. "Benefits and Burdens of Transnational Campaigns: A Comparison of Four Oil Struggles in Ecuador." *Mobilization: An International Quarterly* 12(1): 21–36.

———. 2007b. "Oil Conflict in Ecuador: A Photographic Essay." *Organization & Environment* 20(1): 84–105.

———. 2009a. "Global Links and Environmental Flows: Oil Disputes in Ecuador." *Global Environmental Politics* 9(1): 31–57.

———. 2009b. "Oil Tourism: Disasters and Destinations in Ecuador and the Philippines." *Sociological Inquiry* 79(3): 266–88.

———. 2010. "A Protracted Age of Oil: Pipelines, Refineries and Quiet Conflict in the American Midwest." Paper presented at the International Sociological Association Annual Meeting, Gothenburg, Sweden.

———. 2011. "Governing and Contesting China's Oil Operations in the Global South." In *Environmental Inequalities Beyond Borders*, eds. J. Carmin and J. Agyeman, 159–84. Cambridge, MA: MIT Press.

Williams, William Appleman. 1980. *Empire as a Way of Life*. Oxford: Oxford University Press.

Wilson, E. O. 2002. "Hotspots: Preserving Pieces of Fragile Bioshere." *National Geographic*, July, 86+.

Wong, Otto, and Gerhard K. Raabe. 2000. "A Critical Review of Cancer Epidemiology in the Petroleum Industry, with a Meta-analysis of a Combined Database of More Than 350,000 Workers." *Regulatory Toxicology and Pharmacology* 32: 78–98.

Wood, Lesley J. 2005. "Bridging the Chasms: The Case of Peoples' Global Action." In *Coalitions across Borders: Transnational Protest and the Neoliberal Order*, eds. Joe Bandy and Jackie Smith, 95–117. Lanham, MD: Rowman & Littlefield.

Wunder, Sven. 1999. "Promoting Forest Conservation through Ecotourism Income? A Case Study from the Ecuadorian Amazon Region." Occasional Paper No. 21, March. Bogor, Indonesia: Center for International Forestry Research.

Wyss, Jim. 2001. "OCP Gets Final Okay to Build Ecuador Line." *Platt's Oilgram News* 79(123): 3, 27 June.

Yashar, Deborah J. 2005. *Contesting Citizenship in Latin America: The Rise of Indigenous Movements and the Postliberal Challenge*. New York: Cambridge University Press.

Zamosc, Leon. 2007. "The Indian Movement and Political Democracy in Ecuador." *Latin American Politics and Society* 49(3): 1–34.

Zelezny, Lynnette, and Megan Bailey. 2006. "A Call for Women to Lead a Different Environmental Movement." *Organization & Environment* 19(1): 103–9.

Zhang, Jin. 2004. *Catch-up and Competitiveness in China: The Case of Large Firms in the Oil Industry*. London: RoutledgeCurzon.

Zibechi, Raúl. 2009. "Ecuador: The Logic of Development Clashes with Movements." Translated by E. Brockner from "Ecuador: La lógica del desarrollo choca con los movimientos." Americas Program Report, Center for International Policy (CIP), 17 March.

Zweig, David, and Bi Jianhai. 2005. "China's Global Hunt for Energy." *Foreign Affairs* 84(5): 25–38.

Index

About the Author

Patricia Widener is assistant professor of sociology at Florida Atlantic University. Her research examines environmental disputes, oil disasters, and transnational advocacy from an environmental justice and political economy perspective. She has recently begun research on food justice and food knowledge in Florida. She received a Ph.D. in sociology from Brown University and an M.A. in sociology from the University of New Orleans. Prior to graduate school, she worked as a journalist in Southeast Asia.